THE LEADING FACTS
OF
NEW MEXICAN HISTORY

Volume I

THE LEADING FACTS OF NEW MEXICAN HISTORY

Volume I
Facsimile of Number 1156 of Original 1911 Edition

by
Ralph Emerson Twitchell

New Foreword
by
Richard Melzer, Ph.D.

SANTA FE

New Material © 2007 by Sunstone Press. All Rights Reserved.

No part of this book may be reproduced in any form or by any electronic or mechanical means including information storage and retrieval systems without permission in writing from the publisher, except by a reviewer who may quote brief passages in a review.

Sunstone books may be purchased for educational, business, or sales promotional use. For information please write: Special Markets Department, Sunstone Press, P.O. Box 2321, Santa Fe, New Mexico 87504-2321.

Library of Congress Cataloging-in-Publication Data

Twitchell, Ralph Emerson, 1859–1925.
   The leading facts of New Mexican history : facsimile of original 1911 ed. / by Ralph Emerson Twitchell ; new foreword by Richard Melzer.
     p. cm -- (Southwest heritage series)
   Originally published in 5 v.: Cedar Rapids, Iowa : Torch Press, 1911–17.
   Includes bibliographical references and index.
   ISBN 0-86534-565-1 (v. 1 : softcover : alk. paper) -- ISBN 0-86534-584-8 (v. 1 hardcover)
   ISBN 0-86534-566-X (v. 2 : softcover: alk. paper) -- ISBN 0-86534 -585-6 (v. 2 hardcover)
  1. New Mexico--History. I. Title.

F796. T97 2007
978.9--dc22

                                              2006052281

WWW.SUNSTONEPRESS.COM
SUNSTONE PRESS / POST OFFICE BOX 2321 / SANTA FE, NM 87504-2321 /USA
(505) 988-4418 / ORDERS ONLY (800) 243-5644 / FAX (505) 988-1025

The Southwest Heritage Series is dedicated to Jody Ellis and Marcia Muth Miller, the founders of Sunstone Press, whose original purpose and vision continues to inspire and motivate our publications.

CONTENTS

THE SOUTHWEST HERITAGE SERIES / I

FOREWORD TO THIS EDITION / II

FACSIMILE OF 1911 EDITION / III

I

THE SOUTHWEST HERITAGE SERIES

The history of the United States is written in hundreds of regional histories and literary works. Those letters, essays, memoirs, biographies and even collections of fiction are often first-hand accounts by people who wanted to memorialize an event, a person or simply record for posterity the concerns and issues of the times. Many of these accounts have been lost, destroyed or overlooked. Some are in private or public collections but deemed to be in too fragile condition to permit handling by contemporary readers and researchers.

However, now with the application of twenty-first century technology, nineteenth and twentieth century material can be reprinted and made accessible to the general public. These early writings are the DNA of our history and culture and are essential to understanding the present in terms of the past.

The Southwest Heritage Series is a form of literary preservation. Heritage by definition implies legacy and these early works are our legacy from those who have gone before us. To properly present and preserve that legacy, no changes in style or contents have been made. The material reprinted stands on its own as it first appeared. The point of view is that of the author and the era in which he or she lived. We would not expect photographs of people from the past to be re-imaged with modern clothes, hair styles and backgrounds. We should not, therefore, expect their ideas and personal philosophies to reflect our modern concepts.

Remember, reading their words and sharing their thoughts is a passport back into understanding how the past was shaped and how it influenced today's world.

Our hope is that new access to these older books will provide readers with a challenging and exciting experience.

II

FOREWORD TO THIS EDITION
by
Richard Melzer, Ph.D.

Historians have long admired Ralph Emerson Twitchell's *The Leading Facts of New Mexican History*, considered the first major history of the state. Put succinctly by former State Historian Robert J. Tórrez, Twitchell's five-volume work (of which this is one of the first two volumes Sunstone Press is reprinting in its Southwest Heritage Series) has "become the standard by which all subsequent books on New Mexico history are measured."[1]

As Twitchell wrote in the preface of his first volume, his goal in writing *The Leading Facts* was to respond to the "pressing need" for a history of New Mexico with a commitment to "accuracy of statement, simplicity of style, and impartiality of treatment." Twitchell added that he sought to make his work "available to the person of moderate means," a truly ironic goal as copies of the first edition of *The Leading Facts* sell for well over $500 on the current rare book market, if one can find them.[2]

Ralph Emerson Twitchell was born in Ann Arbor, Michigan, on November 29, 1859. According to a fifty-seven page genealogy he prepared and published privately, the Twitchells (or Twichels or Twichells) date back to the time of William the Conqueror in English history. The earliest Twitchell to emigrate to the American colonies arrived in Massachusetts in 1630, "imbued with the spirit of the Puritans," in Twitchell's words. Twitchell's great grandfather fought on the rebel side in the American Revolutionary battles of Lexington and Bunker Hill.[3]

Twitchell earned his LL.B. degree from the University of Michigan in 1882. By December of that year the twenty-three year old had arrived in Santa Fe to serve as a law clerk to Henry L. Waldo, solicitor of the Atchison, Topeka and Santa Fe Railroad in New Mexico.[4] Upon his arrival, the *Santa Fe New Mexican* described Twitchell as "a pleasant young gentleman of excellent social qualities and fine legal attainments."[5] Twitchell worked for the Santa Fe in increasingly important roles for the balance of his legal career.

Twitchell was involved in political and civic activities from his earliest days in New Mexico. In 1885 he helped organize a new territorial militia in Santa Fe and saw active duty in western New Mexico. Later appointed judge advocate of the Territorial Militia, he attained the rank of colonel, a title he was proud to use for the rest of his life. By 1893 he was elected the mayor of Santa Fe and, thereafter, district attorney of Santa Fe County. He was, in fact, one of the capital city's greatest boosters, supporting the use of traditional Southwest architecture, serving as the president of the local chamber of commerce, and acting as director of the Santa Fe Fiesta when it was rejuvenated shortly after World War I.

Twitchell probably promoted New Mexico as much as any single New Mexican of his generation. An avid supporter of New Mexico statehood, he argued the territory's case for elevated political status, celebrated its final victory in 1912, and even designed New Mexico's first state flag in 1915. He served on the management team of New Mexico's prize-winning state exhibit at the Panama-California Exposition in San Diego and was responsible for suggesting the exhibit's unique design, a replica of a Spanish colonial mission church, which later became the design of Santa Fe's new Museum of Fine Arts. Twitchell served on the board of regents at the Museum of New Mexico and, briefly, on the board of regents at New Mexico A&M (now New Mexico State University).

Active in seemingly countless organizations, from New Mexico's Good Roads Club to the National Irrigation Congress, Twitchell consistently rose to leadership roles in each group he joined. In the Republican Party, he chaired the party's central committee in New Mexico from 1902 to 1903. A life member of the Historical Society of New Mexico, he served as the society's vice president from 1910 to 1924 and its president in 1924.[6] Twitchell was even credited with rescuing the Spanish and Mexican archives when the territorial capitol burned in May 1892. Many of his contemporaries must have reiterated the question that former governor L. Bradford Prince posed in a personal letter to Twitchell in 1919: "How [do you] do it?"[7]

No person could have served so long and have done so much without controversy; Twitchell was no exception. As early as the 1890s he had joined other Republican leaders in the Knights of Liberty, a secret society often identified with the Santa Fe Ring.[8] Twitchell split with several key leaders of his own party, including Max Frost, the editor of the *Santa Fe New Mexican*, whom Twitchell described as "a lying scoundrel,"[9] and Thomas Catron, the most powerful Republican in the territory in the late nineteenth century. In 1892 Catron went so far as to accuse Twitchell of being "under the influence of whiskey and frequenting a very low dive," among other things, at the territorial fair in Albuquerque.[10] Such behavior would have been unusual for Twitchell, if it happened at all, but Catron's charges illustrate the degree of animosity that had developed between the two men within a decade of Twitchell's arrival on the scene.

Twitchell could more accurately be accused of being overly zealous and, as a result, sometimes offensive. In 1901, for example, he wrote to the editor of the *Albuquerque Evening Citizen* with the assertion that any businessman who did not publicly support New Mexico statehood should be "smoke[d] out," implying that those who opposed statehood should no longer be welcomed in the territory.[11] As a result of such statements and poor relations with top Republican leaders like Catron, Twitchell was not included as a delegate to the state constitutional convention of 1910, an affront that undoubtedly bruised his considerable ego.

Twitchell was also involved in two serious controversies regarding Native American rights. In the first of these confrontations, Twitchell had overseen the filming of the sacred Corn Dance, banned to the general public at Taos Pueblo. Without obtaining permission, Twitchell included images of the dance in a movie shown to thousands of visitors to the New Mexico exhibit at the Panama-California Exposition. Convinced that these public showings had caused illness among Indians employed at the exposition, someone broke into the New Mexico building and confiscated the ill-gotten film. Despite an investigation by Pinkerton detectives, the thief was never found. Far worse, Twitchell showed no remorse for betraying the Indians' trust. In fact, he wired Santa Fe for another copy of the film (stored at the Museum of New Mexico), showed the second copy, and blatantly exploited the incident to promote New Mexico and its exhibit at the exposition.[12]

Twitchell became embroiled in a far wider Indian controversy when he served as one of the principal authors of the infamous Bursum Bill in the early 1920s. Introduced by New Mexico's Senator H.O. Bursum, the bill gravely threatened pueblo water rights and considerable portions of Indian lands. Although Twitchell was appointed special assistant to the U.S. Attorney General and traveled to Washington, D.C., to testify before House and Senate committees, the legislation was defeated by the combined effort of pueblo leaders, organized as the All-Pueblo Council, and agitated artists and authors of the Taos and Santa Fe art colonies.[13]

Fortunately for Twitchell, he is less remembered for his involvement in such controversies than for his magnum opus, *The Leading Facts of New Mexican History*. Relying on his own extensive library, the libraries of many colleagues, and every document that might "throw light upon the occurrences of the past," Twitchell created a work in which he "tried to be accurate and fair."[14]

While many contemporaries praised Twitchell's accuracy and fairness, others wondered how fair he could be if one of his major goals, as stated on the first page of his first volume, was to "impress upon the reader's mind the fortitude, the courage, the suffering, and the martyrdom of those who first brought to New Mexico the banner of Christianity and civilization."[15]

Native Americans might well take exception to the idea that only those representing the Catholic faith and Spanish culture displayed fortitude, courage, suffering, and martyrdom in the Spanish colonial period. Spanish newspaper editors also took exception to Twitchell's devotion to English as the preferred language in schools and businesses, at the risk of losing *"el idioma de Cervantes"* and, hence, a major part of their Hispanic culture.[16] Others, like the Hispanic historian Benjamin M. Read, questioned how well Anglo authors like Twitchell could translate Spanish documents and how much accurate historical information was literally lost in their ethnocentric translations.[17] Finally, some questioned Twitchell's objectivity when it was rumored that "the amount of space allocated to contemporaries [in *The Leading Facts*] was weighed by the amount of their subscriptions to help pay for [publication costs]" of at least volumes three, four, and five.[18]

There is no indication that Twitchell heeded this criticism, especially given the near universal acclaim his books received among Anglo peers in New Mexico and across the country.[19] Inspired by this success and truly devoted to the study of history, Twitchell became the most prolific historian of his era, writing several additional histories of the Southwest, making frequent historical addresses, and founding, financing, and editing an ambitious, but short-lived, periodical called, *Old Santa Fe: A Magazine of History, Archaeology, Genealogy, and Biography*.[20]

But *The Leading Facts* remained Twitchell's major contribution to New Mexico history. Limited to fifteen hundred copies in its first edition, *The Leading Facts* had become a rare book by the 1960s when its first two volumes were reissued by Horn and Wallace in 1963. A rare book again by the late twentieth century, a new, affordable edition is long overdue and quite timely. Just as Twitchell's first edition in 1911 helped celebrate New Mexico's entry into statehood in 1912, the newest edition serves as a tribute to the state's centennial celebration of 2012.

Colonel Twitchell would have wanted it that way; boosting New Mexico, its resources and citizens was, after all, the central purpose of Twitchell's long life and productive career. In the apt words of an editorial in the *Santa Fe New Mexican* at the time of Twitchell's death in 1925: "As press agent for the best things of New Mexico, her traditions, history, beauty, glamour, scenery, archaeology, and material resources, he was indefatigable and efficient."[21]

NOTES

1   Robert J. Tórrez, *UFOs Over Galisteo and Other Stories of New Mexico's History* (Albuquerque: University of New Mexico Press, 2004): 131. Also see Howard Robert Lamar, *The Far Southwest* (Albuquerque: University of New Mexico Press, 2000): 457.

2   Ralph Emerson Twitchell, *The Leading Facts of New Mexican History* (Cedar Rapids, Iowa: The Torch Press, 1911): I:ix.

3   Ralph Emerson Twitchell, *Genealogy of the Twitchell Family* (n.c.: privately printed, 1929). A rare copy of Twitchell's genealogy can be found in the Ralph Emerson Twitchell Papers, Box 1, Folder 4, Fray Angélico Chávez Library, Museum of New Mexico, Santa Fe, New Mexico; hereafter cited as the Twitchell Papers. General biographical works on Twitchell include Myra Ellen Jenkins, "Ralph Emerson Twitchell," *Arizona and the West*, vol. 8 (Summer 1966): 102-06; J. Michael Pattison, "Four 'Gentlemen' Historians of New Mexico" (Unpublished M.A. thesis, New Mexico Highlands University, 1992): 43-9.

4   Twitchell so admired Waldo that he named his first and only son after his supervisor. The boy's mother, Twitchell's first wife Margaret, died on January 29, 1900. Twitchell dedicated *The Leading Facts* in Margaret's memory. He married his second wife, Estelle Bennett (1872-1952), in 1916. Twitchell, *Genealogy*, 446.

5   Quoted in the *Santa Fe New Mexican*, August 15, 1999.

6   Appropriately, the Historical Society of New Mexico's annual Ralph Emerson Twitchell Award is given "for significant contributions to the field of history by individuals, organizations, or institutions."

7   L. Bradford Prince to Ralph Emerson Twitchell, Flushing, New York, September 10, 1919, Ralph Emerson Twitchell Collection, New Mexico State Records Center and Archives, Santa Fe, New Mexico; hereafter cited as the NMSRCA.

8   Victor Westphall, *Thomas Benton Catron and His Era* (Tucson: University of Arizona Press, 1973): 208-09.

9   Quoted in ibid, 390n.

10 Quoted in ibid., 261. Twitchell and Catron also argued about a loan Catron had made to Twitchell near the turn of the century. Ibid., 390.

11 *Albuquerque Evening Citizen*, April 25, 1901, quoted in Robert W. Larson, *New Mexico's Quest for Statehood, 1846-1912* (Albuquerque: University of New Mexico Press, 1968): 200.

12 Matthew F. Bokovoy, *The San Diego World Fairs and Southwestern Memory, 1880-1940* (Albuquerque: University of New Mexico Press, 2005): 132-34.

13 The best description of Twitchell's role in drafting and defending the Bursum Bill is found in Lawrence C. Kelly, *The Assault on Assimilation: John Collier and the Origins of Indian Policy Reform* (Albuquerque: University of New Mexico Press, 1983): 203-54. According to Kelly, Twitchell's defense of the bill "crumbled and his composure wilted" under close examination before a Senate committee. "By the time [Twitchell] completed his presentation, there was little doubt that the original Bursum Bill was indeed a dead letter." Ibid., 239. On the *Santa Fe New Mexican*'s coverage of the bill and its fate, see Oliver LaFarge, *Santa Fe* (Norman: University of Oklahoma Press, 1959): 274-81.

14   Twitchell, *The Leading Facts*, I:viii.

15   Ibid.

16   Doris Meyer, *Speaking for Themselves: Neomexicano Cultural Identity and the Spanish Language Press, 1880-1920* (Albuquerque: University of New Mexico Press, 1996): 119-20.

17   Ibid., 200-01. For Twitchell's strong feelings regarding the teaching of English, see *The Leading Facts*, II:508-09, and his address, "The Public School," delivered at high school commencement in Raton, New Mexico, on May 24, 1899. Ralph Emerson Twitchell, Vertical File, Fray Angélico Chávez Library, Museum of New Mexico, Santa Fe, New Mexico.

18   Beatrice Chauvenet, *Hewett and Friends: A Biography of Santa Fe's Vibrant Era* (Santa Fe: Museum of New Mexico Press, 1983): 104. For a sample prepublication subscription card for volumes one and two of *The Leading Facts*, see the Twitchell Papers, Box 2, Folder 7, Twitchell Papers.

19   For a sample of this praise for *The Leading Facts*, see a promotional brochure produced by its publisher, the Torch Press, found in the L. Bradford Prince Collection, NMSRCA.

20   Twitchell's other histories include *Spanish Archives of New Mexico*, 2 vols. (Cedar Rapids, Iowa: The Torch Press, 1914) and *Old Santa Fe: The Story of New Mexico's Ancient Capital* (Santa Fe: Santa Fe New Mexican, 1925). The periodical, *Old Santa Fe*, served as the Historical Society of New Mexico's official bulletin from its inception in 1913 till its demise three years later.

21   Editorial, *Santa Fe New Mexican*, August 26, 1925. Twitchell died at the Clara Barton Hospital in Los Angeles, California, of a paralytic stroke and heart failure on August 26, 1925. He was sixty-five. His last wish, to be buried below the Cross of the Martyrs in Santa Fe, was unanimously approved by the Santa Fe city council, but he was temporarily buried at Fairview Cemetery until a site below the cross could be identified. His funeral was one of the largest in Santa Fe history, with leading members of both major political parties present and a line of cars stretching half a mile. His temporary burial site at Fairview has become permanent and his last wish was never fulfilled. *Santa Fe New Mexican*, August 26-29 and 31, 1925; Paul A.F. Walter, "Obituary: Ralph Emerson Twitchell," *New Mexico Historical Review*, Vol. 1 (January 1926): 78-85; Richard Melzer, *Buried Treasures: Famous and Unusual Gravesites in New Mexico History* (Santa Fe: Sunstone Press).

III

FACSIMILE OF 1911 EDITION

THE LEADING FACTS OF
NEW MEXICAN HISTORY

FRAY JUAN DE TORQUEMADA
A FIRST HISTORIAN

The Leading Facts of New Mexican History

BY

RALPH EMERSON TWITCHELL, Esq.
VICE-PRESIDENT NEW MEXICO HISTORICAL SOCIETY

"HISTORIANS, ONLY THINGS OF WEIGHT,
RESULTS OF PERSONS, OR AFFAIRS OF STATE,
BRIEFLY, WITH TRUTH AND CLEARNESS SHOULD RELATE"
—*Heath*

VOL. I

THE TORCH PRESS
CEDAR RAPIDS, IOWA
1911

COPYRIGHT 1911
BY R. E. TWITCHELL

THE TORCH PRESS
CEDAR RAPIDS
IOWA

TO THE MEMORY OF
MARGARET OLIVIA TWITCHELL
WHOSE LOVE AND APPRECIATION AS A DEVOTED
WIFE CONSTANTLY ENCOURAGED ME IN MY HIS-
TORICAL LABORS THIS WORK IS GRATEFULLY AND
AFFECTIONATELY DEDICATED BY THE AUTHOR

SUBSCRIBERS' EDITION

One Thousand Five Hundred Numbered Autograph Copies

NUMBER **1156**

"*I have discovered a New Mexico as well as a New Viscaya*"
— FRANCISCO DE IBARRA

Las Vegas, New Mexico, January 1, 1911

TO HIS EXCELLENCY, THE HONORABLE WILLIAM J. MILLS
                 Governor of New Mexico

SIR:

    The writing of the history of New Mexico, as found in these volumes, has been accomplished after many years of reading and research. Oftentimes I have been disheartened, owing to my inability to secure accurate information. It has been difficult to harmonize the recorded statements of recognized authorities, varying as they do in many vital particulars.

    It has been my constant endeavor to overlook no book, document, or other source of information calculated to throw light upon the occurrences of the past. I have tried to be accurate and fair.

    Through you, I am giving this work to our people with the hope that careful study will not fail to impress upon the reader's mind the fortitude, the courage, the suffering, and the martyrdom of those who first brought to New Mexico the banner of Christianity and civilization, trusting that present and future generations of New Mexicans may thereby better understand the difficulties surrounding and harassing their predecessors in the maintenance and preservation of that emblem during the periods of isolation which preceded the advent of twentieth century progress and conditions.

                                                 Respectfully yours

                                            R. E. Twitchell

PREFATORY NOTE

THE pressing need of a history of New Mexico from the earliest times to the present, available to the person of moderate means, has been apparent for many years.

In the preparation of these volumes the writer has had in view accuracy of statement, simplicity of style, and impartiality of treatment.

A great many authorities have been read and carefully studied. Such of these as treat of subjects germane to any particular chapter in the book are listed at the conclusion of such chapter. It is hoped that no source of information of prime importance has been overlooked. These authorities have been listed for the purpose of aiding the student desirous of still further research. The majority of the citations and references are from books in the library of the writer. Such as are not, may be found in any of the principal libraries of the country.

Grateful acknowledgements are due to those old friends having in their possession ancient documents, records, and Mss. to which, through their courtesy, access has been had and use of which has been permitted.

Of necessity a great deal of the work found in the pages following may best be termed editing, although entire reliance has not been placed upon the certainty of the citations and references found in other works dealing with the history of New Mexico; nor has the writer depended wholly upon the translations of others, having used his own efforts whenever, in his judgment, it was for the best.

Fortunately, during a period of years, the writer lived at Santa Fé, where he had abundant opportunity for careful examination of the Santa Fé Archives, at that period in the custody of the Territory of New Mexico. Many translations and copies were made at that time. So far as it was possible to learn, the Santa Fé Archives did not ante-date 1680, nearly all of the earlier records having been destroyed by the Pueblos in the uprising of that year. In the office of the Surveyor General for New Mexico are to be found many very valuable ancient documents which may be classed as archives. These contain a wealth of information of rare historical value. In the papers belonging to private families has been found much valuable information, and it is to be hoped that some day all of this class of archives will find way into the possession of the New Mexico Historical Society, where they may be carefully preserved.

The writer does not agree with most of the students of our history that many valuable portions of the Santa Fé Archives were lost during the administration of Governor Pyle. Whatever disappeared at that time had already been combed over by various historians, and at a time when the documents were comparatively intact.

The work performed by Fr. Escalante in 1778, and completed from 1681 to 1717, is of great value, and if anything of that period is lost, the fault can not be laid at the door of the worthy friar. His work contains many copies and extracts from original papers which were available to him, but which have since disappeared. Fr. Escalante's records are found in manuscript in the *Archivo General de Mexico*; they were printed in the year 1856 in the *Doc. Hist. Mex. 3rd series*, part iv, pp. 113-208. Volume xxv of the *Arch. Gen. Mex. Ms.*, entitled *Documentos para la Historia de Nuevo Mexico*, contains the official reports of the friars and other church authorities covering almost all of the eighteenth and some very important documents of the seventeenth century.

Fr. Salmeron's *Relaciones* is a very complete work of the earliest explorations, although at times his accounts appear to be somewhat exaggerated. Fr. Alonso Posada's work is of the greatest value. The fray was custodio of New Mexico in 1660-1664, and had been in New Mexico engaged in missionary work for several years prior to that date. His report was made pursuant to a royal order made in 1678, and was written about eight years later.

The most important work, however, for New Mexican history is that of Torquemada, *Monarquia Indiana,* which brings the records down to 1608. Later authors are Vetancurt, *Crónica,* and *Menologio,* 1691; Mendieta, *Historia Eclesiástica*; Oviedo, *Historia General*; Herrera, *Historia General*; Gomara, *Historia Indiana*; Mota Padilla, *Conquista de Nueva Galicia,* and Villagrá, *Historia de Nuevo Mexico,* probably the best of the earlier writers, particularly upon the occurrences of the period of which he writes.

There are many other authorities upon special subjects, appearing in the foot-notes, whose works appear in the bibliographical list at the conclusion of the chapters.

The best of the earlier modern writers is W. W. H. Davis, at one time United States Attorney for New Mexico, whose work, *The Spanish Conquest of New Mexico,* is a condensation or translation of the early Spanish narratives down nearly to the year 1700.

In 1883, there appeared a very excellent work by L. Bradford Prince, LL. D., entitled *Historical Sketches from the Earliest Records to the American Occupation.* In some respects he has followed the errors of earlier writers, particularly as to the journey of Alvar Nuñez Cabeza de Vaca, the route taken by Francisco Vasquez Coronado, and localities visited by the last named explorer.

Beyond all question the best authorities upon the subjects treated by them are the works of Adolph F. Bandelier, *Con-*

tributions to the History of the Southwestern Portion of the United States; *The Coronado Expedition*, by George Parker Winship; and *Spanish Explorers in the Southern United States*, edited by Frederick W. Hodge, of the Bureau of American Ethnology.

In 1889 appeared the work of Hubert Howe Bancroft, *History of Arizona and New Mexico, 1530-1888*.

There are few publications so elaborate as this great work. The wealth of notes and citations is most attractive to the student or reader. Mr. Bancroft had exceptional opportunity in the preparation of his work, having been the owner of one of the greatest libraries of the country, filled with books and manuscripts touching upon the history of the southwest. The work, however, is one of a set of thirty-nine volumes, and the cost to the individual of moderate means is practically prohibitive.

Some effort has been made by others, but the results, so far as historical writing is concerned, have been very unsatisfactory.

In this work most liberal drafts have been made upon the several monographs published in the *Reports* of the Bureau of American Ethnology, particularly the contributions of the Mindeleff brothers, Mrs. Stephenson, Mr. W. H. Holmes, Mr. Frank H. Cushing, Mr. Frederick W. Hodge, and Dr. Edgar L. Hewett. The facts and deductions contained in the chapter devoted to the archæological and ethnological history of New Mexico are drawn largely from the works of these distinguished workers in special fields of research.

The courteous treatment of the several departments at Washington in supplying information dealing with the history of New Mexico following the American Occupation period is gratefully remembered. The several great public libraries in the West have been of invaluable assistance, and to their librarians the writer tenders his thanks.

Several private libraries in New Mexico and Colorado,

notably those of Hon. Thomas Benton Catron and Dr. L. Bradford Prince, have been open, and to both these distinguished gentlemen the writer is under many obligations.

Special thanks are due to Mr. K. M. Chapman of the School of American Archæology at Santa Fé, whose genius in illustrating and work in copying old documents, engravings, and photographs, has made their reproduction possible.

RALPH EMERSON TWITCHELL

Las Vegas, New Mexico, January 1, 1911

CONTENTS OF VOLUME I

CHAPTER I ANTIQUITY OF NEW MEXICO — THE ORIGIN AND HISTORY OF ITS FIRST INHABITANTS	3
CHAPTER II THE FIRST SPANISH EXPLORERS, 1534-1542 — ALVAR NUÑEZ CABEZA DE VACA AND HIS COMPANIONS .	53
CHAPTER III FRIAR MARCOS DE NIZA — THE NEGRO, ESTEVAN — THEIR JOURNEY TO CIBOLA, 1539 — DEATH OF ESTEVAN — RETURN OF FRIAR MARCOS TO THE CITY OF MEXICO	137
CHAPTER IV FRANCISCO VASQUEZ CORONADO — HIS MARCH AND INVASION, 1540 — HIS FAILURE AND RETURN TO MEXICO, 1542	162
CHAPTER V THE SPANISH FRIARS, AGUSTIN RODRIGUEZ, FRANCISCO LOPEZ, AND JUAN DE SANTA MARIA — THEIR EFFORTS FOR CHRISTIANITY AND CIVILIZATION, 1582 . .	252
CHAPTER VI THE EXPEDITION UNDER DON ANTONIO DE ESPEJO AND FRAY BERNARDINO BELTRÁN UP THE RIO GRANDE DEL NORTE — THEY VISIT MANY PUEBLOS AND RETURN BY WAY OF THE PECOS RIVER, 1582	265
CHAPTER VII THE CONQUEST OF NEW MEXICO BY DON JUAN DE OÑATE, 1595-1598	301
CHAPTER VIII PUEBLO REBELLION AND INDEPENDENCE, 1680-1692 — OTERMIN, CRUZATE, DE VARGAS	354
CHAPTER IX ONE HUNDRED AND TWENTY-TWO YEARS OF SPANISH RULE, 1700-1822	414

LIST OF ILLUSTRATIONS

Fray Juan de Torquemada. A First Historian	*Frontispiece*
The Ruins of Pu-yé	3
Aboriginal Ruins near Santa Fé, N. M.	5
The Rock Trail at Tsan-ka-wi	8
Great Ceremonial Cave, Rito de los Frijoles	10
Doorway of Cavate Dwelling	12
South House at Pu-yé, after Excavation	14
Looking out of Ceremonial Cave, Rito de los Frijoles	16
Indians Entering Cliff Kiva at Pu-yé	18
Cliff Dwellings at Pu-yé	20
Alcoves in Cliff — Back Rooms of Talus Pueblo	22
Excavations — Pueblo of Ty-u-on-yi — Rito de los Frijoles	24
Talus Villages, Cliff of Ty-u-on-yi	26
Tent Rocks near Ot-o-wi	28
Rock Trail at Tsan-ka-wi	32
Portraits of F. W. Hodge, A. F. Bandelier, E. L. Hewett and John W. Powell	34
Ground Plan, Pueblo of Ty-u-on-yi	37
Eastern Mesa, Pueblo of Walpi	38
Masonry of the Pueblo Bonito	40
Ruins of the Pueblo of Hungo Pavie	44
Pre-Spanish Pottery — Moqui	46
Ground Plan of the Pueblo Bonito	47
Typical Navajó Dwelling or "Hogan"	48
Moqui Basket and Pottery	50
Spruce Tree House, Mesa Verde District	53
Fac-simile of Title Page of Relacion of Alvar Nuñez Cabeza de Vaca	54
The Ulpius Globe of 1542	56

MAP OF ROUTES OF SPANISH EXPLORERS	59
SHIPS OF THE NARVAÉZ EXPEDITION	65
BATTLE BETWEEN SPANIARDS AND INDIANS	65
THE BUFFALO OF GOMARA	72
FRAY BARTOLOMÉ DE LAS CASAS	80
THE BUFFALO OF DE BRY	88
SPANISH COINS OF THE SIXTEENTH CENTURY	96
APACHE NECKLACE OF HUMAN FINGERS	98
SANTO DOMINGO PUEBLO INDIAN CLOWN OR DELIGHT-MAKER	104
FAC-SIMILE SIGNATURE OF NUÑO DE GUZMAN	105
THE CASAS GRANDES IN 1850	112
EARLIEST MAP SHOWING CIBOLA-ZUÑI	120
SANTIAGO TRIUMPHING OVER HIS ENEMIES	128
MOQUI BASKETRY AND POTTERY	134
DON ANTONIO DE MENDOZA, FIRST VICEROY OF NEW SPAIN	137
FRAY FRANCISCO DE LOS ANGELES Ó QUIÑONES	144
FRANCISCANS CONVERTING INDIANS	145
FAC-SIMILE OF LAST PAGE OF PATENT TO FRANCISCANS	152
PUEBLO OF ZUÑI	162
MAP SHOWING MARCHES OF CORONADO IN NEW MEXICO	167
THE BATTLE OF HAWAIKÚH	168
TERRACES OF ZUÑI	176
FAC-SIMILE OF PAGE OF RELACION OF CASTAÑEDA	178
ARMS OF THE SPANIARDS UNDER CORONADO	182
DANCERS' ROCK — WALPI	184
MAP OF NEW MEXICO IN 17TH CENTURY	188
INDIAN OF THE PUEBLO OF PECOS, LAST OF HIS RACE	192
WATER VESSELS FROM COCHITÍ	201
SNAKE DANCE OF THE MOQUI	208
GROUND PLAN OF THE PUEBLO OF PECOS	210
WATER VESSELS, TINAJAS — FROM PUEBLO OF TESUQUE	213
GROOVED HAMMERS FROM QUIVIRA	216
OUR LADY OF LIGHT — PAINTING ON WOOD — FROM PECOS PUEBLO	224
ARROW HEADS FROM QUIVIRA	232
GROUND PLAN OF RUINS OF PUEBLO ON EL MORRO	236
FAC-SIMILE OF PAGE OF GRANT TO PUEBLO OF PECOS	240

LIST OF ILLUSTRATIONS

Coat of Arms and Fac-simile Signature of Don Antonio de Mendoza	248
Don Lorenzo Suarez de Mendoza, Condé de la Coruña	256
The Pueblo of Taos	265
Inscription Rock — El Morro	272
Inscriptions on El Morro	280
Fac-simile Signature of the Condé de Coruña	285
Inscriptions on El Morro	288
Don Luis de Velasco	296
Don Gaspar de Zuñiga y Acevedo, Condé de Monterey	304
Don Gaspar de Villagrá	312
Old Spanish Cart	318
Indian Chief, Pueblo of San Juan	320
Fac-simile of Title Page of Narrative by Fr. Montoya	328
Ceremonial Dance, Pueblo of Cochití	336
Pottery Bowls from Pueblo of Zuñi	339
Chapel of San Miguel, Santa Fé, N. M.	344
Woman Dancer, Santo Domingo	352
Fac-simile of Title Page of Narrative of Fr. Estevan de Perea, Custodio of New Mexico	354
Pueblo of Cochití	360
Governor's House, Pueblo of Tesuque	368
Ruins of Mission at Jemez	376
Fac-simile of Title Page of Funeral Oration — Franciscan Martyrs, 1681	384
Carved Leather Horse Furniture of the Reconquistadores	392
Fac-simile of Protest — Last Page and Signatures — as to South Boundary Line of New Mexico	394
Reconquest of New Mexico by De Vargas, Entry into Santa Fé	396
The Condé de Galve, Viceroy of New Spain	400
Fac-simile of Page of Journal of De Vargas	402
A Pecos Indian, from Drawing made in 1849	404
Fac-simile of Page of Journal of De Vargas	408
Fac-simile of Page of Journal of De Vargas	410
Typical Zuñi Indians	414
Fac-simile of Page of Journal of De Vargas	416

LIST OF ILLUSTRATIONS

FAC-SIMILE OF PAGE OF JOURNAL OF DE VARGAS	418
FAC-SIMILE OF PAGE OF JOURNAL OF DE VARGAS	420
FAC-SIMILE SIGNATURE OF DUKE OF ALBURQUERQUE	422
DON FRANCISCO FERNANDEZ DE LA CUEVA ENRIQUEZ, DUKE OF ALBURQUERQUE	424
CHAPEL OF OUR LADY OF GUADALUPE, SANTA FÉ, N. M., 1850	428
VICEROYS OF NEW SPAIN, 1711-1740	430
APACHE MEDICINE SHIRT	432
VICEROYS OF NEW SPAIN, 1740-1760	440
VICEROYS OF NEW SPAIN, 1760-1794	448
FAC-SIMILE OF PAGE OF MUSTER ROLL OF SPANISH GARRISON AT SANTA FÉ	456
VICEROYS OF NEW SPAIN, 1794-1803	464
MAJOR ZEBULON M. PIKE	472
ZUÑI FETICHES OF THE CHASE	480
OLD CHURCH AT LAGUNA, N. M.	482

NEW MEXICO

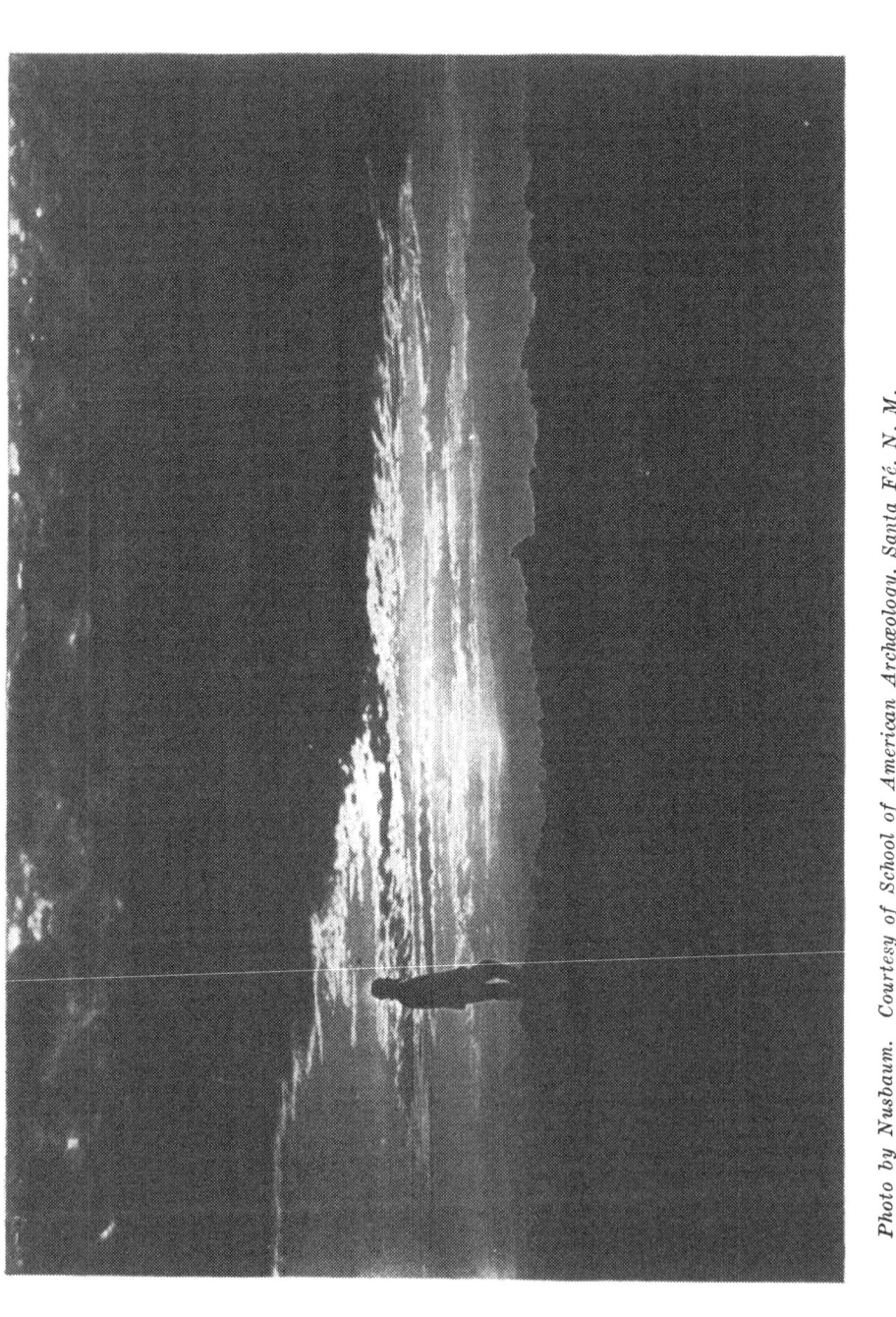

Photo by Nusbaum. Courtesy of School of American Archæology, Santa Fé, N. M.

The Ruins of Pu-yé

"So fleet the works of men, back to their earth again;
Ancient and holy things fade like a dream."—*Kingsley.*

CHAPTER I

Antiquity of New Mexico — The Origin and History of Its First Inhabitants

THE science which treats of antiquity finds abundant material for investigation in New Mexico. The study of oral traditions, inscriptions, ruins, and monuments of all kinds in this portion of the United States is most attractive to the archæologist. This class of historical research and its practical value have only lately become thoroughly recognized in the United States.

The monuments of the past have not appealed strongly to the ordinary American, engaged, as he has been during the past century, in the building of a great nation. He has naturally proceeded along constructive lines. He has occupied himself with the material growth of an advancing and progressive people. He has not cared to investigate or give his time and thought to the history of those whom the European explorers found upon this continent, nor of their predecessors in occupancy.

History is a recital of our knowledge of the development of the human race from the beginning. The history of New Mexico, therefore, rightfully begins with a recital of our present knowledge, not only of the races occupying this portion of our country during the periods of Spanish exploration, but also of their predecessors inhabiting the region named.

The study of archæology is in fact historical research. It aims at a knowledge of the deeds, lives, customs, and habits of the dwellers of the past. In this respect it merges into ethnology. No portion of the United States offers such excellent opportunity for this class of historical research as does New Mexico.

During the first century of our national existence, in his private capacity, the citizen of the republic paid small attention to this most important field of historical research. The government, however, at a very early day, recognized the importance of the subject. In 1795, an agent of the Cherokees, under instructions from the war department, made a careful study of their language and home life, and also collected material for a history of the Indians. President Jefferson, who planned the Lewis and Clark expedition to the northwest in the years 1804-06, "for the purpose of extending the internal commerce of the United States," especially stipulated in his instructions to Lewis, the observations of the native tribes that should be made by the expedition for the use of the national government. These included their names and numbers; the extent and limit of their possessions; their relations with other tribes or nations; their language, traditions, and monuments; their ordinary occupations in agriculture, fishing, hunting, war, arts, and the implements for these; their food, clothing, and domestic accommodations; the diseases prevalent among them and the remedies they used; moral and physical circumstances which distinguished them from known tribes; peculiarities in their laws, customs, and dispositions; and articles of commerce they might need or furnish, and to what extent; "and considering the interest which every nation has in extending and strengthening the authority of reason and justice among the people around them, it will be useful to acquire what knowledge you can of the state of morality, religion, and information among them, as it may better enable those who endeavour to civilize and instruct them to adapt their measures to the existing notions and practices of those on whom they are to operate."

INVESTIGATIONS BY THE GOVERNMENT

During much of his life President Jefferson, like Albert Gallatin, later on, manifested his deep interest in the ethnology of the American tribes by publishing accounts of his observations that are of extreme value today.

In 1820 Rev. Jedediah Morse was commissioned by President Monroe to make a tour for the purpose of "ascertaining, for the use of the government, the actual state of the Indian tribes of our country." The government also aided the publication of Schoolcraft's voluminous work on the Indians. The various war department expeditions

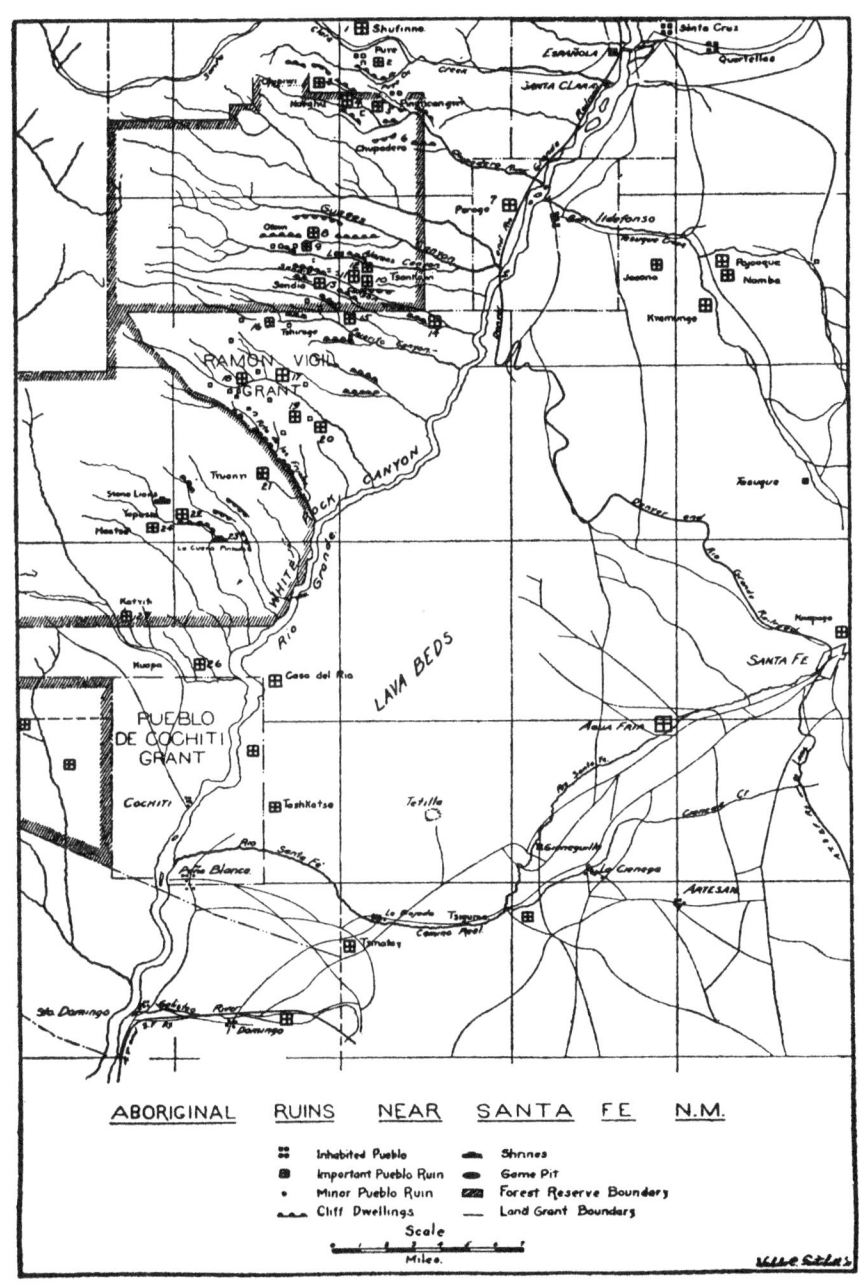

and surveys reported on the tribes and monuments encountered in the west; the Hayden survey of the territories examined and described many of the cliff-dwellings and pueblos, and published papers on the tribes of the Mississippi valley, and Major Powell, chief of the survey of the Rocky mountain region, accomplished much important work among the tribes of the Rio Colorado drainage in connection with his geological and geographical researches. He began the publication, under government auspices, of a series of monographs known as *Contributions to North American Ethnology*. Prior to this period the Smithsonian Institution had also taken a very active part in the publication of the results of researches undertaken by students. The first volume of its *Contributions to Knowledge* is the *Ancient Monuments of the Mississippi Valley*, by Squier and Davis, and, up to the founding of the Bureau of Ethnology in 1879, the Institution had issued upwards of six hundred papers on ethnology and archæology. These early researches took a wide range, but in a way somewhat unsystematic, and it was not until Spencer F. Baird, secretary of the Smithsonian Institution, recognizing the great value of Major John W. Powell's services in initiating researches among the western tribes, selected him as the person best qualified to organize and conduct the work of the Bureau of Ethnology, which congress had put under the supervision of the Smithsonian Institution, that a proper classification of the work was begun. There were numerous subjects of a practical nature that required attention, and these were so involved with the more strictly scientific questions that the two could not be considered separately.

The government, ever since its formation, has had before it problems which have arisen from the presence within the public domain of upwards of three hundred thousand aborigines. Many difficulties have presented themselves on this account, and the solution of the Indian problem has always been one of most serious nature. Within the public domain there were spoken, at one time, over five hundred different Indian languages, as distinct from one another as French is from English. These languages were grouped in more than fifty linguistic families. In addition to the differences in language there were many other distinctions. The investigations by the Bureau demonstrated that tribes allied in language were also often allied in capacity, habits, tastes, social organization, religion, arts, and industries. The researches by the Bureau generally have been of the greatest value. They are especially instructive in the study of the former inhabitants of New Mexico. In this way much progress has been made in understanding the inner life and character of the Indian, as known in post-Spanish times, and also of their ancestors and primitive peoples generally. The results of these researches have been given to the world and are available to the people of all civilized nations.

In New Mexico and the southwest the study of the Indian was greatly restricted until the building of the great railway lines to the Pacific coast. Railway construction in New Mexico and Arizona are contemporaneous with the organization of the Bureau of Ethnology. Ever since the crossing of the continent by Alvar Nuñez Cabeza de Vaca and his companions, at various periods and intervals explorers and students, in a more or less unscientific manner, have recorded the characteristics, habits, and customs of the Indians within the areas now comprising New Mexico and Arizona, but it is only since the advent of the railroads that the obscure characteristics of the present and former dwellers of this region have been scientifically investigated, so that at this time the full significance of many of the relics of the ancient inhabitants is fairly well understood. The study of implements and domestic utensils brought about the investigation of the industrial arts as practised by the Indian in every locality. Special attention has been given to linguistic researches, and in this way it has been ascertained that language is the most certain index of tribal and family relationship.

When the spirit of conquest induced the Romans to lead their legions beyond the Alps, New Mexico had been for centuries preceding the pathway of migratory peoples.[1] The races which submitted to the Roman arms were more barbaric than those which inhabited the table-lands and valleys of New Mexico during the first centuries of

ORIGIN OF THE FIRST INHABITANTS OF NEW MEXICO

[1] Bancroft, H. H., *Native Races*, vol. i, p. 21: "All writers agree in giving to the nations of America a remote antiquity; all admit that there exists a greater uniformity between them than is to be found in the Old World; many deny that all are one race. Traditions, ruins, moral and physical peculiarities, all denote for Americans a remote antiquity. The action of a climate peculiar to America, and of natural surroundings common to all the people of the continent, could not fail to produce in time a similarity of physiological structure."

the Christian era. Buildings sufficiently large to accommodate the inhabitants of a modern American village lie buried or in ruins, mute evidence of the existence of a race whose modes of living, customs, ceremonies, and habits are fruitful subjects of study today. These buried structures, now being uncovered, demonstrate the worth and ability of their builders. The cave- and cliff-dwellings, only lately scientifically explored, have been productive of relics demonstrating a knowledge on the part of their former inhabitants akin to the arts and sciences possessed by those who built the pyramids of Egypt. The construction of any one of the communal houses, the ruins of which are found in many localities in New Mexico, was a more prodigious undertaking for those who built them than was the erection, to their builders, of the Parthenon, the great cathedrals of the Middle Ages, or the steel or concrete structures of the present architecture of our great American cities.

Many theories have been advanced as to the origin of the first inhabitants of this region.[2] They may have been an aboriginal race. More likely they came from Asia. No research yet made overcomes the belief generally entertained by scientists, who have made a careful study of the subject, that the origin of our first inhabitants was Mongolian. Facial resemblance, their customs, ceremonies, industrial implements, ornaments, and weapons bear strong witness of a kinship with the Asiatic people, with our own Esquimaux, as well as also with the dwellers in Mexico, Central America, and Peru.[3]

---

[2] Bancroft, H. H., *Native Races*, vol. i, p. 19: ''There are many advocates for an Asiatic origin, both among ancient and modern speculators. Favorable winds and currents, the short distance between islands, traditions, both Chinese and Indian, refer the peopling of America to that quarter. Similarity in color, features, religion, reckoning of time, absence of heavy beard and innumerable other comparisons, are drawn by enthusiastic advocates, to support a Mongolian origin.''

[3] Bandelier, A. F., *Paper before New York Historical Society*, February 3, 1885: ''No attention is paid as yet to the fact that the religious creeds of the Indians over the whole American continent were moulded on the same pattern, that their social organization was fundamentally the same among the Cherokees, the Pueblos of New Mexico, the Mexicans and the Peruvians, that the system of government of the Iroquois differed from that of the Mexicans but very little, and that the same principles pervade aboriginal architecture from one Arctic circle to the other, varying only in degree and not in kind. It is constantly overlooked that the fact of a certain class of buildings being of stone and another group of wood, does not necessarily imply a superiority of the builders of the former over the builders of the latter, and that the long-house of the Iroquois shows as much mechanical skill, if not more, as the honey-combs in which the New Mexican Indians still live in part, that the carved dwellings of

Courtesy of School of American Archæology, Santa Fé, N. M.

Rock Trail at Tsan-ka-wi

ORIGIN AND HISTORY OF FIRST INHABITANTS

The descendants of five great families, into which the more recent populations since the Spanish conquest are divided, are found in New Mexico, Arizona, Utah, and Colorado. These families consist of the Shoshonean, Zuñian, Keresan, Tanonan, and the Athapascan stocks. The Moquis and Pueblos belong to the first four; the remaining two compose the Apache and Navajó tribes.

It is certainly possible that branches of the Mongolian race may have crossed Behring's Strait. Such a movement was of easy accomplishment. Thence, through the passing years, they could have migrated southward along the Pacific coast and later across the table-lands of New Mexico, where were built the great communal houses, the ruins of which are found from the north forty degrees latitude to the thirty-second parallel; they have thence been traced through southern New Mexico to latitude thirty degrees, in northern Chihuahua, thence along the Pacific slope to Sonora. Likewise, they may have come from northern Asia by way of Greenland.

The compact architecture typified in the communal, many-storied building, made up of hundreds of small rooms, reached its southern limit along the Rio Grande at San Marcial. There the Spaniards found the first villages in 1580, 1582, and 1598. Below that point the detached house type, in clusters, occupies the river banks at intervals, as far south as Doña Ana probably, certainly to old Fort Selden, or latitude thirty-two degrees, thirty minutes north.

Historians all agree that the aboriginal history of our country is properly divided into three distinct periods. The farthest removed is that which fixes the human race with species of animals long extinct. The period following is that of the mound-builders, and the most recent is that during which America was discovered by the Spanish explorers. The last mentioned epoch is the only one of which any historical data are available, other than the weapons, domestic utensils, pottery, and other relics of the mound-builders and their contemporaries in other portions of the continent.

The first peoples inhabiting the table-lands and valleys of New Mexico may have belonged to the same epoch as did the mound-builders. When the Spanish explorers first ventured upon the Atlantic coast, the Cherokees were still burying their dead in mounds.

---

the north-west coast denote an advance in art not behind that of aboriginal Yucatan.''

In the excavations of buried pueblos have been found many sorts of pottery, mummies, skeletons, weapons, and domestic implements which bear out this theory. The first inhabitants of New Mexico were familiar with agriculture; they planted corn, cotton in localities, and raised fruits. The large communal buildings were erected and occupied as a means of protection. Those who lived in these buildings were a sedentary people, and the cliffs, mesas, and canyons of New Mexico proved attractive as places of abode.

The ruins of the domiciles of these people are of two classes, cliff-dwellings, and pueblos. The cliff-dwellings are mostly of the excavated type, and embrace a wide range of habitations. The most primitive is the natural open cave, formed principally by wind erosion, and only slightly, if at all, enlarged by excavation. Wholly artificial dwellings, excavated in the perpendicular face of the cliff, are also found. Others have cased doorways, and some with the front, wholly or in part, of masonry. It is evident that when in use the majority of these dwellings were rendered much more commodious by the building of porches.

ANCIENT HABITATIONS — CLIFF DWELLINGS AND PUEBLOS

These cliff-dwellings occur in vast numbers in the southern faces of the mesas of volcanic tufa that extend out from the base of the mountains toward the valley in that portion of New Mexico known as the Pajarito plateau, the table-lands lying between the Jemez range and the Rio Grande. Occasionally they are found in cliffs with eastern exposures, but they very rarely face either north or west.

The pueblo ruins are those of the many-chambered community houses which are found upon the mesa tops and in the valleys. The pueblo structure is invariably a cluster of rooms or cells.[4] In some cases the rooms are arranged irregularly and in others they have a definite alignment of common wall. The smaller pueblos were but one story high, while the majority were from two to four stories. They were generally built in quadrangular form.

It is believed that the Moquis, and the Pueblos of New Mexico, finding it necessary for economical and defensive reasons, lived in

[4] Hewett, Dr. Edgar L., *Antiquities of the Jemez Plateau*, Bul. 32, B. A. E., 1906, p. 10.

Courtesy of School of American Archæology, Santa Fé, N. M.
Great Ceremonial Cave — Rito de los Frijoles

ORIGIN AND HISTORY OF FIRST INHABITANTS 11

communities, and for the same reasons built their houses one, two, three, and four stories high, of mud or stone, because timber was available only for joists and rafters. In addition, the housetops, covered with mud and solid, furnished look-outs, both in times of peace and war. In the morning the men went out in the fields to work; in the meantime a portion of the people watched on the housetops, looking for enemies or game. They could see the country round about for miles, and give warning of impending danger. This method of community house building is as old as man.

The great number of ruins, deserted pueblos, single houses or small groups of houses, have produced many stories of decayed and passed-away cities and peoples in the region now occupied by the Pueblos. In the neighborhood of the existing Moqui pueblos are found many of these ruins, but the greatest number are in the region about Zuñi, to the west of Acoma, and about the Moqui pueblos in Arizona; also along the streams in southwestern Colorado, northwestern New Mexico, the Pajarito plateau, near Santa Fé, New Mexico, and in southeastern Utah.

Inspection and exploration of some of the ancient ruins are bringing to light pronounced evidence of continued occupation covering many centuries of time. Cut in the rocks in the vicinity of some are found petroglyphs representing human beings and animals in war-like attitudes. Some of the passageways and entrances to these old pueblos are hewn out of solid rock, are very tortuous, and the work was undoubtedly accomplished with the crudest of stone implements and tools.

Ruins of ancient pueblo villages and communal houses are found in the valleys of the Rio Grande, the San Juan, the Chaco, the Animas, and other northern rivers. They are also found on the Gila, and in many parts of southern Arizona and New Mexico.[5]

---
[5] Hewett, Dr. Edgar L., *Historic and Pre-historic Ruins of the Southwest*, p. 5, 1904. Dr. Hewett says: ''The distribution of the pre-historic tribes of the Southwest was determined by the drainage system. The great basins of the Rio Grande, the San Juan, the Little Colorado and the Gila constitute the four great seats of pre-historic culture of the so-called pueblo region. The remains of this ancient culture are scattered extensively over these four areas. . . The majority of the ruins of the four great basins are embraced in twenty districts.

''The districts are grouped as follows:
    I. The Rio Grande Basin:
        1. The Pajarito Park district.

12   LEADING FACTS OF NEW MEXICAN HISTORY

Almost all of the large communal houses are found on the tops of high mesas, far above the valleys. There were very many small rooms in all of these ancient edifices. The masonry varied greatly in material, sometimes being of limestone, at other times of sandstone, and often of lava rock. Each large house had its kivas, and watch-towers for defense were frequent. The walls of the buildings were from three to five feet in thickness. They were plastered with gypsum and painted with red or yellow ochre. The successive stories of the large buildings were reached by ladders. These great buildings, from their lofty sites, commanded magnificent views of the surrounding canyons. The School of American Archæology at Santa Fé, New Mexico, has lately made a systematic excavation of a ruin of one of the ancient pueblos of the Rio Grande valley, the Pu-yé. This is the second ruin in the United States to be scientifically treated with a view to its permanent preservation as a national monument.[6]

        2. The Pecos Pueblo district.
        3. The Gran Quivira district.
        4. The Jemez district.
        5. The Acoma district.
 II. The San Juan Basin:
        1. The Aztec district.
        2. The Mesa Verde district.
        3. The Chaco Canyon district.
        4. The Canyon de Chelly district.
        5. The Bluff district.
III. The Little Colorado Basin:
        1. The Tusayan district.
        2. The Flagstaff district.
        3. The Holbrook district.
        4. The Zuñi district.
IV. The Gila Basin:
        1. The Rio Verde district.
        2. The San Carlos district.
        3. The Lower Gila district.
        4. The Middle Gila district.
        5. The Upper Gila district.
        6. The San Francisco River district.''

[6] Hewett, Dr. Edgar L., *Archæology of the Rio Grande Valley*, Papers of the School of American Archæology, number 4, *The Excavations at Pu-yé, New Mexico, in 1907*:

"Pu-yé: assembling place of cotton-tail rabbits. Pu, cotton-tail rabbit; yé, to assemble, to meet. The word Pu-yé must not be confused with Puye, buck-skin.

"At first, determined opposition to the excavation of the ruins at Pu-yé was offered by the Indians from the nearest Tewa village, Santa Clara, ten miles away in the Rio Grande valley, on whose reservation the site is located. The governor, head men and representatives of the caciques, or religious rulers, were met in council and the whole matter frankly laid before them. It was ex-

Doorway of Cavate Dwelling

ORIGIN AND HISTORY OF FIRST INHABITANTS 13

"Pu-yé is one of the most extensive of the ancient 'Cliff Cities,' " says Dr. Hewett. "It occupies an imposing situation on the Pajarito plateau, ten miles west of the village of Española, and thirty miles northwest of Santa Fé." Since 1880 the place has received some attention in the writings of Powell, Bandelier, Lummis, and Hewett. Through widely published photographs its general appearance has been well known for some years, and much has been said concerning its history, based upon surface evidence and Tewa story. But here, as in archæological research all over the world, it is the spade that must be depended upon to lay bare the irrefutable record.

THE PUEBLO OF PU-YÉ

"It is not an exaggeration to speak of Pu-yé as a 'cliff city,' though it must be understood that the term 'city' does not imply anything of civic organization comparable to that of our modern municipalities. Nevertheless, there were, in the social organization that existed here, elements of collective order that characterize the civic group that we designate by the term of 'city.' There were closely-regulated community life, definite societary obligation, and in point of numbers the population was ample to constitute a modern city.

"Geologically Pu-yé is a rock of grayish-yellow tufa, 5,750 feet long, varying in width from 90 to 700 feet. It is a fragment of the great tufaceous blanket that once covered the entire Pajarito plateau to a thickness of from 50 to 1,500 feet. This covering of tufa has been completely dissected by ages of water and wind erosion. In the northern part not over ten per cent of it remains. These fragments

---

plained to them that this was our way of studying the history of the Indian tribes; that we believed that the thoughts and works of their ancestors and of the other peoples with whom they had been in contact constituted a noble record, worthy of being recovered and preserved for all time. Some appeal was made to their sense of gratitude for assistance rendered them in the past in securing from the government a much-needed and justly-deserved extension of their reservation, and a law releasing them from the payment of taxes on their lands, which at one time threatened the extinction of the titles to their homes. Bare reference was made to the fact that under the permit of the Department of the Interior we were acting entirely within our rights in making excavations upon their reservation, for it was desired to rely mostly upon their higher sentiments in the matter. I greatly regret that I am unable to reproduce the speeches of the head-men on this subject. They abounded in incisive and cogent argument which demanded unequivocal and logical answer. On the whole, their contention was on a high plane, and their deliberation marked by much lofty sentiment. It ended in all objection being withdrawn and most cordial relations established, which were afterwards expressed in a perfectly friendly attitude toward, and interest in, our work."

appear as a multitude of geological islands, some almost circular, but mostly long strips (in Spanish, *potreros*) extending east and west from the base of the Jemez mountains towards the Rio Grande. They present, on the south side, vertical escarpments rising above talus slopes that reach usually almost to the dry arroyos in the valley bottoms. The north side is always less abrupt, presenting only small escarpments and long gentle slopes to the valley. There is scant soil on the tops of these mesas, and vegetation is limited to grass, juniper, and piñon. The valleys are lightly forested with pine of not very ancient growth. The altitude is about 7,000 feet above sea-level.

"The view from the top of the rock of Pu-yé is almost beyond compare. A few miles to the west is the Jemez range, with its rounded contours and heavily forested slopes. On the eastern horizon one sees a hundred and fifty miles of the Santa Fé range, embracing the highest peaks in New Mexico. The northern extremity of the panorama lies in the state of Colorado, and at the south end, near Alburquerque, is the rounded outline of the Sandia mountain, O-kú, the 'Sacred Turtle' of Te-wa mythology. The great synclinal trough of the Rio Grande extends from north to south between the two ranges. The portion of it here seen formed a bed of a Miocene lake. The great expanse of yellowish Santa Fé marl, which the winds have piled into rounded dunes and trimmed into turreted castles, presents at all times a fantastic appearance. In the immediate foreground to the east one looks down upon the level plateau stretching far away to the valley. In the summer and fall this is variegated by masses of yellow flowers, which cover the open parks among the junipers, marking the fields of the ancient inhabitants. Beyond this lie several miles of open grass lands. To the northwest about a mile and a half the yellow rock of Shu-fin-né dominates the plain, and to the west and south lie numbers of the detached masses which I have spoken of as geological islands. Southwest about ten miles the round black bulk of Tu-yó rises from the edge of the Rio Grande valley. Here is an example of the geologically recent basaltic extrusions which characterize the Rio Grande valley from this point south through White Rock canyon. This is the historic 'Black Mesa,' the scene of many stirring events of the early period of Spanish occupation. In Te-wa mythology Tu-yó is the 'Sacred Fire Mountain.' Its top is covered with the remains of semi-subterra-

Courtesy of School of American Archæology, Santa Fé, N. M.

The South House of Pu-yé, after excavation

ORIGIN AND HISTORY OF FIRST INHABITANTS 15

nean dwellings, and fire shrines are still maintained there by the Indians of San Yldefonso.

"Pu-yé was the principal focus of a population that occupied a number of villages in the northern part of this plateau. The distribution of the outlying settlements of this group will be briefly described before considering Pu-yé itself. There are many 'small house' ruins, containing anywhere from two to fifty rooms each, scattered all over the district. The villages are for the most part found on the tops of the mesas, on almost every one of which, of any size, some house remains are found. The large settlements consisted of from one to three quadrangular pueblos, one or more small houses near by, and a village of excavated rooms in the nearest adjacent cliff wall.

"The northernmost settlement is the Shu-fin-né above mentioned. This town lay to the northwest of Pu-yé about a mile and a half, and was separated from it by the deep gorge of the Santa Clara canyon. It occupied a small tufa island, the only one north of the canyon. The rock of Shu-fin-né is a commanding feature of the landscape, being plainly visible from the Tesuque divide, just north of Santa Fé, a distance of about thirty miles. The settlement here consisted of a small pueblo on the top of the rock, and a group of houses built against the vertical wall forming the southern face of the cliff.

"On the next mesa and its adjacent valley south of the Pu-yé are three small pueblos, one on the mesa rim and two in the valley, these being the only valley pueblos of any size in this region. There is also a cliff village of several hundred excavated rooms in the rock wall. There is a lack of certainty in Te-wa tradition with reference to these ruins, but from the most reliable information obtainable, I now believe that these taken together constituted the settlement of Na-va-jú.

"In the second valley south of the great pueblo and cliff village of Pu-yé, in the Pajarito park, New Mexico, is a pueblo ruin known to the Te-wa Indians as Na-va-jú, this being, as they claim, the ancient name of the village. The ruined villages of this plateau are Te-wa of the pre-Spanish period. This particular pueblo was well situated for agriculture, there being a considerable acreage of tillable land near by, far more than this small population would have utilized. The old trail across the neck of the mesa to the north is worn hip-deep in the rock, showing constant, long continued use. I infer that these were the fields of not only the people of Na-va-jú but also of the more populous settlements beyond the great mesa to the north, where tillable land is wanting. The Te-wa Indians assert that the name 'Na-va-jú' refers to the large area of cultivated lands. This suggests an identity with Navajó, which Fray Alonzo de Benavides, in his *Memorial* on New Mexico, published in 1630, applied to that branch of the Apache nation (*Apaches de Navajó*) then living to the west of the Rio Grande beyond the very section above mentioned. Speaking of these people, Benavides says: 'But these [Apaches] of Navajó are very great farmers (*labradores*), for that [is what] Navajó signifies . . "great planted fields" ' (*sementeras grandes*).

"These facts may admit of two interpretations. So far as we know this author was the first to use the name Navajó in literature, and he would have been almost certain to have derived it from the Pueblos of New Mexico among whom he lived as Father Custodian of the Province from 1622 to 1629, since the Navajó never so designated themselves. The expression 'the Apaches of Navajó' may have been used to designate an intrusive band that had invaded Te-wa territory and become intrenched in this particular valley. On the other hand, the Navajó, since the pastoral life of post-Spanish times was not then possible to them, may have been so definitely agriculturists, as Benavides states (although he did not extend his missionary labors to them), and have occupied such areas of cultivated lands that their habitat, wherever it was, would have been known to the Te-wa as Navajó, 'the place of great planted fields.'

"On the next mesa to the south, a *potrero* several miles in length, are two groups of ruins which I now believe constituted the settlement known in Te-wa tradition as Pi-nin-i-can-gwi. The western group is composed of one quadrangle and four small-house ruins, the group occupying a space of not over a quarter of a mile in length. About half a mile to the east is the other group, consisting of one quadrangle and two small houses. All the buildings of this settlement are within a few rods of the mesa rim, and in the face of the escarpments are many excavated cliff-houses.

"Of the next settlement south, the last in the Pu-yé district, we

Courtesy of School of American Archæology, Santa Fé, N. M.

Looking out of Ceremonial Cave, Rito de los Frijoles

ORIGIN AND HISTORY OF FIRST INHABITANTS 17

have no Indian name. The great *potrero* on which the ruins are situated, and the valley to the south of it, are known by the Spanish name Chupadero. The main pueblo is a quadrangle about one hundred and twenty feet square. Near by are three small-house ruins and a reservoir. In the cliff wall below are hundreds of excavated rooms.

"The settlements above described seem to have been rather closely related. The villages are all connected by well-worn trails, some of them of unusual depth. One crosses the mesa of Pi-nin-i-can-gwi. With one exception it is the deepest worn rock trail that I have ever seen. It seems to have been made entirely by the attrition of human feet, being so situated that its depth could not be augmented by water erosion. The net-work of trails to be seen over this entire plateau is one of its most interesting archæological features. The trail is a sharply cut path, usually about eight inches wide, from a few inches to a foot in depth and in many places more. The path narrows but little toward the bottom and is remarkably clean cut. A large part of the surface of the plateau is rock devoid of soil, and these paths afford an imperishable record of ages of coming and going. The well-worn stairways are worthy of particular notice.

"The Pu-yé is a fine example of the ancient Pajaritan community. At this place is found everything that is characteristic of the Pajaritan culture; every form of house ruins, typical in construction and placement; sanctuaries, pictographs, implements, utensils, symbolic decoration, all following a well-defined order, and conforming in all essential particulars to a type of culture to which I have for present convenience given the name Pajaritan.

"The Pu-yé settlement was made up of two aggregations of dwellings: 1. The great quadrangle on the top of the mesa, an arrangement of four huge terraced community houses about a court, forming at once an effective fortress and a capacious dwelling; a compact residential fortress that might not inappropriately be called the citadel; 2. The cliff-villages, consisting of a succession of dwellings, built against and within the wall of the cliff, usually at the level where the talus slope meets the vertical escarpment. The latter will be described first. The cliff is more than a mile in length. We note here three classes of dwellings: 1. Excavated, cave-like rooms, serving as domiciles, without any form of construction in front; 2. Excavated rooms with open rooms or porches built on in front; 3. Houses of stone, one to three stories high, with corresponding number of terraces, built upon the talus against the cliff. In these groups the excavated chambers now seen in the cliff-wall were simply back rooms of the terraced buildings. An examination of the talus shows remains of the walls of several villages of considerable extent that were built upon the talus against the cliff. The row of holes in the cliff wall shows where the ceiling beams of the second story rested. The walls of the first floor rooms are to be found under the debris where the talus meets the vertical cliff. The ruins of a number of excavated back rooms are to be seen in the wall.

"All of section four of the cliff and a great part of section five is broken about mid-way of its height by a ledge which shelves back a few yards and then meets another vertical wall. On this ledge and against and within this upper wall are the remains of another succession of dwellings. These continue for a distance of 2,100 feet. This, added to the line of dwellings on the lower level, gives a continuous extent of house remains of this character about a mile and a half in length. The dwellings of this upper ledge were quite like those below. Here were the simple cave-like houses, the porched chambers, and the terraced pueblo against the cliff, with excavated back-rooms. It was possible to step from the house-tops on to the rim-rock above. In places heavy retaining walls of stone were built on the front of the ledge. Stairways cut in the face of the rock ascend from this upper ledge to the great community house on the top.

"The great community house stands near the edge of the cliff, the southwest corner approaching to within twenty feet of the brink. The huge quadrangular pile of tufa blocks gives at first the impression of great regularity of construction, but on close examination the usual irregularities of pueblo buildings are found. No two exterior walls are exactly parallel, but the orientation of the buildings is approximately with the cardinal points. The wall forming the east side of the court is on a due north and south line. The interior court is not a perfect rectangle, the north side measuring 150 feet; south, 140; east, 158; and west, 143.

"At the southeast corner is the main entrance to the square, 17

Panel by C. Lotave, Old Palace, Santa Fé, N. M.
Indians entering Cliff Kiva at Pu-yé

feet wide at the eastern end but enlarging to double that width before it opens into the court. A narrow passage, 13 feet wide, not known to exist until excavations were begun, was cleared at the southwest corner of the court, thus segregating the 'South House' of the quadrangle from the other four sides. It is probable, however, that this latter was a covered passage. It is possible that excavation will disclose other entrances to the court, but none is now visible. A low oblong mound, its longest diameter about 150 feet in length, lies just outside the main entrance. This has the appearance of neither a general refuse heap nor cemetery, though it occupies the usual position of the latter. It is composed mainly of the refuse produced by the dressing of the stone for the building. A long narrow mound of similar character almost touches the southeast corner of the pueblo.

"One subterranean sanctuary, or kiva, is found just against the outer wall of the east house, and another somewhat larger lies 165 feet slightly north of east of this one. The largest kiva on the mesa top, one apparently about 36 feet in diameter, lies 60 feet west of the southwest corner of the quadrangle. The kivas were all excavated in the rock, there being almost no covering of soil at this place. Others are found on the ledge of the cliff below, and still others in the talus.

"The ruins of an ancient reservoir lie 120 feet west of the pueblo. It is oblong in form, its short diameter being about 75 feet, and the long diameter, 130 feet. The embankment is made of stone and earth, the opening being on the west. It could not have been fed from any living source, and could have been useful only for impounding such surface water as would be conducted to it through the small draw to the west. The supply of potable water for the pueblo must have been derived from what is now the dry arroyo south of the mesa. At one point a meagre supply can still be obtained by the opening of a spring in the sand, but here, as on all parts of this plateau, a much more plentiful supply than that now existing would be absolutely essential to the maintenance of such large settlements as once existed at Pu-yé. An evidence of such supply is to be seen in the irrigation canal which may be traced for nearly two miles along the south side of the Pu-yé arroyo. This ditch heads above the mesa toward the mountain, and must have been used to conduct surface water from the mountain gulches to the level fields below, south and east of the settlements. It is possible that it was constructed during a late occupation of Pu-yé by the Santa Clara Indians, after their knowledge of irrigation had been augmented by contact with the Spaniards of the Rio Grande valley.

"One hundred and forty rooms of the great community house have been excavated by the Southwest Society of the Institute, and may be seen in practically their original condition. This comprises about three-fourths of the south house. The walls of the first floor remain standing in a good state of preservation to a height of from four to seven feet. The latter figure was probably about the height of the ceiling in the first story. That there was much irregularity in the altitude of different parts of the building is shown by the amount of fallen wall material and other debris in the rooms excavated. It is evident that there was an irregular terracing back from the rooms facing the court, and it is likely that small portions of certain terraces were four stories high.

"Large quantities of stone implements and utensils, many articles in bone, and a considerable amount of pottery were found during the excavation work. The pottery found in an apparently hopelessly shattered condition, has been made one of the choicest collections that has been excavated in the southwest. The collection is chiefly characterized by the large amount of a beautiful red ware peculiar to the Pajaritan pottery, and also by elaborate use of ornamental glazing, which was a well-developed art among the Pajaritan people in pre-Spanish times."

Among the several groups of cliff- and cave-dwellings in northern New Mexico which have been but recently brought to notice is the village named by the Pueblo Indians Tsan-ka-wi, the equivalent in the Te-wa language for the "Place of the Round Cactus."

OTHER RUINS OF THE PAJARITO PLATEAU

This remarkable ruin is located about thirty miles northwest from Santa Fé, on the Pajarito plateau. To reach Tsan-ka-wi, an hour's drive in a northeasterly direction brings one to the base of a long, irregularly shaped mesa, the sides of which are strewn with sharp-edged rocks, the volcanic tufa which prevails throughout the locality. On approaching this mesa from the west still another, but smaller, eminence is seen perched upon the larger,

Cliff Dwellings at Pu-yé

ORIGIN AND HISTORY OF FIRST INHABITANTS

probably a thousand feet from its western extremity, occupying a most commanding position and forming a natural citadel.

As one advances, the caves on the sides of the mesa, created partly by erosion and partly by human labor, become more numerous; the trail is worn in places fully one foot in depth in the solid rock. To have accomplished this the wearing process must have been carried on for a long period by a population of hundreds, perhaps thousands; in fact, two of the most remarkable features connected with these ruins are the enormous number of the dwellings and the evidence of continuous occupation for a great period of time.

Following this trail one comes to a great confusion of broken rocks, which appear to have been shaken from the sides of the upper mesa. Proceeding closer to the upper wall, the explorer is confronted by a large and most forbidding group of pictographs or petroglyphs, rock-cut pictures, representing human beings and animals in threatening attitudes, the principal figure having a substantial *macana* in its hand. There can be no question that these rude carvings, cut to a depth of an inch or more, were so placed in order to frighten enemies away from the narrow passage which is located only a few feet further on and which leads to the top of the mesa.

When one enters this passage-way the almost impregnable character of the natural citadel above becomes still more apparent. The opening is about ten feet high, two feet wide at the base and three feet at the top. Immediately after entering the cleft, a slight turn is made to one side, then several more turns in quick succession, and, after a climb of perhaps twenty feet up a gradual incline — there are no steps at this entrance — the top of the upper mesa is reached. Perhaps nowhere in the cliff-dwelling region is there a better evidence of this ancient people's capacity for well-directed, persistent labor than is afforded by this very skilfully made passage-way, hewn out of the solid rock with their crude tools — axes of granite, flint, or obsidian.

From the top of the upper mesa a most magnificent view of the great Pajarito plateau, with its valleys, mountains, and canyons, is afforded, and one is still more impressed with the appreciation of the grand and beautiful, which seems to have been second nature with these primitive peoples in the selection of sites for their dwelling places. To the west is the dark blue Jemez range of mountains;

far to the east the Santa Fé range, while much nearer may be seen portions of the Rio Grande as it flows southward to the Gulf of Mexico. The landscape in every direction is most impressive.

From the upper extremity of the passage-way a path leads to the eastward for another thousand feet along the mesa, which grows gradually narrower until it suddenly widens out and the ruins of the great pueblo are presented to the view.

The regularly hewn stones of which the houses were constructed still lie in great heaps. Very little excavation has been done in this particular ruin. When the debris has been cleared away at all, the walls are found to be standing for only a few feet above the first floor. The arrangement was in the customary quadrilateral form, with a court in the center, 150 to 200 feet across, and with outlets at two opposite corners of the enclosure.

There were probably two hundred rooms on the ground floor; adding two floors above this, each somewhat smaller than the one beneath, would make a structure of perhaps four hundred rooms. Fragments of pottery and arrow-heads are easily found in the ruins, particularly in the vicinity of the graves, some of which have been opened in recent years.

NA-VA-WI AND OT-O-WI Other interesting ruins in this vicinity are those of the ancient communal houses, Na-va-wi and Ot-o-wi. The former is one and one-half miles to the south, and the latter two miles to the west of Tsan-ka-wi. A few miles further is the Pajarito or Tsch-i-re-ge (Little Bird) ruin. There is no doubt that in pre-historic times throughout this region, which is now almost entirely uninhabited, could be seen a very numerous population industriously engaged in the common occupation, agriculture, in which some skill is evidenced by the finding of the remains of irrigating ditches and reservoirs.[7]

The capacity of these communal houses, so far as habitation is concerned, was in some instances as high as fifteen hundred, but, as a general rule, five hundred was the limit. The pueblo of Hungo Pavie, one of the smallest of the ancient pueblos, in the Chaco canyon, was three hundred feet long, one hundred and forty-four feet wide, and three stories high. The walls of Hungo Pavie were built of

---

[7] *National Geographic Magazine*, September, 1909.

Courtesy of School of American Archaeology, Santa Fé, N. M.

Alcoves in Cliff, originally forming back rooms of Talus Pueblo

ORIGIN AND HISTORY OF FIRST INHABITANTS 23

sandstone laid with adobe mortar. In it were one hundred and forty-six apartments, and the building probably accommodated five hundred people.

During the administration of Colonel J. M. Washington, commander of the Ninth Military Department, New Mexico, in 1849, a campaign against the Navajós was undertaken. The course taken by the army in this reconnoissance proceeded by way of the Jemez pueblo, thence by the Chaco river into the Navajó country.[8]

PUEBLOS PINTADO AND BONITO

The historian of this expedition says: [9]

"We found the ruins of the Pueblo Pintado to more than answer our expectations. Forming one structure and built of tabular pieces of hard, fine-grained, compact, gray sand-stone (a material entirely unknown in the present architecture of New Mexico), to which the atmosphere has imparted a reddish tinge, the layers or beds being not thicker than three inches, and sometimes as thin as one-fourth of an inch, it discovers in the masonry a combination of science and art which can only be referred to a higher stage of civilization and refinement than is discoverable in the works of the Mexicans or Pueblos of today. Indeed, so beautifully diminutive and true are the details of the structure as to cause it, at a little distance, to have all the appearance of a magnificent piece of mosaic work.

"In the outer surface of the buildings there are no signs of mortar, the intervals between the beds being chinked with stones of the minutest thinness. The filling and backing are done in rubble masonry, the mortar presenting no indications of lime. The thickness of the main wall at its base is within an inch or two of three feet; higher up it is less, diminishing every story by retreating jogs on the inside, from the bottom to the top. Its elevation at its present highest point is between twenty-five and thirty feet, the series of floor beams indicating that there must have been originally at least three stories. The ground plan, including the court, is about 403 feet. On the ground floor, exclusive of the out-buildings, are fifty-four apartments, some of them as small as five feet square, and the largest about twelve by six feet. These rooms communicate with each other by very small doors, some of them as contracted as

---
[8] Orders for the movement of the troops under Col. Washington were issued August 14, 1849. The command consisted of four companies of the 3rd Infantry, Colonel Alexander; two companies of the 2nd Artillery, Major Kendrick; and one company — mounted — of volunteers. — *Report of an Expedition into the Navajó Country*, Lieut. Simpson, 1850.

[9] Simpson, Lieut. J. H., *Ibid.*

two and a half by two and a half feet. And in the case of the inner suite, the doors communicating with the inner court are as small as three and a half by two feet. The principal rooms, or those most in use, were, on account of their having larger doors and windows, most probably those of the second story. The system of flooring seems to have been large unhewn beams, six inches in diameter, laid transversely from wall to wall, and then a number of smaller ones, about three inches in diameter, laid across them. What was placed on these does not appear, but most probably it was brush, bark or slabs, covered with a layer of mud mortar.

"The beams show no sign of the saw or ax; on the contrary, they appear to have been hacked off by means of some very imperfect instrument. On the west face of the structure the windows, which are only in the second story, are three feet two inches by two feet two inches. On the north side they are only in the second and third stories, and are as small as fourteen by fourteen inches. At different points about the premises were three circular apartments sunk in the ground, the walls being of masonry. These apartments the Pueblos call *estufas*, or places where the people held their political and religious meetings.

"The quarry from which the material was obtained to build the structure seems to have been just back of our camp.

"We came to another old ruin, thirteen miles from our last camp, called We-je-gi, built like the Pueblo Pintado, of very thin, tabular pieces of compact sand-stone. The circuit of the structure, including the court, was near 700 feet. The number of apartments on the ground floor was probably ninety-nine. The highest present elevation of the exterior wall is about twenty-four feet."

Of the Pueblo Bonito, which was also visited by Lieutenant Simpson, he says:

"The circuit of its walls is about 1,300 feet. Its present elevation shows that it had at least four stories of apartments. The number of rooms on the ground floor at present discernible is 139. The apartments in the east portion of the pueblo, not included in this enumeration, would probably swell the number to 200."

Lieutenant Simpson estimates that the four stories, with retreating terraces, had as many as 641 rooms.

"The number of *estufas* is four; the largest being sixty feet in diameter, showing two stories in height, and having a present depth of twelve feet. All these *estufas* are cylindrical in shape, and nicely walled up with thin, tabular stone. Among the ruins are several rooms in a very good state of preservation."

The ruin of the pueblo of Ot-o-wi lies about five miles west of the

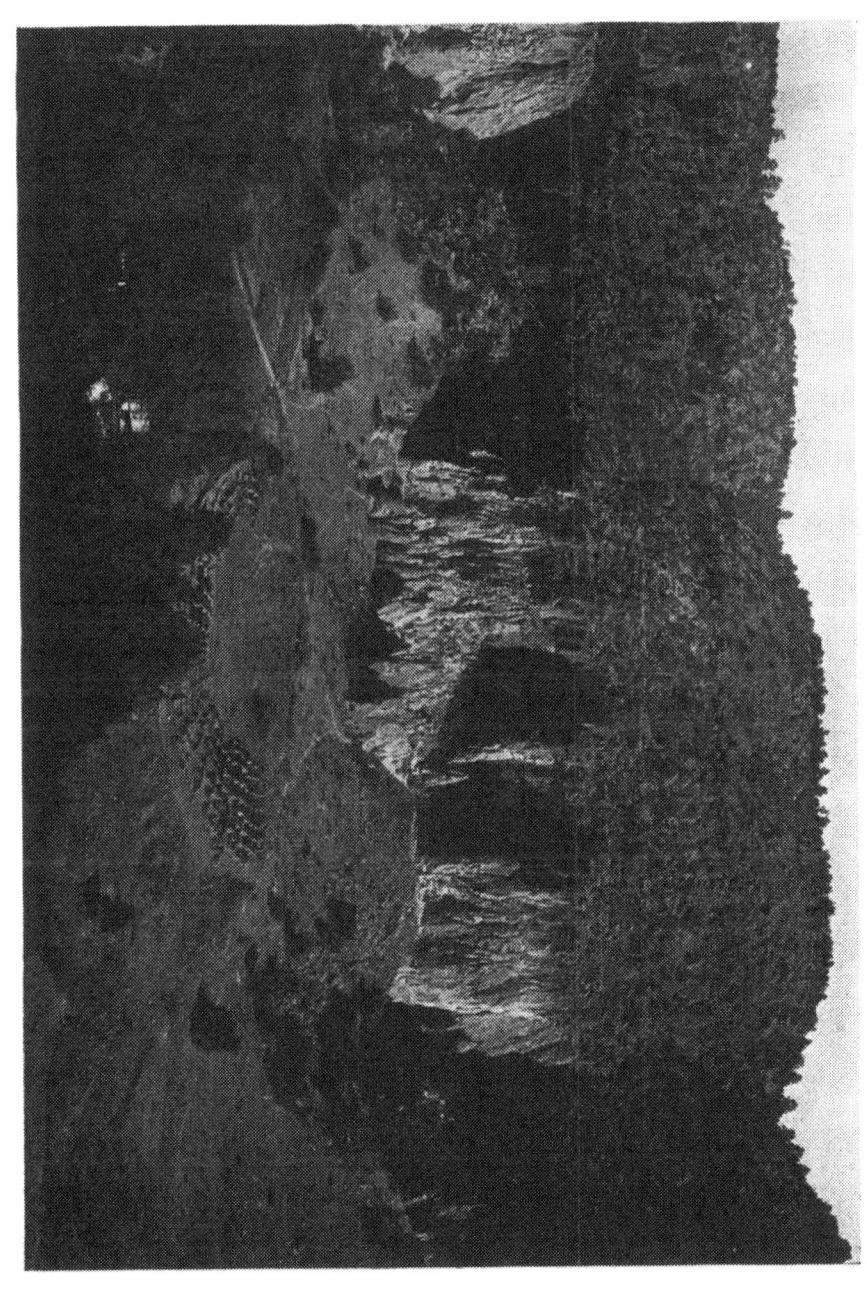

Courtesy of School of American Archæology, Santa Fé, N. M.

Excavations — Pueblo of Ty-u-on-yi — Rito de los Frijoles

ORIGIN AND HISTORY OF FIRST INHABITANTS 25

point where the Rio Grande enters White Rock canyon. The ruin is reached by following up the Alamo canyon from its confluence with the Guages. The top of the mesa is reached at the head of that part of the Alamo canyon known as the Black Gorge. The first canyon entering the Alamo from the north above this point is known as the Ot-o-wi. Following this up about two miles a point is reached where the long, narrow *potrero* bounding the canyon on the north is entirely shut out for a distance of nearly a mile, thus throwing into a squarish open park the width of the two small canyons and the formerly intervening mesa. From the midst of this little park, roughly a mile square, a view of surpassing beauty is to be had. Half a mile to the south the huge mesa which is terminated by Rincon del Pueblo bounds the valley with a high unbroken line, perhaps five hundred feet above the dry arroyo at the bottom. The same distance to the north is the equally high and abrupt Ot-o-wi mesa, and east and west, an equal distance and to about an equal height, rise the wedge-like terminal buttes which define this great gap in the middle of the mesa. Toward the four corners one looks into the beautifully wooded gorges. The entire area is well forested.

The parallel canyons running through this glade are prevented from forming a confluence by a high ridge, the remnant of the intervening mesa. Upon the high point of this ridge is located a large pueblo ruin which formed the nucleus of the Ot-o-wi settlement. In every direction are clusters of excavated cliff-dwellings of contemporaneous occupation, and on a parallel ridge to the south are the ruins of one pueblo of considerable size and seven small ones, all ante-dating the Ot-o-wi settlement.[10]

Two types of excavated cliff-dwellings are found at Ot-o-wi. The first is the open-front dwelling, usually, though not always, single-chambered, in most cases a natural cave enlarged and shaped by excavation.

The second type is wholly artificial, with closed front of the natural rock in situ. Cliff-dwellings of this type are usually multiple chambered, with floors below the level of the threshold; they have generally a crude fire-place beside the doorway, but are seldom provided with smoke-vents. The rooms are commonly rectan-

---

[10] Hewett, Dr. Edgar L., *Antiquities of the Jemez Plateau*, Bul. 32, B. A. E., p. 18, 1906.

gular and well-shaped, with floors plastered always, and walls usually so, to the height of three or four feet. The front walls are from one to two feet thick. In some cases a little masonry has been used in the form of casings about the doorways. In a number of instances, the porches were built over the doorways, but nowhere were complete houses built against the cliffs, as Tsh-i-re-ge.

For the most part the dwellings are found in clusters and at two general levels, that is, at the top of the long, steep slope of the talus, and again in the face of a second terrace far above the talus and exceedingly difficult of access.

From about half a mile to a mile above the main pueblo of Ot-o-wi is a cliff village that is unique. Here is a cluster of conical formation of white tufa, some of which attain a height of thirty feet. These are popularly called "Tent Rocks." They are full of caves, both natural and artificial, some of which have been utilized as human habitations. These dwellings are structurally identical with those found in the cliffs. They present the appearance of enormous bee-hives.

The main pueblo ruin of Ot-o-wi differs in plan from any other in this region. It consists of a cluster of five houses, situated on a sloping ground and connected at one end by a wall. These were terraced structures, probably almost an exact counterpart of the present terraced houses of Taos, though, perhaps, somewhat smaller and containing a less number of stories. No one of the houses at Ot-o-wi had more than four stories and none fewer than two. Altogether the five houses contained about four hundred and fifty rooms on the ground floor. The number of superimposed rooms is largely a matter of conjecture but they may safely be estimated at two hundred and fifty, making a total of about seven hundred rooms.

There were ten circular kivas at Ot-o-wi, all subterranean and outside of the walls of the building, with two exceptions. Kivas within the pueblo walls were unusual in the pueblos of the Pajarito plateau. They exist in the great ruin at the base of Pedernal Peak, and are found also in the older and smaller houses.

A reservoir, which doubtless supplied water for drinking purposes at times, was placed, as was often the case in both ancient and modern pueblos, so as to receive the drainage from the village.

The traditions of Ot-o-wi are fairly well preserved. It was the

Courtesy of School of American Archæology, Santa Fé, N. M.

Talus Villages, Cliff of Ty-u-on-yi

ORIGIN AND HISTORY OF FIRST INHABITANTS 27

oldest village of Pow-ho-ge clans, of which they have definite traditions at San Yldefonso. They hold, in an indefinite way, that prior to the building of this village they occupied scattered "small house" ruins on the adjacent mesa, and they claim that when the mesa life grew unbearable from the lack of water, and removal to the valley became a necessity, a detachment from the Ot-o-wi founded the pueblo of Pe-ra-ge in the valley on the west side of the Rio Grande, about a mile west of their present village site.[11]

There were three principal centers of population situate upon the Pajarito plateau: the Pu-yé, the Pajarito, and the Rito de los Frijoles. Beyond doubt there was some

THE PAJARITAN CULTURE relationship between the inhabitants of these three communities, but just what degree remains to be established. There were certain common characteristics, but it does not follow that they spoke the same language.[12]

---
[11] Hewett, Dr. Edgar L., *Antiquities of the Jemez Plateau*, Bul. 32, B. A. E., p. 18.

Dr. Edgar L. Hewett gave the name to the plateau lying between the Jemez mountains and the Rio Grande and extending from the Chama valley to the Cañada de Cochití. It was largely through his untiring energy that the region was set aside as a national park. In giving it the name of Pajarito plateau the central geographical feature of the area was chosen — the Pajarito canyon — Spanish *pajarito*, a little bird.

The pioneer explorations made in this region were those of Adolph F. Bandelier, but even the scientific work of that noted archæologist in this locality is small when compared with the extensive excavations, scientific study, and investigation given by Dr. Hewett. The Te-wa name, Tch-i-re-ge, the place of the Bird people, is applied to a "cliff city" on the northern rim of the Pajarito canyon. These ruins are still more extensive than those of Pu-yé, and, in all of these, extensive excavation has been done under the direction of Dr. Hewett. His investigations made known a new region and a culture for which a more definite term than "Pueblo," or "Ancient Pueblo," or "Ancient Te-wa" became imperatively necessary. Dr. Hewett does not give assent to the heretofore generally accepted statement that the present Pueblo Indians are the descendants of the ancient cliff-dwellers. He insists that there is a general non-conformity between Te-wa symbolism and Pajaritan symbolism; that they differ in physical types, the ancient inhabitants of the Pu-yé and other pueblo houses and dwellings of this region having been a homogeneous people of dolicocephalic type, while the Te-wa, and all other Pueblos, are non-homogeneous and predominantly brachycephalic. He has given great thought and study to the traditions of the present inhabitants of the valley of the Rio Grande, immediately adjacent to these old sites, and finds that these do not support the hypothesis of identity. For these reasons, which certainly seem to warrant the conclusion, Dr. Hewett has established a culture which, from the community on which the type is based, he has designated as Pajaritan.

[12] Hewett, Dr. Edgar L., *The Pajaritan Culture*, Papers of the School of American Archæology, number 3: "These groups afford exceptional facilities

There is both archæological and physiographic evidence that the earliest inhabitants of this region arrived at a time when climatic conditions were radically different from those of the present day. The proof of slow, progressive desiccation of the Southwest is abundant. This plateau has not been inhabited for ages on account of the almost total lack of water. The great communities, representing the last stages of habitation, clustered about the gradually failing springs. The earlier "small house" communities were found everywhere, indicating a general climatic condition favorable to agriculture.[13]

This diffusion of population would seem to imply a social organization different from that existing among the people of the great community houses, where the system was the prototype of the modern pueblo. Such, however, is not the case. In the dispersed "small house" communities there were fully developed the basic principles of tribal structure that govern in Pueblo organization today.[14]

for the study of the development of culture through a long period of time. The geographical isolation was such as to induce definite, homogeneous development. That this isolation was well preserved is shown in the homogeneity of both the physical type and the cultural remains. In the art of the Pajaritans we may read several centuries of their history. It is entirely pre-Spanish, the excavations having never yet yielded a vestige of European influence, and so distinctly does it reflect the civilization in which it was produced that a specimen of pottery from this region is as unmistakable to the trained eye as is anything Greek, Etruscan, or Egyptian.

"It would seem that some ancient culture wave, traversing the Rio Grande valley in very remote times, must have thrown off detachments which lodged upon this plateau. The cause of the unique localization of these bands is not at first thought clear. It is unlikely that motives of defense directed the choice, as would at first seem obvious, for much evidence tends to show that the modern predatory tribes, Navajó, Apache, and Ute, arrived in the Southwest in comparatively modern times. The construction of the great defensive community houses of the Pajaritans belongs to the latest epoch of their history. For a long period they were dispersed over the plateau. This was the epoch of the 'small houses' of which several thousand have been counted in this region."

[13] Hewett, Dr. Edgar L., *Ibid.*: "The reason for selection of this plateau as a place of residence by those early bands that first settled here was simply that in those times this now desiccated table-land afforded more favorable conditions for subsistence than did the adjacent valley of the Rio Grande; a condition now reversed."

[14] Hewett, Dr. Edgar L., *Ibid.*: "There was lacking only the element of dual organization, a social phenomenon that attended the coming together of numerous clans into great communities. This fact of genetic aggregation persists among the Pueblos today. In the 'small house' communities the groupal unit was the clan. The basic social fact was the matriarchal system, by virtue of which all domestic authority resided in the mother. The fundamental fact of

Courtesy of School of American Archæology, Santa Fé, N. M.

Tent Rocks near Ot-o-wi

ORIGIN AND HISTORY OF FIRST INHABITANTS 29

The study of the subterranean sanctuary of these pre-historic peoples is of great interest. It was the nucleus of the settlement. In some places, even though there remain only the ruins of two or three rooms, the kiva is ever present. It was the germ of every community. The first act on the part of a clan, determining its place of abode, was to build the kiva, and around this were subsequently constructed the rooms in which the members of the clan lived. All over the Pajarito plateau, wherever the small community houses are found, there also is discovered the kiva. With the formation of the great communities a new feature of tribal organization was developed. This was the dual hierarchy, and with this came the dual kiva system, the common sanctuary for each division of the tribe. In it was centered all that was vital to the life and happiness of the people. It was the place of silence, the sanctuary to which those charged with the sacerdotal functions of the clan retired for thought, for prayer, for offering, and for sacrifice.[15] In the kiva of the Rio Grande clans and the observances clustering about it are symbolized the Pueblo conception of human birth, the origin of life, and the ordering of human conduct.

The arts of the residents of the Pajarito plateau were identical

---

the religious order in the modern Pueblos is the dual hierarchy, by virtue of which the sacerdotal authority is lodged in two priests, the *Summer Cacique* and the *Winter Cacique*, who have charge of the ceremonials of their respective seasons. This developed along with the movement toward close community aggregation. But that the basic elements of it existed in the 'small house' communities is disclosed in the house remains. The structural germ of every community house was the *kiva*, the circular subterranean room that is found in conjunction with all the community houses, small and great, of the Rio Grande and the San Juan valleys. This was the clan sanctuary, the place set aside, before the first stone of the dwelling was laid, for prayer and religious ceremony.''

[15] Hewett, Dr. Edgar L., *Ibid.*: ''The kiva was the place for the performance of secret religious rites and preparation for public ceremonials. In gathering about the Si-pa-pu, men again approached the Earth Mother; they sought the channels of ancient wisdom; they were at the portal whence life itself emerged.

''According to the Pueblo priests of today it is not quite correct to speak of the Si-pa-pu as symbolizing the entrance to the underworld.

''In Pueblo organization today, the clan kiva has almost disappeared. It still remains at Taos, but at San Juan, Santa Clara, San Yldefonso, Nambé, and Cochití only tribal kivas remain. There are the kiva of the *Summer People* and the kiva of the *Winter People*. In some cases one of these is subterranean or semi-subterranean, the other wholly above ground. The religious functions of the tribe are in the hands of two priests, the *Summer Cacique* and the *Winter Cacique*. Each one has charge of the ceremonials pertaining to his season, and each one officiates in the sanctuary pertaining to that division. The history and meaning of this dual organization are not yet fully known.''

with those of the other sedentary tribes of the Southwest. They were pottery makers, and in this their only unusual achievement seems to have been in the use of glazing in ornamentation. Upon almost all of the beautiful red and brown pieces of pottery which have been recovered at Pu-yé, Ot-o-wi, and Ty-u-on-yi, the black lines on the vessels are covered with a vitreous coating, which chemical analysis proves to be true glazing.[16]

It cannot be said that the ancient dwellers upon the Pajarito plateau were the immediate ancestors of the tribes now living in the Rio Grande valley. That there was relationship is not questioned, but the degree of relationship is yet to be determined. It is the theory of absolute identity that is not entirely accepted. This general theory concerning the ancestry of the Pueblos was first announced by no less authority than Major J. W. Powell, and for many years was accepted as conclusive. It was based upon facts

---

[16] Hewett, Dr. Edgar L., *Ibid.*: "The process of glazing, as practised by the Pajaritans, was very simple. After the vessel had been decorated and fired in the usual manner, a saturated solution of salt water was laid on over the ornament and the vessel again fired under as great a degree of heat as they were able to produce in their primitive kiln. The soda of the solution combining with the silica of the clay produced over the design, and over all surfaces on which the solution might have been spread, a true, transparent glaze which could never scale or peel off without taking with it the clay of the vessel itself to the full depth to which the salt water had penetrated. The spreading of the solution and the occurrence of oxides in the clay produced beautiful accidental effects, particularly the rich iridescent tints found on the pottery at Pu-yé and Ty-u-on-yi.

"Glazing was practised to some extent in the valley of the Little Colorado but the art was probably carried there in the course of migrations from the Rio Grande drainage. It is of quite an inferior order. In fact, nowhere else on the American continent was the art of glazing so well understood as in this region. It was long held, and may still be held by some American archæologists, that the art of glazing was not indigenous to America, and that wherever found it is an indication of European influence. In fact, by some it has been called the Spanish glaze. We have shown the contrary to be true. It was practised on the plateau west of the Rio Grande for centuries prior to the advent of the Spaniards, and ceased to be practised during the upheaval that occurred with the coming of the conquerors. The art is unknown to the modern Pueblos, is never seen in the specimens of archaic pottery, sacred vessels, and heir-looms that have been handed down among them for many generations, and is not to be found in the refuse heap of their villages which go back over almost the entire historical period. On the other hand it occurs profusely in all the ruins on the western plateau, where no vestige of European influence has ever been found, sites which if occupied at the time of the conquest could not have escaped mention in the ecclesiastical records. It may then be safely affirmed that decorative glazing was an indigenous American art, and I should be inclined to consider the plateaus of the Rio Grande drainage as the place of its origin."

ORIGIN AND HISTORY OF FIRST INHABITANTS 31

of similarity in culture and upon the statements of the living Indians.[17]

The system of symbolism of the Pajaritans was dominated by one definite idea. The prevailing motive throughout all their decoration

[17] Hewett, Dr. Edgar L., *Ibid.*: "My reasons for the rejection of this theory are: First, the symbols with which the ancient people of Pajarito decorated their pottery were entirely different from those of the Pueblos of the present day. This fact was pointed out by me and supported by a large series of illustrations in a paper read before Section H of the American Association for the Advancement of Science, at Washington, in 1902.

"The most convincing testimony on the subject of the non-identity of the Pajaritans with the modern Pueblos is that of their physical characters. The skeletal remains that have been collected, in one case as many as 125 subjects from a single burial place, have been examined by Doctor Herdlicka, and in a preliminary statement he pronounces the ancient Pajaritan people to have been of rather inferior muscular development and of the dolicocephalic type; moreover, a homogeneous people, unmixed in physical characteristics. On the same authority modern Pueblos are predominantly a brachycephalic people. This nonconformity of physical type seems to destroy the hypothesis of identity between the ancient cliff-dwelling people of this region, whom I have called Pajaritans, and the modern Pueblos.

"The evidence on which the hypothesis of identity was mainly based was the testimony of the Pueblo Indians themselves. For example, the Keres of Cochití have always claimed the Rito de los Frijoles as one of their ancestral homes, and the Te-wa of Santa Clara have in like manner laid claim to the ruined towns of Pu-yé. The claim of the latter village was taken for thorough consideration. For over a quarter of a century these Indians have consistently claimed the cliff-dwellings and community homes of Pu-yé as the homes of their ancestors. During this period the Pueblo of Santa Clara has had pending in the courts a claim against the government of the United States for a large tract of land, about 90,000 acres, lying west of their grant and extending to the top of the Jemez range. The basis of the claim was an alleged Spanish grant, and in the support of such documentary proof as could be adduced, their ancient homes scattered over the plateau, particularly the Pu-yé villages, were pointed out.

"This tradition certainly came to be believed in good faith by a majority of the tribe. It was a stock argument in pointing out the injustice of the court in granting them a strip of less than 500 acres along Santa Clara creek in lieu of the large tract claimed by them. This case was recently settled by the setting aside of the original claim and granting in lieu thereof of a new reservation embracing something near half of the tract originally claimed. Since the favorable issue of their suit the old men of Santa Clara are losing their fear that the admission of their exact relationship with the people of Pu-yé will prejudice their claim.

"In a council held with the head men in August, 1907, to consider their opposition to my making excavations at Pu-yé, what I believe to be the exact truth of the matter came out. They do not contend that their people, in their present organization as a village group, were the original builders of the cliff-dwellings and community houses of Pu-yé. They hold consistently to the tradition of a re-occupation of the cliff houses and of some rooms in the great community house by the Santa Clara people during the troublous times of the Spanish invasion. It is possible that after the Pueblo rebellion of 1680, some Santa Clara families lived for a while in the cliff-houses. This could have been but a temporary and limited occupation. The acculturation resulting from contact with

was that of the A-wan-yu. This was the emblem of a mythic power. A-wan-yu was the preserver of water, the guardian of springs and streams, the preserver of life itself, for without water, crops, food, life must fail. The history of the last epoch of the occupation of the Pajarito plateau is one of unceasing struggle against failing nature. Subsistence became constantly more and more uncertain. It was just the condition necessary to the development of ritual and the elaboration of symbolism. It was an ever present fear and thought with the people, and on all their pottery we find the idea perpetuated. In Te-wa tradition there is the belief that the Pajaritans disappeared because they lost favor with A-wan-yu; that he threw himself across the sky, thus accounting to the Indian mind for the origin of the Milky Way.

The ancient cycle of Pajaritan mythology is entirely broken down, and the merest fragments can be recovered from a few of the old men of the different villages. It has been submerged by the more vital mythology of a more recent epoch. The dominant religious symbol of the Pueblos of the present day, seen on all their prayer meal bowls and etched upon the rocks, is the plumed serpent called by them A-wan-yu, but never confused with the A-wan-yu of the ancients. It is a representative figure in reptilian form, furnished with plumes upon head and body, pictured as moving through the

---

European civilization could hardly have failed to manifest itself by that time in their utensils and in decorative motive. The excavations at Pu-yé have as yet yielded no vestige of such influence. It is possible that the irrigating ditch along the south side of the Pu-yé arroyo may belong to this late period. It seems likely that searching investigation of the Pueblo claims with reference to ancient sites will usually result as this case does.

"It is certainly true that some clans in almost every modern Pueblo village trace their origin to the people of the cliffs in a perfectly consistent line, and this would account for the dolicocephalic strain found among all the Pueblos of the Southwest. They are uniformly a composite stock, formed doubtless by the amalgamation of people from the cliffs with incoming bands from outlying regions."

Harrington, John P., *Phonetic and Lexic Resemblance between Kiowan and Tanoan*, Papers of the School of American Archæology, 1910, q. v. Certain phonetic and lexic affinities between Kiowan, Tanoan, and also Shoshonean have been pointed out by Buschmann, Gatschet, and others. In examining the Kiowa vocabulary obtained by Mr. James Mooney and published in the *17th Annual Report of the Bureau of American Ethnology*, part i, pages 391-440, the writer notes to his surprise how strong these Kiowan-Tanoan similarities are. Should it be finally proved that these two "stocks" are really related, either genetically or by mixing, the conclusions would be most interesting, since history traces the migrations of the Kiowa from their former homeland at the headwaters of the Missouri river, while the Tanoans are in every respect a typical Pueblo people.

Courtesy of School of American Archæology, Santa Fé, N. M.
Rock Trail at Tsan-ka-wi

ORIGIN AND HISTORY OF FIRST INHABITANTS 33

air and often drawn with great vigor. It is a symbol that is widely distributed over the American continent, and the being which it represents was doubtless one of the principal deities of the ancient Mexicans. Nowhere else has it been used on so magnificent a scale and with such remarkable effect as a decorative motive as upon the Aztec temple of Xochilcalco, near Cuernavaca, in Mexico. In this connection a myth of the Tlauicas, a branch of the Aztec stock inhabiting Cuernavaca valley, with reference to a mythic power represented by them in serpent form and now seen in the Milky Way, is significant.

It is not to be supposed that the disappearance of this plateau population was due to any catastrophic character. Certain evidences of seismic activity have been observed in this region, but there is nothing to indicate that the dispersion of the people was due to earthquake shocks. There is nothing to indicate any general, sudden exodus, but rather a gradual abandonment of the towns, as the springs and streams dried up and the sites became untenable and the farms worthless because of the failure of the supply of water.

We have as yet no means of knowing to what distance the detachments that migrated from time to time from this plateau may have wandered. We find remnants of them at Hopi and in the villages of the Rio Grande valley, but these small bands do not account for the large numbers that must have at one time occupied the Pajarito plateau. Among the people nearest in physical type to those called Pajaritans are the Tarahumares,[18] a forest people living along the

---

[18] Bandelier, Adolph F., *Investigations among the Indians of the Southwestern United States*, Final Report, part i, p. 98: "The Tarahumares, owing to the nature of the country which they inhabited and to the constant danger to which they were exposed, were in many places cave-dwellers. They lived in natural cavities, as well as in open air dwellings of mud, stone, or wood. These caves they partitioned to suit their convenience; whole families, even small villages, occupying such troglodytan recesses. If the verbal information imparted to me lately is correct, the Tarahumares are, at the present time, in a few secluded localities, still the cave-dwellers of the American continent. The fact that the Tarahumares dwelt at least partly in caves cannot be doubted. Cave-dwelling, on the whole, seems to have been quite common in the mountains of Chihuahua, in those of Sonora bordering on Chihuahua, and in Sinaloa. In the *Libro de Entierros de la Mision de Bacadehuachi*, 1655, it is mentioned that the Janos and Jocomes used to surprise and kill the people of the Sierra Madre in their cave-dwellings. In many places of the Sierra, the formation of rocks favors the existence of

crest of the Sierra Madre and in the barrancas of the Pacific slope in southern Chihuahua and Sinaloa. Also among the California tribes are found those who conform rather closely in physical type to the ancient cliff-dwellers of the Pajarito plateau.

Most remarkable for its antiquities is that section known as the Rito de los Frijoles. From the Pajarito mesa one looks down into the Rito as into a narrow valley. The lower five miles of the Rito are replete with archæological interest. A never-failing streamlet coming from the Jemez mountains carries its waters to the Rio Grande. The former populous condition of this region is attested by the myriad remains of cliff-houses and ancient pueblos that occupy every valley and mesa-top from the Chama river to the Cochití and between the Jemez mountains and the Rio Grande. The northern wall of the Rito is a vertical escarpment of from 200 to 300 feet in height, rising above a sloping talus. The slope of the southern wall is more gentle, and presents none of the vertical escarpments seen on the northern wall.

CAVATE DWELLINGS OF THE RITO DE LOS FRIJOLES

The ancient remains in the Rito consist of four community houses in the valley and one on the mesa rim near the southern brink of the canyon, and a series of cliff-houses extending for a distance of a mile and a quarter along the base of the northern wall. These cliff-houses are of the excavated type. Some of these excavated

natural cavities, therefore ancient cave houses and whole cave pueblos are of common occurrence.

"In regard to the creed and beliefs of the Tarahumares, little is reliably ascertained. We might judge from what is known of the Tepehuanes, who, in addition to being their near neighbors, spoke a kindred language. It is certain that witchcraft played an important part with them. Drunkenness was among them too.

"On the whole the Tarahumares were a numerous, scattered, and quite docile tribe. At the instigation of the Tepehuanes, Tobosos, and of some of their own sorcerers or medicine-men, they rose upon the missionaries several times during the seventeenth century and behaved with as much cruelty as any other Indians. Otherwise they were quiet, and tilled their plots of land, raising the usual kind of crops.

"The oldest census of the Tarahumares, for instance, which is at my command dates back in 1678. There are certainly older ones, and even this one embraces only such Indians as had become Christians. It is found in the *Relacion de las Misiones*, by P. Juan Ortiz Zapata, S. J. According to it the number of persons administered by the Jesuits in the districts of western Chihuahua, almost exclusively Tarahumares, with but a few Tepehuanes and Conchos, was about 8,300."

1. Mr. Frederick W. Hodge, Ethnologist
2. Mr. Adolph F. Bandelier, Ethnologist, Archæologist, Historian
3. Dr. Edgar L. Hewett, Archæologist
4. Major John W. Powell, Naturalist

ORIGIN AND HISTORY OF FIRST INHABITANTS 35

rooms have been used as domiciles independently of any construction upon the talus against the cliff, but through the entire Pajarito region, where this type of cliff-dwelling culture reaches its culmination, the excavated rooms were not generally used as independent domiciles.[19]

Thirteen talus villages have been identified in the Rito de los Frijoles, and sufficient excavation has been done to lay bare foundation walls establishing the existence of houses of from two to four terraces built against the cliff. Nowhere else are the evidences of the existence of the talus pueblos so well preserved as in the Rito. Here we see not only the rows of holes in which rested the floor and ceiling timbers of the building, but in many cases the plaster is still upon the rock which formed the back wall of the house in front. Of the thirteen talus pueblos which have been found in the Rito some contained, perhaps, not to exceed twenty to twenty-five rooms.

The principal focus of population in the Rito was the great com-

---

[19] Hewett, Dr. Edgar L., *Excavations at Tyuonyi, New Mexico*, in 1908.

Bandelier, Adolph F., *Papers of the Archæological Institute of America*, American Series, iv, Final Report, part ii, p. 139, 1892. In his description of the archæological treasures of the Rito, Bandelier, who has been termed the "Pausanias of the Rio Grande Valley" in archæological research, says: "Seen from the brink of the southern mesa, the view of the Rito is surprisingly picturesque. The effect is heightened by the appearance of a great number of little door-ways along the foot of the cliffs, irregularly alternating with larger cavities, indicating caves, the fronts of which have partially or completely crumbled away. The base of the cliff rises and falls, so that the line of caves appears to be at different elevations and not continuous. There are spaces where the rock has not been burrowed into; in some places two, in others three tiers of caves are visible. The whole length of this village of troglodytes is about two miles, rather more than less. The cave dwellings of the Rito are so much like those of the Pu-yé and Shu-fin-né that they scarcely need description; the differences are purely local and accidental. As in the Te-wa country, they have artificial floors and are whitewashed or daubed over with yellow clay. There are the same types of door-ways, air-holes and possibly loop-holes; the same kind of niches and recesses, but the cave-dwellings at the Rito are the most perfect seen by me anywhere. I measured nearly every cave through the whole length of the canyon as far as traces of former habitations extended. . . Against such of the cliffs as rise vertically and the surface of which is almost smooth, terraced houses were built, using the rock for a rear wall. Not only are the holes visible in which the ends of the beams rested that supported roofs and ceilings, but in one or two places portions of beams still protruded. They were round and of the usual size. Along the base of these cliffs extends an apron, which was once approximately leveled, and on this apron the foundations of the walls appear in places. It would seem that a row of houses, one, two and even three stories high, leaning against the cliff had been built; sometimes the upper story consisted of a cave, the lower of a building.

"Chambers nearly circular, larger in size than the majority of caves, are also found in the cliffs, some of which have a low projection around the room like a

munity house of Ty-u-on-yi. This was a terraced structure, roughly circular in form. It was built of blocks of volcanic tufa, and in all probability it was a three-story pueblo. The building was of greater regularity of construction than is usually the case with the community houses. It has the appearance of having been built completely and not to have grown by gradual accretions. The walls are curving and were not produced by a simple change of the direction of the wall from room to room. The walls form curved lines.

THE PUEBLO OF TYUONYI

The thinnest part of the walls of Ty-u-on-yi was at the southwest. They are much thinner than those of the Pu-yé or Tch-i-re-ge; they are not so well laid nor so well plastered. The form of the building was well calculated for defense. The living rooms were entered from the inner court by means of ladders ascending to the roofs, and then through hatchways and by ladders descending into the interior. The court was undoubtedly entered by a single passage-way on the eastern side. This passage-way is about seven feet wide, the side walls being plastered with mud.

One of the most interesting features of the archæological remains in the Rito is the kivas, the circular subterranean chambers which are known to have been the tribal sanctuaries. Three of these ceremonial rooms are found within the court of Ty-u-on-yi. Not far from the pueblo has been excavated a very large kiva. It was long considered as a reservoir. It is a circular room about forty-two feet in diameter, lined with a double wall of tufa blocks. On the

---

bench of stone. These were doubtless *estufas* (*kivas*) as I was told by one of the Indians who accompanied me to the spot. There is a distinct *estufa* not far from the bank of the brook opposite these caves situated in the upper portion of the valley, and a smaller one still higher up. Including the four *estufas* connected with the pueblo ruin . . . I noticed at least ten such constructions at the Rito. In describing the Pu-yé, I spoke of the pueblo ruins which lie on the top of the cliffs of that name. At the Rito de los Frijoles there are at least three similar ruins, but they lie in the river bottom. Two of them are in front of the caves at a short distance from the talus sloping up to them. One was a one-house pueblo of the polygonal type, which probably sheltered several hundred people; the inner court still shows three circular depressions or *estufas*. The other, which lies about 60 meters (96 feet) east of it, shows thirty-nine cells on the ground floor; and 16 meters (23 feet) north of it is an *estufa* 12 meters in diameter.

"A third ruin, situated nearly a mile further down in the gorge, in a grove of pine trees, formed an L, with a rude stone inclosure on its north side and connected with a small *estufa*. It is quite as much decayed as the large polygon, and the potsherds covering its surface are similar."

floor, near the eastern side, is the fire-pit known to the Te-wa Indians as the *sipapu*. In the floor are seen the holes in which stood the four columns that supported the roof of the kiva. The entrance to the kiva was through a trap-door in the roof. If there was an altar it probably occupied a place on the floor between the *sipapu* and the wall back of the fire-pit, constructed in the same manner as the altars which may yet be seen in the *estufas* of the pueblos of the Rio Grande valley now occupied. In the wall adjacent to the fire-pit is a horizontal tunnel forming a passage-way from the kiva to a vertical shaft a short distance outside the walls of the kiva. It is about two feet wide. On each side of the entrance was a stone post, and above a heavy lintel of stone. There are two entrances to

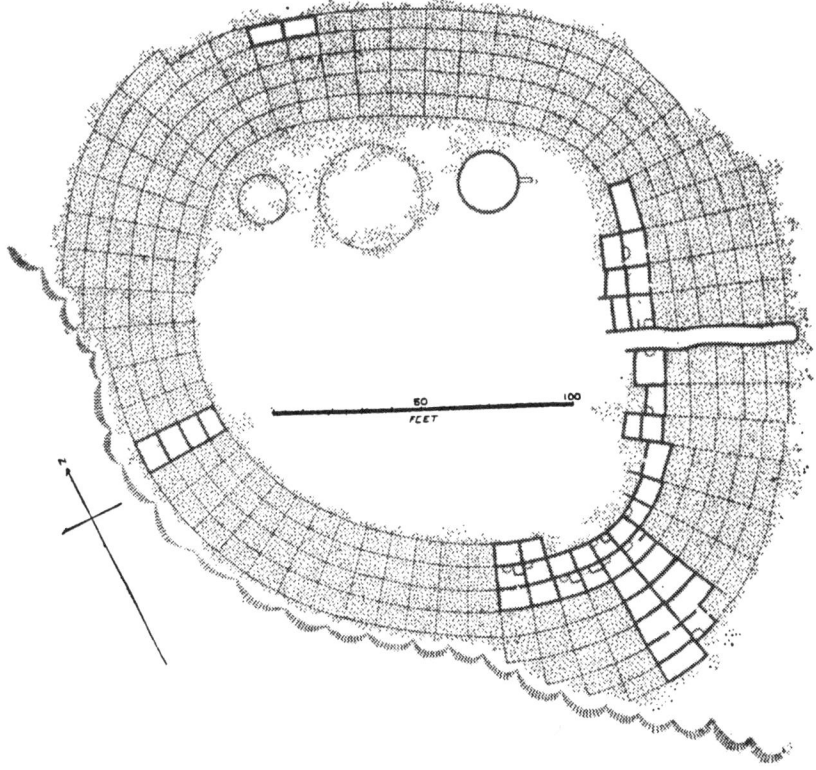

Courtesy of School of American Archæology, Santa Fé, N. M.

Ground Plan Pueblo of Ty-u-on-yi

the kiva, one on the eastern and the other on the western side. In no other kiva has more than one entrance been found.[20]

In the Rito de los Frijoles kivas are found in three situations, viz: contiguous to the pueblos in the valley bottom, sunk in the talus in front of the cliff-villages, and excavated in the walls of the cliff. There is much to indicate that the dual system of tribal organization was in existence here, and it is more than likely that the great kiva before described was the sanctuary of either the *Winter* or the *Summer* people. To the east of the great kiva, probably not more than four hundred yards, is a circular floor made of tufa blocks. This, doubtless, is all that remains of another kiva built above ground, as is the case in some of the present pueblos of the Rio Grande valley. Another interesting feature is the great ceremonial cave, situated high in the cliff just opposite the upper pueblo. The cave has contained several rooms built against the wall, and back of these were excavated rooms. In the bottom of the cave was a kiva excavated in the rock. In this, when it was cleared of the debris, were found pieces of matting in an almost perfect state of preservation and some very well preserved grains of corn. This is one of the very few ceremonial caves found in this region.

What these people of the Rito did with their dead has been a problem for the students of archæology of the region. It has been stated by an eminent authority that cremation was practised.[21] It is more than likely that this belief was based upon the traditions of the Cochití Indians with reference to the custom among their ancestors.[22]

---

[20] Hewett, Dr. Edgar L., *The Excavations at Ty-u-on-yi*: "The function of this feature of the subterranean ceremonial rooms cannot be regarded as finally determined. It is a feature common to all ancient kivas, both in the Rio Grande valley and the San Juan valley, but does not exist in the kivas of the modern Pueblo towns. It is what Dr. J. Walter Fewkes, in his report on the excavation of Spruce-Tree House in Colorado, describes as a device for the ventilation of the kiva. I am not yet prepared to accept Dr. Fewkes's determination, nor am I inclined to oppose any view of my own to that of the distinguished scholar who has long been my teacher in American archæology. . . Whatever may have been its function, it was doubtless the same throughout the Pueblo region. An examination of more than a hundred examples in southern Utah and Colorado, in the Chaco canyon, New Mexico, and the Rio Grande drainage, shows that while this appurtenance of the kiva varied greatly in form and construction, the same principle prevailed throughout."

[21] Bandelier, Adolph F., *The Delight Makers*.

[22] Hewett, Dr. Edgar L., *Excavations at Ty-u-on-yi*: "Traditions of cremation among the Cochití people cannot be accepted as conclusive in their applica-

Eastern Mesa — Pueblo of Walpi

ORIGIN AND HISTORY OF FIRST INHABITANTS 39

The causes of the destruction of the great community houses have given rise to much speculation. Climatic changes and failure of water supply were undoubtedly a factor in causing their abandonment and consequent decay. There is also no doubt that epidemics may have caused the abandonment of some. At various intervals during the passing of the centuries many were destroyed and annihilated by a war-like and predatory race coming from the north. The consensus of opinion has been that the Pueblo Indian of today, but with admixture of alien blood, in all probability is the descendant of the original builder and inhabitant of some of the ancient communal houses. This may be credited as to some of the ancient habitations, but as to the inhabitants of other distinctly pre-Spanish, pre-historic ruins, I cannot say. Present investigation is not bringing any final conclusion other than that the Pueblo Indian of today may be related to the ancient communal house dwellers, but the degree of relationship has not been satisfactorily determined.[23]

CAUSES OF DESTRUCTION OF THE PUEBLO HABITATIONS

---

tion to the ancient people of the Rito until there is some further investigation of the question of their relationship. Exploratory trenches carried in every direction about the great community house of Ty-u-on-yi revealed no general community burial place such as we expect to find in close proximity to every great stone pueblo of this region.''

[23] Hewitt, Dr. Edgar L., *Antiquities of the Jemez Plateau*, p. 12: ''The ruins were the ancient habitations of Indian tribes some descendants of which are today living in the adjacent valley of the Rio Grande and its tributaries; but most of whom are probably dispersed widely over the south-west. In every existing Te-wa tribe (San Juan, Santa Clara, San Yldefonso, Nambé, and Tesuque) it is claimed that certain clans may be traced back through one or more migrations to the ruined pueblos and cliff-villages of the Pajarito plateau. The same may be said of the Keres villages (Cochití, Santo Domingo, San Felipe, Santa Ana, and Zia).''

As heretofore stated, Dr. Hewett is of the opinion that the dwellers of the communal houses were not altogether the ancestors of the present Pueblo Indians. He says: ''Naturally, the first question that arises in the mind of every intelligent visitor to these cliff-dwellings, is — Who were the people who built and lived in these peculiar homes? It has been customary to answer that these were simply the earlier homes of the Pueblo tribes now living in the villages near by. This answer must at least be qualified. It was accepted by the earlier explorers on the evidence of surface appearances and the traditions of the living Pueblo Indians. Subsequent observers merely follow the lead of the predecessors. Extensive excavations made in recent years have brought to light more reliable evidence. Large collections of ancient pottery have been compared with that of the modern Pueblos and but few similarities found in form, color, mode of ornamentation and symbolism. This, in itself, would not be conclusive evidence of lack of identity between the makers, but it is supported by the indisputable evidence of the anatomical characters of the people. The living Pueblo Indians

40   LEADING FACTS OF NEW MEXICAN HISTORY

The pottery found in a vast majority of the ancient ruins, and in the burial places adjacent thereto, in form and color, is similar to the pottery now made by the Pueblos and the Moquis. Vast numbers of these ruins, when excavated in part, have yielded evidence that most of them have been destroyed since the Spanish conquest. Remains of sheep have been found which do not belong to the American fauna anterior to the Columbian period. Moreover, the Indians have preserved traditions, some of which are corroborated by documentary proof, of their ancestors having been driven away from these places, and there is abundant proof, indisputable in kind, that during the Spanish occupancy many pueblos were rebuilt, numbers were moved, and large numbers died out entirely.

There is evidence of a greater water supply than that of today once existing in the region of some of the ruins, which having failed, the pueblos became uninhabitable and were deserted for newly made habitations.[24]

---

are predominantly 50% to 75% brachycephalic or short-headed people, while the ancient people of the cliffs, as shown by the examination of a large collection of skeletal remains excavated by the writer at five different sites on the Pajarito plateau, were practically 100% dolicocephalic, or long-headed. The noticeable proportion of the long-headed people found among the present Pueblo Indians probably represents an infusion of blood from the ancient cliff-dwelling tribes.''
—*Antiquities of the Jemez Plateau*, p. 13.

In my judgment Dr. Hewett is justified in his conclusions insofar as his investigations go; the ''skeletal remains'' from which he has produced his strongest proof were taken from burial places on the Pajarito plateau. Similar remains taken from cliff-houses of the Rio Mancos did not show a long-headed people. Similar remains taken from burial places at Pecos (Cicuyé), the excavations having been made in places that were certainly used for burial places anterior to the coming of the Spaniards, discover the same anatomical characteristic as those taken from the Rio Mancos. The pottery collected by Wetherel in the Rio Mancos, while much better than some taken from graves in the San Juan drainage, bore a marked similarity to the latter.

[24] Bandelier, Adolph F., *Final Report*, part i, p. 32: ''The topography of the country has thus, to a degree, determined the sites of establishments. The Indian looks to a few leading features to decide his settlement, apart from the indications given by superstition. He wants, first of all, water. Then he required a limited amount of fertile soil. If that soil cannot be irrigated, he relies upon rain and snow, for corn will always grow where it rains moderately. Furthermore, he seeks a location where he may feel reasonably safe from an enemy. In judging of defensible locations, we cannot apply to them the principles of modern warfare. A treeless level is often as good a protection to an Indian village, constructed of heavy adobes, against an armed foe equipped only with bows and arrows, as an extensive uncommandable slope is against the artillery of today. Retreats, concealed nooks were as valuable to the Indian as high-perched rocks. Communities could afford to retire into caves, on rocky recesses, where access to water was difficult in the day-time, without thereby exposing themselves to more than usual danger, for it is only of late that the

Masonry of Pueblo Bonito

ORIGIN AND HISTORY OF FIRST INHABITANTS 41

No article of any consequence, of any description, has been found in any of the ruins in New Mexico, other than those taken from the cemeteries on the Pajarito plateau, which may not be traced in a degree to a similar one in the handiwork of the present Pueblos, except in this: in their pottery art the influence of the Spaniard and his customs and even the American succession are apparent. The pottery found in the neighborhood of nearly every pueblo ruin, particularly that which has been taken from the ruins in the valleys, although it does differ somewhat in decorative motive, still is nothing else than the pottery of the Pueblos made prior to Spanish invasion and occupancy. The Indian is an imitator, and this characteristic is most prominently exhibited when the pottery of successive periods is carefully and scientifically compared.

It is my unqualified judgment that the vast majority of ruined pueblos in New Mexico were at one time inhabited by the ancestors of the present Pueblo Indian; that the cause of destruction of most of them may be attributed to the Apache, the Ute, the Navajó, and the Comanche.[25] The pueblo of Acoma, the best of them all, is

---

Indian learned to attack at night. Lastly, the abundance of game, or its absence, and the prevalence of certain nutritive or medicinal plants, influenced the choice of locations.

"The abandonment of villages has been due to various causes. Thus, the Te-was of Santa Clara, assert that their ancestors dwelt in the clusters of artificial grottos excavated in cliffs of pumice-stone west of the Rio Grande. The cave villages of the Pu-yé and Shu-fin-né are claimed by the Te-was as those of their own people. A few years of drought compelled them to abandon these elevated and sparsely watered places, and to descend upon the river banks, where they had resort to irrigation for raising their crops, whereas at the caves they grew corn and squashes by means of the rains alone.

"The Queres of Cochití positively state that similar artificial caves which line the walls of the Rito de los Frijoles, or Ty-u-on-yi, were formerly the habitations of their tribe, and that constant hostilities of the Te-was and the Navajós, as well as the gradual disintegration of the very friable rock, compelled their abandonment. The latter is very plainly visible. In proportion as the material is easy to work, it deteriorates easily and crumbles. The majority of such caves have fallen in on the front, and against such accidents there was no remedy."

Mr. Bandelier overlooks the fact that there may have been more than one occupation of the caves and cliff-dwellings of the Pajarito plateau. The ancestors of the Te-was and those of the Keres may have occupied the places named, and still not be the original builders of the cliff habitations. Late excavations have shown two floors in some of the rooms, one on top of the other, the one above covering up the absolute proof of a prior occupation, corn stalks, corn, and other evidences of an agricultural people.

[25] Smith, Buckingham, *Florida*, p. 65. *Account of what Hernando de Alvarado and Fr. Juan de Padilla Discovered going in Search of the South Sea.* Referring to the destroyed pueblos which he saw in the Rio Grande-Tiguex,

probably the sole pueblo now inhabited which was occupied when the Spaniards came.[26] There is abundant documentary proof of the destruction of pueblo villages by these wandering, marauding tribes. The pueblo of Awatubi was destroyed by war in 1700-1701. The pueblo of Santo Domingo has been destroyed by water and rebuilt on different sites four times in two hundred years.[27] Since the Mexican and American occupancy several pueblos have been rebuilt; others have gone out of existence, the people removing and joining another pueblo, notably the pueblo of Cicuyé-Pecos, which was abandoned about seven years before the American conquest, the remaining inhabitants moving to the pueblo of Jemez.

There is another class of ancient habitation found in New Mexico. The habitations heretofore described have been of the communal house, the detached house, and the cavate types. The cliff-dwelling is a type distinct in itself. The term "cliff-dwelling" is used to designate the houses in the cliffs of the arid region. Their former occupants belonged, at least in the main, to the tribes known today as the Pueblos. The high mesa lands of Arizona, Colorado, New Mexico, and Utah are replete in natural recesses and shallow caverns weathered in the faces of the cliffs; primitive tribes on taking possession of the region, although by preference, no doubt settling in the valleys along the running streams, in many

ANCIENT CLIFF-DWELLINGS

Alvarado says: "In this province there are seven other villages depopulated and destroyed by those Indians who paint their eyes, of whom the guides will tell your Grace; they say that these live in the same region as the cows, and that they have corn and houses of straw."

[26] Bandelier, Adolph F., *Final Report*, part i, p. 34: "With the exception of Acoma, there is not a single pueblo standing where it was at the time of Coronado, or even sixty years later, when Juan de Oñate accomplished the peaceable reduction of the New Mexico village Indians. Such mutations have also been caused by hostilities or merely by fear of them. The great insurrection of 1680 wrought an important change in the numbers and distribution of Indian villages."

[27] Bandelier, Adolph F., says: "The original pueblo, called Gui-pu-y, stood on the banks of the arroyo de Galisteo, more than a mile east of the present station of Domingo. It was partly destroyed by a rise of this arroyo in one night. The next pueblo has completely disappeared, the Rio Grande having washed it away. It was called Uash-Pa-Tze-Na. The village of to-day has suffered three disasters."

Mindeleff, C., *Aboriginal Remains*, 13th Annual Report, Bureau of Am. Eth.: "A band of 500 village-building Indians might leave the ruins of fifty villages in the course of a single century. It is very doubtful whether the total number of Pueblo Indians ever exceeded 30,000."

ORIGIN AND HISTORY OF FIRST INHABITANTS 43

cases naturally occupied the ready-made shelters for residence, storage, and burial, and for hiding and defense, in time of danger. This occupancy led in time to the building of marginal walls for protection and houses within for dwelling, to the enlargement of the rooms by excavation when the formations permitted, and, probably later on, to the excavation of commodious dwellings, such as are now found in many sections of the arid region. It is for this reason that archæologists have divided the cliff-dwellings into two distinct classes, the cliff house proper, constructed of masonry, and the cavate house, excavated in the cliffs.

It is commonly believed that the agricultural tribes of pre-Spanish times, who built large towns and developed an extensive irrigation system, resorted to the cliffs, not from choice, but because of the encroachment of war-like tribes, who were probably non-agricultural, having no well established place of abode. This must be true to some extent, for no people, unless urged by dire necessity, would resort to fastnesses in remote canyon walls or to the margins of barren and almost inaccessible plateaus and there establish their dwellings at enormous cost of time and labor; and it is equally certain that a people once forced to these retreats would, when the stress was removed, descend to the lowlands to re-establish their houses where water is convenient and in the immediate vicinity of arable lands. Although these motives of hiding and defense should not be overlooked, it appears that many of the cliff-dwelling sites were near streams and fields and were occupied because they afforded shelter and were natural dwelling places.

It is important to note also that many of the cliff-houses, both built and excavated, are mere storage places for corn and other property, while many others are out-looks from which the fields below could be watched and the approach of strangers observed. In some districts evidences of post-Spanish occupancy of some sites exist, walls of houses are built on deposits accumulated since sheep were introduced, and adobe bricks, which were not used in pre-historic times, appear in some cases. A well authenticated tradition exists among the Hopi, that about the middle of the 18th century a group of their clans, the Asa people, deserted their village on account of an epidemic and removed to the Canyon de

Chelly, where they occupied the cliff-shelters for a considerable period, inter-marrying with the Navajó.[28]

The area in which the cliff-dwellings occur is practically co-extensive with that in which are now found traces of town building and relics attributable to the Pueblo tribes. The most noteworthy of these groups of built dwellings are found in the canyons of the Mesa Verde, in Colorado, in Hovenweep, McElmo, and Montezuma

---

[28] *Hopi.* The word is a contraction of Ho-pi-tu, meaning "peaceful ones," or Ho-pi-tu Shi-nu-mu, meaning "peaceful all people." It is their own name. These Indians speak a Shoshonean dialect, and occupy six pueblos on a reservation in northeastern Arizona. They are popularly known by the name of "Moki," or "Moqui." The last mentioned appellation means "dead" in the language of the Hopi. Where this tribal name comes from cannot be authoritatively ascertained, but it is undoubtedly of alien origin. It is possible that it came from the Keresan language; like Motsi in the Cochití and San Felipe. Espejo knew them as "Mohace" and "Mohoce" and Juan de Oñate as "Mohoqui." Bandelier says that the Hopi country is the province of Tusayan and is the Totonteac of Friar Marcos.

These people were visited by Pedro de Tovar and Fr. Juan de Padilla, under orders from Francisco Vasquez Coronado, in 1540. At first the Hopi were disposed to be hostile to the visitors, but this was finally overcome and the Spaniards remained several days with them. It was here that Tovar learned of the Grand Canyon, which was afterwards visited by Cardenas. Castañeda does not give the several names of the Tusayan towns, and on this account it is not positively known what villages were at that time occupied, outside of Oraibi, Shongopavi, Mishongnovi, Walpi, and Awatobi. Awatobi was destroyed in the year 1700. The present towns are not the ones visited by the Spaniards. The Hopi were visited by Antonio de Espejo in 1583. The Mohoce or Mohace, as he called them, consisted of five large villages. The Indians gave Espejo a quantity of "towels," kilts, for which they have always been celebrated. Juan de Oñate visited the "Mohoqui" when he was governor of New Mexico and compelled them to take the oath of allegiance and vassalage on the 15th of November, 1598. At this time the villages were called Aguato or Aguatuyba (Awatobi), Gaspe (Gual-pe-Walpi), Comupavi (Shongopavi) Majanani (Mishongnovi), and Ollala or Naybi (Oraibi).

Missions were established among them in 1629. They were all destroyed in the rebellion of 1680. Thereafter no attempt was made to establish any missions until 1700, at Awatobi, but the other Hopi, being greatly angered, fell upon the village one night, killing many people and compelling its abandonment.

The pueblos of Walpi, Mishongnovi, and Shongopovi, situated in the foothills, were probably abandoned about 1680, and new villages built on the mesas nearby; this was done, doubtless, as a means of defense against the Spaniards, whose vengeance was a source of great fear to these Indians. At the time of the reconquest under De Vargas many of the Indians from other tribes came to live with the Hopi. Some of these built the Pay-up-ki, on the Middle Mesa, but were taken back and settled in Sandia about the middle of the 18th century. About the year 1700, Hano was established on the East Mesa, near Walpi, by Te-wa from near Abiquiu, on the Chama river in New Mexico. They were invited by the Hopi and have continued to live and have inter-married with them, although they have retained their native speech and many of their customs. Other Indians, also, came to live with Hopi about this time; these came from the valley of the Rio Grande and settled on the Second Mesa.

Ruins of the Pueblo of Hungo Pavie

ORIGIN AND HISTORY OF FIRST INHABITANTS 45

canyons, in Colorado and Utah, and in Canyon de Chelly and its branches in northeastern Arizona. Although there are local differences in style of building, construction, plan, and finish, the chief characteristics are much the same everywhere. Corresponding differences with general likeness are observed in implements, utensils, and ornaments associated with the ruins, facts which go to show that in early periods, as now, numerous tribal groups were represented in the region, and that then, as now, there was a general community of culture, if not kinship in blood.

Owing to differences in the composition of the rocky strata, the natural shelters occupied by the cliff-dwellings are greatly varied in character. While many are mere horizontal crevices or isolated niches, large enough only for men to crawl into and build small stone lodges, there are extensive chambers, with comparatively level floors, and with roofs opening outward in great sweeps of solid rock surface, more imposing than any structure built by human hands. These latter are capable of accommodating not merely single households but communities of considerable size. The niches occur at all levels in cliffs rising to the height of nearly a thousand feet, and are often approached with great difficulty from below or, in rare cases, from above. Where the way is very steep, niche stairways were cut in the rock face, making approach possible. Ladders of notched logs were also used. In the typical cliff-dwellings of this class, the entire floor of the niche is occupied, the door-way giving entrance through the outer wall, which is built up vertically from the brink of the rocky shelf and rises one, two, or more stories in height, or to the rocky roof, when this is low and over-hanging. In the larger shelters the buildings are much diversified in plan and elevation, owing to irregularities in the conformation of the floor and walls. The first floor was the rock surface, or, if that was uneven, of clay or flag-stones, and upper floors were constructed of poles set in the masonry, often projecting through the walls and over-laid with smaller poles and willows, finished above with adobe mud. Some of the rooms in the larger buildings were round, corresponding in appearance and no doubt in purpose to the kivas, or ceremonial chambers, of the ordinary pueblos. The masonry is excellent, the rather small stones, gathered in many cases from distant sites, being laid in mortar. The stones were rarely dressed, but were carefully selected, so that the wall surface was even, and in some cases a decorative effect was given by alternating layers of smaller and larger pieces and by chinking the crevices with spawls. The walls were sometimes plastered inside and out and finished with clay paint. The door-ways were small and squarish, and often did not extend to the floor, except an opening or square notch in the center of the passage for the feet. The lintels were stone slabs or consisted of a number of sticks or small timbers. Windows or outlook apertures were numerous and generally small.

The antiquity of the cliff-dwellings can only be surmised. That many of them were occupied in comparatively recent times is apparent from their excellent state of preservation, but their great numbers and the extent of the work accomplished suggest very considerable antiquity. Just when the occupancy of the cliffs began, whether five hundred or five thousand years ago will probably always remain a mooted question.

Striking differences in the crania of earlier and later occupants of the cliff-dwellings are cited to prove earlier occupancy by a distinct race, but craniologists observe that equally striking differences exist between tribes living side by side at the present day. It may be safely said that to the present time no evidence of the former general occupancy of the region by peoples other than those now classed as Pueblo Indians, or their neighbors, has been furnished. If we are to judge from results obtained by archæologists studying this interesting subject in other localities, and particularly as to the origin and occupation of the great communal houses of the Pajarito plateau, it is not unlikely that the problem of origin and occupancy of the cliff-dwellings will soon be solved.[29]

[29] Near Flagstaff, Arizona, certain rude habitations may be seen excavated in the slopes of cinder cones and in the steep faces of scoriaceous deposits. These are entered by door-ways excavated in the steep slopes of cliffs, or by shafts descending obliquely or vertically where the slopes are gentle. The rooms are of moderate size and of irregular outline. It is believed that the occupants of these strange dwellings were a part of the great Pueblo family.

In the canyons of the Piedras Verdes river, Chihuahua, Mexico, are cliff-dwellings corresponding in many respects with those of the Pueblo region. These are in ruins, but in other sections of the same state there are similar dwellings occupied today by the Tarahumares Indians. The most southerly cliff-dwellings thus far observed are in the state of Jalisco, in Central Mexico.

Holmes, W. H., *Handbook of American Indians*, Bul. 30, part i, Bureau of American Ethnology. Among the more important examples of the cliff ruins are the so-called Cliff Palace in Walnut Canyon, and the Spruce Tree House in

PRE-SPANISH POTTERY-MOQUI

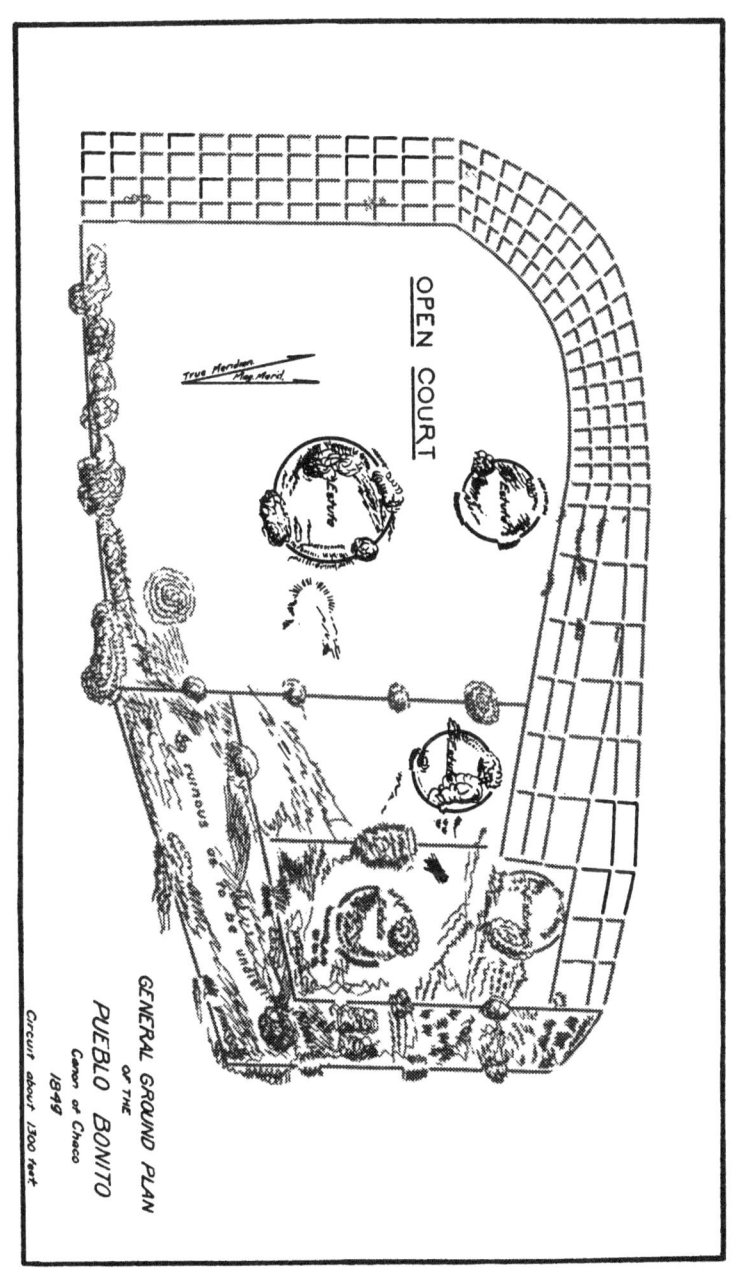

Until a very recent date, the fierce Apache and the Navajó were the constant enemies of the quiet, peaceable Pueblo Indian and his ancestors. These wandering tribes, the Arabs of the plains, together with the elements and climatic conditions, through centuries of time, are responsible, in a great degree, for the destruction of many of the pueblo houses, communal, detached or cliff or cave variety, the ruins of which have been a never-ending cause of inquiry and speculation.

THE ATHAPASCAN RACE — THE NAVAJÓ AND THE APACHE, THE ENEMIES OF THE PUEBLO INDIAN

The Apache and the Navajó are of the Athapascan race,[30] the most widely distributed of all the Indian linguistic families of North America, at one time extending over parts of the continent from near the Arctic coast far into northern Mexico, from the Pacific to Hudson bay, and from the Rio Colorado to the mouth of the Rio Grande, a territory extending for more than forty degrees of lati-

Navajó Canyon, Mesa Verde Colorado; Casa Blanca in Canyon de Chelly, and the so-called Montezuma Castle on Beaver creek, Arizona. Intimately associated with these cliff-dwellings, and situated on the plateaus immediately above or at the base of the cliffs below, are ruins of pueblos in every way identical with the pueblos in the open country.

The so-called Cliff Palace in Walnut Canyon, Mesa Verde, Colorado, consists of a group of houses in a fair state of preservation, all connecting and opening one into the other, the whole forming a crescent about one hundred yards from end to end. It contains ruins of 146 rooms, some of which are on a secondary ledge. The village contained five kivas or estufas.

Some travelers have reported the occurrence of ancient stone houses overwhelmed and destroyed by flows of lava, and have inferred great age from this; verification of these reports is entirely wanting.

The best work treating of these cliff-dwellings is that of Nordenskiold, *Cliff Dwellings of the Mesa Verde*, published in 1893. Other works treating of the same subject are:

Bandelier, A. F., *Papers Archæological Institute of America*, iii, 1890; iv, 1892.
Birdsall, *Bul. Am. Geo. Society*, xxiii, 1891.
Chapin, *Land of the Cliff-Dwellers*, 1892.
Fewkes, J. W., *17th and 22nd Annual Reps.*, Bureau of Am. Eth., 1898, 1904.
Hewett, Dr. E. L., *Smithsonian Report*, 1894.
Holmes, W. H., *U. S. Geological Survey of Territories*, 1876, 1879.
Jackson, *Ibid*, 1874, 1876.
Mindeleff, V., *8th Annual Report*, Bureau Am. Eth., 1891.
Mindeleff, C., *13th Annual Report*, Bureau of Am. Eth., 1896.
Powell, J. W., *7th Annual Report*, Bureau of Am. Eth., xviii, 1901.
[30] Bancroft, H. H., *Native Races*, i, p. 38.

Typical Navajó Dwelling or "Hogan"

ORIGIN AND HISTORY OF FIRST INHABITANTS 49

tude and seventy-five degrees of longitude.[31] The wide differences in language point to a separation for long periods of time of the various branches of this family, certainly covering many centuries.

Geographically the Athapascans inhabited three great divisions of the continent, the Northern, the Pacific, and the Southern. The Northern division covered almost all of the northwest portion of North America, only a narrow strip barring them from Hudson bay and the Arctic ocean. The Pacific division was in the states of Washington and Oregon, while the Southern division held sway over a vast area in the southwest, including most of Arizona and New Mexico, the southern portions of Utah and Colorado, the west borders of Kansas and Texas, and the north portion of Mexico to latitude twenty-four degrees.

Their principal neighbors were the members of the Shoshonean family and the several Pueblo tribes. So far as it has been able to be ascertained the language of this division was quite uniform. The peoples composing it are the Navajós south of the San Juan river in New Mexico and Arizona, the Apaches on all sides of the Navajós, except to the north, and the Lipan, formerly in Texas but now merged with the Mescaleros in New Mexico. The Apaches were, in truth, a number of tribes forming the southernmost part of the Athapascan family. The word "Apache," in all probability, was derived from a Zuñi word, *apachu,* meaning enemy, which was the

---

[31] Hodge, F. W., *Handbook of American Indians*, p. 66: "The Apache are divided into a number of tribal groups which have been so differently named and defined that it is sometimes difficult to determine to which branch writers refer. The most commonly accepted divisions are the Querechos or Vaqueros, consisting of the Mescaleros, Jicarillas, Faraones, Llaneros, and probably the Lipan; the Chiricahua; the Pinaleños; the Coyoteros, comprising the White Mountain and Pinal divisions; the Arivaipa; the Gila Apache, including the Gileños, Mimbreños and Mogollones; and the Tontos. The present official divisions, with their population in 1903, is as follows: White Mountain Apache (comprising the Arivaipa, Tsltaden or Chilion, Chiricahua, Coyoteros, Mimbreños, Mogollones, Pinals, "San Carlos," and Tontos) under Ft. Apache agency, 2,058; Apache, consisting of the same divisions as above under San Carlos agency, 2,275; Apache at Angora, Arizona, 38; Jicarillas under school superintendent in New Mexico, 782; Mescaleros under Mescalero agency, New Mexico, 464; Chiricahua at Ft. Sill, Okla., 298; Kiowa Apache, under Kiowa agency, Okla., 156. Besides these there were 19 Lipan in northwest Chihuahua, some of the survivors of a tribe which, owing to their hostility, was almost destroyed, chiefly by Mexican Kickapoo co-operating with Mexican troops. This remnant was removed from Zaragoza, Mexico, to Chihuahua in October, 1903, and a year later were brought to the United States and placed under the Mescalero agency in New Mexico."

Zuñi name for the Navajó, who were designated *Apaches de Navaju* by the early Spaniards in New Mexico.

The Apaches, Navajós, and the Comanches [32] were beyond question the people whose constant and relentless warfare with the Pueblos, did much to accomplish the overthrow and abandonment of many of their great communal habitations.

Necessarily the destruction of these houses and pueblos was not accomplished in a brief period of time, but it is believed by many scientists that the almost unbroken chain of the remains of permanent aboriginal structures, extending from the north forty degrees latitude to the thirty-second parallel, was at one time inhabited by a race or races which were vanquished and partially obliterated by the war-like, barbarous, and predatory tribes from the north.

Moqui Basket and Pottery

---

[32] The Comanche are of Shoshonean stock, and the only one of the group that lived entirely upon the plains. Their language and traditions show that they are a comparatively recent off-shoot from the Shoshoni of Wyoming, both tribes speaking practically the same dialect and, until very recently, keeping up constant and friendly communication. Within the traditional period the two tribes lived adjacent to each other in southern Wyoming, since which time the Shoshoni have been beaten back into the mountains by the Sioux and other prairie tribes, while the Comanche have been driven steadily southward by the same pressure. The Kiowa say that when they themselves moved southward from the Black Hills region, the Arkansas was the north boundary of the Comanche.

BIBLIOGRAPHY

Bancroft, H. H.	*Native Races*, i, 1886.
Bandelier, A. F.	*Investigations among the Indians of the Southwestern United States*, Final Rep. Papers of the Arch. Inst. of Am., part ii.
	Report of the Ruin of the Pueblo of Pecos. Papers of the Arch. Inst. of Am., American Series, i, 1881.
	Historical Introduction, Arch. Inst. of Am., 1881.
	Investigations, ibid, 1882.
	Historical Archives of the Hemenway S. W. Arch. Ex., Berlin, 1890.
	Documentary History of the Zuñi Tribe. Journal of Am. Eth. and Archae., vol. iii, 1892.
Bureau of American Ethnology	2nd Annual Report, ii, *Catalogue of the Collection obtained from the Indians of New Mexico and Arizona*, 1879-1880, Stephenson.
	3rd Annual Report, *Illustrated Catalogue of the Collection obtained from the pueblos of Zuñi, New Mexico and Walpi, Arizona*, 1881, Ibid.
	4th Annual Report, *Pottery of the Ancient Pueblos*, Holmes.
	8th Annual Report, *A study of Pueblo Architecture, Tusayan and Cibola*, v, Mindeleff.
	17th Annual Report, *Archæological Expedition to Arizona in 1895*, Fewkes.
	22nd Annual Report, *Two Summers' work in the Pueblo Ruins*, Fewkes.
	24th Annual Report, *Work in Mound Exploration*, Thomas.
Bourke, J. G.	*Navajó Legends.* Journal Am. Folk Lore, iii, 1890.
Cushing, F. H.	*Preliminary Notes on the Hemenway Expedition.* Rep. of Congress of Americanists, Berlin, 1890.
Emory, Abert Cooke	*Notes of a Military Reconnoissance, etc., New Mexico and California*, Washington, 1848.
Hewett, Edgar L.	*The Archæology of Pajarito Park*, Pre. Rep., Am. Anthropologist, 1904.
	Studies on Extinct Pueblos of Pecos, Am. Anthropologist, September, 1904.
	Antiquities of the Jemez-Plateau, Bul. 32, B. A. E., 1906.
	The Pajaritan Culture, Papers of the School of American Archæology, iii, 1909.
	The Excavations at El Rito de Los Frijoles, in

	1909, Papers of the School of American Archæology, number 10.
	The Excavations at Tyuonyi, New Mexico, in 1908, Papers of the School of American Archæology, number 5, 1909.
	The Ground Work of American Archæology, Papers of the School of American Archæology, number 1, 1908.
	The Excavations at Pu-yé, New Mexico, in 1907, Papers of the School of American Archæology, number 4, 1909.
Harrington, J. P.	*Introductory Paper on the Tiwa Language, Dialect of Taos, New Mexico*, Papers of the School of American Archæology, number 14, 1910.
	Phonetic and Lexic Resemblances between Kiowan and Tanoan, Papers of the School of American Archæology, number 12, 1910.
Hardesty and Jones	*Smithsonian Report*, 1866-1872.
Hodge, F. W.	*The Verification of a Tradition*, Am. Anthropologist, September, 1897.
	Handbook of American Indians, in B. A. E., Bul. 30, part I.
	National Geographic Magazine, October, 1897.
Holmes, W. H.	*Report on the Ruins of Southwestern Colorado*, Hayden's U. S. Survey, 1876.
Hough, Walter	*Archæological Field Work in Northeastern Arizona*.
Humboldt, Baron A. de	*Essai Politique*.
Morgan, L. H.	*Houses and House Life of the American Aborigines*, 1881.
Mindeleff, Cosmos	*The Cliff Ruins of the Canyon de Chelly*, 16th B. A. E., 1894.
Matthews, W.	*5th Annual Report*, Bureau of American Ethnology.
Memoirs American Museum of Natural History	*American Anthropologist*, vol. iv, 1902.
Pruden, T. M.	*Pre-historic Ruins of the San Juan Water-shed.*
Russell	*Explorations in the Far North*, 1898.
Stevenson, Mrs. C. M.	*The Zia*, 11th Annual Report, Bureau of American Ethnology, 1894.
Simpson, J. H.	*Journal of a Military Reconnoissance from Santa Fé to the Navajó Country*, 1852.

Spruce Tree House, Mesa Verde District

CHAPTER II

THE FIRST SPANISH EXPLORERS, 1534-1542 — ALVAR NUÑEZ
CABEZA DE VACA AND HIS COMPANIONS

ONE of the most marvelous incidents of the sixteenth century, in the way of exploration of the North American continent, was the crossing of the continent by the ship-wrecked survivors of the Narváez expedition.[33]

Don Panfilo Narváez had occupied the position of lieutenant under Don Diego de Velasquez, when the latter was governor of Cuba. Later on he was placed in command of the flotilla sent out by Velasquez for the seizure of Hernando Cortés and his companions. In this he was most unsuccessful, inasmuch as he himself fell into the hands of Cortés but was finally set at liberty by the conqueror of Mexico.

After twenty-six years spent in the service of his royal master in the New World, Narváez returned to Spain, addressed a petition to the king, asking for the grant of a kingdom, and, after due consideration by the Council of the Indies, was authorized to conquer the country from the Rio de las Palmas to the Cape of Florida, and was also granted certain titles and concessions.[34]

Narváez was a native either of Valladolid or of Tudda on the Duro. He was of tall, commanding presence, fair complexion, with a red beard, and had lost an eye in a conflict with Hernando Cortés.[35]

---
[33] Hodge, F. W., *Spanish Explorers in the Southern United States*, p. 3.
[34] Hodge, F. W., *Ibid.*
Smith, Buckingham, *Relation of Alvar Nuñez Cabeza de Vaca; Petition of Narváez to the King of Spain*; Appendix i, p. 207.
[35] Diaz, Bernal, *Memoirs*, Lockhart's trans., vol. i, p. 325: "All at once I heard some one, and it must have been Narváez, cry out in a loud voice: 'Assist me, Oh blessed Virgin! I am a dead man! One of my eyes has been thrust out!' At the same time we all cried out, Victory! Victory! for those of the watchword Espiritu Santo! Narváez is fallen!"

54 LEADING FACTS OF NEW MEXICAN HISTORY

On the seventeenth day of June, 1527, Narváez sailed in five vessels from the port of San Lucar de Barrameda for his province, having on board about six hundred colonists and soldiers.

THE NARVÁEZ EXPEDITION
SAILS FROM SAN LUCAR

The officers of the expedition, other than Narváez, the governor, were Alvar Nuñez Cabeza de Vaca, treasurer and high sheriff, Alonzo Enriquez, comptroller, Alonzo de Solís, asessor, and a Franciscan friar, Juan Xuarez.

Alvar Nuñez Cabeza de Vaca was born of an ancient family and his peculiar name of Cow's Head is said to have originated in the fact that an ancestor had placed a cow's head at the entrance of a mountain pass, which indicated to the king of Navarre a certain trail or roadway, which the king followed and successfully led his army against the Moors, whom he defeated in a tremendous conflict.[36] For this act, the ancestor of Alvar Nuñez, whose name was Martin Aljaha, was ennobled by the king.[37]

After a stormy voyage, in which he lost some ships and a large number of men, on the 14th day of April, 1528, Narváez landed on the coast of Florida, somewhere in the neighborhood of Tampa bay.[38]

[36] Hodge, F. W., *Spanish Explorers in the Southern United States*: "The battle of Las Navas de Tolosa, July, 1212."

[37] Hodge, F. W., *Ibid*: "The author of the narrative was a native of Jeréz de la Frontera, in the province of Cadiz, in southern Spain, but the date of his birth is unknown. His father was Francisco de Vera, son of Pedro de Vera, conqueror of the Grand Canary in 1483; his mother, Teresa Cabeza de Vaca, who was also born in Jerez. Why Alvar Nuñez assumed the matronymic is not known, unless it was with a sense of pride that he desired to perpetuate the name that had been bestowed by the king of Navarre on his maternal ancestor, a shepherd, named Martin Aljaha, for guiding the army through a pass that he marked with the skull of a cow (*cabeza de vaca*), literally 'cow's head', thus leading the Spanish army to success in the battle of Navas de Tolosa, in July, 1212, which led up to the final conquest of the Moors in Spain."

Davis, W. W. H., *Conquest of New Mexico*, note, p. 18, says: "Upon his return from the unfortunate Narváez expedition, the emperor conferred upon him the government of Paraguay, with the title of Adelantado. He sailed from the port of San Lucar de Barrameda on the 2nd of November, 1540, and arrived at Santa Catalina on the 29th of March following. He is described as having the most beautiful and noble figure of all the conquerors of the New World; and in the best days of Spanish chivalry, his valor upon the battle-field, his resolution in danger and his courtesy and resignation in hardship, won for him the appellation 'Illustrious Warrior.' "

[38] Hodge, F. W., *Spanish Explorers in the Southern United States*. St. Clement's Point, near the entrance to Tampa bay, on the west coast of Florida.

Davis, W. W. H., *Conquest of New Mexico*, note, p. 20: "The place where

Fac-simile of Title Page of the *Relacion* of Alvar Nuñez Cabeza de Vaca

From copy of the Zamora Edition, 1542, in New York Public Library

THE FIRST SPANISH EXPLORERS 55

Here he found an Indian village in which was a great communal house capable of sheltering more than three hundred persons.. In the explorations following his landing,
THE EXPEDITION LANDS ON Narváez lost nearly all of the mem-
THE COAST OF FLORIDA bers of his expedition. The only survivors of whom there is any record were Alvar Nuñez Cabeza de Vaca, Andrés Dorantes, a native of Béjar, Alonzo del Castillo Maldonado, a native of Salamanca, and a negro, Estevan by name, a native of Azamor or Asemmur, on the west coast of Morocco, who was the slave of Dorantes,[39] and Juan Ortiz. After many trials and a long captivity by the Indians, the first four [40] found opportunity for escape, crossing from the coast of Texas to the Pacific ocean, arriving on the first day of April, 1536, at San Miguel de Culiacan, where they were received by Melchior Diaz, the alcalde of San Miguel, "with great humanity and with tears, praising God for the marvellous things they had performed." On the 24th day of July, 1536, the survivors finally reached the City of Mexico, where they were most royally entertained by the viceroy, Don Antonio de Mendoza, and by Hernando Cortés, the Marquis del Valle himself. Juan Ortiz, who had been enticed ashore by the Indians, was rescued by De Soto, in 1539, but he died before the expedition returned to civilization.

During his stay in the City of Mexico, Alvar Nuñez and Dorantes occupied themselves in making a report to the Royal Audiencia of

Narváez landed is established without much, if any doubt, as Tampa Bay, on the western coast of Florida, and was named by the Spaniards — the Bay of the Cross. He disembarked on the northern shore, and marched inland towards the north."

[39] Hodge, F. W., *Ibid*, p. 4: "Andrés Dorantes de Carranca, son of Pablo, a native of Béjar del Castañar, in Estremadura, who had received a commission as captain of infantry on the recommendation of Don Alvaro de Zuñiga, Duke of Béjar; Captain Alonzo del Castillo Maldonado, of Salamanca, the son of Doctor Castillo and Aldonza Maldonado; and Estevan, or Estevanico, a blackamoor of Asemmur, or Azamor, on the west coast of Morocco, the slave of Dorantes."

[40] Hodge, F. W., *Ibid*, p. 4: "With the exception of those who returned to the ships, these four men were the only ones of the entire expedition who ever again entered a civilized community."

Hodge, F. W., *Ibid*, p. 10: "There was another survivor of the inland expedition of Narváez, Juan Ortiz by name. This Spaniard, who had been enticed ashore by the Indians of Florida, led practically the life of a slave, like his countrymen on the Texas main, until 1539, when he was rescued by De Soto, but he died before the expedition returned to civilization."

Española of the fate of Narváez and his companions and also a report of their own wanderings across the continent.[41] From this report, undoubtedly, was prepared the narrative of the historian, Oviedo.[42] The relation of Alvar Nuñez Cabeza de Vaca was first printed at Zamora, in the year 1542.[43] They also prepared a map of the region traversed by them and left it with Mendoza.[44]

Finally Alvar Nuñez and Dorantes determined to return to Spain, but upon the request of the viceroy, the ship upon which he had taken passage having proved unseaworthy and having returned to Vera Cruz, Dorantes remained in Mexico.[45] Alvar Nuñez Cabeza de Vaca,

---

[41] Hodge, F. W., *Ibid*, p. 7: ''There are few Spanish narratives that are more unsatisfactory to deal with by reason of the lack of directions, distances and other details, than that of Cabeza de Vaca; consequently there are scarcely two students of the route who agree. His line of travel through Texas was twice crossed by later explorers — in 1541 by the army of Francisco Vasquez Coronado, on the eastern edge of the Stake Plains, and again in 1582 by Antonio de Espejo, on the Rio Grande below the present El Paso. These data, with the clews afforded by the narrative itself, point strongly to a course from the tuna fields, about thirty leagues inland from San Antonio Bay, to the Rio Colorado and perhaps to the Rio Llano, westward across the lower Pecos to the Rio Grande above the junction of the Conchos, thence in an approximately straight line across Chihuahua and Sonora to the Rio Sonora, where we find Cabeza de Vaca's Village of Hearts, which Coronado also visited in 1540, at or in the vicinity of the present Ures.''

[42] Gonzalo Fernandez de Oviedo y Valdez was born in 1478. He belonged to an ancient family of the Asturias. He was early introduced at court, and was appointed page to Prince Juan, the only son of Ferdinand and Isabella, on whom the hopes of the nation rested. Oviedo was present at the siege of Granada. He entered the service of Ferdinand of Naples after the death of his royal master in 1496. In 1513 he was appointed to office in the New World by Ferdinand, the Catholic, and took service under the governor of Darien, sharing in the disastrous fortunes of that colony. In 1526 he published at Madrid his *Sumario*. This work he dedicated to the Emperor Charles the Fifth; it contains an account of the West Indies, the climate, geography, the races living there, and also an account of the animal and vegetable life of the islands. In 1535 Oviedo published his great work, the *Historia de las Indias Occidentales*. The same year he was appointed alcalde of the fortress of Hispañiola, and for the following ten years he remained on the island prosecuting his historical studies. Upon his return to Spain he was appointed Chronicler of the Indies, which post he held until his death, at Valladolid, in 1557, in the 79th year of his age.

[43] Winsor, Justin, *Narr. and Crit. Hist. Am.*, vol. ii, pp. 286-499.

[44] Smith, Buckingham, *Relation of Alvar Nuñez Cabeza de Vaca*, Introduction. Oviedo, *Historia General y Natural de las Indias*, tomo iii, lib. xxxv, ed. 1853.

[45] Hodge, F. W., *Spanish Explorers in the Southern United States*, p. 8: ''Invited to the capital by the viceroy Mendoza, Dorantes was tendered a commission to explore the northern country, but this project was never carried out . . . perhaps because of the projected expedition of Coronado, the way for which was led by Fray Marcos de Niza in 1539 with the negro Estevan as a guide. Dorantes served Mendoza in the conquest

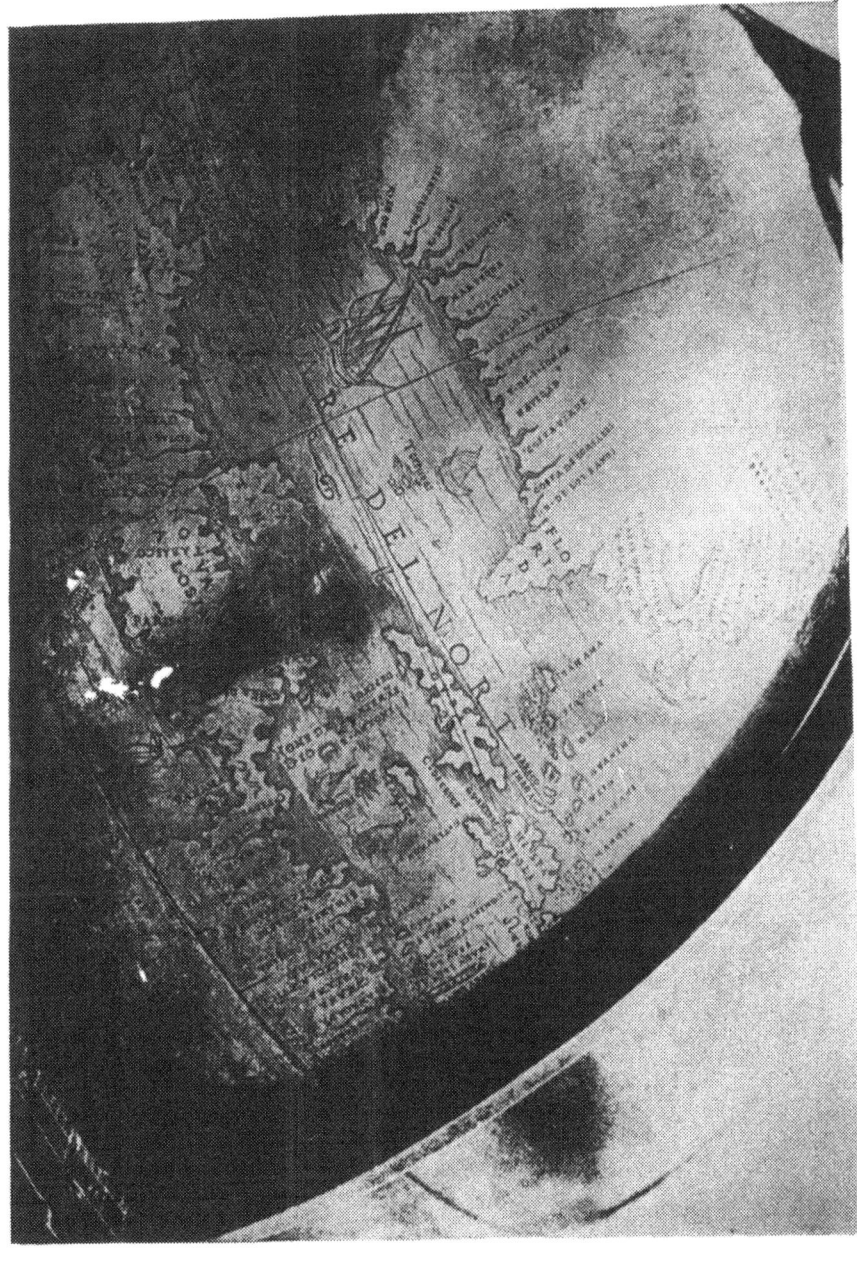

The Ulpius Globe of 1542
In possession of the New York Historical Society

however, sailed from Vera Cruz, reaching the port of Lisbon on the 9th day of August, 1537. During the voyage his ship was pursued by a French corsair.

He had no sooner arrived in Spain than he was promptly summoned to court, at Valladolid, whither he went at once and made his report to the emperor, Charles the Fifth, presenting him also with a buffalo hide, some emeralds, and some turquoises which he had collected during his journey from the Gulf of Mexico to the Pacific coast.[46]

The story of Alvar Nuñez Cabeza de Vaca,[47] published five years

---

of Jalisco, and married Doña Maria de la Torre, a widow, by whom he had a large family. One of his sons, Balthazar, some time king's treasurer of Vera Cruz, was born about the middle of the century, and on the death of his father inherited an *encomienda* that produced an income of five thousand pesos a year. Another son, Gaspar, inherited the *encomienda* of the pueblos of Ocava; and another, Melchior, an *encomienda* of Indians and of very good rents.''

Bancroft, H. H., *North American States*, vol. i, p. 70. See also Letter from Mendoza to Charles the Fifth, of December 10, 1537, *Col. Doc. Flor.*, p. 136.

[46] Hodge, F. W., *Ibid*, pp. 7-8: ''He seems to have been an honest, modest, and humane man, who underestimated rather than exaggerated the many strange things that came under his notice, if we except the account of his marvelous healings, even to the revival of the dead. The expedition of Narváez was in itself a disastrous and dismal failure, reaching 'an end alike forlorn and fatal;' but viewed from the standpoint of present-day civilization, the commander deserved his fate. On the other hand, while one might well hesitate to say that the acomplishment of Cabeza de Vaca and his three companions compensated their untold sufferings, the world eventually became the wiser in more ways than one. The northern continent had been penetrated from shore; the waters of the Mississippi and the bison of the plains were now first seen by white men; and some knowledge of the savage tribes had been gleaned for the benefit of those who should come after. There is no blatant announcement of great mineral wealth — a mountain with scoria of iron, some small bags of mica, a quantity of galena, with which the Indians painted their faces, a little turquoise, a few emeralds, and a small copper bell were all. Yet the effect of the remarkable overland journey was to inspire the expedition of Coronado in 1540; and it is not improbable that De Soto, who endeavoured to enlist the services of Cabeza de Vaca, may likewise have been stimulated to action.''

[47] Hodge, F. W., *Ibid*, pp. 10-11: ''The *Relacion* of Alvar Nuñez Cabeza de Vaca was first printed at Zamora in 1542, and with slight changes was reprinted with the first edition of the *Comentarios* on the Rio de la Plata, at Valladolid, in 1555. The *editio princeps* was translated into Italian by Ramusio, in the third volume of his *Navagationi et Viaggi* (Venice, 1556) and this was paraphrased into English by Samuel Purchase in volume iv of *Purchas His Pilgrimes* (London, 1613, pt. iv, lib. viii, cap. 1). The *Naufragios* (or *Relacion*) and *Comentarios* were reprinted at Madrid in 1736, preceded by the *Examen Apologetico* of Antonio Ardoino, who seemed to feel it his duty to reply to an Austrian monk named Caspar Plutus, who, in 1621, under the name Philoponus, published a treatise in which he maintained that laymen like Cabeza de Vaca should not be permitted to perform miracles. This edition of the narration of Cabeza de Vaca is included in volume i of Barcia's *Historiadores Primitivos*

58   LEADING FACTS OF NEW MEXICAN HISTORY

after his first return to Spain, is unrivalled in the history of the world in its recital of marvelous adventure, shipwreck, captivity by Indians, his escape, and final meeting with the Spaniards on the Pacific coast.

STORY OF ALVAR NUÑEZ CABEZA DE VACA AND HIS COMPANIONS, THE SURVIVORS OF THE NARVÁEZ EXPEDITION

When the so-called armada, composing the expedition of Narváez, had arrived at San Domingo, its commander remained at that port fifty days, procuring horses, provisions, and necessaries for the proper prosecution of his future explorations. While at San Domingo over one hundred and forty of his men deserted him and

---

de las Indias Occidentales, published at Madrid in 1749. The *Naufragios* of Alvar Nuñez, from the edition of 1555, appears in volume i of Vedia's *Historiadores Primitivos de Indias* (Madrid, ed. 1852). The letter to the Audiencia of Española, 'edited' by Oviedo, has already been alluded to. A 'Capitulacion que se tomó con Alvar Nuñez Cabeza de Vaca,' dated Madrid, 18 Marzo, 1540, is found in the *Colecion de Documentos Inéditos del Archivo de Indias* (tomo xxiii, pp. 8-33, 1875). A *Relacion* by Cabeza de Vaca, briefly narrating the story of the expedition until the arrival of its survivors in Espiritu Santo bay, with his instructions as treasurer, is printed in the *Colecion de Documentos de Indias*, xiv, 265-279 (Madrid, 1870). The most recent Spanish edition of the more famous *Relacion* reprinted in the following pages forms a part of volume v of the *Colecion de Libros y Documentos referentes á la Historia de America* (Madrid, 1906), which also contains the *Comentarios*.

"The single French translation was published as volume vii of Henri Ternaux-Compan's *Voyages* (Paris, 1837), from the edition of 1555, while the *Commentaires* form volume vi.

"In 1851 a translation of the edition of 1555 into English by (Thomas) Buckingham Smith, under the title *The Narrative of Alvar Nuñez Cabeza de Vaca*, was published privately at Washington by George W. Riggs; and shortly after Mr. Smith's death, in 1871, another edition, with many additions, was published in New York under the editorial supervision of John Gilmary Shea, and at the expense of Henry C. Murphy. It is this edition of the *Narrative* that is here reprinted. A paraphrase of the 1851 edition of Smith's translation appears in Henry Kingsley's *Tales of Old Travels* (London, 1869). The first fourteen chapters of W. W. H. Davis's *Spanish Conquest of New Mexico* (Doylestown, Pa., 1869) are also a paraphrase of the same work. Chapters xxx-xxxvi of the 1871 edition of Smith, somewhat abridged, were printed in an *Old South Leaflet* (Gen. Ser. No. 39, Boston, 1893). A 'Relation of What Befell the Persons who Escaped from the Disasters that Attended the Armament of Captain Pamphilo de Narváez on the Shores and in the Countries of the North,' translated and condensed from the letter published by Oviedo, is printed in the *Historical Magazine* (vol. xii, pp. 141, 204, 267, 347; September-December, 1867). The most recent English edition of the Cabeza de Vaca *Relacion*, translated from the very rare imprint of 1542 by Mrs. Fanny Bandelier, and edited, with an introduction, by her husband, Ad. F. Bandelier, was published in New York, in 1905, under the title, *The Journey of Alvar Nuñez Cabeza de Vaca*, as one of the volumes of the 'Trail Makers' series.''

THE FIRST SPANISH EXPLORERS

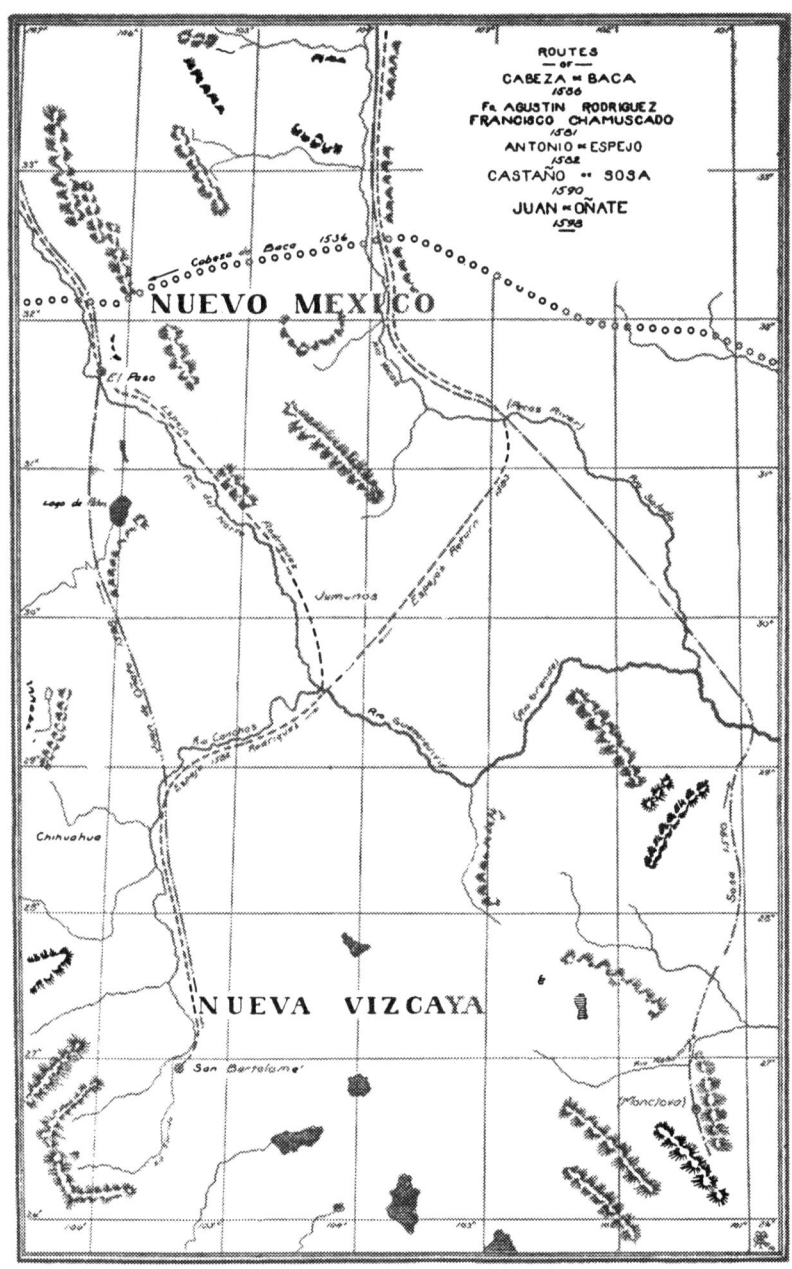

remained upon the island; these were led to this course by the many advantageous offers made to them by the settlers. Leaving San Domingo, Narváez sailed to Santiago, a port on the southern coast of Cuba, where the arrangements for his expedition were completed. Thence he sailed for Trinidad, a hundred leagues distant.

Anchoring his fleet at the port of Cape Santa Cruz, he sent forward two vessels, under the command of Captain Pantoja,[48] for supplies. Pantoja reached Trinidad in safety, but while lying off that harbor a violent storm arose, which wrecked both the vessels and drowned sixty men and forty horses. Alvar Nuñez Cabeza de Vaca was in command of one of the vessels, but having gone ashore with thirty men to secure provisions, they escaped the fate of their companions.

Narváez and his vessels outlived the storm by putting into a harbor near Cape Santa Cruz, where he secured a good anchorage, and, on the 5th of November, joined Alvar Nuñez Cabeza de Vaca at Trinidad. The weather continued most inclement and the commander determined upon spending the winter on the island. The fleet was sent, under the command of Alvar Nuñez Cabeza de Vaca, to the port of Xagua, about twelve miles distant, where there was a safe harbor. Here he remained until the 20th day of February, 1528, when Narváez arrived with a brig which he had purchased, supplying in part the place of the vessels he had lost. He also brought with him a pilot named Miruelo "who was employed because he said he knew the position of the River Palmas, and had been there, and was a thorough pilot for all the coast of the North." Narváez had also purchased and left on the shore of Havana another vessel, which he put in charge of Alvaro de la Cerda, with a force of forty infantry and twelve cavalry.

The second day after his arrival Narváez, having made his preparations rapidly, set sail, having a fleet of four ships and a brigantine, carrying in all four hundred men and eighty horses. Sailing to the

---

[48] Hodge, F. W., *Ibid*, note, p. 15: "One Juan Pantoja, captain of crossbowmen and Lord of Ixtlahuaca, accompanied Narváez on his first expedition to Mexico."

Bandelier, Mrs. Fanny, *The Journey of Alvar Nuñez Cabeza de Vaca*, p. 85, in *The Trail Makers*, A. S. Barnes and Co., New York, 1905: "Moreover, Pantoja, who remained as lieutenant, ill-treated them. On this Sotomayor, brother of Vasco Porcallo (the one from the island of Cuba, who had come in the fleet as Maestro de Campo), unable to stand it longer, quarreled with Pantoja, and struck him a blow with a stick, of which he died."

THE FIRST SPANISH EXPLORERS 61

west, he coasted along the southern shore of the island of Cuba, encountering several very severe storms. After twenty days he rounded Cape San Anton, the westernmost point of the island, and sailed within twelve leagues of Havana. The following day he stood in toward the land, intending to enter the harbor, when a storm suddenly arose and his ships were driven toward the coast of Florida.

On the 12th day of April land was sighted, but Narváez sailed along the coast until Holy Thursday, when the fleet came to anchor at the mouth of a bay, at the head of which some Indian habitations were seen. Alonzo Enriquez, the comptroller, landed upon a small island in the bay and traded with the natives who came to him without fear. The following day, being Good Friday, Narváez himself went ashore, with as many men as the boats would accommodate, and visited the Indian settlements at the head of the bay, which he found deserted. The habitations were generally small rude huts, but one of them was large enough to hold three hundred persons. The only article of value which was found was a small gold bell. Here he remained over night and on the following morning took formal possession of the country for his royal master. This ceremony was performed with great dignity and according to the forms, rules, and regulations of the Spanish crown.[49]

---

[49] Smith, Buckingham, *Relation of Alvar Nuñez Cabeza de Vaca* (ed. 1871), App. iii, 215-217. This is a most remarkable document, bombastic, farcical and yet interesting, as showing how much a Spanish king in that period knew about "claiming" the entire earth. One can readily imagine how much of this was understood by the Indians. This "summons" is as follows: "In behalf of the Catholic Caesarean Majesty of Don Carlos, King of the Romans, and Emperor ever Augustus, and Doña Juana his mother, Sovereigns of Leon and Castilla, Defenders of the Church, ever victors, never vanquished, and rulers of barbarous nations, I, Panfilo de Narváez, his servant, messenger and captain, notify and cause you to know in the best manner I can, that God our Lord, one and eternal, created the heaven and the earth, and one man and one woman of whom we and you and all men in the world have come, are descendants and the generation, as well will those be who come after us; but because of the infinity of off-spring that followed in the five thousand years and more since the world was created, it has become necessary that some men should go in one direction and others in another, dividing into many kingdoms and provinces, since in a single one they could not be subsisted or kept.

"All these nations, God our Lord, gave in charge to one person, called St. Peter, that he might be master and Superior over mankind; to be obeyed and to be head of all the human race, wheresoever they might live and be, of whatever law, sect or belief, giving him the whole world for his kingdom, lordship, and jurisdiction. And He commanded him to place his seat in Rome, as a point most suited whence to rule the world; so He likewise permitted him to have and place his seat on any part of the earth to judge and govern all the

Having made known his authority formally and declared himself as governor of all lands which might be discovered, the officers of people, Christians, Moors, Jews, Gentiles and of whatever creed beside they might be; him they called Papa, which means admirable, greatest, father and preserver, since he is father and governor of all men. Thus St. Peter was obeyed and taken for King, Lord and Superior of the Universe by those who lived at that time, and so likewise have all the rest been held, who to the Pontificate were afterward elected; and thus has it continued until now, and will continue to the end of things.

"One of the Popes who succeeded him to that seat and dignity of which I spake, as Lord of the world, made a gift of these islands and main of the Ocean sea, to the said Emperor and Queen, and their successors, our Lords, in these kingdoms, with all that is in them, as is contained in certain writings that thereupon took place, which may be seen if you desire. Thus are their Highnesses King and Queen of these islands and continent, by virtue of said gift; and as Sovereigns and Masters, some other islands, and nearly all where they have been proclaimed, have received their Majesties, obeyed and served, and do serve them as subjects should, with good will and no resistance, and immediately without delay, directly as they were informed, obeying the religious men whom their Highnesses sent to preach to them and teach our Holy Faith, of their entire free will and pleasure, without reward or condition whatsoever becoming Christians which they are; and their Highnesses received them joyfully and benignly, ordering them to be treated as their subjects and vassals were, and you are held and obliged to act likewise.

"Wherefore, as best you can, I entreat and require you to understand this well which I have told you, taking the time for it that is just you should, to comprehend and reflect, and that you recognize the Church as Mistress and Superior of the Universe, and the High Pontiff, called Papa, in its name, the Queen and King, our masters in their place as Lords, Superiors and Sovereigns of these islands and the main by virtue of these gifts, and you consent and give opportunity that these fathers and religious men, declare and preach to you as stated. If you shall do so you will do well in what you are held and obliged; and their Majesties, and I, in their royal name, will receive you with love and charity, relinquishing in freedom your women, children and estates, without service, that with them and yourselves you may do with perfect liberty all you wish and may deem well. You shall not be required to become Christians, except, when informed of the truth, you desire to be converted to our Holy Catholic Faith, as nearly all the inhabitants of the other islands have done, and when his Highness will confer on you numerous privileges and instruction, with many favors.

"If you do not do this, and of malice you be dilatory, I protest to you, that, with the help of Our Lord, I will enter with force, making war upon you, from all directions, and in every manner that I may be able, when I will subject you to obedience to the Church and the yoke of their Majesties; and I will take the persons of yourselves, your wives and your children, to make slaves, sell and dispose of you, as their Majesties shall think fit, and I will take your goods, doing you all the evil and injury that I may be able; as to vassals who do not obey but reject their master, resist and deny him; and I declare to you that the deaths and damages that arise therefrom, will be your fault and not that of his Majesty, nor mine, nor of these cavaliers who came with me. And so as I proclaim and require this, I ask of the Notary here that he give a certificate; and those present I beseech that they will hereof be witnesses."

THE FIRST SPANISH EXPLORERS 63

the expedition laid before him their commissions, all of which were duly approved by Narváez. Just what effect the reading of the summons to the naked barbarians had upon them is not recorded. It takes no vivid imagination, however, to picture their actions. Little did these savages care about the mighty Don Carlos, and much less did the high-sounding words of the proclamation appeal to them. Their concern was their personal safety, and, according to Alvar Nuñez Cabeza de Vaca, they sought it in flight. There was no interpreter to communicate to them the claim that the Pope was the father and ruler of all men, the king, Lord and Superior of the universe, and this farcical ceremonial only brought forth signs and menaces from the Indians commanding the "servant, messenger and captain" of the "ever victors, never vanquished Sovereigns of Leon and Castilla" to leave the country.

Two days afterwards, Narváez, with a substantial escort, accompanied by Alvar Nuñez Cabeza de Vaca and two other officers, journeyed inland on a short excursion. They marched in a northerly direction until evening, when they came to a large bay, extending far into the interior,[50] upon the shore of which they made camp until the next day, when they returned to the fleet.

Narváez now gave orders that the brigantine should sail along the coast of Florida and make search for the harbor that Miruelo, the pilot, said he knew, although as yet he had failed to find it, and could not inform the officers where they were, nor could he give information as to the location of the port, and that if the harbor were not found, to proceed to Havana and bring provisions from the ship which had been left in command of Alvaro de la Cerda.

After the departure of the brigantine, Narváez returned inland, continuing his explorations. He marched along the coast, with his small party, for a distance of four leagues, capturing four Indians, who conducted them to their town at the head of the bay.

Here was found some unripe corn, and the Spaniards saw four dead bodies covered with deer-skins, and deposited in cases similar to those used in Castile for containing merchandise. The bodies were burned by order of Narváez.[51] They also found some pieces

---

[50] The western arm of Tampa bay.
[51] Bandelier, Mrs. Fanny, *The Journey of Alvar Nuñez Cabeza de Vaca*, note, p. 12:
"There is a discrepancy here between the statement of Cabeza de Vaca

of woolen cloth, bunches of feathers,[52] and a few pieces of gold. The Indians were asked where they obtained these things, their reply being that they came from a distant province called Apalache,[53] which also abounded in many other articles of great value. Narváez continued some ten or twelve leagues further into the interior, being guided by the Indians. No discoveries were made, however, except some ripe corn, and retracing his steps, Narváez returned to the fleet.

What to do was now a problem for Narváez. He, therefore, called

and the letter to the Audiencia. The letter says (*Historia*, etc., iii, p. 583): 'And there they found some large boxes from Castilla, and in each of them a dead man, and the corpses covered with painted hides. It appeared to the Commissary and friars that these were idolatries, so the governor had them burnt. There were also found pieces of shoes and canvas (*lienzo*), of cloth and some iron, and inquiring of the Indians they told us by signs that they had found it in a vessel that had been lost on this coast and in that bay.'

"The text of Oviedo discriminates between the origin of these objects and that of the gold, which it says the Indians declared that there was none in that country, but at Apalache, very far away. The first edition always has Apalachen or Palachen. Oviedo (p. 615) justly blames the friars for having burnt the bodies: 'Since the boxes and other indications might have led them to think that they were the bodies of Christians, and so it is stated in the second relation, that they learned from Indians that these dead people had been Christians.' The *Relacion* (p. 270) mentions briefly the bodies, and also states that gold was found in the province of Apalache.''

[52] Bandelier, Mrs. Fanny, *Ibid*, p. 12: ''Feather head dresses that seemed to be from New Spain.''

Mr. Adolph F. Bandelier, in his notes to the translation of the *Relacion* made by his wife, says: ''The shipwreck mentioned may allude to the loss, in 1526, of one of the two vessels in which Lucas Vasquez de Ayllon made his unlucky voyage to Chicora. This vessel was lost at the mouth of the Rio Jordon.'' Herrera, *Historia General*, etc., 1726, vol. ii, p. 242, *Decada*, iii, lib. vii, cap. xiii.

Mr. F. W. Hodge, commenting upon this suggestion by Bandelier, says: ''As this wreck occurred at the mouth of Cape Fear River, on the southern coast of North Carolina, it does not seem likely that they could have been derived from this source.''

[53] Hodge, F. W., *Spanish Explorers in the Southern United States*, note, p. 21: ''The Apalachee were one of the Muskhogean tribes that occupied northwestern Florida from the vicinity of Pensacola eastward to Ocilla river, their chief seats being in the vicinity of Tallahassee and St. Marks. In 1655 they numbered six or eight thousand, but about the beginning of the eighteenth century they were warred against by the Creeks, instigated by the English of Carolina, and in 1703 and 1704 expeditions by English troops, reinforced by Creek warriors, resulted in the capture and enslavement of about fourteen hundred Apalachee and in practically exterminating the remainder. The town of Apalachicola, on the Savannah river, was inhabited by Apalachee refugees colonized later by the Carolina government, but these were finally merged with the Creeks. Apalachee Bay and the Appalachian Mountains derive their names from this tribe.''

Ships of the Narváez Expedition

THE FIRST SPANISH EXPLORERS

Old Print — Herrera
 Battle between Spaniards and Indians

a council of all the officers of the expedition. The commissary, Father Xuares, and the governor, together with almost all of the officers, were in favor of sending the remaining ships along the coast in search of Panuco, the remainder of the company following along shore. Alvar Nuñez Cabeza de Vaca most strenuously opposed this course, although it was finally determined upon, notwithstanding the latter's statement that the ships would never be seen again. So certain was he of his judgment on this matter that he took the precaution to have a notarial certificate made that he had so advised the governor, and Narváez did the same in order that his course might be justified.

When it became known among the men and women of the expedition that Narváez intended to carry his determination into effect, one of the women [54] aboard the fleet cautioned him not to go inland, as she was confident that neither he nor any going with him could

---

[54] *Naufragios*, cap. xxxviii, p. 43, in *Relacion*, etc., Buckingham Smith's translation. Narváez asked the woman "whence she had learned those things that had passed, as well as those she spoke of that were to come; she replied that in Castilla a Moorish woman of Hornachos had told them to her. When they had betaken themselves to the ships, all of them looking at that woman, they distinctly heard her say to the females, that well, since their husbands had gone inland, putting their persons in such great jeopardy, their wives should in no way take more account of them, but ought soon to be looking after whom they would marry, and that she should do so. She did accordingly."

ever escape. The prophecy of the woman, however, had no effect upon Narváez. He placed the fleet in command of Caravallo, an alcalde of the expedition, and gave him full instructions as to his future course. Narváez mustered his troops upon the shore.[55] There were three hundred infantry and forty cavalry, fully equipped.

On Saturday, the first day of May, Narváez distributed two pounds of biscuit and half a pound of bacon to each man, and thus victualled the command took up its march into the interior.

Very brief indeed is the story of the naval portion of the expedition. The fleet sailed up the coast but failed to find a harbor. Returning, it came over the same course it had pursued, and five leagues below the Baia de la Cruz, the mouth of Tampa bay was discovered. Meanwhile Alvaro de la Cerda arrived with his ship from Havana and the search for Narváez was continued for an entire year, and being entirely unsuccessful, finally Caravallo sailed for New Spain.

Pursuing a northerly course, Narváez began his march. The command was accompanied by Friar Juan Xuares, and another friar, Juan de Palos, and three clergymen. Having traveled along the coast or nearly parallel to it, in a northerly direction, for fifteen days, they arrived at a large river, where the expedition was detained an entire day in crossing. This was accomplished by swimming and with the aid of rafts. This stream was the Withlacoochee,[56] as it is the first large stream north of Tampa bay, emptying into the Gulf of Mexico. After crossing the river they encountered as many as two hundred natives. Narváez met and conversed with them by the use of signs, but the Indians grossly insulted the Spaniards, whereupon five or six were seized and, using them as guides, Narváez went to their homes, about

NARVÁEZ MARCHES INTO THE INTERIOR AND CAPTURES APALACHE

---

[55] Oviedo, *Historia*, etc., iii, p. 584, says, following the letter to the Audiencia, 260 foot and forty horse. The *Relacion* (p. 270) says three hundred men and forty men on horseback.

[56] Smith, Buckingham, *Relation*, p. 34.
Prince, L. B., *Hist. New Mexico*, pp. 49-89.
Hodge, F. W., *Spanish Explorers in the Southern United States*, p. 25, note.
Davis, W. W. H., *Spanish Conquest of New Mexico*, p. 23. "The distance from Tampa is about one hundred miles, and according to their rate of travel, the Spaniards should have reached it in fifteen days, the time they were occupied in making the march."

THE FIRST SPANISH EXPLORERS 67

half a league distant. Here the Spaniards found a large quantity of maize which they gathered, giving thanks to the Lord for having succored them in their great extremity.[57]

Here Narváez remained for several days, sending two exploring parties down to the bay at the mouth of the river, searching unsuccessfully, however, for a harbor. The first party was under the command of Alvar Nuñez Cabeza de Vaca, who, returning, reported that he had marched upon what appeared to be the seashore until he arrived at the river which they had crossed, when he retraced his steps without having discovered the sea. Narváez was dissatisfied with this report and sent out a second party of sixty infantry and six cavalry, under command of Valenzuela, who was directed to cross the river, follow it to its mouth, and look for a good harbor. Valenzuela returned after an absence of two days reporting that the bay was nowhere deeper than to the knee, that he could find no harbor but had seen five or six canoes filled with Indians passing from one shore to the other, wearing many plumes.

Valenzuela having returned, the army resumed its march, continuing in a northerly direction, through a barren and uninhabited country. On the 17th of June the Spaniards were visited by an Indian chief, dressed in painted deer-skins and carried upon the back of a warrior. With him was a very large concourse of his people playing flutes, made of reeds.[58] Narváez held intercourse with him using signs and gave him to understand that he was in search of Apalache. The chief said that his people and those of Apalache were enemies and that he would assist the Spaniards in making war upon them. A few trinkets were given to the Indians and Narváez was presented by the Indian chief with the deer-skin which he wore. Having resumed their march, that night they came to another large river, so broad and so deep that they were obliged to build a large canoe with which to ferry across. This consumed an entire day. The river was the Suwannee.[59] One soldier and his horse were

---
[57] *Relacion* (Bandelier trans.): ''We gave infinite thanks to our Lord for having helped us in such great need, for, as we were not used to such exposures, we felt greatly exhausted, and were much weakened by hunger.''
[58] Hakluyt, *Voyages*, vol. ii, p. 566. It was in this same locality that Hernando de Soto, eleven years later, was also met by Indians who played flutes.
Hodge, F. W., *Spanish Explorers in the Southern United States*, note, p. 26.
[59] Smith, Buckingham, *Relation*, p. 34.
Prince, L. B., *History of New Mexico*, pp. 50-89.

swept away by the current and drowned;[60] the body of the horse was recovered by the Indians and was cooked and eaten by the soldiers. The Spaniards made camp upon the bank of the river until morning, when the march was resumed, and the next day they arrived at the town of the chief. The usual hospitalities of the tribe were extended to Narváez and his army and a substantial supply of corn was also furnished them. During the night the Indians withdrew from the town. The next morning, while on the march, they met a large body of Indians, fully armed and equipped for battle. As the Spaniards came up, however, they fled and then took up a position in the rear of the army. A small party was placed in ambush to surprise them, and in this manner, as the Indians came up, several were captured, and these were compelled to act as guides. Under their direction, Narváez marched until the 24th of June, through a country covered with a heavy growth of timber, the ground covered with fallen trees. Many of the standing trees were riven from top to bottom by bolts of lightning which fall "in that country of frequent storms and tempests." Toiling manfully along until the day of Saint John the Baptist, the army came in sight of Apalache,[61] the inhabitants being

Hodge, F. W., *Spanish Explorers in the Southern United States*, note, p. 27.
Davis, W. W. H., *The Spanish Conquest of New Mexico*, note, p. 25, says: "This river is supposed to have been the Suwannee, which rises in Georgia, flows south and empties into the Gulf. From the length of time employed in marching from the Withlacoochee to the Suwannee, Mr. Smith supposes that Narváez crossed the river pretty high up. As the journal of Vaca makes no mention of having passed any stream between these two rivers, it would naturally be inferred that they crossed the Suwannee below its eastern branch, else some account would have been given of the latter stream. They must have changed their course from the North toward the West before they reached the river. It is the opinion of Mr. Smith, that, in the marching of the Spaniards from the Suwannee to the Gulf, they were conducted by the Indians near the present boundary between Florida and Georgia. Garcillasso de la Vega, who accompanied the expedition of De Soto a few years later, and who appears to have seen Vaca's journal when he wrote his account of De Soto's march, was also of the same opinion."

[60] Bandelier, Mrs. Fanny, *The Journey of Alvar Nuñez Cabeza de Vaca*, p. 22, says: "One horseman, whose name was Juan Velasquez, a native of Cuellar, not willing to wait, rode into the stream, and the strong current swept him from the horse and he took hold of the reins, and was drowned with the animal. His death caused us much grief, since until then we had not lost anybody."

[61] Davis, W. W. H., *The Spanish Conquest of New Mexico*, p. 26, note 3, says: "The exact situation of this place is not known, and it can only be located by conjecture. Narváez was eight days in marching from the Suwannee to Apalachee, and his course must have been west, or nearly so; and I believe

THE FIRST SPANISH EXPLORERS 69

unaware of the approach of the Spaniards; here they gave many thanks to God "that there would be an end to our great hardships, caused as much by the length and badness of the way as by our excessive hunger." Without so much as a grain of corn, they had marched, heavy laden with armor, many weary miles, and "yet, having come to the place desired, and where we had been informed were much food and gold, it appeared to us that we had already recovered in part from our sufferings and fatigue."

Here, again, the Spanish hopes were blasted. They found nothing but an Indian town, and while corn was plentiful, no gold was found. The place was not far from the present city of Tallahassee, situated on one of the larger lakes, surrounded by an almost impenetrable forest, the approach to which was most difficult on account of the fallen timber.

The houses of the village numbered forty, were low, and had thatched roofs. They were occupied only by the women and children. The Indians had fled, but shortly returned and opened fire upon the Spaniards with a great flight of arrows. The battle lasted only a few moments, when they again fled, leaving Alvar Nuñez Cabeza de Vaca and his force of fifty men, who had been sent in by Narváez, in complete possession of the village. No loss was suffered by the Spaniards, with the exception of one horse killed. A few hours after the battle the Indians returned in peaceful attitude and requested that their women and children be delivered up to them.

---

the town to have been situated between that river and the Ocilla, which empties into the bay of Apalachee."

Prince, L. B., *History of New Mexico*, p. 90, believes Apalache to have been in the vicinity of Tallahassee, or farther north in southwestern Georgia, or near the locality of Chattahoochee.

Gatschet, *Migration Legend*, vol. i, p. 74, says the town "was north of Apalachi Bay. This was probably the place after which Apalachie provincia was named in De Soto's time. He says the word is in the Hichiti dialect of the Maskoki and signifies 'Those on the other shore, or river.' This 'Apalache' was nine days' travel from Auté, *Naufragios*, cap. vii, and lay to the north of it, surrounded by lakes of which the largest lay next it. The location on Lake Miccausukee best fills the conditions. I think there can be little doubt it was located among the lakes in the northern ends of Leon and Jefferson counties, north of Tallahassee, Florida."

Herrera, *Historia General*, vol. iii, dec. 6, lib. vii, cap. xii, p. 167.

Bandelier, Ad. F., note to *The Journey of Alvar Nuñez Cabeza de Vaca*, p. 25, says: "This Indian village seems to have been situated west of the peninsula of Florida, not far from the coast. Without presuming to insist upon its location, I would only remark that it might have been on or near what is now the Apalachicola river."

Their request was complied with but Narváez detained one of their chieftains, one who had been most active in stirring up the people against the Spaniards. The following day the savages returned, made a vigorous attack upon the troops, but soon made good their escape in canoes upon the surrounding lakes. Still another attack was made the day following but this also was quickly repulsed.

Narváez remained twenty-five days at Apalache, made frequent excursions into the surrounding country, and satisfied himself that the town was the largest in all that region, and that "thenceforth were great lakes, dense mountains, immense deserts and solitudes."[62] He made frequent inquiries of the captive chief about other towns and was informed that Apalache was the most populous. To the south, he was told, in a journey of nine days, was another town called Auté, where there was plenty of corn, pumpkins, and fish, and that the inhabitants were friendly with those of Apalache. The Indians kept up their attacks upon the army, in one of which they killed a Mexican Indian who had come with Fr. Xuares, Don Pedro by name, a lord of Tescuco.[63]

Narváez determined to march in search of Auté. In the meantime the Indians from all the surrounding country resisted his march to the south. The second day, after leaving Apalache, while crossing a lake, he was attacked by a large body of savages, who fired upon the army from behind trees and from places of concealment in the tall swampy grasses which grew in abundance. They succeeded in checking his advance and fought with great bravery. Several men and horses were wounded, and the Indians were not routed until the cavalry had been dismounted and had charged them on foot, when the Indians broke and fled into the lake. The Indians were all well armed with bows as thick as the arm and about three and one-half feet long; they were good marksmen and shot their arrows long distances with great accuracy, and with such force as to penetrate the coats of mail worn by the soldiers.[64] Having crossed three lakes, the Indians stubbornly disputing their advance at two of them, they

---

[62] *Naufragios*, cap. vii, p. 7, in *Historiadores*, tomo i.

[63] Buckingham, Smith, *Relation of Alvar Nuñez Cabeza de Vaca* (1871), p. 42, n. 7.

[64] Hodge, F. W., *Spanish Explorers in the Southern United States*, pp. 31-32: "There were those this day who swore that they had seen two red oaks, each the thickness of the lower part of the leg, pierced through from side to side by arrows."

came out upon the plain, where they attacked the Indians, killing two and wounding two or three others. They now continued for several days without opposition until they came within a league of Auté, at which place the Indians fell upon the rear guard. In this attack one Spaniard was killed, an hidalgo named Avellañeda, who was struck near the edge of his cuirass with an arrow with such force that the shaft passed entirely through his neck.

Having arrived at Auté,[65] the Spaniards found the village deserted and the huts burned, but there was a plentiful supply of maize, beans, and pumpkins, all beginning to be fit for gathering.

The third day after their arrival Alvar Nuñez Cabeza de Vaca was sent in search of the sea coast, but he returned, reporting his inability to find it owing to the fact that the bays and creeks were so large and lay so far inland that it was difficult to examine them, and that the sea shore was very distant. In his absence the Indians had made an attack upon the camp. He found the commander ill and the soldiers worn out. Treachery among the men was discovered about this time. A plot was discovered among the cavalry to desert the governor and those who were sick. Humanity, however, prevailed, and the persons who were engaged in the conspiracy were dissuaded from their purpose.

After remaining at Auté seven days, Narváez resumed his march toward the coast, and on the evening of the first day, he reached the place where Alvar Nuñez Cabeza de Vaca had ceased his explorations a few days before. Here the army encamped.[66]

BOATS ARE BUILT BY NARVÁEZ AND HE ATTEMPTS TO ESCAPE BY SEA

The misfortunes which beset them made it necessary that imme-

---

[65] Davis, W. W. H., *Spanish Conquest of New Mexico*, says: "The situation of this place is equally uncertain with that of Apalache, but was somewhere in the same region of country."

Prince, L. B., *History of New Mexico*, p. 90, thinks Auté may have been on St. Mark's or the great river, the Appalachicola, and Auté near the site of Ft. Gadsden.

Ship, in his *De Soto and Florida*, thinks it was on the bay of St. Mark's.

Hodge, F. W., *Spanish Explorers in the Southern United States*, p. 33, note, says, "St. Mark's River, which flows into St. Mark's Bay, at the head of which Auté was situated."

[66] Smith, Buckingham, *Relation*, p. 55, says the place was Apalachee bay.

Prince, L. B., *History of New Mexico*, p. 90, thinks so too.

Hakluyt, *Voyages*, vol. ii, p. 565. It was here that De Soto saw remains of the party.

Davis, W. W. H., *Spanish Conquest of New Mexico*, p. 31, note, says. "The

72   LEADING FACTS OF NEW MEXICAN HISTORY

diate steps be taken for their self-preservation. Every officer and soldier of prominence was called to a conference by Narváez and each was asked what, in his judgment, was the best course to be pursued. Calm deliberation was had, and it was determined that the best plan was the building of boats whereby they might escape by means of the sea. As Cabeza de Vaca says, "This appeared [67] impossible to every one; we knew not how to construct, nor were there tools, nor iron, nor forge, nor tow, nor resin, nor rigging; finally, no one thing of so many that are necessary, nor any man who had a knowledge of their manufacture; and, above all there was nothing to eat, while building, for those who should labor." And yet, in spite of all this, it was determined to build the boats, and, embarking, trust their fortunes to the sea, intending to coast along the shore of the bays and gulf until they should reach some Spanish settlements in Mexico.

They commenced to build the boats on the 4th of September,[68] and by the 20th, five were completed, each one being thirty-one feet long.

point where the Spaniards reached the Coast, they called the Bay of Caballos; and from the most reliable data, I am of the opinion that it was one of the coves or inlets of Apalachee Bay; in truth it cannot well be located further west. History seems to have fixed upon this locality with as much certainty as any other upon the whole route. In 1539, a squadron from the army of De Soto, under Juan de Anasco, visited this bay, and the appearance of the shore presented was stated by the Ynca in his account of the expedition. They saw plainly where the furnace had been built and charcoal was still found lying about. The logs the Spaniards had hollowed out and used for horse-troughs were also there. They were told by the Indians that Narváez had encamped at that place and built his boats. They pointed out to Anasco where various events had transpired, and took him all over the ground; and also showed him where the Indians had killed ten of his men as is stated in Vaca's journal. They explained to him by signs all that had occurred there. He and his men searched in holes and under the bark of trees to discover letters or other mementos of Narváez's men, but found nothing. Herrera confirms this location. In 1722, Charlevoix was at San Marcos de Apalache, and, in speaking of the bay, wrote as follows: 'This bay is precisely that which Garcilasso de la Vega, in his history of Florida, calls the port of Auté.' " Letter xxxiv.

[67] Hodge, F. W., *Spanish Explorers in the Southern United States*, p. 34-35.

[68] Hodge, F. W., *Ibid*, p. 35: "'We commenced to build on the fourth, with the only carpenter in the company, and we proceeded with so great diligence that on the twentieth day of September five boats were finished, twenty-two cubits in length, each caulked with the fibre of the palmito. We pitched them with a certain resin, made from the pine trees by a Greek, named Don Theodoro; from the same husk of the palmito, and from the tails and manes of the horses we made ropes and rigging, from our shirts, sails and from the savins growing there we made the oars that appeared to us requisite. Such was the country into which our sins had cast us, that only by very great search could we find stone for ballast and anchors, since in it all we had not seen one."

Courtesy of Bureau of American Ethnology

The Buffalo of Gomara

THE FIRST SPANISH EXPLORERS 73

The tools were of the rudest description. A bellows was made of deer-skins; nails, saws, and axes were made of their stirrups, spurs, bridle bits, and other articles of iron in their equipment. The fibre of the palmetto furnished the rigging for their boats, using also the manes and tails of the horses. The shirts of the officers and men were made into sails and the boats were calked with the palmetto. Every third day a horse was killed and divided among the men and those who were sick; some returned to Auté bringing with them a small supply of corn. The woods swarmed with Indians, who harassed the workmen. A party of ten, while gathering shell-fish in the coves and creeks of the sea, were attacked within sight of the camp and all were killed. Bottles, for the purpose of carrying fresh water aboard the canoes, were made of the tanned skins of the horses' legs.

The whole distance the army had marched from the Bay of the Cross, Baia de la Cruz, to the point where the boats were built, according to the declaration of the pilots under oath, was two hundred and eighty leagues.[69] The number of men lost, through disease and hunger, had been forty, and this did not include those who had been killed by the Indians.

On the twenty-second day of September the horses, all but one, had been consumed, and on that day Narváez and his companions embarked in the following order: in the boat of the governor went forty-nine men; in another, which he gave to the comptroller and the commissary, as many more; the third, he gave to Captain Alonzo del Castillo and Andrés Dorantes, with forty-eight men; and another he gave two captains, Tellez and Peñalosa, with forty-seven men. The last was given to the asessor and Alvar Nuñez Cabeza de Vaca, with forty-nine men. After the provisions and clothes had been taken in, not over a span of the gunwales remained above water and the boats were so crowded that their occupants could not move, "so much can necessity do which drove us to hazard our lives in this

---

[69] Hodge, F. W., *Spanish Explorers in the Southern United States*, note p. 36: "In reality they could not have travelled much more than as many miles in a straight line from Tampa Bay."
Bandelier, A. F., *The Journey of Alvar Nuñez Cabeza de Vaca*, note, p. 38: "The estimate of the distances is of little importance. It is a computation of the length of the line of march, not the distance between two points."

manner, running into a turbulent sea, not a single one who went having a knowledge of navigation."

Sailing to the west, Narváez made his way through bays and sounds, and, finding finally an exit between the islands along the shore, they followed the coast in the direction of the Rio de las Palmas to the southwest. Their horse-hide water bottles soon rotted, their supply of provisions was rapidly decreasing, and they were about reduced to the last extremities of hunger and thirst, when, to increase their difficulties, they were overtaken by a violent storm, which delayed them on one of the islands. Five canoes, loaded with Indians, started from the main land to meet them, but becoming alarmed they deserted their canoes, which fell into the hands of the Spaniards, and were used by them in raising the height of the gunwales, thereby making their boats the safer. On the island they found some mullets and mullet roes. They remained on the island only a short time when they re-embarked and pursued their voyage. They coasted for thirty days, now and again entering the coves and inlets. They suffered greatly from thirst. Five days they were without water and their thirst was so excessive that they were put to the extremity of drinking salt water, by which some of the men became so crazed that four of them died. A very violent storm arose while they were upon one of the islands; they again re-embarked, preferring to trust themselves to the perils of the wind and waves than to remain upon the island enduring such great thirst with no prospect of obtaining relief. The sea ran high, and about sunset they doubled a point of land behind which they found calm water in a sheltered inlet. As they neared the shore some Indians came off to meet them and followed them in to the land. The Indians conducted them to their village, where they offered the Spaniards fish, receiving in exchange some corn and trinkets. The chief invited the governor to his hut, where he tendered him the hospitalities of the tribe. Their friendship was only a pretext to conceal their hostility, for in the night-time they made an attack upon the Spaniards who were in the houses or scattered along the shore and they were with difficulty finally beaten off. Narváez was wounded in the face and hardly a man escaped injury of some sort. The Indian chief was taken prisoner in the conflict, but was afterwards liberated by his people. He left behind him, in his escape, his robe of skins of the

THE FIRST SPANISH EXPLORERS 75

civet-martin, which had a fragrance of amber and musk. The Indians renewed the attack three times and fought fiercely. At the last assault, fifteen men, under Captains Dorantes, Peñalosa, and Tellez, were placed in ambush and attacked them in the rear, when, after a short resistance, the Indians fled and did not return.[70]

The Indians having been repulsed, the Spaniards passed the night quietly and in the morning no sign of the enemy appeared. The weather was cold and, being without shelter, Alvar Nuñez broke up thirty canoes which had belonged to the Indians, using them for fuel. The sea still continued heavy and they were unable to embark. As night came on the sea became calm and on the following morning they continued their voyage. They rowed three days in a westerly direction, and entering an estuary, a canoe filled with Indians came out to meet them. Narváez asked them for water, which they promised to bring if he would furnish something in which to carry it. The Greek and the negro accompanied the Indians for water, against the advice of the governor, the Indians leaving two of their men as hostages. During the night the Indians returned with the vessels empty and without the Greek and the negro.[71]

NARVÁEZ RE-EMBARKS AND THE BOAT IN COMMAND OF ALVAR NUÑEZ CABEZA DE VACA IS CAST UPON THE SHORE

The following day the Indians came in considerable force for the purpose of releasing the hostages left with Narváez, but the Spaniards put out into the gulf and at last the boat commanded by Alvar Nuñez Cabeza de Vaca rounded a cape by which flowed a great river.[72] He cast anchor near a small island, waiting until the gov-

[70] Three men were killed, according to Oviedo.
[71] Mr. Hodge says that this happened in Pensacola bay.
Prince, L. B., *History of New Mexico*, says, p. 90, it was either Pensacola or Mobile bay.
Biedma's Narrative, *Publications of the Hakluyt Society*, ix, 1-83, 1851, says of the De Soto expedition in 1539: "Having set out for this village, we found a large river which we supposed to be that which falls into the Bay of Chuse (Pensacola Bay); we learned that the vessels of Narváez had arrived there in want of water, and that a Christian named Teodoro and an Indian had remained among these Indians; at the same time they showed us a dagger which had belonged to the Christian."
Smith, Buckingham, *Relation*, thinks that Teodoro wandered inland into the country of the buffalo and passed his life among the hunters of that animal.
[72] Hodge, F. W., *Spanish Explorers in the Southern United States*, p. 41, note: "The Mississippi, the waters of which were now seen by white men fourteen years before the 'discovery' of the stream by De Soto."

ernor should come up, but the latter, instead, entered a bay near by filled with small islands. Here all the boats came together and took on a supply of fresh water. This river was undoubtedly the Mississippi. Its powerful current and the wind from the north carried the boats out into the open sea a great distance from land and only after the third day did they see the shore. They were compelled to wait over night, and in the morning it was found that the boats had parted company. The boat commanded by Alvar Nuñez Cabeza de Vaca kept on its way, until, toward evening, the governor's boat was overtaken. Still further on, at sea, another boat was visible. After a short consultation Alvar Nuñez Cabeza de Vaca concluded to follow the governor, but this he was unable to do, as Narváez had all the healthy men and Alvar Nuñez Cabeza de Vaca was unable to keep up with him and joined the boat out at sea, which proved to be the one commanded by Tellez and Peñalosa. For four days the two boats kept company, the men subsisting upon the shortest of rations, when a severe storm parted them also and Alvar Nuñez Cabeza de Vaca was left alone with his men. Soon out of the entire company with Alvar Nuñez Cabeza de Vaca there were only five who were strong enough to handle the oars; as night came on, only two were left, the master and Alvar Nuñez Cabeza de Vaca, and finally the master too gave up and Alvar Nuñez alone remained, steering the frail canoe with a paddle.

In a short time the master revived and took his place at the helm, permitting Alvar Nuñez Cabeza de Vaca to take some rest. Toward morning some breakers were heard, and soon after a wave took the boat and hurled it some distance, into shallow water. From the violence with which the boat struck, nearly all the people were aroused by the shock to consciousness. Crawling into a ravine on shore, they parched some maize and found some rain water which shortly revived their exhausted energies.

Alvar Nuñez Cabeza de Vaca and his crew were cast ashore on the 6th day of November, 1528, and the island upon which they were cast is one not far from Matagorda bay.[73]

[73] Davis, W. W. H., *Spanish Conquest of New Mexico*, says: "From the most careful examination I have been able to give the subject, I believe that the boat of Vaca was cast away west of the Mississippi, upon one of the low, sandy islands that line the coast of Louisiana. There are several reasons for coming to this conclusion. In the first place, the time they were occupied in coasting

THE FIRST SPANISH EXPLORERS 77

The Indians gave the island the name of Auia; it was more than thirteen miles in length, about a mile and a half wide, and was situated in the mouth of a bay where there was another island. The Indians were the Capoques and the Hans. The men pierced their ears, the breasts, and the upper lip, through which they passed a piece of cane. The women were clad in the long Spanish moss, and the young girls wore deer-skins. They were armed with bows and arrows in the use of which they were very dextrous. They lived in houses built on heaps of shells. They subsisted on oysters, fish, roots, and other wild vegetables. As among all the Indians, the women performed most of the work of the household. They were of a kind-hearted disposition and treated the Spaniards with great kindness. Had they been otherwise disposed, resistance would have been use-

along shore would have enabled them to get beyond the mouth of the Mississippi. From the time they embarked at the Bay of Caballos until Vaca's boat was cast upon the island of Malhado, forty-five days elapsed, exclusive of stoppages. They were seven days passing through the shoals after they had embarked, and the other thirty-eight were occupied in rowing toward the west along the coast of the gulf. They did not follow all the windings and indentations of the coast is very evident, for Vaca says they only now and then entered the coves. After rowing thirty-four days, they passed the mouth of a great river, the current of which was so strong that it drove the boats out to sea in spite of all they could do; and four days afterwards the boats were separated in a storm, and that of Vaca wrecked. The Mississippi is the only river that empties into the Gulf of Mexico with a current as strong as the one here described. The mouth of the river was encountered four days before Vaca's boat was wrecked; and Mr. Smith locates the island of Malhado between the Chostawhatchee river and Pensacola Bay, but there is no river, with a current equal to the one the Spaniards encountered, emptying into the gulf at a point four days east of the islands off Pensacola Bay. There is another reason in favor of the conclusion to which I have arrived as to the place of Vaca's shipwreck. After he and his companions started inland in their wanderings through the country, they met with no river the size of the Mississippi, and it is not likely a stream which the Indians called the 'Father of Waters' would have passed unnoticed in the journal. The deepest river Vaca mentions only reached up to the waist, and that stream was encountered far out upon the plains. If they had come to the Mississippi while travelling on land it would have impeded their march unless they could have obtained canoes from the Indians to cross it. The circumstantial evidence already given seems to be sufficient to fix the shipwreck of Vaca at a point west of the Mississippi, in the absence of other testimony. But, in addition to this, we have direct testimony upon the subject. Castañeda, in his narrative of the expedition of Coronado, says the Spaniards passed the mouth of the Mississippi, which they discovered, on the last day of October, about which time they encountered the furious storm which separated the boats and drove that of Narváez out to sea. According to the same chronicler, six days after passing the mouth of the river Vaca's boat was cast upon the shore, which would have allowed them sufficient time to make some of the low sandy islands that skirt the coast of Louisiana.''

less, for among the Spaniards there were not "six that could rise from the ground."

The Spaniards remained on this island several days, recruiting their strength and making preparations to continue their voyage. Having now become well rested and supplied with an abundance of provisions, they determined to re-embark.

ALVAR NUÑEZ CABEZA DE VACA AND HIS COMPANIONS — WHAT BEFELL THEM

Their boat was finally excavated from the sands and in performing this labor they were compelled to work in water a long time without clothing. Having floated the boat, their provisions were put aboard, and having only embarked a fierce wave struck and capsized the boat. The asessor and one man were drowned, while the remainder were cast upon shore, having lost all their clothing, provisions, in fact everything the boat contained. Their condition was now more desperate than ever. A second time they found themselves upon this inhospitable coast, entirely at the mercy of the natives. It was November, and the cold was intense. For six months they had eaten little beside parched corn and shell-fish, and the entire party was so emaciated that they had the appearance of skeletons. Fortunately they were thrown upon the shore upon which they had previously encamped, and finding alive a few embers of the fire they had left in the morning, they kindled the coals anew, warming their chilled and frozen bodies.

The Indians were not aware of the mishap to the Spaniards, not having been told of their intended departure, and when the natives came in to the camp in the evening with the usual supply of food, they were so much surprised at the appearance of the Spaniards that they fled. Calling to them, Alvar Nuñez Cabeza de Vaca finally induced them to return, when they came and sat with him and his men, listening to the new misfortune which had come to them and how two of the party had been drowned. The Indians were very sensibly affected and manifested their grief by loud lamentations for more than an hour. The Spaniards besought the Indians to take them to their huts and give them shelter, which they did. The homes of the Indians were some distance inland and thirty of their number were sent ahead to make preparations for the reception of the Spaniards. Toward evening the weary soldiers were carried in the arms of the natives to the village. Large fires had been kindled, and they were taken to a large hut that had been prepared for them, in which also there was a blazing fire. Here they took up their quarters, while outside the natives held great rejoicings at their rescue, yelling and dancing almost all night, all of which alarmed the Spaniards, as they expected every moment to be taken out and offered up as victims to some heathen rite. They were not molested, however, and in the morning the Indians appeared with roots and fish, and in many ways treated them with great kindness.

The Spaniards were shortly informed by the Indians that there were other white men in the vicinity, whereupon Alvar Nuñez Cabeza de Vaca, having no doubt they were some of his shipwrecked companions, sent out two men in search of them.

MEETING WITH DORANTES, CASTILLO, AND THEIR COMPANIONS

They had not proceeded far, however, when they met a party of their countrymen coming toward the village. They were Andrés Dorantes and Castillo with their boat's crew. Their boat had been capsized on the fifth day of the month about a league and a half from the village, but the entire crew escaped with no loss of life or clothing. The congratulations of meeting having passed, they consulted as to the best means of making their escape. It was agreed to refit the boat of Dorantes and Castillo, and those who were able to go to sea were to ship in her, while the others were to remain until they could have sufficiently recovered their strength to make their way along the coast to some Spanish settlement. Immediate measures were taken to carry out this plan. After much exertion, the boat was launched, but she was hardly afloat when she sank and with it all hopes of the Spaniards of making their escape by water. As the boat went down they turned from the shore and retraced their steps, with heavy hearts, to the village. The Spaniards, finding themselves in no condition to journey westward, the weather being excessively cold, concluded to spend the winter where they were. It was agreed that four men, the most robust of the party and expert swimmers, should be sent forward to search for the Spanish settlement of Panuco. The men selected were Alvaro Fernandez, a Portuguese sailor and carpenter, Mendez, Figueroa, a native of Toledo, and Astudillo, a native of Cafra. They took with them an Indian of the island.[74] A few preparations having been made, these brave hearts started out upon their journey.

The weather continued cold and severe, and the Indians not being able to gather any roots or catch any fish, the Spaniards were confronted with starvation. The huts afforded very little protection and many of the Spaniards became ill and died. Five of them were reduced to such extremity that they were obliged to eat the dead bodies of their companions, in order to preserve their own lives.[75] In a short time only fifteen out of the eighty survivors remained alive. To increase their misery, about this time the Indians were visited by an epidemic of sickness, very fatal in character, and the Spaniards were accused of being the cause of it. This belief made the natives very hostile and they formed a plan to despatch the remaining Spaniards at once. They were prevented from carrying this plot into execution through the efforts of one of their number persuading them that the sickness was not caused by the Spaniards, and as evidence he showed that nearly all of the Spaniards had died of the same disease. The Indians were also much shocked at the cannibalism practiced by the Spaniards and on that account entertained great ill feeling toward them.

The island upon which the Spaniards were wrecked, they gave the name of Malhado or Misfortune. Alvar Nuñez Cabeza de Vaca, in his account [76] of the manners and customs of the people who inhabited the island, says:

THE ISLAND OF MALHADO AND ITS INHABITANTS

"The people on it are tall and well formed; they have no other weapons than bows and arrows with which they are most dextrous. The men have one of their nipples perforated from side to side and sometimes both; through this hole is thrust a reed as long as two and a half hands and as thick as two fingers; they also have the under lip perforated and a piece of cane in it as thin as half the finger. The women do the hard work. People stay on this island from October till the end of February, feed on the roots I have mentioned, taken from under the water in

---

[74] Herrera, *Historia General*, says: "The island of Cuba."

[75] *Relacion*, Bandelier translation: "Their names are: Sierra, Diego Lopez, Corral, Palacios and Gonzalo Ruiz. At this the Indians were so startled, and there was such an uproar among them, that I verily believe if they had seen this at the beginning they would have killed them."

[76] Bandelier, Mrs. Fanny, *The Journey of Alvar Nuñez Cabeza de Vaca*, pp. 65-68.

Fr. Bartolomé de las Casas

November and December. They have channels made of reeds and get fish only during that time; afterwards they subsist on roots. At the end of February they remove to other parts in search of food, because the roots begin to sprout and are not good any more.

"Of all the people in the world, they are those who love their children and treat them best, and should the child of one of them happen to die, parents and relatives bewail it, and the whole settlement, the lament lasting a full year, day after day. Before sunrise the parents begin to weep, after them the tribe, and the same they do at noon and at dawn. At the end of the year of mourning they celebrate the anniversary and wash and cleanse themselves of all their paint. They mourn all their dead in this manner, old people excepted to whom they do not pay any attention, saying that these have had their time and are no longer of any use, but only take space and food from the children.

"Their custom is to bury the dead, except those who are medicine men among them, whom they burn, and while the fire is burning, all dance and make a big festival, grinding the bones to powder. At the end of the year, when they celebrate the anniversary, they scarify themselves and give to the relatives the pulverized bones to drink in water. Every man has a recognized wife, but the medicine men enjoy greater privileges, since they may have two or three, and among these wives there is great friendship and harmony.

"When one takes a woman for his wife, from the day he marries her, whatever he may hunt or fish, she has to fetch it to the home of her father, without daring to touch or to eat of it, and from the home of the father-in-law they bring the food to the husband. All the while neither the wife's father nor her mother enter his abode, nor is he allowed to go to theirs, or to the homes of his brothers-in-law, and should they happen to meet they go out of each other's way a crossbow's shot or so, with bowed heads and eyes cast to the ground, holding it to be an evil thing to look at each other or speak. The women are free to communicate with their parents-in-law or relatives and speak to them. This custom prevails from that island as far as about fifty leagues inland.

"There is another custom, that when a son or brother dies no food is gathered by those of his household for three months, preferring rather to starve, but the relatives and neighbors provide them with victuals. Now, as during the time we were there so many of them died, there was great starvation in most of the lodges, due to their customs and ceremonials, as well as to the weather, which was so rough that such as could go out after food brought in but very little, withal working hard for it. Therefore the Indians by whom I was kept forsook the island and in several canoes went over to the mainland to some bays where there were a great many oysters and during three months of the year they do not eat anything else and drink very bad water. There is lack of fire-wood, but great abundance of mosquitoes. Their lodges are made of matting and built on oyster shells, upon which they sleep in hides, which they only get by chance. There we remained to the end of April, when we went to the seashore, where we ate blackberries for a whole month, during which time they danced and celebrated incessantly.''

The Spaniards had not been on the island a great while, when the natives desired to make physicians of them; they declined all knowledge, however, of the healing art and refused to assume the responsibility of being medicine men. But the Indians were not to be denied, and "they withheld food from us until we should practice what they required," and "at last, finding ourselves in great want we were constrained to obey; but not without fear lest we should be blamed for any failure or success." [77]

In this manner, under duress, the Spaniards became full-fledged disciples of Esculapius and performed some miraculous cures, if we are to believe the story of Alvar Nuñez Cabeza de Vaca. In his *Relacion* he says: "Our method was to bless the sick, breathing upon them, and recite a Pater Noster and an Ave Maria, praying with all earnestness to God our Lord that he would give health and influence to them to make us some good return. In his clemency he willed that all those for whom we supplicated should tell the others that they were sound and in health, directly after we made the sign of the blessed cross over them. For this, the Indians treated us kindly; they deprived themselves of food that they might give to us, and presented us with skins and some trifles." These shipwrecked unfortunates were undoubtedly the first exponents of Christian Science practicing with success upon this continent. Their system seems to have acted like a charm, for it is related that every time they made the sign of the cross the patient immediately recovered. Naturally they became very important personages and great medicine men.

The inhabitants of all this region wore no clothes, with the exception of the women and young girls, and theirs was a very scanty attire. They had no chief. They spoke two languages, those of one being called Capoques, those of the other, Han.[78] "They have

[77] Hodge, F. W., *Spanish Explorers in the Southern United States*, p. 53.
[78] Hodge, F. W., *Spanish Explorers in the Southern United States*, p. 54,

a custom when they meet, or from time to time when they visit, of remaining half an hour before they speak, weeping; and, this over, he that is visited first rises and gives the other all he has, which is received, and after a little while he carries it away, and often goes without saying a word.''

Alvar Nuñez Cabeza de Vaca made up his mind to escape to the mainland. Meanwhile Dorantes, Estevan, the negro from Azamor, and the remainder of the Spaniards, following another band of Indians with whom they had been living, had become separated from him and had gone down the coast leaving Lope de Oviedo and another Spaniard [79] on the island [80] because they were too ill to travel.

DORANTES AND CASTILLO ATTEMPT TO ESCAPE — THEY ARE SEPARATED FROM ALVAR NUÑEZ CABEZA DE VACA

note: ''Important as it is in affording evidence of the route of Cabeza de Vaca and his companions, it is not possible, with our present knowledge of the former tribes of the coast region of Texas, to identify with certainty the various Indians mentioned by the narrator. Whether the names given by him are those which the natives applied to themselves or are those given by other tribes is unknown, and as no remnant of this once considerable coast population now exists, the only hope of the ultimate determination of these Indians lies in the historical archives of Texas, Mexico, and Spain. The two languages and stocks represented on the island of Malhado — the Capoque and the Han — would seem to apply to the Karankawan and Attacapan families respectively. The Capoques (called Cahoques on p. 87) are seemingly identical with the Cocos who lived with the Mayayes on the coast between the Brazos and Colorado Rivers in 1778, and with the Cokes, who as late as 1850, are described as a branch of the Koronks (Karankawa). Of the Han people nothing more definite is known than that which is here recorded.''

[79] Hodge, F. W., *Ibid*, p. 55. Hierronymo de Alvaníz, the notary; also called Alaníz.

[80] Hodge, F. W., *Ibid*, note, p. 57: ''The identification of Malhado island is a difficult problem. On general principles Galveston island would seem to supply the conditions, in that it more likely would have been inhabited by two distinct tribes, perhaps representing distinct linguistic families, as it is known to have been inhabited by Indians (the Karankawa) at a later period, besides having the smaller island or islands behind it. But its size and the other conditions are not in favor of the identification, for its length is at least twice as great as that of Malhado, as given in the narrative, and it is also more than two leagues from its nearest end to the first stream that the Spaniards crossed after departing from the island (Oviedo, p. 593). Mr. James Newton Baskett suggests that the so-called Velasco island, next south of Galveston island, better fulfills the requirements, as indeed it does topographically, except for the fact that it is really a peninsula. Aside from this, it possesses all the physical features — length and width, distance from the first stream to the southward, and having the necessary island or islands (Mud and San Luis) off its northern shore. Accepting Mr. Baskett's determination, it is not difficult to account

Alvar Nuñez Cabeza de Vaca made his escape to the main land and, traveling for forty or fifty leagues along the coast and up into the interior among tribes who lived in the direction of the Red river of Louisiana, he began a traffic among the natives to whom he brought from the coast various kinds of shells, shell ornaments, and small shell beads, in exchange for which he obtained skins and ochre pigments, canes for arrows, flint heads, and tassels of the hair of the deer, dyed red. In this manner he became very well acquainted with the country. Every year he returned to the island, endeavoring always to persuade Oviedo to make his escape with him. The companion of Oviedo having died, these two left the island and traveled south, crossing four rivers, one of which emptied into the gulf; they came upon a bay a league in width, which was supposed to be the bay of Espiritu Santo. This bay they crossed in safety and, resuming their journey, they met some Indians of the Quevenes nation.[81] These told the two Spaniards that there were three

for the four streams, 'very large and of rapid current,' one of which flowed directly into the gulf. Following the journey of the Spaniards from the island, down the coast, in April, when the streams were swollen by flood, the first river was crossed in two leagues after they had reached the main land. This was evidently Oyster creek. Three leagues farther was another river, running so powerfully that one of the rafts was driven to sea more than a league. This fully agrees with the Brazos, which indeed is the only large stream of the landlocked Texas coast that flows directly into the gulf. Four leagues still farther they reached another river, where the boat of the comptroller and the commissary was found. From this fact it may be assumed that this stream also flowed into the open gulf, a condition satisfied by Caney creek. The San Bernardo may well have escaped notice in traveling near the coast from the fact that it flows into Cedar lake. Five or six leagues more brought them to another large river (the Colorado), which the Indians carried them across in a canoe; and in four days they reached the bay of Espiritu Santo (La Vaca bay?). ''The bay was broad, nearly a league across. The side toward Panuco (the south) forms a point running out nearly a quarter of a league, having on it some large white sand stacks which it is reasonable to suppose can be descried from a distance at sea, and were consequently thought to mark the River Espiritu Santo.'' After two days of exertion they succeeded in crossing the bay in a broken canoe; and at the end of twelve leagues they came to a small bay not more than the breadth of a river. Here they found Figueroa, the only survivor of the four who had attempted to return to Mexico. The distance from Malhado island is given as sixty leagues, consequently the journey from the Colorado to the bay now reached, which seems to be no other than San Antonio bay, covered thirty-two to thirty-three leagues. Lofty sand dunes, such as those seen on what we regard as perhaps La Vaca bay, occur on San Antonio bay. See *United States Coast Survey Report* for 1859, p. 325. The western shore of the bay is a bluff or bank of twenty feet. 'At one place on this side, a singular range of sandhills, known as the Sand-mounds approaches the shore. The highest peak is about seventy-five feet above the bay.'''

[81] *Guevenes,* in the edition of 1542 (Bandelier translation). Mr. Hodge

other of their people some distance beyond, the survivors of a considerable number, the others of the company having died of hunger, cold, or had been killed, and that the tribe that held them was treating them very harshly. The Indians, by way of demonstrating to Cabeza de Vaca and Oviedo the cruel manner in which the other Spaniards had been treated, and "that we might know what they told us of the ill usage to be true, slapped my companion and beat him with a stick, and I was not left without my portion. Many times they threw lumps of mud at us and every day they put their arrows to our hearts, saying that they were inclined to kill us in the way they had destroyed our friends." Oviedo became very much frightened at these demonstrations of hostility and desired to return with the women who had come with him. Cabeza de Vaca did everything he possibly could to dissuade Oviedo from his purpose, but he returned with the women and was never heard of afterwards.

Two days after Lope de Oviedo left, the Indians who had Alonzo del Castillo and Andrés Dorantes, came to the place of which he had been told, for the purpose of eating walnuts. An Indian told Cabeza de Vaca that the Christians were coming and said that if he wished to see them he should go to a certain wooded point, and as they came by he and his kindred proposed to visit the Indians and that he would take Cabeza de Vaca with him.

The meeting between the Spaniards was a most joyful one, their delight being mutual. They soon agreed upon a plan of escape, which was to be carried out six months later when the band of Indians who had them as slaves went into another part of the country for the purpose of eating the fruit of the prickly pear. This fruit — the *Opuntia* cactus — Cabeza de Vaca described as being of the size of a hen's egg, vermilion and black in color, and of agreeable flavor, and that the Indians subsisted upon it three months in the year.

Cabeza de Vaca was given to an Indian as his slave and to whom Dorantes already belonged. The Indian was blind of one eye, as were also his wife and sons, and likewise another who was with him.

---

thinks there is reason to believe that these people may have been identical with the Cohani, who lived west of the Colorado river of Texas in the first quarter of the nineteenth century.

These Indians were the Mariames. Castillo was with another and neighboring tribe, called the Iguaces.

From Dorantes, Alvar Nuñez Cabeza de Vaca learned of the fate of two more of the boats which had sailed from the Bay of Horses. Dorantes had learned this from the sole survivor [82] of the party of four which had first left the island of Malhado seeking Panuco, and who had ultimately returned to the coast where he was accustomed to live. He had received his information from another Christian who was a captive among the Quevenes, where Figueroa found him.[83]

CABEZA DE VACA LEARNS OF THE FATE OF NARVÁEZ AND HIS COMPANIONS

According to the story, Narváez, after the parting of his boat and that of Cabeza de Vaca, had come upon the comptroller and Fr. Xuares, with the friars and the crew of the second boat, which had been upset at the confluence of the rivers.[84]

The governor landed his own crew and sailed along the coast, while the remainder of his own men and those of the second boat followed along shore until they came to a bay, across which Narváez carried those on shore in his own boat. The governor remained on board, and, during the night, a heavy gale from the north drove him and those with him out to sea. They had neither food nor water aboard and were never heard of again.[85]

Those who had been left on the shore marched along the coast, feeding upon oysters and shell-fish, and soon became utterly exhausted and one by one died of hunger and cold. The bodies of those who died were eaten [86] by the famished survivors. Finally

---

[82] Figueroa.

[83] Hernando de Esquivel, a native of Bajadóz, who had come in company with the commissary.

[84] The delta of the Mississippi river.

[85] Bandelier, Mrs. Fanny, *The Journey of Alvar Nuñez Cabeza de Vaca*, p. 84: ''The governor did not land that night, but remained on his barge with a pilot and a page who was sick. They had neither water nor anything to eat on board, and at midnight a northerner set in with such violence that it carried the barge out into the sea, without anybody noticing it. They had for anchor only a stone, and never more did they hear of him.''

[86] Hodge, F.W., *The Spanish Explorers in the Southern United States*: ''The living dried the flesh of them who died; and the last that died was Soto-Mayor, when Esquivel preserved his flesh, and, feeding on it, sustained existence until the first of March, when an Indian of those that had fled, coming to see if they were alive, took Esquivel with him. While he was in the possession of the

THE FIRST SPANISH EXPLORERS

all but one met a similar fate and he was pursued by Indians and killed. Dorantes declared that of his own twelve companions four had been drowned, two lost in their journeyings, and three had been killed by the savages. The boat's crew commanded by Tellez and Peñalosa met with death at the hands of the barbarians. The members of the crew came on shore and being too exhausted to offer any resistance were all slain. So, at the time of the meeting of Dorantes and Cabeza de Vaca, there remained only ten of the original expedition of more than four hundred persons, and of these but five were destined ever to meet again with Europeans.

Meanwhile the survivors with great anxiety were awaiting the time when they could escape from the savages who held them as slaves. The Mariames and Yguazes [87] passed their lives between alternate conditions of plenty and starvation. They were not an agricultural people. They had many very peculiar customs, all of which are graphically described by Cabeza de Vaca in his narrative. They destroyed their daughters at birth and also permitted the dogs to devour them, as they were afraid their enemies might raise children from them and thus acquire strength and power sufficient to reduce them to slavery. The men bought their wives of their enemies, the price being a bow and two arrows. They lived in the married state at the will of the parties, separations occurring for the slightest cause. The men were not good hunters, although occasionally they hunted the deer, following the animal on foot all day until it was run down, or killing it by encircling it with fire. They were a merry and cheerful people, and even though they had nothing to eat, never failed to observe their festivities and ceremonials. They seemed to be happiest when gathering the prickly pear. During this time, they danced both day and night.

---

native, Figueroa saw him, and learned all that had been related. He besought Esquivel to come with him, that together they might pursue the way to Panuco; to which Esquivel would not consent, saying that he had understood from the friars that Panuco had been left behind.''

[87] During the time the companions of Dorantes were with the Indians, held in slavery, they were very badly treated, and the Indians, among other things, amused themselves in pulling out their beards. They killed three out of the six without any cause, except that they went from one house to another. Dorantes, fearing he would meet the same fate, made his escape to the Mariames, the people among whom Esquivel tarried. These people informed Dorantes how they had put Esquivel to death, because he tried to run away on account of a woman dreaming that her son would kill him, and to prove their story, they showed him ''his sword, beads, and book, with other things that had been his.''

The pear was prepared for food by squeezing it open, drying it in the sun, and afterwards the skin was beaten into a powder. Their camps were always made near to wood and water. They were a very warlike people and in their campaigns were strategists of no mean order. Cabeza de Vaca writes of their great vigilance, their habits while fighting, their remarkable sight and hearing, as well as of their great powers of physical endurance when confronted with hunger, thirst, or cold.

The first printed mention of the buffalo is made by Cabeza de Vaca. In mentioning this animal, Cabeza de Vaca says: "Cattle come as far as here. Three times I have seen them and eaten of their meat. I think they are about the size of those in Spain. They have small horns like the cows of Morocco; the hair is very long and flocky like the merino's. Some are tawny, others black. To my judgment the flesh is finer and fatter than that of this country. Of the skins of those not full grown the Indians make blankets, and of the larger they make shoes and bucklers. They come as far as the sea-coast of Florida, from a northerly direction, ranging through a tract of more than four hundred leagues; and throughout the whole region over which they run, the people who inhabit near, descend and live upon them, distributing a vast many hides into the interior country."

The Spaniards had agreed among themselves to remain with the Indians a period of six months before making any efforts to escape, and this time having elapsed, they began to put their plans into execution. The Indians made their annual trip, some twenty leagues distant, for the purpose of gathering the fruit of the prickly pear. Just as matters had so shaped themselves as to permit of their carrying out their intentions, the Indians had a quarrel among themselves. They had a great row over a woman, and began beating and kicking each other in a general fight, and finally each one took to his lodge and left for some other part of the country, by which the Spaniards were separated. This unfortunate circumstance compelled them to remain with the Indians another year, during which time they were cruelly beaten and otherwise badly treated by the Indians.

CABEZA DE VACA AND HIS COMPANIONS MAKE THEIR ESCAPE FROM THE INDIANS

Courtesy of Bureau of American Ethnology

The Buffalo of De Bry

Three times Cabeza de Vaca tried to make his escape, but each time he was re-captured. The following year the annual pilgrimage to the district where the prickly pears were to be found was made. Again the Spaniards made plans for escape, when the Indians suddenly separated, and a second time they were disappointed. Cabeza de Vaca now told his companions that he proposed to escape, even though he had to leave without them; that he proposed remaining until the moon was full, when, if they did not join him, he would escape alone. The appointed time was the 13th day of September, and on that day he was joined by Dorantes and Estevan; Castillo was unable to come at that time, as he found it impossible to elude his captors. In a few days, however, he succeeded in escaping and reached his companions at the place agreed upon. This happened in the year 1534. Meanwhile they had joined another tribe from whom it was learned that the Camones tribe of Indians, who lived upon the coast, had slaughtered the commanders, Peñaloza and Tellez, and their entire company. In support of their statement the Indians produced some of the arms and clothing that had belonged to them. It is believed by Bandelier that the locality where these four survivors now found themselves was not far from the coast, somewhere between the Sabine and Trinity rivers.[88]

Now began the journey of these survivors of the ill-fated Narváez expedition across the continent, through the present state of Texas, and westward to the Pacific, the first Europeans to travel from sea to sea. The Indians having changed their camp and moved into another part of the country, the Spaniards remained with them but one day, when, eluding their vigilance, they fled. It was very late in the season; the prickly pears had nearly disappeared, but they hoped with what few remained, they would be able to subsist while making their journey. Speedily they passed over a long distance, when toward evening they saw some "smokes" in the distance. Soon they saw an Indian, who ran away. Estevan was sent after him and soon overtook him. The Indian was informed that they were looking for the people who made the smoke, and asked to be conducted to their lodges. The Indian complied with their request

---

[88] Hodge, F. W., *Spanish Explorers in the Southern United States*, note, p. 71: "Some thirty leagues inland from the coast between latitude 28 and 29 degrees."

and the Spaniards were received with demonstrations of the greatest kindness and were honored by being taken to the lodges of the two native medicine men. These Indians were the Avavares. The Indians knew of the healing powers of the Spaniards. Castillo seems to have been a wonderful healer. One night an Indian came to him saying that he had a great pain in his head and requested him to cure it. Castillo made the sign of the cross and commended the Indian to God, whereupon he announced that the pain had left him. The Indians now brought them venison and the best food that the country afforded. The Spaniards resumed their practice of healing the sick, and each one treated by them speedily or immediately recovered. They made inquiries as to the character of the country beyond them, and when they found out it was uninhabited they concluded to remain with the Indians during the winter.

Shortly after their arrival, the Avavares set out in search of food and in a journey of five days they arrived at a river, but found no pears. In wandering over the country Cabeza de Vaca became separated from his companions and was lost for five days. During this time he was entirely without food. On the evening of the fifth day he reached the bank of the river where he found the Indians encamped, all of whom were rejoiced at his return, as they had given him up for dead.

Shortly after the return of Cabeza de Vaca some Indians brought five sick persons to the camp and insisted that Castillo cure them of their ills, offering him bows and arrows. At sunset he pronounced a blessing over the sick and all the Christians joined in prayer to God, asking Him to restore them to health, and on the following morning there was not a sick person among them. These and other acts established the reputations of the Spaniards as healers, and the Spaniards themselves were impressed with the belief that the blessings of God were resting upon them, and that they would in due season make their escape. In their wanderings they met with a number of tribes of Indians, the Cuthalchuches, Malicones, Coayos, Susolas, and the Atayos.[89]

CASTILLO CURES THE SICK AND PERFORMS MIRACLES

---

[89] Hodge, F. W., *Spanish Explorers in the Southern United States*, note, p. 76-77: ''These were possibly the Adai, or Adaize, although their country was

Among these Avavares the Spaniards remained eight months, going naked during the day and covering themselves with deer-skins at night.

Alvar Nuñez Cabeza de Vaca himself proved an adept in the scientific art of healing. One day Castillo was summoned by some of the Susolas Indians to go to their lodges and cure the sick, one of whom was at death's door. Castillo was somewhat timid and declined to go, when Cabeza de Vaca and the negro, Estevan, went in his stead. Arriving at the lodges of the Indians he "perceived that the sick man was dead. Many persons were around him weeping, and his house was prostrate, the sign that the one who dwelt in it is no more.[90] His eyes were rolled up, and the pulse gone, he having all the appearance of death." Cabeza de Vaca removed the mat that covered him, breathed upon him, and supplicated the Lord to restore him to health. According to the Indians who came to their camp the next day he was restored to life for they said "he who had been dead, and for whom I wrought before them, had got up whole and walked, had eaten and spoken with them, and that all to whom I had ministered were well and much pleased."[91]

CABEZA DE VACA RAISES THE DEAD

During the time when the Spaniards were effecting these marvelous cures they heard the story of a great physician who had been in that country years before.[92]

---

in northeastern Texas, about Red river and the Sabine; nevertheless they may have wandered very far during the prickly pear season. There is evidence that in 1792, fourteen families of the Adai migrated to a region south of San Antonio de Bejar, where they were merged with the tribes living thereabout. The main body although greatly reduced, did not leave their old home until the nineteenth century, when the remnant, who had been missionized, were incorporated with their kindred, the Caddo."

[90] It is a custom among the Navajós at the present time for all the possessions of a member of that tribe to be destroyed at the time of his death.

[91] *The Journey of Alvar Nuñez Cabeza de Vaca* (Bandelier trans.): "Until then Dorantes and the negro had not made any cures, but we found ourselves so pressed by the Indians coming from all sides, that all of us had to become medicine-men . . . and they had such confidence in our skill as to believe that none of them would die as long as we were among them."

[92] *The Journey of Alvar Nuñez Cabeza de Vaca* (Bandelier trans.): "They said there wandered then about the country a man, whom they called 'Bad thing' of small stature and with a beard, although they never could see his features clearly, and whenever he would approach their dwellings their hair would stand on end and they began to tremble. In the doorway of the lodge there would then appear a firebrand. That man thereupon came in and took hold of anyone he chose, and with a sharp knife of flint, as broad as a hand and

Alvar Nuñez Cabeza de Vaca found all the natives whom they met to be the most ignorant and destitute. They were well treated by all the tribes. In the spring when the pears began to ripen, Cabeza de Vaca and the negro visited another tribe called Maliacones,[93] a day's journey further on. In three days they sent for Dorantes and Castillo who soon joined them. The Indians they now were with broke their camp, going into another section where they subsisted off the fruit of a small tree, while the pears were maturing. On their way they were joined by another tribe called the Arbadaos, a weak and miserable people with whom the Spaniards remained after the Maliacones had returned to their own country. While with them the Spaniards suffered greatly, being compelled to buy two dogs which they ate with great relish. The Indians kept them employed a good deal of the time in scraping and softening skins, and Cabeza de Vaca says that this was his season of greatest prosperity, for he preserved the scrapings from the skins, which lasted him for food for several days. The meat that was given them was eaten raw, as it was easier digested. When they had become somewhat replenished in strength, they left the Indians and set out during a heavy fall of rain. They stopped at night in a large wood, and prior to going to sleep, they built an oven in which they placed some of the leaves of the prickly pear, and these were ready to be eaten by morning. Having breakfasted they proceeded on their way and soon came in sight of some lodges, near which were

---

two palms in length, he cut their side, and, thrusting his hand through the gash, took out the entrails, cutting off a piece one palm long, which he threw into the fire. Afterwards he made three cuts in one of the arms, the second one at the place where people are usually bled, and twisted the arm, but reset it soon afterwards. Then he placed his hands on the wounds, and they told us that they closed at once. Many times he appeared among them while they were dancing, sometimes in the dress of a woman and again as a man, and whenever he took a notion to do it he would seize the hut or lodge, take it up into the air and come down with it again with a great crash. They also told us how, many a time, they set food before him, but he never would partake of it, and when they asked him where he came from and where he had his home, he pointed to a rent in the earth and said his house was down below.''

Mr. Adolph F. Bandelier says there is no mention of this story in Oviedo. What may be the basis for it is impossible to conjecture. It may have been a tradition, but completely misunderstood, hence misreported, by the Spaniards.

[93] Hodge, F. W., *Spanish Explorers in the Southern United States*, note, p. 80: ''By the Coast live those called Quitoks, and in front inward on the main are the Chavavares, to whom adjoin the Maliacones, the Cultalchulches and others called Susolas and the Comos. This would seem to indicate that he was journeying in a generally northward or northwestward direction.''

two women and some boys, who fled as the Spaniards approached. They called to them and they returned and soon led the party to their village, which was one of about fifty lodges. They stayed several days with this tribe, and in the meantime other Indians from beyond came to visit at the village. When these returned the Spaniards went with them, much against the wishes of those with whom they were then stopping, who wept at their departure.

The customs and habits of the people with whom the Spaniards were living were nearly the same as those of the inhabitants of the country through which they had been journeying since leaving the island of Malhado. When the Indians traveled in the desert, if one fell sick, they left him behind to perish, unless he were a son or brother, when they would carry him upon their backs. It was the custom for men who were childless to leave their wives at pleasure and unite with another woman, but, having children, they never abandoned their wives. When they fought among themselves they never used the bow and arrow, but beat each other with their fists, and, having ceased fighting, both parties would retire to their lodges or the forest, where they remained until their anger had subsided. When unmarried persons quarreled they went to some neighboring tribe and remained some time before returning to their own people. Even their enemies received them with presents, and, when they returned to their homes, loaded them down with gifts of all kinds.

Cabeza de Vaca mentions the following nations passed by himself and companions: [94]

INDIAN TRIBES MET BY CABEZA DE VACA WHILE CROSSING TEXAS

"I desire to enumerate the natives and tongues that exist from those of Malhado to the farthest Cuchendados, there are. Two languages are found in the island; the people of one are called Cahoques,[95] of the other, Han. On the tierra-firme, over against the island, is another people, called Chorruco, who take their names from the forests where they live. Advancing by the shores of the

---

[94] Smith, Buckingham, *Narrative* (edition 1871), pp. 86-87.

[95] Hodge, F. W., *Spanish Explorers in the Southern United States*, note, p. 87, says: "In the 1542 edition these tribal names are similarly spelled except in the cases of Capoques, Charruco, Deguenes, Yeguaces, Decubados (for Acubados), Quitoles (for Quitoks), Chauauares, and Camolas. None of these Indians have thus far been exclusively identified with later historical tribes, with the possible exception of the Atayos and the Quevenes."

sea, others inhabit who are called the Doguenes, and opposite them others by the name of Mendica. Farther along the coast are the Quevenes, and in front of them, on the main, the Mariames; and continuing by the coast are others called Guaycones; and in front of them, within on the main, the Yguazes. At the close of these are the Atayos; and, in their rear others, the Acubadaos, and beyond them are many in the same direction. By the coast live those called Quitoks, and in front inward on the main are the Chavarares, to whom adjoin the Maliacones, the Cultalchulches, and others called Susolas, and the Comos; and by the coast farther on are the Camoles; and on the same coast in advance are those whom we called People of the Figs.''

These various tribes lived in lodges, and their villages were constructed in various ways; each spoke a different language, although some understood the language of their neighbors. They were great lovers of smoke, with which they stupefied themselves. They made a tea from the leaves of a tree that resembled the oak. In the preparation of this drink, they toasted the leaves in a pot, and after they were well parched, the pot was filled with water and twice boiled, when the liquid was poured into a jar to cool. They drank it as soon as it was covered with a thick froth, and as hot as they could bear it. The color of the liquid was yellow, and while boiling the pot was carefully covered, but if it happened to be open while a woman passed by, they threw the tea away. This tea they drank for three days and a half, and each one drank daily about four and a half gallons. It was customary for the men, while drinking, to cry out, ''Who wants a drink?'' ''When the women hear these cries they instantly stop, without daring to move; and although they be heavily loaded they dare do nothing further. Should the woman move, they dishonor her and beat her with sticks, and, greatly vexed, throw away the liquor they have prepared; while they who have drunk, eject it, which they do readily and without pain. They give as a reason for the usage that when they are about to drink it, if the women move from where they hear the cry, something pernicious enters the body in that liquid, shortly producing death.''

Cabeza de Vaca and companions, after leaving the Arbadaos, were well received by the tribe of Indians with whom it was their fortune next to wander. The members of this tribe brought them food to eat, which consisted of a flour made of the ''mesquiquez,'' mesquite bean. These Indians made a feast for the Spaniards, accompanied by great festivities and dances, which lasted several days.

After they had lived with this tribe for some time, they were visited by the women of a tribe living further on, with whom Cabeza de Vaca proposed to return, but not without much opposition from his present hosts. These women pointed out to the Spaniards the direction in which their village lay, and, bidding farewell to the Indians, they started off to find it. They wandered about for some time, when they were overtaken by the women, who acted as guides. They traveled until sunset, when they came to the village, which consisted of one hundred lodges. On their way they crossed a large river, the water of which, in fording, came up breast high. As they approached the village, the inhabitants came out to welcome them. Many of the savages carried gourds, bored with holes, with pebble stones inside; these were held in great veneration and were only brought out on great occasions.[96] Wonderful virtues were attributed to them, and they were used in effecting cures. The Spaniards were told that they grew in heaven and were washed down to their country by the river.

From all sides the Indians gathered to welcome the strangers. The Indians carried them in their arms into their lodges. Permission was asked of Cabeza de Vaca to perform some ceremony in their honor, but this was declined by the Spaniards. They were asked by the entire population to bless them in the same manner they had done to others through whose countries they had passed. They remained here two days and then departed, accompanied by all the inhabitants who escorted them to the next village. Here again they were met with rejoicing and abundant provisions, including a portion of a deer that had been killed that day. Their services as healers were required at this place, and in return for their services the Indians gave them bows and arrows, shoes and beads, the Indians who accompanied the Spaniards being presented with the last two articles.

---

[96] Hodge, F. W., in note, pp. 90-91, of *Spanish Explorers in the Southern United States*, says: ''The Pueblo Indians of New Mexico have cultivated gourds for use as rattles and receptacles, especially dippers, from time immemorial. If the Pecos were the stream, or one of the streams, whence the gourds were derived they might have come from the pueblo of Pecos, southeast of the present Santa Fé; if from the Rio Grande, they might have come from various villages along that river and its tributaries in the north.''

Setting out from this village Cabeza de Vaca and his companions continued their journey, crossing river and plain, passing numerous tribes. Among others they came to a people who dwelt in fixed habitations. These were of a fairer complexion than any yet seen, but some of them had but one eye and some of them were blind. Here they observed a new and singular custom which prevailed among nearly all the tribes they met thereafter. When they arrived at a village the Indians who accompanied them immediately began to ransack the houses and steal everything upon which they could lay their hands. The Spaniards became very much alarmed at this, fearing that it would bring them into trouble; but they were assured by the Indians that they were so much pleased at seeing them that they considered their goods well disposed of and that further on there were other rich tribes from whom they would amply repay themselves. The entire population was blessed by the Spaniards.

THE SPANIARDS RESUME THEIR WANDERINGS

The entire aspect of the country now changed. In the far distance could be seen the peaks of high mountains. Guided by the Indians the Spaniards took a course in the direction of these mountains. They soon arrived among another people, when immediately the plundering was resumed by the Indians. They were welcomed in a very friendly manner, however, and their coming was celebrated with great rejoicing. One day they remained with these people and then left. It was the desire of the Indians that they visit some friends who lived on top of the mountains, but the Spaniards continued along the plain at the foot of the mountains. The women carried a supply of water and no one was allowed to drink without permission of the Spaniards. The Indians were very insistent that the journey proceed by way of the mountains but Cabeza de Vaca refused, whereupon the Indians left them and "returned down the river to their houses, while we ascended along by it." They marched up the river all day and in the evening arrived at a town containing a small number of people, who were greatly concerned, fearing that they were about to be plundered by the Indians who accompanied them, but when they saw that the Spaniards were alone they felt re-assured and their weeping was turned into joy. That night the village was attacked by the Indians

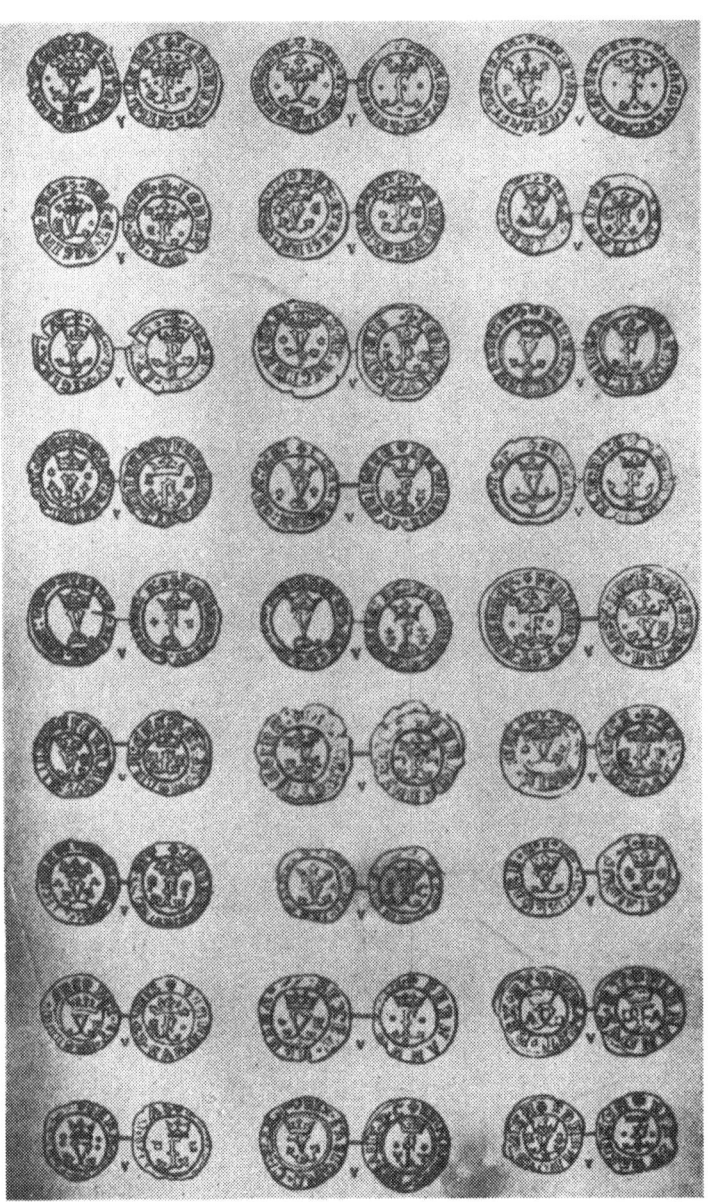

Spanish Coins of the Sixteenth Century

who had left the Spaniards the day before and the villagers were robbed of everything they had. The marauders, however, told them that the Spaniards were children of the sun, with the power of life and death in their hands. They advised the Indians to take the Spaniards where the population was numerous and that the Spaniards must not be offended in any way. The following day the Spaniards resumed their march through a very well inhabited country, and at the expiration of three days, came to a village to the people of whom the Indians related wonderful stories about the Spaniards. Here they were made numerous presents, one to Dorantes being a copper bell, with a human face engraved upon it.[97]

---

[97] Hodge, F. W., *Spanish Explorers in the Southern United States*, p. 95: "Among the articles given us, Andrés Dorantes received a hawk-bell of copper, thick and large, figured with a face, which the natives had shown, greatly prizing it. They told him they had received it from others, their neighbors; we asked them whence the others had received it, and they said it had been brought from the northern direction, where there was much copper, which was highly esteemed."

Mr. Hodge, *Ibid*, note p. 97, in reference to a subsequent inquiry made of the Indians as to where they obtained the copper bell, says: "The allusion is probably to Mexico rather than to a northern country, as previously asserted by the Indians." Upon what authority, contained in the *Narrative*, or elsewhere, Mr. Hodge feels called upon to suggest "Mexico" as the place where the bell came from, I can not imagine, particularly when it is well known that most extensive deposits of native copper are found in Grant and Sierra counties, New Mexico; that lead is found in Socorro county, and copper also; that in all the mountain ranges on either side of the valley of the Rio Grande, from the Organ mountains, in Doña Ana county, as far north as the Colorado line, are found silver, copper, and lead. When the Indians told the Spaniards that in the place whence the hawk-bell had come "were buried many plates of the same material," they undoubtedly intended to convey the idea, using the word "buried," that there were deposits of copper in sheets, such as have been taken out in New Mexico in many localities, but particularly in Grant county. I have seen "plates" of native copper taken from the deposits in that county "buried" as the Indians said, which were two and three feet in length, half an inch in thickness and twelve to fifteen inches in width, and all comparatively near the surface. Yet, in their efforts to keep Cabeza de Vaca and his companions out of New Mexico, some historians have been willing to ignore all these well-known facts, and like Mr. Hodge, in the face of the statement deliberately made that the copper bell came from the north, say that probably the Indians meant to say from the south — Mexico.

Again, it must be remembered that there is preserved to us the record of the journey of Coronado in 1541, and that while on his search for Quivira, after he had crossed the Pecos river, in New Mexico, and at some point in eastern New Mexico or northwestern Texas, at least thirty days' journey in a southerly direction from the point where Coronado crossed the Arkansas, and at a time prior to the date when the army under Arellano was ordered back to Tiguex, Coronado sent Rodrigo Maldonado on an exploring expedition, and the latter in a journey of four days reached a deep ravine or canyon in the bottom of which he found a village that Cabeza de Vaca had visited and whose inhabitants

The next day they crossed a mountain range about seven leagues broad upon which they found indications of iron, and in the evening arrived at a village located upon the bank of a beautiful river. Here they were given many presents including mica, pulverized galena, and many beads and robes of cow-skins.

"There are in that country," says Cabeza de Vaca, "small pine trees and the cones of them are like small eggs; but the seeds are better than those of Castile, as the husks are very thin, and while green it is beat and made into balls and thus eaten. If dry it is pounded in its husk, and consumed in the form of flour."

The Spaniards were furnished with food, and after awhile the Indians brought to Cabeza de Vaca a man who had been wounded some time before with an arrow, the head remaining in the wound, and requested that he be cured. Here Cabeza de Vaca again demonstrated wonderful capabilities, this time as a surgeon. He extracted the arrow head, sewed up the wound, and the next day he cut the stitches he had made and the Indian was well. The wound made by Cabeza de Vaca "appeared only like a seam in the palm of the hand." They showed these Indians the copper bell that had been given them, and they were informed that in the place where the bell had come from "were buried many plates of the same material."

They shortly left this village and "travelled through so many sorts of people, of such diverse languages, the memory fails to recall them. They ever plundered each other, and those that lost, like

---

presented Maldonado with a lot of tanned buffalo hides and other things and that the members of Maldonado's command rushed upon the pile of buffalo robes and took possession of them. That thereupon the "women and some others were left crying, because they thought that the strangers were not going to take anything, but would bless them as Cabeza de Vaca and Dorantes had done *when they passed through here.*" Cabeza de Vaca and Dorantes did not take the many gifts of the kind here mentioned although they were offered to them, and because they did not take them, but gave them back, was one of the reasons why the Indians had so much confidence in them. It will also be remembered that Castañeda relates the circumstance, hearsay to him, that while on this march Coronado met a wandering band of Querechos Indians, among whom was one who was blind who told them that "he had seen four others like us many days before, whom he had seen near there and rather more toward New Spain." We are as much justified in believing that these places mentioned by these Indians were far north of the mouth of the Pecos river, and not upon the Colorado river, as are some historians in coming to the conclusion that the route of Cabeza de Vaca did not proceed across any portion of the present confines of New Mexico.

Courtesy of Bureau of American Ethnology

Apache Necklace of Human Fingers

those that gained, were fully content." All of these Indians carried clubs and, on the discovery of hares (jack-rabbits), the Indians killed them, using the clubs with astonishing accuracy. The hares were very abundant; everything they killed they brought to the Spaniards. The women carried mats, of which lodges were built for the Spaniards, each one having his own house; the deer and hares were roasted in ovens, and after partaking of some of the food prepared for them, they distributed it among the principal Indians, who were asked to divide it among the others, but they would not touch it until the Spaniards had blessed it.

On their route they crossed a great river *which came from the north* [98] and traversed a plain thirty leagues broad. Here they were met by other Indians, who had come from a great distance to meet and extend them welcome. They stood in great awe of the Spaniards, and for several days after their arrival dared not speak nor raise their eyes to heaven.

The Indians who had accompanied them thus far now returned, and the new tribe conducted them through a desert and mountainous country for fifty leagues, when they came to a very large river, which in fording was breast-deep.[99] From the river onward, many of the people accompanying the Spaniards began to sicken from the great privation and labor they had undergone in the passage of the "ridges," which were sterile and difficult in the extreme. Thence they entered upon great plains with mountains in the distance, and

---

[98] This river from the north is undoubtedly the Pecos.

[99] This river was the Rio Grande, and I believe that the Spaniards crossed it at a point not further south than old Ft. Selden, New Mexico, near the present town of Doña Ana. The distance from the Pecos to the Rio Grande, if they crossed near this point, is about eighty leagues; the intervening country is of the kind described by Cabeza de Vaca; from the Pecos to the first "ridges" is about thirty leagues, and thence in a westerly direction to the Rio Grande, one passes over leagues of desert plain and mountain ranges.

There is no doubt in my mind that the word "ridges" was not used by Cabeza de Vaca to indicate the walls of canyons; it was evidently meant to describe ranges of mountains. If we are to conclude that Bandelier, and Hodge, who accepts Bandelier's map of the route of these travelers, are correct, the distance from the point where the Pecos was crossed to the point where the Rio Grande was forded, the Spaniards did not travel one hundred miles in making the journey, instead of eighty leagues as the narrative recites. There is just as much reason to believe that they met the Jumanos Indians in this neighborhood, those who mentioned the circumstance to Espejo in 1582, as there is in refusing to believe that it was far north of the mouth of the Pecos river that Cabeza de Vaca and companions journeyed.

were met by still other Indians who came from a great distance beyond. The Spaniards were again given presents, more than they could carry, and when requested to take part of them back, the Indians replied that such was not the custom and the gifts were left upon the ground.

It was now the desire of Cabeza de Vaca that he be conducted toward the setting sun, for, as he says, "we ever held it certain that going towards the sunset we must find what we desired." The Indians were requested to send messengers ahead to announce the coming of the Spaniards. This the Indians did not care to do, saying that the country was too remote and the inhabitants were their enemies. Not daring to disobey them, the Indians finally sent two women, one of their own, the other a captive from the people beyond, it having been found out by the Spaniards that the women could negotiate, even though there be war. These the Spaniards and Indians followed, but tarried at a certain point, awaiting the return of the women; here they remained five days.

THE SPANIARDS ARRIVE AMONG A PEOPLE OF FIXED HABITATIONS

The Spaniards now requested that they be conducted to the north, but the Indians declined to do this, saying that in that direction there was neither water to drink nor food to eat. Cabeza de Vaca became very angry, at which the Indians became very much alarmed, and finally promised to guide them in whatever direction they chose, even though they lost their lives in doing so.

After a lapse of eighteen days the women returned, reporting that they had seen very few Indians as it was the season of the "cows,"[100] and that they had nearly all gone in pursuit of them. The next morning the Spaniards began their journey forward, and after traveling three days through an uninhabited country, they made camp. Castillo and Estevan started the next morning, accompanied by the women, in search of the inhabitants of that portion of the country. One of the women conducted them to the town where her father lived, situate upon a river which ran between mountains, the habitations being the first they had seen with the appear-

---

[100] No buffalo ever came as far west or southwest as this portion of the Rio Grande, but the inhabitants of the Rio Grande valley and its tributaries hunted the buffalo on the plains; the "cows" roamed as far as the plains through which the Pecos river flows.

ance and structure of houses. At the end of five days Castillo took five or six of the principal Indians and returned to Cabeza de Vaca, reporting that they had found a people living in civilized dwellings and subsisting upon beans, pumpkins, and corn. The entire company immediately set out for this village and, after traveling a league and a half, met Estevan with the entire population [101] coming to receive them.

The Indians who had accompanied them thus far were now sent back, after receiving many presents from Cabeza de Vaca and his companions; the journey was resumed and, after travelling about six leagues, in the evening, they reached the village, their arrival being the cause of great rejoicing. Here they remained two nights and one day, when they were conducted to another village where lived a people whose manners and customs were different. The inhabitants did not go out to receive them as the others had done, but waited for them in their houses, with their heads cast down, faces turned to the wall, and their hair pulled over their eyes, and their property placed in a heap in the middle of the house. From this place they gave the Spaniards many tanned skins and everything else that they had. They were a very intelligent and active people, of fine form, who understood the Spaniards and intelligently answered their questions. The Spaniards called them the Cow nation, because "most of the cattle killed are slaughtered in their neighborhood, and along up that river [102] for over fifty leagues they destroy great numbers." These people went entirely naked, except the women and old men, who dressed in deer-skins. Seeing corn, the Spaniards asked them where it had been obtained, and ascertained that it came from where the sun sets, and that it was found all over that country and the shortest way to it was in that direction. Being asked in what direction we must go to reach that country they replied, "up by that river towards the north, for otherwise in a journey of seventeen days we should find nothing to

---

[101] Sometimes as many as three or four thousand Indians followed the Spaniards, according to the *Narrative*, Smith, Buckingham, ed. 1871: "And as we had to breathe upon and sanctify the food and drink for each, and grant permission to do the many things they would come to ask, it may be seen how great was the annoyance."

[102] Not the river which the Spaniards had last crossed; the buffalo roamed on the Pecos. The Indians of the Rio Grande valley hunted the buffalo on the plains annually.

eat, except a fruit they called *chacan*, that is ground between stones. They showed this food to the Spaniards and they could not eat it. After remaining here two days they determined to go in search of the country where the corn grew. As Cabeza de Vaca says: "So we went on our way and traversed the whole country to the South Sea, and our resolution was not shaken by the fear of great starvation, which the Indians said we should suffer (and indeed suffered) during the first seventeen days of travel. All along the river, and in the course of these seventeen days we received plenty of cow hides and did not eat of their famous fruit (*chacan*), but our food consisted (for each day) of a handful of deer tallow, which for that purpose we always sought to keep, and so endured those seventeen days,[103] at the end of which we crossed the river [104] and marched for seventeen days more." At sunset on a high plain, between two very high mountains, the Spaniards met people who, for one-third of the year, subsisted on powdered straw, of which they also ate, and at the end of their journey they came to a village of permanent houses, with plenty of harvested grain, of which and its meal they gave the Spaniards great quantities; also squashes and beans, and blankets of cotton, all of which the Spaniards gave to their Indian guides "so that they went home the most contented people upon earth."[105] From this point the Spaniards traveled "more than a hundred leagues, always meeting permanent houses and a great stock of maize and beans;" they were presented with many deer-skins and blankets of cotton better than those of New Spain. They also received from the Indians plenty of beads made out of the coral found in the South Sea; many good turquoises,[106] which they get from the north, and Dorantes was presented with five emeralds,[107] shaped as arrow points, which arrows they use in

---

[103] If this part of the journey had been along the left bank of the Rio Grande, they would have had plenty to eat, as the locality was populated.

[104] Not the Rio Grande but some river seventeen days' journey to the west and southwest from where they left the Rio Grande; undoubtedly some river in the present state of Chihuahua, Mexico.

[105] *The Journey of Alvar Nuñez Cabeza de Vaca*, Bandelier trans., p. 156.

[106] The finest turquoises found in New Mexico are those found in Grant county, in the southwestern part of the state. The turquoise mines of that county have been known to the Indians from time immemorial. Turquoise is also found in the Chalchiuitl mountain, near Los Cerrillos, twenty miles from Santa Fé. This was a famous place and one from which the Indians secured many turquoises.

[107] Bandelier thinks these may have been malachites. Many fine specimens

their feasts and dances. As they appeared to be of very good quality the Indians were asked whence they got them, and they said it was from some very high mountains toward the north, where they traded for them with feathers and parrot plumes, and where there were villages with many people and very big houses.[108]

In their travels through this section of the country everywhere the Spaniards met with evidences of an advanced degree of civilization. The women were better treated and better dressed than those among the tribes they had already visited. They wore cotton skirts, with half sleeves, and skirts of dressed deer-skin, reaching to the ground, open in front and confined with leather straps. They washed their clothing with a certain soapy root [109] and they wore shoes. It was their belief that the Spaniards came from heaven. The negro, Estevan, kept up a constant conversation with them and found out a great many things his companions were desirous of knowing. They left all the tribes through whose country they passed, at peace; they were told that in heaven there was a Great Being whom they called God, who made the sky, the earth and all other things; that He was their master, and they worshiped and obeyed Him and received from Him all good things. It was difficult for the Indians to comprehend the teachings of the Spaniards, but at the rising and going down of the sun, they would open their hands towards the heavens, with loud shoutings, and afterwards draw them down over their bodies. Although the Spaniards spoke six different languages, the people they were now with could understand no one of them, and they only conversed with each other by means of signs.

The Spaniards remained in the village where they obtained the emeralds three days. Here the Indians gave Dorantes over six hundred hearts of deer, opened, of which they kept on hand a large supply. For this reason, the Spaniards gave to the settlement the name of "Village of Hearts."[110]

THEY REACH THE SETTLEMENTS; THEY GO TO THE CITY OF MEXICO

---

of malachite have been taken from Grant county, New Mexico. Bandelier also says that he saw in the possession of a prominent medicine-man from the pueblo of San Juan, in New Mexico, a plate of malachite, shaped like a large, blunt knife, which he said had come from Chihuahua. Grant county has for its south boundary line the state of Chihuahua, Mexico.

[108] The Pueblo Indians of New Mexico.
[109] The Amole-root of the Yucca.
[110] Oviedo, *Historia*, vol. iii, lib. xxxv, cap. vi, p. 610 (ed. 1853): "Pues

In a day's journey beyond this village, they arrived at another town where they were detained fifteen days on account of heavy floods which raised the river so high that it was impossible to make a crossing for some time. It was here that Castillo saw upon the neck of an Indian the buckle of a sword-belt and the nail of a horse's shoe. Having been asked how they obtained these things, the Indians replied that they had got them from men who wore beards like the Spaniards, who came from heaven, and had arrived at the river with horses, lances, and swords, where they killed two of their people; that they had gone to sea and returned home where the sun sets.

This was the first information that the Spaniards received of their countrymen; they were greatly rejoiced and, as they advanced, heard more rumors of white men having been in the country, and, in order to conciliate the Indians, they were informed that the Spaniards were going to find the white people in order to persuade them to no longer hurt or make slaves of the natives.

In the account of their further journeyings, the meetings with their countrymen, and their final arrival at the City of Mexico, and their reception by the viceroy, Don Antonio de Mendoza, Alvar Nuñez Cabeza de Vaca says:[111]

"We travelled over a great part of the country, and found it all deserted as the people had fled to the mountains, leaving houses and fields, out of fear of the Christians. This filled our hearts with sorrow, seeing the land so fertile and beautiful, so full of water and streams, but abandoned and the places burned down, and the people so thin and wan, fleeing and hiding; and as they did not raise any crops, their destitution had become so great that they ate tree-bark and roots. Of this distress we had our share all the way along, because they could provide little for us in their indigence, and it looked as if they were going to die. They brought us blankets, which they had been concealing from the Christians, and gave them

---

pasadas las tierras ques dicho, llegaron estos cuatro christianos . . . á tres pueblos que estaban juntos é pequeños, en que avia hasta veynte casas en ellos, las cuales eran como las pasadas é juntas . . . á ere pueblo, ó mejor diciendo pueblos juntos, nombraron los christianos la Villa de los Corazones, porques les dieron alli mas de seiscientos corazones de venados escalados ó secos.''

The Village of Hearts is a place well established in southern Central Sonora, says Bandelier.

[111] *The Journey of Alvar Nuñez Cabeza de Vaca*, Bandelier trans., p. 163 et seq.

Santo Domingo Pueblo Indian Clown or Delight-maker

to us, and told us how the Christians had penetrated the country before, and had destroyed and burnt the villages, taking with them half of the men and all the women and children, and how those who could escaped by flight. Seeing them in this plight, afraid to stay anywhere, and that they neither would nor could cultivate the soil, preferring to die rather than suffer such cruelties, while they showed the greatest pleasure at being with us, we began to apprehend that the Indians who were in arms against the Christians might ill-treat us in retaliation for what the Christians did to them. But when it pleased God, our Lord, to take us to those Indians, they respected and held us precious, as the former had done and even a little more, at which we were not a little astonished, while it clearly shows how, in order to bring those people to Christianity and obedience to your Imperial Majesty, they should be well treated, and not otherwise.

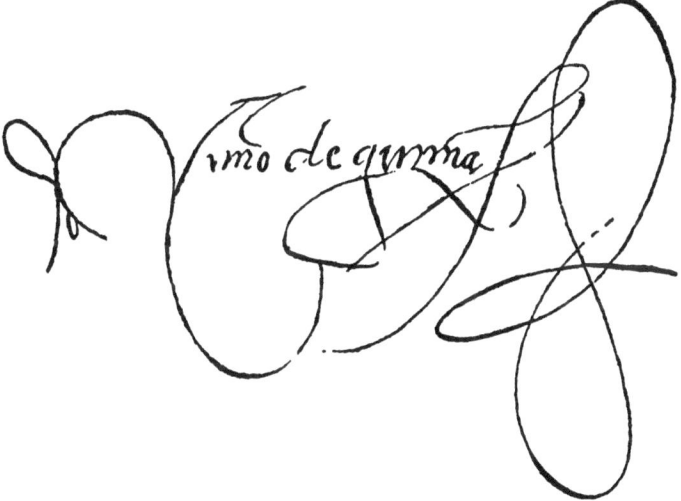

Fac-simile of signature of Nuño de Guzman, governor of New Galicia

"They took us to a village on the crest of a mountain, which can be reached only by a very steep trail, where we found a great many people, who had gathered there out of dread of the Christians. These received us very well, giving us all they had; over two thousand loads of maize, which we distributed among the poor, famished people who led us to this place. The next day we despatched (as we were wont to do) four runners, to call together as many as could be reached to a village three journeys away; and on the next day we followed with all the people that were at the place, always meeting with signs and vestiges where the Christians had slept.

"At noon we met our messengers, who told us they had not found anybody, because all were hidden in the woods lest the Christians might kill or enslave them; also that, on the night before, they had seen the Christians and watched their movements, under cover of some trees, behind which they concealed themselves, and saw the Christians take many Indians along in chains. At this the people who were with us became frightened and some turned back to give the alarm through the land that the Christians were coming, and many more would have done the same had we not told them to stay and have no fear, at which they quieted down and were comforted. We had Indians with us at the time who came from a distance of a hundred leagues, and whom we could not induce to go back to their homes. So, in order to reassure them, we slept there that night, and the next day went further, and slept on the road; and the day after, those we had sent to explore guided us to where they had seen the Christians. Reaching the place in the evening, we saw clearly they had told the truth, and also, from the stakes to which the horses had been tied, that there were horsemen among them.

"From here, which is called the river of Petután [112] to the river which Diego de Guzman reached, there may be, from the place where we first heard of the Christians, eighty leagues; thence to the village where the rain overtook us, twelve leagues; and from there to the South Sea,[113] twelve leagues. Throughout all that country, wherever it is mountainous, we saw many signs of gold, antimony, iron, copper and other metals. Where the permanent houses are it is so hot that even in January the air is very warm. From there to the southward the land, which is uninhabited as far as the Sea of the North, is very barren and poor. There we suffered great and almost incredible starvation; and those who roam through that country and dwell in it are very cruel people, of evil inclinations and habits. The Indians who live in permanent houses and those in the rear pay no attention to gold or silver, nor have they any use for either of the metals.

"Having seen positive traces of the Christians and become satisfied they were very near, we gave many thanks to our Lord for redeeming us from our sad and gloomy condition. Anyone can imagine our delight when he reflects how long we had been in that land, and how many dangers and hardships we had suffered. That night I entreated one of my companions to go after the Christians, who were moving through the part of the country pacified and quieted by us, and who were three days ahead of where we were. They did not like my suggestion, and excused themselves from going

---
[112] Petlatlan. This is the Rio Sinaloa.
[113] The Gulf of California. Cabeza de Vaca did not go to the coast.

THE FIRST SPANISH EXPLORERS 107

on the ground of being tired and worn out, although any of them might have done it better than I, being younger and stronger.

"Seeing their reluctance, in the morning I took with me the negro and eleven Indians and, following the trail, went in search of the Christians. On that day we made ten leagues, passing three places where they slept. The next morning I came upon four Christians on horseback, who, seeing me in such a strange attire and in company with Indians, were greatly startled. They stared at me for quite awhile, speechless, and so great was their surprise that they could not find words to ask me anything. I spoke first, and told them to lead me to their captain, and we went to Diego de Alcaraz, their commander.[114]

"After I had addressed him he said that he himself was in a plight, as for many days he had been unable to capture Indians, and did not know where to go, also that starvation was beginning to place them in great distress. I stated to him that, in the rear of me, at a distance of ten leagues, were Dorantes and Castillo, with many people who had guided us through the country. He at once despatched three horsemen, with fifty of his Indians, and the negro went with them as guide, while I remained and asked them to give me a certified statement of the date, year and day — when I had met them, also the condition in which I had come, with which request they complied.

"From this river [115] to the village called San Miguel,[116] which pertains to the government called New Galicia, there are thirty leagues.

"Five days later Andrés Dorantes and Alonzo del Castillo came with those who had gone in quest of them. They brought along more than six hundred Indians, from the village, the people of which the Christians had caused to flee to the woods, and who were in hiding about the country.

"Those who had come with us as far as that place had taken them out of their places of concealment, turning them over to the Christians. They had also despatched the others who had come that far. When they arrived where I was, Alcaraz begged me to send for the people of the villages along the banks of the river, who were hiding in the timber, and he also requested me to order them to fetch supplies. There was no occasion for the latter, as the Indians always took good care to bring us whatever they could; nevertheless, we sent our messengers at once to call them, and six hundred

---

[114] Bandelier, A. F., note, p. 168, *The Journey of Alvar Nuñez Cabeza de Vaca*: "He was an officer of Nuño de Guzman, and a worthy one, trained in the school of arbitrariness and cruelty of his commander."
Oviedo, *Letter*, iii, p. 612, says that there were twenty Spaniards on horseback, according to the report to the Audiencia.
[115] The Rio Sinaloa.
[116] San Miguel de Culiacan.

persons came with all the maize they had, in pots closed with clay, which they had buried for concealment. They also brought nearly everything else they possessed, but we only took the food, giving the rest to the Christians for distribution among themselves.

"Thereupon we had many and bitter quarrels [117] with the Christians, for they wanted to make slaves of our Indians, and we grew so angry that, at our departure, we forgot to take along many bows, pouches and arrows, also the five emeralds, and so they were left and lost to us. We gave the Christians a great many cowskins, robes, and other objects, and had much trouble in persuading the Indians to return home and plant their crops in peace. They insisted upon accompanying us until, according to their custom, we should be in the custody of other Indians, because otherwise they were afraid to die; besides, as long as we were with them, they had no fear of the Christians and their lances. At all this the Christians were greatly vexed and told their own interpreter to say to the Indians how we were of their own race, but had gone astray for a long while, and were people of no luck and little heart, whereas they were the lords of the land, whom they should obey and serve.

"The Indians gave all that talk little attention. They parleyed among themselves, saying that the Christians lied, for we had come from the sunrise, while the others came from where the sun sets; that we cured the sick, while the others killed those who were healthy; that we went naked and shoeless, whereas the others wore clothes and went on horseback and with lances. Also, that we asked for nothing, but gave away all we were presented with, meanwhile the others seemed to have no other sin than to steal what they could, and never gave anything to anybody. In short they recalled all our deeds and praised them highly, contrasting them with the conduct of the others.

"This they told the interpreter of the Christians, and made understood to the others by means of a language they have among them, and by which we understood each other. We call those who use that language properly *Primahaitu*,[118] which means the same as say-

---

[117] Buckingham Smith, *Narrative* (ed. 1871), says that they told the Indians that Cabeza and his companions "were persons of mean condition."

[118] Hodge, F. W., note, p. 115, *Spanish Explorers in the Southern United States*, says: "Evidently intended for *Pimahaitu*, through misunderstanding. These tribes who lived in permanent habitations, from the village of the Corazones (Hearts) to Culiacan, were all of the Piman family, and consequently spoke related languages. The Pima do not call themselves Pima, but O-otam, 'men,' 'people.' *Pima* means 'no'; *pimahaitu*, 'no thing.'"

Bandelier, A. F., in note, p. 172, *The Journey of Alvar Nuñez Cabeza de Vaca*, says: "No mention of such an idiom in Oviedo, and I do not venture any sugestion as to what language it might have been. The references to the Basque language may mean that it was as difficult to understand as that idiom."

ing Biscayans. For more than four hundred leagues, of those we travelled, we found this language in use, and the only one among them over that extent of country. Finally we never could convince the Indians that we belonged to the other Christians, and only with much trouble and insistency could we prevail upon them to go home.

"We recommended to them to rest easy and settle in their villages, tilling and planting their fields as usual, which, from laying waste, were overgrown with shrubbery, while it is beyond all doubt the best land in these Indies, the most fertile and productive of food, where they raise three crops every year. It has an abundance of fruit, very handsome rivers and other waters of good virtues. There are many evidences and traces of gold and silver; the inhabitants are well conditioned, and willingly attend to the Christians, that is those of the natives who are friendly. They are much better inclined than the natives of Mexico; in short, it is a country that lacks nothing to make it very good. When the Indians took leave of us they said they would do as we had told them and settle in their villages, provided the Christians would not interfere, and so I say and affirm that, if they should not do it, it will be the fault of the Christians.

"After we had despatched the Indians in peace, and with thanks for what they had gone through with us, the Christians (out of mistrust) sent us to a certain alcalde, Cebreros, who had with him two other men. He took us through forests and uninhabited country in order to prevent our communicating with the Indians, in reality, also, to prevent us from seeing or hearing what the Christians were carrying on.

"This clearly shows how the designs of men sometimes miscarry. We went on with the idea of insuring liberty of the Indians, and, when we believed it to be assured, the opposite took place. The Spaniards had planned to fall upon those Indians we had sent back in fancied security and in peace, and that plan they carried out.

"They took us through the timber for two days, with no trail, bewildered and without water, so we all expected to die from thirst. Seven of our men perished, and many friends whom the Christians had taken along could not reach before noon the following day the place where we found water that same night. We travelled with them twenty-five leagues, more or less, and at last came to a settlement of peaceable Indians. There the alcalde left us and went ahead, three leagues further, to a place called Culiacan, where Melchior Diaz [119] was chief alcalde and the captain of the province.

---

[119] Melchior Diaz was not the same sort of man as Nuño de Guzman or his subaltern officers, Alcaraz and Cebreros. He was kind-hearted, and did not believe in the enslaving of the natives, except as distinctly provided by law.

Bandelier, A. F., *Investigations in the Southwest*, Final Report, part 1, p.

"As soon as the chief alcalde became informed of our arrival, on the same night he came to where we were. He was deeply moved,

---

192, says: "Spanish justice was slow, but it was sure, and no official, however exalted his position, escaped the dreaded 'Residencia' or the still more dangerous 'Visita.' On such occasions a functionary had his misdeeds charged against him, and, if nobody else would accuse him of cruelty against the natives, there was surely some priest ready to drag him to trial for misconduct of that sort. It was not easy to escape punishment for cruelty to Indians under Spanish regime.

"The Spanish government recognized at an early day, not merely that the Indian was a human being, but that he was, after all, the chief resource which the New World presented to its new-comers. The tendency of Spanish legislation is therefore marked towards insuring the preservation and progress of the natives. The first great step in this direction was the promulgation of the celebrated 'New Laws and Ordinances for the government of the Indies' finally established in 1543, by which the aborigines were declared direct vassals of the crown. Stipulations in their favor, as, for instance, enfranchisement from personal servitude and from compulsory labor, became the subject of subsequent modifications and local changes, but the disposition first announced, that of direct vassalage, remained a fixed dogma in Spanish American law.

"It may not be amiss here to glance at the great question of Indian servitude and labor. The question was one of utmost vitality, for the obvious reason that upon its solution depended the future prosperity of the colonies. We must not forget that, as I have already stated, Spain was a small nation, that it had over-run a territory enormous in extent, extremely varied in resources as well as in natural obstacles, and that Spanish immigration could in no manner suffice for the imperative demand for labor which the resources of the land presented. In order to improve the Indies, the Indian must work, and work was as distasteful to him then as it is today. Furthermore, he had to be taught to perform this work with implements the mere material of which was to him a mystery, and therefore a source of mistrust and superstitious fear. The reluctance on the part of the native to work was, therefore, for reasons paramount to him, but utterly incomprehensible to the Spaniard, or to any other European of the time. Hence the Crown decrees in regard to compulsory labor changed in tone frequently, and finally measures were adopted which, if properly executed, would have responded to all the demands of humanity and statesmanship combined.

"In the last will and testament of Queen Isabella of Spain, see Vasco de Puga, *Cedulario*, vol. i, p. 2, the following appears: 'Supplico al Rey mi señor muy efectuosamente y mando á la dicha Princesa mi hija, y al dicho Principe su marido, que ansí lo hagan cumplan; y que este sea su principal fin; y que en ello pongan mucha diligencia, y no consientan ni den lugar á que los yndios vezinos y moradores de las dichas yndias y tierra firma, ganadas y por ganar, reciban agrauio alguno en sus personas y bienes; mas manden que sean bien y justamente tratados; y si algun agrauio han recibido, lo remedien y preuan, por manera que no se exceda cosa alguna lo que por las letras apostólicas de la dicha concesion nos es injugido y mandado.'

"The concession referred to in the will of Queen Isabella is the famous bull of Pope Alexander VI. The royal decree of the 9th of November, 1526 (*Ibid*), provided that no Indians of New Spain should be enslaved without a proceeding information conducted in presence of the governors and their officials. The pretext then used for obtaining slaves was: 'Socolor que dicen que los tienen los naturales entre sí por esclauos cautiados en las guerras que han tenido y tienen vnos con otros.' This decree was repeated in 1529 (p. 36). Stronger

and praised God for having delivered us in His great pity. He spoke to us and treated us very well, tendering us, in his name, and

yet is the *Cédula* of January 10, 1528, reiterated on August 2, 1530 (pp. 230-231). Severe punishment was enjoined against such as might illtreat the natives. *Cédula* of March 20, 1532 (p. 254). Further decrees for the protection of the Indians of New Spain are those of January 7, 1549, April 16, 1550, August 28, 1552, etc. A detailed statement concerning legislation on the treatment and personal service of the Indians is found in Juan de Solorzano-Pereyra, *Politica Indiana*, ed. of 1703, lib. ii, cap. i-4. It would take too long to copy all he says on the subject. The famous decree of May 26, 1609, bears exclusively on the good treatment of the aborigines. See Francisco de Montemayor, *Sumarios de las Cédulas, Ordenes y Provisiones Reales*, 1678 (sum. 48, fol. 216), which contains the complete text. This decree authorized the employment of Indians in the mines, provided they were specially cared for and remunerated for the work they performed. The principle of remuneration of mining work was rather a local measure. The Indians attached to ''Encomiendas'' were compelled to labor in the mines in the early days. Mining was regarded as a public work, and as such the Indians were called upon to perform it, but every precaution was taken by the law for their welfare. Hospitals were required to be established for their special benefit. Still, in a long decree directed to the Condé de Villar (predecessor in the viceroyalty of New Castile, or Peru, to Don Francisco de Toledo), the king writes as follows: (Solorzano, *Politica-Indiana*, p. 76): 'E porque aviendose platicado sobre este, he parecido, que sin embargo de lo proveido por cédulas antiguas; cerca de que no fuesen compellidos á este travajo contra su voluntad, se les podria mandar, que vayan á ellas lo haren de aqui adelante, no mudando templo de que se les siga daño en la salud, é teniendo dotrina, á justicia que les ampare, é comida con que se sustenen é buena paga de sus jornales, y hospital donde se curen y sean bien tratados los que enfermaren.' The expense of these arrangements was at the cost of the miner.''

Bandelier, A. F., *Ibid*, says: ''In regard to New Mexico, a very instructive case occurred in 1709. The viceroy of New Spain, having been secretly informed that the governor of New Mexico (at that time the Marques de la Peñuela) was making liberal use of the personal services of the Indians for his own benefit, wrote at once to that functionary, enjoining him from further abuse of this sort, and threatening him with a fine of two thousand pesos, and damages to the Indians, in case of disobedience to the royal edicts on that point. See Fray Juan de la Peña, *Carta Patente*, May 18, 1709 (Ms). It gives the order of the viceroy to the custodian of the Franciscans, in which the Duke of Alburquerque states: 'Se despachó esta en este dia ordenando al Govr de aquellas partes y Provas qe peña de dos mil pesos qe he aplicado á mi distribucion, demas de lo qe importaren los daños qe se causaren á los Yndios se contengan y mando contener á los Maiores pa qe no executen hi hagan semejantes extorsiones.' Another case occurred in 1784. A bitter strife prevailed between the governor, Juan Bautista de Anza, and the Franciscans, and the commander in chief at Arizpe had to intervene. He sent peremptory orders that all personal services of Indians to the governor and his lieutenants should cease. Fray Santiago Fernandez de Sierra, *Memorial presentado al Señor Comandante General en Arizpe* (Ms. 1784).''

Bandelier, A. F., *Ibid*, p. 194, says: ''In New Mexico, there were no mines until after 1725, and compulsory labor on the part of the Indians even after that date was limited to service in the Missions, and, by abuse of authority, to personal attendance upon higher magistrates. The latter was time and again severely checked and strong penalties threatened the governor who ventured to

in behalf of the governor, Nuño de Guzman, all he had and whatever he might be able to do. He appeared much grieved at the bad reception and evil treatment we had met at the hands of Alcaraz and the others, and we verily believe that, had he been there at the time, the things done to us and the Indians would not have occurred.

"Passing the night there, we were about to leave in the morning of the next day, but the chief alcalde entreated us to stay. He said that by remaining we would render a great service to God and to Your Majesty, as the country was depopulated, lying waste, and well nigh destroyed. That the Indians were hiding in the woods, refusing to come out and settle again in the villages. He suggested that we should have them sent for, and urge them, in the name of God and of Your Majesty, to return to the plain and cultivate the soil again. This struck us as difficult of execution. We had none of our Indians with us, nor any of those who usually accompanied us and understood such matters. At last we ventured to select two Indians from among those held there as captives, and who were from that part of the country. These had been with the Christians whom we first met, and had seen the people that came in our company and knew, through the latter, of the great power and authority we exercised all through the land, the miracles we had worked, the cures we had performed, and many other particulars. With these Indians we sent others from the village to jointly call those who had taken refuge in the mountains, as well as those from the river of Petlatlán, where we had met the Christians first, and tell them to come, as we wished to talk to them. In order to insure their coming, we gave the messengers one of the large gourds we had carried in our hands (which were our chief insignia and tokens of great power.)

"Thus provided and instructed, they left and were absent seven days. Then they came back, and with them three chiefs of those

---

infringe the royal decrees prohibiting personal service to him and to his assistants. The solicitude of royal officers went so far as to abolish, in 1784, any and all personal services for church matters; a measure that called forth well grounded and effective protests.

"Slavery was considered in the light of a punishment, and as war against Spain was a crime against the state and its subjects, prisoners of war made in campaigns against hostile tribes could be sold as slaves. The immediate result of this custom was, in New Mexico, frequent intermixture of the different aboriginal stocks, and hence a gradual modification of physical type.

"By declaring the Indian to be a crown vassal, the laws placed him on an equal footing with the native of Spain in one sense, and yet, practically, he enjoyed a much more favorable position. He became a special ward of the royal government, and the complaint by Spanish settlers is very well grounded, that everything was done for the Indian, and but little for them."

This complaint is uttered as late as 1793. See Fernando de la Concha, Ms. (governor of New Mexico): "Emanadas, presisamente de la abundancia, comodidad, y ventajas que logran estos Yndios mui superiores en ellas á los Españoles que se hallan establesidos en sus ynmediaciones."

The Casas Grandes in 1850

who had been in the mountains and with these were fifteen men. They presented us with beads, turquoises and feathers and the messengers said the people from the river whence we had started could not be found, as the Christians had again driven them into the wilderness.

"Melchior Diaz told the interpreter to speak to the Indians in our name and say that he came in the name of God, Who is in Heaven, and that we had travelled the world over for many years, telling all the people we met to believe in God and serve Him, for He was the Lord of everything upon earth, Who rewarded the good, whereas to the bad ones He meted out eternal punishment of fire. That when the good ones died He took them up to heaven, where all lived forever and there was neither hunger nor thirst, nor any other wants — only the greatest imaginable glory. But that those who would not believe in Him nor obey His commandments He thrust into a huge fire beneath the earth and into the company of demons, where the fire never went out, but tormented them forever. Moreover, he said that if they became Christians and served God in the manner we directed, the Christians would look upon them as brethren and treat them very well, while we would command that no harm should be done them; neither should they be taken out of their country, and the Christians would become their great friends. If they refused to do so, then the Christians would ill-treat them and carry them away into slavery.

"To this they replied, through the interpreter, that they would be very good Christians and serve God.[120]

"Upon being asked whom they worshipped and to whom they offered sacrifices, to whom they prayed for health and water for the fields, they said, to a man in Heaven. We asked what was his name, and they said Aguar, and that they believed he had created the world and everything in it. We again asked how they came to know this, and they said their fathers and grandfathers had told them, and they had known it for a very long time; that water and all good things came from him. We explained that this being of whom they spoke was the same we called God, and that thereafter they should give Him that name and worship and serve Him as we commanded, when they would fare very well. They replied that they understood us thoroughly and would do as we had told.

"So we bade them come out of the mountains and be at ease, peaceable and settle the land again, rebuilding their houses. Among these houses they should rear one to God, placing at its entrance a cross like the one we had, and when Christians came, they should go out to receive them with crosses in their hands, in place of bows and arrows and other weapons, and take the Christians to their homes,

---

[120] These people were the ancestors of the Yaqui Indians of today.

giving them to eat of what they had. If they did so, the Christians would do them no harm but be their friends. They promised to do as we ordered, and the captain gave them blankets, treating them handsomely, and they went away, taking along the two captives that had acted as our messengers. This took place in the presence of a scribe (notary) and of a great many witnesses.

"As soon as the Indians had left for their homes and the people of that province got news of what had taken place with us, they, being friends of the Christians, came to see us, bringing beads and feathers. We ordered them to build churches and put crosses in them, which, until then, they had not done. We also sent for the women of the chiefs to be baptized, and then the captain pledged himself before God not to make any raid, or allow any to be made, or slaves captured from the people and in the country we had set at peace again. This vow he promised to keep so long until His Majesty and the Governor, Nuño de Guzman, or the Viceroy, in his name, would ordain something else better adapted to the service of God and of His Majesty.

"After baptizing the children we left for the village of San Miguel, where, on our arrival, Indians came and told how many people were coming down from the mountains settling the plains, building churches and erecting crosses. In short, complying with what we had sent them word to do. Day after day we were getting news of how all was being done and completed.

"Fifteen days after our arrival Alcaraz came in with the Christians who had been raiding, and they told the captain how the Indians had descended from the mountains and settled on the plain; also that villages formerly deserted, were now well populated, and how the Indians had come out to receive them with crosses in their hands, had taken them to their houses, giving them of what they had and how they slept the night there. Amazed at these changes and at the sayings of the Indians, who said they felt secure, he ordered that no harm be done to them and with this they departed. May God in His Infinite mercy grant that in the days of Your Majesty, and under your power and sway these people become willingly and sincerely subjects of the True Lord Who created and redeemed them. We believe they will be, and that Your Majesty is destined to bring it about, as it will not be at all difficult.

"For two thousand leagues did we travel on land, and by sea in barges, besides ten months more after our rescue from captivity; untiringly did we walk across the land, but nowhere did we meet either sacrifice or idolatry. During all that time we crossed from one ocean to the other, and from what we very carefully ascertained there may be, from one coast to the other and across the greatest width, two hundred leagues.[121] We heard that on the shores of the South Sea there are pearls and great wealth, and that the richest and best is near there.

"At the village of San Miguel we remained until after the fifteenth of May,[122] because from there to the town of Compostella, where the Governor Nuño de Guzman resided, there are one hundred leagues of deserted country, threatened by hostiles, and we had to take an escort along. There went with us twenty horsemen, accompanying us as many as forty leagues; afterwards we had with us six Christians, who escorted five hundred Indian captives. When we reached Compostella, the Governor received us very well, giving us of what he had, for us to dress in; but for many days I could bear no clothing, nor could we sleep, except on the bare floor. Ten or twelve days later we left for Mexico. On the whole trip we were well treated by the Christians; many came to see us on the road, praising God for having delivered us from so many dangers. We reached Mexico on Sunday, the day before the vespers of Saint James,[123] and were well received by the Viceroy and the Marquis of the Valley,[124] who presented us with clothing, offering all they had. On the day of Saint James there was a festival, with a bull-fight and tournament."

In his report to the king, Alvar Nuñez Cabeza de Vaca gives small hope of the discovery of gold or precious stones, magnificent kingdoms or cities in the far-distant lands through which he had traveled, and yet its relation to the court served to inflame the ambitions and greed of the Spaniards, who were fully alive to the possibilities of conquest and glory in the New World.

Alvar Nuñez Cabeza de Vaca sought to obtain from his royal master the governorship of Florida, but, notwithstanding the stories of his wanderings and the excellent recommendations which he brought from the viceroy, Mendoza, he was unsuccessful. This had been given to Hernando de Soto three months before. During the three years subsequent to his return to Spain, little is known of the life or work of Alvar Nuñez Cabeza de Vaca. In the year 1540, the news came to Spain that Ayolas, commander of a colony in South America, had been slain by the natives. The colonists sent urgent requests to the home government for assistance, and Cabeza de Vaca

---
[121] Evidently a mis-print; the Buckingham Smith translation (ed. 1871) says "two thousand leagues."
[122] 1536.
[123] July 25, 1536.
[124] Hernando Cortés.

was given command of the relief expedition and was named governor, captain-general, and adelantado of all the territories he might be able to reduce. In the preparations for this expedition he spent his entire fortune. The tribe of Indians he was specifically commissioned to conquer was the Pariembos, a wild tribe of Paraguay Indians, living on the great plains bordering on the Rio de la Plata.

After many difficulties Cabeza de Vaca landed at St. Catherine's, in Brazil, in March, 1541, marching from that point across an utterly unknown country to the river Parana. In this march, although he encountered dangers which exceeded anything he had ever experienced in North America, he showed the same enterprise and determination and the identical disposition and policy toward the natives which he had exhibited in his treatment of the savages whom he had met on his journey from the Gulf to San Miguel de Culiacan. He arrived at his capital on the 11th day of March, 1542. Here he encountered the opposition and hostility of the lieutenant-governor, Irala, who secretly worked against him and finally succeeded in raising an insurrection, in which Alvar Nuñez was seized and thrown into prison. He was kept under guard for two years, when he was sent to Spain. He was accused by Irala of the gravest crimes. He was thrown into prison to await trial, and while constantly petitioning for his release upon bond, he remained in jail for six years. Finally, in 1551, the Council of the Indies rendered judgment by which he was deprived of all his titles and the privileges which pertained to them. The decree included banishment to Africa for a term of eight years — a judgment which undoubtedly was not carried into effect, for, it is said, the emperor granted him a pension of two thousand crowns and gave him a place in the Royal Audiencia [125] of Seville, in which city he died at an advanced

---

[125] Charlevoix, *Letters*: "I have, indeed, seen a memorial in which it is said that he was immediately gratified with a seat in the Council of the Indies." Smith, Buckingham, *Relation*, p. 251, note.

Bandelier, A. F., *Contributions*, p. 27, and note i, says: "On his career in Paraguay there is ample material in Oviedo, Herrera, and Gomara. In addition to these there is Cabeza de Vaca's own statement, printed in 1555, under the title *Comentarios de Alvar Nuñez Cabeza de Vaca, Adelantado y Gobernador del Rio de la Plata* (reprint in Vedia, vol. i). The statement about the latter days of Cabeza de Vaca is from Vedia, *Historiadores primitivos* (p. xxi): 'Fue tambien condenado Alvar Nuñez Cabeza de Vaca á privacion de oficio y á seis años de destierro en Oran, con seis lanzas; apeló, y en revista salió libre, señalan-

age. Thus ended the career of a most remarkable man. His life's portion was little less than the "stings and arrows of outrageous fortune." His courage and powers of endurance were most remarkable; he was gentle, kind, and considerate, and entirely unlike the great majority of Spanish explorers, whose greed for gold and the spoils of conquest are exemplified in the methods of Cortés, Alvarado, Nuño de Guzman, Pizarro, and many others, the record of whose deeds is a story of outrage, slavery, plunder, and rapine.

Castillo returned to New Spain, resided in the City of Mexico, married a widow, and was granted half the rents of the Indian town of Tehuacan.

Alvar Nuñez Cabeza de Vaca and his three companions were the first men of alien birth to set foot upon the soil of what is today New Mexico. To the student of New Mexican history the question whether or not these survivors of the ill-fated Narváez expedition ever passed over New Mexican soil is interesting. Without discussing several points reached by Narváez prior to his embarkation at the Bay of Horses (Apalachee bay) there is no doubt and the historian is justified in declaring that the great river which emptied such great quantities of water into the Gulf of Mexico, with such a powerful current, was the Mississippi. The island of Malhado was

---

dole dos mil ducados de pension en Sevilla. Retirose á aquella ciudad en la cual faleció ejerciendo la primacia del consulado con mucha honra y quietud de su persona, ignorandose en año de su muerte.' The consulate of Seville was quite a responsible office. It consisted of a 'prior' and one consul, who were annually elected by those who traded with the Indies, freighters and ship-owners. Their duty was to regulate and superintend the fitting out of vessels, the cargo and the trading with America in general.''

Bandelier, A. F., *Ibid.*: ''In regard to Cabeza de Vaca's personal character, the opinions of older writers differ; still it is noteworthy that the leading chroniclers, Herrera, Oviedo, and Gomara, speak well of him. Were I to formulate a judgment, I would qualify him as a well-intentioned man, rather visionary, ready for any personal sacrifice, but out of place at the head of an expeditionary corps. It was probably injudicious to intrust Cabeza de Vaca, who had never been a military man, with such a difficult position as the one he occupied in Paraguay. On the other hand it is clear that the Crown desired to reward him for all the hardships and sufferings he had gone through in North America. But the position with which he was rewarded was above his ability, and, like a great many others, his failure to perform what he was incompetent to undertake, put an end to his career. It is stated that he was at first banished to Oran. The fact that this sentence was cancelled, and that he was completely absolved, tends to show that he was rather a victim than a cause of the disorders which occurred in Paraguay during his administration.''

one of the low islands, somewhere on the coast of Texas, near Galveston.[126]

The course pursued by Alvar Nuñez Cabeza de Vaca and his companions, after leaving the coast of Texas, was generally in a northwesterly direction. Many distinguished historians and translators of the narrative have endeavored to mark and trace, with some degree of plausibility or certainty, the course of the wanderers after they had reached the western portion of the present state of Texas. Not one of these, by personal exploration or inspection, so far as the writer is advised, ever acquainted himself with the actual physical conditions of that section of the state, nor has any one of them, with the possible exception of Dr. Prince, ever visited or traveled over the country now embraced within the limits of eastern and southeastern New Mexico. Mr. Winship [127] in his historical introduction to his monograph on the Coronado expedition has undoubtedly fol-

[126] Prince, L. B., *History of New Mexico*, p. 91, says: "The island of Malhado and Espiritu Santo bay have been located by different historians in widely varying localities. Buckingham Smith, in his first edition of his translation of Cabeza de Vaca's *Narrative*, places them as far east as Mobile bay, and traces the travelers' route north to the Muscle Shoals in the Tennessee river. And in the edition of 1871, he has changed his views so far as to suggest that the locality may have been as far west as San Antonio bay, in Texas.''

Davis, W. W. H., *Spanish Conquest of New Mexico*, expresses the opinion that Malhado was one of the low islands on the coast of Louisiana; and the mention of a tribe called Atayos in the narrative, who are probably identical with the Adayes, who lived, in 1805, about forty miles from Nachitoches, and the Hadaies, who years before were reported as being between Nachitoches and Sabine rivers — adds plausibility to this view. It is possible the island may have been at or near Galveston, or as far west as the beaches or islands known as Matagorda beach and Matagorda island, which are the outer protections of Matagorda and San Antonio bays.

But see *ante*, this volume, Hodge, F. W., p. 83, note 80.

The Atayos, mentioned by Cabeza de Vaca, in his *Narrative*, and mentioned by Prince, were a part of the Caddo confederacy, speaking a dialect closely related to that of the Kadohadacho, Hainai and Anadarko. De Soto also encountered some of the Caddo Indians in 1540, but the people did not become known until met by La Salle in 1687. At that time the Caddo villages were scattered along Red river and its tributaries in what are now Louisiana and Arkansas and also on the banks of the Sabine, Neches, Trinity, Brazos, and Colorado rivers in eastern Texas.

[127] Winship, George Parker, *The Coronado Expedition*, 14th Ann. Rep., B. A. E., p. 347, note: "The best study of the route followed by the survivors of the expedition, after they landed in Texas, is that of Bandelier, in the second chapter of his *Contributions to the History of the Southwest*. In this essay, Bandelier has brought together all the documentary evidence, and he writes with the knowledge obtained by travelling through the different portions of the country which Cabeza de Vaca must have traversed.''

THE FIRST SPANISH EXPLORERS 119

lowed the course and adopted the one as described by Mr. Bandelier. Mr. F. W. Hodge [128] is also impressed with the solution offered by Mr. Bandelier. While it is true that the last named did traverse portions of the route probably taken by Alvar Nuñez Cabeza de Vaca, he began his travels at the point where Cabeza de Vaca had concluded his wanderings across the continent. Mr. Bandelier is entirely familiar with western and southwestern New Mexico, Arizona, and the states of the Mexican Republic which join the American southern border, still he had no personal acquaintance with the topography of middle or western Texas, nor of eastern or southeastern New Mexico.

The same may be said of Buckingham Smith, W. W. H. Davis, Dr. J. G. Shea, Hubert Howe Bancroft, and others. Mr. Smith was clearly in error when he fixed one of the large rivers crossed by Cabeza de Vaca as being the Arkansas, near its junction with the Canadian fork. Mr. Davis also erred when he stated that in his judgment the wanderers were as far north as the Canadian. Francisco Vasquez Coronado, in 1542, after leaving the pueblo of Ci-cu-yé, going toward the plains, after a four days' journey came to a "river with a large, deep current which flowed down toward Ci-cu-yé, and they named this the Ci-cu-yé river." This river was beyond all doubt the Pecos of the present day. Across this river they built a bridge which took them four days to construct. This bridge could not have been built across the Canadian at any point where Coronado and his army could have been traveling in the direction described by Castañeda for the reason that the Canadian at any point in the direction taken by Coronado is not a river "having a large, deep current," nor does it flow down towards Ci-cu-yé. It was somewhere in the vicinity of the Pecos crossing, in an easterly direction on the plains, certainly within two or three days' marching, that Coronado was informed by Indians whom he met that Cabeza de Vaca and Dorantes had visited that portion of the country some years before, and also near the place where Maldonado was informed that Cabeza de Vaca [129] and Dorantes "passed through here." It is the judgment of the writer that the Indians who gave this information to

---
[128] Hodge, F. W., *The Spanish Explorers in the Southern United States.*
[129] Winship, George Parker, *Coronado Expedition*, 14th Ann. Rep. B. A. E., p. 505.

Coronado, either themselves had seen Cabeza de Vaca and his companions, or had information from other Indians who were cognizant of the crossing of the Pecos river, to the south, by Cabeza de Vaca, who in his narrative states that while traveling "we crossed a big river coming from the north and, traversing about thirty leagues of plains, met a number of people that came from afar to meet us on the trail." [130]

Afterwards Cabeza de Vaca was guided more than fifty leagues through a desert of rugged mountains, and so arid that there was no game. Later the same Indians led them to a plain beyond the chain of mountains where people came to meet them from a long distance. These people were told by the Spaniards that their route was toward the sunset, and the Indians replied that in that direction people lived very far away; that they did not care to go to them as they were their enemies, yet they did finally send two women, one of their own and the other a captive from the country itself; these women returned saying that they had met very few people, nearly all having gone after the "cows," as it was the season. The following day, the woman who was a captive took Castillo and Estevan to a "river that flows between mountains, where there was a village, in which her father lived, and these were the first abodes we saw that were like unto real houses." Castillo and Estevan went to these and, after holding parley with the Indians, at the end of three days Castillo returned to where he had left the other two, bringing with him five or six of the Indians, telling how he had found permanent houses, inhabited, the people living in them eating beans, squashes, and that he had also seen maize.

Instead of carrying the wanderers far into the north to the Arkansas, or even to Red river, or making them cross the Rio Grande far to the south near and above the point where the Pecos empties into it, why, while indulging *in mere speculation*, is it not equally satisfactory, taking into consideration the now well known topography of western Texas, until recent years the domain of hostile and cruel savages, to arrive at the conclusion that the survivors of the Narváez expedition crossed the Pecos at some point far enough above its

---
[130] Bandelier, Mrs. Fanny, *The Journey of Alvar Nuñez Cabeza de Vaca*, trans., p. 144.

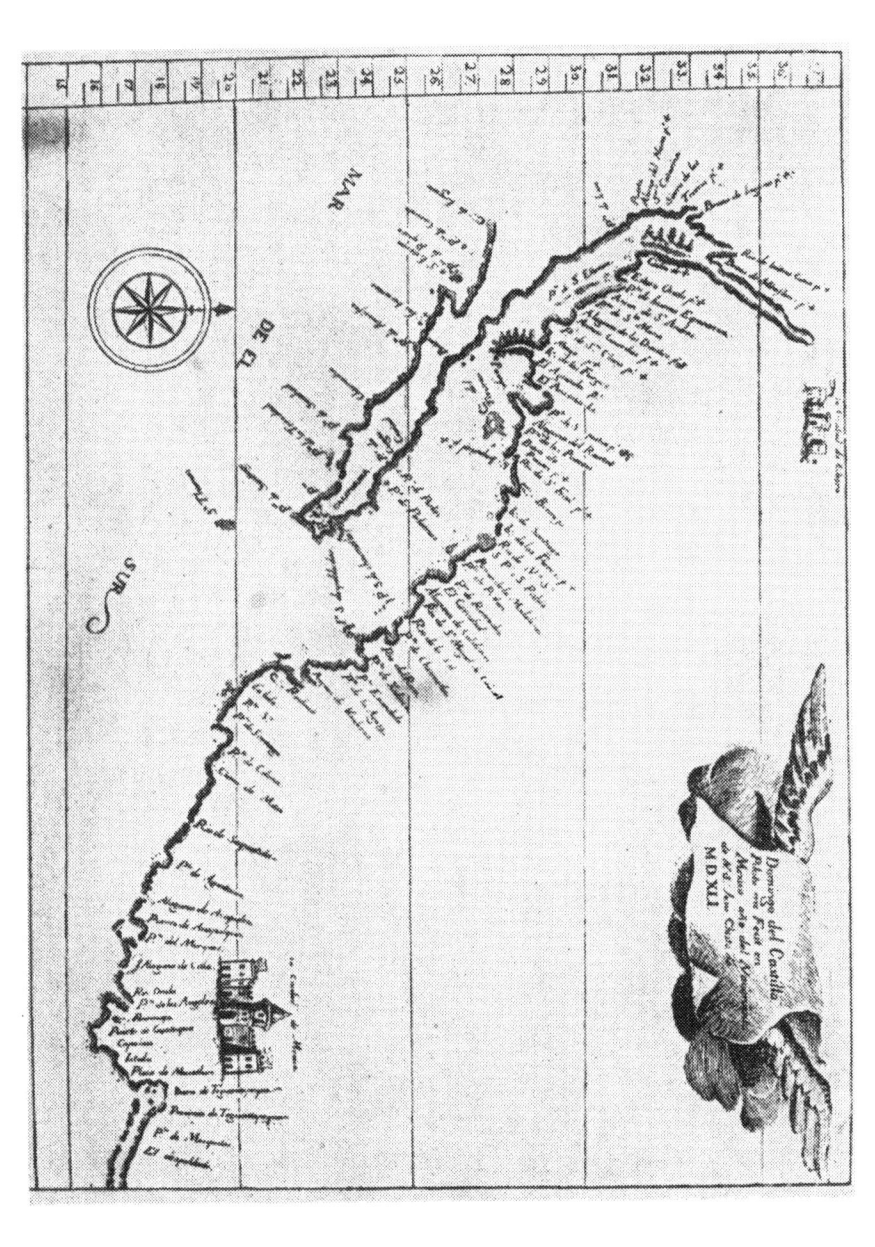

Earliest Map showing Cibola-Zuñi. This map belonged to Herman Cortés and was made by the pilot, Domingo del Castillo

confluence with the Rio Grande to permit of their traveling a distance of eighty leagues, over plains and mountains, before reaching the Rio Grande and the place where they first saw permanent houses. If Bandelier's route is correct, then the distance between the Pecos and the Rio Grande is a great deal less than eighty leagues, and if they followed along the left bank of the Rio Grande to a point beyond the mouth of the Concho, they would have had something to eat from the natives other than *chacan*, which the wanderers found impossible for them to eat. The fact that the *pinus edulis* — the "piñones," so exactly described by Cabeza de Vaca, is not to be found below the mouth of the Pecos, in truth not for many miles above its mouth, nor at any point on the Colorado river, where Bandelier would have it appear the survivors crossed that stream, is very persuasive, at least, that the Spaniards must have been in the areas and in the altitudes where that tree is found; this would compel a crossing of the Pecos river far above the point desired by Bandelier in his argument as to the probable route of the wanderers. Their presence in the locality where the piñon grows justifies the conclusion that they were in western Texas in localities far to the north of the Rio Grande at the mouth of the Pecos. It is also possible that the Jumanos Indians may have seen them at points much farther north than Mr. Bandelier wishes to place them. The Jumanos roamed and lived as far north as the present county of Torrance, in New Mexico, at some periods much farther north. After reaching the Rio Grande where the permanent habitations were found, the wanderers followed up that stream, as the narrative states, seventeen days, but Cabeza de Vaca, all things being taken into consideration, the lapse of time, the fact that he wrote entirely from memory, is just as apt to be in error as to time as he was as to distance. The writer cannot agree with Dr. Prince on this subject, who carries them as far north as the Rio Puerco or the San José, for in that event they would have passed by the communal houses near San Marcial, which were visited by the Spaniards in 1580, 1582, and 1598. Cabeza de Vaca would certainly have mentioned these houses had he seen them, for the reason that he does recite that he was told by the Indians that further to the north houses of this character of construction could be found, while south of San Marcial, the detached house-type, in

122 LEADING FACTS OF NEW MEXICAN HISTORY

clusters, occupied the river banks at intervals, as far south as Doña Ana county, New Mexico, and in all probability, much farther.

So far as the mention of turquoises [131] and the locality from which they were obtained is concerned, it does not necessarily follow that the Indians secured all of their supplies of this stone from the Chalchuitl mountain near Los Cerrillos, in Santa Fé county, as there are places in the counties of Otero and Grant, in New Mexico, and other places in Arizona, where this stone could have been obtained, and which places were known to the Indians, at least to those of more modern times. Mr. Bandelier cannot be taken as infallible in this matter. He certainly is in error in his conclusions as to the route taken by Francisco Vasquez Coronado after that explorer left the pueblo of Ci-cu-yé in his march in search of Quivira, and it is possible that he may be in error in stating positively that Cabeza de Vaca was never upon New Mexican soil.

The narrative and the other proofs are not conclusive and, in the judgment of the writer, there is no way of ascertaining whether he was upon New Mexican soil or not. The best evidence, and that was only a sort of tradition, that they crossed the Rio Grande into the state of Chihuahua, is the statement made by the Indians to Espejo in 1582, that many years before some Spaniards had passed through their country. These Indians were the Jumanos. In 1541, Francisco Vasquez Coronado also heard from an old Indian about the passing of the Spaniards through the country. The point where Coronado had

---

[131] Prince, L. B., *History of New Mexico*, p. 92, says: "Just how far up the Rio Grande Cabeza de Vaca came we shall probably never know; but evidently not further than central New Mexico, as the turquoises which were presented to him, and which certainly came from the great Chalchuitl mountains in the Cerrillos, south of Santa Fé, he mentions as coming from the north. From the highest point reached, the party seems to have turned abruptly west, probably as soon as they had passed by the desert regions on the west of the river; and then marched for more than a hundred leagues, continually finding settled domiciles, with plenty of maize and beans. It may be well conjectured that this was along the line of the Puerco and San José, and among the numerous pueblo towns of which we have such full descriptions a few years later, in the time of Coronado; although the route may have been further south."

The communal house near San Marcial was visited by a party of friars, Spanish soldiers, and Mexican and Indian guides and servants in 1581. The commander of the soldiers was Chamuscado. The village consisted of forty-five houses, two and three stories high, and there was plenty of corn and beans and other vegetables to be had at that point. The inhabitants wore cotton garments; they were the Piros.

THE FIRST SPANISH EXPLORERS 123

the interview with the Indian was more than seven hundred miles north of the point mentioned by Espejo, and Coronado's native informant said that he had seen them further south toward New Spain.

Inasmuch as Mr. Bandelier is so positive in his declaration as to the route of Cabeza de Vaca, it is no more than right to present his argument and conclusions, as the judgment of so distinguished an authority is entitled to great weight and consideration. He says:

"It remains to be investigated which route the adventurous wanderers took, and that investigation will, in turn, determine whether or not it is true, as has hitherto been admitted, that Cabeza de Vaca was the first European, writing of the event, to tread New Mexican soil. I have already stated, as a result of previous studies, that the prevailing notions are incorrect, and that he never set foot on New Mexican territory, as the term is understood to-day. I shall add here, that he never claimed, as little as did his companions, to have seen or visited any of the sedentary tribes whose peculiar culture and condition have become so characteristic of New Mexico.

"There are a few points in the itinerary which are of decisive value in the discussion of it, and are placed beyond all controversy by the statements of the travellers. These are:

"1. That they began their journey in eastern Texas, and near the coast.

"2. That during their peregrination, they always remained south of the range where the buffalo was wont to roam.

"3. That the mean direction of their course was from east to west.

"4. That until they entered the broad mountain chain, through whose gaps or valleys they emerged upon the slope of the Pacific, they had constantly been travelling among and with roaming savages, and that the first clusters of more permanent settlements were met with by them in that great mountain region, as well as to the west of it, near the shores of the South Sea.

"5. That the place where they received the first intimation of the proximity of the Spaniards, was situated on the Yaqui river of Sonora, and at no great distance from the coast.

"No. 1 and No. 5 give us the terminal points of the journey. No. 2 limits the belt through which they travelled to a zone in the southern part of the United States of to-day. It also excludes all possibility of their having impinged upon southern New Mexico, and particularly upon the part inhabited by the Pueblo Indians.

"To re-establish the itinerary with complete accuracy is quite impossible. It was written, not as a journal, for they had no means of recording anything on their trip, but as recollections sufficiently fresh, however, to admit of tolerable accuracy, provided it was done in good faith. Nothing in their report indicates that they wilfully exaggerated or misrepresented, taking into consideration their extraordinary sufferings and the state of physical as well as mental exaltation which the terrible strain upon body and mind cannot but have produced. The wonderful cures which they relate are no evidence of studied deception on their part. The interpretation given by them to their unexpected success in the art of healing and curing was in accordance with the spirit of the times, and the conditions of knowledge at that epoch. I therefore regard their relations as reliable in the main, though of necessity confused, and often unsatisfactory in precision and detail. This lack of prolixity speaks in favor of their truthfulness.

"It is worthy of note, that after the four castaways had met, and had determined upon striving to reach the part of America where they might find settlements of their own people, they did not in all their wanderings, cross any river of such proportions as might correspond to the width and depth of the Mississippi, or of any other large stream in the Central and Southern states of the Union. One river, particularly, is mentioned as being 'wider than the Guadalquivir in Seville, and they crossed it all up to the knee and thigh, and for a length of more than two lances up to the breast, but without peril.'[132]

"Of this same character all the other rivers which they crossed must have been, else they would have mentioned any notable difference. They consequently did not have to cross the Mississippi, but found themselves beyond its mouth even previous to their meeting. The last remnants of the expedition to which they belonged perished probably in the neighborhood of the Mississippi delta and somewhat west of it, and the survivors, completely at the mercy of the Indians, were tossed to and fro between bands moving no great distance from the coast or to the west. Once united and bent upon their westward progress, they took care to note, not only the size, but also the number, of the streams they had to cross, and this number is given by

[132] *Historia*, p. 604: " 'É antes que el sol se pusiesse llegaron á un rio, que á su parescer era mas ancho que Guadalquivir en Sevilla, é passaronlo todo á larodillo é al muslo, é obra de dos lancas en luengo á los pechos, pero sin peligro.' *Naufragios*, p. 538: 'Partimos de allí llevandolas por guia, y pasamos un rio quando ya vino la tarde, que nos daba el agua á los pechos; seria tan ancho como el de Sevilla, y coria muy mucho.' It is the general character of Southwestern streams to have wide beds in proportion to their depth. It is noteworthy also, that they lay stress upon this particular river for its size and the depth of its current, as well as its velocity. Neither corresponds with the Mississippi, nor with the Red river, taking into consideration (as far as the latter is concerned) that they were still close to the coast, whereas the Red river empties into the Mississippi at a distance of 110 miles north of the nearest point on the shore. Neither did the expedition of Narváez, as long as it was together, cross the Mississippi. That they should have passed its mouth without

them as four. They were the Trinity, the Brazos, the Colorado, and the Rio Grande del Norte.[133]

noticing it, is quite possible, from the state of utter helplessness in which they were, completely adrift and at the mercy of the wind and waves in their frail boats.

"Only twice there is a qualification: *Naufragios*, p. 540, 'á la ribera de un muy hermoso rio'; p. 541, 'Y al cabo dellas un rio muy grande, que nos daba á los pechos.'"

[133] *Ibid*: "Previous to their meeting, many bays, lagunes and streams are mentioned. All were, however, in the vicinity of the shore. Afterwards during their peregrinations we find only four rivers which they crossed, the last of the four being the one near the region where the buffalos were said to roam.

"It must be borne in mind, that the average direction of their wanderings was from east to west. Consequently the streams which they crossed must have flowed, on an average also, from north to south. The only country in the southern part of North America where four water-courses of the particular kind mentioned by Cabeza de Vaca and his companions would have to be crossed successively on a journey from east to west is Texas, and they can only have been the Trinity, the Brazos, the Colorado, and the Rio Grande. That the Nueces should not be counted will appear from the direction they took, which carried them to the mouth of the Pecos, consequently so far north that the Nueces must have appeared to them as a mere creek. That the Pecos would not be mentioned becomes evident from what I shall develop further on, so that the Trinity as the first, and the Rio Grande as the last, of the four rivers indicated, are the only identifications possible. The Trinity was the one described as being as large as the Guadalquivir at Seville (see note 1, page 51). The Brazos was the next, of which Cabeza de Vaca says (*Naufragios*, p. 539): 'Y nosotros caminamos por el rio arriba.' And the joint report preserved in Oviedo (*Historia*, p. 604): 'Hasta un rio que estaba al pie de la punta, donde comencaba la dicha tierra.' The river which the joint report in Oviedo (*Historia*, p. 606) mentions as within a mountainous region is the Colorado, which indeed traverses a series of heights (appearing like low mountains in comparison with the extensive levels of Texas) between Austin and San Saba. Of it Cabeza de Vaca says (p. 540): 'Y atravesamos una sierra de siete leguas y las piedras de ella eran de escorias de hierro; y á la noche llegamos á muchas casas, que estaban asentadas á la ribera de un hermoso rio.' This would also indicate volcanic rocks. Finally, the last river mentioned (*Naufragios*, p. 542, *Historia*, pp. 608, 609) after traversing a very dry expanse of mountainous country, was the Rio Grande. At the end of this region, whose width is given at fifty leagues, he mentions another river, 'muy grande, que el agua nos daba á los pechos.' The joint report does not mention it, and I have only accepted what is contained in both sources. In case Cabeza de Vaca is right, then there were five streams, the first of which was the Nechez, the second the Trinity, the Brazos the third, the Colorado the fourth, and the Rio Grande the last. In either case, the ultimate geographical result is the same.— *Alvar Nuñez Cabeza de Vaca, the first overland Traveller of European Descent, and His Journeys from Florida to the Pacific Coast*, 1528-1536, in the *Magazine of Western History*, July, 1886, p. 330 et seq.

"There is abundant proof of this. In 1581, Francisco Sanches Chamuscado with eight soldiers accompanied three Franciscan friars up the Rio Grande to New Mexico, and they met the buffalo quite far east of that river, in the great plains east of the Sierra de Sandia, and the Sierra del Manzano, *Testimonio dado en Mejico sobre el Descubrimiento de doscientas leguas adelante, de las Minas de Santa Barbola*, etc. (Doc. de Indias, vol. xv). In the following year, Antonio de Espejo marched up the Rio Grande from near the mouth of the

"All these streams are fordable during the winter months, and it was in fall and winter that the Spaniards performed their journey through Texas. In another place I have written as follows on this subject, and I have nothing to alter in the opinions there expressed:
"They travelled five days, crossing a river 'wider than the Guadalquivir at Seville,' and quite deep. This was the Trinity. Three days' march west of this river they began to see mountains, one range of which seemed to sweep directly northward. One day farther, or 'five leagues farther on' they reached another river 'at the foot of the point where the said mountains commenced.' That river was the Brazos, and by 'mountains' the hills of Central Texas must be understood. Cabeza de Vaca says he estimated the distance of these mountains from the sea to be fifteen leagues (forty miles). People from the coast came in one day to visit them.

"Here they changed their direction, and moved northwards along the base of a mountain chain and partly away from water-courses, eighty leagues according to the joint report, fifty according to Cabeza de Vaca. The last estimate is more likely, for the journey was painful and slow, and they experienced great scarcity of food, as well as of water. In this manner they reached the vicinity of Fort Graham. Here they changed their route, making towards sunset again.

Conchos to Bernalillo, in New Mexico, and found no trace of the great quadruped, whereas, upon his return down the Rio Pecos he saw large herds of them along the latter stream. In 1590 Gaspar Castaño de Sosa marched up the Pecos river, after crossing the Rio Grande and he saw tracks of the buffalo only on the former. In 1598, Oñate again followed the Rio Grande upwards, from a considerable distance below El Paso del Norte, and saw no trace of the buffalo along its banks.

"In *Naufragios*, p. 542: 'Y porque aquel rio arriba mas de cincuenta leguas, van matando muchas de ellas.' Further on we find the following passage: 'Passados dos dias que allí estuvimos, determinamos de ir á buscar el maiz; y no quesimos seguir el camino de las vacas porque es hacia el norte y esto era para nosotros muy gran rodeo.' They therefore followed the river for seventeen days. 'Y ansi pasamos todas las diez y siete jornadas, y al cabo de ellas atrevesamos el rio.' This shows that the river on which were the cows was not the same as the one which the Spaniards followed. *Historia*, p. 609: 'E assí fueron por este rio arriba las nueve jornadas, cada dia caminando hasta la noche, con grandissima hambre.' The Indians on that river told them 'que eran ydos á comer las vacas, tres jornadas de alla en unos llanos entre las sierras que decian venian de arriba hacia la mar.' The plain which is here mentioned corresponds to the level through which the Pecos flows in northwestern Texas. The mountains are the Sierra Apache, Sierra Guadalupe, Pahcut, and the others of that wild and arid region between the Pecos and the Rio Grande, south of the New Mexican boundary.

"In 1684, Juan Domingo de Mendoza crossed over from the mouth of the Conchos to the Pecos river, and on the 10th of January, ten days after leaving the Rio Grande, he saw the first signs of buffalo. *Diario del Viage á la Junta de los Rios y hasta el Rio de Pecos*, Ms., fol. 8.''

THE FIRST SPANISH EXPLORERS   127

"Including prolonged stays among the Indian hordes, our Spaniards consumed nearly two months in these wanderings, so that it was November when they began to move westward again. Guided by sunrise and by sunset they consequently followed a line south of west, it being now late in the fall. The farther they advanced, the greater became that southern deflection. They crossed the Colorado, and finally struck a large river, to which they gave the name 'Rio de las Vacas,' or river of the Cows, since the buffalo herds were said to roam more than fifty leagues up the river.

"This is the last stream mentioned in either of the relations. It was evidently the Rio Grande.

"Here both reports become extraordinarily diffuse, although the joint narrative is less so than Cabeza de Vaca's book, still, it is easily discernible that the Spaniards struck the Rio Grande, without crossing the Pecos, therefore below or very near the mouth of the latter. Refusing to go due north where the cows were, they followed the eastern bank for fifteen (*Naufragios* have seventeen) days. The mountains were to the north, and during this tramp they suffered much from hunger. At the end of fifteen or of seventeen days, they crossed the river to the west. The distance from the mouth of the Pecos to Presidio del Norte (where the Rio Conchos empties into the Rio Grande) is about two hundred and fifty miles, a reasonable stretch for fifteen days of wearisome and difficult foot travel. I conclude, therefore, that they crossed the Rio Grande about Fort Seaton. Thereafter their route lay towards the sunset again, and no more water-courses are mentioned. That is, until they reached the banks of the Yaqui.

"In the sixteenth century, the buffalo never reached the shores of the Rio Grande del Norte. This seems to militate against the assumption that that river was the last stream which they met (of any importance) previous to their striking Sonora. But the text of both the main sources indicate that the cows were not on the river which they followed for about seventeen days. It is certain that they never saw the buffalo themselves, except Cabeza de Vaca, who saw them in the Red River country, but the Indians on the Rio Grande told them that they roamed 'three days distance from there.' It is well ascertained that the buffalo used to descend along the Pecos to near the mouth of that river. Therefore the Spaniards must have struck the Rio Grande a little below its junction with the Pecos and the reports which they gathered concerning the vicinity of the great quadruped applied to the Pecos, owing to the near proximity of both rivers, of which, however, they saw but the larger one. Furthermore, their journey up the river exposed them to many hardships, owing to the lack of food. The Indians had hardly anything to eat, still less wherewith to feed guests, and while buffalo robes were plentiful, the animal itself was said to exist 'three days' journey from there in plains among mountains which they said descended from higher up towards the sea, and that they themselves went thither also. These plains between mountains are the plains through the western edge of which the Pecos approaches the Rio Grande; the mountains are the maze of arid chains covering the triangle formed in the extreme northwest of Texas by the Rio Grande and the Pecos.

"The upper course of the Rio Brazos, perhaps on the thirty-second parallel of latitude, appears therefore to have been the most northerly point reached by the wanderers on their peregrinations. This is also the latitude of the southern boundary of New Mexico; but they struck that parallel at least four degrees of longitude east of the southeastern corner of the New Mexican territory, and thence declined to the southwest to two and a half degrees farther south. As long as they were east of the Rio Grande, or on the soil of the United States of today, Cabeza de Vaca and his friends remained far out of reach of New Mexico. In addition to the geographical and zoographical evidences given, there is further proof derived from the statements of the travellers concerning the flora of the country, and the condition of the aborigines with whom they came in contact. As long as they were together on the coast, and even for some time afterward, they place much stress upon several nutritive plants which were characteristic of the vegetation, and at the same time prominent means of subsistence for the Indians. Prominent among these are the mesquite [134] (Prosopis juliflora) and the cactus pear (Opuntia). Neither of these plants appears in Eastern Texas towards the Indian Territory in any great abundance, and yet the natives were wont to leave the coast and go inland in order to subsist for months on the tuna or cactus fruit; and the beans of the mesquite are mentioned time and again, as one of the principal means of subsistence of these hordes during certain periods of the year. Such statements can only apply to Southern and Central Texas.

"Again a small tree or shrub is mentioned bearing edible nuts.[135] At first glance, the Piñon, or Pinus Edulis, may be thought of, a

---

[134] "The descriptions are full and accurate. Not only the Tuna is mentioned, but the name Mesquite, also Mesquisez, appears in both reports. *Historia*, p. 604, and possibly p. 609; *Naufragios*, p. 538: 'Este Mesquisez es una fruta que cuando está en el arbol es muy amarga, y es de la manera de algarraobas y comese con tierra, y con ella está dulce, y bueno de comer.'

[135] "That these cannot have been the New Mexican Piñones is quite clear, *Naufragios*, p. 540: 'Hay por aquella tierra piños chicos, y las piñas de ellas son como pequeños huevos, mas los piñones son mejores que los de Castilla, porque tienen las cascaras muy delgadas; y cuando estan verdes muelenlos y

Santiago Triumphing over His Enemies. Painted on Elk Skin
In Collections of New Mexico Historical Society

tree which is almost specifically New Mexican; but the shell of these 'Piñoñes' was soft and edible also. This proves that the tree must have been a cedar, the fruit of which is also used by the Pueblo Indians and other tribes of New Mexico. This tree or shrub occurs in Northern Texas. The travellers strongly insist upon the almost total absence of maize or Indian corn as long as they remained to the east of the Rio Grande. On the banks of that stream they were finally told that to find corn in any abundance, it was necessary for them to go westward, and also to the north a long distance.

"What the Indians planted were beans and calabashes, and even these grew only in small quantities, as the soil was very poor. Had they ever come in contact with the New Mexican Pueblos, they would have told a different story. The Indians themselves whom the castaways met and cured, and who voluntarily accompanied them as escort from band to band, or from camp to camp, are plainly described as being the merest savages. Nowhere is there any mention of houses of mud or stone.[136] Only lodges made of boughs or leaves, the rudest huts, are spoken of. These Indians led an erratic life,

hacenlos pellas, y ansí los comen; y si estan secos, los muelen con cascaras de manera que los comen con lo demas; las piñas de ellas son muy chiquitas, é los arboles llenos en aquellas serranias en cantidad.' This does not at all agree with the New Mexican piñon. I am unable as yet to find out whether there is a species of piñon in Texas. At all events, if there is, it appears to be different from the northern kind.

"In the vicinity, or on the banks of the Rio Grande, perhaps, there was a little corn, but there were no plantations of it. *Naufragios*, p. 542: 'Preguntamosles como no sembraban maiz; respondierronnos que lo hacian por no perder lo que sembrasen, porque dos años atras les habian faltado las aguas y habia sido el tiempo tan seco, que á todos les habian perdido los maices los topos, y que no usurian tornar á sembrar sin que primero hubiese llovido mucho; . . . tambien nosotros quesimos saber de donde habian traido aquél maiz, y ellos nos dijeron que de donde el sol se ponia, y que lo habia por toda aquella tierra; mas que lo mas cerca de alli era por aquel camino.'

[136] "The only place where they found dwellings slightly more substantial was on the Rio Grande. *Historia*, p. 608: 'Los cuales lo llevaron á un rio donde hallaron gente é casas á assiento; á algunos fesoles é calabacas que comian, aunque mui poco.' *Naufragios*, p. 542. It is not surprising that on the Rio Grande there should have lived Indians in more permanent abodes. It was in this vicinity that, forty-six years later, Espejo met the Jumanos Indians, of whom he says (*Relacion del Viage*, Doc. de Indias, vol. xv, p. 168): 'En que parecia habia mucha gente y con pueblos formados, grandes en que vimos cinco pueblos con mas de diez mil indios y casas de azutea, bajas, y con buena traza de pueblos.' These Jumanos recollected the passage of Cabeza de Vaca and his companions through their country: 'Respondieron que de tres Christianos, y un negro que auian passado por allí, y detennidose algunos dias en su tierra, etc.' It is very significant also, that they mention houses of mud for the first time in the Sierra Madre. *Historia*, p. 609: 'É tenian casas estos indios algunas pequeñas de tierra.' *Naufragios*, p. 543. "Entre estas casas habia algunas de ellas que era de tierra." Had these not been the *first* ones which the Spanards saw on the whole journey, they would scarcely have made such special mention of them. It is also stated in *Historia*, p. 610: 'É tambien les

wandering to and fro at will, or according to the necessities of life. Nothing in the picture made of these nomads corresponds in the least to the sedentary tribes of New Mexico. There is not even an indication that the Spaniards, while east of the Rio Grande, heard of the Pueblos and their strange, characteristic many-storied dwellings.

"Cabeza de Vaca has given a list of tribes (*Naufragios*, cap. xxvi), which contains a great number of names. I have not as yet been able to identify a single one of them. This is not surprising. Texas was not explored by the Spaniards until one hundred and fifty years later, and among roaming Indians it is extremely difficult to recognize the name of a band or horde after such a lapse of time. Besides, we do not know to what extent the appelatives left us by Cabeza de Vaca, surnames — to what extent they were recognized by the tribe, or only applied to it by some neighbor, whether friend or enemy.

"It remains now to trace the course of the Spaniards on the west side of the Rio Grande, and to see whether, perhaps, on that side they penetrated New Mexico.

"I believe that I have established that the crossing of the stream which now divides the state of Texas from the Mexican States of Chihuahua and Coahuila was effected at the junction of the Rio Conchos with the Rio Grande, or near Presidio del Norte, in Chihuahua. Thence onward their course was westward, declining to the south, Presidio del Norte, itself, is more than two degrees south of the New Mexican boundary line; it lies even outside the limits of the territory as they were during the Spanish domination. It is therefore equally impossible that Cabeza de Vaca ever could have trod New Mexican soil on the west side of the Rio Grande. His route led him across the central portions of the State of Chihua-

---

paresció que aquellos terradillos é andar las mugeres en habito tan honesto, lo aprendian é tomaban della (from the coast of the Pacific).' This shows that until then they had not seen any houses of earth or stone.

"Another point which is itself almost decisive is the statement that until they entered the Sierra Madre they nowhere saw pottery in use or in the hands of the natives. On the Rio Grande, where they found the most substantial dwellings, Cabeza de Vaca remarks (*Naufragios*, p. 542): 'Ellos no alcanzan ollas, y para cocer lo que ellos quieren comer hinchen media calabaza grande con agua, y en fuego echas muchas piedras de las que mas facilmente ellos pueden encender, y toman el fuego; y cuando ven que estan ardiendo, tomanlas con unas tenasas de palo, y echanlas en aquella agua que eta en la calabaza hasta que la hacen hervir con el fuego que las piedras llevan; y cuando ven que el agua hierve, echan en ella lo que han de cocer, y en todo este tiempo no hacen sino sacar unas piedras y echar otras ardiendo para que el agua hierva para cocer lo que quieren, y asi lo cuecen.' *Historia*, p. 608. Had the travellers met the New Mexican Pueblos, they would have seen pottery, and undoubtedly have mentioned it."

hua to the Pass of the Mulatos in the Sierra Madre. The time spent in traversing that arid country, twenty days, agrees with the distance fairly well, and the short description of the condition of the aborigines whom the Spaniards met on their passage is very well put. And from there they went to the west, or setting sun, more than twenty days more, through people that were famished, though not as much (as those previously spoken of) because they ate powdered herbs and killed a great many hares.'' [137]

"In a straight line the eastern flanks of the Sierra Madre are not more than two hundred miles from the mouth of the Conchos. It is self evident that the route taken was not a perfect air-line, and that consequently they travelled a greater distance. They must have kept on the north side of the Conchos river, else they would have mentioned it. The country has some beautiful valleys, at least now, when such spots have been improved for sites of ranchos, haciendas, and a few settlements. But by far the greater portion of the country which the Spaniards then traversed must have produced upon them the impression of an arid waste. It was only when they ascended the foot-hills of the Sierra Madre and penetrated into the deep gorges and valleys of that extensive mountain area, that a fertile land met their eyes and at last they found Indians who cultivated maize, who owned turquoises, although in small quantities and who traded parrot's feathers for green stones, far in the north. The houses of these Indians were made of palm leaves tressed and plaited, and some of the buildings had earthen walls and a dirt roof.

"All this is significant, and enables us to identify the region though not the exact locality. A species of large green parrot inhabits the pine forests of the Sierra Madre as far north as latitude 30 degrees. Palms are found in the Sierra Madre and its tributary chains. They are especially fan-palms and the houses of the aborigines of Sonora were often made of that material.

"The interior of the Sierra Madre is strewn with remains of Indian hamlets and cave dwellings, and with traces of small garden-beds. Not all of these ruins ante-date the time of Spanish occupation. The Jovas, a branch and dialect of the Opatas, dwelt in scattered clusters in the interior of the chain, almost due west of

---

[137] "The limits were the Boquillas, 40 leagues (108) miles south of El Paso. Rivera, *Diario*, p. 27. In 1836 Pedro Garcia Condé fixes the northern limits of Chihuahua at latitude 32 degrees 57 minutes. *Ensayo Estadistico sobre el Estado de Chihuahua*, p 7. Presidio del Norte is south of that line. *Historia*, p. 609. For a description of that part of Chihuahua as it was sixty years after Cabeza de Vaca's passage, compare Juan de Oñate, *Discurso de Las Jornadas*, pp. 236-243; also Gaspar Perez de Villagrán, *Historia de la Nueva Mejico*, 1610, fol. 85-115.''

Presidio del Norte. It is more than likely that Cabeza de Vaca and his friends fell in with these Jovas, and that the 'houses of sod with dirt roofs' were those of Jova or Opata hamlets scattered through the valleys in the mountain fastnesses between the sources of the Rio Aros and the Rio de Mulatos, both of which, by the way, are tributaries of the Yaqui, and belong, therefore, to the drainage of the Pacific slope.

"My main object is, I believe, attained; namely, to establish nowhere, on their long and painful journey, did Cabeza de Vaca, Dorantes, Castillo Maldonado, and Estevan, the negro, touch upon New Mexico; that, therefore, the wide-spread notion which ascribes to the first-named the discovery of that Territory is without any foundation whatever. Furthermore, the assertion that he claimed to have discovered it, and to have seen its sedentary inhabitants and their strange buildings is absolutely gratuitous. Neither Cabeza de Vaca, in his book, nor the three Spaniards jointly, in their official report, make the slightest allusion to such a claim on their part. It may be, that the large houses or villages of which they claim to have heard, while in the Sierra Madre, and four degrees of latitude south of the southern limit of the Pueblos in the sixteenth century, were those of the Pueblos; but it might also be that the Jovas (whom by the way they could hardly understand) referred to past reminiscences, alluding to the remains of Casa Grande in Arizona, or to those of Casas Grandes in northwestern Chihuahua.[138]

"Thence it is comparatively easy to follow their course to the southwest, and finally to points in Sonora where they first heard of the presence of people of their own race, and were finally taken to Compostella, and, afterwards, to the City of Mexico."

Thus was concluded an expedition begun with all the prospects of success which had crowned the efforts of the conquerors of the Montezumas and the Incas, and which "though doomed to disaster from its very inception, and utterly unsuccessful in accomplishing its design, still lives in history through the sufferings and endur-

---

[138] "The Casa Grande in Arizona was a Pima town, and the Casas Grandes in Chihuahua were probably Opata settlements. Both had been in ruins for long years previous to the sixteenth century. The southern Pimas, however, dwelt in houses similar to those of the ruins as late as the middle of the seventeenth century. (Ribas, *Historia*, pp. 360, 371.) There is a passage in Oviedo's synopsis of the joint report that deserves to be noticed (*Historia*, p. 610): 'Decianles aquellos indios que por toda aquella costa del Sur hacia el Norte (que mejor se puede é debe llamar, no del Sur sino septrional) avia mucha gente é mucha comida é mucha algoden, é las casas grandes; é que tenian muchas piedras turquesas, quellos las traian de alla por rescate.' This would indicate that the great houses were those of Nebomes or Pimas, and not New Mexican Pueblos."

THE FIRST SPANISH EXPLORERS 133

ance of the four men who were the first to cross the continent north of the comparatively narrow domains of Mexico."[139]

The negro, Estevan, the slave of Dorantes, of all the survivors, was the only one whose destiny was an active participation in future explorations of New Mexico, and foreordained to live in the traditions of the Zuñis.[140]

The colophon[141] of the first edition of the *Narrative* of Alvar Nuñez Cabeza de Vaca is as follows:

"The present tract was imprinted in the very magnificent, noble and very ancient city of Zamora, by the honored residents Augustin de Paz and Juan Picardo, partners, printers of books, at the cost

---

[139] Prince, L. B., *History of New Mexico*, p. 89.

[140] Cushing, F. H., *Extract from a Lecture*, by: "It is to be believed that a long time ago, when roofs lay over the walls of Kya-ki-mé, when smoke hung over the house-tops, and the ladder-rounds were still unbroken in Kya-ki-mé, then the black Mexicans came from their abodes in Everlasting Summerland. One day, unexpectedly, out of Hemlock canyon they came, and descended to Kya-ki-mé. But when they said they would enter the covered way, it seems that our ancients looked not gently at them; for with these Black Mexicans came many Indians of So-no-lí, as they call it now, who carried war feathers and long bows and cane arrows like the Apaches, who were enemies of our ancients. Therefore, these our ancients, being always bad-tempered, and quick to anger, made fools of themselves after their fashion, rushed into their town and out of their town, skipping, shouting and shooting with sling-stones and arrows and tossing their war-clubs. Then the Indians of So-no-lí set up a great howl, and thus they and our ancients, right where the stone stands down by the arroyo of Kya-ki-mé, did much ill to one another. Then and thus was killed by our ancients, one of the Black Mexicans, a large man, with chilli lips, and some of the Indians they killed, catching others. Then the rest ran away, chased by our grand-fathers, and went back toward their country in the land of Everlasting Summer. But after they had steadied themselves and stopped talking, our ancients felt sorry, for they thought 'Now we have made bad business, for after awhile these black people and the So-no-lí Indians, being angered, will come again.' So they felt always in danger from fear, and went about watching the bushes. By and by they did come back, these Black Mexicans, and with them many sons of So-no-lí. They wore coats of iron, and war-bonnets of metal, and carried for weapons short canes that spit fire and made thunder, so said our ancients, but they were guns, you know. They frightened our bad-tempered fathers so badly that their hands hung down by their sides like the hands of women. And this time these black, curly-bearded people drove our ancients like slave-creatures.

"One of these coats of iron was hung a long time in Isleta, and there people say you may see it. After that the Black Mexicans were peaceful, they say; but they went away, and sometimes came back, it seems, and never finished making anger with our ancients, it seems. Thus it was in the days of Kya-ki-mé. That is why there are two kinds of Mexicans, good and bad, white and black. And the white are good to our people; but the black ones like troublesome beasts.''

[141] Hodge, F. W., *The Spanish Explorers in the Southern United States*, p. 126.

134   LEADING FACTS OF NEW MEXICAN HISTORY

and outlay of the virtuous Juan Pedro Musetti, book merchant of Medina del Campo, having been finished the sixth day of the month of October, in the year one thousand five hundred and forty-two of the birth of our Saviour Jesus Christ.''

Moqui basket and pottery

BIBLIOGRAPHY

Bancroft, Hubert Howe	*History of Arizona and New Mexico*, pp. 1-73.
Bandelier, A. F.	*Historical Introduction to Studies among the Sedentary Indians of New Mexico*, Santa Fé, N. M., September, 1880. Papers of the Archæological Institute of America, edition 1883, pp. 1-33.
	Report on his Investigations in New Mexico in the Spring and Summer of 1882. Bul. of the Arch. Inst. of Am., i. Boston, 1883, pp. 13-33.
	Contributions to the History of the Southwestern Portion of the United States. Papers Arch. Inst. of Am., American Series, v.
	Final Report of Investigations among the Indians of the Southwestern United States, 1880-1885.
	Alvar Nuñez Cabeza de Vaca, the First Overland Traveller of European Descent, and his Journey from Florida to the Pacific Coast, 1528-1536. Magazine of Western History, iv. Cleveland, July, 1886, pp. 327-336.
	His Editorial Notes to translation of the *Journey of Alvar Nuñez Cabeza de Vaca*, translation by Mrs. Fanny Bandelier, New York, A. S. Barnes & Co., 1905.
Blackmar, F. W.	*Spanish Colonization in the Southwest*. Johns Hopkins University Studies, viii,, April, 1890.
Davis, W. W. H.	*The Spanish Conquest of New Mexico*.
Hakluyt, Richard	*The Principal Navigations, Voyages, Trafficks and Discoveries of the English Nation*, etc. Edinburg ed., 1885-1890, vol. xiv, America, part iii, pp. 59-137.
Herrera, Antonio de	*Historia General*. Madrid, 1730.
Hodge, Frederick W,	*Spanish Explorers in the Southern United States*, pp. 3-126, Charles Scribner's Sons, New York, 1907.
Diaz, Bernal	*Historia Verdadera, de la conquista de la Nueva España*.
Las Casas, Bartolome	*Historia de las Indias*.
Mendoza, Antonio de	*Carta á la emperatriz, participando que vienen á España Cabeza de Vaca y Francisco Dorantes, que se Escaparon de la armada de Panfilo Narvaez, á hacer Relacion de lo que en ella sucedio*. Mexico, Feb. 11, 1537., Doc. de Indies, xiv, 236.
Mota Padilla, Matias de la	*Historia de la conquista de la provincia de la Nueva Galicia, escrita en 1742*. Mexico, 1870.

Oviedo y Valdes, Gonzalo Fernandes de	*Historia General.*
Prince, L. Bradford	*History of New Mexico.* 1883, pp. 40-148.
Smith, (Thomas) Buckingham	*Alvar Nuñez Cabeza de Vaca, Narrative,* New York, 1871.
Ternaux-Compans, H.	*Voyages,* etc. Paris, 1837-1841, vol. ix.
Winship, George Parker	*The Coronado Expedition,* 14th Ann. Rep., B. A. E., 1896.

Don Antonio de Mendoza, First Viceroy of New Spain

CHAPTER III

FRIAR MARCOS DE NIZA—THE NEGRO, ESTEVAN—THEIR JOURNEY TO
CIBOLA, 1539—DEATH OF ESTEVAN—RETURN OF FRIAR
MARCOS TO THE CITY OF MEXICO

HERNANDO CORTES, governor, captain-general, and chief justice of New Spain, was succeeded in office, in 1526, by Luis Ponce de Leon. The latter had been sent out from Spain to prefer charges against the conqueror of Mexico. In 1528, Cortés left Mexico for Spain. Nuño de Guzman, meanwhile, had been appointed governor, and, in the year following his appointment, organized an expedition for the exploration of the lands and countries lying far to the north. Nuño de Guzman was of a most cruel and avaricious disposition, and, having learned from a Tejos Indian that, in the countries far to the north, gold and silver were obtainable in great quantities, determined upon the exploration of that country. The Indian had told him that he had seen towns that were of a size equal to the City of Mexico. These towns were seven in number, and in them were streets, the houses along which were occupied entirely by workers in the precious metals. These cities, he said, could be reached by traveling north and crossing a desert covered with grass, after a journey of forty days' duration.

This expedition started in the month of December, 1529, and, during the ensuing two years, Guzman conquered Sinaloa, founded the settlement of San Miguel and also that of Culiacan, lying farther north. He did not find the Seven Cities, however, and gave to the countries he had subdued the name of New Galicia.

EXPEDITION SENT OUT BY
NUÑO DE GUZMAN

In the year 1530, Cortés returned from Spain, bringing with him the title of Marques del Valle de Oajaca, together with extensive privileges and rights of exploration, and, during the four years following, made several attempts at exploration of the coast northward, with no more important result, however, than the discovery of Lower California.

Previous to the year 1536, Cortés set on foot not less than four distinct attempts to navigate the South Sea. The first one, in 1522, failed on account of the supplies and building material having been set on fire and destroyed in the port of Zacatula, where the ships were being constructed.

The ships commanded by Alvaro Saavedra Ceron, which sailed from Zihuátlan in November, 1527, were destined for the Spice Islands, and were lost on the voyage thither.

In 1532, Diego Hurtado de Mendoza sailed from Acapulco with two vessels. The one commanded by him was lost, and the other was thrown on the coast of Jalisco.

In 1533, two other ships sailed from Tehuantepec. One of these, in charge of Hernando Grijalva, came in sight of the southern extremity of Lower California, and immediately returned to New Spain. The other was commanded by Diego Becerra de Mendoza, a relative of Cortés. When at sea, the pilot, Fortuno Jimenez, murdered the captain, landed the two priests on the shores of Jalisco, and with the crew sailed as far as the harbor of La Paz, in Lower California, where the natives surprised and killed him and twenty of his men.

The expedition which Cortés commanded in person took place in the year 1534. It accomplished nothing.[142]

In 1535, Antonio de Mendoza was commissioned viceroy of New Spain. During the year following his appointment Alvar Nuñez Cabeza de Vaca and his companions reached the City of Mexico. They were royally entertained by Mendoza, and the story of their wanderings undoubtedly produced a marked impression upon the

---

[142] Oviedo, *Historia General*, ed. 1853, vol. iii, p. 434; *Doc. de Indias*, p. 65 et seq.; Ycazbalceta, J. G., *Historia de Mexico*, p. 35 et seq.; *Doc. de Indias*, p. 128 et seq.; Herrera, *Historia*, dec. v, vol. ii, p. 197 et seq.; *Memorial contra Don Antonio de Mendoza*, June 25, 1540.

Bandelier, A. F., *Contributions*, p. 17, says: "None of these expeditions increased the knowledge of the northern regions to any extent. And yet, in 1540, Cortés boldly asserted that he had informed Fray Marcos of Niza of what the latter reported concerning the coast of Sonora and the Californian Gulf, accusing the friar of speaking about what he never saw."

JOURNEY TO CIBOLA 139

mind of the representative of the crown. Shortly he purchased from Dorantes the negro slave, Estevan, and forthwith began the organization of an expedition for the prosecution of discoveries in the lands of the far north which had been so attractively described to him by the survivors of the Narváez expedition. For some reason Mendoza's project never materialized and finally fell through altogether.[143]

The next attempt to reach the unknown north occurred in 1538, when the provincial of the Franciscans in New Spain, Fray Antonio de Ciudad Rodrigo, sent Fray Juan de la
THE EXPEDITION OF FR. Asuncion and another friar on a mission
JUAN DE LA ASUNCION beyond New Galicia-Sinaloa.[144] The best of authority [145] says with reference to this expedition, after a careful review, "the present condition of the case leads me to believe that the journey was really made, that Fray Juan de la Asuncion was the man who performed it, and that he reached as far north as the Lower Gila, and perhaps the lower course of the Colorado of the West; that consequently there was a discovery of southern Arizona one year previous to that of New Mexico by Fray Marcos de Niza.

Mendoza, for the glory of the church and the imperial crown, was determined to explore the regions of the north, and for that purpose conferred with Don Francisco Vasquez Coronado as to the best plan for carrying his wishes into effect. It was agreed that a peaceful subjugation of the countries [146] was best.

At this period a certain Friar Marcos de Niza, of Savoy, was holding the office of vice-commissioner-general of New Spain.[147] He

---
[143] Hakluyt, *Voyages*, vol. iii, p. 61; Bandelier, A. F., *Contributions*, p. 80. Bancroft, *N. A. States*, vol. iv, 70.

[144] Mendieta, *Historia Ecclesiastica*, lib. vi, cap. xi, p. 398 et seq.

[145] Bandelier, A. F., *Contributions*, p. 101; Coues, Dr. E., *On the Trail of a Spanish Pioneer*, p. 479; *Comms. on Fr. Juan de la Asuncion*, Ibid, p. 505 et seq.

[146] Herrera, *Historia*, vol. iii, dec. 6, lib. vii, p. 155.
Bandelier, A. F., *Contributions*, Instruccion de Don Antonio de Mendoza, Visorey de Nueva España.

[147] Bandelier, A. F., *Contributions*, says: "Mendoza, the viceroy, had been engaged in attempts to educate a large number of Indians, teaching them the Spanish language and the Christian religion. This was done with the view of using them as interpreters in the event of his undertaking certain explorations in the far north. These Indians had been placed in charge of a Franciscan missionary, Fray Marcos, born in the city of Nizza, which at that

was a man of distinguished attainments, had accompanied Pizzaro in the conquest of Peru, and had been present at the death of Atahualpa. He was much beloved, not only by the members of his order, but by all who knew him. Fray Marcos made a personal investigation of the expedition of Fray Juan de la Asuncion in order to satisfy himself of the truth of what the friar had published, determined to suffer any exposure by taking the lead, before any others should conclude to do it, and so he went as quickly as possible himself; and finding that the report and indications of the friar were true, he returned to Mexico and confirmed what the other had said.[148]

FRIAR MARCOS DE NIZA

time was included in the Duchy of Savoy. On account of his origin, the friar, whose other name is never mentioned, was and has remained known as Fray Marcos of Nizza.

"Beyond the place of birth, nothing is known as yet of the career of this ecclesiastic previous to his appearance in the New World. This took place in 1531, when he went to the island of Santo Domingo with six other monks, and thence to Peru in the year following. He was present at the capture of the Peruvian war-chief, Atahualpa, at Caxamarca. After remaining several years in Peru and Quito, he returned to Mexico via Nicaragua and the Isthmus (probably with Pedro Alvarado). His first work in New Spain seems to have been in Jalisco, where he officiated as missionary. He soon assumed a position of prominence among the regular clergy of his order in Mexico, to such an extent as to be elected Provincial in 1540, or after a residence of only a few years in the country. He had already written, according to his translator and detractor, Ternaux-Compans, three works or reports on the Indians of Peru and Quito, the accuracy of which was strongly impugned by Cortés. The reasons for the severity of Cortés in regard to the writings of the monk, who never did him any harm, become plain, when we consider that Cortés was then claiming, as discoveries of his own, the countries which Fray Marcos visited in North America. The conqueror of Mexico, after his failures in California, shrunk from nothing, stooped to anything, that might re-establish his waning prestige. At all events the Provincial of the Franciscan Order in Mexico, Fray Antonio de Ciudad Rodrigo, issued to Fray Marcos the following testimonial, under date of August 29, 1539, after the latter's return from his trip in quest of the Seven Cities: 'I, the undersigned, etc., certify that it is true that I have despatched Fray Marcos of Nizza, a regular priest, pious, endowed with every virtue and utter devotion; that I have approved of him, I and my brothers, the Deputed Definers, whose advice I take in important and difficult cases, and that he was approved and acknowledged as capable of making this journey of discovery, not only on account of the qualities above mentioned, but also owing to his knowledge in theology, and even in cosmography and in navigation.' "— *Doc. de Indias*, vol. iii, p. 328.

"With the appearance of Fray Marcos upon the scene of explorations in the north, a certain confusion sets in about events immediately following, and he, himself, has been the subject of misrepresentation for three centuries. It may well be said, that for more than three hundred and thirty-three years Fray Marcos of Nizza has been the worst slandered man known in history."

[148] Mendieta, *Historia Ecclesiastica*, lib. iv, cap. x, p. 398 et seq.; Bandelier, A. F., *Contributions*, p. 90.

JOURNEY TO CIBOLA 141

Fray Marcos came to America in 1531, and after his service with Pizarro in Peru, served in Nicaragua and accompanied Don Pedro Alvarado to the north. From 1540 to 1543 he was provincial of the Serafic order in New Spain. He lost his health through his strenuous service for the good of Christianity, and, having retired to Jalapa, later in the year 1558, died at the City of Mexico.

At this time, 1538, Francisco Vasquez Coronado was the governor of New Galicia-Sinaloa. The viceroy, a very religious man,[149] under the influence of the Fray Bartolomé de Las Casas,[150] was

---
[149] Bancroft, Hubert Howe, *North American States*, vol. i, p. 71.

[150] Fray Bartolomé de las Casas, bishop of Chiapa, was one of the most remarkable men of the sixteenth century. He was born in Seville in 1474. His father accompanied Columbus as a common soldier, in his first voyage to the New World. He was educated at the University of Salamanca. In 1498 he completed his studies in law and divinity, took his degree of licentiate, and, in 1502, accompanied Oviedo in the most brilliant armada which had yet been equipped for the New World. Eight years later he was admitted to priest's orders, a memorable event, as he was the first person consecrated in that holy office in the New World. During his first years in the western world, he became very much impressed with the manner in which the natives were treated by the Spanish conquerors and officials. He returned to Spain to see if some means could not be had to stop this sort of oppression. Cardinal Ximenes listened to the complaints made by Las Casas and authorized a commission to reform the abuses. Las Casas was honored, for his exertions, with the title ''Protector General of the Indians.'' He is accused of having been the first European to cause the introduction of negro slavery in the New World. He died at Madrid, in 1566, at the age of ninety-two.

Prescott says of his character: ''He was one of those, to whose gifted minds are revealed those glorious moral truths, which, like the lights of heaven, are fixed and the same forever; but which, though now familiar, were hidden from all but a few penetrating intellects by the general darkness of the time in which he lived. He was a reformer, and had the virtues and errors of a reformer. He was inspired by one glorious idea. This was the key to all his thoughts, all that he said and wrote, to every act of his long life. It was this which urged him to lift the voice of rebuke in the presence of princes, to brave the menaces of an infuriated populace, to cross seas, to traverse mountains and deserts, to incur the alienation of friends, the hostilities of enemies, to endure obloquy, insult and persecution. It was this, too, which made him reckless of obstacles, led him to count too confidently on the co-operation of others, animated his discussion, sharpened his invective, too often steeped his pen in the gall of personal vituperation, led him into gross exaggeration and overcoloring his statements and a blind credulity of evil that rendered him unsafe as a counsellor, and unsuccessful in the practical concerns of life. His motives were pure and elevated. But his manner of enforcing them was not always so commendable. Las Casas, in short, was a man. But, if he had the errors of humanity, he had virtues that rarely belong to it. The best commentary on his character is the estimation which he obtained from his sovereign. No measure of importance, relating to the Indians, was taken without his advice. He lived to see the fruits of his efforts in the amelioration of their condition, and in the popular admission of those great truths which it had been the object of his life to unfold. And who shall say how much of the successful

fully convinced that the natives of the far northern countries, which he intended to explore, should be brought into subjection "rather by the preaching of religious men than by force of arms."

For the purpose of carrying out his policies, the viceroy determined upon the selection of the Friar Marcos de Niza.[151] He gave

efforts and arguments since made in behalf of persecuted humanity may be traced to the example and the writings of this illustrious philanthropist?''

The great work of Las Casas is the *Historia General de las Indias*. He was engaged thirty years in the preparation of this work. Herrera, in 1601, copied most of his work from the manuscript of Las Casas. Quintana, in his work, *Españoles Celebres*, gives a good estimate of the character and life of Las Casas.

[151] Bandelier, A. F., *Contributions*, p. 80: "In a letter to the emperor, relative to the journey of Fray Marcos, the viceroy, Mendoza, says: 'Of all these preparations which I had made, I had nothing left me but a negro who came with Dorantes, a few slaves I had bought, and Indians, natives of the country, whom I had caused to be gathered. I despatched them with the Friar Marcos of Nizza and another ecclesiastic of the Order of St. Francis. These friars had long resided in the neighboring countries, were inured to hardships, experienced in matters of the Indies, conscientious, and of good morals. I requested their provincial to grant them to me. They left with Francisco Vasquez Coronado, governor of New Galicia, and went to San Miguel de Culiacan, the most remote place in that government inhabited by Spaniards, and two hundred leagues from Mexico. When the governor arrived there with the friars, he commanded some Indians whom I had given to him to act as his guides to inform the natives that your Majesty had forbidden that they should be reduced to slavery. I induced them to be no longer afraid to come back to their homes and live quietly. They had, indeed, been much ill-treated in the beginning. He told them that your Majesty had chastised the guilty ones. Ten days afterwards, these Indians returned, to the number of about four hundred, appeared before the governor, and told him that they came in behalf of all the inhabitants, to see and to know those who did them so much good, allowing them to return to their homes and plant corn; for it was a long time that they had been scattered through the mountains, hiding like wild beasts, for fear of being reduced to slavery. They added that they and their companions were ready to comply with the orders that would be given them. The governor consoled them, had supplies distributed among them, and kept three or four of their number. The priests taught these to make the sign of the cross and to pronounce the name of Jesus Christ, our Lord. These people displayed much good will to learn. A few days afterwards they were sent back to their homes with the assurance that they would not be disturbed. Clothing, knives, agnus and other similar objects, which I had sent for the purpose, were given to them, and these Indians returned home well pleased, saying that any time they were sent for, they would come at once to obey the orders which they might receive.

"'When the journey of discovery was thus securely prepared, Friar Marcos, his friend, the negro, other slaves and Indians whom I had given to them, left, after having spent twelve days in making their preparations. I had also heard of a province called Topira, situated in the heart of the mountains, and had ordered the governor to take information in regard to that country. Considering that it was a matter of importance, I determined upon setting out in person to visit it. I had arranged with the ecclesiastic to rejoin him in the mountains, at a town called Corazones, one hundred and twenty leagues from Culiacan. When he reached that province, he saw, as I stated in my letters,

orders to the governor to accompany the friar as far as the town of San Miguel de Culiacan. Strongly he impressed upon the friar the necessity of a conciliatory policy toward the natives. He was instructed to take with him the negro, Estevan. The negro was enjoined to obey implicitly the orders of the friar, who was author-

that there was lack of food. The mountains were so steep that he found no way of crossing them, and was compelled to return to San Miguel. So it seems that God, either through the choice that was made of the road, or the difficulty of finding a path, has opposed Himself to all those who intended to carry out the enterprise with human power, and has reserved it for an humble, bare-footed friar. He is beginning to penetrate into the interior of the country, has been very well received, as he has written below the instructions which I gave him, adding an account of everything that has happened on his last journey. I shall not continue any further on the subject and will transcribe to your Majesty what he himself has reported.'"

This letter of Mendoza has no date, but it was at all events posterior to the 20th of December, 1538, and prior to September of the year following.

The fray, Toribio de Paredes, writing during the year that Coronado was exploring New Mexico, better known as Motolinia, says of the journey of Fray Marcos: "In this same year, the said provincial, Fray Antonio de Ciudad Rodrigo, sent two friars by the coast of the South Sea around to the north, through Jalisco and New Galicia, with a captain who was on a voyage of discovery. As soon as they were beyond the part of that coast that is discovered, known and conquered, they met with two roads, well open and plain. The captain made the choice and went by the right-hand road that deflected towards the interior, and after a few days' journey got into mountains so rugged that his party could not cross them, and he was obliged to turn back by the same road he had come. Of the two friars, one fell sick, and the other with two interpreters, took the road to the left that led towards the coast, finding it always open and plain, and in a few days' march reached a country inhabited by poor people, who came out to receive him, calling him a messenger from Heaven, and as such they all touched him and kissed his garments. From day to day he was accompanied by three and four hundred persons, and sometimes by more, of whom, when it was time to eat, some went out to hunt game, of which there was an abundance, chiefly hares, rabbits and deer; and they, who are so expert in hunting, in a short time got all they wanted, and, giving first to the friar, divided among themselves what they had. In this manner he travelled more than three hundred leagues, and on nearly the whole route had notice of a country inhabited by many people who were clothed, and who have houses constructed of sod and of many stories. It is said that these people are settled on the shores of a great river, where there are enclosed villages, and at times the chiefs of those villages are at war with the others; and it is said that beyond that river there are other villages, larger and more wealthy. What they say that there are in the villages on the first shores are small cows, smaller than those of Spain, and other animals different from those of Castile; good clothing, not only of cotton, but also of wool; and that there are sheep from which that wool is taken. It is not known what kind of sheep they might be. These people use shirts and dresses with which they cover their bodies. They have shoes that cover the whole foot, a thing thus far met with nowhere else. From these villages also many turquoises are obtained, of which, and of all the other things I have mentioned here, there were some among the poor people where the friar was. Not that such objects would be produced in the lands of these poor Indians, but because they brought it from

ized to take with him the Indians who came with Dorantes, and who were to form a part of Coronado's expedition.

The friar was instructed to note carefully the kind of people, their numerical strength, and their mode of living; the quality and fertility of the land, its climate, the trees and plants, domestic or savage animals, the aspect of the country, whether rugged or level, the streams, if large or small, and the rocks and metals. He was also advised that if a large settlement be found, suitable for the erection of a monastery, he was secretly to advise the viceroy of this fact, "in order that everything be prepared without commotion, and that, in the pacification of what may be discovered, the service of our Lord and the good of the people of the country be properly secured."

Friar Marcos left San Miguel de Culiacan on the 7th day of March, 1539, accompanied by Friar Onorato, Estevan, and some of the Indians who had gone to the City of Mexico with Cabeza de Vaca, where they had espoused the cause of Christ, learned the Spanish language, and had been given their freedom by Mendoza expressly for the purpose of taking part in his explorations. Friar Onorato was taken ill when the village of Petatlán was reached, and there he was left by Friar Marcos. Leaving Petatlán in company with the Indian guides and the negro, Estevan, Friar Marcos proceeded on his journey, and was received at all times and places by the natives with great rejoicing, owing to the statements made to them by him that no more Indians would be stolen by the Spaniards for purposes of slavery.

---

the large villages whither they at times went to work and earn their living, as day-laborers are wont to do in Spain."

When the above was written by Motolinia, Fray Marcos was the provincial of the Franciscans, to which order Motolinia belonged.

"In appealing to the religious zeal of the Franciscans, the Viceroy acted very judiciously. He knew that it would have jeopardized his own position had he engaged the credit of the Crown in any doubtful enterprise. By securing monks as explorers or scouts, he saved a great deal of expense, and accomplished more. The friars were bound to report the truth. No worldly interest was to bias their judgment and they travelled very economically. Accustomed to receive charity, they knew also how to do charity to such as were poorer than they. A double end could be obtained; first, an inexpensive and yet profitable journey; second, an impression could be made upon the feelings of unknown and therefore doubtful tribes, through the meekness and pliability of the emissary. That Fray Marcos should have been selected for this task certainly speaks in his favor."—Bandelier, A. F., *Contributions*, p. 108.

Fr. Francisco de los Angeles ó Quiñones, General of the Order of Franciscans, 1521

Reprint from Beaumont
Franciscans converting Indians

Beyond the Rio Mayo, possibly the Yaqui, he left the coast, and turning toward the north reached the town of Vacapa, in all probability the town of Matapa,[152] not far south of the valley of the Sonora river.

At Vacapa he rested until Easter, having despatched messengers to the sea coast, only forty leagues distant, and at the same time ordered the negro, Estevan, to proceed to the north fifty or sixty leagues and in the event he heard of rich and populous countries, either to return in person, or to await his arrival, sending him by the Indians a cross the size of which should indicate the character

---

[152] Bandelier, A. F., *Contributions*, pp. 122-125: "An Indian village in Central Sonora." This is not the place known as San Ludovic de Vacapa, although Father Kuehne was under the impression that it was. Fr. Marcos, in the course of a month could not possibly have traveled so far north. The inhabitants of Matapa spoke the Opata or Pima language, in the opinion of Bandelier. A Jesuit Mission was founded here in 1629.

146 LEADING FACTS OF NEW MEXICAN HISTORY

and importance of the information he desired to communicate.[153] If nothing of consequence was discovered during his journey, the negro was instructed to send back a cross, the size of a hand; if any great matter should be ascertained, the cross returned was to be two handfuls in length, and if the country he was exploring was greater or better than New Spain, a great cross should be returned.[154] Within four days after leaving the friar, the Indian messengers returned bearing a cross as large as a man and notifying the friar

[153] Davis, W. W. H., *The Spanish Conquest of New Mexico*, pp. 114-115, note 2, says: ''The route taken by Niza and Stephen can be traced with much greater accuracy than that of Vaca and his companions. They travelled nearly parallel with the Gulf of California, until they arrived near the head of it, when they changed direction to the northeast, crossed the river Gila, and traversed the extensive stretch of barren country that lies to the north of that stream. This region is almost a desert waste, with a light, sandy soil, covered for the most part with a growth of stunted pine trees and with little water.

''It is the opinion of some who have examined the subject that the route of Niza was further inland than I have located it, among whom are Lieutenant Whipple of the U. S. Topographical Engineers, and Mr. Bartlett. It is supposed that the 'desert of four days' journey' first crossed by Niza, lies between the Rio Yaqui and Rio Sonora. Thence he passed through the valley of Sonora and continued in a course nearly north. The town of Vapupa, 'of reasonable bigness,' is supposed to have been identical with Magdalena on the river San Miguel. He is thought to have passed near the present site of Tuscon, a small town in the Territory of Arizona, and continuing north struck the Gila, through the valley of which he travelled five days' journey; he then crossed over to the Rio Azul, which he ascended, and so continued on to the great desert, which he passed, until he came in sight of Cibola. Upon reflection I believe that Niza travelled some distance up the valley of the Gila, but that he did not ascend it to a point so high up as the Azul, as that would have obliged him to cross the Mogollon mountains, of which no mention is made. He must have followed up the Rio Francisco or Salt river further to the west and thus escaped the mountains.''

[154] Hakluyt, Richard, *Voyages*, etc., vol. iii, p. 70: ''To wit; that if it were but a meane thing, hee should send mee a white cross of one handfull long; and if it were any great matter, one of two handfulls long. And if it were a Countrey greater and better than Nueva Espana, hee should send mee a greate crosse. So the sayde (negro) Stephan departed from me on Passion Sunday, after dinner.''

Bandelier, A. F., *Contributions*, p. 128, says: ''He showed them the sign of the cross, and here, as everywhere else, the Indian was at once struck by the token. The cross is an original symbol of the American aborigines. It is used by them to indicate a star, and the crosses of the morning and evening stars are particularly distinguished, among the Pueblos of New Mexico, at least, by shape and color. The crucifix which the friar carried, and his manner of crossing himself, attracted the natives; and not only did they see no harm in imitating the gesture and in manufacturing small crosses for themselves, but they considered it profitable, as a reinforcement of the charm which their own primitive token of the cross was supposed to possess under certain circumstances . . . that figure hereafter remained as a manifestation of peace and friendly welcome.''

to come to him at once, as he had found people who gave him information of the "greatest thing in the world." One of the people from whom the negro had obtained this information was sent back to the friar to whom he related that it was "thirty days' journey" from the town where the negro then was to the first city of the province of Cibola; that there were seven great cities in the first province, all under the rule of one lord, and that the houses were constructed of stone and lime, the smallest being of one story with a flat roof, and others of two and three stories, while the house of the lord contained four stories, all connected in order; that the portals of these houses were decorated with turquoises which were abundant; that the inhabitants were very well dressed, as well those of the seven cities as the cities of the province further on, each of which, the friar was informed, was much greater than those of the seven cities.

Friar Marcos did not immediately take up his journey to overtake Estevan, but awaited the return of his messengers to the coast, and, on the second day after Easter, he set out to overtake the negro.

He ascended the valley of the Sonora,[155] as it is believed, through a beautiful valley hemmed in by mountains, at times passing through great canyons whose walls towered to the sky. "Here I raised two crosses and took possession," says the friar, "for it appeared to me suitable from here on to perform acts of possession."

Later on he met with the Opatas,[156] from whom he secured much

---

[155] Bandelier, A. F., *Contributions*, p. 133; Bartlett, *Personal Narrative*, p. 278.

[156] Bandelier, A. F., *Final Report*, part i, pp. 114, 117: "From the Opatas the Friar learned of the three distant kingdoms of Marata, Acus and Totonteac. Marata is Ma-tya-ta, a cluster of pueblos which at that time had been but recently abandoned, lying between Zuñi and Acoma. Acus is the pueblo of Acoma, and Totonteac was the Moqui in northeastern Arizona.

"The Opatas, a formerly very important group of Indians, have become so 'hispanicised' as to have almost forgotten their native tongue. They are also known by the name of Sonora, Teguima and Hures. They lived in the State of Sonora, Mexico, and held sway over fully one-fourth of that state. O-Pa-Ta seems to be a Pima word, a corruption of Oop, enemy, and Ootam-people, that is, people of our own stock with whom we are at war. The Opata language, as well known, is closely allied to the Pima; both are but members of one family. The bulk of the Opatas were settled in the valley of the Sonora river, from north of Bacuachi river as far south as Ures. West of this channel, the water supply grows scant and scantier, towards the arid coast of the Gulf of California. Indian settlements, therefore, became less numerous,

information, and in the valley of the Sonora, where the Opatas lived, he set up another great cross.

The Opatas told him of the distant kingdoms of Marata, a group of pueblos now abandoned, but lying southeast of modern Zuñi, Acus, the Acoma of today, and Totonteac, the Moquis.[157] They also

---

and they were no longer of pure Opata stock. The villages of the Opatas were small, their houses detached, and only for one family. In the Sierra Madre proper, where the Yaqui gushes out of the picturesque gorge descending from its sources at Chu-ui-chu-pa, there are remains of Opata villages recalling, on a lesser scale, the stately architecture of Casas Grandes. The houses are connected so as to form an interior square, and appear as if raised on artificial platforms. Mutual protection from enemies, which threatened the Opatas on the Chihuahua side of the great central chain, from the inhabitants of the valley of Casas Grandes, is stated as having caused this superior and defensive mode of building. Such is the common opinion of the Opatas of the villages from Huassabas to Baserac and Bapispe. There are sites of hamlets which, according to tradition, had been deserted on account of the constant danger threatening from the Chihuahua side. Whether the enemies who compelled this abandonment were the Sumas of Casas Grandes, or some other tribe who, perhaps, built the villages whose ruins have given the name to the valley and settlements, is not known. Some say that the builders of Casas Grandes were the Opatas.

"In dress and ornaments the Opatas resemble the Pimas as well as the Yaquis; but owing to their more northerly home, their costume was more substantial. Deer skins and cotton mantles constituted it in the main. If Fr. Marcos was correctly informed we might even suspect that an occasional buffalo robe found its way into the valley of the Sonora river. Still the hide of the large red deer, or of the mule deer, so common in Lower California, may have given rise, through imperfect and still more imperfectly understood descriptions of the animal, to the supposition that the Opatas obtained buffalo hides from the Zuñi Indians."

[157] Bandelier, A. F., *Investigations in the Southwest*, part i, p. 114: "Longest, and above all, best known among the Indians of Arizona, are the Pueblo Indians of the north, the Moquis or Shi-nu-mo. They were mentioned to Fray Marcos de Niza in 1539 under the name of Totonteac, a corruption of a Zuñi term which applied to a cluster of twelve pueblos lying in the direction of Moqui, and already abandoned in the sixteenth century, but the reminiscence of which still remained in the name. The ruins of the villages whose name, as given by the Indians of Zuñi in their idiom, has been corrupted into Totonteac, lie between Zuñi and Moqui. It is interesting to note how the reports which Fray Marcos gathered in Sonora concerning the northern pueblos frequently relate to events which had occurred some time previous to his coming. Tribes were mentioned to him, like 'Marata' and 'Totonteac' who had ceased to exist, though the distant southern Indians had no knowledge of their disappearance. This is very instructive in regard to the value of historical tradition in point of chronology.

"In 1540, one of Coronado's lieutenants, Don Pedro de Tovar, visited the seven cities of Tusayan, a few days' journey northwest or west of Zuñi. There is not the slightest doubt that the Tusayan of Castañeda is the Moqui of today. The group consisted of seven pueblos, and that same number subsisted until the beginning of the past century, when one of the seven disappeared, Ahuatu, although it was promptly replaced by a village founded mostly by Tanos fugitives from New Mexico, and to which, in deference to the language

gave him a description of the Seven Cities of Cibola, but could tell him nothing of the negro, Estevan. Here it was that the friar first heard reports of the wearing of the turquoises [158] in the ears and noses of the natives, as well as of their full-sleeved cotton gowns. The Indians of the last village through which he passed before leaving the Sonora valley, also informed him that in To-ton-teac, Moqui, there were stuffs like the woolen frock which he wore, made from material obtained from small animals about the size of a grey-hound.[159]

Leaving the high table-lands adjacent to the Sonora valley, Friar Marcos descended into the valley of the San Pedro, which he says was well irrigated, the small villages extending down the valley a distance of a quarter of a league to half a league apart, and that the turquoises were so plentiful that the men wore three or four strings of them about the neck and the women ornamented their ears and noses with them.[160]

there spoken, the name of Tehua was given. Ahuatu was destroyed by the Moquis of Oraibe in the year 1700. In June of that year, it still existed. In 1701, Cubero made an unsuccessful expedition against the Moquis. The cause for this military movement is stated in the declaration of the New Mexican clergy, November 20, 1722, as follows: 'Se mobió (Cubero) con las armas de este Rl Presidio á la venganza del estrago qe dhos apostatas executaron contra los indios del puo de Aguatubi de su misma Nazion, que pacíficos y combertidos á ñra Sta Fee passaron á sangre y fuego las vidas bienes y alajas, del culto diuino de los miserables qe solo con la firmeza con qe se hallauan de nra Sta Fee otro motibo hizieron en ellos tan pernissiosos estragos.' It appears, therefore, that Ahuatu was destroyed either towards the end of the year 1700, or in the beginning of 1701.

''Not much importance can always be attached to the numbers and names of Indian villages, according to Spanish sources of an older date. Thus, at the time of Coronado, the seven pueblos of Tusayan Moqui admit of no doubt. Forty years afterward, the Asay or Osay of Chamuscado had, according to statements made to that explorer by Zuñi Indians, he himself never visited the locality — only five.''

[158] *Doc. Inédit.*, vol. iii, p. 136.

[159] Winship, George Parker, *Coronado Expedition*, 14th B. A. E., p. 357, says: ''The strange thing about all these reports is not that they are true, and that we can identify them by what is known concerning these Indians, but the hard thing to understand is how the Friar could have comprehended so well what the natives must have tried to tell him. When one considers the difficulties of language, with all its technicalities, and of radically different conceptions of every phase of life and of thought, the result must be an increased confidence in the common sense and the inherent intelligence of mankind.''

[160] Winship, George Parker, *Ibid*, p. 357, says: ''Friar Marcos tried to find out how these Indians bartered for the things they brought from the northern country, but all he could understand was that 'with the sweat and

The men clothed themselves in skins and blankets and the women wore chemises and skirts. It was here the friar saw his first buffalo robe, which he describes as being half as big again as the hide of a great ox.[161] As he progressed, there was still no news of the negro, except that in places he found shelter and provisions which Estevan had provided along the route for his use.

In due course of travel Fray Marcos reached the Gila river,[162] most likely at a point east of its confluence with the San Pedro, above which it flows through deep valleys, hemmed in by mountains whose sides were covered with many kinds of cactus. Here he received news of Estevan, who, escorted with a force of three hundred natives, was on his way to the northeast, through that portion of Arizona where the Apache Indian reservation is located.[163]

Friar Marcos now rested, having received word from the negro that he had not yet surprised a native in telling lies and that they were absolutely truthful. He took formal possession of the valley

---

service of their persons they went to the first city, which is called Cibola, and that they labored there by digging the earth and other services, and that for what they did, they received turquoises and the skins of cows, such as these people had.' We now know, whatever Friar Marcos may have thought, that they doubtless obtained their turquoises by digging them out of the rocky ground in which they are still found in New Mexico, and this may easily have seemed to them perspiring labor. It is not clear just how they obtained the buffalo skins, although it was doubtless by barter. The friar noticed fine turquoises suspended in the ears and noses of many people whom he saw, and he was again informed that the principal door-ways of Cibola were ceremonially ornamented with designs made of these stones. Mr. Cushing has since learned through tradition, that this was their custom. The dress of these people of Cibola, including the belts of turquoises around the waist, as it was described to the friar, seemed to him to resemble that of the Bohemians, or gypsies. The cow skins, some of which were given to him, were tanned and finished so well that he thought it was evident that they had been prepared by men who were skilled in this work.''

Fray Marcos de Niza, *Descubrimiento de las Siete Ciudades* (Doc. de Indias, vol. iii, p. 338) says: ''Salieron á mi muchos hombres y mugeres con comida; y todas traian muchas turquesas que les colgaban de las narices y de las orejas, y algunos traian colares turquesas.''

[161] Fr. Marcos de Niza, *Descubrimiento*, etc., p. 341: ''Aqúi es este valle, me truxeron un cuero, tanto y medio mayor que de una gran vaca, y me dixeron que es de un animál, que tiene solo un cuerno en la frente y que este cuerno es corbo hacia los pechos, y que alli sale una punta derecha, en la cual dice que tiene tanta fuerza, que ninguna cosa, por recia que sea, dexa de romper, si topa con ella; y dicen que hay muchos destos animales en aquella tierra; la color del cuero es á manera de cabron y el pelo tan largo como el dedo.''

[162] Bandelier, A. F., *Final Report*, part ii, pp. 405, 469, 470.

[163] Winship, George Parker, *Coronado Expedition*, p. 359: ''The White Mountain Apache.''

and made final preparations for the last fifteen days of travel which lay between him and Cibola. A great multitude of Indians presented themselves for the purpose of accompanying him to Cibola as an escort, but the friar was content with selecting thirty of the most influential and wealthiest, concluding that those who were best dressed and wore the most turquoises were of this class; he also selected a number of others who acted as servants, accustomed to labor and able to carry his provisions across the desert which confronted him.

On the 9th day of May, 1539, he started on the journey, finding a broad and well beaten road, each noon and night stopping at places where some of his party in advance had prepared resting places for him, and several times recognizing houses which had been prepared for the negro who had but a short time before preceded him. For twelve days his course was through rough mountains, the crests of which were still covered with snow. This portion of his journey must have been in the Mogollon mountains in western Socorro county, New Mexico, now a portion of the Gila forest. His Indian guides now had no trouble in supplying him with plenty of game, deer, rabbits, and partridges (quail), which reminded him of Spain. He had now reached the Continental Divide, and here he was met by an Indian, the son of one of the chiefs accompanying the friar, greatly frightened, who informed him that Estevan had reached Cibola and that he had been seized, plundered of all his possessions, and imprisoned along with his Indian attendants, and that he, himself, had escaped, after going all night without food or drink.

The effect produced by this unexpected news was startling. The Indians burst into tears, and for a while the friar was afraid for his life. However, by giving the escort additional gifts, he induced them to advance. Within a day's march of Cibola they met two more Indians, wounded and covered with blood, who said that they had escaped from the killing of three hundred of their companions. They gave the friar a full account of the treatment which had been accorded Estevan and of his probable death.

FRIAR MARCOS HEARS OF THE DEATH OF ESTEVAN

Again the friar sought to appease his escort by gifts of merchandise, and personally sought consolation in prayer. He was determined to get sight of the great Cibola, and, after much argument and a further distribution of all his remaining merchandise, he succeeded in persuading two of the chiefs to accompany him. Journeying as rapidly as he could, he soon came within sight of Cibola, "which is situate on a plain at the foot of a round hill and seems to be a fair city, and is better situated than any I have seen in these parts. The houses are builded in order, according as the Indians told me, all made of stone with divers stories and flat roofs, as far as I could discern from a mountain, whither I ascended to view the cities.''[164]

The city which the friar saw was undoubtedly the pueblo of Ha-wai-kúh.[165] The friar appears not to have been lacking in cour-

---

[164] Winship, George Parker, *Ibid*, pp. 362-363, says: "In his official report it is evident that Friar Marcos distinguished with care between what he had himself seen and what the Indians had told him. But Cortés began the practice of attacking the veracity and good faith of the friar, Castañeda continued it, and scarcely a writer on these events failed to follow their guidance until Mr. Bandelier undertook to examine the facts of the case, and applied rules of ordinary fairness to his historical judgment. This vigorous defender of the friar has successfully maintained his strenuous contention that Fr. Marcos neither lied nor exaggerated, even when he said that the Cibola pueblo appeared to him to be larger than the City of Mexico. All the witnesses agree that these light stone and adobe villages impress one who first sees them from a distance as being much larger than they really are. Mexico, in 1539, on the other hand, was neither imposing nor populous. The great communal house, the 'palace of Montezuma,' had been destroyed during or soon after the siege of 1521. The pueblo of Hawaikúh, the one which the friar doubtless saw, contained about 200 houses, or between 700 and 1,000 inhabitants. There is something naive in Mr. Bandelier's comparison of this with Robert Tomson's report that the City of Mexico, in 1556, contained 1,500 Spanish households. He ought to have added, what we may be quite sure was true, that the population of Mexico probably doubled in the fifteen years preceding Tomson's visit, a fact which makes Niza's comparison even more reasonable.''

[165] Hodge, F. W., *The First Discovered City of Cibola*, p. 3: "It is regarding the identity of the village at which Estevan lost his life and which Niza observed from a distant height that question has arisen. The name of one of the Cibolan villages the friar learned from an old Zuñi whom he found living with one of the Pimas tribes and who had been a fugitive from Cibola for many years. This name was Ahacus, and is identical with Hawaikúh, a pueblo occupied by the Zuñis until about 1670, when the Apaches compelled its abandonment. It should be remembered, however, that the name, Ahacus, was not applied by Niza to the pueblo visited by Estevan and seen by himself, nor indeed, to any other pueblo; hence the question as to which of the cities of Cibola was first discovered.

"The place of the killing of the 'Black Mexican' is fixed by Zuñi tradition at Ki-ak-ki-ma, and this tradition Mr. Bandelier has attempted to substantiate by applying thereto the description by Niza, as well as by other documentary testimony bearing on the point. It is my purpose to show that not Ki-ak-ki-ma but Hawaikúh was the town of Cibola discovered by Niza, that the latter

Fac-simile of Last Page of Original Patent to the Order of Franciscans, given by the General of the Order to the first twelve friars who came to America to convert, baptize, and pacify the natives

age, for at this point he raised a heap of stones and placed at the top a small cross and formally took possession of the country in the name

village alone corresponds substantially with the settlement described by the friar, and that Zuñi traditional accounts of events which occurred over three centuries ago are not worthy of consideration as historical or scientific evidence.

"In order that there may be no difference in terms employed I will recite Mr. Bandelier's own translation from the Spanish of the description of the Cibolan village seen by Niza when he took possession in the name of the king of Spain of the territory now forming Arizona and New Mexico.

"Reviewing that portion of the friar's narrative relating to his desire to continue onward to Cibola, after the death of Estevan and some of his companions, Mr. Bandelier says: 'His Indians were unwilling to accompany him. They not only resisted his entreaties, but threatened his life, in atonement for the lives of their relatives slaughtered at Cibola. He pleaded and remonstrated, but they remained stubborn. At last two of their number, "principal men," he says, consented to lead him to a place whence he could see Cibola from afar (then quoting Niza): "With them and with my Indians and interpreters, I followed my road till we came in sight of Cibola, which lies in a plain on the slope of a round height. Its appearance is very good for a settlement, the handsomest I have seen in these parts. The houses are, as the Indians had told me, all of stone, with three stories and flat roofs. As far as I could see from a height where I placed myself to observe, the settlement is larger than the City of Mexico." Here again, in sight of Cibola (now continues Bandelier), his Indian guides re-iterated the statement that the village now in view was the smallest one of the seven, and that Totonteac (Tusayan) was much more important than the so-called Seven Cities. After taking possession of Cibola, Totonteac, Acus and Marata for the Spanish Crown, raising a stone heap, and placing a wooden cross on top of it, with the aid of the natives, and naming the new land the "New Kingdom of St. Francis," the friar turned back, "with more fright than food," as he very dryly but truthfully remarks.'

"The natural approach to Zuñi from the southwestward, the direction whence Niza came, is by way of the Little Colorado and Zuñi river valleys. Any other route from that direction would lead through a region of utter desolation, extremely difficult of travel by reason of its broken and arid character. The valley through which Zuñi river flows on to the Little Colorado part of the year, is easy to travel, and it may be reasonably assumed that water was abundant at or within easy reach of the sandy river bed when Niza's little force wended its way toward Cibola, late in May of the year 1539. To have left the valley would have increased the distance which the barefooted friar must traverse, besides leading him over an indescribably dreary and rugged stretch. It therefore would seem that Niza, as well as Estevan, approached Zuñi by the valley route over which Coronado, guided by Niza, went a year later, a route leading directly to Hawaikúh, the southwesternmost of the Cibolan towns, and one of the two largest of the group. From the southwest Ki-ak-i-ma, which lies at the southwestern foot of Taaiyalone or Thunder Mountain, in the eastern part of the plain, can be reached only by the tortuous route alluded to. Moreover, Ki-ak-i-ma was the most remote of all the Cibolan pueblos when approached from the southwest, Matsaki alone excepted.

"In the light of these facts, then, what would have been Niza's object in visiting Ki-ak-i-ma, particularly when guided by unwilling natives, who evidently had visited Cibola before? Had he made a detour before reaching the vicinity of Hawaikúh for the purpose of viewing Ki-ak-i-ma from the adjacent

of the viceroy and the emperor, and gave to it the name of the Kingdom of St. Francis, in honor of the founder of his order.

mesas, Niza scarcely would have used the words: 'I followed my road until we came in sight of Cibola;' that is, the road he was following; the *only* road.

"The friar describes the pueblo as 'lying in a plain at the slope of a round height.' This is one of the most significant points in the narrative in favor of Hawaikúh. This ruin was surveyed by Mr. Cosmos Mindeleff, and a carefully prepared ground-plan is reproduced in the Memoir *Architecture of Tusayan and Cibola*, by Victor Mindeleff, in the Eighth Annual Report of the Bureau of American Ethnology. This author describes (p. 80) the ruin of Hawaikúh as 'occupying the point of a spur projecting from a low rounded hill,' a description coinciding precisely with that by Niza. Moreover, Hawaikúh is so situated in a plain as to command a view for miles in every direction, a situation worthy of the enthusiasm of even the undemonstrative Niza, who described it as 'the handsomest I have seen in these parts.' Ki-ak-i-ma, perched on its inconvenient knoll of talus and cowering under the projection of old Taaiyalone, could not have conjured up this outburst of praise from the honest old friar.

"Ki-ak-i-ma, it will be seen, is not in a plain. A view toward that pueblo from the southern heights is completely closed by Thunder Mountain, which here seems to wall the very Universe. Furthermore, I am confident, through personal observation, that the mountain does not appear to be round from either the west or the south.

"Niza could never have been so deceived in the appearance of Ki-ak-i-ma as to have said: 'Where I placed myself to observe, the settlement is larger than the City of Mexico.' Such a comparison might truthfully have been made with Hawaikúh, however, situated as it was in a broad plain, with no beetling height to be-little it.

"Mr. Cosmos Mindeleff, who made a careful survey and study of the Ki-ak-i-ma ruin, informs me that in all probability the houses did not exceed one story. Those of Hawaikúh, in the language of Mr. Victor Mindeleff, considering 'the large amount of debris and the comparative thinness of such walls as are found, suggest that the dwellings had been densely clustered and carried to the height of several stories.' In this connection it is of moment to observe that Niza speaks of the houses as 'all of stone, *with their stories* and flat roofs,' a reference that under the circumstances could not pertain to Ki-ak-i-ma.

"The re-iteration of the Indians 'that the village now in view was the smallest one of the seven' I believe to have been mere braggadocio, and contained as much truth as their allegation in the same breath that Tusayan was much more important than Cibola. Any statement to the effect that the smallest village of the Cibolan group was larger than the City of Mexico is incredible. Niza has shown himself to have been a man of truth. The many groundless assertions of the Indians as recorded throughout this and subsequent Spanish narratives speak for themselves.

"Yet the clause 'the village now in view' is of the utmost importance. Indeed, if there were no other evidence that Hawaikúh was the village seen by Niza this would suffice, for inasmuch as Ki-ak-i-ma is visible only from the southeast and south, there is no point of view from these directions that would not include Halona (the site of the present Zuñi), and from any point farther westward along the southern eminences Matsaki also would have been seen. From the heights south of the plain on which Hawaikúh was situated, however, one village only was observable in the sixteenth century. That village was Hawaikúh and the massive walls of the ruined adobe church erected in the seventeenth century still rise above the plain. T'kanawe (a triple pueblo of which Kechipauan formed a part). on the mesa to the southeastward, the nearest settlement to Hawaikúh when that village was inhabited, could be seen neither

These formalities having been gone through with, the friar turned his face southward, anxious to return to Mexico. His escort had left him and, making all the haste possible, he passed through the valley of the San Pedro where, to his terror, he found that he was in poor repute with the natives, all of which frightened him, but not to such a degree as to prevent his again claiming possession of the entire country for the viceroy.

"With far more fright than food," says the friar, the return journey was made in great haste, traveling at the rate of eight or ten leagues each day. On his way to the Seven Cities, the friar had heard of a large valley among the mountains. This valley was off the route which he traveled but he had been told that in the valley were very large settlements and that the people wore garments made of cotton. Desiring to ascertain whether there was any gold in this valley or the adjacent mountains, he showed the Indians some metals which he had and they picked out the gold, telling him that the inhabitants of the valley had vessels of that metal and also wore ornaments made of the same kind. That they also had some little shovels with which they scraped themselves to be rid of their per-

---

from the valley below nor from the adjacent heights. Hawaikúh, therefore, necessarily must have been the 'village now in view.'

"Mr. Bandelier's belief that Ki-ak-i-ma was discovered by Niza, it appears was based mainly on tradition. Concerning the visit of Estevan to the Zuñis, two accounts have been recorded by Mr. Cushing, each of which places the scene of the killing at Ki-ak-i-ma. The text of one of these stories is approximately accurate; the other maintains that the wise men of the Ka-Ka order took Estevan 'out of the pueblo during the night and gave him a powerful kick that sped him through the air back to the south, whence he had come.' A tradition so contorted by its authors that it bears little semblance of its original form is worthy of serious consideration only in so far as it aids in establishing the maximum age at which authenticity of Zuñi tradition ceases.

"In view then of the untrustworthiness of Zuñi tradition, as above exemplified, can the persistent myth of the natives that Ki-ak-i-ma was the pueblo where Estevan met his death stand in the way of such overpowering testimony to the contrary? Should the story of the negro who, by a powerful kick, was sped through the air back whence he had come, a story suspended by a single strand of truth, take precedence as historical evidence over the statement of Jaramillo, who visited Hawaikúh with Coronado only a year later and specifically recorded that 'here was where they killed Estevanillo,' or of the declaration in 1626 of Fray Geronimo de Zarate Salmeron, who mentions Hawaikúh positively as the Cibola of Fray Marcos and of Coronado.

"That Hawaikúh was the village first seen by Estevan, who there met death; that it was the 'City of Cibola' rising from the plain which Niza and his Piman guides viewed from the southern heights in 1539, and that it was the pueblo which Coronado stormed in the summer of the following year, seems indisputable."

spiration. On the way back he determined to see this valley. He did not dare to venture into it, because, as he says, he believed that those who would come after him to settle the country, could do it safely. That he could not further risk his life and thereby, if anything should happen to him, prevent the world from knowing what he had already witnessed. He went as far as the entrance, and says that he saw seven good looking settlements in the distance, from which arose a good deal of smoke.

From this point the friar returned to San Miguel and thence to Compostella, where he found the governor and made a report of the wonderful things he had seen and heard. This report, reduced to writing, was sent to the viceroy, who, in turn, sent it to the emperor, accompanying it with a full account of the ill success of several other attempts to discover countries abounding in gold, and adding, "It seemeth unto all men that it was God's will to shut up the gate to all those who by strength of human force have gone about to attempt this enterprise, and to reveal it to a poor and bare-footed friar." Friar Marcos also sent a report or notification of his return to the provincial of his order and asked for further instructions. While at Compostella he certified, under oath, before the viceroy and Coronado, that everything contained in his report of the journey to the Seven Cities was the truth.[166]

There is no doubt that the negro, Estevan, met with a deserved fate. He paid no attention to the orders of the viceroy, who had commanded him implicitly to obey the instructions of the friar.[167] After leaving the friar he took upon himself all the authority usually accompanying an ambassador and gave out that he was an envoy of the viceroy; gaily bedecked in bells and

THE MANNER OF THE DEATH OF ESTEVAN

---

[166] Winship, George Parker, *Coronado Expedition*, p. 363: "The credit and esteem in which the friar was held by the viceroy is as convincing proof of his integrity as that derived from a close scrutiny of the text of his narrative. Mendoza's testimony was given in a letter which he sent to the king of Spain, inclosing the report written by Friar Marcos, the *premiere lettre* which Ternaux translated from Ramusio. This letter spoke in laudatory terms of the friar and of course is not wholly un-biased evidence. It is at least sufficient to counterbalance the hostile declarations of Cortés and Castañeda, both of whom had far less creditable reasons for traducing the friar than Mendoza had for praising him."

[167] Winship, George Parker, *Ibid*, p. 355: "The negro, Estevan, had been ordered by the viceroy to obey Friar Marcos in everything, under pain of serious

feathers around his arms and legs, he traveled in state. Carrying with him a gourd, decorated with two bells and feathers, one white and one red, he sent messengers ahead, displaying the gourd as a symbol of his authority. This he had seen done in his travels across the state of Texas, when with Cabeza de Vaca. He was also attended by a large number of handsome women, whom he had attached to his party along the route. He also carried turquoises, and the Indians who accompanied him were fully convinced that while in his company and under his protection no danger or ill could befall them.

Arriving within a day's journey of Cibola, the negro again disobeyed the orders of Friar Marcos, for, instead of awaiting the coming of the friar, he sent messengers, bearing his gourd, to the city to notify the chief that he came seeking peace and to cure the sick.[168] When the gourd had been delivered to the chief and he had observed the bells he became very angry, cast the gourd upon the ground, and cried: "I know those people, for those bells are not of our fashion; tell them to return at once, or not a single man of them will be left alive." Sadly the messengers returned to the negro, fearing to tell him what had been the character of their reception, but finally they decided to advise him fully. Estevan, however, was far from dismayed, and told them to have no fear, as he intended to go to Cibola and that he would be well received. Accordingly he proceeded on his way and reached Cibola at sunset, with more than three hundred attendants, men and women. The chief would not permit him to enter the town, but he was given a lodging place outside its limits. Then, by order of the chief of Cibola, the negro was deprived of everything he had, and both food and drink were refused to him and his company.[169]

punishment. . . Castañeda preserves a story that Estevan was sent ahead, not only to explore and pacify the country, but also because he did not get on well with his superior, who objected to his eagerness in collecting the turquoises and other things which the natives prized and to the moral effect of his relations with the women who followed him from the tribes which they met on their way. Friar Marcos says nothing about this in his narrative, but he had different and much more important ends to accomplish by his report, compared with those of Castañeda, who may easily have gathered the gossip from some native."

[168] Alarcon, *Rel. du Voyage de Cibola*, Appendice iv, p. 331; Herrera, vol. iii, dec. 6, lib. ix, cap. xv, p. 211.

[169] Winship, George Parker, *Coronado Expedition*, p. 360: "While Cabeza de Vaca and his companions were travelling through Texas, the natives had

The next morning, shortly after sunrise, Estevan left the house in company with some of the chiefs, when suddenly a great number of the inhabitants appeared, seeing whom, the negro and his companion sought safety in flight. They were pursued, however, and slain, only the Indians who brought the news to Friar Marcos escaping with their lives.

Authorities differ as to why the negro was slain by the Indians. Castañeda says that they believed him to be a spy sent from some nation for the purpose of conquest.[170] Bandelier believes that the

---

flocked to see these strange white men and soon began to worship them, pressing about them for even a touch of their hands and garments, from which the Indians trusted to receive some healing power. While taking advantage of the prestige which was thus obtained, Cabeza de Vaca says that he secured some gourds or rattles which were greatly reverenced among these Indians and which never failed to produce a most respectful behaviour whenever they were exhibited. It was also among these southern plains Indians that Cabeza de Vaca heard of the permanent settlements toward the north. Castañeda says that some of these plains Indians came each year to Cibola to pass the winter under the shelter of the adobe villages, but that they were distrusted and feared so much that they were not admitted into the villages unless unarmed, and under no conditions were they allowed to spend the night within the flat-roofed houses. The connection between these Indian rattles and the gourd which Estevan prized so highly can not be proven, but it is not unlikely that the negro announced his arrival to the Cibola chiefs by sending them an important part of the paraphernalia of a medicine man of a tribe with which they were at enmity.''

Prince, L. B., *History of New Mexico*, p. 110, says: ''At the moment when he (Estevan) was about to enter, he was met by a party of Indians, who took him to a large house just outside of the city, and forthwith despoiled him of all that he had with him, including the articles he had brought for trading purposes, some turquoises and many other presents that he had received during the journey. He passed the night in the place, without anything either to eat or to drink being given to himself or his companions, who were lodged with him. The next morning the narrator (who was one of them), being very thirsty, started out of the house in order to get some water which flowed in a river near by. Soon after, he saw Stephen running away, pursued by the Cibolans, who were killing the Indians who were with the negro. As soon as the narrator saw this, he hid himself by the river, and at the first opportunity, started back through the desert.''

Winship, George Parker, *Coronado Expedition*, p. 360, says: ''There are several versions of the story of Estevan's death, besides the one given in Friar Marcos's narrative, which were derived from the natives of Cibola. Castañeda, who lived among these people for a while the next year, states that the Indians kept the negro a prisoner for three days 'questioning him' before they killed him. He adds that Estevan had demanded from the Indians treasure and women, and this agrees with the legends still current among the people. When Alarcon ascended the Colorado river a year later, and tried to co-operate, he heard of Estevan, who was described as a black man with a beard, wearing things that sounded, rattles, bells and plumes, on his feet and arms, the regular outfit of a southwestern medicine man.''

[170] Castañeda, *Relacion de la Jornada de Cibola*, etc., Winship's trans., p. 475: ''As I said, Stephen reached Cibola loaded with the large quantity of turquoises

JOURNEY TO CIBOLA 159

gourd and rattles irritated the natives, and that the chiefs, in council, determined to put him to death.[171]

There is no certainty as to the manner in which he was killed, but it is said that his body was cut in pieces and given to the chiefs to satisfy them that the negro had been killed.[172] The particular pueblo where the negro was slain was most likely Hawaikúh, although this has been disputed.[173] Coronado in his letter of 1540, from Granada, says the Indians "killed him here."[174] The same

they had given him and several pretty women who had been given him. The Indians who accompanied him carried his things. These had followed him from all the settlements he had passed, believing that under his protection they could traverse the whole world without danger. But as the people in this country were more intelligent than those who followed Stephen, they lodged him in a little hut they had outside the village, and the older men and the governors heard his story and took steps to find out the reason he had come to that country. For three days they made inquiries about him and held council. The account which the negro gave them of two white men who were following him, sent by a great lord, who knew about the things in the sky, and how these were coming to instruct them in divine matters, made them think that he must be a spy or a guide from some nations who wished to come and conquer them, because it seemed to them unreasonable to say that the people were white in the country from which he came and that he was sent by them, he being black. Besides other reasons, they thought it was hard of him to ask them for turquoises and women, and so they decided to kill him. They did this, but they did not kill any of those who went with him, although they kept some young fellows and let the others, about 60 persons, return freely to their own country."

[171] Bandelier, A. F., *Contributions*, p. 116.
[172] Alarcon, *Relacion du Voyage de Cibola*, p. 331.
[173] Jaramillo, *Col. Doc. Flo.*, p. 157.
[174] *Letter from Coronado to Mendoza*, August 3, 1540: "The death of the negro is perfectly certain, because many of the things which he wore have been found, and the Indians of Chichilticalli said that he was a bad man, and not like the Christians, because the Christians never kill women, and he killed them, and because he assaulted their women, whom the Indians love better than themselves. Therefore, they determined to kill him, but they did not do it in the way that was reported because they did not kill any of the others who came with him, nor did they kill the lad from the Province of Petatlán, who was with him, but they took him and kept him in safe custody until now. When I tried to secure him, they made excuses for not giving him to me, for two or three days, saying that he was dead, and at other times that the Indians of Acúco had taken him away. But when I finally told them that I should be very angry if they did not give him to me, they gave him to me. He is an interpreter; for although he can not talk much, he understands very well."

That Friar Marcos has been most undeservedly abused by contemporaneous writers, notably Cortés, Coronado, and Castañeda, is becoming to be an accepted fact, owing to the studies of later writers who have given his story careful consideration. Some of the historians, immediately following those of the time of Cortés, were also most uncharitable in their estimate of the friar. For centuries he has been known as the "lying monk." In the light of late investigation it is impossible for anyone justly to agree with his contemporaries nor with those who followed in giving Friar Marcos the reputation for untruthfulness which he has had. There was nothing for the friar to gain by making false reports, when

statement is made by Fray Geronimo Zarate-Salmeron, who wrote in 1626.

---

he, above all others, knew that an expedition would follow his return, organized for the exploration and conquest of the very country about which he was making report. Cortés, Coronado, and Castañeda, however, in their statements about the friar can not escape the rightful suspicion of being insincere. Mr. Bandelier has made the first careful study into the facts and his judgment is of great weight. Cortés wanted it to appear that the friar was untruthful; he was actively engaged in explorations along the Pacific coast, was supposed to have certain rights and privileges, and, naturally, was claiming everything in sight which might in any way add to the glory of his name or increase his personal fortune, and if anyone was personally interested it was the Marquis del Valle, himself. The proof is available that Cortés did not hesitate to distort the truth, and he was surely mendacious when he said, "Y al tiempo que yo viene de la dicha tierra, el dicho Fr. Marcos hablo conmigo . . . é yo le dí noticia de esta dicha tierra y descubrimiento de ella,'' etc. . . . "y despues que volvió el dicho fraile ha publicado que diz que llego á vista de la dicha tierra; la cual yo neigo haber el visto ni descubierto,'' etc. "y en haber se en esta adelantado el dicho Fr. Marcos fingiendo y refieriendo lo que no sabe ni vió.''

So far as Francisco Vasquez Coronado is concerned he was a very much disappointed man, and was looking for some one upon whose shoulders he might place the responsibility for the failure of the expedition which had been placed under his command.

Castañeda never was in position to know just what Fr. Marcos had reported when he returned from Cibola. All that Castañeda knew he probably picked up as common gossip, and if his own veracity is to be questioned, there are certainly many statements that will not bear the light of strict investigation. As has been said, "Friar Marcos's narrative may be somewhat colored, and this doubtless came about from the fact that he wanted to believe what the natives told him, but, in his report, he carefully discriminates as to what the natives told him and that which he personally witnessed through signs and other imperfect means of communication.''

There has been a wide difference of opinion as to the location of a portion, at least, of the route followed by Fr. Marcos. It may be taken as conclusive, however, that Cibola was the Zuñi country of today. The difference of opinion as to the route taken by the friar seems to exist as to the point where he entered the last desert before reaching the immediate vicinity of Hawaikúh. Bancroft and some others seem to think that the friar entered the last desert near Chichilticalli, at the Casas Grandes of the Gila, for at this place, Castañeda says, "is where the wilderness begins, 220 leagues from Culiacan.'' Mr. Bandelier thinks that Coronado's Chichilticalli was near Ft. Grant, at the foot of Mt. Graham. In his *Contributions*, p. 150, note 2, he points out what seems like the most probable route. Mr. Bandelier personally traveled over this entire section of country for the express purpose of ascertaining present physical conditions, all of which information was of great use to him in making up his judgment as to the route which Friar Marcos followed.

BIBLIOGRAPHY

Alarcon, Hernando	*Relacion du Voyage de Cibola* — Ramusio.
Bancroft, Hubert Howe	*North American States; Mexico; Arizona and New Mexico.*
Bandelier, Adolph F.	*Contributions*, etc.
Bartlett, John Russell	*Personal Narrative of Explorations and Incidents in Texas, New Mexico, California, Sonora and Chihuahua*, New York, 1854, 2 volumes.
Coronado, Francisco Vasquez	*Relacion del Suceso de la Jornada que hizo en el Descubrimiento de Cibola; año de 1531*, translation by Buckingham Smith.
Davis, W. W. H.	*The Spanish Conquest of New Mexico.*
Hakluyt, Richard	*The Principal Navigations*, etc.
Herrera, Antonio de	*Historia General*, Stevens translation.
Hodge, F. W.	*The First Discovered City of Cibola*, Am. Anthro., April, 1895.
Mendieta, Fr. Geronimo de	*Historia Ecclesiastica Indiana*; Joaquin Garcia Ycazbalceta, Mexico, 1870.
Niza, Fr. Marcos de	*Relacion del Descubrimiento de la Siete Ciudades*, Doc. de Indias.
Prescott, William H.	*Conquest of Mexico.*
Winship, George Parker	*The Coronado Expedition*, 14th B. A. E., pp. 345-546.
Whipple, A. W.	*Report of Explorations*, etc., Pac. R. R. Reports, vols. iii and iv.

CHAPTER IV

FRANCISCO VASQUEZ CORONADO—HIS MARCH AND INVASION, 1540—
HIS FAILURE AND RETURN TO MEXICO, 1542

THE City of Mexico, in the year 1540, did not contain more than two thousand inhabitants.[175] These consisted of two classes, sharply divided and almost antagonistic, the soldiers of fortune and the settlers, the former, says Mota Padilla, "floating about like corks upon water," unemployed, restless spirits, longing for campaigns, conquest, and consequent adventure, fame and fortune.[176]

The return of Friar Marcos, accompanied by the governor of New Galicia, and the report made to the viceroy, Mendoza, by the friar, produced a tremendous sensation among the many cavaliers then sojourning and idling away their time at the ancient capital of Montezuma. The Seven Cities had been discovered. Justly proud of the great achievement of Friar Marcos, his friends in the priesthood and the members of his order took advantage of every opportunity to laud his single-handed efforts in behalf of the church and the crown.[177]

---

[175] Bandelier, A. F., *Contributions*, p. 172, and notes: "The Spanish town of Mexico, founded in 1524, contained, fifteen years after its foundation, barely one thousand people."

[176] Mota Padilla, *Historia*, cap. xxii, sec. 2, p. 3, Mexico, 1870.

[177] Winship, George Parker, *Relacion de la Jornada de Cibola compuesta por Pedro Castañeda de Naçera*, 14th B. A. E., p. 420: "He (Coronado) found the friars who had just arrived, and who told such great things about what the negro, Stephen, had discovered and what they had heard from the Indians, and other things they had heard about the South Sea and islands and other riches that, without stopping for anything, the Governor set off at once for the City of Mexico, taking Friar Marcos with him, to tell the Viceroy about it. He made the things seem more important by not talking about them to anyone except his particular friends, under promise of the greatest secrecy, until after he had reached the City of Mexico and seen Don Antonio de Mendoza. Then he began to announce that they had really found the Seven Cities which Nuño de Guzman had tried to find, and for the conquest of which he had collected a

Pueblo of Picuri

There was no public press in those days to herald far and wide the news of this latest discovery so promising to the church and crown. This was the office of the representatives of the church. The viceroy had endeavored to maintain secrecy as to the facts contained in the report of the friar, but all in vain.[178] Rivalry and jealousy were apparent on all sides. Before the emperor were laid petitions from the Marquis del Valle, Nuño de Guzman, Alvarado, and others, each urging a right to the coveted prize.

These petitions failed of their purpose. The conqueror of Mexico, himself, was blinded by jealousy and charged the friar with wilful deception.[179] Cortés, probably from information obtained relative

force. The noble Viceroy arranged with the friars of the order of Saint Francis so that Friar Marcos was made father provincial, as a result of which the pulpits of that order were filled with such accounts of marvels and wonders that more than 300 Spaniards and about 800 natives of New Spain collected in a few days.''

[178] Winship, George Parker, *Coronado Expedition*, p. 386: ''Friar Marcos undoubtedly never wilfully told an untruth about the country of Cibola, even in a barber's chair. But there seems to be little chance for doubting that the reports which he brought to New Spain were the cause of much talk as well as many sermons, which gave rise to a considerable amount of excitement among the settlers, whose old-world notions had been upset by the reputed glory of the Montezumas and the wealth of the Incas. Very many, though perhaps not all, of the colonists were stirred with an eager desire to participate in the rich harvest awaiting the conquerors of these new lands. Friar Marcos was not a liar, but it is impossible to ignore the charges against him quite as easily as Mr. Bandelier has done.''

The use of the words ''even in a barber's chair'' by Mr. Winship refers to a statement, under oath, made by a man named Andrés Garcia, relative to statements supposed to have been made by Friar Marcos. In Garcia's deposition he states that ''he had a son-in-law who was a barber, who had shaved the friar after he came back from the new country. The son-in-law had told the witness that the friar, while being shaved, had talked about the country which he had discovered beyond the mountains. After crossing the mountains, the friar said there was a river, and that many settlements were there, in cities and towns, and that the cities were surrounded by walls, with their gates guarded, and were very wealthy, having silver-smiths, and that the women wore strings of gold beads and the men girdles of gold and white woolen dresses; and that they had sheep and cows and partridges and slaughter houses and iron forges.''

It may be noticed that in the days of the Spanish conquest and in the exploration and colonization periods, it was very popular to have certificates made before notaries. It seems also that the custom of procuring affidavits, in the time of Cortés, as well as in more modern times, was easy and quite popular.

[179] In one of the documents submitted in the litigation between the rival claimants for the privilege of exploring the country discovered by Friar Marcos, Hernando Cortés sets forth in detail the ill treatment which he claimed to have received from Mendoza. In this document or memorial, he declared that after the viceroy had ordered him to withdraw his men from their station on the coast of the mainland towards the north, where they were engaged in making ready for extended inland explorations, he had a talk with Friar Marcos.

to the expedition of Fray Juan de la Asuncion, long before the friar Marcos had returned from his trip to Cibola, in July, 1539, despatched Francisco de Ulloa on an expedition by sea. Ulloa sailed from Acapulco and, in due course, ascended the Gulf of Cali-

"And I gave him," said Cortés, "an account of this said country and of its discovery, because I had determined to send him in my ships to follow up the said northern coast and conquer that country, because he seemed to understand something about matters of navigation. The said friar communicated this to the said viceroy, and he says that, with his permission, he went by land in search of the same coast and country as that which I had discovered, and which it was and is my right to conquer. And since his return, the said friar has published the statement that he came within sight of the said country, which I deny that he has either seen or discovered; but, instead, in all that the said friar reports that he has seen, he only repeats the account I had given him regarding the information which I obtained from the Indians of the said country of Santa Cruz, because everything which the friar said that he discovered is just the same as what the Indians had told me; and, in enlarging upon this, and, in pretending to report what he neither saw nor learned, the said Friar Marcos does nothing new, because he has done this many other times, and this was his regular habit as is notorious in the provinces of Peru and Guatamala; and sufficient evidence regarding this will be given to the court, whenever it is necessary."

Bancroft, H. H., in *North American States and Texas*, vol. i, p. 77, says: "Cortés claimed the exclusive right to make explorations in the north. In September, 1538, he wrote to the Council of the Indies that he had nine good vessels ready for a voyage, only lacking pilots. (*Col. Doc. Inédit*, iv, 193; Cortés, *Escritos*, 280-1). Mendoza's act in despatching Niza, to whom Cortés had confided all he had learned about the north, was strenuously but vainly opposed by the captain-general, who, on hearing the friar's marvelous tales, became alarmed lest another should reap the fame and wealth for which he had toiled so earnestly, and resolved to get the start of his rival by sending out a fleet at once."

Hernando Cortés, in his *Escritos*, 303-5; *Col. Doc. Inédit*, iv, 213, says that the viceroy, hearing of Ulloa's departure, sent men to the ports where the fleet might touch, to prevent the voyage; and also on the return to hear what had been accomplished. Thus a messenger sent from Santiago to Cortés was seized and tortured with a view of obtaining information. The viceroy also ordered that no person be allowed to leave New Spain without his permission so that no aid could be sent to Ulloa. Bernal Diaz, however, *Historia Verdadera*, p. 234, says the expedition was sent by the express order of the Audiencia. In his memorial of 1539, Cortés announces that Ulloa is ready to sail and asks that no restrictions be placed on his sending expeditions to the countries he has discovered.— *Escritos*, 294-5. The state of feeling between the different would-be conquerors after the receipt of Niza's report is best shown by the papers in the legal proceedings in Spain in 1540-1.— *Proceso del Marqués*, 300-408. Cortés, Guzman, Alvarado, and De Soto, each, by an attorney, urged upon the royal council his title to Cibola. Each had a license for northern discovery, obtained in the hope that in the vague northern somewhere was a mighty nation, etc., to make the finder famous, powerful, and rich. Now this prize had been found by a fifth party, the viceroy, through Niza, and Mendoza was said to be preparing to follow up the discovery. Something must be done. De Soto was authorized to conquer and govern 200 leagues on the Florida coast and was at the time engaged in active explorations. That Cibola was included in his territory was a fact known to all the world, so clear

fornia but failed to find the country for which he was seeking. Cortés demanded of the crown that the expeditions being contemplated and sent out by the viceroy should be prevented by royal decree, and asked for authority to continue his own efforts as explorer and conqueror.

There is no doubt, whatever, upon the question of the activity of the viceroy in guarding his own interests and circumventing, if possible, all efforts on the part of his rivals. He not only took active steps in preventing the organization of expeditions from his own jurisdiction, but, when he received the report from Friar Marcos, he immediately took precautions against the news of the discovery being made known in other portions of the world. He was fearful that Hernando de Soto, who had recently received a license to explore the country between the Rio de las Palmas, in the present state of Texas, and Florida, might conclude to direct his explorations toward the western portions of his territory.[180]

---

that a child might comprehend it As yet, his obtuse adversaries had the assurance to deny that Cibola was in Florida.

Cortés, who, in general terms, would admit the right of no other to make northern discoveries at all, had authority to explore and conquer on the South Sea coasts toward the Gran China; he had spent large sums of money, had sent several armadas, and had another ready; indeed, he had already discovered Cibola or the lands immediately adjoining. It was doubtful whether Niza had found anything, but he had probably repeated the reports obtained from Cortés. Had it not been for Guzman's opposition, he would now be in full possession of Cibola and the country far beyond. Everybody knew that De Soto's claim was absurd, Florida being a long way off. As for Don Nuño, he was simply governor of New Galicia, and would do well to attend to his own business. Guzman, for his part, was also licensed to make northern *conquistas*, and had done so for many leagues. Both the lands discovered by Cortés (Santa Cruz) and Cibola were notoriously in his jurisdiction, just adjoining in fact his actual settlements. Cortés never had any right to go north, his license being for the west, or toward India; but if he had any such right he had forfeited it by not retaining possession of the island he claimed to have discovered. He could not have made the voyage any way without Guzman's aid; nor could Niza have gone so far north but for Guzman's earlier conquest. Alvarado figured less prominently but he too had a license for South Sea exploration and thought it well to keep his claim alive before the consejo. All agreed on one point, that Mendoza had no right to continue his efforts.

[180] Winship, George Parker, *Coronado Expedition*, citing as authority, *Doc. de Indias*, vol. iv, pp. 354-363, says: "Although Mendoza did not know it, De Soto had sailed from Havana in May, 1539, and, in July, sending back his largest ships, began the long march through the Everglades of Florida, which was to end in the Mississippi. Mendoza, with all the formality of the viceregal authority, ordered that no vessel sailing from New Spain should touch at any port in the New World on its way back to the home peninsula, and this notice was duly served on all departing ship-masters by the secretaries of the viceroy. By the middle of November, however, despite all his care, a ship from

The viceroy was a very wise man, understood fully the opposition which was making against him and was always on the alert for aid in bringing about the successful issue of his undertakings. He had arranged with Pedro de Alvarado for the use of the latter's fleet. By this arrangement, the viceroy and Alvarado were to share equally in the fruits of all expeditions and conquests. Alvarado had been one of the most vigorous of the lieutenants of Cortés, and was a soldier of great ability. He held the position of governor of Guatamala at one time and had explored the South Sea as early as 1526. He took no part in the Coronado expedition. He lost his life in the Indian insurrection of 1540 and later the entire fleet became the property of Mendoza, or at least was under his control.

When the news of the discoveries of Friar Marcos reached Europe, together with the reports of the preparations being made by Mendoza, the representatives of all the governors and explorers in the New World, at the court and the bureaus of the government, began filing protests against the action being taken by the viceroy.

The Council of the Indies referred the entire controversy to the licentiate, Villabolos, April 21, 1540, who made a report in which he says that the most conclusive reason in favor of the advice which he offers to the Council, is that each of the parties has clearly proved that none of the others has any right to claim a share in the newly

---

Vera Cruz sailed into the harbor of Havana. The master declared, on oath, that he had been forced to put in here, because sickness had broken out aboard his vessel soon after the departure from New Spain, and because he had discovered that his stock of provisions and water was insufficient for the voyage across the Atlantic. Curiously enough, one of the crew, possibly one of those who had been seized with the sickness, had in his possession some letters which he had been asked to deliver to Hernando De Soto, in Havana. Apparently the agent or friend of De Soto living in Mexico, one Francisco de Billegas, did not know that the adelantado had left Cuba and had arranged to have the letters carried to Spain and given to the representative of the adelantado there if De Soto was not found at Havana ''

Pacheco-Cardenas, *Colecion de documentos inéditos relativos al descubrimiento conquista y colonizacion de las posessiones españolas en America, y Oceanica, sacados bajo la direcion de D. Joaquin Pacheco y D. Francisco de Cardenas,* Madrid, 1864-1884: ''Petitions, testimony, narratives of explorations and discoveries, acts taking possession of new lands, notifications and decisions, appeals and counter-charges, were filed and referred, each claimant watching his rivals so closely and objecting to their claims so strenuously that the fiscal, Villabolos, in his report on the case, May 25, 1540, gives as one of the most conclusive reasons in favor of the advice which he offers the Council, that each of the parties has clearly proved that none of the others have any right to claim a share in the newly discovered region by virtue of any grants, licenses or achievements whatsoever.''

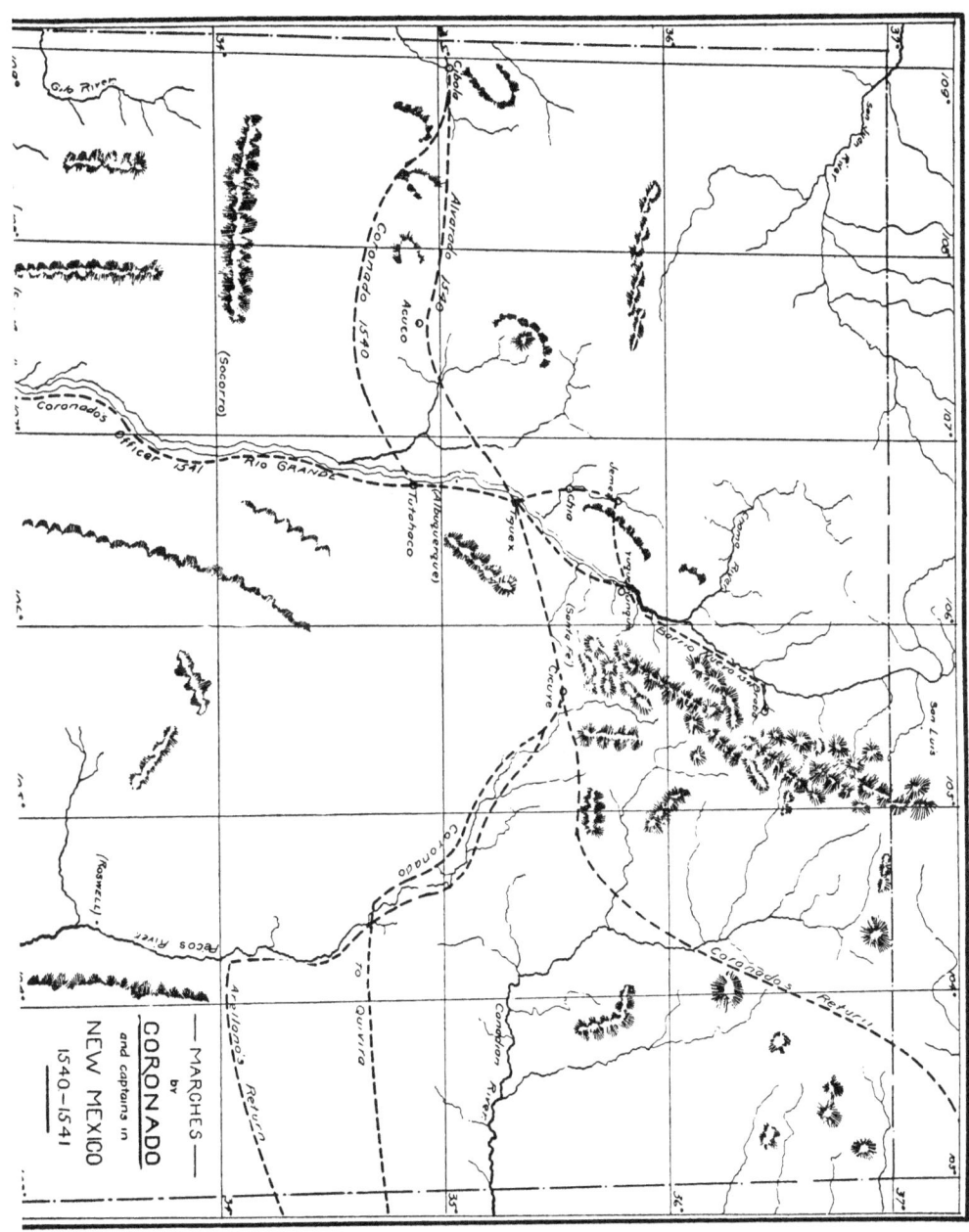

discovered region by virtue of any grants, licenses, or achievements whatsoever.

The rivalries and jealousies which existed upon the return of Friar Marcos can be readily appreciated and understood. The stories which he told or was supposed to have told in his report awakened the liveliest interest throughout New Spain. A writer, in his narrative of conditions existing at that time and commenting upon the statements of the friar, says: "that the country was so stirred up by the news which the friar had brought from the Seven Cities that nothing else was thought about. For he said that the city of Cibola was big enough to contain two Sevilles and over, and the other places were not much smaller; and that the houses were very fine edifices, four stories high; that everybody was for going there and leaving Mexico depopulated; that the news from the Seven Cities inspired so eager a desire in every one that not only did the viceroy and the marquis (Cortés) make ready to start for there, but the whole country wanted to follow them so much that they traded for the licenses which permitted them to go as soldiers, and people sold these as a favor, and whoever obtained one of these thought it was as good as a title of nobility at the least." [181]

Even if only a hundredth part of what the friar is supposed to have said in relation to his journey was really stated by him, and from all accounts he was not backward in proclaiming what he had heard and seen, one can readily comprehend the feelings which must have stirred the hearts of such men as Hernando Cortés. During the first years of Mendoza's administration Cortés and the viceroy were not overly friendly. As soon as it could be done, Mendoza had asked the king for permission to make explorations.[182] The marquis evidently fully understood that his power and prestige with his royal master at home were on the wane, and it was but natural that he should look upon the viceroy with distrust and regard him as an interloper. This feeling was greatly enhanced when Mendoza, urged on by the Audiencia, undertook to execute the royal orders which instructed him to investigate as to the lands held by Cortés and the number of Indians in his service. These

---

[181] Zaragoza, Justo, *Noticias Historicas de la Nueva España*, Madrid, 1878.

[182] In the earliest letters of the viceroy this request appears and is repeated in his letter of December, 1537.

The Battle of Hawaikúh

two were the leading men in New Spain, and the friction existing between them was known to all.[183]

It is certain that the feeling between them was very bitter, and when Cortés finally realized that he could do nothing to prevent the expedition which Mendoza was organizing, he left Mexico and sailed for Spain, believing that his claims would be recognized by his royal master if presented in person.[184]

What had been the plans of Cortés, prior to his departure, and just how much he had done to carry his plans into execution, cannot be ascertained with any certainty. He was naturally unwilling to give up all hope of benefit from his previous efforts, and he was doubtless convinced that his expectations would never be realized when he ascertained that the viceroy had sent the friar and Estevan to the north in search of the Seven Cities, and to verify the reports which had been brought to New Spain by Alvar Nuñez Cabeza de Vaca, and his companions. We have only Cortés's own statement as to many of his claims, and there is no means of knowing whether he had learned of the actual discovery of Cibola when he ordered Ulloa to take three vessels and sail up the coast toward the head of the Gulf of California. In the statement of his grievances, he declared that Mendoza not only threw every possible obstacle in his way, seizing six or seven vessels which failed to get away with Ulloa, but that even after Ulloa had gone, the viceroy sent a strong force up the coast to prevent the ships from entering any of the ports.[185]

Mendoza was a very active and a very able man. Immediately he began the formation of plans for the organization of the expedition which, in his judgment, meant so much for the glory of the church, the crown, and himself.

In a very short period of time, public excitement being at such a high pitch, he was able to organize a company of more than three hundred Spaniards, a large number of whom were mounted. There were also upwards of eight hundred Indian allies. He equipped the expedition with some light artillery which, as is stated by the

---
[183] Suarez de Peralta, Joan, *Tratado del Descubrimiento de las Yndias y su Conquista.*
[184] Winship, George Parker, *Coronado Expedition*, 14th B. A. E., p. 369.
[185] Winship, George Parker, *ibid.*

historian of the expedition, was of little service when used against the walls of the Pueblo villages. Large numbers of cattle and sheep were also taken with the expedition.[186]

The command was composed largely of soldiers of fortune, who had been living in Mexico. Among them were the sons of many Spanish noblemen. Their presence in the New World has been easily accounted for. A great portion of the discovery and conquest by the Spaniards was due to this class of individuals. They were good soldiers; by personal valor and ability they held the positions of leadership everywhere among men who followed whom and when they chose; they always served under the banner of the successful leader and explorer.

"There had been few attractions to draw these adventurers away from Mexico," says Winship, "for some time previous to 1539. Peru still offered excitement for those who had nothing to gain or lose, but the purely personal struggle going on between Pizarro and Almagro could not arouse the energies of those who were in search of glory as well as employment. A considerable part of the rabble which followed Nuño de Guzman, during the conquest of New Galicia, went to Peru after their chief had been superseded by the licentiate de la Torre, so that one town is said to have disappeared entirely from this cause. But among these were men of good blood and spirit. Mendoza had been able, at first, to accommodate and employ those who accompanied him from Spain, like Vasquez Coronado, "being chiefly young gentlemen." But every vessel coming from home brought some companion or friend of those who were already in New Spain, and after Cabeza de Vaca carried reports of his discoveries to the Spanish court, an increasing number came each season to join the already burdensome body of useless members of the viceregal household.

The viceroy recognized the necessity of relieving the community of this burden very soon after he had established himself in Mexico, and was continually on the watch for some suitable means of freeing himself from these guests. By 1539, the problem of looking after these "young gentlemen" whose number is determined quite accurately by the two hundred and fifty or three hundred "gentlemen

---

[186] Castañeda, Winship's translation, 14th B. A. E., pp. 420, 469.

on horseback" who left New Spain with Coronado in the spring of 1540, had become a very serious one to the viceroy.[187]

Consequently, in September, 1539, after the return of Friar Marcos, with the news of his great discovery of the Seven Cities, the viceroy had no difficulty in organizing the expedition and within a month and a half an urgent, restless, but light-hearted band of conquest-loving cavaliers was ready to be led into the unknown regions of the north. In the entire army there were only two or three men who had ever been settled residents of New Spain.[188]

Compostella, on the Pacific coast, was announced as the point where the intended army of invasion and conquest would be mobilized, and Don Francisco Vasquez Coronado[189] was named as the commander of the expedition.

Mendoza spared neither pains nor expense to insure the success

[187] Winship, George Parker, *Coronado Expedition*, 14th B. A. E., p 376.

[188] Pacheco y Cardenas, *Doc. de Indias*, vol. xxv, p. 373, Testimony concerning those who went on the Expedition with Francisco Vasquez Coronado, Winship's translation.

"At Compostella, on February 21, 1540, Coronado presented a petition to the viceroy, Mendoza, declaring that he had observed that certain persons who were not well disposed toward the expedition which was about to start for the newly discovered country had said that many of the inhabitants of the City of Mexico and of the other cities and towns of New Spain, and also of Compostella and other places in this province of New Galicia were going on the expedition at his request or because of inducements offered by him, as a result of which the City of Mexico and New Spain were left deserted, or almost so. Therefore, he asked the viceroy to order that information be obtained, in order that the truth might be known about the citizens of New Spain and of his province who were going to accompany him. He declared that there were very few of them, and that they were not going on account of any attraction or inducement offered by him, but of their own free will, and as there were few of them, there would not be any lack of people in New Spain. And as Gonzalo de Salazar, the factor or royal agent, and Pedro Almides Cherino, the veedor or royal inspector of His Majesty for New Spain, and other citizens of Mexico who knew all the facts and had the necessary information, were present there, Coronado asked His Grace to provide and order that which would best serve His Majesty's interests and the welfare and security of New Spain.

"The viceroy instructed the licentiate, Maldonado, oidor of the royal audiencia, to procure this information. To facilitate the hearing he provided that the said factor and veedor and the regidores, and others who were there, should attend the review of the army, which was to be held the following day. Nine of the desired witnesses were also commanded by Maldonado to attend the review and observe those whom they knew in the army.

"On the 26th day of February the licentiate, Maldonado, took the oaths of the witnesses in proper form and their testimony as to the personnel of the army has been preserved."

[189] Don Francisco Vasquez Coronado — de Coronado, it is sometimes written, was born in Salamanca, as is stated by Herrera, in his *Historia General*, and by Tello in Icazbalceta's *Mexico*. "Who he is, what he has already done, and

of the expedition. Arms, horses and supplies were furnished in abundance; money was advanced from the royal chest to anyone

his personal qualities and abilities, which may be made useful in the various affairs which arise in these parts of the Indies, I have already written to your Majesty,'' says Mendoza, in his letter to the emperor, dated December 10, 1537. It is known that he came to New Spain with Mendoza two years previous to the writing of this letter. He was always upon good terms with the viceroy, until after his return from the expedition to Quivira. His wife was Beatriz de Estrada, a cousin by blood, as it was said at the time, of the emperor, Charles V. Her father, Alonzo, had been royal treasurer of New Spain. From his mother-in-law Coronado received as a marriage gift a very large estate, which was confirmed by royal grant. He also obtained another estate, that of Juan de Burgos. This acquisition was also confirmed by royal grant. At least, so it is said in Icazbalceta's *Mexico*, vol. ii, p. 95. Later on, when Coronado had returned from his unfortunate expedition, an order was received from Spain, a part of the ''New Laws and Ordinances for the Indies,'' calling for an investigation into the value and extent of his estates.

In the year 1537, a revolt occurred among the negroes working in the mines at Amatapeque. Thither the viceroy sent Coronado, who quickly quelled the revolt with the aid of some friendly Indians. This exploit Mendoza reported to the emperor at the time.

In 1538, Coronado became a legally recognized citizen of the City of Mexico, where he was a witness chosen to testify to the formal recognition by the Marquis del Valle of the royal order which gave Hernando De Soto the right to explore and conquer Florida. In September, of that year, the representative of De Soto, Alvaro de Sanjurlo, summoned Coronado himself to recognize and promise obedience to the same royal order ''as governor, as Sanjurlo declared him to be, of New Galicia.'' Coronado promised his obedience to his emperor, but said that the matter presented by Sanjurlo did not concern him at all, inasmuch as he was not governor nor was he at that time advised that his Majesty desired him to have such a position; but, if his Majesty should desire his services in that position he would obey and submit to the royal provision for him whenever he was called on and would do what was most serviceable to the royal interests. He also says that he knows nothing about the government of Ayllon or that of Narváez, which were mentioned in the grant to De Soto. Coronado evidently knew something of the art of dissimulation. At any rate his answer was not satisfactory to the representative of the discoverer of the Mississippi, who informed Coronado that he had received information that Coronado was to be appointed governor of New Galicia. Coronado declined to make further answer, whereupon Sanjurlo formally protested that the blame for any expenditures, damages, scandals, or other injurious results which might come from a failure to observe the royal order must be laid at the door of the one to whom they rightfully belonged, and that they would not result from any fault or omission on the part of De Soto. It is likely that Mendoza had already suggested to the king that Coronado be appointed governor, but no action was taken by the crown until after the death of de la Torre. The confirmation was signed April 18, 1539. He was allowed a salary of one thousand ducats from the royal treasure chest and one thousand five hundred more from the province, with a proviso that the royal revenues would not be laid liable for the latter sum in the event he was unable to collect the amount from his province. He immediately began the performance of his gubernatorial duties by appointing judges and magistrates for Compostella and Guadalajara.

Coronado was actively engaged in handling the reins of government, and when Friar Marcos came north on his journey of exploration, together with the negro, Estevan, under the authority of the viceroy, Coronado accompanied the

who had debts to pay before he could depart, and provision was made for the support of those who were about to be left behind by fathers, brothers, or husbands. The equipment of the force was all that the viceroy could desire. Beside the commander-in-chief, Don Francisco Vasquez Coronado, the officers of the expedition, as given by Castañeda, were: Standard-bearer, Don Pedro de Tobar, a young cavalier, son of Don Fernando de Tobar, mayor-domo of the late queen, Joana; master-at-arms, Lope de Samaniego, governor of the arsenal of Mexico; captains, Don Tristan de Arellano, Don Pedro de Guevara, Don Garcia Lopez de Cardenas, Don Rodrigo Maldonado, brother-in-law of the Duke de Infantado, Diego Lopez, member of the city council of Seville, and Diego Gutierrez. The remaining "gentlemen" were placed directly under the orders of the general, because they were men of distinction, and a number of them were afterwards appointed captains. The commander of the infantry was Pablo de Melgoza, and the chief of artillery Hernando de Alvarado. The historian of the expedition was Pedro de Castañeda [190] de Naçera, who accompanied the expedition in all its

---

friar as far as Culiacan, the furthest north of all the Spanish settlements at that time.

Coronado was the leader in the improvement of the city of Guadalajara, and on account of his services and activities in this respect, the city was able to obtain, by royal grant, a coat of arms, which was done at Madrid, November 8, 1539, as is declared by Icazbalceta in his history of Mexico. It was he, in the following year, who promulgated the order, dated December 20, 1538, by which it was decreed that thereafter no settler should build a house of any material except stone, brick, or un-baked brick, and that the houses should be built after the style of those in Spain, having in view the permanency thereof, and the adornment of the cities.

When Friar Marcos returned from his trip to Cibola, he was met by Coronado and with the friar he went to the City of Mexico, where he told the viceroy what Marcos had witnessed on his journey to the north. He remained at the capital assisting the viceroy in making preparations for the expedition of which he was later placed in command, under the title of captain-general.

Upon his return from this expedition, attended by scarce one hundred faithful followers, he presented himself before Mendoza, by whom he was ill received, says Castañeda. The viceroy gave him his discharge, however, but his reputation was gone and soon afterward he lost the government of New Galicia. It is not known what thereafter became of him. There is no doubt that Mendoza was filled with disappointment over the outcome of the enterprise.—Winship, *Coronado Expedition.*

[190] Pedro de Castañeda de Nacera, the historian of the Coronado expedition, was a private soldier in the army of Coronado. Very little is known of him. He was evidently a man of very considerable education and accustomed to writing, as his account and style are far superior to that of most of the narratives of the sixteenth century relative to the Spanish conquerors and their explorations. Upon the return of the Spaniards to New Spain from the Cibola

wanderings. He mentions a number of illustrious names, among them, whom he remembered, being "Francisco de Barrionuevo, a gentleman from Granada; Juan de Salvidar, Francisco de Ovando Juan Gallego, and Melchior Diaz, a captain who had been mayor of Culiacan, who, although he was not a gentleman, merited the position he held. The other gentlemen who were worthy substitutes, were Don Alonzo Manrique de Lara, Don Lope de Urrea, a gentleman from Aragon, Gomez Suarez de Figueroa, Luis Ramirez de Vargas, Juan de Sotomayor, Francisco Gorbalan, the commissioner Riberos, and other gentlemen, of high quality, whom I do not now recall. As I say, since then I have forgotten the names of many good fellows. It would be well if I could name some of them, so that it might be clearly seen what cause I had for saying that they had on this expedition the most brilliant company ever collected in the Indies to go in search of new lands. But they were unfortunate in having a captain who left in New Spain estates and a pretty wife, a noble and excellent lady, which were not the least causes for what was to happen."

The equipment of the army was of the same character as was usual where expeditions were made up largely of volunteers.[191] Arms and military supplies had been among the things greatly needed in New Spain when Mendoza reported its condition in his first letters to the home government. It was a most dazzling and splendid array as the army passed in review before Mendoza and

---

country, Castañeda remained at Culiacan, where he wrote the *Relacion de la Jornada de Cibola*. The work left by him is in manuscript covering one hundred and forty-seven pages, written on paper in characters of the times. It was preserved in the collection of D'Uguina, Paris, and was translated and published in French for the first time by H. Ternaux-Compans, in 1838. This copy is now in the Lenox Library, New York. It is not the original but a copy made in 1596. Although diligent inquiry has been made of the custodians of the large Spanish libraries at Simancas, Madrid, and at Seville nothing has as yet been learned of the original. The best translation in English is that of George Parker Winship. The Ternaux version or translation was made with great freedom and in some respects is far from accurate.

[191] Castañeda, *Relacion*, etc.: "As each one was obliged to transport his own baggage and all did not know how to fasten packs, and as the horses started off fat and plump, they had a good deal of difficulty and labor during the first few days, and many left many valuable things, giving them to anyone who wanted them, in order to get rid of carrying them. In the end, necessity, which is all powerful, made them skillful, so that one could see many gentlemen become carriers, and anybody who despised this work was not considered a man."

the officials who helped and watched him govern New Spain on this day, February, 1540.

The young cavaliers curbed the picked horses from the large stock farms of the viceroy, each resplendent in long blankets flowing to the ground. Each rider held his lance erect, while his sword and other weapons hung in their proper places at his side. Some were arrayed in coats of mail polished to shine like that of the general, whose gilded armor, with its brilliant trappings, was to bring him many hard blows a few months later. Others wore iron helmets or vizored head-pieces of the tough bull-hide for which the country has ever been famous. The foot-men carried cross-bows and arquebusses, while some of them were armed with sword and shield. Looking on at these white men, carrying their weapons of European warfare, was the crowd of native allies, in their paint and holiday attire, armed with the bow and club of the Indian warrior. When all these started off the next morning, in duly ordered companies, with their banners flying, upward of a thousand servants and followers, black and red men, went with them, leading the spare horses, driving the pack animals, bearing the extra baggage of their masters, or herding the large droves of oxen, cows, and sheep which had been collected by the viceroy to assure fresh food for the army on its march.[192] There were more than a thousand horses in the train, besides the mules, loaded with camp supplies and provisions, and carrying half a dozen pieces of light artillery, the pedreros, or swivel guns of the period.[193]

Awe-inspiring was the spectacle of this army of volunteers, caparisoned in all the panoply of war, as it started on its northward march from Compostella on Monday,[194] February 23, 1540. Not

---

[192] Winship, George Parker, *Coronado Expedition*, pp. 378-379.

[193] Icazbalceta, J. Garcia, *Documentos para La Historia de Mexico*, ii, 72. This author gives all the details of the expedition. ''199. *Item*, si saben etc. que la gente que salio de la villa de S. Miguel de Culiacan, que es el postrer lugar de Galicia de la Nueva España, para ir en descubrimiento de la tierra nueva de Cibola con el capitan general Francisco Vasquez Coronado, fueron hasta doscientos y cincuenta españoles de á caballo, los cuales asi para sus personas, como par su carruaje, armas, y bastimientos, y municiones y otras cosas necesarias para el dicho viaje, llevaron mas de mil caballos y acemilas, y asi lo diran los testigos, porque lo vieron y hallaron presentes, y fueron al dicho viaje.''

[194] It is a very difficult matter to ascertain positively the exact date of the departure of the army from Compostella. The several writers do not agree, and Castañeda does not give a date other than the force was assembled on the ''dia

even the conqueror of Mexico had ever commanded so brilliant a company. The distance to Culiacan, along the coast was eighty leagues, and notwithstanding the desire on the part of officer and man to reach the point of destination at the earliest opportunity the march was necessarily slow. Several days of delay were made necessary on account of the fording of the Centizpac river.

THE DEPARTURE OF
THE EXPEDITION

de carnes tollendas,'' the carnival preceding Shrove-tide, which, in 1540, fell on February 10, Easter being March 28. Mr. Winship has gone into this discrepancy with his usual analytical skill and in a note, at page 382 of his *Coronado Expedition*, says: ''This march from Compostella to Culiacan according to a letter which Coronado wrote from Granada — Zuñi — on August 3, occupied eighty days. The same letter gives April 22 as the date when Coronado left Culiacan, after stopping for several days in that town, and this date is corroborated by another account, the *Traslado de las Nuevas*. April 22 is only sixty days after February 23, the date of the departure, which is fixed almost beyond question by the legal formalities of the *Testimonio* of February 21-26. We have only Ramusio's Italian text of Coronado's letter of August 3, so that it is easy to suspect that a slip on the part of the translator causes the trouble. But to complicate matters, eighty days previous to April 22 is about the 1st of February. Mota Padilla, who used material of great value in his *Historia de la Nueva Galicia*, says that the army marched from Compostella 'el 10 de Febrero del año de 1540.' . . . Mendoza, who had spent the New Year's season at Pasquaro, the seat of the bishopric of Michoacan, did not hasten his journey across the country, and we know only that the whole force had assembled before he arrived at Compostella. At least a fortnight would have been necessary for completing the organization of the force, and for collecting and arranging all the supplies.''

Another combination of dates makes it hard to decide how rapidly the army marched. Mendoza was at Compostella February 26. He presumably started on his return to Mexico very soon after that date. He went down the coast to Colima, where he was detained by an attack of fever for some days. Thence he proceeded to Jacona, where he wrote a letter to the king, April 17, 1540. March 20, Mendoza received the report from Melchior Diaz, who had spent the preceding winter in the country through which Friar Marcos had traveled trying to verify the friar's report. Diaz, and Salvidar, his lieutenant, on their return from the north, met the army at Chiametla, as it was about to resume its march, after a few days' delay. Diaz stopped at Chiametla, while Salvidar carried the report to the viceroy, and he must have traveled very rapidly to deliver his packets on March 20, when Mendoza had left Colima, although he probably had not arrived at Jacona.

Everything points to the very slow progress of the force, hampered by the long baggage and provision trains. Castañeda says that they reached Culiacan just before Easter, March 28, less than thirty-five days after February 23. Here Coronado stopped for a fortnight's entertainment and rest, according to Castañeda, who was present. Mota Padilla says that the army stayed here a month and this agrees with Castañeda's statement that the main body started a fortnight later than their general.

The attempt to arrange an itinerary of the expedition is perplexing, and has not been made easier by modern students. Professor Haynes, in his *Early Explorations of New Mexico*, Windsor's *Narrative and Critical History*, vol. ii, p. 481, following Bandelier's statement on page 26 of his *Documentary History of Zuñi*, says that the start from Compostella was made ''in the last days of

Terraces of Zuñi

When the army arrived at Chiametla, camp was made at the ruins of a village which had been established by Nuño de Guzman. The settlers had been driven away by a pestilence caught from the Indians, and by fierce attacks from the natives who lived in the surrounding mountains.

There was a growing scarcity in the food supply for the army, and Coronado sent a force into the mountains to obtain provisions, if possible. The foraging party was put in command of Lope de Samaniego.[195] After leaving the clearing the force under Samaniego entered a dense thicket, when one of his soldiers became separated from his command. The Indians, out of sight, attacked him, and the commander, hearing his cries, hastened to his assistance. The Indians, who had tried to seize him, disappeared, and Samaniego, believing himself entirely safe, raised his visor. Without warning of any sort an arrow shot from among the bushes pierced his eye and passed through his skull. The death of this officer was a great loss to the army, and was avenged by Coronado who captured a number of natives and hung them to trees in the vicinity for the

February, 1540.'' Mr. Bandelier, however, who has given much more time to the study of everything connected with this expedition than has been possible for any other investigator, in his work, *The Gilded Man*, p. 164, adopts the date which is given by Mota Padilla. The best and the safest way out of this tangle in chronology is gained by accepting the three specific dates, February 23, or possibly 24, Easter, and April 22, disregarding every statement about the number of days intervening.

[195] This is from the account of Mota Padilla. Castañeda, however, who was on the ground at the time and ought to know what happened, says: ''During this time, the army-master, Lope de Samaniego, went off with some soldiers to find food and at one village, a cross-bowman having entered it indiscreetly in pursuit of the enemies, they shot him through the eye and it passed through his brain, so that he died on the spot. They also shot five or six of his companions before Diego Lopez, the alderman of Seville, since the commander was dead, collected the men and sent word to the general. He put a guard in the village and over the provisions. There was great confusion in the army when this news became known. He was buried here. Several sorties were made by which food was obtained and several of the natives taken prisoners. They hanged those who seemed to belong to the district where the army-master was killed.''

Mota Padilla says: ''A Chametla . . . hallaron la tierra alzada, de suerte que fue preciso entrar á la sierra en busca maiz, y por cabo el maese de campo, Lopez de Samaniego; internaronse en la espatura de un monte, en donde un soldado que inadvertiente se apartó, fue aprehendido por los indios, dió voces, á las que como vigilante, acudio el maese de campo, y libro del peligro a! soldado, y pareciendole estar seguro, alzo la vista á tiempo que de entre unos matoralles se le desparó una flecha, que entrandole por un ojo, le atravesó el cerebro. Samaniego (era) uno de los mas enforzados y amado de todos; enterrose en una ramada, de donde despues sus huesos fueron translados á Compostela.''

purpose of counteracting the bad augury which followed from the loss of the first life.

Just as the army was about to resume its march from Chiametla, Melchior Diaz and Juan de Salvidar returned from their trip to the north, having been sent thither by Mendoza the year before to see if the account which Friar Marcos brought back agreed with what they could observe. Leaving Culiacan on November 17th of the year previous, Diaz, with a command of fifteen horsemen, had traveled as far north as the wilderness, or desert, beyond which lay the far-famed Cibola. He had followed the route taken by the friar and had examined all the natives whom he met, questioning them with the greatest care. A great deal that Friar Marcos had stated was verified, but nowhere did he find any foundation for the tales of wealth, except in the descriptions given by the natives.

ARRIVAL OF MELCHIOR DIAZ AND JUAN DE SALVIDAR AT CHIAMETLA

This report was placed in the hands of Mendoza by Salvidar and, on the 17th of the following month, Mendoza, in his letter to the king, makes use of this report and incorporates it in full.

The captain-general was unwilling that Diaz communicate to the soldiers of his army the results of his reconnoissance, but rumor had it that the friar was guilty of gross exaggeration and that his report was visionary. The friar, however, was equal to the emergency, and the mutterings of discontent among the soldiers coming to his ears, he exhorted them in a special sermon and by his eloquence and position — he was now provincial of his order — succeeded in persuading them that all their hardships and labors would soon be repaid.

Leaving Chiametla, the army resumed its march and a day or two before Easter, March 28, 1540, arrived before Culiacan.[196] A little over a month had been consumed in this portion of the journey.

---

[196] Winship, George Parker, *Coronado Expedition*, p. 384: "The town of San Miguel de Culiacan in the spring of 1540, was one of the most prosperous in New Spain. Nuño de Guzman had founded the settlement some years before and had placed Melchior Diaz in charge of it. The appointment was a most admirable one. Diaz was not of gentle birth, but he had established his right to a position of considerable power and responsibility by virtue of much natural ability. He was a hard worker and a skillful organizer and leader. He inspired confidence in his companions and followers, and always maintained the best of order and of diligence among those who were under his charge. Rarely does one meet with a man whose record for every position and every duty assigned to him shows such uniform and thorough efficiency."

Fac-simile of Page of the Relacion of Castañeda

The viceroy seems to have been a man of prodigious energy and foresight. He was determined, so far as he was concerned, in the matter of the disposition of the naval or military forces at his command, to allow no stone to be unturned in the support of his expedition.

THE EXPEDITION BY SEA UNDER HERNANDO DE ALARCON

In all probability he was possessed of the idea, obtained, perhaps, from conversations with Friar Marcos, that Coronado would follow a route along the western coast. With this idea in view, he ordered two vessels, under the command of Hernando de Alarcon, to call at Jalisco and take on all of the equipment which Coronado had been unable to transport and to keep in communication with the captain-general, if possible. Accordingly Alarcon set sail on the 9th of May, 1540, in command of the San Pedro and the Santa Catalina, from the port of Natividad, or possibly from Acapulco.[197] He proceeded to the port of Aguaauale, where he learned of the departure of Coronado. At this point the San Gabriel joined his fleet and he proceeded up the coast and, after great difficulties in navigation, owing to powerful currents, entered the Gulf of California. To the east were high mountains. Ahead, through sandy wastes, flowed the Colorado of the West. His ships could hardly hold their own, so strong was the tide and incoming rush of the waters of the great river.

Alarcon finally concluded to proceed up the river in two small boats, leaving the third with his ships, awaiting his return. With twenty men and some small cannon, he began his journey up stream, dragging his boats a distance of six leagues the first day.[198] The

[197] Alarcon, H., *Voyage de Cibola*, p. 302.
[198] The complete text of Alarcon's report was translated into Italian by Ramusio (vol. iii, fol. 363, ed. 1556), and the Spanish original is not known to exist. Herrera, however, gives an account which, from the close similarity to Ramusio's text and from the personality of the style, must have been copied from Alarcon's own narrative. The Ramusio text does not give the port of departure. Herrera says that the ships sailed from Acapulco. Castañeda implies that the start was made from Natividad, but his information could hardly have been better than second hand. He may have known what the viceroy intended to do, when he bade the army farewell, two days north of Compostella. Alarcon reports that he put into the port of Santiago de Buena Esperanza, and as the only Santiago on the coast hereabout is south of La Natividad, which is on the coast of the district of Colima, H. H. Bancroft, *North Mexican States*, vol. i, p. 90, says the fleet probably started from Acapulco. Bancroft does not mention Herrera, who is, I suppose, the conclusive authority. Gen.

next day he saw some Indians along the river bank, who at first seemed greatly frightened, but soon began making hostile threats. An arquebus was fired by one of the men to the terror of all except one or two old men, who showed no signs of fear. Alarcon landed and was struck in the chest by one of the old men, whereupon, not desiring trouble, he withdrew to his boat and continued up-stream and at night anchored in the middle of the river, as many of the Indians had gathered on its banks.

These Indians were the Cocopas, who lived along the lower course of the Rio Colorado; they were gaily decorated with feathers and small sticks, rings and pendants hung from their ears and noses. Some were blackened with charcoal; others were tattooed with fire, and all wore a bunch of feathers which hung from a cord which encircled the waist. The women were naked, except for two great bunches of feathers which hung in front and behind, and both men and women wore the hair cut short in front and down to the waist behind. They carried wooden clubs and bows and arrows.

On his way up the river Alarcon maintained strictly his attitude of peace, distributed little crosses among the natives, who now crowded to the river banks to see him, and, day after day, they helped to drag his boats against the current.

In conversation with some of the Indians, Alarcon learned of an ancient tradition to the effect that in a distant country there lived white and bearded men like himself. He met with many tribes along the river, with a great variety of dialects. They lived on the mountain side in communal huts [199] made of wood and plastered

---

J. H. Simpson, *Smithsonian Report for 1869*, p. 315, accepted the start from La Natividad, and then identified this Santiago with the port of Compostella, which was well known under the name of Xalisco. The distance of Acapulco from Colima would explain the considerable lapse of time before Alarcon was ready to start.

[199] The Cocopas are a division of the Yuman family, which in 1604-5 and earlier lived on the Rio Colorado five leagues above its mouth. At a later period they also extended into the mountains of Lower California, hence were confined almost exclusively to Mexico. The tribe was once very strong in numbers and, according to some authorities, could muster three hundred warriors. In 1775-6, Fr. Francisco Garcés estimated them at 3,000, but there are now only 800 in Lower California, in the valley of the Rio Colorado. The Cocopa were reputed to be less hostile than the Yuma or the Mohave, who frequently raided their villages; nevertheless they were sufficiently warlike to retaliate when necessary. Garcés said of them in 1776 that they had always been enemies of the Papago, Jalliquamai, and Cajuenche, but friendly to the Cuneil. Although spoken of as being physically inferior to the cognate tribes,

inside with mud, coming to the river in the summer to plant and returning after the harvest was over. A mountain was pointed out to him where lived a people who were at war with them, and who dressed in deer-skins, which they sewed with needles made from the bones of the deer, and who traded these hides for corn.

Alarcon now began to hear reports of Cibola, which he was told was distant a journey of thirty days. Further on he heard the story of the death of Estevan and that of the hounds which had accompanied him. He also met with natives who had visited Cibola, and later he heard the details of the death of Estevan and, much to his concern, that men with beards like himself, armed with swords and firearms, calling themselves Christians, had arrived at Cibola.

ALARCON HEARS REPORTS OF CIBOLA AND OF THE DEATH OF ESTEVAN

It was now only ten days' march to Cibola, but the region to be crossed was a wilderness. He tried to prevail upon his soldiers to carry the news to Coronado, but not a man would undertake the journey, except a negro slave, to whom, however, Alarcon would not give his consent.

Alarcon seems to have been well liked by his hosts, and they were loth to see him return, but, fearing that his identity would be discovered, he determined upon a return voyage, and, in two days and a half, with the rapid current of the river assisting him, he returned to his ships, where he found all on board well but anxious on account of his prolonged absence.

The companions of Alarcon were not disposed to make a second

---

the males are fully up to and in some cases rather above normal stature, and are well proportioned, while the females appear to be at least of ordinary size and are also well developed. Heintzlemann says: "They do so much resemble the Cuchan (Yuma) in arms, dress, manners, and customs it is difficult to distinguish one from the other. They depended for subsistence chiefly on corn, melons, pumpkins and beans, which they cultivated, adding native grass seeds, roots, mesquite beans, etc." The Cocopa houses of recent times range in character from the brush arbor for summer use to the wattled hut, plastered outside and inside with mud, for winter occupancy. Polygamy was formerly practised to some extent. They universally cremate their dead.— Hodge, F. W., *Handbook of American Indians.*

For an account of the Indians of Lower California in the eighteenth century, see the translation of Father Jacob Baegert's Narrative, by Charles Rau, in the *Report of the Smithsonian Institution,* for 1863 and 1864.

effort to unite with Coronado, but the commander was equally determined that he would, if within the range of possibilities, and, on the 14th day of September he again started up the river, accompanied by his head pilot, Camorano. On this occasion he went further than on his previous voyage, passing by the picturesque mountain range above the mouth of the Gila. The Indians made no attempt to prevent his advance except the planting of a barrier of reeds on

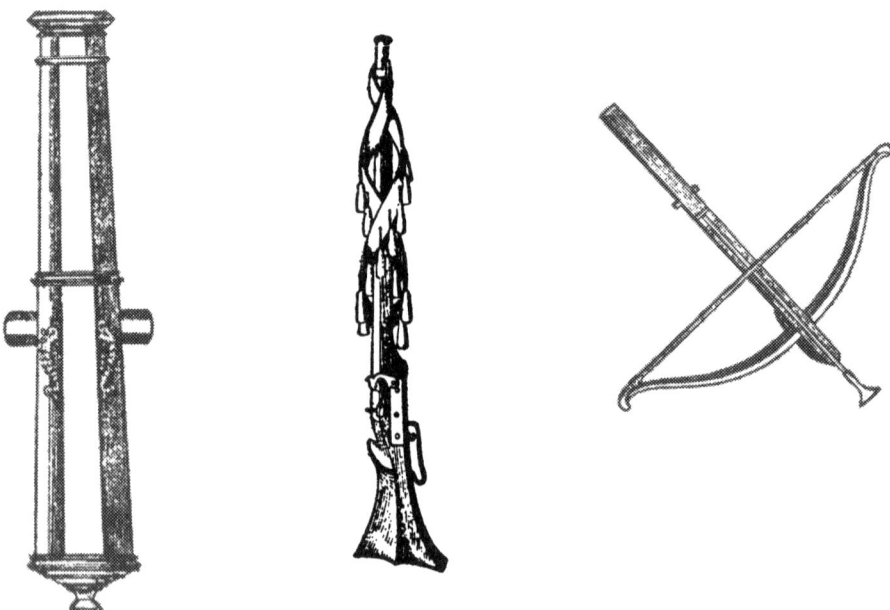

Arms of the Spaniards under Coronado

each side of the stream, through which he passed unharmed. It was here that Alarcon erected a great cross and secreted the letters which were afterwards found by Melchior Diaz. He also obtained from an Indian a rough map traced on paper of the course of the river and of the manner of distribution of the inhabitants along its banks.

Alarcon now determined to return to his ships; the voyage being uneventful, except that, while sailing down stream, an Indian woman came aboard his boat and refused to leave, saying that her husband had taken to himself another wife, by whom he had children, and that she would no longer live with him.[200]

Alarcon soon rejoined his ships and started on his return journey, keeping in sight of the coast and sending in land parties in a vain endeavor to find Coronado. In his story of the journey, Alarcon says: "I bring with me a great number of acts of possession made on that shore and river.[201]

---

[200] Bandelier, A. F., *Final Report*, part i, page 107, says: "The fact that Alarcon came up as high as Long Bend, that is higher than the mouth of the Gila, is doubted. But there is no reason to doubt the accuracy of his statement that he proceeded eighty-five leagues up the Colorado of the West coming from its mouth. It is alleged that Alarcon failed to notice the mouth of the Gila; and that he must have seen and noticed it in case he had gone higher up the Rio Colorado. But at the time of the year when Alarcon made his exploring expedition (August, September and the beginning of October) the Gila is so low that it would scarcely attract attention from anyone who, like Alarcon, was ascending the main stream in boats."

Bancroft, Hubert Howe, *North Mexican States*, p. 93, says: "Before turning back Alarcon says he passed a place where the river flowed between high mountains; he states also that he went eighty-five leagues — which may mean any distance from 100 to 250 miles, up the river; and further that he advanced four degrees beyond the latitude reached by Ulloa. The mountain pass with a medium estimate of distance would seem to indicate a part of the Colorado above the Gila and below Bill Williams Fork; but Melchior Diaz found Alarcon's letters two months later at a distance which he estimated to be only fifteen leagues from the mouth, so that if these were the only letters deposited, Alarcon's statement of distance is grossly exaggerated. It may also be noted that he mentions no stream corresponding to the Gila, as he naturally would have done had he passed its mouth."

Vanegas and other writers say that Alarcon reached 36 degrees. This comes from his instructions or from the statement that he went four degrees farther than Ulloa.

Mr. Bancroft, *ibid*, p. 94, says that most writers state that Mendoza was exceedingly displeased at Alarcon's want of success, though it is not easy to understand in what respect he failed to carry out the spirit of his instructions. Torquemada affirms that one cause of Mendoza's dissatisfaction was that fuller reports of the voyage were sent to the king than to himself, and that Alarcon claimed the honor that was due to the viceroy. He says further that Alarcon retired in great disgrace and sorrow to Cuernavaca, where he fell sick and died. But the current statements on this subject are doubtless erroneous, for there are extant, and bearing date of May 31, 1541, instructions (*Florida*, Col. Doc., i, 1-6) from Mendoza to Alarcon for a second voyage and a new attempt to communicate with Coronado and Melchior Diaz, whose departure from San Geronimo was already known. In the document Alarcon is spoken of as the discoverer of the Buena Guia, of which river he is ordered to make further explorations, as also of an estero said to exist at the head of the gulf. Another proposed voyage is mentioned, probably to be directed up the outer or Pacific Coast, under Zuñiga, with whom Alarcon was to communicate if possible. From another document, *Visita á Mendoza*, in Icazbalceta, Col. Doc., ii, 110, we learn that three vessels were made ready for this second voyage, which was prevented by the breaking out of the Guadalajara revolt, and during which Alarcon was stationed with thirty men at Autlan.

[201] Alarcon, *Voyage de Cibola*, p. 342.

Arriving at the port of Colima, Alarcon came across the fleet of Pedro Alvarado, and on account of some conflict of authority, he delivered his report to Don Luis del Castillo and sailed away at night, as he says "to avoid scandal." Afterwards he was directed by the viceroy to renew his efforts to communicate with Coronado but the expedition never sailed.

Coronado's command was most anxious to proceed with the march to the north. The experiences they had gone through in the journey from Compostella to Culiacan were of the greatest value. The "young gentlemen" of the army had left Compostella with an abundant supply of luxurious furnishings and extra equipment. Many of them had received their first lessons in campaigning, and many of their notions as to what properly constituted a soldier's comfort and ease had changed, for, when the preparations for leaving Culiacan were under way, the citizens of that town received from their guests much of the clothing and other surplus baggage which was left behind because it was apparent that the expedition could not advance rapidly if encumbered in this manner and beside the pack animals were needed for the transportation of provisions and other necessary equipment for the soldiers.

CORONADO'S JOURNEY FROM CULIACAN TO CIBOLA

In the account given him by Melchior Diaz of the conditions and difficulties to be encountered in traveling through the country which he was about to enter, the food supply was declared to be so insufficient for the support of his army that the captain-general determined upon a division of his forces for this part of the journey. He made selection of seventy-five or eighty cavaliers, principally his personal friends, and twenty-five or thirty foot-soldiers and, with these, equipped for rapid marching, he hastened forward, clearing the way for the main body of the army, which was to follow more slowly, starting a fortnight after his departure. Under the orders of the viceroy, he named Hernandarias Saavedra, his lieutenant, to replace him in the government of the province during his absence, and Don Tristan de Arellano was appointed to succeed him in command of the army.

Accompanying this advance party were four priests, whose zealous eagerness to reach the unconverted natives of the Seven Cities was

Dancers' Rock — Pueblo of Walpi

so great that they were willing to leave the main portion of the army without a spiritual guide. Fortunately for those in the rear, after marching three days, one of the friars, Antonio Victorio, broke his leg and was sent back to Culiacan, which caused a little delay. The captain-general also endeavored to take with him a few sheep but these made the traveling so slow that he left them at the river Yaquimi. Again putting themselves en route, they traveled through the country without interruption, meeting with Indians who were invariably friendly, many of them having seen the friar Marcos on his previous journey, and all of whom expressed the greatest friendship for the Spaniards. They passed through the whole of the inhabited country and finally reached Chichilticalli. In arriving at this place, which had been described to them by Friar Marcos, Coronado followed the coast "bearing off to the left," as Mota Padilla says, "by an extremely rough way" to the river Sinaloa. The physical conditions encountered made it necessary to follow up the valley of this stream until he could find a passage across the mountains to the Yaquimi. He traveled along this river for some distance and then crossed to the Sonora.[202] At Chichilticalli [203] the party made camp for two days, in order to secure rest for the horses, which had begun to give out, as a result of over-loading, rough roads, and poor food. The captain-general was very much disheartened for

---

[202] Winship, George Parker, *Coronado Expedition*, note p. 386, says: "Coronado's description of this portion of the route, in the letter of August 3, is abbreviated, he says, because it was accompanied by a map. As this is lost, I am following here, as I shall do throughout the introduction, Bandelier's identification of the route in his *Historical Introduction*, p. 10, and in his *Final Report*, part ii, pp. 407-409."

Mr. Bandelier, of all the modern writers, is the only one who personally traveled over and made every effort to identify the route taken by Coronado.

[203] Winship, George Parker, *ibid*, note, p. 387, says that "This 'red house' in the Nahuatl tongue, has been identified with the Casa Grande ruins in Arizona ever since the revival of interest in Coronado's journey, which followed the explorations in the southwestern portions of the United States during the second quarter of the last century. Bandelier's study of the descriptions given by those who saw the 'Red House' in 1539 and 1540, however, shows conclusively that the conditions at Casa Grande do not meet the requirements for Chichilticalli. Bandelier objects to Casa Grande because it is white, although he admits that it may once have been covered with the reddish paint of the Indians. This would suit Mota Padilla's explanation that the place was named from a house there which was daubed over with colored earth — *almagre*, as the natives called it. This is the Indian name for red ochre. Bandelier thinks that Coronado reached the edge of the wilderness, the White Mountain Apache reservation in Arizona, by way of the San Pedro river and Arivaypa creek."

he had as yet seen nothing that was encouraging. The country, for the most part, was mountainous and barren and inhabited by miserable Indians. Chichilticalli, instead of being a fine large town, as he had been led to believe, dwindled down to a single ruin. The assurances which he received from his companions that wonderful things were further on did not restore his spirits, for he had been so often deceived that he could no longer believe them.

The prospect was very gloomy, but Coronado determined to advance and left Chichilticalli and entering the wilderness traveled to the northeast. During fifteen days they marched across the sandy and barren desert, almost dead with thirst and wearied by fatigues of the terrible march. At the end of fifteen days they came to a narrow river where they camped and called the stream the Rio Vermejo on account of the reddish color of the water.

Here they saw the first Indians of the country who fled as soon as they were discovered. The next evening when within about two leagues of Cibola, they saw some Indians watching their movements from a high mesa that could not be reached. When the army came into view the natives raised piercing cries that spread alarm among the Spaniards, and Castañeda says that some of the soldiers were so frightened that they "saddled their horses wrong-end foremost." The soldiers did their utmost to capture some of these Indians, but were unsuccessful. The following day Coronado entered the inhabited country and came in sight of the far-famed Cibola, but they were so much disappointed in its appearance that the soldiers broke out in maledictions against the friar Marcos.[204]

The next day the captain-general ordered an advance upon the first town, which was Hawaikúh, a small village of two hundred houses, about fifteen miles southwest of the present Zuñi. The disappoint-

---

[204] Castañeda, Pedro de, *Relacion*: "Such were the curses that some hurled at Friar Marcos that I pray God may protect him from them."

Mota Padilla, p. 113, says: "They reached Tzibola, which was a village divided into two parts, which were encircled in such a way as to make the village round, and the houses adjoining three and four stories high, with doors opening on a great court or plaza, leaving one or two doors in the wall, so as to go in and out. In the middle of the plaza there is a hatch-way or trap-door, by which they go down to a subterranean hall, the roof of which was of large pine beams, and a little hearth in the floor, and the walls plastered. The Indian men stayed there days and nights playing (gaming) and the women brought them food, and this was the way the Indians of the neighboring villages lived."

This *kiva* of Hawaikúh was probably the first ever seen by the Spaniards.

ment of the soldiers was great, as the historian of the expedition says, "it looked as if it had been crumpled up altogether. There are mansions in New Spain which make a better appearance at a distance." The village stood upon a rocky mesa of no very great height and overlooked the plains that extended on the southern side of the Rio Zuñi. The entrance was narrow and crooked, and, in the plain below, were the irrigated "fields" mentioned by Coronado. No women or children were to be seen but warriors were there in plenty to defend the town. As the Spaniards drew near the Indians came out to meet them. The captain-general sent forward two friars and two officers and a body of cavalry, but, as these approached, they were met with a volley of arrows, and were so closely pressed that Coronado, giving the war cry of "Santiago," charged upon them and drove them into the town. This was next attacked but was not taken without great effort. Its only approach consisted of a narrow and steep pathway that led from the valley to the top of the rock, and this the Indians had prepared to defend. As Coronado advanced he was received with a volley of arrows, and large stones were hurled down upon his men. Coronado himself was stricken to the earth and would have been killed had it not been for Don Garcia Lopez de Cardenas, who came to his aid. As Coronado describes this: "I ordered the musketeers and cross-bowmen to begin the attack and drive back the enemy from the defenses, so that they could not do us any injury. I assaulted the walls on one side, where I was told there was a scaling ladder, and there was also a gate. But the cross-bowmen broke all the strings of their cross-bows and the musketeers could do nothing, because they had arrived so weak and feeble that they could scarcely stand on their feet. On this account the people who were on top were not prevented at all from defending themselves and doing us whatever injury they were able. Thus, for myself, they knocked me down to the ground twice with countless great stones which they threw down from above, and if I had not been protected by the very good head-piece I wore, I think that the outcome would have been bad for me. They picked me up from the ground, however, with two small wounds in my face and an arrow in my foot, and with many bruises on my arms and legs, and in this condition I retired from the battle, very weak. I think that if Don Garcia Lopez de Cardenas had not come to my

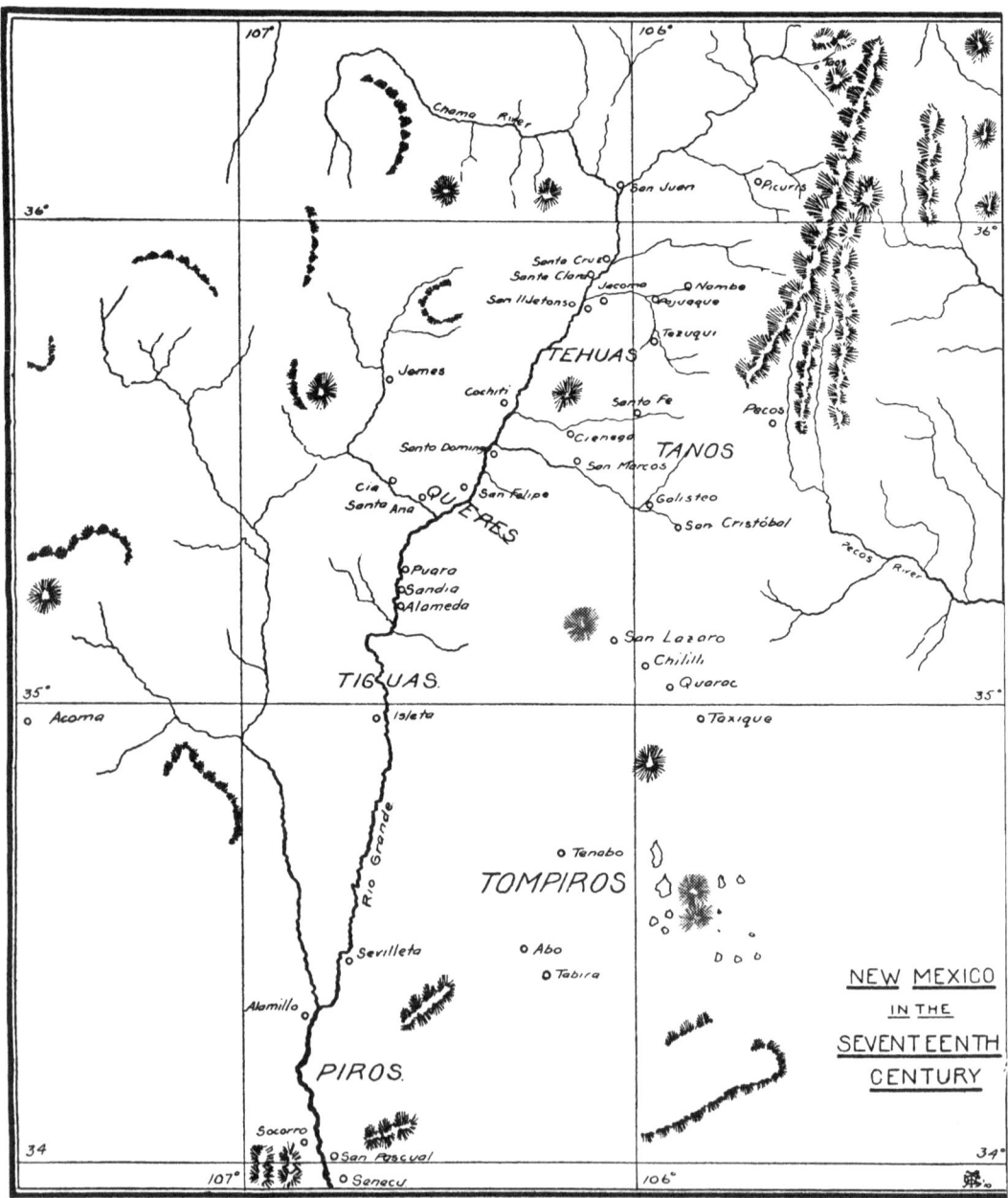

help, like a good cavalier, the second time that they knocked me to the ground, by placing his own body above mine, I should have been in much greater danger than I was. But, by the pleasure of God, these Indians surrendered, and their city was taken with the help of our Lord, and a sufficient supply of corn was found there to relieve our necessities. The army-master and Don Pedro de Tobar and Hernando de Alvarado and Pablo de Melgoza, the infantry captain, sustained some bruises, although none of them were wounded. Agoniez Quarez was hit in the arm by an arrow, and one Torres, who lived in Panuco, in the face by another, and two other footmen received slight arrow wounds. They all directed their attack against me because my armor was gilded and glittered and on this account I was hurt more than the rest, and not because I had done more or was farther in advance than the others; for all these gentlemen and soldiers bore themselves well, as was expected of them. I praise God that I am now well, although somewhat sore from the stones. Two or three other soldiers were hurt in the battle which we had on the plain, and three horses were killed, one that of Don Lopez and another that of Vigliega, and the third that of Don Alonzo Manrich, and seven or eight other horses were wounded; but the men, as well as the horses, have now recovered and are well.''[205]

Happy, indeed, were the travel-worn and battle-bruised explorers, when they found shelter in the abandoned pueblo, for there they also found food in plenty. Disappointed in the character of the village, led on as they had been by the stories of the friar Marcos, still they made careful examination and report of all they saw; the

---

[205] *Letter* from Coronado to Mendoza, August 3, 1540; *Relacion del Suceso*, Doc. de Indias, vol. xiv, p. 318, Account of what happened on the Journey which Francisco Vasquez made to discover Cibola, states:

"The day we reached the first village, part of them came out to fight us, and the rest stayed in the village and fortified themselves. It was not possible to make peace with these, although we tried hard enough, so it was necessary to attack them and kill some of them. The rest then drew back to the village, which was then surrounded and attacked. We had to withdraw, on account of the great damage they did us from the flat roofs, and we began to assault them from a distance with the artillery and muskets, and that afternoon they surrendered. Francisco Vasquez came out of it badly hurt by some stones, and I am certain, indeed, that he would have been there yet, if it had not been for the army-master, D. Garcia Lopez de Cardenas, who rescued him. When the Indians surrendered, they abandoned the village and went to the other villages, and as they left the houses we made ourselves at home in them.''

customs of the people, their manners of dress and living, and everything of consequence that would be of possible interest to the viceroy and the king. Within a very few days Coronado found time to write a letter to the viceroy, in which he calls attention to the misrepresentations of the friar.[206]

As the captain-general says in his letter to the viceroy, he found these natives to be well bred. In truth, the people were more civilized and intelligent than any with whom the Spaniards had met since leaving Mexico. Their clothing was made of skins and of cotton. The costume of the women differed from that of the men. The former wore a mantle over the shoulder fastened around the neck and passing under the right arm. The skins of which their garments were made were beautifully dressed. The hair was ar-

---

[206] Coronado, *Letter* to Mendoza, August 3, 1540: "It now remains for me to tell about this city and kingdom and province, of which the Father Provincial gave your Lordship an account. In brief, I can assure you in reality he has not told the truth in a single thing that he said, but everything is the reverse of what he said, except the name of the city and the large stone houses. For, although they are not decorated with turquoises, nor made of lime nor of good bricks, nevertheless they are very good houses, with three and four and five stories, where there are very good apartments and good rooms with corridors, and some very good rooms underground and paved, which are made for winter, and are something like a sort of hot baths. The ladders which they have for their houses are all movable and portable, which are taken up and placed wherever they please. They are made of two pieces of wood with rounds like ours. The Seven Cities are seven little villages, all having the kind of houses I have described. They are all within a radius of five leagues. They are all called the kingdom of Cevola, and each has its own name and no single one is called Cevola, but altogether are called Cevola. This one which I have called a city I have named Granada, partly because it has some similarity to it, as well as out of regard to your Lordship. In this place where I am now lodged, there are perhaps 200 houses, all surrounded by a wall, and it seems to me that with the other houses, which are not so surrounded, there might be altogether 500 families. There is another town nearby, which is one of the seven, but somewhat larger than this, and another of the same size as this, and the other four are somewhat smaller. I send them all to your Lordship, painted with the route. The skin on which the painting is made was found here with other skins. The people of the towns seem to me to be of ordinary size and intelligent, although I do not think that they have the judgment and intelligence which they ought to have to build these houses in the way which they have, for most of them are entirely naked . . . and they have painted mantles like the one which I send to your Lordship. They do not raise cotton, because the country is very cold, but they wear mantles, as may be seen by the exhibits which I send. It is also true that some cotton thread was found in their houses. They wear the hair on their heads like the Mexicans. They have all good figures, and are well bred. I think that they have a quantity of turquoises which they have removed with the rest of their goods, except the corn, when I arrived, because I did not find any women nor any men under 15 years or over 60, except two or three old men who remained in command of all the other men and warriors."

ranged in a peculiar manner, being done up behind the ear "in the shape of a wheel which resembles the handle of a cup." Corn was raised as an article of food, the stalks being very short, the ears starting out very near the ground, and containing seven or eight hundred grains. This was a matter of great astonishment to the Spaniards, and was said to excel anything seen in the Indies. Many wild and ferocious animals were found, including bears, in great numbers, lions, wild-cats, hyenas, and beavers. A few turquoises were found but no gold or silver.

The customs and manners of the people attracted a great deal of attention and were carefully noted. A man married but once, and if he lost his wife, he was condemned to a life of single-blessedness forever thereafter. The women were well treated, but two of them were not permitted to enter a place at the same time, such conduct being considered sacrilegious. They had very little government and no caciques or councilors. It was believed that their religion was related to the worship of the Aztecs. They had priests, who were selected from among the older persons, and it was the duty of these to regulate the manner of living for the people. They preached every morning at sunrise. They were a peaceful and laborious people. The cross was known to them, and was an emblem of peace. The dead were cremated, and with them the instruments of their trade.

The captain-general remained at Cibola for some time and during this period received a delegation of Indians who came to him asking for peace. Naturally Coronado was pleased with their offer, but on the very day following their coming, the Indians abandoned their towns and escaped to the mountains, taking with them their women, children, and all their goods and supplies.[207]

Not long after this interview with the natives, the captain-general was advised that the Indians were fortifying a pueblo situate on a mesa or high table land near by. Coronado was not long in reducing

---

[207] Coronado, *Letter* to Mendoza, August 3, 1540: "Three days after I captured this city, some of the Indians who lived here came to offer to make peace. They brought me some turquoises and poor mantles, and I received them in his Majesty's name with as good speech as I could, making them understand the purpose of my coming to this country. . . After this they returned to their houses and suddenly, the next day, they packed up their goods and property, their women and children and fled to the hills, leaving their towns deserted, with only some few remaining in them."

this province, and thereafter he despatched Don Pedro de Tovar, with a company of cavalry and foot-men, to visit the province [208] of Tusayan, of which he had heard from the natives of Cibola. This was the modern Moqui. This province, he was told, contained seven cities like those of Cibola; that the houses were several stories high, and that the inhabitants were great warriors. Accompanying the

---

[208] The Moqui Pueblo Indians are in Apache county, Arizona; this section is the Tusayan of Coronado, to which he sent Tovar. The nearest railroad station to the Moquis is Holbrook, Arizona. They are known among themselves by the name of Hopi, or Ho-pi-tuh-lei-nyu-muh, meaning a peaceful people. In the Moqui language, the word ''Moki'' means dead. Their homes, consisting of seven pueblos, or villages, are situated at an elevation of from 700 to 800 feet above the valleys on the almost level tops of three long mesas or table-lands. These three mesas project in a southwesterly direction from the main table-land into the desert south. On the first or eastern mesa, about three miles in length, are the pueblos of Si-kum-na-vi, Tewa, and Walpi; on the second, or middle, about three and one-half miles long, are the pueblos of Mishongnovi, Shimpovi, and Shipaulovi; on the third, or western, is Oraibi, which is the largest, containing about one thousand inhabitants.

The erection and final abandonment of their villages by the various Hopi clans during their migrations and successive shiftings have left many ruins, now consisting largely of mounds, some near the present pueblos and others remote from them. Ruins of villages, which the Hopi traditions ascribe to their ancestors, are found as far north as the Rio Colorado, west of Flagstaff, Arizona, south to the valleys of the Verde and the Gila rivers and east to the Rio Grande in New Mexico. Therefore, although Shoshonean in language, the present Hopi population and culture are composite, made up of accretions from widely divergent sources and from people of different linguistic stocks. Some of the Hopi ruins have been explored by the Bureau of American Ethnology. One of the most celebrated of these is Awatobi on the Antelope Mesa, the walls of whose mission church, built probably in 1629, are still partly standing.

Sik-yat-ki, another large and well-known ruin, in the foot-hills of the East Mesa, was occupied in pre-historic times by Kokop clans of Keresan people from the Rio Grande; they had attained a very highly artistic development, as exhibited by their pottery, which is probably the finest ware ever manufactured by Indians north of Mexico.

The original clans of Walpi are said to have occupied three sites after their arrival in the Hopi country, settling first on the terrace west of the East Mesa, then higher up and toward the south where the foundation walls of a Spanish mission church can still be traced. From this point they moved to the present Walpi on the summit of the mesa, apparently soon after the Pueblo revolt of 1680.

The old pueblo of Shon-go-po-vi lay in the foot-hills at the base of the Middle Mesa, below the present pueblo of that name. This town was inhabited at the time of the Coronado expedition, and near it was built a church, the old walls of which, up to a few years since, were used as a corral for sheep and goats.

The ruins of old Mish-ong-no-vi lie below the present pueblo. The walls are barely traceable. From graves near this old pueblo many fine specimens of pottery have been taken. There are many other ruins located on the Antelope Mesa; others on the Little Colorado, and near Winslow are ruins known by the name of Ho-mo-lo-bi.

Indian of the Pueblo of Pecos, now living at Jemez, one of the last of his race

command under Tovar was a friar named Juan de Padilla, who had been a soldier in his youth, but now belonged to the order of Franciscans.

The coming of the Spaniards, the conflict with the inhabitants of Cibola, the horses which the Spaniards rode, the firearms which discharged the lightning, all had been noised around the country in a very brief space of time. Knowing that the news of their coming had spread far and wide, Tovar was of the opinion that the people of Tusayan would be carefully watching whether or not they were to be visited by the "ferocious Spaniards who rode great animals and devoured men." Great was his surprise, then, that he was able to march to their province without being discovered. Tovar and his command came within sight of one of the Moqui villages about dark, and, crossing some cultivated fields, approached so near to the houses that they heard people talking within. Here, still undiscovered, they camped for the night. The following morning they were seen by the Indians, who immediately sounded the alarm throughout the village. The warriors turned out armed with bows and arrows and advanced against the Spaniards. The latter sent forward their interpreter to hold a talk. He was received in a friendly manner, but was informed that they would not permit the strangers to enter their village. The Indians traced a line upon the sand, which they forbid any of the Spaniards to cross, but one of the soldiers rode his horse over the line, when he was assaulted by one of the Indians. The friar, Juan de Padilla, could not restrain the military ardor of his youth and advised his captain to attack the Indians at once, saying, "In truth, I know not why we have come hither." The order to advance was given, the charge was made at full speed, when the Indians broke and fled to their village but did not reach it before a large number had been slain by the Spaniards. The latter did not at once seek to enter the village, but made camp at a convenient place near by. Shortly the Indians came out to see them, loaded with presents, and gave in their submission in the name of the entire province and asked for an alliance. The presents included tanned leather, flour, fir-nuts, corn, poultry (turkeys), and some turquoises, all of which they desired Tovar to accept as a mark of their good will. Toward evening the Spaniards entered and took possession of the village. The inhabitants lived much the same as did those of

Cibola, and were governed by a council of wise men; they also had governors and captains of war. Some of the chiefs informed Tovar that to the west there ran a great river and by ascending it they would find a nation with people of great stature. Having now accomplished the mission on which they had been sent, the Spaniards returned to Cibola and reported to the captain-general the result of the expedition.

The captain-general caused two skins to be painted by the Indians, showing the beasts, birds, and fish of the region, and a picture of the town of Cibola. These, with some other specimens of semi-precious stones, garnets, turquoises, and peridots, together with a letter to the viceroy, he put in the hands of Juan Gallego, whom he sent to Mexico; with him went Melchior Diaz, sent by the captain-general to join the army left in command of Arellano. They were accompanied by the friar Marcos, who, as Castañeda remarks, "did not think it was safe for him to stay in Cibola, seeing that his report had turned out to be entirely false; because the kingdoms that he had told about had not been found, nor the populous cities, nor the wealth of gold, nor the precious stones which he had reported, nor the fine clothes, nor other things that had been proclaimed from the pulpits."

MELCHIOR DIAZ, ACCOMPANIED BY FR. MARCOS, RETURNS TO THE ARMY, LEFT IN COMMAND OF ARELLANO

About the middle of September, Gallego, Diaz, and the friar joined Arellano on the Sonora river, where the latter had established a settlement and from which he had sent an expedition down the river toward the sea in search of the fleet under Alarcon. Soon after the arrival of Diaz, who brought orders from Coronado to that effect, Arellano and the army started on its march to join the captain-general at Cibola.

After the departure of Arellano with the army, Diaz, who had been left in command of the settlement, which consisted of about eighty persons, determined to go in search of the fleet under Alarcon. For this purpose he fitted out a company of twenty-five selected men and started in a northwesterly direction from the river Sonora, and traveled until he reached the Colorado river. Here he found the Yuma Indians living in great subterranean houses with straw-covered roofs, in some of which as many as one hundred people gathered at one time. These Indians were of great height and very strong.[209]

During the winter season these Indians carried with them a firebrand with which they warmed their bodies, and it was for this reason that Diaz called the river Rio del Tizon or Firebrand.

It was at this point on the Colorado river that Diaz heard that vessels had been seen at a point three days' journey down the river.

MELCHIOR DIAZ HEARS OF THE FLEET OF ALARCON AND FINDS HIS LETTERS

He immediately commenced a march down stream, and later found a tree upon which was cut: "Alarcon came as far as this; there are letters at the foot of this tree." He began a rigid search for other evidences of Alarcon's visit, and in digging around this tree found the letters concealed by Alarcon, which informed him that the fleet had returned to New Spain. Diaz was greatly disappointed at not finding the commander of the fleet, and immediately began a journey up stream, looking for a suitable ford. After a march consuming five or six days, a place was found where they attempted to cross the river on rafts. While the command was crossing, armed Indians began gathering in force. Diaz was equal to the emergency, however; seizing one of the friendly Indians, who was helping in the building of the rafts, he put him to the torture and, in this manner, ascertained that an attack had been planned while the Spanish forces were divided, one-half on either side of the river, and that the Indians on the rafts were to cast overboard those of the Spaniards who were on the rafts with them.[210]

---

[209] Castañeda, *Relacion*, Winship, *Coronado Expedition*, p. 485: "When they carry anything, they can take a load of more than three or four hundred weight on their heads. Once when our men wished to fetch a log for the fire and six men were unable to carry it, one of these Indians is reported to have come and raised it in his arms, put it on his head alone and carried it very easily."

Mota Padilla, cap. xxxii, p. 158, describes an attempt to catch one of these Indians.

[210] Castañeda, *Relacion*, Winship's translation: "While the rafts were being made, a soldier who had been out around the camp saw a large number of armed men go across to a mountain, where they were waiting till the soldiers should cross the river. He reported this, and an Indian was quietly shut up, in order to find out the truth, and, when they tortured him, he told all the arrangements that had been made. These were, that when our men were crossing and part of them had got over and part were on the river and part were waiting to cross, those who were on the rafts should drown those whom they were taking across and the rest of their force should make an attack on both sides of the

This Indian was drowned by order of Diaz so that the savages would not know that he had discovered their plot, and, the following day, the attack was made, Diaz driving them into the mountains and successfully crossing the river with his men and horses. He then followed the right bank of the river in a southeasterly direction in search of the coast.[211]

Having proceeded on his journey, one day a greyhound belonging to one of the soldiers chased some sheep which were being taken along for food. When the captain noticed this he threw his lance at the dog while his horse was running, so that it stuck up in the ground, and not being able to stop his horse he went over the lance so that it nailed him through the thighs, and the iron came out behind, rupturing his bladder. On account of this accident to Diaz, the command turned back and were compelled each day to battle with Indians. Diaz lived twenty days and was buried in the sandy wastes of the desert. The soldiers quickly returned to Sonora, which they reached in safety. Upon their arrival, Alcaraz, who had been left in command by Diaz, sent word to Coronado of the death of Diaz,[212] also notifying him that some of the soldiers had been mutin-

DEATH OF MELCHIOR DIAZ

---

river. If they had as much discretion and courage as they had strength and power, the attempt would have succeeded."

[211] Castañeda, *Relacion*, p. 501: "Continuing in the direction they had been going, they came to some sand-banks of hot ashes which it was impossible to cross without being drowned as in the sea. The ground they were standing on trembled like a sheet of paper, so that it seemed as if there were lakes underneath them. It seemed wonderful and like something infernal, for the ashes to bubble up here in several places."

[212] Mota Padilla, p. 158, gives an account of the journey and death of Diaz, as follows: "He started before the end of September, going into the rough country west of Corazones valley, and, finding only a few naked, weak-spirited Indians, who had come, as he understood, from the land on the farther side of the water, i. e., Lower California. He hurried across this region and descended the mountains on the west, where he encountered the Indian giants, some of whom the army had already seen. Turning toward the north, or northwest, he proceeded to the sea coast and spent several days among the Indians who fed him with corn which they raised and with fish. He travelled slowly up the coast until he reached the mouth of a river which was large enough for vessels to enter. The country was cold, and the Spaniards observed that when the natives thereabouts wished to keep warm, they took a burning stick and held it to their abdomens and shoulders. This curious habit led the Spaniards to name the river Firebrand — Rio del Tizon. Near the mouth of the river was a tree on which was written, 'A letter is at the foot of this.' Diaz dug down and found a jar wrapped so carefully that it was not even moist. The enclosed papers stated that 'Hernando de Alarcon reached this place in the year '40 with three ships, having been sent in search of Francisco Vasquez Coronado by the viceroy,

ous; that he had been compelled to sentence two of them to be hanged, but both had escaped.

Upon his return from the province of Tusayan, Captain Pedro de Tovar related to the captain-general all he had seen and heard of the Colorado river and the race of giants who lived along its banks. Coronado, without delay, sent Don Garcia Lopez de Cardenas and twelve companions to discover the river. Cardenas proceeded on his journey by way of the Moqui pueblos, who furnished him with guides, carrying with him provisions for twenty days' travel, as there was a great desert lying between Tusayan and the river which had to be crossed. They passed this desert in safety, suffering much from the cold, however, although it was in the summer time. The country was covered with a growth of low, stunted pine trees. Arriving at the banks of the river, they found these so high and rugged that it was impossible to reach the water. From the top of the bank the stream did not appear more than a fathom in breadth, while the Indians told them it was half a league wide. Cardenas and his command marched several days along the ridge of mountains searching for an opening by which they might descend to the stream; but there appeared one continuous barrier of almost perpendicular rock on either side, and far below the river could be seen like a silver thread. At one point the bank

DON GARCIA LOPEZ DE CARDENAS DISCOVERS THE GRAND CANYON OF THE COLORADO

D. Antonio Mendoza; and after crossing the bar at the mouth of the river and waiting many days without obtaining any news, he was obliged to depart, because the ships were being eaten by worms,' the terrible *teredo navalis*.

"Diaz determined to cross the river, hoping that the country might become more attractive. The passage was accomplished with considerable danger, by means of certain large wicker baskets, which the natives coated with a sort of bitumen, so that the water could not leak through. Five or six Indians caught hold of each of these and swam across, guiding it and transporting the Spaniards with their baggage and being supported in turn by the raft. Diaz marched inland for four days, but not finding any people in the country, which became steadily more barren, he decided to return to Corazones valley. The party made its way back to the country of the giants without accident, and then one night while Diaz was watching the camp, a small dog began to bark and chase the flock of sheep which the men had taken with them for food. Unable to call the dog off, Diaz started after him on horseback and threw his lance while on the gallop. The weapon stuck up in the ground, and before Diaz could stop or turn his horse, which was running loose, the socket pierced his groin. The soldiers could do little to relieve his sufferings and he died before they reached the settlement, where they arrived January 18, 1541.''

seemed less precipitous and an attempt was made to descend. Three of the party, Captain Melgoza, Juan Galeras, and a private soldier made the effort, and descended until those on the rim above lost sight of them. They did not return until four o'clock in the afternoon and reported that they were unable to accomplish one-third of the distance; that the descent was very dangerous and difficult, and that the rocks which, from the top appeared no taller than a man, were found, when they reached them, to be higher than the tower of the cathedral of Seville, and that the river appeared very large to them at that point.[213] Finding the grand canyon an impassable barrier to further progress westward, Cardenas returned and made his report to the captain-general.

While Cardenas was off in search of the Grand Canyon and the race of giants, a deputation of Indians from the province of Cicuyé [214] came to visit Coronado. They informed him that they had heard of his arrival and came to offer their services, and asked that if the Spaniards intended visiting their country, they be treated as allies and friends. They were accompanied by one of their chiefs, a very handsome man, whom the Spaniards called "Bigotes," on account of the long mustaches which he wore. They brought many presents of tanned

CORONADO HEARS OF THE PROVINCE OF CICUYÉ AND SENDS HERNANDO DE ALVARADO IN SEARCH OF IT

---

[213] Castañeda, *Relacion*, Winship's trans., p. 429; *Rel. del Suceso*, Winship, p. 574: "Having gone 50 leagues west of Tuzan, and 80 from Cibola, he (Cardenas) found the edge of the river down which it was impossible to find a path for a horse in any direction, or even for a man on foot, except in one very difficult place, where there was a descent for almost two leagues. The sides were such a steep rocky precipice that it was scarcely possible to see the river, which looks like a brook from above, although it is half as large again as that of Seville, according to what they say, so that although they sought for a passage with great diligence, none was found for a long distance, during which for several days they were in great need of water, which could not be found, and they could not approach that of the river, although they could see it, and on this account Don Garcia Lopez was forced to return."

[214] Brower's *Memoirs*, Hodge, F. W., vol. ii, p. 59: "Pecos is the only new Mexican pueblo that answers these descriptions of Cicuyé."

Bandelier, A. F., *Final Report*, part i, p. 127, says Cicuyé is Tshi-qui-te or Tzi-quit-e of the Pecos.

For a complete description of the pueblo of Cicuyé see *Ruins in the Valley of the Rio Pecos*, Bandelier.

Cicuyé, now almost entirely obliterated, lies about a mile and a half from the station of Rowe, in the county of San Miguel, New Mexico, on the line of the Atchison, Topeka and Santa Fé Railway.

skins and bucklers for the captain-general, who gave them in return some necklaces of beads and some bells, with which they were greatly pleased, as they had never seen any such ornaments before. They gave Coronado much information about the country from which they came, particularly of the buffalo, a picture of which was painted on the body of one of the Indians. The captain-general was much interested in their story and resolved to send an expedition into their country for the purpose of exploring it.

The captain-general placed Hernando de Alvarado in command of this expedition, who, with twenty men, at the end of August, 1540, together with the friar Juan de Padilla, set out upon the journey. They followed a trail which led from Hawaikúh almost directly to Acoma,[215] passing by a number of abandoned pueblos, among the others that of "Marata," which had been described by Friar Marcos.

---

[215] The people of Acoma are a tribe of the Keresan family, whose village or pueblo is situate on a rock mesa, 357 feet in height, about sixty miles west of the Rio Grande, in Valencia county, New Mexico. The native name is A-ko-me, people of the white rock, and is now commonly pronounced A-ko-ma. The native name for the town is A-ko. Friar Marcos de Niza reported this town to the viceroy Mendoza by the name of Acus. Coronado called the place Acuco. The strength of the place was noted by the Spaniards from the time of Coronado down. It is the oldest inhabited village in the United States. When visited by Hernando de Alvarado it was supposed to contain about two hundred houses. In the year 1583, Antonio de Espejo also visited Acoma; he mentions the dizzy trail cut in the rock and the cultivated fields, two leagues distant. In 1598, the village was visited by Juan de Oñate, at that time governor of New Mexico. The Indians, in the time of Coronado, living in the other pueblos visited by him, regarded the Acoma as very warlike and "feared by the whole country round about." Castañeda says they were robbers or regarded as such. Juan de Salvidar visited the pueblo in December, 1598, with thirty men; they were surprised by the Indians, fourteen of the Spaniards being killed outright, including Salvidar and two other captains. Four of the Spaniards were compelled to leap over the cliff, three of whom were miraculously saved. In January, 1599, an avenging party of seventy Spaniards were sent under command of a brother of Salvidar, who, after a battle, which lasted three days, succeeded in killing about half of the tribe of about three thousand and in partly burning the town. The first missionary labor performed at Acoma was by Fr. Geronimo Zarate-Salmeron, prior to 1629, but Fray Juan Ramirez, who went to Acoma in the spring of 1629 and remained there many years, was its first permanent missionary and the builder of the first church, which was replaced in or after 1699 by the present great adobe structure. The Indians of Acoma took part in the great uprising of 1680, killing their priest, Fr. Lucas Maldonado, but, largely on account of their isolation, and the inaccessibility of the village, they were not so severely dealt with by the Spaniards under De Vargas, as were some of the eastern pueblos. De Vargas made an attempt to reconquer the village in August, 1696, but he succeeded only in destroying their crops and in capturing five warriors. The Indians held out until July 6, 1699, when they submitted to Governor Cubero, who changed the name of the pueblo from

After a journey of five days Alvarado arrived at Acoma, a very strong place built upon a rock, the inhabitants of which were great "robbers" and much dreaded by the people of the surrounding country. The rock upon which the town stood was very high, and on three sides the ascent was perpendicular. The only means of reaching the top was by ascending a stairway cut in the solid rock. The first flight of steps numbered two hundred, which could be ascended without much difficulty, when a second flight of one hundred more commenced. These were narrower and more difficult of ascent than the first; and when surmounted there still remained about twelve feet to the top, which could only be ascended by putting the hands and feet in holes cut in the rock. On the top was a large pile of stones for the purpose of hurling down upon an enemy who should attempt the ascent of the stairway. There was space enough on top to store a great quantity of provisions and to build cisterns for the purpose of holding water and snow.

The Indians came down off the mesa brandishing their bows and arrows and marched out on the plain to meet the Spaniards, and refused to receive any proposition from them whatever. Like the Moquis, they drew a mark in the sand and ordered the Spaniards

---

San Estevan de Acoma to San Pedro; but the former name was afterwards restored and is now retained. The population of the Acoma dwindled from about 1,500 in 1680 to 1,052 in 1760. In 1782 the mission was reduced to a *visita* of Laguna, and by the close of the century its population was only a few more than eight hundred. At present (1910) the pueblo has about five hundred and fifty inhabitants. The Acoma are agriculturists, cultivating their lands by irrigation; they raise corn, wheat, melons, squashes, and hay crops of all kinds. They have quite large herds of sheep, goats, burros, and horses, and some cattle. In early historic times, and in pre-historic as well, they raised large flocks of domesticated turkeys. They make excellent pottery but do very little weaving. The villages which, according to tradition, were occupied by these people after leaving Shi-pa-pu, their mythical place of origin in the north, were Kash-ka-chu-ti, Wash-pa-chu-ka, Ku-cjt-ya, Tsi-a-ma, Ta-pit-si-a-ma, and Kat-si-mo, the Enchanted Mesa. Katsimo is the name of a very precipitous mesa rising 430 feet above the basin of Acoma and about three miles northeast of the present pueblo. According to tradition its summit was the site of one of several prehistoric villages which the Acoma successively occupied during their southwesterly migration from Shi-pa-pu. The tradition relates that during a storm a part of the rock fell and some of the inhabitants, cut off from the valley beneath, perished. The site was thenceforth abandoned, the survivors moving to another mesa on the summit of which they erected the present pueblo of Acoma. Katsimo is inaccessible by ordinary means, but it was scaled in 1897 by a party representing the Bureau of American Ethnology, and evidences of its former occupancy observed, thus verifying the native tradition.

Hodge, F. W., in *Century Magazine*, lvi, 15 May, 1898.
Lummis, Charles F., *The Enchanted Mesa*, New Mexico David, 39, 1891.

Courtesy Bureau American Ethnology
Water Vessels from Cochití

not to cross it. Alvarado, seeing that there was no chance for a peaceable occupation of the place, determined to attack the Indians. He began making his preparations, when the Indians came forward and sued for peace. Castañeda says that the Indians went through the forms of making peace, which were to "touch the horses and take their sweat and rub themselves with it and to make crosses with the fingers of their hands. But to make the most secure peace, they put their hands across each other, and they keep this peace inviolably." After the surrender the Indians presented the Spaniards with turkeys, bread, dressed deer-skins, grains of the fir-cone, flour, and corn.

Continuing on, Alvarado, in due time, arrived at Tiguex.[216]

[216] The official account of the journey to Cicuyé is given by Alvarado himself in his *Account of what Hernando de Alvarado and Friar Juan de Padilla Discovered going in Search of the South Sea*, Pacheco y Cardenas, *Doc. de Ind.*, vol. iii, p. 511. Translation found in *Transcript*, Boston, Oct. 14, 1893. Alvarado says: "We set out from Granada (Civola) on Sunday, the day of the beheading of Saint John the Baptist, the 29th of August, in the year 1540, on the way to Coco (Acoma). After we had gone two leagues, we came to an ancient building like a fortress, and a league beyond this we found another one, and yet farther on another, and beyond these we found an ancient city, very large, entirely destroyed, although a large part of the wall was standing, which was six times as tall as a man, the wall well made of good worked stone, with gates and gutters like a city in Castile. Half a league or more beyond this we found another ruined city, the walls of which must have been very fine, built of very large granite rocks, as high as a man and from there up of very good quarried stone. Here two roads separate, one to Chia (Cia) and the other to Coco (Acoma); we took this latter and reached that place, which is one of the strongest places that we have seen, because the city is on a high rock, with such a rough ascent that we repented having gone up to the place. The houses have three or four stories; the people are the same sort as those of the province of Cibola; they have plenty of food, of corn and beans, and fowls like those of New Spain. From here we went to a very good lake or marsh, where there are trees like those of Castile, and from there we went to a river, which we named Our Lady (Nuestra Señora), because we reached it the evening before her day in the month of September (September 8th). We sent the cross by a guide to the villages in advance, and the next day people came from twelve villages, the chief men and the people in order, those of one village behind those of another, and they approached the tent to the sound of a pipe, and with an old man for spokesman. In this fashion they came into the tent and gave me food and clothes and skins they had brought, and I gave them some trinkets, and with this they went off.

"This river of Our Lady (Rio Grande) flows through a very wide, open plain sowed with corn plants; there are several groves, and there are twelve villages. The houses are of earth, two stories high; the people have a good appearance, more like laborers than a war-like rare; they have a large supply of corn, beans, melons and fowl in great plenty; they clothe themselves with cotton and the skins of cows and dresses of the feathers of birds; they wear their hair short. Those who have the most authority among them are the old men; we regarded them as witches because they say that they go up into the sky and other things

Here the inhabitants received him with peaceful demonstrations, largely because Bigotes was with him, he being a powerful chief and much feared in that country. Alvarado was so much pleased with the appearance of Tiguex that he sent a messenger to Coronado recommending that he bring the army and spend the winter at that place. Thence the Spaniards continued their march, and in five days arrived at Cicuyé, a large and strongly fortified village. Here, also, they were received in a most friendly manner. When the inhabitants saw them approach they marched out to receive them, and escorted them into town to the music of drums and flutes. Alvarado was presented with goods and turquoises, of which latter there were many in the province. Here Alvarado remained for some days recovering from the fatigues of his march from Cibola. While at Cicuyé [217] they met

ALVARADO PROCEEDS TO TIGUEX AND CICUYÉ

---

of the same sort. In this province there are seven other villages, destroyed and depopulated by those Indians who paint their eyes, of whom the guides will tell your Grace; they say that these live in the same region as the cows, and that they have corn and houses of straw.

"Here the people from the outlying provinces came to make peace with me, and as your Grace may see in this memorandum, there are 80 villages there of the same sort as I have described, and among them one which is located on some streams; it is divided into twenty divisions, which is something remarkable; the houses have three stories of mud walls and three others made of small wooden boards, and on the outside of the three stories with the mud wall, they have three balconies; it seemed to us that there were nearly 15,000 persons in this village. The country is very cold; they do not raise fowls nor cotton; they worship the sun and water. We found mounds of dirt outside of the place, where they are buried.

"In the places where crosses were raised, we saw them worship these. They made offerings to these of their powder and feathers, and some left the blankets they had on. They showed so much zeal that some climbed up on the others bringing ladders, while some held them, went up to tie strings, so as to fasten the flowers and feathers.''

[217] Castañeda, *Relacion*, etc. This historian's account of the pueblo of Cicuyé is very accurate, when one compares the foundation and old wall remains of this ruin as they appear today. He says: "Cicuyé is a village of nearly five hundred warriors, who are feared throughout that country. It is square, situated on a rock with a large court-yard in the middle, containing the estufas. The houses are all alike, four stories high. One can go over the top of the whole village without there being a street to hinder. There are corridors going all around it at the first two stories, by which one can go around the whole village. They are like outside balconies, and they are able to protect themselves under these. The houses do not have doors below, but they use ladders, which can be lifted up like a draw-bridge, and so go up to the corridors which are on the inside of the village. As the doors of the houses open on the corridor of that story, the corridor serves as a street. The houses that open on the plain are right back of those that open on the court, and in time of war they

an Indian from a far-distant province, toward the east, whom they called the "Turk," because of his great resemblance to the people of that nation. He gave a most glowing account of the famous cities to be found in the country whence he came and of the abundance of gold and silver to be found there. His story so interested Alvarado that he felt but little interest in completing his expedition into the country where the buffalo abounded. However, taking this Indian for a guide, he continued his march until he obtained a view of the buffaloes, and then quickly hastened back to report to Coronado the result of his explorations.

The messenger despatched by Alvarado from Tiguex [218] reached

---

go through those behind them. The village is enclosed by a low wall of stone. There is a spring of water inside, which they are able to divert. The people of this village boast that no one has been able to conquer them and that they conquer whatever villages they wish. The people and their customs are like those of the other villages. Their virgins also go nude until they take husbands, because they say that if they do anything wrong then it will be seen, and so they do not do it. They do not need to be ashamed because they go around as they were born.''

[218] Castañeda's account of the province of Tiguex is very complete and very interesting; he says: ''The province of Tiguex contains twelve villages, situated on the bank of a great river; it is a valley about two leagues broad and bounded on the east by very high mountains covered with snow. Four villages are built at the foot of these mountains and three others on the heights.

''There are seven villages 7 leagues to the north, at Quirix, and the seven villages of the province of Hemes are 40 leagues northwest. It is 40 leagues north or east of Acha (Picurís) and 4 leagues southeast to Tutahaco, a province with eight villages. In general, these villages all have the same habits and customs, although some have some things in particular which the others have not. They are governed by the opinions of the elders. They all work together to build the villages, the women being engaged in making the mixture and the walls, while the men bring the wood and put it in place. They have no lime, but they make a mixture of ashes, coals and dirt which is almost as good as mortar, for when the house is to have four stories, they do not make the walls more than half a yard thick. They gather a great pile of twigs of thyme and sedge grass and set it afire, and when it is half coals and ashes they throw a quantity of dirt and water on it and mix it all together. They make round balls of this, which they use instead of stones after they are dry, fixing them with the same mixture, which comes to be like a stiff clay. Before they are married the young men serve the whole village in general, and fetch the wood that is needed for use, putting it in a pile in the court-yard of the villages, from which the women carry it to their houses. The young men live in the *estufas*, which are in the yards of the villages. They are underground, square or round, with pine pillars. Some were seen with twelve pillars and with four in the center as large as two men could stretch around. They usually had three or four pillars. The floor was made of large, smooth stones, like the baths which they have in Europe. They have a hearth made like the binnacle or compass box of a ship, in which they burn a handful of thyme at a time to keep up the heat, and they can stay in there just as in a bath. The top was on a level with the ground. Some that were seen were large enough for a game of ball. When

Coronado in safety and the captain-general was so much pleased
with the account given by him
of the place that he at once determined to winter the army
there. He immediately sent
Garcia Lopez de Cardenas thither to prepare quarters for the troops.
When Cardenas arrived at Tiguex, he turned all the inhabitants out
of their houses so that they could be used as quarters for the soldiers.
They were not allowed to carry anything away with them but their
clothing and were obliged to find shelter in the adjoining villages.
This action on the part of the Spanish captain greatly incensed the
Indians, who now became very hostile.

CORONADO DETERMINES TO WINTER
HIS ARMY AT TIGUEX

In the meantime the army under Arellano, leaving Sonora in the
latter part of October, had reached Cibola, joining Coronado at the
pueblo of Hawaikúh. Having determined to visit another province of
eight villages of which he had heard
before going to Tiguex, with thirty of
his best men, the captain-general started upon his journey, leaving
instructions with Arellano to follow with the army in twenty
days. On this journey they saw snow-covered mountains, toward
which they went in search of water. After a march of eight days,
the command reached Tutahaco,[219] where they learned there were

THE ARMY UNDER ARELLANO
REACHES CIBOLA

---

any man wishes to marry it has to be arranged by those who govern. The man
has to spin and weave a blanket and place it before the woman, who covers
herself with it and becomes his wife. The houses belong to the women, the
estufas to the men. If a man repudiates his woman, he has to go to the *estufa*.
It is forbidden for women to sleep in the *estufas* or to enter these for any purpose except to give their husbands or sons something to eat. The men spin
and weave. The women bring up the children and prepare the food. The
country is so fertile that they do not have to break up the ground the year
round, but only have to sow the seed, which is presently covered by the fall of
snow, and the ears come up under the snow. In one year they gather enough
for seven. There are a great many native fowl in these provinces, and cocks
(turkeys) with great hanging chins. When dead, these keep for sixty days, and
longer in winter, without losing their feathers or opening, and without any bad
smell and the same is true of dead men.''

[219] In all probability this was a village or group of villages near Isleta, on
the Rio Grande. Bandelier, A. F., *Final Report*, part ii, pp. 234, 235, and
note, says this point on the Rio Grande was the location of Tutahaco. He says
that Castañeda may have mistaken the name, which sounds like the Tigua name
for the pueblo of Acoma. Messrs. Davis and Prince are in error as to the
route taken either by Alvarado or Coronado in their marches to Tiguex. Bancroft says that Tutahaco was in the neighborhood of the present pueblo of
Isleta, probably farther south. Prince and Davis thought that Tutahaco was a

other towns down the river. The inhabitants were peaceful; the villages were terraced. Coronado visited all of the villages of this province, and resuming his march to Tiguex,[220] reached that place, where he met Alvarado, Cardenas, and El Turco, waiting for him in the village that had been prepared as winter quarters for the army.

part of the Laguna group, north of Acoma. In this they certainly err, because Castañeda says Tutahaco was down the river southeast of Tiguex.

[220] Bancroft, Hubert Howe, *History of Arizona and New Mexico*, identifies the province of Tiguex with the valley of the Rio Grande, and Cicuyé, at the edge of the buffalo plains, from the vicinity of which a river flowed southeastward, with the now ruined pueblo of Pecos. In a very elaborate note he cites many authorities. He says: ''Tiguex, also printed Tihuex and Tihuek, is 40 l. N(E?) of Cibola. *Castañeda* 3. d. eastward, of Acuco. *Id.* It has twelve villages on a great river; the valley is about 2 l. wide and bounded on the w. by high snowy mts. 4 villages at the foot of the mts. 3 others on the heights. *Id.* Tiguex is the central point of all the pueblos; 4 villages on the river below Tiguex are S. E. because the river makes a bend to the east (no such bend appears on the modern maps); up and down the valley the region explored extends about 130 l. all inhabited. *Id.* 20 l. east of the peñol of Acuco, a river flowing from N. to S., well settled, with 70 pueblos, large and small, in its whole extent (and branches?); the settled region extends 50 l. N. and S. and there are some villages 15 or 20 l. away on either side. *Rel. del Suceso*, 323. On the river are 15 villages within 20 l. and others on the branches, *Jaramillo*, 309. *Coronado*, Pacheco, doc. iii, 368, says Tiguex was the best province found; yet not desirable for Spanish occupation. Gallatin, followed by Prince, 128, and Davis, 185, puts Tiguex on the Puerco. The reasons are, the N. E. direction of Jemez from Tiguex and the great river crossed after passing Cicuyé, which these authors identify with the Rio Grande. In my opinion these points are of slight weight in opposition to the general tenor of all the narratives. It seems incredible that the Spaniards should have described the valley of the Puerco as the broad valley of a large river on which and on its branches for over 100 l. on the right and left were situated most of the pueblos. Davis admits that the Puerco was but a small stream, but suggests that it may have been full or flooded at the time; yet, in a year and more the Spaniards had ample time to learn its comparative size. They went in their explorations far below the junction, and if the river Tiguex had been the Puerco, its junction with a larger river would naturally have been noted. If, however, any further proof is needed, we have the fact that Espejo, ascending the Rio Grande forty years later, found the province of Tiguas with reports of Coronado's visits and fights with the natives. Espejo, *Relacion*, 112-113. This province of the Tiguas, distinct from the Teguas, or Tehuas, was well known at the end of the 16th and in the 17th centuries, being on the Rio Grande and almost certainly in the region of Sandia. Bandelier, *Historical Introduction*, 18-20, after a study of documentary evidence which he cites, has no hesitation in locating Tiguex on the Rio Grande above the Puerco junction, at or near Bernalillo. Squier, Kern and Morgan had previously located Tiguex on the Rio Grande above the Puerco junction. Simpson, *Coronado's March*, 334-335, while admitting that some of the evidence points to the northern location, yet chooses to find Tiguex below the mouth of the Puerco, because only there is the valley bounded on the west by snowy mountains, the Socorro range, citing also Jeffery's Atlas of 1773, which puts Tigua at the foot of those mts. Simpson's view of this matter would remove some of the difficulties in connection with Espejo's trip . . . but it would also create other and greater difficulties.''

Upon his arrival at Tiguex, the captain-general had an interview with El Turco, whose stories sounded good to the credulous ear of Coronado. Already the Turk had evolved a plan by which, trusting to the well-known desire of the Spaniards for gold, he would lead them over the mountains on to the staked plains, where they would die of thirst.

The Turk was blessed with an imagination far more vivid than any possessed by the ordinary Indian, and, in his conversation with the Spanish captain, led them to believe that in his country the yellow metal was a very common affair. Naturally the Spaniards, filled with disappointment at not finding the statements of the friar Marcos verified, were ready to believe almost anything the Turk had to relate, and became very enthusiastic in their hopes of a great future conquest.

"In his country," said El Turco, "there was a river in the level country which was two leagues wide, in which there were fishes as big as horses and large numbers of very big canoes, with more than twenty rowers on the side, and that they carried sails; and their lords sat on the poop, under awnings, and on the prow they had a great golden eagle. He said also that the lord of that country took his afternoon nap under a great tree on which were hung a great number of little gold bells, which put him to sleep as they swung in the air. He said also that everyone had their ordinary dishes made of wrought plate, and the jugs, plates, and bowls were of gold."[221] El Turco even had a name for the yellow metal, which he called *acochis*. He also told them that when he was captured by the Indians of Cicuyé, the latter had deprived him of his golden bracelets. When the captain-general heard this statement, he immediately sent Alvarado to Cicuyé to secure the bracelets; upon arrival Alvarado ascertained that El Turco was a great liar. He then succeeded in decoying the chief of the Cicuyé, Bigotes, and the cacique, who was an old man, into his tent, where he put them in chains, took them to Tiguex, where they were held in confinement for six months. When Alvarado left Cicuyé, taking with him their

---

[221] Castañeda, *Relacion*, Winship's trans., p. 493: "For the present he was believed, on account of the ease with which he told it and because they showed him metal ornaments and he recognized them and said they were not gold, and he knew gold and silver very well and did not care anything about other metals."

chieftain fettered [222] with chains, the natives became very angry, accusing him of faithlessness and lack of friendly appreciation, and gave evidence of their pronounced hostility by letting fly a great shower of arrows. Thus early were the natives learning that the Spaniards were not to be trusted. The doctrines of Christianity and Spanish civilization did not now appeal strongly to the native mind, and when Arellano and the main body of the expedition arrived at Tiguex, the whole province was in arms against them.

This state of affairs grew out of the open violation of the instructions of the viceroy. The Spanish soldiers deprived the natives of their houses and turned them out without ceremony, and, in many ways, disregarded the property rights of the Indians who had so kindly received them in their midst. Before the army had arrived Coronado called upon the Indians for a large amount of clothing, and, as they were somewhat dilatory in responding to his commands, sent his soldiers to take the clothing by force. One of his officers, having asked an Indian to hold his horse, ascended a ladder to an apartment in one of the houses, where he violated the wife of the Indian and the latter received no justice because he could not satisfactorily identify the man who had committed this heinous crime. This last offense was the culmination of the indignities heaped upon them by the soldiery. Coronado sent Cardenas to parley with the natives, but he found their villages barricaded, and later on, being commanded to lay siege to the village, he took possession of the house-tops by surprising the natives; here a battle raged with great fury during an entire day and night, and throughout a portion of the day following. At last, the poor Indians, exhausted by their efforts for defense of their homes, were smoked out by the Mexican allies, who, protected by the Spanish cavalry, undermined the outside walls of the village, and, building smudges, soon compelled the natives to sue for peace. This was granted them by two Spanish officers,[223] who responded by folding their arms.

When the Indians saw the Spanish officers cross their arms, this being the Indian signal for an inviolable peace, they all surrendered. The captives were led into the tent of Don Garcia Lopez de Cardenas,

---

[222] Castañeda, *Relacion*, p. 493: "This began the want of confidence in the word of the Spaniards whenever there was talk of peace from this time on."

[223] Castañeda, *ibid*, Winship's translation, p. 496. These officers were Pablo de Melgosa and Diego Lopez, the alderman from Seville.

Courtesy Walton's Studio, Alburquerque, N. M.

Snake Dance of the Moqui

who, as Castañeda relates, "according to what he said, did not know about the peace and thought that they had given themselves up of their own accord, because they had been conquered. As he had been ordered by the general not to take them alive, but to make an example of them so that the other natives would fear the Spaniards, he ordered 200 stakes to be prepared at once to burn them alive. Nobody told him about the peace that had been granted them, for the soldiers knew as little as he, and those who should have told him about it remained silent, not thinking that it was any of their business. Then when the enemies saw that the Spaniards were binding them and beginning to roast them, about a hundred men who were in the tent began to struggle and defend themselves with what there was there and with the stakes they could seize. Our men who were on foot attacked them on all sides, so that there was great confusion around it, and then the horsemen chased those who escaped. As the country was level, not a man of them remained alive, unless it was some who remained hidden in the village and escaped that night to spread throughout the country the news that the strangers did not respect the peace they had made, which afterwards proved a great misfortune."[224]

DON GARCIA LOPEZ DE CARDENAS ORDERS THE MASSACRE OF THE INDIANS

---

[224] Don Garcia Lopez de Cardenas, returning to Spain, afterwards, in order to secure an inheritance, was imprisoned for this enormous act of cruelty and perfidy.

Mota Padilla, xxxii, 6, p. 161, relates that "Esta accion se tuvo en España por mala, y con razon, porque fue una crueldad considerable; y habiendo el maese de campo, Garcia Lopez, pasado á España á heredar un mayorazgo, estuvo preso en una fortaleza por este cargo."

See also Bandelier, *Final Report*, part ii, p. 223. Also Escudero, *Noticias Estadisticas de Sonora y Sinaloa*, pp. 27-29.

In the *Relacion del Suceso*, a different account of this affair is given; in that account it is said: "When Hernando de Alvarado returned from these plains to the river which was called Tiguex, he found the army-master Don Garcia Lopez de Cardenas getting ready for the whole army, which was coming there. When it arrived, although all these people had met Hernando de Alvarado peacefully, part of them rebelled when all the force came. There were twelve villages near together, and one night they killed 40 of our horses and mules which were loose in the camp. They fortified themselves in their villages and war was declared against them. Don Garcia Lopez went to the first and took it and executed justice on many of them. When the rest saw this, they abandoned all except two of the villages, one of these the strongest of them all, around which the army was kept for two months. And although after we invested it, we entered it one day and occupied a part of the flat roof, we were forced to abandon this on account of the many wounds that were received and

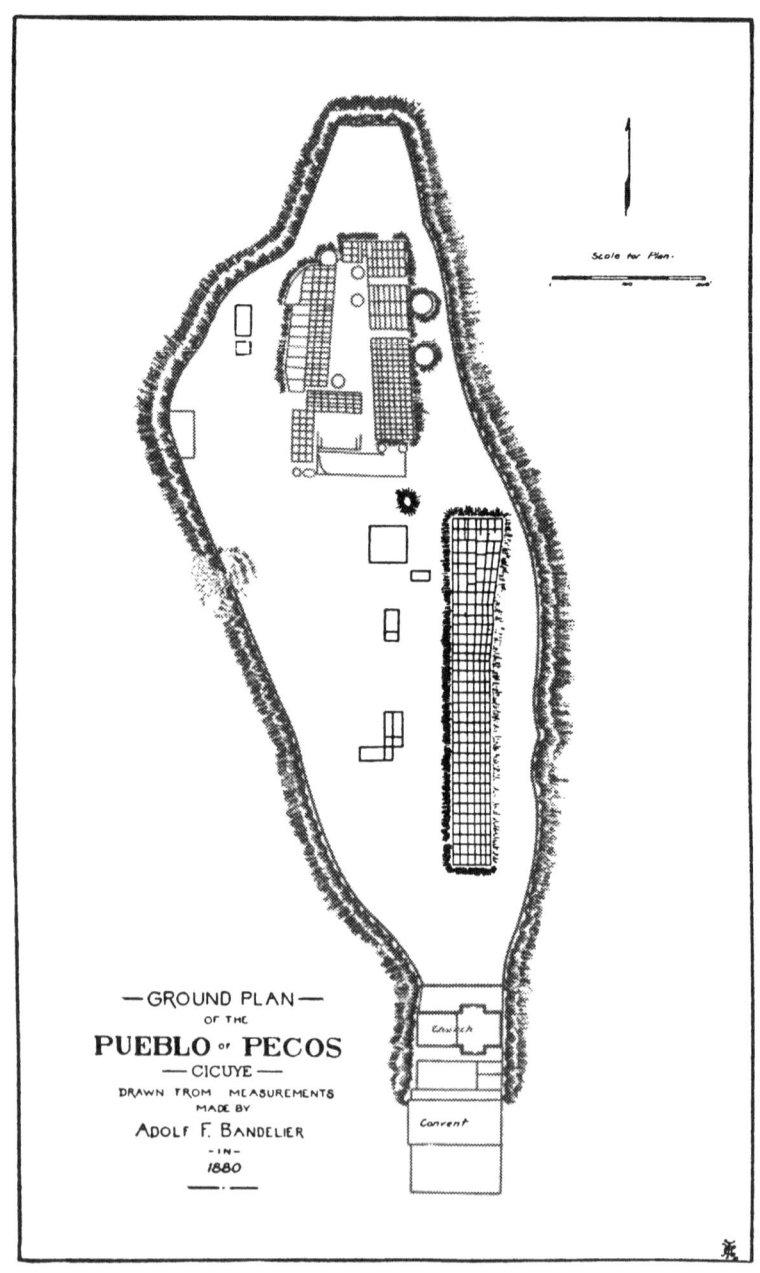

The immediate consequences of this "great misfortune" were very serious. The entire province rose; the Indians would not trust the Spaniards in word or deed, for those who had escaped this frightful massacre proclaimed throughout the country that this sort of action was customary with the Spaniards and that they invariably violated their treaties and agreements.

In the latter part of December, 1540, shortly after the massacre of the Indians, the main body of the army, under Arellano, arrived from Hawaikúh. Nearly a month was consumed in the march. On the first day out they made camp in the best, largest, and finest village of the province of Cibola. This was the village of Matsaki,[225] at the northwestern base of Thunder Mountain, about eighteen miles from Hawaikúh.

Matsaki had houses seven stories in height, some of which were used as fortresses, and these were higher than the others and rose

because it was so dangerous to maintain ourselves there, and although we again entered it soon afterwards, in the end it was not possible to get it all, and so it was surrounded all this time. We finally captured it because of their thirst, and they held out so long because it snowed twice when they were just about to give themselves up. In the end we captured it, and many of them were killed because they tried to get away in the night."

An account of the events transpiring at this time is also given by Gomara, cap. ccxiii, who says: "Fueronse los Indios una noche y amanecieron muertos treynta caballos, que puso temor al Exercito. Caminando, quemaron un lugar, y en otro que acometieron, les mataron ciertos, Españoles, y hierieron cinquenta cavallos, y metieron dentro los vezinos á Francisco de Ovando, herido, ó muerto, para comer, y sacrificar, á lo que pensaron, ó quiça para mejor ver, que hombres eran los Españoles, ca no se hallo por alli rastro de sacrificio humano. Pusieron cerco los nuestros al lugar, pero no lo pudieron tomar en mas de cuarenta, y cinco dias. Beuian nieue los cercados por falta de agua, y viendose perdidos, hizieron una hoguera, echaron en ella sus matas, plumajes, turquesas, y cosas preciadas, por que no las gozassen aquellos estrangeros. Salieron en escuadron, con los niños, y mugeres en medio, para abrir camino por fuerza, y salvarse; mas pocos escaparon de las espadas, y cavallos, y de un rio q cerca estava. Murieron en la pelea siete Españoles y quedaron heridos ochenta, y muchos cavallos porq veays quanto vale la determinacion en la necessidad. Muchos Indios se bouieron al pueblo, con la gente menuda, y se defiendieron hasta que se puso fuego."

[225] Matsaki derives its name, "Salt City," because the Zuñi Goddess of Salt is said to have made a white lake there. It is now a ruined pueblo of the Zuñi near the northwest base of Thunder Mountain, in the county of Valencia, New Mexico. It was the Macaque of Castañeda, and formed one of the Seven Cities of Cibola province. It was occupied until August, 1680, the time of the great Pueblo revolt, at which time it was permanently abandoned, the inhabitants fleeing to the mountains, remaining on top of Thunder Mountain for several years.

See Mindeleff, in 8th B. A. E., 86, 1891; Bandelier, in *Arch. Inst. Papers*, iv, 337, 1892; Cushing, *Zuñi Folk Tales*, I, 32, 1901.

above the rest like towers. There were embrazures and loop-holes in them for defending the roofs of the different stories, because of there being no streets. As is stated by Castañeda, "the flat roofs are all of a height and are used in common. The roofs have to be reached first, and these upper houses are the means of defending them."

The army continued its march from Matsaki, having been delayed ten days on account of a continuous fall of snow. The country round about was covered with junipers and stunted pines which the soldiers used for firewood. The snow was a very dry fall, covering the baggage two and three feet deep, but not injuring it. Castañeda says that "it fell all night long, covering the baggage and the soldiers and their beds, piling up in the air, so that if anyone had suddenly come upon the army nothing would have been seen but mountains of snow." The horses were half buried in it, but it served to keep those who were underneath quite warm. The army passed by the great rock of Acoma, to the top of which some of them climbed with great difficulty, although the natives could go up and down quite easily, carrying loads, and the women carrying water. The soldiers marveled at these feats in climbing because, in making the ascent themselves, they were compelled to pass their weapons up from one another, while the natives would not touch the rocky sides of the precipice even with their hands.

Finally the army reached Tiguex and occupied the quarters that had been prepared for them at such a tremendous sacrifice of honor and fair dealing. The winter was so severe that nothing was accomplished until late in February, 1541, at which time Coronado sent messengers to every pueblo asking that the natives make peace. He met with only poor success for, pointing to the slaughter of their friends who had surrendered, they answered that they had no faith in the word of the Christians. Thus almost the entire winter was passed in vain endeavor to restore conditions to their former status.

The captain-general despatched Don Garcia Lopez de Cardenas, with thirty men, to Tiguex to propose terms of peace. Although the natives were very hostile, they talked with him and said that if he cared to treat with them he must dismount and they would come and confer with him; they also required that his cavalry be sent

Courtesy Bureau American Ethnology
Water Vessels, Tinajas — from Pueblo of Tesuque

away, saying that one of their own number, who was now known by the name of Juan Aleman,[226] and another captain would come out and make a treaty of peace. The army-master consented to this arrangement for the purpose of regaining confidence and on account of his great desire for peace.

CORONADO BEGINS THE SIEGE OF TIGUEX — CARDENAS BARELY ESCAPES DEATH

When he met them, Juan Aleman approached and embraced him vigorously, while the other two who had come with him drew two war-clubs from behind their backs, and gave him two such blows over the helmet as to almost knock him senseless. Seeing this assault, two of the soldiers on horseback, who had been unwilling to go a great distance off, even though the army-master had so ordered them, rode up quickly, rescuing the captain, although they were unable to catch the treacherous Indians, even though they were followed to the walls of their village, from the roofs of which the pursuers were greeted with a great shower of arrows, one of which struck a horse, going entirely through his nose. A number of Spaniards composing the escort of Cardenas soon came up and participated in the battle, accomplishing very little and finally passing on to another village where the people, in response to the invitation to treat for peace, again greeted Don Garcia Lopez de Cardenas and his soldiers with arrows and with jeers.[227]

When the captain-general was advised of this affair, he ordered the army to surround the village of Tiguex. He set out with his men in good order, having made several scaling ladders with which he expected to gain the roofs of the houses. When he reached the

---

[226] Castañeda, *Relacion*, Winship's translation, p. 495: "This Indian was one of the chiefs of Tiguex, with whom Coronado had already had much intercourse and with whom he was on good terms, who was called Juan Aleman by our men, after a Juan Aleman, who lived in Mexico, whom he was said to resemble."

[227] This fight is described by Mota Padilla: "D. Garcia pasó al pueblo mayor á requirir al principal cacique, que se llamba D. Juan Loman, aunque no estaba bautizado, y se dejó ver por los muros sin querer bajar de paz, y á instancias de D. Garcia, ofreció salirle á hablar, como dejase el caballo y espada, porque tenia mucho miedo; y en este conformidad, desmontó D. Garcia del cavallo, entregó é con la espada á sus soldados, á quienes hizo retirar, y acercandose á los muros, luego que Juan Loma se afrontó, se abrazó de el, y al punto, entre seis indios que habia dejado apercibidos, lo llevaron en peso y lo entraron en el pueblo si la puerta no es pequeña, por lo que en ella hizo hincapie, y pudo resistir hasta llegaron soldados de á caballo, que le defendieron. Quisieron los indios hacer alguna crueldad con dicho D. Garcia, por lo que intentaron llevarlo vivo, que si los indios salen con macanas ó porras que usaban le quitan la vida."

village, he made camp near by and commenced the siege, but the enemy, having provided themselves with a great quantity of stores, resisted the assaults which were made with great bravery, throwing down upon the Spaniards great quantities of stones. Almost a hundred Spaniards were wounded with arrows, several of whom died shortly afterwards. The siege lasted fifty days, during which time several assaults were made. The Indians were greatly distressed for want of water. They dug a very deep well inside the village, but were not able to get water, but while they were sinking it, the earth caved in and thirty of their number were killed. Two hundred lost their lives defending the village against the assaults of the Spaniards. On one occasion there was a particularly fierce engagement, in which Francisco de Ovando was killed. He was a captain, and had acted as army-master during the absence of Don Garcia Lopez de Cardenas. Another Spanish gentleman, Francisco Pobares, also fell. The Spaniards were unable to prevent the Indians from carrying Obando inside their village. His loss was much regretted as he was a most distinguished person, affable and much beloved by his soldiers. Shortly before the town was reduced, the Indians asked to have a parley with the Spaniards and said that knowing we would not harm the women and children, they wished to surrender them, as they were using up the water. It was impossible to persuade them to make peace; so they gave up about one hundred women and boys, who were unwilling to leave their village. As Castañeda relates this occurrence, "Don Lope de Urrea rode up in front of the town without his helmet and received the boys and girls in his arms, and when all these had been surrendered, Don Lope begged them to make peace, giving them the strongest promises for their safety. They told him to go away, as they did not trust themselves to people who had no regard for friendship or their own word, which they had pledged. As he seemed unwilling to go away, one of them put an arrow in his bow, ready to shoot, and threatened to shoot him with it unless he went off, and they warned him to put on his helmet, but he was unwilling to do so, saying that they would not hurt him so long as he stayed there. When the Indian saw that he did not want to go away, he shot and planted his arrow between the forefeet of his horse, and then put another arrow in his bow and repeated that if he did not go away he would really shoot him. Don Lope put on his helmet and slowly rode back to where the horsemen were, without receiving any harm from them. When they saw that he was really in safety, they began to shoot arrows in showers, with loud yells and cries. The general did not want to make an assault that day, in order to see if they could be brought in some way to make peace, which they would not consider.''

Having withstood this siege for a period of two weeks longer, owing to the scarcity of provisions and particularly of water, the Indians determined to abandon the village. This was attempted during the night time. They came out of the village on the side where the cavalry was stationed. An alarm was quickly sounded in the camp of Don Rodrigo Maldonado. The Indians boldly attacked the Spanish cavalry, killing one soldier, one horse, and wounding several, but they were soon driven back with great execution, until they came to the river, where the current flowed swiftly and very cold. Into the water the Indians threw themselves. Only a few escaped the merciless onslaught of the Spaniards. Some succeeded in getting across the river, but were so benumbed that they could proceed no further and were captured the following day, brought to the Spanish camp, and reduced to slavery.[228]

---

[228] Castañeda, *Relacion*, Winship's translation, p. 499-500.

Mota Padilla gives a very full account of the reduction of the village of Tiguex. In vol. xxxii, 8, p. 161, we find: ''Habiendose puesto el cerco, estuvieron los indios rebeldes á los requerimientos, por lo que se intento abrir brecha, y rota la argamasa superficial, se advertió que el centro del muro era de palaizada, troncos y mimbres bien hincados en la tierra, por lo que resistian los golpes que daban con unas malas barras, en cuyo tiempo hacian de las azoteas mucho daño en los nuestros con las piedras y con las flechas por las troneras; y quoriendo un soldado tapar con lodo una tronera de donde se hacia mucho daño, por un ojo le entraron una flecha, de que cayó muerto; llamabase Francisco Pobares; y á otro que se llamaba Juan Paniagua, muy bien cristiano y persona noble, le dieron otro flechazo en el parpado de un ojo, y publicaba que á la devocion del rosario, que siempre razaba, debio la vida; otro soldado, llamado Francisco de Ovando, se entro de bruzas por una portalnueva, y apenas hubo asomado la cabeza, cuando le asieron y le tiraron para adentro, quitandole la vida; pusose una escala por donde á todo trance subieron algunos; pero con arte, los indios tenian muchas piezas á cielo descubierto, para que se no comunicasen; y como á cortas distancias habia torrecillas con muchas saeteras y troneras, hacian mucho daño, de suerte que hierrieron mas de sesenta, de los que murieron tres: un fulano, Carbajal, hermano de Hernando Trejo, quien fue despuez tentiente de gobernador por Francisco de Ibarra, en Chametla; tambien murió un vizcaino, llamado Alonzo de Castañeda y un fulano Benitezy esto fue por culpa de ellos, pues ya que habia pocas armas de fuego con que ofender, pudieron haber pegado fuego a los muros, pues eran de troncones y palizadas con solo el embarrado de tierra.

''Viendo el gobernador el poco efecto de su invasion, mandó se tocase a

Grooved Hammers from Quivira

There was one other village which the Indians had occupied and barricaded; this was reduced by a force under the captains, Diego de Guevara and Juan de Salvidar. At this village, some of the Spaniards having started out one morning for the purpose of an ambuscade by which they thought to capture some of the warriors who were accustomed every morning to come out in a vain endeavor to frighten the Spanish soldiery, the guards who had been placed where they could see when the Indians left the village, saw the natives come out and proceed toward the country. The soldiers left their ambuscade and going to the village saw the people in full flight. They were pursued and large numbers were mercilessly slain. The town was then plundered by the Spaniards and prisoners were made of all who were in it, numbering about one hundred women and children.

During the siege of these two villages the captain-general had found time to visit Cicuyé, where he replaced in power the cacique whom Alvarado had brought to Tiguex in chains, because he would not reveal the whereabouts of the golden bracelets taken from El Turco by the natives of that pueblo. He also promised the Indians that as soon as he started for the country of El Turco he would restore to them their chief, Bigotes.

After the reduction of the two villages, Coronado sent a captain and a small force to the pueblo of Cia,[229] which had already given in its submission.

---

recoger, con animo de rendirlos por falta de agua, ya que no por hambre, porque sabia tenian buenas trojes de maiz. Trataron de curar los heridos, aunque se enconaron, y se cicatrizaban; y segun se supo, era la causa el que en unas vasijas de mimbre encerraban los indios vivoras, y con las flechas las tocaban para que mordiesen las puntas y quedasen venenosas; y habiendose mentenido algun tiempo, cuando se esperaba padeciesen falta de agua, comenzó a nevar, con cuya nieve se socorrieron y mantuvieron dos meses, en los que ententaron los nuestros muchos desatinos; el uno fue formar undos ingenios con unos maderos que llamaban vaivenes, y son los entiguous arietes con que se batian las fortalezas en tiempo que no se conocia la polvera; mas no se acetaron; despues, por falta de artilleria, intentaron hacer unos cañones de madera bien liados de cordeles á modo de cohetes; mas tampoco sirvio; y no arbitraron el arrimar lena á los muros y prenderles fuego; á mi ver entiendo que la crueldad con que quitaron la vida a los ciento y treita gandules, los hizo indignos del triunfo; y asi, en una noche los sitiados salieron y se pusieron en fuga, dejando a los nuestros burlados y sin cosa de provecho que lohrassen por despojos de la plaza sitiada y se salieron los indios con su valeroso hecho."

[229] The Pueblo of Cia still stands in about the place indicated. The present village is surrounded by ruins of old pueblos formerly inhabited by the same stock. In 1582, Espejo says, *Relacion del Viage*, p. 178: "Hallamos otro

He sent another substantial force to Quirix,[230] a province of seven villages on the Rio Grande, near the present pueblo of San Felipe. Peace was now restored throughout the region, although the Tiguas declined to return to their homes in the villages which they had deserted.

The captain-general was in frequent conversation with El Turco relative to the country from which he came, but notwithstanding the statements made by him, since his reputation as a liar had become known to the soldiers, there were many who put little faith in his promises. Castañeda relates that "a Spaniard, named Cervantes, who had charge of El Turco during the siege, solemnly swore that he had seen the Turk talking with the devil in a pitcher of water, and also that while he had him under lock and key, so that no one could speak to him, the Turk had asked him what Christians had been killed by the people at Tiguex. He told him 'nobody,' and then the Turk answered: 'You lie; five Christians are dead, including a captain.' And as Cervantes knew that he told the truth, he confessed it so as to find out who had told him about it, and the Turk said he knew it himself and that he did not need to have anyone tell him in order to know it. And it was on account of this that he watched him and saw him speaking to the devil in a pitcher."

However, Coronado was determined to ascertain the truth or falsity of the Turk's statements, although his captains advised that it would be best to make a reconnoissance in the direction desired to be taken before moving the entire command.[231] Before starting he

---

provincia que llaman los Punames, que son cinco pueblos, que la cabecera se dice Sia.''

[230] Bandelier, A. F., *Final Report*, part i, p. 125, says: "Skirting the course of the Rio Grande, the most easterly villages of the numerous (comparatively speaking, of course) Queres stock were scattered on the banks of the river. Twenty-seven miles southwest of Santa Fé is Cochití, or Ko-tyi-ti. Three miles east of the stream, on the dangerous Galisteo creek, was the old pueblo of Santo Domingo, or Gui-pu-y, the predecessor of the village of to-day. On the same side, but directly on the river banks, stood Kat-ish-tya, the antecessor of the present San Felipe. This exhausts the list of the Rio Grande Queres, but farther west, along the Jemez river, the tribe inhabited several sites. There was the cluster of the Cia, or Tzia towns, of which but one remains, and old Santa Ana, or Ta-ma-ya. The first pueblo of Ta-ma-ya stood near the Mesa del Cangelon and far from the mouth of the Rio de Jemez. The historic pueblo that was stormed by Pedro Reneros de Posada in 1687, was on the summit of what is called to-day the 'Mesa de Santa Ana.'"

[231] *Relacion del Suceso*, 14th B. A. E., p. 577.

sent Don Pedro de Tovar to Sonora with a report for the emperor and directions to return with the remainder of the expedition. At this time some Indians came to see him from Cibola, and Coronado charged them to take good care of the Spaniards who would come with Tovar, and also gave them some letters to give to Don Pedro, informing him of his plans and that he would find letters under the crosses which the army would put up along the way.[232]

In the latter part of April or the first days of May,[233] as soon as the ice on the Rio Grande had broken [234] up, the captain-general set out for Cicuyé, and on his arrival at that point set Bigotes at liberty, which caused great rejoicing among the Indians, who were now very friendly and brought him great quantities of food for his journey out on the plains. The Turk was opposed to accepting this supply of food for the reason, as Castañeda says, that "it was useless to fatigue the horses with loads of supplies, so that they could not bring back the gold and silver." [235]

The army started from Cicuyé, leaving the village at peace and well contented because their governor and cacique had been restored to them. They had as guides a young man named Xabe, who was said to be a native of Quivira and who was given to Coronado by the cacique of Pecos; also a Quivira Indian called Ysopete, and El Turco. They started in a southeasterly direction, and after a journey of four days reached the Pecos river, which they were compelled to bridge. This bridge was completed in four days' time, whereupon the entire army with the animals was able to cross in safety.[236]

---

[232] Castañeda, *Relacion*, Winship's translation, p. 503.

[233] Castañeda says they started on May 5th. Coronado, in his letter of October 20, states that he started on the 23rd of April.

[234] Bancroft, Hubert H., *History of Arizona and New Mexico*, p. 59, note, says: "It must have been a most extraordinary winter, but probably the floods following the breaking up of the ice, may have been as formidable obstacles to fording as the ice."

There is nothing extraordinary in seeing the Rio Grande filled with floating ice in great quantities in the early spring, far south of Alburquerque.

[235] Castañeda, *Relacion*, Winship's translation: "Decia el turco quando salió de tiguex el campo que para cargauan los cauallos tanto de bastimentos que se cansarian y no podrian despues trae el oro y la plata donde parese bien andaba con engaño."

[236] Brower's *Memoirs*, F. W. Hodge, says the river crossed was the Pecos, somewhere in the vicinity of Puerto de Luna, Guadalupe county, New Mexico.

Castañeda, *Relacion*, says that "after four days'" journey they came to a river, with a large deep current, which flowed down toward Cicuyé, and they named this the Cicuyé river.

The only river which flows down from Cicuyé (Pecos) is the Pecos river. The

It was but a short distance now until Coronado was upon the plains, where he came upon some settlements inhabited by people "who lived like Arabs" and were known as Querechos. These people lived in tents made of the tanned skins of the buffalo. When they saw the army they did not appear to be at all alarmed and came out of their tents to witness its approach. Fearlessly they advanced to the horsemen in front, and asked the Spaniards who they were. [237] Presently Coronado came up and talked with them. The conversation was carried on by means of signs, by which they made themselves very well understood, in fact there was no need of an interpreter. They informed the general that there was a very large river over toward the rising sun, and that it was possible to go along this stream for ninety days without a break from settlement to settlement; that

THE ARMY REACHES THE PLAINS AND THEY SEE BUFFALO AND INDIANS CALLED QUERECHOS

---

natural and accustomed route for the Indians of the Rio Grande and of the several pueblo villages northeast of the present pueblo of Santo Domingo and those of Cicuyé to take when going to the plains in search of buffalo was by way of the Pecos river, particularly those who lived in the neighborhood of Cicuyé.

Bancroft, Hubert H., *History of Arizona and New Mexico*, p. 59, thinks this river was the Gallinas, the eastern and larger branch of the Pecos. In a note he says, "as we have seen, the size of this stream has to be explained by the season of the flood, with the possible addition of earlier exploration by Alvarado. To thus explain away the difficulty is a very different matter from Davis's similar theory about the Rio Puerco, because on the Puerco the army spent, if D. and the others are right, two winters, and had ample time to learn its size and its connection with the Rio Grande; while the Cicuyé was merely crossed at this point once in May, and was once or twice explored below and shown to be really a large river. D.'s position that the Cicuyé was the Rio Grande is wholly untenable." Prince undoubtedly followed Davis and thus fell into this error.

Bancroft is clearly in error. To have reached the left bank of the Gallinas, the army would have to cross the Pecos; the Gallinas is not the larger branch of the Pecos. Bandelier also errs when he thinks that the bridge was built across the Canadian. No Indian or *cibolero* ever left the locality of the old Pecos pueblo, going to the "buffalo plains," except by the route down the Pecos river, and at the time that Coronado went out upon the plains, the Pecos was at a flood season, and difficult to cross.

[237] Hodge, F. W., *Spanish Explorers in the Southern United States*, note p. 330: "The name by which the eastern Apaches, or Apaches Vaqueros of later times were known to the Pecos Indians. The first Querechos were met near the eastern boundary of New Mexico."

Hodge, F. W., *The Early Navajó and Apache*, Am. Anthrop., p. 235, July, 1895, says: "Mr. James Mooney has discovered that 'Querecho' is an old Comanche name of the Tonkawa, who ranged the buffalo plains of western Texas and eastern New Mexico."

the first of these settlements was called Haxa, and that the river was more than a league in width and that there were many canoes on the river.[238] During the two days' march after this meeting with the Querechos, the Spaniards saw many others of the same tribe and such great numbers of buffalo that it seemed almost incredible. The Turk told them that it was a two days' journey to Haxa, and Coronado sent Captain Diego Lopez with a command of ten men, lightly equipped, in search of the place. The army followed over a section of country, the *llano estacado*, "without sight of mountain range, nor a hill, nor a hillock, which was three times as high as a man." Diego Lopez was lost for two days, at the end of which he returned with the news that although he had traveled a distance of twenty leagues he had seen "nothing but buffalo and sky."

While on the march the army came across a wandering band of Indians, among whom was one who was blind, who told them, using the sign language, that "he had seen four others like us many days before, whom he had seen near there and rather more toward New Spain," believed by the soldiers to have been Alvar Nuñez Cabeza de Vaca and his companions.

Later on other Indians of the plains were encountered, who called themselves Teyas, an intelligent, well-formed people, who lived like the Querechos.

At this time it was estimated that the army had marched upwards of two hundred and fifty leagues since leaving the province of Tiguex. The captain-general, who by this time had come to have great doubts as to the sincerity of the Turk,[239] called a council of his captains. At this meeting it was concluded that it was best that

---

[238] This river was the Arkansas near the Mississippi probably.

[239] Jaramillo, in his *Relacion*, etc., says: "We all went forward one day to a stream which was down in a ravine in the midst of good meadows, to agree on who should go ahead and how the rest should return. Here, the Indian Ysopete, as we had called the companion of the said Turk, was asked to tell us the truth, and to lead us to that country which we had come in search of. He said he would do it, and that it was not as the Turk had said, because those were certainly fine things which he had said and given us to understand at Tihuex, about gold and how it was obtained, and the buildings, and the style of them, and their trade, and many other things told for the sake of the prolixity, which had led us to go in search of them, with the advice of all who gave it and of the priests. He asked us to leave him afterward in that country, because it was his native country, as a reward for guiding us, and also, that the Turk might not go along with him, because he would quarrel and try to restrain him in everything that he wanted to do for our advantage; and the general promised him this, and said he would be one of the thirty, and he went in this way."

Arellano return to Tiguex, but that the general, with an escort of thirty cavalry-men and six foot-soldiers, should push on to Quivira. [240]

Accordingly the captain-general, willing to incur almost any risk, provided he succeeded in his efforts, placed Arellano in command

---

[240] Coronado to the king, *Letter* of October 20, 1541: "It seemed to me best in order to see if there was anything there of service to your Majesty, to go forward with only 30 horsemen until I should be able to see the country, so as to give your Majesty a true account of what was to be found in it. I sent all the rest of the force I had with me to this province (Tiguex) with Don Tristan de Arellano in command, because it would have been impossible to prevent the loss of many men, if all had gone on, owing to the lack of water and because they also had to kill bulls and cows on which to sustain themselves. And with only the thirty horsemen whom I took for my escort, I travelled forty-two days after I left the force, living all this while solely on the flesh of the bulls and cows which we killed, at the cost of several of our horses which they killed, because, as I wrote your Majesty, they are very brave and fierce animals; and going many days without water, and cooking the food with cow-dung, because there is not any kind of wood in all these plains, away from the gullies and rivers, which are very few. It was the Lord's pleasure that, after having journeyed across these deserts seventy-seven days, I arrived at the province they call Quivira, to which the guides were conducting me, and where they had described to me houses of stone, with many stories; and not only are they not of stone, but of straw, but the people in them are as barbarous as all those whom I have seen and passed before this; they do not have cloaks, nor cotton of which to make these, but use the skins of the cattle they kill, which they tan, because they are settled among these on a very large river. They eat the raw flesh like the Querechos and the Teyas; they are enemies of one another, but are all of the same sort of people, and these at Quivira have the advantage in the houses they build and in planting corn. In this province of which the guides who brought me are natives, they received me peaceably, and although they told me when I set out for it that I could not succeed in seeing it all in two months, there are not more than twenty-five villages of straw houses there, and in all the rest of the country that I saw and learned about, which gave their obedience to your Majesty and placed themselves under your Majesty's overlordship. The people here are large. I had several Indians measured, and found that they were ten palms in height; the women are well proportioned and their features are more like Moorish women than Indians. The Indians here gave me a piece of copper which an Indian chief wore hung around his neck: I sent it to the viceroy of New Spain, because I have not seen any other metal in these parts except this and some little copper bells which I sent him and a bit of metal which looks like gold. I do not know where this came from, although I believe that the Indians who gave it to me obtained it from those whom I brought here in my service, because I cannot find any other origin for it nor where it came from. The diversity of languages which exists in this country and my not having anyone who understood them, because they speak their own language in each village, has hindered me, because I have been forced to send captains and men in many directions to find out whether there was anything in the country which could be of service to your Majesty. And although I have searched with all diligence I have not found nor heard of anything, unless it be these provinces, which are a very small affair. The province of Quivira is 950 leagues from Mexico. Where I reached it, it is in the fortieth degree. The country itself is the best I have

of the army, directing him to return, and, guided by some Teyas Indians, accompanied by an escort of thirty cavalry-men, proceeded in a northerly direction. He also took with him the friar Juan de Padilla, El Turco, and Ysopete, as he had promised to do. He had not been long on the march before his Indian guides deserted him, and for six weeks this intrepid band of cavaliers, living entirely off of the buffalo, pursued their journey northward. Having traveled thirty days Coronado came to a river which he called the "St. Peter and St. Paul." More than likely this stream was the Arkansas, and the crossing was made somewhere near its southern bend, east of Dodge City, Kansas. Coronado followed the northern bank of this stream, in a northeasterly direction, for three days and, in a journey of three days farther on, reached Quivira, which Coronado states was in 40° of latitude.

The location of the Quivira, sought for by Coronado, has long been a subject of much speculation, and many writers have en-

---

ever seen for producing all the products of Spain, for besides the land itself being very fat and black and being well watered by the rivulets and springs and rivers, I found prunes like those of Spain (or I found everything they have in Spain) and nuts and very good sweet grapes and mulberries. I have treated the natives of this province, and all the others whom I found wherever I went, as well as was possible, agreeable to what your Majesty had commanded, and they have received no harm in any way from me or from those who went in my company. I remained twenty-five days in this province of Quivira so as to see and explore the country and also to find out whether there was anything beyond which could be of service to your Majesty; because the guides who had brought me had given me an account of other provinces beyond this. And what I am sure of is that there is not any gold nor any other metal in all that country, and the other things of which they had told me are nothing but little villages, and in many of these they do not plant anything and do not have any houses except of skins and sticks, and they wander around with the cows; so that the account they gave me was false, because they wanted to persuade me to go there with the whole force, believing that as the way was through such uninhabited districts, and from the lack of water, they would get us where we and our horses would die of hunger. And the guides confessed this and said they had done it by the advice and orders of the natives of these provinces. At this, after having heard the account of what was beyond, which I have given above, I returned to these provinces to provide for the force I had sent back here and to give to your Majesty an account of what this country amounts to, because I wrote your Majesty I would do so when I went there. I have done all that I possibly could to serve your Majesty and to discover a country where God, our Lord, might be served and the royal patrimony of your Majesty increased, as your loyal servant and vassal. For since I reached the province of Cibola, to which the viceroy of New Spain sent me in the name of your Majesty, seeing that there were none of the things there of which Friar Marcos had told, I have managed to explore this country for 200 leagues and more around Cibola, and the best place I have found is the river of Tiguex where I am now, and the settlements here."

deavored, approximately at least, to determine its site. Mr. A. F. Bandelier, in discussing the route taken by the captain-general and the army, after leaving the valley of the Rio Grande-Tiguex, says:

THE LOCATION OF QUIVIRA

"A careful examination of the route taken by the Spaniards on their trip to and from Quivira, and identifications of the localities and of the tribes met, are indispensable. Quivira was the place where, subsequently, Father Juan de Padilla sacrificed his life as a missionary. We must, therefore, ascertain where Quivira was, what it was and what people were its inhabitants. The data at our command, while comparatively meagre, are still, perhaps, more complete than any yet brought to bear upon the subject, and we therefore don't hesitate in undertaking the task. Should subsequent investigations alter our conclusions or confirm them we shall only feel too happy.

"It is unimportant to follow the route taken by Coronado from Bernalillo to Pecos. From [241] Pecos he marched to the north-east, and, after crossing a deep river, found himself on the plains on the 12th of May. The deep river was the Canadian. Between it and the Pecos village he had, according to the eye-witness, Jaramillo, crossed two creeks; one of these was the Rio Pecos, the other the Gallinas. To cross the Canadian it was necessary to build a bridge. No other river four days' march to the north-east of Pecos, is wide and deep enough to require such preparations for its crossing. Beyond the Canadian the plains were reached, and ten days after the crossing had been effected the first Indians of the plains, the Querechos or Apaches (subsequently called Vaqueros) were met. Here the Spaniards changed their course from north-east toward the rising sun, that is almost due east. Very soon they met enormous herds of American bison or buffaloes. It is well to note this change in direction; it is also well to observe that soon the Spaniards found out that their Indian guides had lost their reckoning.

"It is a constant fact that anyone lost on the plains inclines to the right and finally describes a circle. After thirty-seven days of

---

[241] Bandelier, A. F., *American Catholic Quarterly Review*, vol. xv, p. 551, 1890.

Hodge, F. W., *Spanish Explorers in the Southern United States*, p. 337, note, says: "For additional details respecting the route pursued by Coronado after the main army was sent back, consult the narrative of Jaramillo, the *Relacion del Suceso*, and other documents pertaining to the expedition, in Winship's *Coronado Expedition* (1896) and *Journey of Coronado* (1904), and in connection therewith a discussion of the route by F. W. Hodge, in J. V. Brower's *Memoirs of Explorations in the Basin of the Mississippi*, ii (St. Paul, 1899). Continuing due north from the upper waters of the Rio Colorado of Texas, Coronado's immediate force in thirty days' march, according to the *Relacion del*

Our Lady of Light

Painting on wood, in relief. Originally in the mission at Pecos. Now in possession of Dr. L. Bradford Prince, Santa Fé, N. M.

march, the Spanish army halted on the banks of a stream which flowed at the bottom of a deep and broad ravine. For several days past the appearance of the country had begun to change; a more exuberant vegetation had made its appearance, and Indian villages were met with whose inhabitants were clothed. There was in the Spanish troop one man specially charged with counting the steps in order to approximate the distances. According to his reckoning, they were then, at the end of thirty-seven days, two hundred and fifty leagues or six hundred and seventy-five miles from Bernalillo. But this distance cannot be taken as an air line. Coronado had marched to the north-east for seventeen days, thence, first east, afterwards, slightly south of east. We must also note that no other river has been met with since the crossing of the Canadian, except a small one at the bottom of a deep ravine, and which had been struck a few days previous. Owing to the direction and manner in which Coronado advanced, after crossing the Canadian, the only water-course which he could have met at that distance was the Canadian again. The first stream was probably the north fork of that river, and the second where the army came to a halt, was the main branch below the junction in the eastern part of the Indian Territory.

"The place was occupied or roamed over by a tribe which is called Teyas. Who these Indians were we cannot attempt to decide. They tattooed themselves either with paint or with incisions. This custom would tell in favor of their being Jumanos, a semi-sedentary

Suceso (or 'more than thirty days' march, although not long marches,' according to Jaramillo), reached the river of St. Peter and St. Paul the last of June, 1541. This was the 'river of Quivira' of the *Relacion del Suceso*, the present Arkansas river in Kansas, which was crossed at its southern bend, just east of the present Dodge City. The party continued thence northeast, down stream, and in thirty leagues, or six or seven days' march, reached the first of the Quivira settlements. This was at or near the present Great Bend, Kansas, before reaching the site of which the Turk was 'made example of.' That the inhabitants of Quivira were the Wichita Indians there can be no reasonable doubt. The Quivira people lived in grass or straw lodges, according to the Spaniards, a fact that was true of the Wichitas only of all the northern plains tribes. The habitations of their congeners and northern neighbors, the Pawnee (who may be regarded as the inhabitants of the province of Harahey), were earth lodges. The word *acochis*, mentioned by Castañeda as the Quivira term for 'gold,' is merely the Spanish adaptation of *hakwichis*, which signifies 'metal,' for of gold our Indians knew nothing until after the advent of the white man. After exploring Quivira for twenty-five leagues, Coronado sent 'captains and men in many directions,' but they failed to find that of which they went in search. There is no reason to suppose that Coronado's party went beyond the limits of the present State of Kansas."

Mr. Hodge is undoubtedly correct in his theory as to the route taken by Coronado, as Mr. Bandelier has evidently overlooked the fact that the bridge was built across a river which came down from Cicuyé; this could not be the Canadian; in flood times, the Pecos is as large as the Canadian; in ordinary seasons the flow of either is about the same in New Mexico.

tribe shifting to and fro across the eastern part of New Mexico at that time. Leaving this matter undecided, we must remark that the Teyas signified to Coronado that his guides had led him completely astray, the Quiviras being far north of the place. Castañeda adds that those guides had led Coronado in too southerly a direction, 'too near to Florida.' This is a further confirmation of what we have said, namely that the Spaniards marched like people losing their reckoning on the plains, in a circle or arc of a circle, first, north-east, then east, afterwards even south of east.

"At this place Coronado left the main body and with twenty-nine horsemen, and probably Father Padilla, struck out for Quivira. He moved northward, and, at the end of about forty days (the number is variously given) a large river was reached which he crossed to its northerly bank and followed its course to the northeast for upwards of twenty days. Finally, turning to the north inland, he reached, after sixty-seven days of short marches and occasional delays, the region called Quivira. The great river north of the Canadian can only have been the Arkansas, and they struck it some point below Fort Dodge, whence the river flows to the north-east. It is noteworthy also that Jaramillo states, while going in that direction, they descended the course of the stream.[242]

"It is therefore in northeastern Kansas, not far from the boundary of Nebraska, that we must look for the homes of the Quiviras in the years 1541 and 1543. The descriptions of the country furnished by Coronado himself, by his lieutenant, Jaramillo, and (from hearsay) by Castañeda, agree very well with the appearance of that country. As long as they remained south of the Arkansas the land was one great plain, without timber and very little water; north of the Arkansas, its aspect changed."

The writings of all the historians of the expedition under Coronado, from Mexico to the valley of the Kansas and its tributaries, do not disclose sufficient facts to determine with certainty the situs of the terminal point reached in 1541, but it is safe to conclude that Mr. Hodge has arrived at the most satisfactory solution of the problem. The opinions and conclusions of the earlier writers are entirely conflicting.[243] Mr. Winship quite closely agrees with the route marked

---

[242] Simpson, Gen. J. H., in *Smithsonian Report*, pp. 309-340, discusses the march of Coronado. He does not agree with Mr. Bandelier nor with Mr. Hodge. He takes Coronado across the Kansas river as well as the Arkansas. In doing this he is governed by the statement of the captain-general that he had reached 40° of latitude, and therefore locates Quivira on the Missouri in northeastern Kansas and southeastern Nebraska.

[243] That the reader may know how conflicting these conclusions are, the following list will afford some light:

Bandelier, A. F., *Final Report*, part i, pp. 44, 169, note 4, and p. 170, says

out by Mr. Bandelier. On the map which accompanies his *Memoir*, the province of Quivira covers central Kansas from a point not far

that the Quiviras were a band of roving Indians in northeastern Kansas, beyond the Arkansas, and more than one hundred miles northeast of Grand Bend.

Simpson, Gen. J. H., *Smithsonian Report*, 1869, says Quivira was the boundary between the states of Kansas and Nebraska, well on towards the Missouri river.

Bancroft, Hubert H., *History of Arizona and New Mexico*, p. 62, says: "There is nothing in the Spaniards' description of the region, or of the journey, to shake confidence in Simpson's conclusion that it was in the modern Kansas, between the Arkansas and Missouri Rivers."

Prince, L. B., *Historical Sketches*, p. 141, says that it was on the borders of the Missouri, somewhere between Kansas City and Council Bluffs.

Haynes, *Narr. and Crit. Hist. Am.*, vol. ii, p. 494, note, does not agree with the earlier writers, Gallatin, Squier, Kern, Abert, nor does he quite agree with Simpson, Bandelier, Hodge, or Prince, as he says, in his opinion, Coronado crossed the Kansas plains and came out at a point much farther west than latitude 40 degrees, upon the Platte river.

Winship, George Parker, *Coronado Expedition*, 14th B. A. E., p. 398, note, says: "Bandelier accounts for sixty-seven days of short marches and occasional delays between the separation of the force on the Canadian river and the arrival at Quivira. It may be that the seventy-seven days of desert marching which Coronado mentions in his letter of October 20, 1541, refers to this part of the journey, instead of to the whole journey from the bridge (near Mora on the Canadian) to Quivira. But the number sixty-seven originated in a blunder of Ternaux-Compans, who substituted it for seventy-seven, in translating this letter. The mistake evidently influenced Bandelier to extend the journey over more than it really took. But this need not affect his results materially, if we extend the amount of ground covered by each day's march and omit numerous halts, which were very unlikely, considering the condition of his party and the desire to solve the mystery of Quivira. If the Spaniards crossed the Arkansas somewhere below Fort Dodge, and followed it until the river turns toward the southeast, Quivira can hardly have been east of the middle part of the state of Kansas. It was more probably somewhere between the main forks of the Kansas river, in the central part of that state. Bandelier seems to have abandoned his documents as he approached the goal, and to have transported Coronado across several branches of the Kansas river, in order to fill out his sixty-seven days, which should have been seventy-seven, and perhaps to reach the region fixed on by previous conceptions of the limit of exploration. He may have realized that the difficulty in his explanation of the route was that it required a reduction of about one-fourth of the distance covered by the army in the eastward march as plotted by General Simpson. This can be accounted for by the wandering path which the army followed."

Mr. Hodge himself, at one time, believed that Coronado reached the Kansas river, for in Brower's *Memoirs* he says that Great Bend or its vicinity is the site of the first village of the province of Quivira and that Coronado, after leaving the village at or near Great Bend, continued in a northeasterly course, and either followed down the Smoky Hill, or crossed that stream and also the Saline, Solomon, and Republican Forks, reaching Kansas river not far from Junction City.

Davis, W. W. H., *Conquest of New Mexico*, thinks that Quivira was about one hundred and fifty miles due south of Santa Fé. The old pueblo which gave this idea to Mr. Davis is that of Tabira, often called the Gran Quivira.

Brower, J. V., *Quivira, Memoirs*, etc., pp. xii and xiii, also thinks that Quivira was on the Kansas river. See for description of village sites and weapons of

north of Dodge City to the bend of the Republican river, near Concordia, in Cloud county.

The captain-general, as a result of his visit to Quivira, derived small satisfaction, enjoying only the empty honor of taking possession in the name of his royal master. He erected a cross with the inscription, "Francisco Vasquez Coronado, general of an expedition, reached this place," and doubtless enjoyed also the manner in which he disposed of El Turco, who had been the cause of all his trials and who, as Jaramillo says, "called on all these people to attack and kill us. We learned of it, and put him under guard and strangled him that night so that he never waked up."[244]

Some time after the middle of August, 1541, Coronado and his little escort, totally unprepared for passing the winter at Quivira, and anxious to know the fate of the army which had been sent back under Arellano, started on the return trip. They left the Indian, Ysopete, in the village where the captain-general had erected the cross, and having secured Indian guides, the Spaniards soon reached the Arkansas. Arriving here, Coronado did not follow the route which he had taken when he came, but turned to the right and marched to the west, soon coming to the country of the Querechos, where the Turk had led them astray. After a march of forty days, traveling southwest, the captain-general reached Tiguex, in time to make preparations for spending the winter, and determining to pursue his explorations further, along with the entire army, the coming spring and summer.

CORONADO LEAVES QUIVIRA AND RETURNS TO TIGUEX

The army, the command of which had been given to Don Tristan de Arellano, when Coronado started north to discover the province of Quivira, reached Tiguex about the middle of July, 1541, having on the return trip, accomplished in twenty-five days' marching what

---

war and the chase found at places indicated by him, which "present such an array of facts that it does not seem possible that Coronado and his followers could have passed a hundred miles northeast from the Great Bend of the Arkansas without hearing of and discovering a great group of aboriginal villages, the inhabitants of which, for untold decades, occupied the valley of the Kansas, subsisting on an abundant natural wealth, which was permanently available and of the easiest possible access, conditions which were never willingly ignored by the North American Indians."

[244] Jaramillo, *Col. Doc. Flo.*, p. 161.

had taken thirty-seven days in going. In this journey they passed by many salt lakes upon which were pieces of salt "bigger than tables, as thick as four or five fingers." On the plains they passed many prairie-dog villages, and finally reached the Pecos river more than thirty leagues below where they had built the bridge on their outward march. The Indian guides informed them that this river, the Pecos, flowed into the river Tiguex, the Rio Grande, "more than twenty days from here and that its course turned toward the east."[245]

THE RETURN OF THE ARMY UNDER COMMAND OF ARELLANO

During the progress of the army across the plains the Indian guides in directing the course pursued, in the morning, at sunrise, would shoot an arrow forward, and thereafter shoot other arrows as the ones which had been shot were reached. When the army finally arrived at the pueblo of Cicuyé (Pecos) the Indians were found in revolt and refused to furnish the Spaniards with food.

Arriving at Tiguex, Arellano sent out foraging parties collecting supplies of food for the winter; some of these parties, in their wanderings, explored countries and found villages which had not before been known by the Spaniards. Captain Francisco Barrionuevo ascended the Rio Grande, where he came to two provinces, one of which was called Jemez, and the other Yuqueyunque.[246]

---

[245] Additional proof that it was the Pecos that was bridged, because the Pecos flows into the Rio Grande, which was the river of Tiguex.

Hodge, F. W., *Spanish Explorers in the Southern United States*, p. 338, note, thinks the army on its return reached the Pecos about eighty miles below Puerto de Luna, or not far from the present town of Roswell.

This was the second time the army had crossed this river; this time at a point more than thirty leagues below where they had built the bridge on their outward journey. The guides told them that it flowed into the Tiguex. How can Mr. Bandelier or Mr. Winship reconcile this fact with their conclusions that the bridge had been built over the Canadian, which finally flows into the Mississippi? Castañeda says that they followed up this river as far as Cicuyé. Had they followed up the Canadian the army never would have reached Cicuyé but would have gone into western Colfax county, or across the range into Taos.

It seems strange, however, if the army crossed the Pecos in the neighborhood of Roswell, that the beautiful streams of water near that place, and the springs, all so different from the brackish water of the Pecos, are not mentioned by Castañeda. I incline to the belief that the army crossed the Pecos further north than Roswell, else the Spring rivers would have been noticed and mentioned.

[246] Bandelier, A. F., *Final Report*, part i, note, p. 123: "Yuge-uinge-ge is the Yuqueyunque of Castañeda. The Tehuas occupied, says he, two pueblos on the Rio Grande, and four in the mountains. The four in the mountains may have

When Barrionuevo reached the last named province the entire nation left their villages, which were on either side of the river, and fled into the mountains, where they had four other villages, but so located that they could not be reached by horsemen. In these villages the Spaniards found some very fine pottery and many bowls "full of a carefully selected shining metal with which they glazed the earthenware."

THE SPANIARDS VISIT THE PUEBLO OF TAOS

Following up the Rio Grande from this point the Spaniards came to a village which they called Braba,[247] and which the Spaniards named Valladolid. This river was crossed by the natives upon wooden bridges, made of very long, squared logs. Here the Spaniards saw the largest and finest "hot rooms or estufas that there were in the entire country, for they had a dozen pillars, each one of which was twice as large around as one could reach and twice as tall as a man."[248] Castañeda says that Hernando de Alvarado also visited Taos at the time he discovered Cicuyé. Leaving the people of this province entirely at peace, Captain Barrionuevo and his party returned by quick marches down the valley to the winter quarters at Tiguex.

Another captain went down the Rio Grande a distance of eighty leagues until he reached a point where the river lost itself in the sands.[249] He passed by the pueblos in the vicinity of San Marcial

included, in addition to the three mentioned further on, Cu-ya-mungé. The information is of course imperfect, as Barrionuevo had no intercourse with the people, who fled at his approach. Yuge-uinge-ge is now in ruins and its site is occupied by the little hamlet of Chamita, opposite San Juan."
It was near Yuge-uing-ge that Juan de Oñate built his capital.
Today there remains but one pueblo of the Jemez; this is on the river Jemez, in Sandoval county, New Mexico. In the time of Coronado there were Giusiwa, Amushungkwa, Patoqua, and Astyalakwa. Near old Giusiwa are the ruins of the old Jemez church.

[247] Bandelier, A. F., *Final Report*, part i, p. 123. Taos is the "Braba" of Castañeda. His description, taken from the reports of Francisco Barrionuevo, is excellent, and can only apply to Taos; he also says that Braba was the most northerly of all the pueblos. No mention of Taos is found, as nobody visited it until 1598, when Oñate went there on the 14th of July (*Discurso*, p. 257). But in this document, as well as in the *Obediencia y Vassalje*, etc., *de San Juan Baptista*, p. 114, Taos is called a province. It is also named Tayberon. In 1630 Benavides speaks of only one pueblo of Taos, and thus it appears in all posterior documents.

[248] It was a very easy matter for these Indians to have secured large pine logs of this size in the pine-clad mountains lying immediately east of Taos.

[249] Bandelier, A. F., *Final Report*, part i, p. 130: "South of that place (Isleta) and almost touching the land of the Tiguas, began the range of the

and Socorro. At or very near San Marcial they came to the most southerly pueblo which was inhabited during the sixteenth century. It was the village of Tre-na-qúel, at which village was situate the furthest south of all the large communal houses [250] of the Pueblos.

Piros, which reached as far south as San Marcial, and consisted of at least ten settlements in sight of the river bank. Conspicuous among them were Alamillo north of Socorro, Pilabó on the site of Socorro itself, and Se-ne-cú, whose ruins are now covered by the present town of San Antonio. Alamillo was a conspicuous pueblo as late as 1680. It was then abandoned. The name of Pilabó, for the old pueblo on the present site of the town of Socorro, is taken from Benavides (*Memorial*, p. 16) 'el otro es el pueblo Pilabó, á la Virgen del Socorro.' The village of San Antonio de Senecú was the first mission founded on the southern Rio Grande on New Mexican soil. According to Vetancurt (*Cronica*, p. 309) it was established in 1630. Its founder was the Capuchin Fray Antonio de Arteaga. Benavides (*Memorial*, p. 15) places the foundation of the mission as early as 1626. It was abandoned and the pueblo destroyed in the year 1675, on the 23rd day of January. The Apaches pounced upon it, killing the priest, Fray Alonzo Gil de Avila, and many of the people. The remainder fled to Socorro or to El Paso. Fray Juan Alvarez, *Carta al Gobernador Francisco Cubero y Valdez*, 28th April, 1705 (Ms), says: 'Tambien el pueblo Senecú, mataron al Pe. Por. Fr. Alonzo Gil de Avila, y destruieron lo mas de la gentte Indiana.''

[250] Bandelier, A. F., *Final Report*, part i, p. 131: ''The Piros had crept up towards the coveted salt lagunes of the Manzano. The picturesque valley of A-bó, northeast of Socorro, contained at least two of their villages, A-bó proper, and Ten-a-bó, probably the ruin called to-day 'El Pueblo de los Siete Arroyos.' Lastly, still east of it, at the foot of the Mesa de los Jumanos, there was Tabira, now famous under the mis-leading name of 'La Gran Quivira.' It lay very near the range of the New Mexican Jumanos, so that it is not unlikely that the pueblo de los Jumanos, mentioned as a Piros village, is but another name given to Tabira.''

Oñate (*Discursos*, p. 240) says that the second pueblo after passing the ''mesilla de guinea, por ser de piedra negra'' was Qualacú. This black mesa is that of San Marcial, a very conspicuous object in that region for anyone coming up the river or through the ''Jornada del Muerto.'' In *Obediencia de San Juan* (p. 115) he speaks of ''Trenaquel de la mesilla, que es la primera poblacion de este reyno, hacia parte del sur y Nueva España.''

Of these three, or four, pueblos, it is only known that they were abandoned between 1670 and 1680, probably about 1675, or a little previously. The descendants of their inhabitants today live at Senecú in Chihuahua. Of the cause of their abandonment there is but one report, namely, that the Apaches compelled the people to leave. Fr. Juan Alvares (*Carta* Ms.) places the loss of the six pueblos of the Salines immediately before the slaughter at Senecú, and after the massacre at Hauicú in 1672. Fray Sylvestre Veles de Escalante (*Carta al Padre Morfi*, 1778) mentions the event as follows: ''Pocos años antes de la dicha sublevacion, destruyeron los enemigos apaches con casi continuas invasiones, siete pueblos de los cuarenta y seis dichos; que fueron Chilili, Tajique y Quarac, de Indios Tehuas; Abó, Jumancas y Tabira de Tompiros, todos los cuales estaban en la falda oriental de la sierra de Sandia, menos dos que estaban distantes de dicha sierra hacia las Salinas.'' Of these it seems that Cuaray or Quarac fell first. The people fled to Tajique. Those of the Piros villages retired to Socorro and Alamillo, or to El Paso, for safety.

The chief interest, historically, centers in the ruins called La Gran Quivira.

The inhabitants were Piros, whose villages extended up the Rio Grande to a point somewhere in the neighborhood of the present town of Belen.

There is no doubt that they are simply the remains of the pueblo of Ta-bi-ra. The name of Quivira was given to them in the latter part of the last century (18th) in consequence of a misunderstanding. The mission at Tabira was founded, and the older and smaller of the two churches built by Fray Francisco de Acevedo, between 1625 and 1644. Vetancurt (*Menologio*, p. 260). The large church and convent are posterior to that date, and were evidently never used, not even finished. There were Indians (Piros) from Tabira at El Paso in 1684. *Causa Criminal por Denunciacion de Andrés Jopita* Ms. p. 4.

Whether the pueblo ''de Jumanos'' was the same as Tabira it is difficult to determine. I suspect it to have been the same. In the document entitled *Confessiones y Declaraciones de varios Indios de los Pueblos del Nuevo Mexico*, 1683 (Ms., fol. 6) there is the deposition of an Indian calling himself Juan, and ''de nacion piro natural del pueblo de Jumanos en el nuebo Mejico.'' There was one Jumano village, if not more, but this particular one strikes me as being possibly a surname given to Tabira, owing to the latter being situated on the southern declivity of the ''Mesa de los Jumanos.''

Hodge, F. W., *The Language of the Piro*, Introduction, Am. Anthrop., vol. ii, note 3, July-September, 1909: ''In the early part of the seventeenth century the Piro, who have been classed as belonging to the Tanoan linguistic family, consisted of two divisions, one inhabiting the Rio Grande valley from the present town of San Marcial, Socorro county, New Mexico, northward to within about fifty miles of Albuquerque, where the Tigua settlements began; the other division, sometimes called Tompiros and Salineros, occupying the desert stretches east of the river in the vicinity of the salt lagoons, or salinas, where they bordered the eastern group of Tigua settlements on the south. The western or Rio Grande branch of the Piro was visited in 1540 (1541) by members of the Coronado Expedition, in 1580 by Chamuscado, in 1583 by Espejo (who found them occupying ten villages along the river and in others near by), in 1598 by Oñate, and in 1621-1630 by Fray Alonzo Benavides, who relates that they were settled in fourteen pueblos along the river.

''The establishment of missions among the Piro began in 1626. In that year the most southerly church and monastery in New Mexico were built at Senecú by Arteaga and Zuñiga (to whom are attributed the planting of the first vines and the manufacture of wine in this region), and during the same year missions at Sevilleta, Socorro, and probably also at Alamillo were founded. It is not improbable that the Piro of the Rio Grande, although said to number 6,000 in 1630, had been already seriously harassed by the Apache, for Servilleta had been depopulated and burned in consequence of inter-tribal wars prior to the founding of the missions, and was not re-settled until the missionaries arrived. Moreover the fourteen villages along the Rio Grande occupied by the Piro in 1630 were reduced to four half a century later. 'This was due not only to the efforts of the missionaries to gather their flocks into larger pueblos,' says Bandelier, 'but also to the danger to which these Indians were exposed from the Apaches of the ''Perillo'' and the ''Gila,'' as the southern bands of that restless tribe were called.'

''The area occupied by the Piro of the Salinas extended from the pueblo of Abó southeastward to and including the pueblo of Tabira, commonly but improperly called 'Gran Quivira,' a distance of about 25 miles. The habitat of the eastern Piro was even more desert in character than that of the eastern Tigua, which bounded it on the north, for the Arroyo de Abó, on which Abó pueblo was situated, is the only perennial stream in that region, the inhabitants of Tabira

Arrow Heads from Quivira

This captain did not proceed beyond where the river sank into the sands, because he was commissioned by Arellano to go only a distance of eighty leagues, and therefore he returned to Tiguex, where he found the commander much exercised because of the failure of Coronado to return within the promised time, which had already expired. Owing to this fact, Arellano placed Barrionuevo in com-

and Tenabó depending entirely on the storage of rainwater for their supply. In addition to the three pueblos named, Bandelier has concluded that the now ruined villages known by the Spanish names Pueblo Blanco, Pueblo Colorado and the Pueblo de la Parida, were probably the eleven inhabited settlements of the Salinas seen by Chamuscado in 1580, but at least three of this number were occupied by the Tigua. Juan de Oñate, in 1598, also visited the pueblos of the Salinas, and to Fr. Francisco de San Miguel, a chaplain of Oñate's forces, was assigned the Piro country as part of his mission district. The headquarters of this priest being at Pecos, many miles to the northward, it is not likely that much active mission work was done among the Piro during his incumbency, which covered only about three years.

''The first actual missions among the Piro pueblos of the Salinas were established in 1629 by Francisco de Acevedo at Abó and Tabira, and probably also at Tenabó; but before the massive-walled churches and monasteries were completed, the village dwellers of both the Salinas and the Rio Grande suffered so seriously from the depredations of the Apaches, that Senecú on the Rio Grande, as well as every pueblo of the Salinas, was deserted before the great pueblo insurrection of 1680. Prior to the raid on Senecú by the Apache, in 1675, six of the inhabitants of that village were executed for the murder of the alcalde mayor and four other Spaniards. Probably on account of the fear with which the Spaniards were known to be regarded by the Piro after this occurrence, they were not invited by the northern pueblos to participate in the revolt against the Spaniards in 1680; consequently when Otermin, the governor, retreated from Santa Fé to El Paso in that year, he was joined by nearly all the inhabitants of Socorro, Sevilleta and Alamillo. These, with the former inhabitants of Senecú, who, since the destruction of their village by the Apache, had resided at Socorro, were afterwards established in the new villages of Socorro, Texas, and Senecú del Sur ('Senecú of the South') in Chihuahua, on the Rio Grande below El Paso, where their remnant still survives.

''In attempting to re-conquer New Mexico in the following year, Otermin caused Alamillo to be burned, because the few remaining inhabitants fled at his approach. Only three families remained at Sevilleta when the Spaniards retreated, but these had departed and the pueblo was almost in ruins on their return in 1681.

''The entire Piro division of the Tanoan family probably numbered 9,000 early in the seventeenth century. Now, only about sixty individuals are known to survive, and although these still retain a shadow of their aboriginal customs, they are 'Mexicans' to all intents and purposes, and perhaps only one or two have any remembrance of their native language.''

Bancroft, Hubert H., *Native Races*, vol. iii, p. 714, gives the Lord's Prayer in the Piro language. It is as follows:

''Quitatac nasaul e yapolhua tol huy quiagiana mi quiamnarinu. Jaquie mugilley nasamagui hikiey quiamsamae, hikiey, hiquiquiamo quia inae, huskilley nafoleguey, gimorey, y apol y ahuley, quialiey, nasan e pomo llekey, quiale mahimnague yo se mahi kana rohoy, se teman quiennatehui mukilley, nani, nani emolley quinaroy zetasi, nasan quianatehuey pemcihipompo y, qui solaquey quifollohipuca. Kuey maihua atellan, folliquitey. Amen.''

mand, and with forty selected men started out in search of the captain-general. When he reached Cicuyé the inhabitants of that stronghold came out to fight, the engagement lasting about four days, during which time he threw some cannon balls into the pueblo, killing several men, among them two of their principal chiefs. After this affair it was learned that Coronado was coming and he was welcomed with great joy, and together they returned with their commands to Tiguex.

The captain-general was given a great welcome when he arrived at Tiguex. The Indian, Xabe, who had been given to Coronado at Cicuyé, when he started off in search of Qui-

CORONADO ARRIVES AT TIGUEX

vira, was with Don Tristan de Arellano when it was announced that Coronado was coming and was greatly pleased, saying to all, "now when the general comes, you will see that there is gold and silver in Quivira, although not so much as the Turk said." When Coronado arrived, and Xabe saw that they had found nothing, he was sad and silent and kept declaring that there was some. As Castañeda remarks, "he made many believe that it was so, because the general had not dared to enter into the country on account of its being thickly settled, and that he would lead the army there after the rains were over." This declaration of the Indian had much to do with the subsequent dissensions in the army. The men were not ready to believe, as Castañeda says, that "there was no gold there, but instead had suspicions that there was some further back in the country, because, although this was denied they knew what the thing was and had a name for it among themselves — *acochis*."

The inactivities of camp life during the winter season gave much opportunity for gossip, discussion, and consequent dissatisfaction and dissension. The captain-general made every effort to induce the Indians to return to their villages, but was uniformly unsuccessful. Foraging parties were sent out. The army was in great need of clothing and, as Castañeda remarks, "necessity knows no law, and the captains, who collected the cloth divided it badly, taking the best for themselves and their friends and soldiers, and leaving the rest for the soldiers, and so there began to be some angry murmurings on account of this. Others also complained because they noticed that some favored ones were spared in the work and in the watches and received better portions of what was divided, both of cloth and food." In this manner the entire winter was passed, when an accident happened to the captain-general which fixed his determination and gave him a good excuse for returning to Mexico.

Coronado had already announced that he proposed returning to Quivira with the army, and the men began their preparations for the journey. As the historian of the expedition states, "since nothing in this life is at the disposition of men but all is under the ordination of God, it was His will that we should not accomplish this, and so it happened that one feast day the general went out on horseback to amuse himself, as usual, riding with the Captain Don Rodrigo Maldonado. He was on a powerful horse, and his servants had put on a new girth, which must have been rotten at the time, for it broke during the race and he fell over on the side where Don Rodrigo was, and as his horse passed over him it hit his head with its hoof, which laid him at the point of death, and his recovery was slow and doubtful." [251]

It was said that a friend of the captain-general, in Spain, had prophesied that Coronado would some day become a powerful lord in a far-distant country, but would receive a fall which would cause his death. During his illness, it is said that this prediction so influenced Coronado that he gave up all desire to go to Quivira, and only longed to return to his family, where he might die surrounded by his wife and children.

During the time that Coronado was recovering from this accident, Don Garcia Lopez de Cardenas, who had started to go to Mexico, came back in flight from Suya, bringing the news that the town was deserted and the people, horses, and cattle were all dead. This news was brought to Coronado only after he had so fully recovered as

---

[251] Mota Padilla, cap. xxxiii, 6, p. 166: "así el (gobernador) como los demas caiptanes del ejercito, debian estar tan ciegos de la pasion de la codicia de riquesas, que no trataban de radicarse poblando en aquel paraje que veian tan abastecido, ni de reducir á los indios é instruirlos en algo de la fé, que es la que debian propagar; solo trataron de negordar sus caballos para lo que se ofresiese pasado el invierno; y andando adiestrando el gobernador uno que tenia muy brioso se le fue la silla, y dando la boca en el suelo, quedo sin sentido, y aunque despues se recobro, el juicio le quedo diminuto, con lo cual trataron todos de desistir de la empresa."

Gomara, cap. ccxiv: "Cayó en Tiguex del cauallo Francisco Vasques, y con el golpe salió de sentido, y deuaneaua; lo qual unos tuniero por dolor, y otros por fingido, ca estauan mal con el, porque no pablaua."

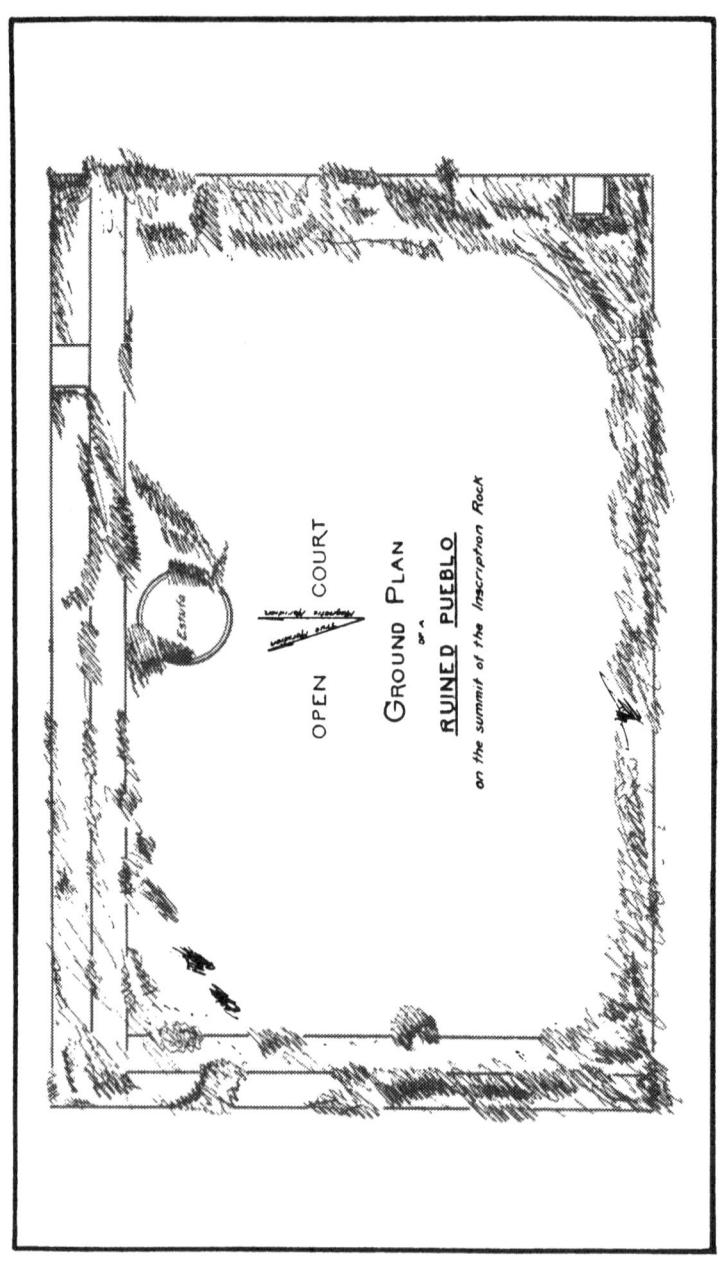

to be up and about the camp, and it so affected him that he was compelled to return to his bed. Meanwhile, as Castañeda says, Coronado made up his mind to return to New Spain and through the influence of certain friends the soldiers began talking and holding consultations about it, and finally sent a petition to the captain-general asking him to return with the army to their homes in Mexico. When Coronado was approached upon the subject and had read the petition, he was opposed to making an order for the return of the army, apparently, but all the gentlemen and captains "supported them, giving him their signed opinions, and as some were in this, they could give it at once, and they even persuaded others to do the same." In this manner it was made to appear that "they ought to return to New Spain, because they had not found any riches, nor had they discovered any settled country out of which estates could be formed for all the army." [252]

As before stated, the news brought by Don Garcia Lopez de Cardenas, who had received permission from Coronado to return to New Spain, a letter having been brought to him by Don Pedro de Tovar announcing the death of a brother, had a very pronounced effect upon the mind of the captain-general. Cardenas related how he had found the town of Suya deserted; that a revolt had occurred

---

[252] Castañeda, *Relacion*, etc., Winship's translation, p. 532: "When he had obtained their signatures, the return to New Spain was at once announced, and since nothing can ever be concealed, the double dealing began to be understood, and many of the gentlemen found that they had been deceived and had made a mistake. They tried in every way to get their signatures back again from the general, who guarded them so carefully that he did not go out of one room, making his sickness seem very much worse, and putting guards about his person and room, and at night about the floor on which he slept. In spite of all this they stole his chest, and it is said that they did not find their signatures in it, because he kept them in his mattress; on the other hand, it is said that they did recover them. They asked the general to give them 60 picked men, with whom they would remain and hold the country until the viceroy could send them support, or recall them, or else that the general would leave them the army and pick out 60 men to go back with him. But the soldiers did not want to remain either way, some because they had turned their prow toward New Spain, and others because they saw clearly the trouble that would arise over who should have command. The gentlemen, I do not know whether because they had sworn fidelity or because they feared that the soldiers would not support them, did what had been decided upon, although with an ill will, and from this time on they did not obey the general as readily as formerly and they did not show any affection for him. He made much of the soldiers and humored them, with the result that he did what he desired and secured the return of the whole army."

Jaramillo says that after the fall from his horse Coronado "conceived the idea of returning, which ten or twelve of us were unable to prevent by dissuading him from it."

under the leadership of one, Pedro de Avila; that these had gone back to Culiacan, leaving the captain, Diego de Alcaraz, very ill, with only a few men to guard the town. Alcaraz, owing to the limited number of men at his disposal, was unable to compel the return of the deserters under de Avila. On their way to Culiacan the force under de Avila killed a number of people, and, finally reaching Culiacan, where Hernandarias Saavedra detained them by means of promises, hoping for the arrival of Juan Gallego from New Spain with a force sufficient to take them back to San Hieronimo. After the departure of de Avila and the others, the natives, watching their opportunity, early one morning before day, began an attack upon the village. So sudden was the assault that the Indians were not seen until they had begun to kill and plunder. In their endeavors to escape from the village, the captain was mortally wounded; afterwards several Spaniards came back on horseback and attacked the Indians, rescuing a few of their friends who had been taken captive. In this affair three Spaniards were killed, besides many of the servants and more than twenty horses. The following day, the survivors, not having any horses, started on foot toward Culiacan, keeping away from the highways, and not having any food until they reached Corazones. These refugees finally reached Culiacan where they were received by the mayor, Saavedra, and entertained as best he could until the arrival of Juan Gallego.

In the first part of the month of April, 1542, the captain-general and his army began their homeward march to Mexico. Before starting he gave orders to the soldiers to release all of the natives who were held as servants, permitting them to return to their villages, if they so desired.[253]

THE ARMY STARTS ON ITS RETURN TO MEXICO — FR. JUAN DE PADILLA AND OTHERS REMAIN BEHIND

Several were left behind, among the rest the Franciscan friar Juan de Padilla, a lay brother named Luis Descalona, a Portuguese named Campo, three negro slaves, one of whom had already become a Franciscan novice, a half breed, and two Mexican Indians.[254]

---
[253] Castañeda, *Relacion*, Winship's translation, 14th B. A. E., p. 536.

[254] Jaramillo, *Narrative*, Winship's translation, 14th B. A. E., p. 592: "When this return had been ordered, the Franciscan Friars who were with us,

According to the historian, Castañeda, Coronado was very happy and contented when the time came for them to start on the journey from Tiguex to Cibola. On this part of the march many of the horses belonging to the army died, the journey being a very severe one and consuming ten days. After the army reached Cibola a long rest was taken before starting across the sandy wilderness between that place and Sonora. Finally the army left, leaving the whole country well disposed and at peace. Several of the Indian allies who had come from Mexico with Coronado remained at the pueblo of Hawaikúh.[255]

The courage and devotion of the two friars, Juan de Padilla [256]

---

one of them a regular and the other a lay brother, who were called, the regular one, Friar Juan de Padilla and the lay one, Friar Luis de Escalona, were told to get ready, although they had permission from their provincial so that they could remain. Friar Luis wished to remain in these flat-roofed houses, saying that he would raise crosses for those villagers with a chizel and adze they left him, and would baptize several poor creatures who could be led, on the point of death, so as to send them to heaven, for which he did not desire any other company than a little slave named Christopher to be his so as to help him; and he brought up so many things in favor of this that he could not be denied, and so nothing more has been heard from him. The knowledge that this friar would remain there was the reason that many Indians from hereabouts stayed there and also two negroes, one of them mine, who was called Sebastian, and the other one Melchior Perez, the son of the licentiate, la Torre. This negro was married and had his wife and children. I also recall that several Indians remained behind in the Quivira region, besides a Tarascan belonging to my company, who was named Andrew. Friar Juan de Padilla preferred to return to Quivira and persuaded them to give him those Indians whom I said we had brought as guides. They gave him these, and he also took a Portuguese and a free, Spanish-speaking Indian, who was the interpreter, and who passed as a Franciscan Friar, and a half-blood and two Indians from Capottan or thereabouts, I believe. He had brought these up and took them in the habits of friars, and he took some sheep and mules and a horse and ornaments and other trifles. I do not know whether it was for the sale of these or for what reason, but it seems that they killed him, and those who did it were the lay servants, or these same Indians whom he took back from Tiguex, in return for the good deeds he had done them. When he was dead, the Portuguese whom I have mentioned fled and also one of the Indians that I said he took in the habits of friars, or both of them, I believe. I mention this because they came back to this country of New Spain by another way and a shorter route than the one of which I have told, and they came out in the valley of Panuco.''

[255] Castañeda, *Relacion*, Winship's translation, p. 536.

Antonio de Espejo, in the *Relacion* of his visit to New Mexico in 1582 (Pacheco y Cardenas, *Doc. de Ind.*, vol. xv, p. 180), states that at Zuñi-Cibola, ''hallamos tres indios cristianos que se digeron llamar Andrés de Cuyacan, y Gaspár de Mexico, y Anton de Guadalajara, que digeron haber entrado con Francisco Vasquez, y reformandolos en la lengua mexicana que ya casi al tenian olvidada; destos supimos que habia llegado alli el dicho Francisco Vasquez Coronado.''

[256] Davis, W. W. H., *Spanish Conquest of New Mexico*, p. 231, gives the fol-

and Luis de Escalona, true soldiers of the cross, is evidenced by
their determination to remain among the
FRIAR JUAN DE PADILLA savages after the departure of the army.
Willing to remain alone, unarmed, among
the savage tribes, they displayed a zeal in the work of salvation
seldom equaled in the history of Christianity. Separated from

lowing extract translated from an old Spanish Ms. at Santa Fé: "When
Coronado returned to Mexico, he left behind him, among the Indians of Cibola,
the father Fray Francisco Juan de Padilla, the father Fray Juan de la Cruz,
and a Portuguese named Andrés del Campo. Soon after the Spaniards departed,
Padilla and the Portuguese set off in search of the country of the Grand Quivira,
where the former understood there were innumerable souls to be saved. After
travelling several days, they reached a large settlement in the Quivira country.
The Indians came out to receive them in battle array, when the friar, knowing
their intentions, told the Portuguese and his attendants to take to flight, while
he would wait their coming, in order that they might vent their fury on him as
they ran. The former took to flight and, placing themselves on a height within
view, saw what happened to the friar. Padilla awaited their coming on his
knees, and when they arrived where he was they immediately put him to death.
The same happened to Juan de la Cruz, who was left behind at Cibola, which
people killed him. The Portuguese and his attendants made their escape and
ultimately arrived safely in Mexico, where he told what had occurred."

General Davis, when asked, some years since, regarding this manuscript, stated
that when he re-visited Santa Fé, a few years ago, he learned that one of his
successors in the post of governor of the territory, having despaired of disposing
of the immense mass of old documents and records deposited in his office, by
the slow process of using them to kindle fires, had sold the entire lot, an invaluable collection of material bearing on the history of the southwest and its early
European and native inhabitants, as junk.

I may remark, that if the "old documents" sold as "junk" included the
"manuscript" used by General Davis in bringing out the above story of the
death of Fr. Juan de Padilla, it is just as well that they were lost to the world
in the manner named. I do not believe that any such "manuscript" was ever
in the Santa Fé archives; the fact that the "Grand Quivira" is mentioned by
Davis is clear proof to my mind that some one either made a poor translation
of some old document, written long after 1680, or a large part of the Davis
story is the product of a very romantic imagination.

What he says about the disposition of some of the old archives is partially
true; the official who "disposed" of them was Governor Pyle; but it is not
believed that much was used to kindle fires or sold as junk. It is true that some
of the papers were disposed of, but, in these later years, and about the time of
the establishment of the Court of Private Land Claims, and at the time when
interests in old Spanish and Mexican land grants were being purchased by various persons, and still later when old documents were valuable and found a ready
sale as curios, etc., from various sources, large numbers of these old papers which,
at one time had undoubtedly been in the archives and which it was supposed
had been used to kindle fires, began to see the light of day. No matter how
much truth there may be in the destruction of the archives during the Pyle
administration, nothing was destroyed which ante-dated 1680. Nearly everything prior to that date was destroyed during the revolt among the Pueblos of
that year.

The archives which were "saved" from the Pyle administration, minus all
that did not fall into the hands of interested persons purchasing interests in

Fac-simile of Page of Ms., Grant of Lands to the Pueblo of Pecos, 1689

home and friends by pathless wastes these martyrs seemed to be only too willing to suffer death if by so doing they could rescue the souls of these benighted barbarians. Fr. Juan de Padilla had been a soldier in his earlier years, "hombre belicoso," as Castañeda says, and was, at the time he came with Coronado, a regular friar of the Lesser Order of Franciscans. He had come from Andalusia to Mexico, and had been stationed at Tulanzinco and at Tzapotla in Xalisco, where he was first guardian and had performed great service with the natives for the cause of Christianity. As before stated in this volume, he accompanied Pedro de Tovar to Moqui, where he aroused the soldiers under Tovar to begin the attack upon the natives. When he had returned to Hawaikúh, he also accompanied Hernando de Alvarado on the expedition to Tiguex, and later on when Coronado and the army set out in search of the province of Quivira, the fray accompanied him and set up the emblem of Christianity in that far off country.[257]

land grants, or falling into the hands of persons who claimed interests in lands in New Mexico, who found among these archives documents which aided them in the courts in establishing title, and minus also some carried off by curio hunters, are now in the custody of the general government at Washington, whence they were taken during the administration of Governor M. A. Otero.

Before the destruction by fire of the capitol building at Santa Fé, these archives were in the territorial library, on the first floor of the capitol, at that time being chronologically arranged and indexed by A. F. Bandelier and Mrs. Anita J. Chapman. On the night of the fire, the writer helped carry them to a place of safety.

[257] Mota Padilla, cap. xxxiii, 7, p. 167, gives the story of these friars. This historian says: "Pero porque el padre Fr. Juan de Padilla, cuando acompanó á D. Francisco Vasquez Coronado hasta el pueblo de Quivira, puso en el una cruz, protestando no desempararla aunque le costase la vida, por tener entendido hacer fruto en aquellos indios y en los comarcanos, determinó volverse, y no bastaron las instancias del gobernador y demas capitanes para que desisteiese por entonces del pensamiento. El Padre Fr. Luis de Ubeda rogó tambien le dejasen volver con el padre Fr. Juan de Padilla hasta el pueblo de Coquite, en donde le parecia podrian servir de domesticar algo aquellos indios por paracerle se hallaban con alguna disposicion; y que pues el era viejo, emplearia la corta vida que le quedase en procurar la salvacion de las almas de aquellos miserables. Á su imitacion tambien el padre Fr. Juan de la Cruz, religioso lego (como lo era Fr. Luis de Ubeda) pretendio quedarse en aquellas provincias de Tiguex, y porque se discurrio que con el tiempo se conseguirria la poblacion de aquellas tierras, condescendió el gobernador á los deseos de aquellos apostolicos varones, y les dejaron proveidos de lo que por entonces pareció necessaria; y tambien quiso quedarse un soldado, de nacion portugues, llamado Andrés del Campo, con ánimo de servir al padre Padilla, y tambien dos indizuelos que en el exercito hacian oficios de sacritanes, y otro muchacho mestizo; de jarinle á dicho padre Padilla ornamentos y provision para que celebrase en santo sacrificio de la misa, y algunos biencillos que pudiese dar á los indios para atraerlos á su voluntad.

"Quedaron estos benditos religiosos como corderos entre lobos; y viendose

Of no less noble and fearless character was the Fray Luis de Escalona. Among the first to participate in the conflict with the natives at Hawaikúh, he too wished to remain so that he could "raise crosses for those villagers with a chisel and adze . . . and would baptize several poor creatures who could be led, on the point of death, so as to send them to heaven." This friar selected

solos trato el pardre Fr. Juan de Padilla con los Tiguex, el fin que le movia á quedarse ellos, que no era otro que el de tratar de la salvacion de sus almas; que ya los soldados se habian ido, que no les serian molestos, que el pasaba á otras poblaciones y les dejaba al padre Juan de la Cruz para que les fuese intruyendo en lo que debian saber para ser cristianos é hijos de la Santa Iglesia, como necessario para salvar sus almas, que les tratasen bien, y que el procuraria volver á consolarles; despidese con gran tenura, dejando, como prelado, lleno de bendiciones, á Fr. Juan de la Cruz, y los indios de Tiguex señalaron una escuadra de sus soldados que guiasen á dichos padres Fr. Juan de Padilla y Fr. Luis de Ubeda hasta el pueblo de Coquite, en donde les recibieron con demonstraciones de alegria, y haciendo la misma recomendacion por el padre Fr. Luis de Ubeda, le dejó, y guiadó de otros naturales del mismo pueblo, salió para Quivira con Andrés del Campo, donados indizuelos y el muchacho mestizo; llego á Quivira y se postro al pie de la cruz, que hallo en donde le habia colocado; y con limpieza, toda la circunferencia, como lo habia encargado, de que se alegro, y luego comenzo á hacer los oficios de padre maestro y apostol de aquellas gentes; y ahlandolos dociles y con buen animo, se inflamo, su corazon, y le pareció corto numero de almas para Dios las de aquel pueblo, y trato de ensanchar los seños de nuestra madre la Santa Iglesia, para que acogiese á cuantos se le decia haber en mayores distancias.

"Salió de Quivira, acompañado de su corta comitiva, contra voluntad de los indios de aquel pueblo, que le amaban como á su padre, mas á una jornada le salieron indios de guerra, y conociendo mal ánimo de aquellos barbaros, le rogo al portugues, que pues iba á caballo huyese, y que en su conserva llevase aquellos donados y muchachos, que como tales podrian correr y escaparse; hicieronlo asi por no hallarse capaces de otro modo para la defensa, y el bendito padre, hincado de rodillas afrecio la vida, que por reducir almas á Dios tenia sacrificada, logrando los ardientes deseos de su corazon, la felicidad de ser muerto flechando por aquellos indios barbaros, quienes le arrojaron en un joyo, cubriendo el cuerpo con inumerables piedras. Y vuelto el Portugues con los indizuelos á Quivira, dieron la noticia, la que sintieron mucho aquellos naturales, por el amor que tenian á dicho padre, y mas lo sintieran si hubieran tenido pleno conocimiento de la falta que les hacia; no sabe el dia de su muerto, aunque si se tiene por cierto haber sido en el año de 1542; y en algunos papeles que dejó escritos D. Pedro de Tovar en la villa de Culiacan, se dice que los indios habian salido á matar á este bendito padre, por robar los ornamentos, y que habia memoria de que en su muerte se vieron grandes prodigios, como fue inundarse la tierra, verse globos de fuego, cometas y oscurecerse el sol.

"Del padre Fr. Juan de la Cruz, la noticia que tiene es, que despues de haber trabajado en la instruccion de los indios en Tiguex y en Coquite, murió flechando de indios, porque no todos abrazaron su doctrina y consejos, con los que trataba detestasen sus barbaras costumbres, aunque por lo general era muy estimado de los caciques y demas naturales, que habian visto la veneracion con que el general, capitanes y soldados trataban. El padre, Fr. Luis de Ubeda se mantenia en una choza por celda ó cueva, en donde le ministraban los indios, con un poco de atole, tortillas y frijoles, el limitado sustento, y no se supo de su muerte; si quedó entre cuantos le conocieron la memoria de su perfecta vida."

the pueblo of Cicuyé as the scene of his future labors, and being known in the army and among the Indians and servants as a "mui santa persona," several of the Mexican Indians and negroes determined to remain with him.

The friars were ready and anxious to start on their journey, and for that purpose Coronado furnished them with an escort which accompanied them as far as Cicuyé. Everything that was needed for the celebration of mass was given to the friars, besides some trinkets, which it was intended to use in maintaining the good will of the Indians. When they arrived at Cicuyé, the friars were gladly received by the inhabitants. Friar Luis remained at Cicuyé, and the last that was ever heard of him came through some soldiers, who, before the army left Tiguex for Hawaikúh, had gone to Cicuyé "to take him some sheep that were left for him to keep, met him as he was on his way to some other villages that were fifteen or twenty leagues from Cicuyé, accompanied by some followers." The friar sent word to the army that he felt very hopeful that he was liked at the village and that his teachings would bear fruit, although he complained that the old men were falling away from him, and, he believed, would finally kill him.

It is a difficult matter for the present age to understand or realize the true character of these missionaries, or to appreciate the quality of their courage. Physically, their courage was something marvelous; no soldier, officer, or man could exceed them, for theirs was based upon an implicit and unwavering faith in the doctrines of Christianity. Imbued with the ideas which they had, they gloried in the destruction, at their own hands, of the temples of idolatry which the natives used for their worship. As is said by Fr. Zarate-Salmeron, "It is worth consideration that there has been no corner discovered in this New Spain in which the first Columbus was not a fraile of Saint Francis. They have ever been first to shed their blood, that with such good mortar the edifice should be lasting and eternal." While it was not the policy of the Spanish government to send these missionaries to the New World purely from philanthropic motives, still as far as the friars themselves were concerned, their work was simply the salvation of souls. The friar Luis, whose gown was pierced by the hostile arrow, was only one of hundreds who succeeded him, possessing the courage and qualities of a soldier, only too glad to offer up his life, if necessary, that souls of the heathen might be saved. Kind, gentle, and considerate, still they possessed that fighting spirit which gave them influence with all brave men, and this quality attached the natives to them and gave them influence in converting the savage to the religion of Christ. They quickly grasped the methods of thought of these barbarians; they grafted the Christian religion upon the Pagan wherever it was possible, without an assault upon their own consciences; they gave them the cross with the result that this symbol was worshiped with even as much veneration if not more than that which had been accorded their own idols, for as Alvarado says, with reference to the cross, "in the places where crosses were raised, we saw them worship these. They made offerings to these of their powder and feathers, and some left the blankets they had on. They showed so much zeal that some climbed up on the others to grasp the arms of the cross, to place feathers and flowers there; and others bringing ladders, while some held them, went up to tie strings, so as to fasten the flowers and the feathers."

Although we do not know what became of the friar Luis, let us believe with Castañeda, "that as he was a man of good and holy life, our Lord will protect him and give him grace to convert many of those peoples, and end his days in guiding them in the faith."

Friar Juan de Padilla left Cicuyé, escorted only by a few Pecos Indians, the soldiers with whom he had come from Tiguex returning to that place and rejoining the army, to cross the pathless plains for Quivira. After many days' travel, he reached the province and prostrated himself at the foot of the cross which he had erected there a few months before. According to Mota Padilla, he found this emblem "all around it clean, as he had charged them to keep it, which rejoiced him, and then he began the duties of a teacher and apostle of that people; and finding them teachable and well disposed, his heart burned within him, and it seemed to him that the number of souls of that village was but a small offering to God and he sought to enlarge the bosom of our mother, the Holy Church, that she might receive all those he was told were to be found at greater distances. He left Quivira, attended by his small company, against the will of the village Indians, who loved him as their father. At more than a day's journey the Indians met him on the war-path, and knowing the evil intent of those barbarians, he asked the Portuguese, that as he was on horseback he should flee and take under his protection the oblates and the lads who could thus run away and escape . . . and the blessed father, kneeling down, offered up his life which he had sacrificed for the winning of souls to God, attaining the ardent longings of his soul, the felicity of being killed by the arrows of those barbarous Indians, who threw him into a pit, covering his body with innumerable stones. . . It is said that the Indians had gone out to murder the blessed father in order to steal the ornaments, and it was remembered that at his death were seen great prodigies, as it were, the earth flooded, globes of fire, comets and obscuration of the sun.'' [258]

Thus perished the first white man, known to have met his death at the hands of savages, in what is now the state of Kansas. His crown of martyrdom rests safely.[259]

Coronado set out into the wilderness, leaving behind him the settlements of Cibola. The natives followed the army for two or three days, picking up the cast-off baggage of the soldiers and detaining those of the Mexican Indians whom it was possible to persuade to remain in the country. Altogether the natives succeeded in carrying off several people besides those who remained of their

---

[258] Winship, George Parker, *Castañeda*, Introduction: ''The friar was successful in his labors until he endeavoured to enlarge the sphere of his influence, when the jealousy, or possibly the cupidity of the Indians led them to kill him, rather than permit the transference to some other tribe of the blessings which he had brought them.''

Vetancurt in the *Menologio*, gives the date of the martyrdom of Fray Juan de Padilla as November 30, 1544, and I see no reason to prefer the general statements of Jaramillo, Castañeda, and Mota Padilla, which seem to imply that it took place in 1542. De Campo and the other companions of the friar brought the news to Mexico. They must have returned some time previous to 1552, for Gomara mentions their arrival in Tampico, on the Gulf of Mexico, in his *Conquista de Mexico*, published in that year. Herrera and Gomara say that the fugitives had been captured by Indians and detained as slaves for ten months. The historians state also that a dog accompanied the fugitives. Further mention of dogs in connection with the Coronado expedition is in the stories of one accompanying Estevan which Alarcon heard along the Colorado river; also in the account of the death of Melchior Diaz, and in the reference by Castañeda to the use of these animals as beasts of burden by certain plains tribes.

Mendieta and Vetancurt say that, of the two donados, Sebastian died soon after his return, and the other lived long as a missionary among the Zacatecas.

[259] Hodge, F. W., *Notes to Translation of Benavides' ''Memorial,''* Land of Sunshine, September-October, 1900, p. 288, declares that Fr. Padilla met his death in 1544. It is to be remembered that Coronado left Tiguex for New Spain in 1542, and Vetancurt says that ''Despues de dos años procuro entrar mas adentro el P. Padilla.''

own accord. The journey across the desert was accomplished without the occurrence of any event of note, and on the second day before reaching Chichilticalli, they met Juan Gallego, with reënforcements from New Spain and necessary supplies for Coronado's army. When Gallego saw that the army was on its homeward march, he told the captain-general that he was glad of it, and after reaching army headquarters, according to Castañeda, there was considerable agitation among the soldiers composing Gallego's force, who were desirous of continuing their march into the country from whence Coronado had returned, or else establish a settlement somewhere in that region until the viceroy could receive an account of what had occurred.

However, the soldiers under Coronado would listen to nothing except an immediate return to Mexico, which was then determined upon. It was now apparent that the authority of the captain-general was waning, as Castañeda says, "he had been disobeyed already and was not much respected."

When the army reached the Spanish settlements of New Galicia there were frequent desertions from the ranks, and it was only with the greatest effort that the captain-general was able to keep together even a respectable command with which to enter the City of Mexico, where he made his report to the viceroy.

When Coronado reached the city he appeared "very sad and very weary, completely worn out and shame faced." As Mr. Winship says,[260] "Suarez de Peralta was a boy on the streets of the capital. His recollections give a vivid picture of the return of the expedition, when Coronado came to kiss the hand of the viceroy, and did not receive so good a reception as he would have liked for he found him very sad." For many days after the general reached the city the men who had followed him came straggling in, all of them worn out with their toils, clothed in the skins of animals, and showing the marks of their misfortunes and sufferings. "The country had been very joyous when the news of the discovery of the Seven Cities spread abroad, and this was now supplanted by the greatest sadness on the part of all, for many had lost their friends and their fortunes, since those who remained behind had entered into partnerships with

---

[260] Winship, George Parker, *Coronado Expedition*, Introduction, p. 402.
Suarez de Peralta, J., *Tratado del Descubrimiento de las Yndias*, etc.

those who went, mortgaging their estates and their property in order to procure a share in what was to be gained, and drawing up papers so that those who were to be present should have power to take possession of mines and enter claims in the name of those who were left behind, in accordance with the custom and the ordinances which the viceroy had made in New Spain. Many sent their slaves also, since there were many of these in the country at this time. Thus the loss and the grief were general, but the viceroy felt it most of all, for two reasons; because this was the outcome of something about which he had felt so sure, which he thought would make him more powerful than the greatest lord in Spain, and because his estates were ruined, for he had labored hard and spent much money in sending off the army. Finally, as things go, he succeeded in forgetting it, and devoted himself to the government of his province, and in this he became the best of governors, being trusted by the King and loved by all his subjects.''

There is no record of what became of Francisco Vasquez Coronado. Even the viceroy, who had more at stake than anyone else, did not hold him to blame for the failure of the expedition which had been put in his charge.[261] It was not long after his return that he gave up his position as governor of New Galicia. Later on, doubtless owing to the fact that he did not enjoy his former reputation at the court of Spain, accusations were filed against him because it was claimed

---

[261] Hodge, F. W., *Spanish Explorers in the Southern United States*, Introduction, pp. 276-280: ''The elaborate expedition of Coronado is the subject of the narrative of a private soldier in his army, Pedro de Castañeda, a native of Najera, in the province of Logrono, in the upper valley of the Ebro, in Old Castile. Of the narrator little is known beyond the fact that he was one of the colonists who settled at San Miguel de Culiacan, founded by Nuño de Guzman in 1531, where he doubtless lived when Coronado's force reached that point in its northward journey, and where, more than twenty years later, he wrote his account of the expedition and its achievements. The dates of Castañeda's birth and death are not known, but he was born probably between 1510 and 1518. In 1554, according to a document published in the *Colecion de Documentos Inéditos del Archivo de Indias* (XIV, 206), his wife, Maria de Acosta, with her four sons and four daughters, filed a claim against the treasury of New Spain for payment for the service of the husband and father had rendered in behalf of the King.

''The Coronado expedition was of far-reaching importance from a geographical point of view, for it combined with the journey of De Soto in giving to the world an insight into the hitherto unknown vast interior of the northern continent and formed the basis of the cartography of that region. It was the means also of making known the sedentary Pueblo tribes of our Southwest and the hunting tribes of the Great Plains, the Grand Canyon of the Colorado and the lower reaches of that stream, and the teeming herds of bison and the abso-

that he had more Indians in his service, working on his estates, than the regulations of the crown permitted. So far as the records show, he disappeared from official and public life, after he made his report to the viceroy in the fall of 1542.

Coat of Arms and fac-simile of signature of Don Antonio de Mendoza

---

lute dependence on them by the hunting Indians for every want. But alas for the Spaniards, the grand pageant resulted in disappointment for all, and its indefatigable leader ended his days practically forgotten by his country for which he had accomplished so much.''

BIBLIOGRAPHY

Alarcon, Hernando	*De lo que hizo por la mar Hernando de Alarcon, que con dos nauios andaua por la costa por orden del Visorey don Antonio de Mendoza,* 14th B. A. E.; *Coronado Expedition,* Winship, George Parker.
Alvarado, Hernando de	*Relacion de lo que Hernando de Alvarado y Fray Juan de Padilla descubrieron en demanda de la mar del Sur,* 14th B. A. E., *ibid.*
Bancroft, Hubert Howe	*History of the Pacific States of North America,* Vol. V; *Mexico,* Vol. X; *North Mexican States,* Vol. XII; *Arizona and New Mexico.*
Bandelier, A. F.	*Historical Introduction to Studies among the sedentary Indians of New Mexico,* Santa Fé, N. M., Sept. 19, 1880. Papers of the Arch. Inst. of Am., American Series, I, Boston, 1881. This relates specially to the Coronado Expedition.
	A visit to the Aboriginal Ruins in the Valley of the Pecos, Papers of the Arch. Inst. of Am., American Series, I, 1881. *Contributions to the history of the southwestern portion of the United States,* Papers of the Arch. Inst. of Am., American Series, V, and, *The Hemenway Southwestern Archæological Expedition,* Cambridge, 1890.
	Fray Juan de Padilla, The First Catholic Missionary and Martyr in Eastern Kansas, 1542, American Catholic Quarterly Review, Phila., July, 1890.
	Final Report of Investigations among the Indians of the Southwestern United States, Carried on mainly in the years 1880-1885, Papers of the Arch. Inst. of Am., Part I, 1890, Part II, 1892, Cambridge.
	The Discovery of New Mexico by Fray Marcos de Nizza, Magazine of Western History, iv, Cleveland, Sept., 1886.
Bandelier, Mrs. Fanny	*The Journey of Alvar Nuñez Cabeza de Vaca,* with notes by A. F. Bandelier; *The Trail Makers,* A. S. Barnes and Co., New York, 1905.
Barcia, Andrés Gonzales	*Historiadores primativos de las Indias Occidentales, que junto traduxo en parte, y saco á luz, ilustrados con eruditas notas, y copiosos indices, el ilustrissimo Señor D. Andrés Gonzales Barcia, del Consejo, y Camara de S. M. Divididos en tres tomos. Madrid, Año MDCCXLIX. The*

	Naufragios and *Comentarios*, of Cabeza de Vaca, are in the first volume.
Benavides, Alonzo de	*Memorial*, etc., Madrid, MDCXXX.
Cabeza de Vaca, Alvar Nuñez	*Relation of*, translated by Buckingham Smith, New York, 1871.
Castañeda, Pedro de	*Relacion de la jornada de Cibola compuesta por Pedro de Castañeda de Naçera donde se trata de todos aquellos poblados y ritos, y costumbres la cual fue el año de 1540*, 14th Annual Report, Bureau of American Ethnology, pp. 414-469, from the manuscript in the Lenox Library, New York, Winship, George Parker.
Coronado, Francisco Vasquez	*The relation of*, Hakluyt, iii, 373-380. *Carta de Francisco Vasquez Coronado al Emperador, dandole cuenta de la expidicion á la provincia de Quivira*, etc., Oct. 20, 1541, 14th B. A. E., 580-583, Winship, *ibid*. *Traslado de las nuevas y noticias que dieron sobre el descubrimiento de una ciudad, que llamaron de Cibola, situada en la tierra nueva*, Año de 1541, 14th B. A. E., *ibid*, pp. 564-565. *Relacion del Suceso de la jornada que Francisco Vasquez hizo en el descubrimiento de Cibola*, 14th B. A. E., pp. 572-579.
Cortés, Hernan	*Memorial que dio al Rey el Marquis del Valle en Madrid 25 de Junio 1540 sobre agravios que la habia hecho el Virey de Nueva España D. Antonio de Mendoza estorbandole la prosecucion del descubrimiento de las costas é islas del mar del Sur que le pertenecia al mismo Marques segun la capitulacion hecha con S. M. en año de 1529*, etc., Doc. Inédit. España, iv, 209, 217.
Davis, W. W. H.	*The Spanish Conquest of New Mexico*, Doylestown, Pa., 1869.
Diaz del Castillo, Bernal	*Historia Verdadera de la conquista de la Nueva España escrita por uno de sus conquistadores*, Madrid, 1632.
Espejo, Antonio de	*El Viaje que hizo Antonio de Espejo en al añño de ochenta tres; el cual con sus compañeros descubrieron una tierra en que hallaron quinze provincias todas llenas de pueblos y de casas de cuatro y cinco altos, a quien pusieron por nombre El Nuevo Mexico*, Hakluyt, iii, 383-389.
Gomara, Francisco Lopez de	*Primera y Segunda parte de la historia general de las Indias con todo el descubrimiento y cosas notables que han aceido donde que se ganaron ata el añño de 1551*, Hakluyt, iii, 380-382.
Hakluyt, Richard	*The Principal Voyages*, etc., Edinburg, 1885, vol. xiv.
Herrera, Antonio de	*Historia General*, d. vi, l. v. cap. ix and d. vi, lib. ix, cap. xi-xv.
Hodge, F. W.	*The First Discovered City of Cibola*, Am. Anthro., viii, July, 1895.

BIBLIOGRAPHY

	Spanish Explorers in the Southern United States, Charles Scribner's Sons, New York, 1907.
Icazbalceta, J. G.	*Mexico*, 1886-1892.
Informacion	*Del Virey de Nueva España, D. Antonio Mendoza*, etc., Doc. de Indias, 14th B. A. E., pp. 596-7.
Jaramillo, Juan	*Relacion hecha por el capitan Juan Jaramillo*, 14th B. A. E., pp. 584-593.
Lummis, Charles F.	*The Spanish Pioneers*, Chicago, 1893.
Mendieta, Fr. G. De	*Historia Eclesiástica, etc.*, Mexico, 11 Febrero, 1537. Doc. de Indias, xiv, 235.
	Instruccion de Don Antonio de Mendoza al Fray Marcos de Niza, Bandelier, *Contributions*, 109-112.
Mota Padilla, Matias de la	*Historia de la conquista*, Mexico, 1870.
Niza, Fr. Marcos de	*Relacion, etc.*, Doc. de Indias, iii, 325-351.
Oviedo Y Valdez, Gonzalo Fernandes de	*Historia General de las Indias*, Madrid, 1851.
Pacheco y Cardenas, Colecion	*Colecion de documentos*, etc. Cited as Doc. de Indias
Prince, L. Bradford	*Historical Sketches of New Mexico*, New York, 1883.
Simpson, James Hervey	*Journal of a Military Reconnoissance from Santa Fé*, etc., Sen. Ex. Doc. 64, 31st Congress, 1st Session.
	Coronado's March in Search of the "Seven Cities" of Cibola, Smithsonian Report for 1869, pp. 309-340.
Smith, Thomas Buckingham	*Florida*.
Suarez de Peralta, J.	*Tratado, etc.*, Madrid, 1878.
Ternaux-Compans, H.	*Voyages, etc.*, Paris, 1837-1841.
Vetancurt, Aug. de	*Teatro Mexicano, etc.*, Mexico, 1898.
Villagrá, Gaspar de	*Historia de Nuevo Mexico*, Alcala, 1610.
Winship, George Parker	*The Coronado Expedition, 1540-1542*, 14th Annual Report B. A. E., Washington, 1896.
Winsor, Justin	*Narrative and Critical History of America*, Boston, 1869.
Zaragoza, Justo	*Noticias Historicas de la Nueva España*, Madrid, 1878.

CHAPTER V

THE SPANISH FRIARS, AGUSTIN RODRIGUEZ, FRANCISCO LOPEZ, AND
JUAN DE SANTA MARIA — THEIR EFFORTS FOR CHRISTIANITY
AND CIVILIZATION — 1582

THE expedition led by Coronado had been so disastrous in its results that nothing in the way of exploration was done, in the countries visited by him, for forty years. Discoveries which promised rich returns to the Spanish arms were constantly being made in Central and South America, and in those regions the adventurous cavaliers found wondrous fields for the exhibition of their enterprise and martial ability. The Seven Cities of Cibola had been almost forgotten. Colonization of the northern portions of New Spain, during this period, however, was carried on and many settlements were established. Spanish occupation had gradually extended northward from Nueva Galicia to the latitude of Southern Chihuahua. When we take into consideration the great distance from the City of Mexico to these northern settlements, the number of Indian tribes that had to be subdued, the rapidity with which the Spaniard brought these people under the yoke is little short of marvelous. It is true that the Spaniard was charged with something other than religious zeal in his efforts to Christianize the natives of the New World, for it was early said that "under color of religion they but seek the gold and silver of an undiscovered treasure." But with the Spanish soldiery cheering them on, administering to their spiritual wants, ready, if necessary, to carry the sword and use it, too, were the friars, brave, devoted, gentle, whose greed was not for gold, but whose most supreme delight was the salvation of souls.[262] The king of Spain required that every

---

[262] Mendoza, in his instructions to the friar Marcos, evidently had in mind the establishment of missions in the countries that were to be explored. He

expedition be accompanied by representatives of the church, and all principal officers of the king's armies were enjoined to preach the Holy Catholic faith to the natives of the countries explored and subjugated, and, in this way, under royal order, not by papal bull, the explorers of the new world were accompanied by priests and monks who endured all the privations and hardships of a soldier's life.

The Spaniards claimed at this time the empire of the whole world, notwithstanding the fact that the Holy Father had only given them one-half, and many expeditions, ostensibly undertaken for the glory of God and prosecuted at the expense of the church, were really sent out for the purpose of extending this magnificent empire, and incidentally increasing the royal revenues and patrimony. Many times the good viceroy, Mendoza, sent appeals to Spain for more friars, and the Franciscans and Dominicans were constantly urged to send out representatives of their orders to reap the harvest which the Lord had provided.[263] In recording the failure of the Coronado expedition,

---

specifically instructed the friar that if large settlements be found, suitable in the opinion of the friar for the erection of a monastery, whither priests could be sent, fitted for the work of conversion, Friar Marcos was to advise him with due secrecy.

But it was not the Spanish policy nor was it the intention of the government to found missions in the New World solely for the benefit of the savages. Philanthropic motives no doubt existed and influenced the rulers, but to civilize and convert the natives to the faith meant not only the rescue of savages from perdition, but the enlargement of the church influence and wealth, preparation for future colonization, and naturally an extension of Spanish power. This was the end in view, but the "benditos padres," who had charge of these enterprises were almost, without exception, consecrated to one idea, and that was the inculcation of the faith and the consequent salvation of souls.

These missions were religious establishments, under the control of the laws but directly governed and directed by a padre presidente. The ultimate design of the crown, in the establishment of these missions, was that as soon as the Indians were Christianized, civilized, and self-supporting, they (missions) would be converted into civil pueblos, the missions into churches, and the missionary would be supplanted by a regular priest.

A *visita* was a sort of Christian outpost, visited or to be visited by a padre who resided elsewhere, and having no resident representative of the clergy. The word "Padre" means "Father." Fr. stands for "Fray," Spanish for Fra, Italian, and the Latin Frater, which indicates that the person so designated belonged to a religious brotherhood, particularly some one of the mendicant orders, Dominicans, Franciscans, Capuchins, but the word is not applicable to all of the religious orders. The Jesuit fathers are never so designated. All the members of the mendicant orders were Frailes (pl.); when "P. Fr." was used it was one fray speaking or writing of another fray.

[263] Icazbalceta, Zummaraga, p. 82.

Mota Padilla gives expression, in a lamentable way, to the sentiment which seems to have prevailed in court circles in Spain, as to the real benefits which the crown would reap by these conquests in the New World, for he says: "It is most likely the chastisement of God that riches were not found on this expedition, because, when this ought to have been the secondary object of the expedition, and the conversion of all those heathen their first aim, they bartered with fate and struggled after the secondary; and thus the misfortune is not so much that all those labors were without fruit, but the worst is that such a number of souls have remained in their blindness."[264]

When the news reached Spain of the martyrdom of the friar, Juan de Padilla, a number of Franciscans were fired with the zeal of entering the country and carrying on the work thus begun. Several received the royal permission and went to the Pueblo country. It is said that one of them was killed at Tiguex, where most of them settled. A few went on to Cicuyé or Pecos, where they found a cross which the friar Juan de Padilla had erected. Proceeding to Quivira, the natives there counseled them not to proceed further. They were given an account of the manner in which the friar Juan de Padilla had been put to death, and said, that if he had taken their advice, he would not have been killed.[265] Every facility was granted to these friars, by the government, for their coming to New Spain and other portions[266] of the newly discovered countries. These appeals from New Spain were nearly always addressed to the mendicant orders. These friars were sent by their superiors, whose sole object in view was the conversion of the barbarians. Their vows of poverty protected them against the temptations which were not resisted by the soldiers themselves. In 1522, Pope Adrian VI invested the Franciscans with his own apostolic authority in everything which the friars, being on the ground, thought necessary for the salvation of the souls of the savages, when there were no bishops or where the bishops, if there were any, resided at

---

[264] Mota Padilla, cap. xxxiii, 4, p. 166. It is not difficult to understand the sentiments of Mota Padilla, for he was a Franciscan himself, and thoroughly imbued with the idea of a peaceful conquest of the natives and their salvation through the medium of the members of his order.

[265] Winship, George Parker, *Coronado Expedition*, 14th B. A. E., note, p. 536.

[266] Herrera, *Historia*, vol. i., dec. 1, lib. vi, cap. xx, p. 174.

a distance of a two days' journey.[267] It was the glory of the Franciscan order that Fr. Juan de Padilla had sealed with his blood the cause of Christianity while attached to the expedition under Coronado. The Franciscans were by far the most popular of the orders, as they were also the most powerful, and the members were greatly beloved by the Indians. The relative position of the Spanish soldier and the Franciscan friar, so far as the esteem of the poor Indians was manifest, is expressed by Nuño de Guzman, one of the most cruel hearted of all the Spanish conquerors, who said that "the poor natives were well disposed to receive the friars, while they flee from us as stags fly in the forest."[268]

As has been said, the Spanish settlements, during the forty years succeeding the Coronado expedition, had gradually proceeded northward from New Galicia to the southern portion of Chihuahua. In this state, in the neighborhood of the present Jimenez, known at that time by the various names of San Bartolomé, Santa Barbola, and San Gregorio, rich mines were being worked by the Spaniards. At the settlement, as was always the case, the Franciscans were present working for the cross, and, at this particular place, there was also a small military force, maintained for the protection of the settlers and miners.

At this settlement, there was living a Franciscan friar, named Agustin Rodriguez.[269] This good friar, after the fashion of those of his order of that day, was filled with an ardent desire for martyrdom, as a fitting close and reward for his work in the salvation of souls. This soldier of the cross had read the narrative of Alvar Nuñez Cabeza de Vaca, and had also received much information from the Conchos and Passaguate Indians, who told him that far to the north were some large cities and kingdoms which had not yet been discovered or explored by the Spaniards. Moved by the usual desire for the conversion of these heathen people, the friar determined, if possible, to secure permission to visit this far-off region. Therefore in November, 1580, he made application to the

---

[267] Icazbalceta, Zummaraga, p. 111. This papal bull was called the *Omnimoda*.

[268] *Doc. Inédit.*, vol. ii, p. 356.

[269] In the narrative attached to the *Relacion* of Espejo, this friar is called Agustin Ruiz, but he is known by the name of Rodriguez by Torquemada, Mota Padilla, and Aparicio. Being a Franciscan, Mota Padilla ought to know.

Condé de Coruña, at that time viceroy of New Spain, for permission to explore the new country, to learn the language and to bring about the conversion of the Indians to the Holy Catholic faith. Although contrary to the royal command, the king having ordered that no privilege of exploration be given without the royal sanction, the viceroy authorized the organization of a volunteer escort, not to exceed twenty in number. The provincial of the Franciscan order also granted him permission, and the friar immediately began the preparations for the journey.

Selection was made of two brothers of his order to accompany him, whose names were Friar Francisco Lopez and Friar Juan de Santa Maria. In addition there were twelve soldiers, under the command of Francisco Sanchez Chamuscado; there were also ten or fifteen Indians, servants of the Spaniards, and a mestizo, named Juan Bautista.[270]

In addition to the soldiers being a defense against attacks from the Indians, they went along because it was stated that there were mines abounding with the precious metals in the regions which they intended to visit.

The friar and his companions set out from San Bartolomé on the 6th of June, 1581, and, following the Conchos river down stream to its junction with the Rio Grande, which they called the Rio Guadalquivir, they turned to the northwest and passed up the Rio Grande a journey of twenty days, by way of the present city of El Paso, the Mesilla valley in New Mexico, finally reaching a province in which there were large communal houses, to which province they gave the name of San Felipe, reaching this place in the month of August. The village which they first reached containing the large communal house was located about where the town of San Marcial is now situated, and is the same Piro village visited by one of Coronado's captains in 1542. According to Bandelier, the name of this village was Tre-na-quél.

FRAY RODRIGUEZ AND COMPANIONS BEGIN THEIR JOURNEY TO NEW MEXICO

---

[270] Bancroft, H. H., *History of Arizona and New Mexico*, says that there were only eight or nine soldiers in the party and that their names were Pedro Bustamante, Hernan Gallegos, Felipe Escalante, Hernando Barrundo, and (according to Villagrá) Pedro Sanchez de Chavez, Juan Sanchez Herrera, and Buensalida.

Don Lorenzo Suarez de Mendoza, Condé de la Coruña, Viceroy of New Spain, 1580-1583

From this point they journeyed up the valley of the Rio Grande, visiting almost all of the pueblos along its banks and on its branches.[271]

Pedro Bustamante and Hernan Gallegos, soldiers in the expedition, in their narratives, say they heard of many pueblos on both sides of the river which they visited and that they reached a province where a different language was spoken and where the inhabitants wore a different sort of clothing and where they had better habitations. This was in all probability the Tiguex of Coronado.[272] Leaving the river they visited a very large pueblo containing four or five hundred houses, some of which were four and five stories in height, which place they called Tlascala. Here they heard of many other fine villages to the north, but they did not visit them, but, turning back, crossed the river and going up one of its branches, visited three others, whose inhabitants told them of eleven others. They then visited many other places, going in search of buffalo and

---

[271] The friar passed through and crossed the route taken by Alvar Nuñez Cabeza de Vaca. He met no Indians who had ever heard of Alvar Nuñez, as did Espejo later.

Escalona and Barrundo, *Relacion*, 1582, Cartas de Indias, 230, say that the friar and his companions traveled thirty-one days among tribes of Indians, then nineteen days through a desert, uninhabited country, and, on August 15th, found an Indian who told of a corn-producing country ahead; that they reached the first pueblo on the 21st day of August; that this pueblo had forty-five houses and half a league farther on were five more towns and that in the whole province, for a space of fifty leagues, there were sixty-one towns, with a population of over 130,000.

[272] This was the pueblo of Puara, situate in the vicinity of the present town of Bernalillo, but not near its present location, as Bandelier says. Puara was undoubtedly on the opposite side of the Rio Grande. As late as the first years of the nineteenth century, the Rio Grande had its channel about where the town of Bernalillo is now located, and that town, before the independence of Mexico from Spain, was located over two miles west, where the course of the Rio Grande is found today. These facts were ascertained in the investigation before the Court of Private Land Claims, when the title to lands at Bernalillo was being determined by the court.

Mr. Bandelier says: "Speaking of Puaray . . . which pueblo stood directly opposite the present town of Bernalillo," and again he says, "where Bernalillo stands to-day, there were probably two."

Espejo, at page 175 of his *Relacion del Viage*, says: "A donde hallamos relacion muy verdadera; que estuvo en esta provincia Francisco Vasquez Coronado y le mataron en ella nueve soldados y cuarenta caballos, y que por este respeto habia asolado la gente de un pueblo desta provincia, y destos nos dieron razon los naturales destos pueblos por señas que entendimos."

This corresponds exactly with what Castañeda relates concerning events at Tiguex. Puaray meant village of worms or insects. The site of this pueblo is well known to the Indians of Sandia. Vetancurt says, *Cronica*, p. 132, it was "cerca de una legua de Zandia, á la orilla del rio."

finding a great many, particularly at some springs and on the plains which they called Llanos de San Francisco y Aguas Zarcas. From the plains they returned to the pueblo of Puara, and afterwards heard of a valley called Asay or Osay — the Zuñis — which they did not visit, because of the depth of the snow. Later, they journeyed to the salt lakes across the mountains to the east and returning to Puara, where the friars had remained, made up their minds to return to San Bartolomé, which they did, leaving the courageous friars alone and unprotected.

The soldiers were insistent that the friars return with them, but this the missionaries steadily refused to do. They were not alarmed at the departure of the soldiers, but remained cheerfully with the Indians, hoping for the Christian's reward.

CAPTAIN CHAMUSCADO RETURNS
TO SAN BARTOLOMÉ

When Chamuscado had arrived at San Bartolomé, he, in company with some of his men, started to the City of Mexico to make their report, particularly as to some mines which they had discovered while in the Indian country. Chamuscado, however, died on the way, and, in the month of May following, the testimony of the two soldiers, Bustamante and Gallegos, was taken before the viceroy, and this testimony is probably the best account of the expedition conducted by Friar Rodriguez.[273]

Barrundo, another of the soldiers, testified that of the southern Indians who had gone with them on the expedition, three had remained at Puara; these were named Andrés, Francisco, and Geronimo, the last named being a servant of the witness. Francisco

---

[273] Pacheco, Doc. xv, 80-150, *Testimonio dado en Mejico sobre el Descubrimiento de doscientas leguas adelante de las minas de Santa Barbola, gobernacion de Diego de Ibarra; cuyo descubrimiento se hizo en virtud de cierta licencia que pidió Fr. Augustin Rodriguez y otros religiosos Franciscanos. Acompanan relaciones de este descubrimiento y otros documentos, Años, 1582-3.*

Bancroft, H. H., *History of Arizona and New Mexico*, note, p. 78, where he gives a brief of the investigation which was held concerning what was to be done account of news received of the death of Friar Lopez.

Escalona and Barrundo, *Relacion*, p. 149, make mention of the mines, as follows: "Asi mismo descubrimos en la dicha tierra once descubrimientos de minas con venas muy poderosas, todas ellas de metales de plata, que de los tres dellos se truxo el metal á esta ciudad, y se dió á Su Excelencia; el lo mando ensayar al ensayador de la casa de la moneda, el cual los ensayo y les hallo, al un metal dellos a la mitad de plata; al otro hallo a viente marcos por quintal, y al otro cinco marcos."

had made his appearance at San Bartolomé and stated that the friar had been killed by the Indians, whereupon he and his companions had made their escape, believing that the other two friars had also been murdered. Andrés was killed on his way back, but Geronimo was found in the mines of Zacatecas and confirmed all that Francisco had related.

The story of the martyrdom of these friars, as told by Zarate-Salmeron,[274] differs somewhat from the testimony taken in the City of Mexico before the viceroy. According to this historian, after the departure of the soldiers, the friars continued their journey to the north, and, after traveling a few leagues, arrived at the pueblo of Galisteo,[275] a village of the Tanos nation. This pueblo has long since disappeared. Throughout their entire journey they had found the Indians very peaceable and friendly and willing, at all times, to furnish them food and other necessities. Being highly pleased with the provinces through which they had passed, the friars decided to send one of their number back to New Spain to make a full report of their observations and to invite other friars to come to that country. The friar Juan de Santa Maria volunteered to undertake the journey, and, having made the necessary preparations, set out on his return.

He was accompanied some distance by Friar Rodriguez, called Ruiz by Zarate-Salmeron, and Friar Lopez, who returned to Puara, where they established themselves for the purpose of learning the language of the country. After bidding his companions farewell, Friar Juan de Santa Maria crossed the Sandia mountains, intending to pass by the salt lakes and thence, by a direct course, to El Paso del Norte, one hundred leagues to the south, which was a shorter and speedier route than the one by which they had come into the country. The third day, when near the pueblo afterwards

---

[274] P. Zarate-Salmeron, *Relaciones*, 9-10.

[275] Twenty-two miles south of the city of Santa Fé began the Galisteo group of the Tanos nation, consisting of Galisteo or Ta-ge-uing-ge proper, of San Lazaro or I-per-e, of San Cristoval, or Yam-p-hamba, all of which clustered in a radius of ten miles on or about the water-shed of the Rio Galisteo, and possibly the pueblo Largo or Hish-i. These villages were all inhabited during the 16th century, as were also some west and south toward the Sandias, notably the village of Tung-que, ruins of which are still visible; there was also one near Golden, and at San Pedro, the ruins of Ku-kua are still visible. All of these are in Santa Fé county, New Mexico.

called San Pablo, in the Teguas province, he stopped to rest under a tree, where the Indians killed him and burned his remains.

The two remaining friars lived some time in peace and quiet at Puara, and pursued their labors without interruption. One afternoon Friar Lopez retired about a league from the village to engage in his devotions, and, while occupied in prayer, was killed by an Indian, who inflicted two mortal wounds upon his temples. The Indians [276] afterwards pointed out to Friar Rodriguez the place where the body of his companion had been buried, which he caused to be disinterred and re-buried in the pueblo, according to the forms of the Catholic religion. The death of Friar Lopez was a sore affliction to the sole survivor, who mourned his loss in bitterness of spirit. He felt now, in truth, that he was alone in the midst of these barbarians, with no one upon whom he could rely save Him whose cause he most earnestly espoused.

The war-captain of the pueblo of Puara was much grieved over the death of the friars and, in order to save Friar Rodriguez from the same fate, he removed him to the pueblo of Santiago, a league and a half further up the river. But his death had been resolved upon and it was impossible to save him. A few days afterward he met the same fate as his brethren, and almost before the breath of life was out of his body, it was thrown into the Rio Grande, at that time in flood.

"From the sacrifice of these three friars," says Davis, "the old chroniclers contend there sprung a plentiful harvest of souls. They record that from that time down to the year 1629, there were baptized thirty-four thousand six hundred and fifty Indians, and many others were in a state of conversion; and that in the same period the friars had erected, without cost to the government or king, forty-three churches in New Mexico."

The body of the friar Lopez remained buried at Puara for thirty-three years, when the place of interment was pointed out to Estevan

---

[276] Torquemada, Fr. Juan de, *Monarquia Indiana*, iii, 459, 626-8, gives the story of the death of the friars about as it is given by Fr. Zarate-Salmeron. He says that Fr. Rodriguez was a lay friar, a native of Niebla, in Spain, who had penetrated some distance northward before he went to Mexico to get a license for his expedition. Fr. Lopez was an Andalusian and superior of the band. Fr. Juan de Santa Maria was a Catalan, versed in astrology, which particularly led him to try a new route for his return. The friars went on 150 leagues after the soldiers left them to New Mexico, so named by Torquemada.

de Perea, commissary of the province.[277] The remains were disinterred in the month of February, 1614, and deposited in the church at the Sandia pueblo,[278] with great ceremony, a number of priests marching on foot, dressed in full robes. It is related in one of the writings of one of the priests who was present, that when the procession began to move the saint in the church commenced to perform miracles.

The brothers of the order of Franciscans who were at the time located in the province of Nueva Biscaya, hearing of the accounts of the death of Friar Rodriguez, were very much troubled over the fate of the remaining friars,[279] at that time not knowing of their

[277] In this locality has lived the Perea family for many generations.
[278] The old church at Sandia, now a ruin.
[279] The correct location of Puaray, the place of the death of Friar Rodriguez, is of considerable importance. It is one of the most historical of all the pueblos. It lay in front of the southern portion of the present town of Bernalillo, on a gravelly bluff overlooking the river, which at that time had its course very near the present located line of the Atchison, Topeka and Santa Fé Railway, at the town of Bernalillo. From this point a magnificent view of the towering Sandia is to be had. The pueblo of Puara was the pueblo of the Worm or the Insect. Vetancurt in his *Cronica*, at page 312, says: ''El nombre Puray quiere decir gusanos, que es un genero de que abunda aquel lugar.'' Just what kind of a ''worm'' or ''insect'' is meant is difficult to tell, but it must have been a peculiar kind of beetle, of which there are specimens along the Rio Grande in that locality, of a singular species. Bandelier says that the pueblo never had to exceed five hundred inhabitants, and quotes Vetancurt as authority, who says it had ''doscientas personas de nacion Tiguas.'' Nothing but foundations and mounds are now to be seen, but there have been excavated a number of rooms, covered up with the vast rubbish. Lying south and east of the larger ruin were two smaller structures, which appear to have been built of lava rock, of which there is plenty in that vicinity. It is possible that the one east may have been the chapel which was standing at the time of the Pueblo rebellion in 1680.
The village has also been known as the Pueblo de Santiago, although I think this is a mistake, although the war-captain at Puara removed Fr. Rodriguez from Puara to Santiago, which was up the river, shortly before he was killed. The patron saint of Puara is St. Bartholomew. Vetancurt says: ''La Yglesia es al apostól San Bartolomé dedicada.''
I am of the opinion that the Friar Juan de Santa Maria was killed very near the site of old San Pedro, in Santa Fé county. Bandelier thinks that there was an old pueblo near this place. Zarate-Salmeron says, in writing of the death of Fr. Juan de Santa Maria: ''Por que al tercero dia que se despidio de sus compañeros hermanos llegando á sestear debajo de un arbol los Indios Tiguas del pueblo que ahora se llama Sn Pablo lo mataron, y quemaron sus huesos.''
Zarate-Salmeron says that Puara and Santiago were two different pueblos, *Relaciones de todas las cosas*, par. 7. After stating that Fr. Francisco Lopez and Fray Agustin Rodriguez had established themselves at Puaray and that the former had been killed at Puaray, he says: ''El capitan del pueblo dio muestras de sentimiento por la muerte del religioso y porque no sucedie se lo mismo con

death. As a consequence they did everything possible to secure the services of a company of soldiers to march to their relief. One

el religioso lego quedaba, se lo llevo consigno al pueblo que se llama Santiago, legua y media el rio arriba.'' On the other hand Espejo, who followed the tracks of the murdered missionaries less than one year after their death, says of the Tigua pueblos, ''one of which is called Puala, where we found that the Indians of this province had killed Fray Francisco Lopez and Fray Agustin Ruiz.'' Villagrá, who was at Puara eighteen years after the death of the friars, says that at least two of them were killed there. — *Historia de la Nueva Mexico*, 1610, canto xv, fol. 137.

Castaño de Sosa also visited this part of the country in 1591, for in *Memoria del Descubrimiento*, p. 256, we find: ''Y por lo que alli habia y en toda la tierra nos habian dado, que eran estos pueblos los que habian muerto los padres que á nos dieron, habian andado por aqui.''

Juan de Oñate was at Puara on June 27, 1598. He stayed all night at the pueblo. In one of the larger rooms, in which priests who came with Oñate were quartered, they discovered a painting on the walls partially effaced representing the killing of the missionaries in 1580. Oñate gave strict orders not to show any resentment at the sight, but to act as if the painting had not been noticed.

Captain Villagrá also tells the story of the discovery of this painting on the walls of the room at Puara. In these words this poet historian sings:

''Y haziendo jornada en vn buen pueblo,
Que Puarai llamauan sus vezinos,
En el á todos bien nos recibieron,
Y en vnos corredores jaluegados,
Con vn blanco jaluegue recien puesto,
Barridos y reados con limpeca,
Lleuaron á los padres, y alli justos,
ueron muy bien seruidos, y otro dia,
Por auerse el jaluegue ya sacado,
Dios que á su santa Iglesia siepre muestra
Los Santos que ella padezieron,
Hizo se trasluziesse la pintura,
Mudo Predicador, aqui encubrieron
Con el blanco barniz, porque no viessen
La fuerza del martirio que passaron,
Aquellos Santos Padres Religosos,
Fray Agustin, Fray Juan, y Fray Francisco.
Quios cuerpos ilustres retratados,
Los Baruaros tenian tan al viuo,
Que porque vuestra gente no los viese
Quisieronlos borrar con aquel blanco,
Quia pureza grande luego quiso
Nostrar con euidencia manifiesta,
Que á furo azote, palo, a piedra fueron,
Los tres Santos varones consumidos.''

From the time of Oñate down to the Pueblo rebellion of 1680 there is little known of Puara. The Indians of this locality took part in the rebellion. When it became known to Otermin that his efforts to negotiate with the Indians at Cochití had failed owing to their duplicity, he ordered the three villages of Puaray, Sandia, and Alameda burned, and they were so destroyed. Puaray was never reoccupied. It became the property of Captain Juan de Ulibarri, and later

friar, Benardino Beltrán, was particularly active in his efforts to secure the accomplishment of this design on their part.

At this time there was a cavalier at the mines of Santa Barbara named Antonio de Espejo, a native of Cordova, and a man of wealth, courage, and industry. He offered his services to the Franciscans for the purpose of the rescue of their brethren, declaring he was willing to risk his life and fortune in the enterprise, provided he should be authorized by some person in authority to undertake it. The offer was accepted, and the governor, or chief alcalde of Cuatro Cienegas, took it upon himself to issue the license and commission. Espejo was authorized to take with him as many soldiers as might be willing to follow his fortunes, or would be required to carry out the objects of the expedition.

---

of Captain Juan Gonzales. This was known as the Gonzales land grant.—*Venta Real al Capitan Juan Gonzales*, 1711, Ms.

There were discovered near where the school and church of the Christian Brothers are located near Bernalillo the remains of a pueblo that had been destroyed by fire; metates were found; also skeletons and jars filled with corn meal.

BIBLIOGRAPHY

Bandelier, A. F.	*Final Report*, part ii, Cambridge, 1892.
Bancroft, H. H.	*History of Arizona and New Mexico.*
Davis, W. W. H.	*Spanish Conquest of New Mexico*, Doylestown, Pa., 1869.
Espejo, Antonio de	*Relacion*, etc., 1584. In Pacheco, doc. xv, 151.
Frejes, Francisco	*Hist. Breve*, Mexico, 1839.
Hakluyt, Richard	*Voyages*, etc.
Holmes, A.	*Annals of America.*
Prince, L. Bradford	*Historical Sketches*, etc.
Pino, Pedro Bautista	*History of New Mexico*, Mexico, 1849. (*Noticias Hist.*)
Mendieta, Geronimo	*Hist. Eccle.*
Villagrá, Gaspar de	*Hist. of New Mexico*, Alcala, 1610. *Reprint*, Mexico, 1900.
Zarate-Salmeron, P.	*Relaciones*, etc.

The Pueblo of Taos

CHAPTER VI

THE EXPEDITION UNDER DON ANTONIO DE ESPEJO AND FRAY BERNARDINO BELTRÁN UP THE RIO GRANDE DEL NORTE — THEY VISIT MANY PUEBLOS AND RETURN BY WAY OF THE PECOS RIVER — 1582

THE arrangements for the expedition into New Mexico, for the rescue of the friars, were made by Espejo with all the rapidity possible under the circumstances. Espejo was a very energetic man and, in a comparatively short period, all the necessary arrangements had been perfected. Fourteen soldiers volunteered for the entrada.[280] The explorer furnished an abundant supply of arms and ammunition, taking with him also one hundred and fifteen horses and mules. A large number of Indian servants and camp followers were also attached to this expedition. The commander and his small company left San Bartolomé on the 10th of November, 1582. They followed the same route down the Conchos that had been taken by the friar Rodriguez and his brothers, and reached the junction with the Rio Grande, a distance of fifty-nine leagues, after a journey of fifteen days.[281]

---

[280] The names of the soldiers who accompanied Espejo were Juan Lopez de Ibarra, Diego Perez de Lujan, Gaspar de Lujan, Cristobal Sanchez, Gregorio Hernandez, Juan Hernandez, Miguel Sanchez, Valenciano, with his wife and two sons, Lazaro Sanchez, and Miguel Sanchez Nevado, Pedro Hernandez de Almansa, Francisco Barreto (Barrero or Barroto), Bernardo de Luna (or Cuna), Juan de Frias, and Alonzo Miranda.

Aparicio says there were one hundred horsemen. Vargas, 131-2, says there were seventeen men and a woman; and he names Padre Pedro de Herredia. Espejo, himself, in one letter, *Expediente*, 151, says he had fifteen men. Arlegui and Mota Padilla say there were two friars, the latter naming the second Juan de la Cruz.

[281] Espejo, Antonio de, *Relacion del Viage*, etc., is the best authority for the expedition and its members and equipment. The *Relacion* was written by Espejo personally, at San Bartolomé, in October, 1583, immediately after his return from the north.

In the course of this march to the Rio Bravo they passed through a province inhabited by the Conchos Indians, who lived in villages, the houses of which were made of straw. All of the inhabitants of these villages gave the Spaniards a cordial welcome. These people wore very few clothes, going about almost naked. Their government was about the same as that of the other Mexican Indians. They were agriculturists and raised great quantities of corn, gourds, squashes, and melons of fine quality. From the Rio Conchos they brought to the Spaniards fine fish which were enjoyed exceedingly. Their principal articles of diet were rabbits, jack-rabbits, and bears, the last named being very plentiful. They were killed by the Indians in great numbers. The Indians were not idolatrous, nor was any form of religious worship found among them. The Spaniards erected crosses, the natives making no objection, and the friars explained to them the meaning of the cross and how it was an emblem of religion. The Indians told them of other towns of their nation twenty leagues down the river, and conducted them thither. The chiefs sent word, one place to another, in advance, and upon the arrival of Espejo, the inhabitants were waiting to receive him.

Leaving the Conchos Indians, Espejo arrived among the Passaguates, their immediate neighbors, who lived in much the same manner as the Conchos. The Spaniards remained with them but a short time, and were accompanied by the Indians further down the river, a four days' march. In passing through this country, they found indications of silver mines, but made no effort to prospect them, although some of the company, who were posted on such matters, pronounced the ore very rich. Continuing their march they came to the land of the Tobosos, whose inhabitants fled to the mountains on the approach of the Spaniards. In later years, these Toboso Indians rivalled the Apache in cruelty, making many raids, and giving as reason that they had received very bad treatment at one time from a party of Spaniards, seeking slaves in their country.

After leaving the mouth of the Conchos, the Spaniards passed into the country of the Patarabueyes, or Jumanos,[282] who, like the

---

[282] Hodge, F. W., *Handbook of American Indians*, vol. i, p. 636. A tribe of unknown affinity, first seen, although not mentioned by name, about the beginning of 1536 by Cabeza de Vaca and his companions in the vicinity of the Conchos, at its junction with the Rio Grande, or northward to about the south boundary of New Mexico. They were next visited in 1582, by Antonio de Espejo, who called

Tobosos,[283] were hostile at first, attacking the Spaniards, killing some horses, and afterward fleeing to the mountains. They, afterwards, having been approached by the Spaniards, through interpreters, listened to explanations, received gifts from them Jumanos and Patarabueyes, stating that they numbered 10,000, in five villages along the Rio Grande from the Conchos junction northward for 12 days' journey. Most of their houses were built of sod or earth and grass, with flat roofs; they cultivated maize, beans, calabashes, etc. When visited in 1598 by Juan de Oñate, who called them Rayados, on account of their striated faces, a part at least of the Jumanos resided in several villages east of the Rio Grande, in New Mexico, the four principal ones being called Atripuy, Genobey, Quelotetrey and Pataotrey. From about 1622 these were administered to by the Franciscan Fray Juan de Salas, missionary at the Tigua pueblo of Isleta, New Mexico. In response to the request of 50 Jumanos who visited Isleta in July 1629, an independent mission, under the name of San Isidoro, was established among them in

[283] The Tobosos were evidently a very prominent and a very warlike tribe of Indians. They first appear in the *Relacion* of Espejo at page 167. He calls them Tobozos. He states that they were shy and shiftless: ''Son esquivos y asi se fueron de todas las partes que estaban pobladas, en Xacales, por donde pasabamos . . . sustentase con lo que los dichos Pazaguates; usan de arcos y flechas; andan sin vestiduras; pasamos por esta nacion que parecia haber pocos indios, tres jornadas, que habria en ellas once leguas.''

Mr. Bandelier, *Final Report*, note, p. 82, in writing of this tribe, says: ''Gaspar Castaño de Sosa, who marched from Nuevo Leon to New Mexico, in 1590, makes no mention of the Tobosos in his *Journal*. Neither does Juan de Oñate in his Diary of 1596. The Tobosos were, then, to be found mainly in Coahuila and Nuevo Leon, and also in Tamaulipas. They became formidable to Chihuahua only in the seventeenth century, after missions had been established and the contact with civilization gave some pretext for depredations. I say pretext, for in most cases, as with the Apaches, for instance, such tribes only waited for some opportunity to resort to murder and rapine. In his *Carta Etnografica*, Orozco y Berra localizes, so to say, the Tobosos in Coahuila and Nuevo Leon. It seems certain that they most habitually infested those districts, but they were also a terrible scourge in Chihuahua. On the whole, it would be as difficult to assign to them a definite territory as it would be to the Apaches in former times, previously to their reduction to reservations. In 1630, Fray Alonzo de Benavides mentions again the Tobosos, *Memorial que Fray Ivan de Santador de la Orden de San Francisco, Comisario General de Indias, presento á la Majestad Catolica del Rey don Felipe Cuarto Nuestro Señor*, Madrid, 1630, p. 7. He speaks of the Tobosos along with a number of other tribes of Chihuahua, like the Tarahumares, Sumas, Janos, etc., and says of them collectively: 'Gente muy feróz, barbara, y indomita; porque andan siempre totalmente desnudosin tener casa, ni sementera alguna, viven de lo que cacan, que es todo genero de animales, aunque sean inmudos, mudandose para esto de unos cerros á otros; y sobre el juego suelen estas naciones tener guerras ciuile. v se matan brutalmente. sus armas son arco y flecha, que son las generales de todas las naciones.'

''The historian of the Jesuit missions in Mexico, P. Francisco Xavier Alegre, says of the Tobosos, speaking of their first appearance as fomenters and leaders in the insurrection of contiguous tribes, *Historia de la Compania de Jesus en Nueva España*, vol. ii, p. 244: 'Comenzaron las hostilidades por los tobosos, gentes belicosas y barbaras, y que servian como de asilo á todos los foragidos y mal contentos de aquellas provincias. Los robos y las muertes

the Spaniards and became friendly, furnishing escorts and guides, as well as provisions, to Espejo and his command. These Indians, in many respects, were superior to the southern tribes which had become known to the Spaniards, as was evidenced by the class of

the Salinas, but the main body of the tribe, at this time, seems to have resided 300 miles east of Santa Fé, probably on the Arkansas, within the present Kansas, where they were said to be also in 1632. Forty years later there were Jumanos fifteen leagues east of the Piros and Tigua villages of the Salinas, not far from Pecos river, who were administered to by the priest at Quairai. About this time the Salinas pueblos were abandoned on account of Apache depredations. The Jumano did not participate in the Pueblo rebellion of 1680-92, but before it was quelled, i. e., in October, 1683, 200 of this tribe visited the Spaniards at El Paso, to request missionaries, but owing to the unsettled conditions of affairs, by reason of the revolt in the north, the request was not granted. In the following year, friars visited the Jumano in southern Texas, and, within this

eran ordinarias no so lo en los carros y españoles que encontraban en los caminos, pero aun en las poblaciones y en los reales de minas mas pobladas. En los reales de Mapimi, del Parral y en San Miguel de las Bocas se vivio en un continuo sobresalto, especialmente en las crescientes de las lunas, en que solian juntarse.' This recalls vividly the condition of New Mexico and of Arizona not more than twenty-five years ago. The same custom of starting on forays and killing expeditions with the waxing moon, is well known to exist also among the Apaches. What Father Alegre says refers to 1644, however. A witness of the times, the Jesuit P. Nicolas de Zepeda, says, *Relacion de lo Sucedio en esto Reino de Vizcaya desde el Año de 1644 hasta el de 1645*, etc., Doc. para La Historia de Mejico, series 2: 'Como tambien tan cercano á las cosas tan nobles que an sucedio de los años á esta parte que comenzaron a malograrse los indios de la nacion taboz, que es y hasido siempre la mas cruel bellicosa y guerrera pues no obstante que casi cada año de nuevo les bajaban de paz los señores gobernadores y capitanes de presidios.' The historian of the province of San Francisco de Zacatecas, Fr. Francisco de Arlegui, devotes several chapters to dissertations on the manners and customs of the Indians inhabiting or roaming over the various regions through which the missions of that province were scattered. He enumerates a long list of tribes, and without special reference to any one of them.

"The constant hostilities of the Tobosos were, for more than a century, the greatest obstacle to the colonization of Chihuahua, and they seriously impeded communication between Parral and New Mexico. The authors of the past century designate them as the scourge of Chihuahua. It was only after a century of frequently unsuccessful warfare, very similar to that which the United States troops have had to carry on against the Apaches, that the Tobosos were finally exterminated and the Apaches took their place as the curse of the unfortunate provinces. In 1748, the Tobosos, according to Villa-Señor y Sanchez, *Teatro Americano*, vol. ii, lib. v, cap. xi, p. 297, were reduced to not over one hundred families. It is not unreasonable to suppose that the few remaining Tobosos, if any, joined the Apaches, when the latter began to infest Chihuahua. But this would be no proof of the assumption by Orozco y Berra that the language of the Tobosos belonged to Apache or Tinneh stock. See *Geografia de Lenguas*, pp. 309, 325, 327. It is perfectly true, as the author just quoted says, that the Tobosos prepared the road for the Apaches in central and southern Chihuahua, in Coahuila, and in neighboring states; but while it is not at all impossible that they were a kindred tribe, there is as yet, to my knowledge, no evidence to that effect."

houses which they had in places. Some of them were probably built of adobe brick, or of stone, possibly. They told Espejo of a tradition that many years before "three Christians and a negro"

decade, they became known to the French under the name of Choumans. Various references to them are made during the 18th century, including perhaps the significant statement by Cabello (*Informe*, 1784, Ms. cited by H. E. Bolton, inf'n, 1906) that the Taguayazes (Wichitas) are known in Mexico by the name of Jumanes also. As late as the middle of the 19th century, they are mentioned in connection with the Kiowa, and again as living near Lampazas, Nuevo Leon, Mexico. The tribal name was once applied to the Wichita mountains, in Oklahoma, and it is still preserved in the "'Mesa Jumanos'" of New Mexico.

F. W. Hodge, in his monograph, *The Jumano Indians*, pages 8-9, says: "The Salinas referred to are situated in the central portion of that part of Valencia county, New Mexico, lying east of the Rio Grande. Bounding the salt lagoon area on the south is the Mesa de los Jumanos, or, as it is termed on present-day if not altogether 'modern' maps, 'Mesa Jumanes.' This landmark, of course, derived its name from the tribe which formerly occupied the vicinity, a fact illustrating the persistency with which aboriginal names are sometimes retained in the Southwest, even where good excuse may exist for forgetting them.

"The Salinas country, although known far and wide for its generally inhospitable and forbidding character, was inhabited at the opening of the seventeenth century and for twenty-five years later, by the eastern divisions of the Tigua and Piro (the latter being sometimes known as Tompiro), as well as by the Jumano. The former two groups belong to the Tanoan linguistic family and inhabited several pueblos similar to those of their Rio Grande congeners. When, in 1626, Fray Alonzo Benavides, the Father Custodian of the missions of New Mexico, appealed for additional missionaries, he had particularly in mind the conversion of the tribes of the Salinas region, especially the Jumano, among whom Fray Juan de Salas had already been. Says Benavides, writing in 1630, 'I kept putting off the Xumanas who were asking for him (Salas), until God should send more laborers.'

"Through their affection for Salas, the founder of the mission of Isleta, the Jumano went year after year for some six years prior to 1629 to visit him at that Rio Grande mission station in the hope, they asserted, that he might come to live among them. Finally, on July 22, 1629, a delegation of some fifty Jumano visited the pueblo of San Antonio de Isleta, where the custodian (probably Estevan de Perea) was then staying, for the purpose of again asking for friars; and 'being questioned as to what induced them to make this demand, they said that a woman wearing the habit had urged them to come; and being shown a picture of Mother Luisa de Carrion, they rejoiced, and speaking to each other said that the lady who had sent them resembled the picture, except that she was younger and more beautiful.'

"Fray Juan de Salas and Fray Diego Lopez volunteered to go, accompanied by an escort of three soldiers. They found the Jumano this time more than 112 leagues (about 300 miles) to the eastward from Santa Fé, or possibly in the western part of the present Kansas in the vicinity of what later became known as El Quartelejo. The cause of this shifting may have been due to the hostility among the tribes of the Salinas about this time, of which Benavides speaks, for subsequent history seems to indicate that the Jumano were never an aggressive people . . . . . .

"There has been much discussion regarding the location of the 'pueblo' occupied by the Jumano that was dedicated to 'the glorious Isidoro'. We may

had passed through their country, and it is from this statement
largely that Bandelier, Bancroft, Hodge, and some others believe
that Alvar Nuñez Cabeza de Vaca and his companions passed
through the country below El Paso, Texas, and the mouth of the
Conchos river, forgetting that the Jumanos province extended

assume that it was not until after the visit of Salas to the Jumano on the plains in July-August, 1629, that this mission was founded, since the new friars did not arrive from Mexico until Easter of that year, and prior to that time no permanent missionaries were available even had the Jumano not been three hundred miles away on the prairies. We learn from the *Relacion* of Fray Estevan Perea, the successor of Benavides as Custodian of the missions of New Mexico, and under whose guidance the new missionaries came in the spring of 1629, that there were sent to the pueblos of the Salinas —'in the great pueblo of the Xumanas, and in those called Pyros and Tompiros'—six priests and two lay religious, one of whom, Franciso de Letrado, is known to have been assigned to the Jumano alone. It does not seem necessary to look for the 'great pueblo of the Xumanos' of which Benavides speaks, among the ruins of eastern New Mexico, from amongst the debris of which the massive walls of former Spanish churches and monasteries still rise, for it is scarcely likely that the Jumano occupied a village other than their own, or that the settlement was anything but an aggregation of dwellings of the more or less temporary kind which they were found to occupy when visited by Cabeza de Vaca and by Espejo on the lower Rio Grande.''

In concluding his monograph Mr. Hodge says: ''We may now summarize the testimony as follows: In 1535 and again in 1582 the Spaniards found a semi-agricultural tribe living in more or less permanent houses, some of them built of grass, on the Rio Grande at the junction of the Conchos in Chihuahua and along the former stream northward for a number of leagues. They subsisted partly by hunting the buffalo, and raised beans, calabashes, and corn. At the date last mentioned they were called Jumano, and the Spainards named them Patarabueyes. A distinguishing feature of the tribe was its tattooing, for which reason, when found east of the Rio Grande in New Mexico in 1598, they were called 'Rayados' by the Spaniards. They were erratic in their movements. The Franciscans established a mission among them in New Mexico in 1629, but it does not seem to have been successful, for the Indians appear to have been here today but elsewhere tomorrow. In the seventeenth century they were found on the plains of Texas, and again living on the prairies to the northward, evidently in Kansas, the name seemingly being applied to each of two divisions of the same tribe or confederacy. Their custom of tattooing, the character of their houses, and their semi-agricultural mode of life during the century they were first known, suggests relationship, if not identification with the Wichita people. References in unpublished Spanish documents of the seventeenth and eighteenth centuries indicate that the Jumano of the Spaniards of New Mexico were the Tawehash of Texas; and it is known that Tawehash, the name of a division of the Wichita, was also the term by which other Caddoan tribes knew the Wichita tribe proper. There is direct information from the beginning of the nineteenth century that the Wichita mountains, which received their name because the Wichita tribe dwelt thereabouts, were also called 'Jumanes mountains' and 'Tawehash mountains,' thus further substantiating the testimony that the Jumano and the Tawehash were one people. The Tawehash have been absorbed by the Wichita proper, and their divisional name is now practically lost. Likewise the term Jumano, which originating in Chihuahua and New Mexico, passed into Texas but seems to have been

far up into New Mexico; at least, there were villages of this tribe as far north as the Abó pass, east of Belen, in Valencia county, and beyond as far as the state of Kansas.

After leaving this portion of the country of the Jumanos, the Spaniards continued up the river, but Espejo does not record

gradually replaced by the name 'Tawehash,' which in turn was superseded by 'Wichita.'

"Thus is accounted for the disappearance of a tribe that has long been an enigma to ethnologists and historians."

Bandelier, than whom there is no better authority, in a note on page 80 of his *Investigations among the Indians of the Southwestern United States*, Final Report, part i, quotes from Espejo's *Relacion del Viage*, etc., as follows: "Acabadas de salir de esta nacion, entramos en otra que se llama de dos Xumarias, que por otro nombre los llamaban los españoles, los Patarabueyes, en que parecia habia mucha gente y con pueblos formados grandes, en que vimos cinco pueblos con mas de diez mil indios, y casas de azotea, bajas, y con buen a traza de pueblos; y la gente de este nacion está rayada en los rostros; y es gente crecida, tienen maiz y calabazas, y casa de pie y vuelo, y frijoles y pescados de muchas maneras, de dos rios caudalosos, que es el ono que dicen viene derechamente del Norte y entra en el rio de los Conchos, que este será como la mitad de Guadalquibi, y el de Conchos será como Guadalquibi, el cual entra en el mar del norte," and says, "A better and clearer description of the delta formed by the junction of the Rio Grande and the Conchos could not be wished." The other copy of Espejo's report, in the same volume of the *Documentos de Indias*, p. 105, has distinctly "que se llama de los Jumanos."

"It is strange," says Mr. Bandelier, "that there should be, so far as anything appears, such a long silence on the Jumanos of Chihuahua, after Espejo's journey, for it is more than likely, it is almost certain, that they continued to inhabit the delta above mentioned. They were there in 1683, and of their own choice; no missionary had induced them to settle there. This is clearly established by the documents relative to the reconnoissance made by Juan Dominguez de Mendoza as far as the Rio Nueces in Texas in the year 1683. See *El Diario del Viaje de Juan Dominguez de Mendoza á la junta de dos rios y Hasta el Rio Nueces*, Ms., copy in my possession, and more particularly by the documents annexed to it. See also Felipe Romero, *Carta al Gobernador Don Domingo Gironza Petriz de Cruzate*, and, *Pedimento al Maestre de Campo Juan Dominguez Mendoza*. Father Nicolás Lopez, who accompanied Dominguez, says the same in his *Memorial acerca de la Repoblacion de Nuevo Mexico y Ventajas que ofrece en Reino de Quivira*, April 24, 1686: 'Y en la sazon halle, treinta y tres capitanes infieles de la nacion Jumanas y otras que venian á pedir el baptismo . . . nos fuimos caminando á pie y descalzos en compania de dichos infieles sin escolta de españoles, hasta llegar á la Junta de los Rios . . . á donde nos tenian estos infieles fabricados dos ermitas aseadas,' etc. Also Fray Alonzo de Posadas, *Informe al Rey sobre las Tierras de Nuevo Mejico, Quivira y Teguayo, 1686*. It is true that Dominguez calls these Indians Julimes, but from the context I must conclude that they were also Jumanos. It looks as if the two tribes had lived together at the 'Junta de los Rios.' In 1715, when the missions were re-established, the following tribes or clusters are mentioned as living at the 'Junta' in *Los Titulos y Advocaciones de los once Pueblos contenidos en esta Relacion*, Documentos para la historia de Mejico, cuarte seria, vol. iv, p. 169: Mesquites, Calcalotes, Oposines, Conejos, Polames and Sivlos, Puliquis, Conchos, Pasalmes. These names are repeated, with many others, as those of tribes inhabiting New Biscay in 1726, by the Brigadier Pedro de Rivera

definitely the time consumed in the journey nor the distance. Two large provinces of friendly Indians were passed, which were a journey of eight days' distance apart, of whom nothing could be

(*Diario y Derrotero de lo Caminado visto y observado*, etc., p. 22). Juan Dominguez de Mendoza (*Diario*, fol. 46) gives the names of a number of tribes connected at least with the Jumanos, which he met in northwestern Texas, and among that list the 'Poliches' (Puliquis?) are mentioned. I suspect, however, that these names are not always those of separate tribes, but rather names of clans or bands. The Jumanos are ranked among the Chihuahua tribes by Orozco y Berra (*Geografía*, etc., p. 386). But he considers them as a branch of the Apaches-Faraones. There are no grounds for such a conclusion beyond the possible fact, that the remnants of the Jumanos may have become absorbed by the Apaches, upon the latter obtaining sway over Chihuahua. This is only a possibility, and as yet not a certainty. Of the language of the Jumanos we know nothing. Fray Nicolas Lopez asserts (*Memorial*) that he composed a vocabulary of the Jumano idiom, but we have no knowledge of its existence. He says: 'Yo, Señor, saldria deesta ciudad á fines del que viene para aquella custodia; llevo dispuesto el animo á entrar segunda vez á dichas naciones, por saber ya la lengua jumana y haberla predicada á aquellos y haber hecho vocabulario muy copioso de dicha lengua, como consta juridicamente en los instrumentos que tengo presentados. Father Lopez is not an absolutely reliable authority. He took the part of Juan Dominguez Mendoza in the latter's quarrels with nine of his men, who subsequently deserted his camp, returning to El Paso del Norte at their own risk. Compare his *Diario*, fol. 14, *Auto*, fol. 15, *Peticion*, etc., also Felipe Romero and others, *Carta al Gobernador*, fol. i-3; *Pedimento*, p. 2. He was even accused of conspiring with Dominguez against the Governor Petriz de Cruzate in 1685, *Testimonio á la letra de la causa criminal que se á seguido contra el Maestre de Campo, Juan Dominguez de Mendoza y los demas*, etc., September, 1685, Ms. Some of his claims to services performed may be exaggerated.

"There were many contradictory reports about the Indians of the Junta de los Rios, dating from 1683 to 1686. Juan Dominguez Mendoza, in his *Diario*, fol. 5, calls them 'Jente de la nasion Julimes jente politica en la lengua mexicana y que todos siembran mais y trigo y otras semillas.' Also Felipe Romero (*Carta*, p. 1) 'á este puesto de Xulimes.' But Fray Nicolas Lopez, *Memorial*, calls them Jumanos. So, on the other hand, Fray Sylvestre Velez de Escalante, *Carta al Padre Fray Augustin Morfi*, April 2, 1778, paragraph 7, says: 'Legaron á la junta de los dos rios Norte y Conchos, predicaron á los indios que alli estaban, que eran de las tres naciones, Conchos, Julimes y Chocolomes.' The documents of 1715 do not mention the Jumanos as living there. It may be that, as Sabeata, the Jumano Indian who guided Dominguez, considered the people living at the Junta as his own, and as Espejo had, in 1582, met the Jumanos at that very place, that the Julimes were in fact a branch of the Jumanos. In a witchcraft trial of 1732 (*Causa Criminal contra unos indios del Pueblo de Santa Ana denunciados por Echiseros*, Ms.) there appears a Jumano Indian from El Paso, but whose relatives lived at Julimes. Orozco y Berra, *Geografía*, p. 326, classifies the Julime with the Tepehuan, without giving any authority for so doing."

Mr. Bandelier says further: "The Jumanos have disappeared from the surface and strange to say, although mentioned as an important and even numerous tribe in the sixteenth and seventeenth centuries, I have not as yet been able to trace any description of the customs, manners, etc., of that northern branch of them which belonged to New Mexico proper. They ranged in the southeastern part of the Territory, south and southeast of the salt lagunes

Inscription Rock — El Morro — Valencia County, N. M.

learned, not even the names of the provinces and towns, owing to their having no interpreter. In the first of these provinces the people used cotton cloth and feather-work, which the Spaniards

of the Manzano, where the name of 'Mesa de los Jumanos' still commemorates their former presence. About their abodes, their mode of dress, their rites and creed, we know as little as of their language—nothing.

"'In 1598, Oñate visited the three great villages of the Jumanos, or 'Rayados' in the vicinity of the Salines and of Abó, consequently on or near the 'Mesa de los Jumanos' of to-day, *Discurso de las Jornadas*, p. 266. 'Uno muy grande.' In the *Obediencia de San Juan Baptista*, p. 114, are mentioned 'Los tres Pueblos grandes de Xumanos ó Rayados, llamados en su lengua, Atripuy, Genobey, Quelontetrenuy, Pataotrey con sus sujetos.' This would make four instead of three. The *Obediencia y Vassalaje á su Majestad por los Indios del Pueblo de Cueloce*, Doc. de Indias, vol. xvi, p. 126, mentions the pueblo of Cueloce as 'que llaman de los rayados.' Cueloce may be another version of Cuelotetrey. In the same document Xenopuey is mentioned and Patasce. The former is most likely the same as Genobey, and the latter may stand for Pataotrey. I place some stress on these local names, as they may be authentic remains of the language. Oñate, *Carta escripta*, 1599, p. 306, mentions the Xumanas as the second tribe encountered in New Mexico, coming to that country from the south. In 1630 Benavides, *Memorial*, p. 771, locates the Jumanos 112 leagues east of Santa Fé. Fray Alonzo de Posadas (*Informe al Rey*, 1686) locates them on the upper river Nueces, in Texas, 80 leagues east or northeast of the Junta de los Rios, or mouth of the Conchos. Dominguez Mendoza, *Diario*, 1684, fol. 12, also places them in that vicinity. In connection with the location of the Jumanos, I may be permitted here to recall the mention made of the Teyas, a tribe of the plains, which tribe Coronado met on his adventurous trip to Quivira, *Carta á Su Magestad*, 20th October, 1541, old style, Doc. de Indias, vol. xiii, p. 263: 'Y otra nacion de gente que se llaman los Teyas, todos lobrados los cuerpos y rostros.' The fact that the Teyas tattooed their faces and bodies might possibly indicate that they were the Jumanos, who, in quest of buffalo, had gone as far north as eastern or northeastern New Mexico.

"Benavides states that the Jumanos of New Mexico subsisted on the buffalo almost exclusively, and I have not been able to find any documentary evidence that they cultivated the soil.

"And yet Espejo found their kindred in Chihuahua living in permanent abodes and raising the same crops as the Pueblo Indians. It is not unlikely that the northern branch of the tribe succumbed to the remarkable influence which the great quadruped exerted over the aborigines, who attached themselves to its immense hordes and, becoming accustomed to the life which the following of the buffalo required, discarded permanence of abode, exchanging it for vagrancy, with its consequences. The Jumanos were lost sight of after the great convulsions of 1680 and succeeding years, and their ultimate fate is as unknown as their original numbers."

Mr. Bandelier made great effort in his researches as to this great tribe of Indians. They were the only Indians in New Mexico who were accustomed to striate the face, either to paint it or to tattoo it. He says: "From the word 'rayado' it is not quite certain whether this was done merely with paint or whether it was done by incising. It may be the latter. It is certain that as late as 1697, a Jumano Indian, a female described as 'a striated one of the Jumano nation' was sold at Santa Fé for a house containing three rooms and a small tract of land besides. This woman had been sold to the Spaniards by other Indians who had captured her. *Escritura de Uennta de una Casa de las*

understood from the inhabitants were obtained by them in trade with a people living farther west, in exchange for buffalo hides and deer-skins. The Spaniards also received information that plenty of silver could be obtained by traveling farther west a journey of five days.

In the second province, where the rancherias were near lakes on both sides of the Rio Grande, probably near the present towns of Rincon and Hatch, they were told by a Conchos Indian that fifteen days westward there was another large lake, on the borders of which were many towns containing houses several stories high. He offered to take the Spaniards there, but they continued their journey north.

Following the course of the Rio Grande, Espejo journeyed for fifteen days, a distance of eighty leagues, without meeting any inhabitants; and, finally, beyond a village of straw huts, they reached the pueblos, where the houses were from three to four stories high, and where ten towns were visited, situated on both sides of the Rio Grande; other towns were seen in the distance, and all containing a population of about 12,000, all of whom were friendly, as Espejo says, in describing the manner in which they were received and the manners and customs of the natives. These pueblos must have been located in the valley beginning with the site of the

---

Hijas de Fco. Lucero que isieron al Sargento Mayor Fco. Anaya Almazan, Ms.: 'Por una india rayada de nazion Jumana auida y comprada de los amigos cristianos.' In regard to the inhabitants of the Jumanos I can find nothing precise; that is, so far as the New Mexican Jumanos are concerned.

"From the statements of Benavides, it might be inferred that they had no fixed abodes, but lived almost exclusively on the buffalo. *Memorial*, p. 79, 'Viendo el demonio, enemigo de las almas, que aquellos religiosos ivan á librar de sus unas las que alli gozaua, quiso defenderse, y vso de vn ardid de los que suele, y fue, que seco las lagunas del agua que bebian, á cuya causa tambien se auyento el mucho ganado de Sibola que por alli auia, de que todas estas naciones se sustentauan, y luego, por medio de los Indios hechizeros, echo la voz, que mudassen puesto, para buscar de comer.' This intimates an erratic life. On the other hand, however, Oñate, as I have shown above, mentions at least three large villages. . In 1700, a village of the Jumanos re-appears, and that village cannot have been situated outside of New Mexico, as the news of its destruction (by the French) was carried to Taos in the most northerly part of the Territory by the Jicarilla Apaches, *Relacion Anónima de la Re-conquista*, Ms. Sesto Cuaderno, 'El año de 1700 refirio un apache de los llanos, que los franceses habian destruido el pueblo de los Jumanos, y esta noticia, que el alcalde mayor del pueblo de Taos comunicó á Cubero, hizo temer á todos los del reino que los franceses podian hacer suya esta tierra.' The village of Jumanos here mentioned cannot have had any connection with the pueblo of Jumanos, which had been abandoned previously to 1680.''

present town of San Marcial, just after passing the Jornada del Muerto.

These were the pueblos that had been visited by one of Coronado's captains and by the fray Rodriguez.

Not far beyond the limits of this district the Spaniards came to another, the Tiguas, the Tiguex of Coronado, and, in a short time, had arrived at the pueblo of Puara, one of sixteen towns constituting the province.

Upon the arrival of the Spaniards at Puara, the news that the friars, Rodriguez and Lopez, with some of their attendants, had been murdered, was confirmed. The recollections of the vengeance of the Spaniards under Coronado and Garcia Lopez de Cardenas of forty years before caused the Indians to take to flight upon the approach of Espejo, and, although he offered every inducement to them to return, they refused to do so.

The abandonment of Puara was effected very quickly, the Indians leaving behind large quantities of provisions, of which the Spaniards stood in sore need. It is said by one historian that Puara was sacked by Espejo and the murderers of the friars garroted.[284] Another writes [285] that several thousand Indians were slain, but Espejo says nothing of this in his account. The Indians also informed Espejo as to Coronado having been at Tiguex and that they had killed nine of his soldiers and forty horses and on this account he had destroyed one of the pueblos of the province.[286]

The primary object of the expedition was now accomplished, but the commander, after consultation with the friar Beltrán, determined that he would make further explorations before returning to New Biscay. Espejo had been advised by the Indians that, in the eastern portion of the province, there were great and rich towns, and he was anxious to make explorations in that direction, thus becoming eye-witnesses to the true facts and in this way en-

[284] Zarate-Salmeron, *Relacion*, ii.
[285] Arlegui, *Cronica Zac.*, p. 221.
[286] Bancroft, H. H., *History of Arizona and New Mexico*, p. 84, says that in Hakluyt version of the Espejo narrative the information gained by Espejo that Francisco Vasquez Coronado had been there and that the Indians had killed nine of his men and horses does not appear, and that this doubtless accounts for the errors of Gallatin, Davis, Prince, and others in locating Coronado's Tiguex on the Rio Puerco.

abled to give true reports on their return. In this he was supported by the friar, as well as by the soldiers.

It was determined that the command should remain at Tiguex while some of these places were explored by the commander, and setting out with only two men, he traveled eastward for two days, finally arriving in a province which contained eleven towns; these contained upwards of forty thousand inhabitants, according to Espejo. The province was that of Maguas,[287] or Magrinas, and was particularly fertile, all of the necessaries of life being produced in abundance. There were a great many cattle, with the hides of which, and with cotton, they made their clothing, the style of dress being very much like that of their nearest neighbors. There were indications of rich mines, and they found some considerable quantity of metal in the houses. The inhabitants worshiped idols. The Spaniards were given a friendly welcome and provisions were furnished. Returning to the camp at Puara, Espejo gave an account of what had been seen to those who had remained behind at that place. Espejo was undoubtedly in error in his estimates of the population of these provinces.[288]

---

[287] Bancroft, H. H., *ibid*, note, p. 85. In Espejo Exped., 156, the province of Magrias is said to adjoin that of the Tiguas on the northeast. Thus it would seem to have been in the Galisteo region though I know of no ruins to indicate so large a province, and some other difficulties will appear in connection with later wanderings. Davis and Prince, misled probably by the word cibola (esta provincia confina con las vacas que llaman de Civola) or buffalo represent this expedition as having been led to the west.

[288] Bandelier, A. F., *Final Report*, part i, note, p. 121: "If we sum up the number of souls attributed to them by him (Espejo), we arrive at about a quarter of a million. Wherever we go into details, however, and compare his estimates for certain well known villages with the possibilities and the true conditions, or with other statements of older sources about them, it becomes clear how this otherwise acute observer was misled in his estimate of the numbers of the people. Thus, for instance, Acoma (*Relacion del Viage*, p. 179) is reckoned at 'mas de seis mil animas,' whereas, Castañeda (*Cibola*, p. 69) says that it can place on foot about 200 warriors, and on the rock of Acoma there is furthermore, not room for much over 1,000 people. The Pecos or the Tanos, as he calls them, are credited with 40,000 (p. 185), but the pueblo of Tshi-quit-e, or the old Pecos village, shows that over 2,000 souls could never have lived in it. Indeed, Castañeda, (p. 176) asserts that the people of Cicuyé might place on foot 500 warriors all told. Such evidences of very gross exaggeration could be multiplied. Espejo has consistently exaggerated, but not intentionally. He was led astray by the appearance of the pueblos, most of which he saw at a distance, in the first place, and then still more by the custom of the Indians flocking to the place where strangers arrive, in great numbers, and remaining about these strangers so long as they are new and interesting visitors. Also out of suspicion. Wherever Espejo stopped, he found not merely the inhabi-

Having returned to the Rio Grande, after a short rest, Espejo determined upon an exploration of the country up that river to the province of the Queres, and, after some preparation, departed, taking with him his entire command. This province had five pueblos, and, as Espejo states, 15,000 inhabitants. The Spaniards were given a friendly reception, and, from observations taken, Espejo states that they were in latitude 37 degrees 30 minutes, which is undoubtedly an error by at least two degrees. From this point,

tants of that particular pueblo, but nearly the whole tribe, congregated, and having once begun to form his estimates, he applied the same criterions to every place. His figures are, therefore, to be absolutely rejected, without invalidating thereby the exactitude of other parts of his valuable report.

"I am not in possession of official data emanating from Oñate directly, and establishing the population of the pueblos about the year 1600, but the investigations into his administration, made at the instigation of the viceroy Condé de Monterey, contain some information at least on the ideas then prevalent on the subject. The factor, Don Francisco de Valverde, examined five witnesses on the subject, *Memorial sobre el Descubrimiento del Nuevo Mexico y sus Cacontecimientos, 1595 to 1602* (*Doc. de Indias*, vol. xvi, p. 210). 'Se colige que realmente para labranza y crianza hay tierras y poastos apropositos; y no es aquella tan esteril como la gente que se vino pintaba, ni tan próspero como otros ó hacen y ó represento al gobernador en las relaciones del año de noventa y nueve, que algo mejor informado con mas moderacion escribe de esto, y con la misma hablan los suyospaqui por donde se dexa de entender, que debe de ser cosa corta lo de alli . . . coliegese tambien que hay razonable numero de indios.'

"In 1630 Benavides gives an approximate enumeration of the Pueblos, and he figures their numbers at about 70,000. Acoma appears in that list with 2,000. (*Memorial*, p. 32.) We know what to think of such an estimate; it is twice as much as the rock will hold conveniently. There are other equally glaring inaccuracies. On page 26, the Tehuas are credited with eight villages whereas they had only seven. On page 33, the Zuñi pueblos are set down as 'eleven or twelve,' whereas there were only half that number. The population of Taos, given at 2,000, is also vastly exaggerated. In short, the *Memorial* is, in many respects, a 'campaign document.' Its purpose was to induce the King to favor the Missions, to create a better impression of the missionaries than the Spanish government had at that time, after their constant quarrels with the governors of New Mexico, and to obtain the establishment of a bishopric at Santa Fé. The latter fact is very plainly established in the *Real Cedula* of May 19, 1631, Ms. in which the King, among other matters touching the proposed establishment of an episcopal see, says: 'Fray Franco de Sosa, Comisario de Corte y Secreto General del Orden de San Francisco se me ha hecho relacion . . . y estan oy convertidos mas de quientos mil Indios y de ellos bautizados mas de ochenta mil.' This is said of New Mexico.

"The earliest actual census of the Pueblos, which I know of, dates back to 1660. Vetancurt (*Cronica*, p. 314): 'Pues el año de 1660 se hizo padron general, en que se hallaron mas de veinte cuatro mil personas, chicas y grandes, idios y españoles.' There were then about 1,000 Spaniards in all of New Mexico, so that the number of Pueblo Indians was a little over 23,000. This corresponds very well with the statements of Castañeda, one hundred and twenty years previously.''

they traveled two days, and, in a distance of fourteen leagues, arrived in the province of Cunames or Punames. Here they found five towns, the largest of which was called Cia. The town of Cia was quite extensive, containing eight market places and the houses were better built than any others which had yet come to the notice of the Spaniards, as they were plastered and painted in many colors. Espejo estimates the population at twenty thousand. They made the Spaniards presents of provisions and some handsome mantles. Here they were also shown some specimens of the precious metals and were shown the mountains from which they had been taken. From Cia the Spaniards went in a northwesterly direction, probably up the river of that name, to the pueblo of Jemez, called by them Emexes, Emeges, or Amejes; this province contained seven pueblos altogether, and contained some thirty thousand inhabitants; one of the towns, a large one, situated in the mountains, was not visited. The people of this province resembled those of Cunames, being well provided with the necessaries of life and possessing a good form of government.

Espejo left the Jemez country and pursued a westerly course for fifteen leagues to the pueblo of Acoma, situated upon a high rock, and accessible only by steps cut in the solid rock, and containing a population which was estimated at over six thousand. Upon the approach of the Spaniards the principal men of the place came down to meet them, bringing with them many presents and an abundance of provisions. The cultivated fields of the Acoma were located two leagues from the town, and were irrigated from a small river that flowed nearby, along the banks of which were growing great clusters of roses like those of Castile. In this vicinity were several mountains, said to contain metals, but they were inhabited by a warlike people and were not visited by the Spaniards. At Acoma they remained three days, and during their stay the Indians performed a solemn dance before them. They came out dressed in good apparel and gave many amusing exercises and performances. On the morning of the fourth day after their arrival at Acoma, Espejo resumed his journey, still continuing westerly, and at a distance of twenty-four leagues reached the province of Zuñi, which the Spaniards called Cibola, having, as the

ESPEJO VISITS ACOMA, ZUÑI, AND MOQUI

commander says, six pueblos and twenty thousand inhabitants. Here they found still standing the crosses which had been erected by the Spaniards forty years before under Coronado's command. They also found the Mexican Indians whom Coronado had left behind when he returned to New Spain still living; they were named Andrés de Culiacan, Gaspar de Mejico, and Antonio de Guadalajara. They had been so long among the Zuñis that they had almost forgotten their mother tongue and spoke the language of the Zuñis with great fluency. They told Espejo of the journey undertaken by Don Pedro de Tovar, but, what was of greater interest to the Spaniards, they informed them that in a journey of sixty days to the west, far beyond where Coronado's captains had been compelled to return on account of the lack of water and the great canyon, there was a lake with many settlements upon its banks, where the people had gold in abundance, wearing that metal in the form of ear-rings and bracelets. They said that Coronado had heard of this province, but after attempting to reach it failed and came back to Cibola and never made a second attempt. Espejo was very anxious to attempt the discovery of this lake and the populous towns, and proposed to his men and officers that they undertake the journey. Some of them were willing, but the majority, including the friar, Beltrán, was opposed and advocated a return to New Biscay. Nine of his soldiers agreed to accompany him, and, having made the necessary preparations, he left Cibola on his journey to the west. In a distance of twenty-eight leagues, they approached a large and populous province which was estimated to contain fifty thousand inhabitants. This was the country of the Moqui. The Indians were alarmed when they heard of the approach of Espejo and his companions, and immediately sent a messenger to warn him not to come nearer their towns under penalty of death. They were assured by Espejo that his coming was for a peaceful purpose and that no harm could come to his people. He gave the messenger several presents to carry to the Indians. He made such a favorable report of the Spaniards and the presents had so much influence in quieting the fears of the natives that they gave Espejo permission to enter their towns. When the Spaniards arrived within a league of the first town, they were met by about two thousand Indians who had come out to give them welcome, and bringing with them great loads of provisions. In return Espejo gave them a few articles of small value, which greatly pleased them. As they drew nearer the town, the caciques, with a multitude of other Indians, came out to meet them. They manifested great pleasure at the visit of the Christians, in testimony of which they cast corn meal on the ground under the feet of the horses. Escorted by this immense throng of natives the nine soldiers and their commander entered the town where they were well lodged and entertained. Espejo, not to be excelled in generosity, again distributed among them some glass beads and other small articles. Word was sent by the cacique to the whole province, announcing the arrival of the strangers, who were represented as being a very courteous people, and for which reason he had not offered them any harm. The Indians came from all over the province to visit the Spaniards, loaded them with presents, which they gave with an invitation to come to their towns and enjoy themselves. Notwithstanding this apparent display of friendship, Espejo feared that treachery might be lurking at the bottom of so much hospitality, and, to be better prepared in case of necessity he wanted some place of defense to rally upon. Using considerable strategy he represented to the chiefs that his horses were very fierce animals and might do some of the Indians harm in case they should become enraged, and that it was necessary to have an enclosure in which to confine them and thereby prevent the occurrence of any accident. The cacique, believing this to be true, assembled the Indians, and, in a short time, a rude fort of lime and stone was constructed, being just such an enclosure as the Spaniards desired in the event the Indians should show any signs of hostility. The name of this town was Zaguato-Awatobi.[289]

The Spaniards remained several days at Awatobi, receiving the hospitalities of the Indians, but, having received additional information here as to the great lake of which he was in search, Espejo began making his preparations for the continuation of his journey to the westward. He sent two Spaniards and some of the Indians,

---

[289] This place which Espejo called Zaguato was Awatobi or Aguatuvi or Aguitobi; it was destroyed by the Moquis of Oraibi in the year 1700. It existed in the month of June of that year. Fray Juan Garayochea, *Carta al Gobernador Pedro Rodriguez Cubero*, June 9, 1700. In 1701, Cubero made an unsuccessful expedition against the Moquis, *Relacion Anónima de la Reconquista del Nuevo Mejico* (Ms. Sesto Cuaderno).

Inscriptions on El Morro

who had accompanied him, back to Zuñi, and, with only four companions, Espejo set out upon his journey. When the natives were advised that he was going to leave them, they brought him numerous presents, among which were a great many mantas and some specimens of silver ore.

Espejo took with him some Moqui guides, and after a journey of forty-five leagues over a mountainous country, he found the mines and with his own hands obtained rich samples of silver ore. On the streams he found large quantities of wild grapes, walnut trees, flax, and Indian figs. He visited several settlements of the mountain tribes, where corn was raised and whose people were found friendly. These natives told of a great river beyond the mountains and told of its great width and the great towns which were to be found upon its banks. The river, they said, flowed into the north sea and the natives used canoes to cross it. From the mines Espejo returned to Zuñi, returning by a more direct route, and traveling only sixty leagues. It is believed that the mining section visited by Espejo was somewhere in the neighborhood of Bill Williams Mountain, forty or fifty miles north of Prescott, Arizona.[290]

When the Spaniards had returned to Zuñi, they not only found the five soldiers who had been sent back by Espejo, with his baggage, but Friar Beltrán and his companions as well, as the friar had not yet started on his return to New Biscay, but soon did so, by the same route, or possibly direct from Acoma southeastward to the Rio Grande, and thence down the river.[291]

Espejo, with his eight remaining soldiers, with a view of making further exploration of the upper Rio Grande, took up his march to the valley of that river and, after a march of ten days, arrived at

---

[290] Bancroft, H. H., *History of Arizona and New Mexico*, p. 88: "It will be remembered that Coronado had reached the Colorado by a westerly or northwesterly course from Moqui; and it is probable that Espejo's route was rather to the southwest, as he only heard of the great river beyond the mountains. Taking his distances of 45 leagues from Moqui and 60 leagues from Zuñi, we might locate his mine in the region of Bill Williams Mountain, 40 or 50 miles north of Prescott. The record hardly justifies any more definite location."

[291] Bancroft, H. H., *ibid*: "In the statement of Escalante and Barrundo, in *New Mex. Testim.*, p. 148-9, made before Espejo's return, but at a date not given, allusion is made to the return of Beltrán, leaving Espejo in the north. The returning party at first consisted of Miguel Sanchez and his two sons, Gregorio Hernandez, Cristoval Sanchez, and Frias, or six in all, leaving Espejo nine for the Moqui trip; later, on Espejo's return, Gregorio Hernandez is said to have joined Beltrán's party."

the province of the Queres, and thence eastward in two days, or twelve leagues, to the province of the Ubates, or Hubates, which had five pueblos containing 20,000 inhabitants. These were undoubtedly the pueblos lying north of Santa Fé, and to reach these from the Queres province, Espejo traveled northeast instead of east.

ESPEJO RETURNS TO THE RIO GRANDE—THENCE HOME BY WAY OF THE PECOS RIVER

From these pueblos it was possible for him to reach the pueblo of Cicuyé, which he next visited, in one day's journey. Cicuyé, according to Espejo, was in the province of the Tamos, which, with its three large pueblos, contained forty thousand people. There is no doubt that the Cicuyé of Espejo is the Pecos of today, as it was situate half a league from the Rio de las Vacas, by which name the Pecos river was known to Espejo.

The Tanos, different from the other natives visited by Espejo, were very unfriendly, refusing to admit the Spaniards to their pueblos and declining to furnish them with any provisions whatever. Some of the soldiers in his command were taken ill, and Espejo determined to make quick return to New Biscay. Taking with him a Pecos Indian, and leaving the pueblo of Cicuyé, after having traveled half a league, they reached the Rio Pecos, down which they journeyed for one hundred and twenty leagues. On this portion of the journey they saw many herds of buffalo. Meeting with some Indians of the tribe of Jumanos, Espejo was escorted by them to the Rio Concho in twelve days of travel, covering some forty leagues. Espejo left Cicuyé in the month of July, 1583, and arrived at San Bartolomé, in New Biscay, on the 20th day of September of that year. Here, during the month of October he made up his report. Friar Beltrán and his party had arrived some months before, and the friar had left and gone to Durango. The viceroy, to whom the report was sent, forwarded the same to the king and the Council of the Indies.

When we take into consideration the size of the force under Espejo, the conditions which existed, the purposes for which he came to New Mexico, the feelings of hostility which necessarily must have prevailed among the Indians who had recollections of the visit of Coronado years before, this entrada was little short of remarkable. Without the loss of a single life, without a conflict with the natives of a single province, he accomplished as much, if not more than had been effected by Coronado and his great expedition, confessedly the most brilliant and completely equipped of any that had ever left the City of Mexico. Coronado's treatment of the natives, in many respects, was most barbarous, and the reception and treatment of Espejo by the natives of Tiguex, who had suffered most at Coronado's hands, is a fair commentary upon the peaceful disposition of the Indians had they been accorded the treatment which the instructions of the viceroy, Mendoza, had demanded. The practical results of this entrada were far more important and satisfactory than the efforts of Coronado forty years before. Castañeda, the historian of the early expedition, realized what a great section of country had been lost to the members of the expedition under Coronado, and the reports of the subsequent exploring parties only confirmed what Castañeda deplored.[292]

There is no means of knowing with certainty whether or not Francisco de Ibarra ever entered what is now the territory of New Mexico. As has been said, after the Coronado expedition, the Spaniard gradually extended his conquests northward toward the Rio Grande and the Rio Gila. This progress was most constant, and was carried on by miners and missionaries. Just how far Ibarra penetrated the unknown north is not positively known. At any rate, on his return Ibarra boasted that he had discovered a "New Mexico" as well as a

ORIGIN OF THE NAME OF NEW MEXICO —
EXPEDITION OF IBARRA, 1563-5

---

[292] Castañeda, *Relacion*, etc., Winship's translation, p. 472: "I always notice and it is a fact, that for the most part, when we have something valuable in our hands, and deal with it without hindrance, we do not value or prize it as highly as if we understood how much we would miss it after we had lost it, and the longer we continue to have it the less we value it; but after we have lost it and miss the advantages of it, we have a great pain in the heart and we are all the time imagining and trying to find ways and means by which to get it back again. It seems to me that this has happened to all or most of those who went on the expedition which, in the year of our Saviour, Jesus Christ, 1540, Francisco Vasquez led in search of the Seven Cities. Granted that they did not find the riches of which they had been told, they found a place in which to search for them and the beginning of a good country to settle in, so as to go on farther from there. Since they came back from the country which they conquered and abandoned, time has given them a chance to understand the direction and locality in which they were, and the borders of the good country they had in their hands, and their hearts weep for having lost so favorable an opportunity."

new Biscaya. It is not unlikely that from this circumstance, the name New Mexico came to be applied in later years to a country that Governor Ibarra had never seen. The application of this name to the country has been attributed by a good many authorities, early and modern, both to Friar Rodriguez and Don Antonio de Espejo, although the former called the country which he visited San Felipe, and Espejo, Nueva Andalucia. The truth would seem to be that the name was applied in Mexico, under circumstances not fully recorded, after the return of Chamuscado and while Espejo was still journeying through the land of the pueblos. The first occurrence of the name is in Rio de Losa's essay written about this time. San Felipe de Nuevo Mexico appears occasionally in early documents. It was obviously natural that such a name should have suggested itself as appropriate for any newly discovered province whose people and buildings resembled, in a general way, that is in comparison with the wild tribes and the huts, those of the valley of Mexico.[293]

[293] Bancroft, H. H., *History of Arizona and New Mexico*, pp. 72 and 73-91 and notes: ''While Coronado's was the last of the grand military expeditions for half a century, and while for much longer the far north was left almost exclusively to the theorists, yet toward the north there was a constant progress in the interior through the efforts of miners and missionaries in Nueva Galicia and Nueva Viscaya, destined to cross the line of our Territory in time. It was forty years before the line was again passed, unless there may have been one exception in the expeditions of Francisco de Ibarra in 1563-5. From a point not very definitely fixed in the sierra between Sinaloa and Durango, Ibarra marched for eight days to a point from which he saw a large town of several-storied buildings; and later, having gone to Sinaloa, he says he 'went 300 leagues from Chametla, in which entrada he found large settlements of natives clothed and well provided with maize and other things for their support; and they also had many houses of several stories. But because it was so far from New Spain and the Spanish settlements, and because the governor had not enough people for settlement, and the natives were hostile, using poisoned arrows, he was obliged to return.' Beaumont, deriving his information from unknown sources, adds that 'Ibarra was accompanied by fifty soldiers, by Pedro de Tovar, of Coronado's expedition, and by Padre Acevedo and other friars.' His course was to the right of that followed by Coronado and nearer New Mexico. He reached some great plains adjoining those of the *vacas*, the buffalo plains, and there found an abandoned pueblo whose houses were of several stories, which was called Paguemi, and where there were traces of metals having been melted. A few days later, Ibarra reached the great city of Pagme, a most .beautiful city adorned with very sumptuous edifices, extending over three leagues, with houses of three stories, very grand, with various and extensive plazas, and the houses surrounded with walls that appear to be of masonry. This town was also abandoned, and the people were said to have gone eastward. It is difficult to determine what reliance should be placed on Beaumont's narrative; and there appears to be no grounds for more than

In the month of November, 1582, the viceroy, the Condé de Coruña, reported to his king the results of his investigations relative to the journey and probable fate of the friar Rodriguez and his companions. At this time nothing whatever was known in the City of Mexico of the expedition under Don Antonio de Espejo, starting from Nueva Biscaya. In his report to the king, the viceroy attached for his information a communication from Don Rodrigo del Rio de Losa, lieutenant captain-general of Nueva Galicia, whom he had consulted. This officer, as the viceroy says, was a man of great experience in explorations, having served with Arellano in Florida, and with Ibarra in Nueva Biscaya.

THE EXPEDITIONS OF HUMANA AND CASTAÑO

Fac-simile of Signature of the Condé de Coruña

He was under the impression that the people of New Mexico were very hostile owing to the fact that the friars had been murdered and insisted that a force sufficient for the proper reduction of the natives should be sent, thereby inspiring respect for the Spanish arms and preventing future revolts and outrages; that the force should consist of not less than three hundred men, each provided with seven mules and horses. It was his opinion that after the death of the friars had been avenged and the country placed

the vaguest conjecture as to what region was thus explored by Ibarra. He may have visited some of the abandoned pueblos of the Gila valley; or may, as Beaumont seems to think, have gone farther to the region of the Moqui towns; or, perhaps, he went more to the east and reached the Casas Grandes of Chihuahua.''

Bancroft, H. H., *Hist. North Mex. States*, i, 105-10; also Ibarra, *Relacion*, 482. Vargas, *N. Mex. Testim.*, 129 (about 1583), tells us that Ibarra ''revolvió sobre la parte del norte hasta que dió en los valles de las vacas.''

Bancroft, H. H., *Hist. Ariz. and New Mexico*, p. 73, says: ''Another noteworthy circumstance in this connection was the discovery in 1568 by a party of mining prospectors from Mazapii, in northern Zacatecas, of a lake which was formally named Laguna del Nueva Mejico. This lake was apparently one of those in the modern Coahuila, but the tendency to find a 'New Mexico' in the north is noticeable.''

upon a peace footing, a few settlers should be left, the main body of the expedition should proceed across the buffalo plains to Quivira and beyond, even to the shores of the north or south sea, or to the strait "which is near China, in latitude 57 degrees, the occupation thereof by the English or French being in this manner prevented."

Don Rodrigo was also of the opinion that the expedition should carry with it the material necessary for building two small ships, so that rivers and straits might be safely and easily crossed, or possibly for use in sending news to the viceroy, in the event any great discoveries should be made. The officer goes into all the details, suggests that friars be sent along and proposes that the officers and men be encouraged in their effort thus to explore the country by having their property exempt from taxation, the giving of titles, and very liberal encomiendas of the Indians of New Mexico.[294]

The report of the viceroy and its accompanying communication from De Losa received a favorable reception at the hands of his royal master, and in the month of March, 1583, an order was made by the king, instructing the viceroy to enter into a contract with some suitable person to undertake the expedition, in accordance with the laws and regulations, but without any cost to the royal treasury, the contract to be submitted to the Council of the Indies before anything was actually undertaken. This order was received in Mexico some time during the following month of August.[295]

About one month after a copy of this royal order was received by the viceroy, Beltrán and Espejo returned from their expedition to the north, and the reports made by them awakened a lively interest in New Mexico and adjacent lands and provinces. The friar and Espejo both reported that the people were not hostile; that they had received a most friendly reception, and that the country was well worth settling and colonizing; that the natives knew nothing of the use of the precious metals, but ores, rich in silver, had been found at several places, which, with proper development, would doubtless result in good producing mines. The friar

---
[294] *New Mexico Testim.*, pp. 96-97-99, viceroy to the king, November 1st, 1582.
[295] Pacheco, *Doc.*, xv, 100; xvi, 297.

Beltrán was most enthusiastic in his description of the people and the prospects of saving the souls of over a quarter of a million natives whose intelligence was of a superior character. Furthermore, the Spaniards had never failed to remember the tales of the wealth of Quivira, and Espejo's report of the big lake, the populous villages, and plenty of gold was all that was required to arouse great interest in the prospects of any expedition which might receive the royal sanction.

Again, Rio del Losa, in his communication to the viceroy, had made allusion to the necessity of further exploration and conquest because of the possible activity of other powers, and, as he says, to prevent "otras naciones de franceses ó ingleses luteranos no la ocupen." One, Padre Diego Marqués, had fallen into the hands of the English and had been closely questioned by them respecting his knowledge of the countries then being explored in the north by the Spaniards.

There was living in the vicinity of the City of Mexico at this time a man by the name of Cristobal Martin, wealthy and prominent, who, having heard of the royal cedula and the reports brought to the country by the friar, Beltrán, and Don Antonio de Espejo, made application to the audiencia for a contract of exploration under the laws and regulations. He was willing to head an expedition of two or three hundred men and would spend fifty thousand dollars in the enterprise. He desired a missionary force of not less than six Franciscans and two secular clergymen, and wished that he be supplied with certain arms and ammunition at the cost of the crown. Don Cristoval was evidently an ambitious individual. He also asked that he receive the title of captain-general and governor for himself and family during three lives of the kingdom which he should be able to conquer. He also wanted the right to distribute as encomiendas to his soldiers all of the natives of the conquered provinces for ten lives. He had ideas of power that are somewhat amusing to those who know how jealous was the Spanish crown at this time, for he gave as a condition of his undertaking the enterprise that he be given the right to appoint and remove all officials, and to grant lands. He thought that the royal one-fifth of the product of all mines should be reduced to one-twentieth for a period of one hundred years; that all products be exempt from taxation for a like period. Again, he wanted to be vested with the chief judicial authority in his capacity as governor, and also have the right to discover and settle all lands for one thousand leagues beyond the first New Mexican towns, to occupy ports on either ocean, and to trade, with two ships, from one of these ports, without paying any duties. It was also to be his right and privilege to call upon the viceroy for more men, provided that he paid the cost. He was to be given the right to found a mayorazgo, or entail, for his heirs, with enough revenue to perpetuate the family name and glory, as well as many other things too numerous to mention in full.

Don Cristoval renewed his petition several times during the months of October to December, 1583, and, according to the record, his contract was finally approved and sent to the Council of the Indies for confirmation, pursuant to the royal cedula.[296]

Don Antonio de Espejo, who had made the successful journey to the far north, now made application to the king direct for the right to colonize the lands he had visited, claiming that his service, experience, knowledge, and success entitled him to the preference over all others. He was insistent in his requests that the viceroy be not allowed any part in the enterprise whatever. That if his plan was followed out and the right be given to him, without any interference on the part of the vice-regal authorities, there would be no wrangles or delays; that the natives would be well treated and that, under his policies and plans, the new country would soon become a flourishing community and add much to the royal revenues.

ESPEJO APPLIES TO THE KING FOR THE RIGHT TO COLONIZE THE LANDS HE HAD VISITED

When Espejo made his report of his journey to the north and in the statement of what he had seen and accomplished he gave expression to the desire to spend his life and fortune in the service

---

[296] Pacheco, *Doc.* xvi, 277-301, *Martin, Asiento con Cristobal Martin por el que se ofrece á ir en persona al descubrimiento, pacificacion y poblacion del Nuevo Mexico, bajo las condiciones que expone*, Mexico á 26 Octubre de 1583.

This is the expediente of the proceedings had at the City of Mexico, which was sent to Spain; the date does not appear, but it was soon after December 24th, as that is the date of the certificate. It nowhere appears in the document that the contract was signed, but in the beginning, Don Cristoval says that "el fue el primero que capituló ó asento en virtud de una Real Cedula de V. A., el negocio de la poblacion y descubrimiento del N. Mexico y fue remetido á Vuestra Real Consejo de Yndias."

Inscriptions on El Morro

of his royal master, and stated that in anticipation of the future colonization or exploration of the countries he had visited, he had brought with him to New Biscay two Indians, one from Moqui and the other from Pecos, who might become useful as interpreters, if properly educated in the Spanish language. Espejo also wrote to the archbishop and stated that it was his intention to apply for a royal commission to explore and conquer the countries he had visited in company with Fray Beltrán.[297]

Don Antonio was a man of family, and his son-in-law, Don Pedro Gonzales de Mendoza, being about to start for Spain, was, in the month of April, 1584, duly empowered by Espejo to represent him at the court of Spain and obtain, if possible, the right to the "conquista y pacificacion y gobernacion" of the provinces of New Mexico or Nueva Andalucia, which Espejo had discovered and taken possession of the year before, in the name of the crown. Gonzales de Mendoza took with him a copy of Espejo's *Relacion*, which was attached to the formal petition.

The proposition advanced by Espejo was the organization of an expedition consisting of not less than four hundred men, the most of whom were to be brought from Spain, and one hundred of whom should be married and having children. The expedition was to be organized into four companies, and each well supplied with all necessaries, whether soldier or settler. A portion of the force was to consist of cavalry, and with them should be taken mares, cattle, and sheep. He declared that twenty-four Franciscans were necessary for the spiritual welfare of the new kingdom. Having been over both routes which he mentioned, he would take a portion of the expedition by way of the Rio del Norte and the other by way of the Rio de Vacas, the Pecos. For the safety of the settlers, it was his idea that the garrison should be stationed in the neighborhood of the Rock of Acoma, that being, in his judgment, the best center for military or other operations. Espejo believed in carrying out the plan inaugurated by himself on his first trip to the north in the matter of the treatment of the natives; his policy would be one of conciliation and justice, always looking forward to the preservation of peaceful relations. In the enterprise, Espejo declared himself willing to expend more than one hundred thousand ducats, in addi-

---

[297] Espejo, *Relacion*, in Pacheco, doc. xv, 151-191.

tion to the ten thousand which had already been expended by him in his journey with Friar Beltrán. In the expedition he could rely upon twenty associates, all of whom were men of considerable wealth, and that he was ready to give bonds in the sum of two hundred thousand dollars for the faithful performance of his contract. It is supposed that, as was usual with the so-called governors, Espejo asked for the several titles of captain-general, governor, and all the privileges which, under the laws, accompanied those positions in the New World.

We have seen that Espejo made his request direct to the king and it is not believed that his intentions were known by the authorities at the City of Mexico. It is possible, that, owing to the fact that Don Cristoval Martin had made application for a contract of exploration, some sort of an investigation was had, for about that time the alguacil mayor and regidor of Puebla addressed the king upon the subject of exploration of the lands visited by Espejo. He was of the opinion that the country was not worth much, and was generally undesirable and offered but slight inducements to the settler and colonizer. The name of this officer was Francisco Diaz de Vargas. He believed, however, having heard the latest reports from the countries desired to be explored, that, inasmuch as there appeared to be evidences of rich mineral deposits in the country, it would be well to send an expedition of exploration, not for colonization purposes, into the country and, in this way, confirm the reports that had been made by the friar and Espejo. To accomplish this, a force of fifty or sixty men was entirely sufficient and to that end he was entirely willing to head such an expedition himself. That, in the event the exploring expedition thus by him recommended, confirmed what had been reported, he, accepting the titles and usual emoluments which the law and the regulations gave, would be willing to take charge of a greater expedition, having for its object the settlement and colonization of the lands in question.

There is no record of anything having come out of these various propositions. However, no expedition was organized either by Martin, Espejo, or de Vargas, and for the next five years nothing is known, which is of record, concerning New Mexico.

Early in the year 1589, Don Juan Bauptista de Lomas y Colmenares, a resident of the Nieves Minas, presented a petition to the

viceroy, Villamanrique, in which he proposed to undertake the conquest of New Mexico. His requirements of the crown were almost as exacting as was possi-
JUAN BAUPTISTA DE LOMAS Y COL- ble to be suggested by a sub-
MENARES MAKES A PROPOSITION FOR ject. He proposed that he be
THE CONQUEST OF NEW MEXICO given a commission as captain-
general and governor, with al-
most unlimited authority for a period of six lives, to which there was to be attached a salary of eight thousand ducats, coupled with entire jurisdiction beyond the Conchos river. All other explorers must be excluded from the territory, and he was to have the title of count or marqués for himself and his descendants, together with forty thousand vassals. He also desired the privilege of granting three pueblos as entailed encomiendas, and another for the descendants of explorers who had not been provided for; also the right to fortify ports and build ships on either ocean. Associated with him were his sons. Don Juan Bauptista, in his petition, claimed to have rendered services at his own expense on the northern frontier.[298]

This contract was approved by the viceroy, and although he had no authority to grant entradas, the contract was sent to the king for his approval, by whom, in the matter of approval or disapproval, nothing appears to have been done. In the year 1595, Don Juan Bauptista renewed his petition, addressing the same to the then viceroy, Monterey, but it appears that nothing was done by this representative of the crown, and nothing is heard of the project thereafter, so far as the records show.

Gaspar Castaño de Sosa had been alcalde mayor of San Luis Potosi in the year 1575, and, in 1590 was the lieutenant governor
of Nuevo Leon. This explorer
GASPAR CASTAÑO DE SOSA LEADS made up his mind to lead an
AN EXPEDITION INTO NEW MEXICO expedition without consulting
the viceroy or obtaining the
authority of the king in any way. Castaño de Sosa claimed some

---

[298] Pacheco, *Doc.*, xv, 54-80. Here we find the *Expediente* sent from Mexico by the viceroy in 1592 and attached to the second petition of Lomas in 1595. In the record it is entitled: "Lomas, Asiento y capitulaciones que el virey de la nueva España, Marques de Villamanrique, hizo con Juan Bautista de Lomas Colmenares, sobre el descubrimiento y poblacion de las provincias del Nueva Mejico á 15 de Febrero de 1589."

sort of authority, but, judging from subsequent events, all of his acts were regarded as irregular and illegal. His original diary has been preserved.[299]

Castaño de Sosa started on the 27th day of July, 1590, from the village of Almaden, somewhere in Nuevo Leon, and in his command there were over one hundred and seventy persons, including women and children. Accompanying the expedition was a wagon train of supplies deemed necessary for the prospective settlements. After a trip covering some two weeks, the party arrived at the Rio Grande, where the remainder of the month of August was spent awaiting the return of messengers who had been sent to the City of Mexico.[300]

---

[299] Pacheco, *Doc.*, iv, 283-354; *Idem*, xv, 191-261: "Castaño de Sosa, Memoria del descubrimiento que Gaspar Cataño de Sosa, teniente de gobernador y capitan general del nuevo reino de Leon por el rey D. Felipe nuestro señor, va á hacer, al cumplimiento de las provisiones que el dicho gobernador les han concedido, y á el como su lugar teniente, como mas largamente se verá por la dicha provisione é cedulas reales y libro de nuevas leyes de pobladores concedidas á todos los vecinos del dicho reino," etc., etc.

Bancroft, H. H., *History of Arizona and New Mexico*, note, p. 101, says: "From the Munoz collection, and at the end, was a note as follows: 'Hizose relacion dello, y viose por los señores del Consejo en 10 de Noviembre de 1592 — Sant Andres.' It would seem to be a copy of the original diary made in some official book of records, probably in connection with legal difficulties in which the leader became involved."

[300] Bancroft, H. H., *History of Arizona and New Mexico*, p. 101-102, notes 14 and 15: "It is a somewhat perplexing narrative; long, verbose and complicated; requiring close study, but rewarding that study with only the most meagre general results. If a man lost his way, we have all the details of his wanderings back to camp; we know exactly the day and hour when the dog of Juan Perez was killed by the kick of an ox; we have all the discussions and diplomatic maneuvers resulting from a difference of opinion as to whether a bushel of corn might safely be distributed as rations; but we rarely find the course or distance of a day's journey. Were it not for the vicinity of two great rivers, the reader might be in doubt whether the travellers were going northwest in Guatamala or southeast in New England.

"The following names appear scattered in the narrative, most evidently those of leading men in the company: Cris. de Herredia (captain and mæstro de campo), Andrés Perez (secretary), Manuel de Medreras, Fran. Lopez de Recalde, Juan de Carabajal, Juan de Contreras, Domingo de Santistevan, Diego Diaz de Verlanda, Alonzo Jaimes y Ponce, Fran. de Mancha, Fran. Salado, Juan Perez de los Rios, Martin de Salazar, Juan Rodriguez de Nieto, Pedro Flores, Blas Martinez de Mederos, Cris. Martin, Jusepe Rodriguez, Juan de Estrada, Gonzalo de Lares, Diego de Biruega, Cris. de Biruega, Pedro de Inigo, Juan Rodriguez de Avalos, Hernan Ponce de Leon, Pedro Pinto, Juan de Vega, Alonzo Lucas, Domingo Hernandez, Franco. De Bascones and Juan Sanchez."

The most definite statement contained in the narrative is on page 289, while they were on the Rio Grande del Norte. One exploring party had found a stream which could not be crossed; whereupon Captain Heredia was sent out "el cual salió en demanda del dicho rio Salado, y llegó al rio que estaba descubrimiento hallo paso en el dicho rio para poder pasar las caretas, porque

From this place several exploring expeditions were sent out from the main command and, finally, in October, they started for a river which they called the Salado, undoubtedly the Pecos of today. The command followed the course of the Pecos throughout its entire length to a point near the pueblo of Cicuyé, which was reached about the last of the month of December. A small party of explorers, during the course of the journey, was attacked, as they claimed, by some natives of a pueblo situate on the river some distance ahead. It appears that this party had been out stealing some corn and were driven off by the natives on that account, losing a part of their arms and luggage and having three of the party seriously wounded.

When the news of this so-called attack upon members of his party reached the commander, he left the women and children with the wagons, all properly guarded, at a place called Urraca, and with the remainder of his command set out for the pueblo of Cicuyé, or Pecos, which was situated about half a league from the river. It was a large town, having houses of four and five stories. Upon the roofs of the houses the natives were stationed, brandishing their weapons, which consisted of bows, arrows, stones, and slings. The Spanish commander tried every means to conciliate the Indians but was unsuccessful, consuming the greater part of the day. Finally, and late in the afternoon, he made an attack upon the village, which was taken without any serious loss to either side. Although the greatest precautions were taken to prevent insult or outrage, it was impossible to overcome the suspicions and fears of the Indians, and during the following night they all abandoned the pueblo. The Spaniards, however, remained in the pueblo for five or six days. The narrative recites that there were five plazas and sixteen estufas in the village as well as immense stores of corn, amounting to 30,000 fanegas in all, of which the Spaniards took possession.

A portion of the supplies taken from the Indians of Pecos was sent back to Urraca, and, on the 6th day of January, 1591, Castaño started out upon another exploring expedition. Two days he journeyed across a mountainous snow-covered country to a small pueblo, the inhabitants of which were friendly and readily submitted

hasta entonces no se habia hallado. Y descubierto el dicho paso, fue atravesando aquela lomeria que habia hasta el Rio Bravo, y llegó al dicho rio Bravo; y se volvió al dicho real, diciendo que por alli podiamos pasar y ir atravesando el rio Salado.''

to the appointment of the officials named by the commander. The Spaniards visited four other pueblos, all of the same kind. These were doubtless the Tehua pueblos north of Santa Fé. In each a cross was set up. The seventh village visited contained a large communal house of two or three stories, in the plaza of which village there was a large structure, half under ground, which seemed to serve as a kind of temple. The eighth and ninth pueblos were a day's march up a large river — the Rio Grande — but the tenth was the largest of all, being a journey of five leagues beyond the last, the buildings being seven to nine stories in height. This pueblo the Spaniards did not enter, because the people were not altogether friendly. This pueblo was undoubtedly Taos.[301] The snow at this time was very

[301] The Taos valley is one of the finest in New Mexico. Fernandez de Taos is the county seat of Taos county. It is most romantically situated in this valley, surrounded by mountains which rise to a height of 14,000 feet. The town is very interesting, quaintly built around a large plaza. Its church possesses considerable antiquity. The population is about two thousand. Before the advent of the railroads, Taos was a place of very considerable commercial activity. Only three miles to the northeast, under the shadows of the great mountains, and occupying both sides of a bright, clear river, is the pueblo of Taos, undoubtedly the most interesting native settlement in all America. Scores of tourists visit it annually, particularly on its feast day, San Geronimo, September 30. The Jicarilla Apaches, the Navajós, as well as the Pueblo Indians from the south send delegations to this annual festival. The population of the pueblo has been decreasing in large numbers during the past decades, and now numbers about 400. The Taos Indians cling tenaciously to their primitive customs. The pyramid houses of this historic pueblo stand today as they did sixty-nine years before there was an English-speaking resident in the New World, on the two sides of a beautiful stream, in a valley among the last vertebrae of the Rocky mountains. Close on the north the massive peaks spring abruptly from the little plain; to the east and south are the ranges of Picurés and Santa Fé; on the west the grand canyon of the Rio Grande splits the valley from the timbered uplands to the southern extremity. It is one of the finest landscapes in the whole southwest, and despite its altitude of over seven thousand feet, one of the fairest valleys. Nowhere in all the world is there a more startling page of history brought down to date. All of Europe has nothing which remotely suggests these human bee-hives, these pyramidal fortress-homes of the northern Tiguas. It is only in America, and only in New Mexico, that such things are to be seen. Acoma and the pueblos of Moqui are only diminished specimens of the same development. But Taos is the most perfect remaining type of the terraced communal house of the ancient Pueblos, which was in its turn the most astonishing domestic architecture ever invented by man, savage or civilized.

The Indians of Taos have a tradition as to the founding of their pueblo; the story smacks strongly of the tale of Posenueve and the so-called legend of Montezuma. According to the story, as given by the *principales* and the governor of the pueblo, it seems that many hundreds of years since the Indians of Taos lived in the northwest; long before the coming of the Spaniard, an epidemic broke out among them, carrying off more than half of the nation; they

deep and forage for the horses was not to be obtained, the Spaniards returned to the south, where they visited pueblos eleven and twelve, situate to the west of the Rio Grande, a league apart, and then an-

do not know the site of the old pueblo; it was far away to the north and west by a great lake and river.

The pestilence raged; many of their *principales* died, and finally their *cacique* fell a victim. An election to name his successor was held, a very important affair, as without a *cacique* the pueblo could not exist as a unit, and would soon be merged into some other pueblo. Many meetings had been held in their *kivas*, but without result. All of the immediate family of the *cacique* had died, and it was necessary to elect his successor from the council of the nation; such an event had never occurred in the history of their people, and the council which was called hesitated to act; a hive of bees without a queen, however, could exist easier than a pueblo without a *cacique*.

One day, as the council entered the *kiva*, a boy, known as Bah-tak-ko, a lad of about twelve years, and known in the pueblo as a sort of Simple Simon, entered also, though the rule prohibited anyone entering on such an important occasion, under no less a penalty than death, unless by right. The boy took his seat as though he had this right, and acted as though he were one of the council.

The boy's history was well known to everyone in the pueblo. His mother, Ah-za-za, a maiden of perhaps sixteen years, was sent one day to the hills to gather piñones, and herbs with which to color feather robes. When her task was finished, she became weary and laid down under a piñon tree, where she fell asleep.

When she awoke her lap was filled with piñon nuts, and the ground around about was covered with them. In the course of time a son was born, who was called Bah-tah-ko. He was always a strange child and from infancy grew up uninstructed, as he had no father. He was shunned by other children, had no playmates, and other than his mother, Ah-za-za, had no friends in the pueblo.

Often, as he grew older, he would wander in the forest, remaining there for days; he had been heard talking to himself, in a strange language; he was seen in company with great birds and wild beasts, which seemed to like rather than to fear him; it was said his closest companion was a great grizzly bear, and he had been seen talking with the beast, the enemy of the tribe. These, and many other stories were told of Bah-tah-ko. He had escaped the plague; in fact, had not been ill, though all the others had been at the doors of death. Ah-za-za had, with others, been gathered to her fathers, where the Apache could not enter, and where the corn was always ripening.

When the council had assembled, so goes the story from our ancients, it was seen that Bah-tah-ko was seated by the everlasting fire. Someone, whether in jest or otherwise, many votes already having been taken without result, nominated Bah-tah-ko for *cacique*. The council assented to the nomination, when Bah-tah-ko arose and addressed the old men in words of great wisdom; told them he had known of his mission for many years; that it had been revealed to him by an eagle, which came to talk to him often.

The council was astounded at the words and wisdom of Bah-tah-ko, for they had believed him half-witted; unanimously he was made *cacique*, and from the walls of the pueblo the criers announced the election of the new *cacique*. A celebration of many days followed. A new house was built for his *caciqueshin*; the *cacique* lands were tilled for him, and a general hunt for the *cacique* brought him much meat. Great strings of turquoise were sent him as gifts from other nations; he slept on feather robes; the mothers of the pueblo vied with each other in presenting the charms of their daughters, for the *cacique* must have a

other, number thirteen, situated on the east bank of the same river. At this point the Spaniards left the river and marched over a snowy route to another valley, two days' journey. Here they found, in sight of one another, four more pueblos, the Quereses, as Castaño calls them, apparently the Quirix of Coronado, and the Queres of Espejo. These were situate somewhere near the junction of the Galisteo with the Rio Grande. The eighteenth, nineteenth, and twentieth pueblos, about a league apart, were visited and submitted to the Spaniards, who called them respectively, San Marcos, San Lucas, and San Cristobal. The ruins of these old pueblos are to be

---

wife, but the *principales* selected his partner for him, a custom since the earliest days; she was a woman wiser than many and more beautiful than the moon, and their home was happy with many children.

The pueblo prospered; it was strong in battle, and defeated its enemies; they took many captives, who worked in the fields and brought the pine trees from the forest. Bah-tah-ko was wise, and his rule was famous.

One day, Bāh-tah-ko, who was now old and infirm, called the council together in the great *kiva*; he had returned from a hunting trip in the mountains; he told that he had again seen the eagle of his boyhood; that the eagle had said that he and his people must move or else they would be destroyed by another pestilence; that they must abandon their fields; must wall up the entrances to their pueblo, so that, were it afterwards necessary, they could return to their old homes. He told them they must travel to the east till they came to a great river, now known to be the Rio del Norte, which ran in a deep canyon on a great plain; that a ford would be found above the entrance on the opposite side; that they must cross at this ford, the sign of which would be an eagle, hovering high in the air above them; then they would travel for two days, when they would come to a crystal stream running down from the everlasting snows of the high mountains into a beautiful valley that would be rich with fruit; that the mountains were filled with game and the rivers full of fish. This was to be their home and here they would build a great pueblo, which the eagle said should be called Taos.

Some of the council did not care to leave their homes and abandon the old pueblo; they said the *cacique* was growing old and childish; that he feared the Apache. But Bah-tah-ko was strong, and the people decided to follow his instructions, and the order was given from the walls of the pueblo.

The sun rose seven times and on the eighth day the people started for the east, and in a journey of twenty days arrived at the spot which the eagle had described to Bah-tah-ko; two days the people saw the eagle, high above the mountains, soaring near the clouds. One day Bah-tah-ko saw the eagle drop a feather as he circled high above the spot where the pueblo now stands; Bah-tah-ko watched the feather as it fell; he picked it up and on the spot the building of the pueblo was commenced. For many days our ancients kept the feather in the *kiva*, but it is gone now.

Some of their people refused to abandon the old pueblo; the Apache came and drove them away; they wandered over hills and mountains for many days as they had no *cacique* to lead them; they finally came to a great river in the south and built a great pueblo called Isleta. They know this because in Isleta the old men know the story of Bah-tah-ko, and they speak the same language as at Taos.

Don Luis de Velasco, Viceroy of New Spain

found south of Santa Fé; near the old San Marcos are located the mines of the Cerrillos district. The Spaniards found indications of mineral near this pueblo at the time of this visit.

On the 24th day of January, the Spaniards started eastward, with Indian guides, for the purpose of bringing up the remainder of the army, the colonists, and the wagon-trains from Uracca. In their journey, they passed through pine forests, and for drinking purposes for men and horses were compelled to melt the snow which covered the ground to a considerable depth. They crossed the Pecos river two days later and the following day came to Uracca, finding the colonists much alarmed as the food supply was about exhausted. Here they remained four days, when the entire command started on the return, leaving the Pecos on the eighth day of February and reaching San Marcos ten days later. For a short time they made this town the center of operations, visiting a pueblo, the twenty-first, two leagues distant. In the month of March, Castaño again visited the pueblo of Cicuyé, where he found the inhabitants much more friendly than on his first visit. Afterwards he visited the twenty-second pueblo, known as Santo Domingo, on the Rio Grande, to which place later the headquarters of the command were moved.

The men, owing to the strict rules which Castaño enforced relative to the plundering of the natives, became very restless, and according to the chronicler entered into a conspiracy to abandon him and return to Mexico.

Before anything was accomplished, however, Castaño was advised of this plot and promptly suppressed it. In the month of March, while searching for mining prospects, Castaño found two more pueblos, twenty-three and twenty-four, both of which had been abandoned by the natives on account of conflicts with the wandering tribes of the plains. The Spaniards now explored the province of Tiguex and found fourteen pueblos, nine of which were visited. Upon the approach of the Spanish army the natives fled to the hills, because, as the commander says, they were afraid of being punished for having killed the friars.

While on these exploring expeditions down the Rio Grande, the Indians brought news of other Spaniards coming up the river. Later on Castaño met some of his own men, who informed him of the arrival of Captain Juan Morlete, with a force of fifty men. Castaño hastened to the camp of Morlete, thinking that reënforcements had been sent to him, but was much surprised to learn that he had come for the purpose of arresting him for having entered the country without a license. Don Gaspar was put in chains and, along with his entire command, was returned to Mexico.

When Don Juan Oñate entered the country, in 1598, he found traces of the wagons, showing that the return route was down the Rio Grande.

Zarate-Salmeron, in writing of this expedition, says, "and of those of Captain Nemorcete (Morlete) [302] and of Humana, I do not write, because they all saw the same things, and one telling suffices." [303]

Some time during the years 1594 and 1596 Captain Francisco Leiva Bonilla, a native of Portugal, and Juan de Humana, were at the head of an expedition, sent out under THE EXPEDITION UNDER the instructions of the governor of Nueva BONILLA AND HUMANA Biscaya, to suppress the warlike and rebellious tribes in the northern part of his province. Being successful in this, Captain Bonilla, who was cognizant of the current reports as to the wealth of the lands to the far north, determined to continue his operations by exploring New Mexico and Quivira. The governor of Nueva Biscaya heard of Bonilla's intentions and immediately despatched Pedro de Cazorla to overtake him and notify the men in his command that such an expedition was forbidden and declaring Captain Bonilla a traitor if he disobeyed the mandate. Bonilla, however, refused to pay any

---

[302] Castaño calls him Morlete, which is doubtless correct.
[303] Villagrá, *History of New Mexico*, 1610, Alcala, 36-7, says:
"Y por el de nouenta entro Castaño,
Por ser alla teniente mas antiguo,
Del Reyno de Leon á quien siguieron
Muchos nobles soldados valerosos,
Cuio Maese de campo see Lamaua
Cristoval de Herredia bien prouado
En cosas de la guerra y de buen tino
Para correr muy grandes despoblados,
A los cuales mando el Virey prendiese
El Capitan Morlete, y sin tendarse,
Socorrido de mucha soldadesca;
Brava dispuesta, y bien exercitada,
A todos los prendio, y bolvio del puesto."

attention to the order, although six of his men refused to continue with him and returned to Nueva Bizcaya. There is no record of this expedition or what was done except in small particulars. After reaching New Mexico, the next heard of Bonilla was at Quivira, or out on the plains in the neighborhood of that place. Bonilla and Humana quarreled, and in the conflict Bonilla was slain. After the death of Bonilla, Humana assumed command, and a short while afterward, when his party had passed through an immense settlement and reached a broad river, which was to be crossed on balsas, three of the Mexican Indians in the party deserted, one of whom, José, became the sole survivor of this expedition and told the tale to Juan de Oñate in 1598. After having proceeded to Quivira, so the story goes, and on their return, the command was attacked by thousands of Indians, the conflict commencing just before dawn. All were massacred except Alonzo Sanchez and a mulatto girl. It was said that Sanchez became a great chief among the Indians of the plains, but nothing definite is known as to this, as he was never seen afterwards by any white man.[304]

---

[304] Bancroft, H. H., *History of Arizona and New Mexico*, note, pp. 108-109, says:

"The authority for the first part of this expedition is Villagrá, *Hist. of New Mexico*, 37, 142. Villagrá was an eye-witness to the telling by the Indian deserter, José, of the story to Juan de Oñate. Oñate, *Carta de 1599*, 303, 309, says that he was instructed to free the province from traitors by arresting Humana and his men; also, that one of Humana's Indians (José) joined his force. Gregg, *Commerce of the Prairies*, i, 117, seems to have seen a copy of this communication or another containing similar statements at Santa Fé. Niel, *Apunt.*, 89, 95, calls Humana, Adelantado and governor; says that he killed Captain Leiva, his bravest officer and that his Indian, José, was found by Oñate among the Picuriés. Davis, *Spanish Conquest*, 260, seems to follow Niel for the most part, without naming that author.

BIBLIOGRAPHY

Alegre, Francisco Javier	*Historia de la Compania de Jesus*, Mexico, 1841.
Aparicio, Manuel R.	*Los Conventos Suprimidos en Mexico*, Mexico, 1861.
Bandelier, A. F.	*Historical Introduction.*
Barreiro, Antonio	*Ojeada sobre Nuevo Mexico*, Puebla, 1832.
Espejo, Antonio de	*Relacion del Viage que hizo*, etc., in Pacheco, 100. Also in Hakluyt's *Voyages*, iii, 383.
Frejes, Francisco	*Historia Breve de la Conquista*, Mexico, 1839.
Gregg, Josiah	*Commerce of the Prairies*, New York, 1844.
Mendieta, Geronimo	*Historia Eclesiastica Indiana*, Mexico, 1870.
Mota Padilla	*Conquest of Nueva Galicia*, Mexico, 1870.
Niel, Juan A.	*Apuntaciones*, in Doc. Hist. Mex., 3rd ser., iv, 56.
Pino, Pedro Bautista	*Exposicion Sucinta*, Cadiz, 1812; *Not. Hist.*, Mexico, 1849.
Pacheco, Joaquin F.	*Coleccion de Documentos Inéditos*, Madrid, 1864-1881. Cited as Pacheco, *Doc.*
Salmeron, P. Zarate de	*Relaciones de N. Mexico*, in Doc. Hist. of Mex., 3rd ser., iv.
Torquemada, Juan	*Monarquia Indiana*, Madrid, 1723. 3 vols.
Villagrá, Gaspar de	*Historia de Nuevo Mexico*, 1610, Alcala, Reprint, Mexico.

CHAPTER VII

THE CONQUEST OF NEW MEXICO BY DON JUAN DE OÑATE, 1595-1598

THE actual conquest of New Mexico was accomplished by Don Juan de Oñate in the years 1598 and 1599. In making his preparations for his journey to the far north he was engaged several years. His is the prominent name in the history of New Mexico for the following twenty years. He was well fitted for his task of giving civilization to the country, and undertook the enterprise in a most systematic manner. His achievement is one of the most important in the annals of the country and, until the appearance of Bancroft's account of his entry and march, very little had been published in the English language in relation to this most important event. The early standard writers were very brief and generally inaccurate in their story of this conquest.[305]

---
[305] Bancroft, H. H., *History of Arizona and New Mexico*, p. 110: "Nearly all gave the date as 1595-6, fixing it by that of Oñate's preparations; and greatly underestimating the delays that ensued; and only Mariana, the historian of Spain, seems to have given a correct date. The sum and substance of all these versions, rejecting errors, would be hardly more than a statement that in 1595 Oñate undertook the enterprise, and soon, with the aid of Franciscan friars, succeeded in occupying the province, and even made a tour to the Quivira region in the northeastern plains."

That later writers, consulting only a part of these earlier authorities, should not have materially improved the accuracy and completeness of the record, is not surprising. They have made a few slight additions from documentary sources; but they have retained, for the most part, the erroneous dates, and have introduced some new errors, the latest and best of them, Davis and Prince, having copied the blunder of some faulty document consulted, and moved the conquest back to 1591.

In an elaborate note, Mr. Bancroft gives a résumé of the statements made by the earlier writers. He says: Torquemada, *Monarquia Indiana*, i, 670 et seq., mentions the confirmations of Oñate's contract in 1595 by viceroy Monterey, the enlistment of men in Mexico and the appointment of a comisario of the Franciscan band, but gives no further details or dates until after New Mexico was occupied, that is, after 1600. "Pasaron todos, hasta llegar á las poblaciones que llaman N. Mexico, y alli asentaron Real, y oi Dia permanece, y de la que ha ido sucediendo se dira en sus lugares." This is virtually Torque-

Mr. Adolph F. Bandelier, writing in 1881 of Oñate's entrada, is the first authority, in the English language, to use the poem of Gaspar de Villagrá, a companion of Oñate, which was published only eleven years after the conquest. Later, the facts narrated in this poem were used by Bancroft, and at a still earlier date, in 1882, a Spanish investigator gave to the world a résumé of the book, which, for historical accuracy as demonstrated by the inspection of documents in the Spanish archives, found in modern times, is really remarkable.[306]

mada's history of the conquest. Mendieta, *Hist. Ecles.*, 402, writing in 1596, merely notes that the viceroy is now fitting out Oñate's expedition. Vetancurt, *Cronica*, 95, notes the contract made by Velasco and confirmed by Monterey, the appointment of friars, as in Torquemada, and then says: ''Llegaron con facilidad, y entre los dos rios fundaron una Villa á San Gabriel dedicada.'' Calle, *Noticias*, 102, after noting the contract ratified September 30, 1595, the Franciscans, etc., like the rest, thus records the conquest: ''Llegó al Nuevo Mejico y iso asiento, tomo posesion del por la Magestad Catolica del Rey N. Señor, y puso su Real en el pueblo que se intituló San Gabriel cuyo sitio está en 37 de altura al Norte, situada entre dos rios, donde fundaron Convento luego los Religiosos, y hasta el año de 1608 bautizaron 8,000 almas.'' Salmeron, *Relaciones*, 23-4, recording the start in 1596, the names of the friars, number of soldiers, etc., tells us ''dejadas largas historias, que no hacen á mi intento,'' that Oñate with over 400 men went 400 miles north, pitched his camp in latitude 37° 30', and went on to make further entradas and explorations. But he adds an account of the Quivira expedition, pp. 26, et seq.

[306] Villagrá, *Historia de La Nueva Mexico, del Capitan Gaspar de Villagrá. Dirigida el Rey D. Felipe nuestro señor Tercero deste nombre Año 1610.* Con Privilegio, en Alcala, por Luys Martinez Grande. Á costa de Baptista Lopez mercador de libros.

The writer has had the privilege of using a copy of Villagrá's work, made by Mr. Bandelier and by him presented to Hon. T. B. Catron, of Santa Fé, N. M. The copy is a beautiful specimen of Bandelier's work with the pen and brush; a reprint of Villagrá was published in Mexico in 1900 by the Museo Nacional de Mexico. The book contains a wood-cut print (portrait) of Villagrá; the usual certificates of license and approval by the clergy; a dedication to the king; prologue; quite a number of *canciones* and *sonétos* by different authors, addressed either to Captain Villagrá or to Oñate, and also a table of contents.

The first canto is as follows:

HISTORIA DE LA NUEVA MEXICO

Del Capitan Gaspar de Villagrá

Canto Primero

Que declara el argumento de la historia
y sitio de la nueva Mexico, y noticia
q della se tuvo, en cuanto la antigualla
de los Indios, y de la salida y decendencia
de los verdaderos Mexicanos.

Las armas y el varon heroico canto,
El ser, valor, prudencia, y alto esfuerço,

Don Juan de Oñate was a resident of Zacatécas, a man of very considerable wealth, and ambitious to be known as one of the discov-

> De aquel cuya paciencia no rendida,
> Por un mar de disgustos arrojada,
> Á pesar de la inuidia ponçoñosa.
> Los hechos y prohesas va encumbrando.
> De aquellos Españoles valerosos,
> Que en la Occidental India remontados,
> Descubriendo del mundo lo que esconde,
> Plus vltra con baauesa van diziendo,
> A fuerça de valor y braços fuertes,
> En armas y quebrantos tan sufridos,
> Quanto de tosca pluma celebrados;
> Suplicosos Cristianissimo Filipo,
> Que pues de Nueva Mexico soys fenix,
> Neuamente salido y producido,
> De aquellas viuas llamas y cenizas,
> De ardentíssima fee, en cuyas brazas,
> A vuestro sacro Padre, y señor nuestro,
> Todo deschecho y abrasado vimos,
> Suspendais algun tanto de los hombres (hombros),
> El grande y graue peso que os impide,
> De aqese inmenso globo que en justicia,
> Por solo vuestro braço se sustenta,
> Y prestando gray Rey atento oido,
> Vereis aqui la fuerça de trabajos,
> Calumnias y afliciones con que planta,
> El evangelico santo y Fé de Cristo,
> Aquel Christiano Achiles que quisiestes
> Que en obra tan heroica se ocupase,
> Y si por qual que buena suerte alcanço,
> A tenernos Monarco por oiente,
> Quien duda que con admirable espanto,
> La redondez del mundo todo escuche,
> Lo que a tan alto Rey atento tiene,
> Pues siendo assi de vos fauorecido,
> No siendo menos escriuir los hechos,
> Dignos de que la pluma los leuante
> Que emprender los q no son menos dignos
> De que la misma pluma los escruia,
> Solo resta que aquellas valerosos.
> Por quien este cuydado yo he tomado,
> Alienten con su gran valor heroico,
> El atreuido buelo de mi pluma,
> Porque desta vez pienzo que veremos,
> Yguales las palabras con las obras.
> Escuchadme gran Rey que soi testigo,
> De todo quanto aqui señor os digo.

Villagrá was procurador general of the Oñate expedition as well as captain. He was of the family of Perez of Villagrá, a town in the province of Campos, Spain, a family of many valiant soldiers, among them Don Francisco de Villagrá, well known in the conquest of the Araucanos in South America.

Bancroft says of the poem: "I found it a most complete narrative, very little, if at all, the less useful for being in verse. The subject is well enough

erers of the unexplored lands of the New World. His father had been an officer in the army of Nuño de Guzman, and his wife's grandfather was one of the founders of Zacatecas and a large owner in the mines at that place. Oñate offered to equip and at his own expense pay the wages of at least two hundred soldiers.

The king was not to pay [307] any portion of the expenses [308] of this expedition, as proposed by Oñate, and in the month of September, 1595, the viceroy, Don Luis de Velasco, signed the contract, accepting all of Oñate's proposals except some of his most extravagant demands, the agreement as entered into being a stipulation for "the discovery, pacification and settlement of the provinces of New Mexico, which are in New Spain." [309]

---

adapted to epic narration, and in the generally smooth-flowing endecasylabic lines of Villagrá loses nothing of its intrinsic fascination. Occasionally the author quits the realms of poesy to give us a document in plain prose; and, while enthusiastic in praise of his leader and his companions, our New Mexican Homer is modest in recounting his own exploits. Of all the territories of America, or of the world, so far as my knowledge goes, New Mexico alone may point to a poem as the original authority for its early annals. Not less remarkable is the historic accuracy of the muse in this production, or the long concealment of the book from the eye of students."

[307] Fernandez Duro says that Oñate was married to Doña Isabel Cortés Montezuma, daughter of Hernando Cortés. Villagrá says he was married to Doña Isabel, daughter of Juan de Tolosa, granddaughter of Hernando Cortés, and great granddaughter of Montezuma, and Bernardes, *Zac.*, 31-4, agrees with Villagrá.

[308] According to Gregg, who claims to have seen Oñate's petition with marginal notes of approval and dissent, at Santa Fé, Oñate offered to raise 200 men and to supply, at his own expense, live-stock, implements, merchandise, and one year's provisions for the colony. In return he asked for himself the titles of governor, adelantado, and captain-general, for five lives; 30 leagues of land with all the vassals thereon, a salary of 8,000 ducats and exemption from the crown tax for working mines; for his family, hereditary nobility and liberal encomiendas; for his army, arms and ammunition; for his officers, repartimientos of native laborers; for his colony, a loan of 20,000 pesos from the royal treasury; and for the spiritual well-being of all, six friars and the fitting church accoutrements.

[309] The following is a copy of the original decree of the king of Spain in favor of Oñate:

"Don Felipe, by the grace of God, King of Castile, of Aragón, of the Sicilies, of Jerusalem, of Portugal, of Granada, of Toledo, of Valencia, of Galecia, Mayoria, Sevilla, of Yerdina, Cordova, Coreega, Murrisa, Jaen, Algarbes, of Algesir á Gibraltar, Canary Islands, East and West Indies, Islands, and Tierra Firma of the Ocean, Arch-duque of Austria, Duque of Borgora and Milan, Count of Traspur Flanders, and Tirol, of Barcelona, Lord of Viscaya and Molisa, etc., etc.:

"Whereas, the viceroy, Don Louis of Velasco, by virtue of a decree of the King, my Lord — may he live in glory — entered into an agreement and capitulation with Don Juan de Oñate, relative to the discovery, pacification and settlement of the provinces of New Mexico, which is in New Spain, and

Don Gaspar de Zuñiga y Acevedo, Condé de Monterey, Viceroy of New Spain, 1595

By virtue of the acceptance of Oñate's proposition, he was to obtain the title of adelantado, governor and captain-general, to-

among other things he granted to him what is contained in one of the chapters or instructions of new discoveries and settlements of the Indies, which is as follows: 'To those who bind themselves to form said settlements, and shall have done the same, and shall have complied with the agreement, in honor of their own persons and their descendants and of them as first settlers, laudable memory may remain, we make them and their legitimate descendants Hijosdalgos of the lands owned by them, in order that in the settlement established by them, and in any other part of the Indies they may be Hijosdalgos and persons of noble lineage and Lord paramount, and as such they shall be known, held and considered, and enjoy all the honors and pre-eminences, and may do all things that noblemen and gentlemen of the Kingdom of Castile can do, according to the privileges, laws and customs of Spain, should or ought to do and enjoy. And in behalf of the said Juan de Oñate, I have been requested to grant him the grace to command him to approve, notwithstanding the moderation which the Duque of Monterey used relative thereto, and published by him, my Council of the Indies, I have thought proper that the said prerogatives should be understood to continue during the time occupied in said conquest, for five years, and if the said conquerors should terminate the conquest thereof before the expiration of the five years, they, their sons, and descendants shall enjoy the said prerogatives as herein set forth. And I do hereby command that all who may have gone and shall go on the said conquest, pacification and settlement, according to, and in conformity with, the provisions of the said chapter, and shall continue in the conquest for five years; and those who shall prosecute the same who should die before the expiration of five years, there shall be reserved and secured unto their sons and descendants all the pre-eminences and prerogatives, exemptions, and liberties as aforesaid in conformity to, and as is granted and conferred upon them in the said chapter, entirely and completely, failing in nothing, and charge the Infantes, Prelates, Duques, Marquises, Counts, Nobles, Subjects and Priors of Royal Orders, Prefects, Alcaldes of the Castiles, houses surrounded with a moat, and country houses (casas fuertes y lanas), and those of my councils, Presidents, Judges, Alcaldes, High Constables of my household and court, and chancery to my viceroys and Governors, and to all of my authorities and Judges, as well those of my Kingdom and Seignories as those of the Indies and Tierra Firma of the Ocean, and other persons of whatever condition or quality, to observe and comply, and to have obeyed and executed this my franchise and grace, confirmed to the aforesaid, without restricting or increasing, nor consent to any infraction of the contents of this my determination, which I desire and it is my will that it shall have the force of law as though it had been decreed and promulgated in court, and it be published in all proper parts and places.

" 'Given at San Lorenzo, on the 8th day of July, 1602.
(Signed) " 'I, THE KING.
"'Laguna, Armenteros, Doc. Eugenio de Salazar, Benabente de Venavides, Louis de Salcedo. By order of the King, my Lord. Juan de Ibarra. Recorded, Gabriel de Ochoa, Chancellor, Sebastian de la Vega.'

"ACT OF AUDIENCE

"In the City of Mexico, June 20, 1604, the President and Judge of the Royal Audience of New Spain being present at the session, also the Mariscal de Campo, Vicente de Salvidar, presented the Royal decree governing to the opposite party and asked that it be complied with; and being seen by the said Audience, they obeyed the same with all reverence and respects, and replied

gether with high official titles for his two cousins, as well as for his son, Cristoval Oñate, who was to accompany him.

As soon as the contract had been signed by the viceroy, Oñate began, along with his four brothers, and his four nephews, the Salvidars, and other powerful friends, to recruit for his army. Recruiting stations were established in the City of Mexico, to which came adventurers from all portions of the country, anxious to enlist under the banner of the brave Oñate, and particularly attracted by the terms offered, which gave great promise of wealth, fame, and fortune in the far north. There were many very influential men engaged in promoting this grand enterprise, among them being Don Diego Velasco, governor of Nueva Viscaya, Rodrigo del Rio de Losa, Santiago del Riego, and Maldonado of the Audiencia, Loquetio, Antonio de Figueroa, the Banuelos, Ruy Blas de Mendoza, Juan Cortés, the great grandson of the conqueror, Juan de Guevara, and Salas, the alcalde of Zacatécas. The brothers of Don Juan were Fernando, Cristoval, Alonso and Luis Nuñes Perez. The brothers Salvidar were Cristobal, Francisco, Juan, and Vicente. They were sons of Don Juan Salvidar, who had been a captain in the army of Don Francisco Vasquez Coronado, nearly half a century before.

Already six or seven hundred men had enlisted, and the preparations for departure were about concluded when the count de Monterey succeeded Don Luis de Velasco, as viceroy. The new viceroy arrived at the City of Mexico on the 5th day of November, and immediately began investigating the fitness of Don Juan for the enterprise, and on the 20th day of December wrote to the king asking that a ratification of the project be deferred until he could secure additional information. Many charges were filed against Oñate by his enemies and others who were jealous of Oñate's brilliant opportunities and the most unusual privileges and prerogatives which had been granted to him under the contract.[310]

---

that it should be observed and complied with, and executed in all its parts as His Majesty commanded; and this it was recorded as their act, and they approved the same by placing their rubric thereto in my presence.
(Signed) ''CRITOBAL OROSIO.''

[310] All of the facts concerning the conquest by Oñate, confirming what is found in the poem by Villagrá, are to be found in Pacheco, *Doc.* xvi, pp. 188-227. There is a resumé of the documents, all correspondence, and a lot of testimony taken in Mexico on the achievements of Oñate and the great necessity for continuing the conquest. On pages 98-141 appear the formal acts of the taking possession of New Mexico for Spain, followed by the acts

Finally, after the many charges against Oñate had been thoroughly canvassed and considered by the viceroy, he came to the conclusion that he would approve the contract made by Don Luis de Velasco, but insisted upon certain modifications which, when they became known to those who had enlisted in the enterprise, caused Oñate a great deal of annoyance and trouble. But, undaunted, Oñate made additional haste in his preparations and started for the north, halting at Zacatécas. With him at this time went several Franciscans, under P. Rodrigo Duran as comisario, whose names were Baltazar, Cristoval de Salazar, and Diego Martinez.

In June, 1596, Lope de Ulloa y Lemos was commissioned by the viceroy to make an inspection and inventory. He was also instructed to remove the army from the settlements on account of complaints of disorderly conduct; this caused some delay, but finally the army moved on to the mines in Durango and a portion still farther on to the valley of San Bartolomé.

A courier arrived on the 9th of September, carrying a royal order of the 8th of May, which directed a suspension of the entrada until further instructions were received. Ulloa's letter from the viceroy, dated August 12th, came with the same packet, and in this he was ordered to instruct Oñate, under the severest penalties, not to advance. Oñate promised to obey the order but kept the news from the army for a long time. The order from the viceroy in no manner kept him from his purpose of continuing the enterprise, and, aided by Juan Guerra, who most generously offered to bear a share of the expense incident to the delay, he kept up a brave front during the delay, which lasted nearly a year. During all this period, soldiers were constantly deserting, and failure at times seemed certain. Inspection followed inspection, but each time Oñate was able to keep his force up to the required standard. His foes spared nothing in their efforts to break up the expedition, and at times it seems that the government entertained this policy also. Father Duran became greatly disheartened, and notwithstanding the most vigorous protests left with most of his friars. During this period, and particularly between the months of November, 1596, and February, 1597,

---

of submission of the Pueblo Indians, giving dates and witnesses. See *post*, note 314.

many communications passed between Ulloa and Oñate, relative to the inspections which were being made as to his forces and supplies.[311]

Some of the soldiers became very mutinous, but the leader was tried and beheaded.

On the 17th day of December, 1597, orders came finally to prepare for a last inspection and to proceed to New Mexico. The final inspection was made at the mines of Santa Barbara. This inspection and review was made by Juan Frias de Salazar, who had been com-

---

[311] Palacio, *Mexico*, tomo ii, pp. 454-455: "Concertada ya la marcha de la expedicion de Oñate, habia salido la gente de este de algunas de las poblaciones de Nueva Vizcaya reuniendose en las minas de Caxco en el mes de Junio de 1596, en cuya fecha el virey dió comision á don Lope de Ulloa y Lemos para que pasase visita á la gente, caballos, armas, municiones y pertrechos que Oñate habia reunido y tenia dispuestos para aquella entrada, y para que sacase la gente fuera de poblado para que no hiciese daño. Ulloa nombró en representacion suya, para este ultimo encargo, á Francisco de Esquibel y el comenzó á practicar la visita el 29 de julio de 1596."

Orozco y Berra, in his work *Apuntes para la Historia*, etc., par. x, says: "Siguiendo á Cavo, que Velasco concibió la idea de enviar una colonia á Nuevo Mexico, que capitulo primero con Francisco de Urdinola y luego mudo de parecer y envió a don Juan de Oñate:— que la expedicion salió de Mexico en 1596;— que el real de Caxco se amontinó la gente por falta de avio:— que el virey mando á Ulloa á calmar la sedicion y que este, con dadivas y energia, obligó á los colonos á seguir á Oñate. Como se ve por documentos autenticos, nada de esto paso, sino que fue como se refiere en el texto de esta obra, citando los comprobantes respectivos."

Documentos inéditos de Indias, vol. xvi, p. 188 et seq: "El Itinerario seguido por esa expedicion se marca por los puntos siguientes: San Juan del Rio, Nazas, Caxco, la Zarca, Cerro Gordo, la Parida, Rio Flórido, Pilar de Conchos, San Pedro, Nombre de Dios (near Chihuahua), San Buenaventura, un lago, quiza Patos, los Medanos (el Rio del Norte)."

Palacio says of these inspections, etc.: "Don Lope de Ulloa encontró conformes á la capitulacion todos los preparativos, y solo dió auto para que llevase quiientos escudos de medicinas, en lo que convino Oñate sin dificuldad, y parece que el visitador regreso á Zacatécas y emprendió su marcha la expedicion; pero el 12 de Agosto en virey cominsiono al mismo Ulloa para que alcanzase á Oñate y le notificase que se suspendia la expedicion en virtud de una cedula real que asi lo disponia, fecha el 8 de mayo de 1596. Detuvose Oñate, y á pesar de que represento los grandes perjuicios que se seguian, porque la gente podia desertar, huirse la caballada y los bueyes y perderse los bastimentos y otras muchas cosas que llevaba, no consiguió permiso para continuar su marcha hasta diez y seis meses despues, tiempo en que tanto habia perdido que tuvo necessidad de perdir refuerzos al virey obligandosele á reponer lo que faltaba para cubrir su compromiso. Salió por fin con dosientos y un hombres, atravesó, buscando y llevando siempre camino de carretas, lo que forma hoy el Estado de Chihuahua, hasta llegar a Paso del Norte, y desde allí comenzó á extender sus conquistas."

N. Mex. Mem., pp. 192-7. A portion of Oñate's army was at Caxco and the balance at Santa Barbara. Altogether there were about 200 soldiers (colonists), besides negro slaves and Indians.

missioned as visitador. It was believed by Oñate's enemies that he could not pass this final inspection, and the viceroy advised him not to attempt it, but to disband his forces; this he refused to do and successfully passed through the official ordeal. The records show that there were deficiencies at this time and that his force only amounted to 130 men, and it was determined that the viceroy should raise 80 men, Oñate to bear the expense, and it appears that about this number were sent north at the time the expedition finally left for New Mexico.[312]

Everything having been placed in readiness, on the 20th day of January, 1598, the army left for the northward, and six days later reached the Rio Conchos.

OÑATE LEAVES SAN BARTOLOMÉ FOR NEW MEXICO, JANUARY 20, 1598

Here they remained for a week, at the same time parting from the visitador and Friar Marquez, the confessor. On March 3rd, a new band of Franciscans joined the army, having come under the leadership of Padre Alonzo Martinez, comisario, and escorted by Captain Farfan and party. The names of these Franciscans were Alonzo Martinez, Francisco de Zamora, Juan Rosas, Alonzo Lugo, Francisco de San Miguel, Andrés Corchando, Cristobal Salazar (a cousin of Oñate), Juan Claros, Pedro Vergara, and Juan de San Buenaventura, the last two lay-friars; also brothers Martin, Francisco, and Juan de Dios. One writer, Barreiro, says that Oñate had sixty-five Franciscans

---

[312] Bancroft, H. H., *History of Arizona and New Mexico*, note, p. 122, says: "Villagrá does not name Salazar, but calls the successor of Ulloa, who was sent to China, Captain Guerrero, with Jaime Fernandez as secretary. This may be an error, or Guerrero may have been intermediate between Ulloa and Salazar. The new *visitador*, according to Villagrá, was a bitter foe of Oñate and the quarrel between the two waxed very hot. As a sample of the obstacles thrown in the way of the colony, I note the following: Instead of permitting a halt while the inspection was being made, as was usual and expected, the *visitador* ordered an immediate march; then, in some most unsuitable place he would order a halt, forbid the men for several days to leave their tents to look after the live-stock, forbid the purchase of any animals, and then suddenly order the goats or some other class to be presented immediately at his office for inspection.— Villagrá, *Hist. of N. M.*, 72-4; *N. M. Mem.*, 197-8; *Id., Discurso*, 44. Many of the authorities mention the delays as being very short and insist that the expedition started for New Mexico in the summer of 1596. Salmeron and Niel attribute the delays to the devil, who trembled at the prospect of losing his grasp on so many thousands of souls. Cavo, *Tres Siglos*, i, 225-9, says that the delay was caused by a mutiny at Caxco, which was quelled by the inspector, Ulloa.''

with him, but this is undoubtedly a mistake. According to Salmeron and Niel, there were 400 men in the party, 130 of whom were accompanied by their families. Villagrá also intimates that this was the number composing the expedition. Don Cristobal Oñate, son of the conquistador, only ten years of age, was teniente de gobernador of the expedition; Juan de Salvidar was the maestro de campo, his brother, Don Vicente, sargento mayor, Captain Villagrá, procurador-general; Captain Bartolomé Romeros, contador; Zubia or Cubia, proveedor, and Juan Velarde and Juan Perez Doñiz, secretaries. There were 83 wagons in the train and seven thousand head of cattle.[313]

In Oñate's march to the north occurred the really first exploration of the present state of Chihuahua. Captain Villagrá was at the head of one of the two parties under Oñate after the start was made, neither one of the two divisions going down the Conchos river as previous exploring parties had done.

[313] Bancroft, H. H., *History of Arizona and New Mexico*, has given a list of the first settlers of New Mexico, arranged alphabetically, as follows:

Captain Pablo de Aguilar, Araujo, Ascencio de Archuleta, Ayarde, Alf. Dionisio de Banuelos, Bartol, Juan Benitez, Bibero, Capt. Juan Gutierres de Bocanegra, Juan Perez de Bustillo, Cesar Ortiz Cadimo, Juan Camacho, Estevan Carabajal, Carrera, Juan de Caso, Ald. (Capt.) Bernabe de Las Casas, Castillo, Juan Catalan, Cavanillas, Capt. Gregorio Cesar, Cordero, Alf. Juan Cortés, Marcos Cortés, Pedro Sanchez Damiero, Juan Diaz, Sec. Juan Perez de Doñis, Capt. Felipe Escalante, Juan Encarramajal, Capt. Marcelo de Espinosa, Capt. Marcos Farfan de los Godos, Juan Fernandes, Manuel Francisco, Alvaro Garcia, Francisco Garcia, Marcos Garcia, Simon Garcia, Luis Gascon, Bartolome Gonzales, Juan Gonzalés, Juan Griego, Guevarra, Francisco Guillen, Antonio Gutierres, Alf. Geronimo de Herredia, Antonio Hernandes, Francisco Hernandes, Gonzalo Hernandes, Pedro Hernandes, Antonio Conde de Herrera, Cristobal de Herrera, Juan de Herrera, Alonzo Nuñez de Hinojosa, Leon de Isasti, Jimines, Captain Diego Landin, Francisco de Ledesman, Alf. Juan de Leon, Domingo de Lisana, Cristoval Lopez, Juan Lopes, Alonzo Lopez, Lucio, Mallea, Francisco Marquez, Capt. Geronimo Marques, Hernan Martin, Juan Martinez, Juan Medel, Medina, Monroi, Alonzo Gomez Montesino, Baltazar de Monson Morales, Juan Moran, Munuera, Naranjo, Capt. Diego Nuñez, Juan de Olague, Ten. Gen. Cristoval Oñate, Captain General Juan de Oñate, Juan de Ortega, Ortiz, Regundo Paladin, Simon de Paz, Juan de Pedraza, Alf. Peyreyra, Simon Perez, Capt. Juan Pinero, Alf. Fran. de Posa y Peñalosa, Capt. Alonzo de Quesada, Fran. Guillen Quesada, Martin Ramirez, Juan R. Angel, Rason, Pedro de los Reyes, Pedro de Ribera, Alonzo del Rio, Diego Robledo, Francisco Robledo, Pedro Rodriguez, Sebastian Rodriguez, Bartolomé Romeros, Captain Moreno de la Rua, Capt. Ruiz, Juan Ruiz, Lorenzo Salado, Juan de Salas, Alonzo Salas, Cristobal Sanchez, Francisco Sanchez, Antonio Sariana, Juan de Segura, Serrano, Sosa, Capt. Tabora, Capt. Francisco Baca, Varela, Francisco Vasquez, Jorge de la Vega, Sec. Juan Velarde, Francisco Vida, Juan de Victorio Vida, Capt. Gaspar de Villagrá, Villaba, Villaviciosa, Capt. Juan de Salvidar, Capt. Vicente de Salvidar, Alf. Leon Zapata, Prof. Zubia, Zumaia.

THE CONQUEST OF NEW MEXICO 311

The Rio Grande was not reached until the 30th day of April, 1598, at which time the expedition proceeded up the western bank, after very formal religious ceremonies had been had, and the formal taking possession for God, for the king, as well as for himself, of all New Mexico and the adjoining provinces.[314]

[314] Palacio, *Mexico, Tráves de los Siglos*, pp. 455-456: ''Tomo Oñate posesion del Nuevo Mexico, sentados ya sus reales del otro lado del rio Bravo, el dia 30 de abril de 1598, con solemne aparato y hiciendo extender una acta que dice en su parte mas importante y curiosa: . . . Y por tanto, fundado en el solido fundamento sobre dicho, se tome la sobredcha posesion; y asi lo haciendo, en presencia del Reverendissimo Padre Fray Alonzo Martinez, Comisario Apostolico con plenitudine potestatis desta jornada del Nuevo Mexico y sus provincias y de los reverendos padres de la orden del Señor Sant Francisco sus compañeros predicadores del Santo Evangelico que son, Fray Francisco de Sant Miguel, Fray Francisco de Zamorra, Fray Joan de Rosas, Fray Alonzo de Lugo, Fray Andres Corchado, Fray Joan Claros y Fray Cristobal de Salazar; y de los amados Padres y hermanos Fray Joan de San Buenaventura, y Fray Pedro de Vergara, frayles legos religiosos que van en esta jornada y conversion; y del Maese de Campo General, Don Juan Zaldivar Oñate, y de los oficiales mayores, y de lo mayor parte de los demas capitanes y oficiales del campo y gente de paz y guerra del, digo; que en voz y nombre del cristinaísimo Rey Don Fhelipe nuestro Señor, unico defensor y amparo de la Santa Madre Inglesia y su verdadero hijo, y para la corona de Castilla y Reyes que de su gloriosa estirpe reynaren en ellas, y por la dicha y para la dicha de mi Gobernacion, tomó y aprehendo, uno y dos y tres veces, uno y dos y tres vezes, y todas las que de derecho puedo y debo, la Tenencia y posecion real y actual, cevil ó natural en este dicho Rio del Norte, sin exceptuar cosa alguna y sin alguna limitacion, con los montes, riberas, vegas, cañadas y sus pastos y abrevederos; y esta dicha posesion tomo y aprehendo, en voz y en nombre de las demas tierras, pueblos, Ciudades, Villas, Castillos y casas fuertes y llanas, que agora estan fundadas en los dichos Reynos y provincias de la Nueva-Mexico, y las á ellas circunvecinas y comercanas y adelante, y adelante; por tiempo se fundaron en ellos, con sus montes, rios, y viveros, aguas, pastos, vegas, cañadas, abrevaderos y minerales de oro, plata, cobre, azogues, estano, hierro, piedras preciosas, sal, morales, alumbres, y todos los veneros de cualesquier suerte, calidad o condicion que sean ó ser puedan, con todos los Yndios naturales que en ellas y en cada una dellas se incluyeren, y con juridicion civil y criminal, alta y baja horca y cuchillo, mero mixto imperior, desde la oja del arbol y monte, hasta la piedra y arenas del rio, y desde la piedra y arenas del rio, hasta la oja del monte; é yo el dicho Joan Perez de Donis, escribano de Su Magestad y Secretario susodicho, certificó y doy fee: que el dicho Señor Gobernador, Capitan General y Adelantado de los dichos Reynos y provincias, en señal de verdadera y pacifica posesion, y continuando los autos della, puso y clavo con sus proprias manos, en un arbol fijo que para dicho efecto se aderezo, la Santa Cruz de Nuestro Redemptor Jesucristo y bolviendose á ella, de rodillas por el suelo, dijo: Cruz I santa que soys, divina puerta del cielo, altar del unico y esencial sacrificio del cuerpo y sangre del Hijo de Dios, camino de los Santos y posesion de su gloria, abrid la puerta del cielo a estos ynfieles fundad la iglesia y altares en que se ofrescan el cuerpo y sangre del hijo de Dios, abridnos camino de seguridad y paz para la conservacion dellos y conservacion nuestra, y dad á nuestro Rey y ansi en su Real nombre, pacifica posesion destos Reynos y provincias para su Santíssima gloria, amen. Y luego yncontinenti, pendió y fixó asi mismo con sus proprias manos el estandarte real, con las armas del Cristianismo Rey Don

In the evening of the same day, there was given a performance of an original comedy, written by Captain Farfan, relative to the conquest of New Mexico.

Having crossed the Rio Grande at a point very near the location of the present city of El Paso on the 4th day of May, for fifteen days thereafter Oñate marched up the river on the eastern bank, a distance of fifteen and a half leagues, during which time several of the colonists died. Captain Aguilar, who had been sent forward on an exploring expedition, returned about this time, having gone as far north as San Marcial, beyond the Jornada del Muerto. This officer, contrary to his orders from Oñate, had entered one of the pueblos, his disobedience being overlooked by the captain-general when his men had interceded for him. Oñate was very much concerned for fear that the natives, having been apprized of his approach, would desert their homes, carrying with them all of the available food supply. As a consequence the commander, together with the Salvidars, Captain Villagrá, and the friars Salazar and Martinez, with an escort of seventy men, left the main army on the 22nd, and, after a journey of six days, traveling about twenty-six leagues, reached the first group of pueblos, their arrival occurring during a great storm.

ONATE MARCHES UP THE RIO GRANDE

Oñate was given a kindly welcome by the Indians, entertained by the governor, and furnished with an abundant supply of maize. He remained here until about the middle of June, when an advance was made up the river to a small pueblo located near the mouth of the Rio Puerco, and called by the Spaniards Nueva Sevilla. Here they remained a week, while the Salvidars went in search of the pueblos of Abó, and Captain Villagrá on a foraging expedition. On the 22nd day of June they continued up the river four leagues to an abandoned pueblo, which they called San Juan Bautista, inas-

Fhelipe, Nuestro Señor, que estaban bordadas de la una parte las Imperiales, y de la otra las Reales; y al mismo tiempo y cuando se hizo lo susodicho, se tocó el clarin y disparó la arcabuseria con grandisima demonstracion de alegria, a lo que notoriamente parecio, y Señoria, el dicho Señor Gobernador, Capitan General y Adelantado para perpetua memoria, mandó se autorize y selle y con sello mayor de su oficio, y signado y firmado de my nombre y signo, se guarde con los papeles de la jornada y gobernacion y se sacen de este original, uno dos ó mas testimonios con la dicha autoridad, asentandose en el libro de la Gobernacion ante todas cosas.''

Don Gaspar de Villagrá

Fac-simile of Page in his History of New Mexico, 1610, Alcalá Edition

THE CONQUEST OF NEW MEXICO   313

much as the locality was reached on the 24th of June, Saint John's day; here they were advised that up the river could be found two Mexican Indians who had been left in the country by Castaño de Sosa, and Oñate immediately started north in search of them, and reached the pueblo of Puara, after a journey of sixteen leagues. At this place the friars occupied the same room in the building which the Indians had given to Espejo and those friars who accompanied him in his entrada, for on the walls of the room the friars with Oñate discovered the same pictures outlining the death of the frailes Rodriguez and Lopez, seventeen years before, and which the Indians had attempted to cover up with whitewash. Oñate was here told that the two Mexican Indians were at another pueblo, and having asked that they be brought to him, the Indians granted his request, and thereafter they were of invaluable aid to the commander as interpreters. From this point Oñate visited several pueblos in the vicinity, notably one called Tria.[315] Leaving Puara, they came to a pueblo which they called San Felipe,[316] and from this point, after a journey of four leagues to the pueblo of Gi-pu-y. At this last named Oñate remained for a considerable period, awaiting the coming of the main army and colonists. This occurred after the 4th day of July, as on this date Captain Juan de Salvidar was sent back to bring them up, this being accomplished some time in August.

Going from pueblo to pueblo, Oñate in each established the Spanish authority and introduced the religion of the Holy Faith. The tact and friendliness which had been exhibited by the several explorers who had come into the country since the expedition under Coronado, helped him very materially in dealing with the natives. He was also most ably assisted by the two Mexican Indians, acting as his interpreters.

A conference of the pueblo tribes was held at Santo Domingo on the 7th day of July, at which time they gave in their allegiance to the Spanish crown. A second conference was held on the 9th of September, at which time the religious missions of New Mexico were definitely located, and the presidents of the missions designated.[317]

---
[315] This may have been the pueblo of Cia.
[316] Bancroft thinks that this is the San Felipe of today, but I do not think so, as the present San Felipe was built some time in the seventeenth century.
[317] Palacio, tomo ii, *Mexico, Tráves de los Siglos*, p. 456, says: ''Los

314 LEADING FACTS OF NEW MEXICAN HISTORY

There were seven of the frailes thus commissioned to most dangerous and difficult charges, including the Apaches and other wandering tribes, as well as the Pueblo or sedentary Indians. It is remarkable how efficient was the work of these soldiers of the cross, when we take into consideration that the tribes themselves were almost always at war; the frailes knew nothing of their language, and it was indeed almost a superhuman task imposed upon these priests, in this manner and under such circumstances to convert these barbarians to the Christian religion. There was no power to protect them when they left the protecting wing of the army, and yet, trusting in the power of God, they departed to their separate fields of endeavor. They were received by the natives as instructors and prophets, and acted as intermediaries for things both spiritual and material.

A CONFERENCE IS HELD AT SANTO DOMINGO WITH THE PUEBLOS

Having been at the pueblo of Bové for two days, on the 9th day of July the army left this pueblo and proceeded to San Juan, the wagons going by the way of the pueblo of San Marcos,[318] in

caciques volvieron á jurar y prometer, bajo graves peñas, que cuidarian y respectarian á los religiosos, y estos salieron del campamento á predicar cada uno en las tribus que le habian tocado, y fueron asi: á fray Francisco de San Miguel, los *pecos* y los que tenian ganado de cibolo hasta la sierra nevada; á fray Francisco de Zamora los *cicuris* y los *apaches*, al norte y poniente de la sierra nevada, y los *taos*; á fray Juan de Rosas los *cheros* y los pueblos *castixes*; á fray Alonzo de Lugo los *emenes*, los *apades* y *cocoyes*; á fray Andrés Corchado, los *trias*, los *acomas*, los *truñi* y los *mohou*; á fray Juan Claros los *tiguas* o *ohiguas*, y á fray Cristobal de Salazar los *tepuas*. Ademas de estas, que eran las principales tribus que cada uno de esos religiosos tenia por encargo convertir, agregabanseles muchos pueblos y tribus mas reducidas, de manera que comprendia si jurisdiccion espiritual un territorio tan extenso, que numero decuplo de misioneros no hubiera sido suficiente para aquella empresa.'

[318] Bandelier, A. F., *Final Report*, part ii, p. 93: "Near San Marcos lies the celebrated locality of Callaite, called popularly the 'turquoise mines.' The turquoises are imbedded in a white porphyritic rock, and a high authority on gems, Mr. George F. Kunz, has informed me that the New Mexican turquoise bears greater resemblance to the Egyptian than to the Persian specimens of that mineral. Beautiful stones have been found occasionally; also very large masses of an inferior quality. The Tanos of Santo Domingo regard themselves as the owners of the site and visit it frequently to procure the stones that are so much esteemed by them. As to the popular belief in ancient mining of turquoises, it is, like many others of the kind, a myth. The Tanos obtained the mineral by knocking it out of the rock with stone mauls, axes and hammers, many of which have been found in the locality. They also dug and burrowed, but their excavations were made at random, and went but little beneath the

southern Santa Fé county, and almost in sight of the present city of Santa Fé. The inhabitants of San Juan received the Spaniards with great courtesy, and thereafter the pueblo was known as that of San Juan de los Caballeros.

Across the Rio Grande from San Juan, Oñate established his capital and gave it the name of San Gabriel. This was upon the present site of Chamita, and there is a tradition among the people living in the vicinity that the place was once called San Gabriel del Yunque. This location is in a most fertile valley, and the lands enjoy exceptional facilities for irrigation. Today some old walls show that unhewn stones and rubble laid in adobe mortar entered largely into the composition of the structures. Cultivated fields now extend all around the ruin of the old Indian village which Oñate found there and adjoining which he erected the chapel of San Gabriel in 1598. There is some question as to the name given by Oñate to this first settlement made by him; some historians say that he called it San Francisco, and others San Gabriel.[319] Villagrá describes the pueblo which was at this point.[320]

---

surface. Still less did the Spaniards compel the Indians to 'mine' the turquoise for them. Very little attention was paid by the whites to the green and blue stones, the latter of which are comparatively rare; since they regarded the New Mexican Callaite as of a base quality, and therefore as of no commercial value. Nevertheless the turquoises of the Cerrillos were quite a resource for the Tanos, so far as aboriginal commerce went.

"Castañeda says nothing of the turquoise of the Cerrillos; neither does Espejo, who visited the Tanos. While Oñate personally did not pass by San Marcos, still no mention is made by him of the turquoise.

"The first writer of the turquoise mines is Fr. Zarate-Salmeron, who in his *Relaciones*, says: 'Y minas de Chalchihuites que los Indios benefician dese ó su gentilidad, que para ellos son Diamantes y piedras preciosas. De todo esto se rien los Españoles que alla estan.'

"Vetancurt mentions isinglass but nothing of the turquoises; he says: 'Y una de talco trasparente á modo de yeso, que lo sacan como tablas, y adornan las ventanas con ellas como si fueran de cristal.'— *Cronica*, p. 286.

"Benavides, in his *Memorial*, however, mentions the turquoise; at page 44 he says 'Toda esta gente . . . con gargantillas y oregeras de turquesas, que tienen minas dellas, y las labran, aunque imperfectamente.'

[319] In *Obediencia y Vasalaje de San Juan Baptista*, Doc. de Indias, vol. xvi, p. 116, we find: "Y este pueblo de Sant Joan Baptista y el de San Gabriel el de Troomaxiaquino . . . y mas, la Ciudad de Sant Francisco de los Españoles, que al presente se edifican." This might indicate, says Mr. Bandelier, "that it was Oñate's intention to call the new settlement San Francisco. But

---

[320] Villagrá, *Historia de la Nueva Mexico*, Canto xxvii, fol. 228:
"El Pueblo, no constaua ni tenia,
Mas que vna sola plaça bien quadrada,
Con quatro entradas solas cuios puestos,

Mr. Bancroft is in great error as to the exact location of the capital first established by Oñate, when he says that it was at San Juan de los Caballeros. He also is mistaken as to the place where the chapel of San Gabriel was located. He would have both on the left bank of the Rio Grande, while as a matter of fact they were on the right bank, and north of the confluence of the Chama with the Rio Grande. It was the village of Yuque-Yunque,[321] and was com-

it is abundantly proved that its patron saint was San Gabriel from the very beginning.'' Zalvidar, *Memorial, ibid*, p. 198: ''Parece que con este aparato entro hasta el asiento y Villa de San Gabriel.'' Zalvidar was an eye-witness. Torquemada, *Monarquia*, vol. i, p. 672: ''Despachados Don Juan de Oñate, y los suios, para la jornada del Nuevo Mexico, siguieron su camino, en demanda de aquellas tierras, y en llegando á aquells partes, tomaron posesion, por el Rei, en ellas, y el pueblo donde Don Juan de Oñate, Gobernador, y Capitan-General de esta entrada hico asiento y puso su Real, se llama San Gabriel, el qual sitio esta en treinta y siete grados de altura al Norte, y esta situado entre dos rios, y con las aguas del menor de los dos, se riegan los trigos, cevada, y maiz. El otro rio es grande, que llaman del Norte, que es de mucho, y mui buen pescado.'' Torquemada wrote not later than 1609 (*carta Nuncupatoria, ibid*), and he was a contemporary of the events. Fr. Geronimo Zarate-Salmeron, *Relaciones de Todas las Cosas*, Ms., par. 34: ''Planto su real entre este rio y el de Zama.'' Par. 44: ''Año de 1604, á 7 dias del mes de Octubre, salio D. J. de Oñate de la villa de Sn Gabriel a descubrir la mar del Sur.''

Also:
Despues de auerlos bien fortalecido,
Con tiros de campana, y con mosquetes.''
''Al arma dando todos con gran priessa,
Requieieron los puestos, y notaron,
Que estaban ya los altos de las casas.''
Also: ''Los techos y terrados lebantados.''

[321] Bandelier, A. F., *Final Report*, p. 60: ''Indian folk lore has much to say about Yuque-Yunque (Yuge-uingge). The Tehuas relate that when their ancestors journeyed southward from Cibobe, and the division into summer and winter people occurred . . . the summer people, under the guidance of the Pay-oj-ke or Po-a-tuyo, settled at Yuge-uingge; but the winter people, after wandering over the eastern plains for a long while, at last went in search of their brethren, and established themselves near San Juan, in sight of the other's village at Chamita. Finally it was agreed upon that a bridge should be built across the Rio Grande, and the official wizards went to work and constructed it by laying a long feather of a parrot over the stream from one side, and a long feather of a magpie from the other. As soon as the plumes met over the middle of the stream, people began to cross on this remarkable bridge; but bad sorcerers caused the delicate structure to turn over, and many people fell into the river, where they instantly became changed into fishes. For this reason the Navajós, Apaches, and some of the Pueblos, refuse to eat fish to this day.

''The story goes on to tell that both factions united and lived together at Oj-ke on the west bank. It seems, however, that Yuge-uingge was not abandoned, since Poseueve in that pueblo met with an affront that caused him to forsake this earth. . . The village was definitely forsaken in 1598, for the benefit of the Spaniards, who established themselves in the houses temporarily, until they could build their own abodes. This occurred with consent of the Indians, who voluntarily relinquished the place to join their brethren at San Juan.''

pletely forsaken by the Indians when Oñate came there, the inhabitants joining their brethren across the river at San Juan, and it was partly on this account that the title of "de los Caballeros" was bestowed upon the Tehuas of the latter village.[322]

The site of Chamita [323] does not seem to have been much occupied during the seventeenth century, and it was about the year 1605 that Oñate changed the location of his capital to Santa Fé. Although the Utes and the Comanches in the eighteenth century were constantly harassing the settlers of San Pedro de Chama, as the locality was called after the re-conquest by De Vargas, the number of Spanish inhabitants increased very considerably. The Indians of San Juan today hold a portion of the cultivated fields about Chamita, and a few of them live on the west side of the Rio Grande, at a place called El Pueblito.

The commander was highly pleased with the locality in which he made his first settlement. The fertility of the soil, and the healthful climate were very attractive, and reminded the colonists of the

[322] Villagrá, *Historia de Nueva Mexico*, fol. 141:
"Aqui los Indios mui gustosos,
Con nosotros sus casas dividieron.
Y luego que alojados y de asiento,
Haziendo vezindad nos asentamos."
Also: "Hazia un gracioso Pueblo bien trazado
A quien San Juan por nombre le pusieron,
Y de los caualleros por memoria,
De aquellos que primero lebantaron,
Por estas nuevas tierras y regiones,
El sangriento estandarte donde Cristo,
Por la salud de todos fue arbolado."
This disposes of the fable that the title of "Caballeros" was given to the San Juan Indians for their loyalty to Spain during the insurrection of 1680. On the contrary, the Indians of San Juan were among the most bitter and cruel of the rebels; and their participation in the risings of 1694 and 1696 is well known.

[323] The name Chamita dates from the eighteenth century, and was given in order to distinguish it from the settlements higher up on the Chama river. Morfi, *Descripcion Geografica*, fol. 99, says that seventeen families lived there in 1744. A list nearly complete of the murders committed by the roaming Indians in the Chamita district is contained in the *Libro de entierros de Santa Clara*, Ms. In 1748 the people of Chamita applied for permission to abandon their homes owing to these hostilities. *Peticion y auto sobre abandonar los Puestos de Abiquiu, Ojo Caliente y Pueblo Quemado*, 148, Ms. This was refused.— Thomas Velez Cachupin, *Auto prohibiendo el despueble de Chama como pretendian sus moradores por ostilidades de los Yutas*, 1749, Ms. In 1781 the district was visited by a terrible epidemic, which lasted about two months, and carried off a frightful number of victims.— *Libro de Difuntos de Santa Clara*, 1781, Ms.

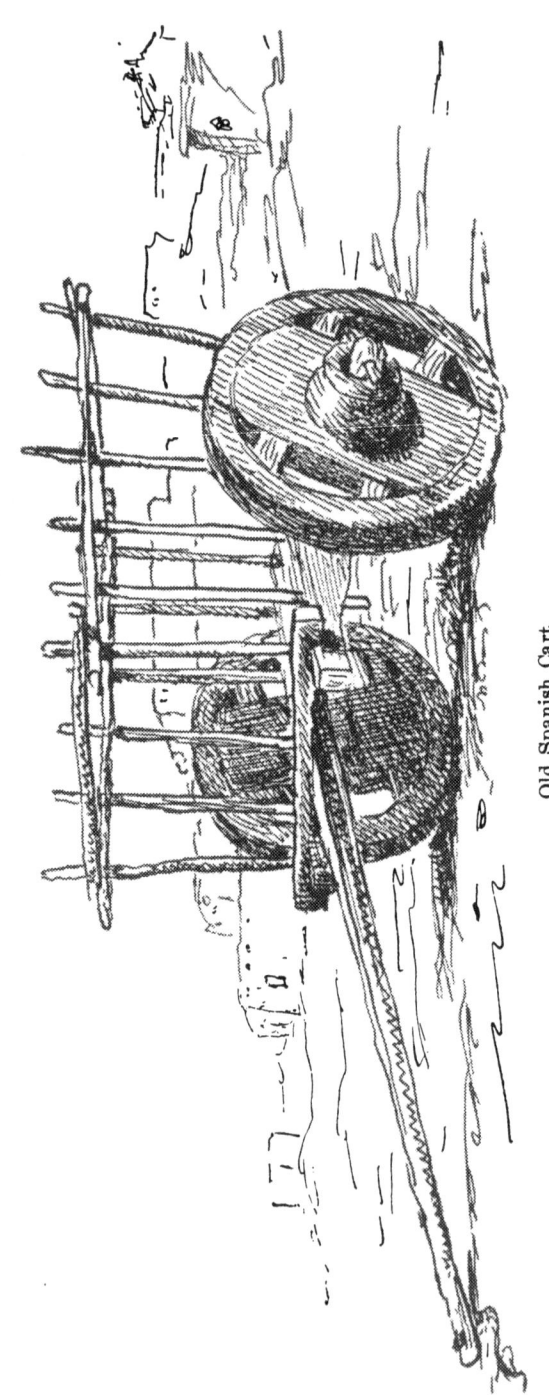
Old Spanish Cart

THE CONQUEST OF NEW MEXICO 319

valleys of their native country. Some, however, became discouraged, owing to the great hardships incident to life in this far-off country, and a few returned to New Spain. Immigration, however, increased gradually and settlements were made to the north, almost to the present boundary line of the state of Colorado.

The representatives of the church were indefatigable in their labors but were poorly rewarded. The harvest of souls did not meet with the expectations of the frailes; they made but few converts, and owing to the fact that the missions were so far distant from each other, the trials, both physical and spiritual, of these missionaries, were many; they also suffered in some localities from the improvidence of the natives, upon whom they had to rely for subsistence. The Indians proved but poor students of the new religion, and it was a very difficult matter to induce them to abandon the pagan rites conducted in their kivas.

Oñate, however, maintained a stout heart and was very confident of the ultimate success of his enterprise. He was unwearied in his efforts to explore the country and bring into obedience and submission the several tribes of the adjacent and outlying districts. He made journeys to Picuriés, a distance of six leagues, and thence to Taos, or San Miguel, an equal distance to the north. Taos was also called Tayberon. In the same month, he returned and visited San Ildefonso,[324] and thence a distance of five leagues to the pueblos of San Marcos and San Cristobal.

OÑATE CONTINUES HIS EXPLORATIONS

On the 24th and 26th days of July, Oñate journeyed to the pueblo of Pecos, going by way of Galisteo, and returning to San Cristobal[325] and San Marcos on the last named day; the following day

---

[324] Bandelier, A. F., *Final Report*, part ii, p. 82: "The pueblo of San Ildefonso or Po-juo-ge, offers nothing of archæological interest. After the uprising of 1696, when the church was ruined by fire, and two priests, Fr. Francisco Corbera and Fr. Antonio Moreno, were cruelly murdered and cremated, the village was moved a short distance north, and the present church at the pueblo is located almost in front of the site of the older one, to the north of it."

[325] In going from San Ildefonso to San Marcos, physical conditions and water supply compelled him to travel in a direction which would have made him pass by the present location of the city of Santa Fé. Leaving San Ildefonso, the natural route would have been up the river, now known as the Pojoaque; thence up the river which comes down past the present pueblo of Tesuque, and thence over a "divide" a distance of about two leagues, and he would reach the Rio Santa Fé, down which he would have proceeded for a few miles on the way to San Marcos. This is the route which any Indian would have taken,

he went south to the pueblo of Santo Domingo, where he met the main army under the command of Salvidar, whom he had sent south for the purpose of bringing them to San Gabriel.

In the first week of August Oñate explored the country in the neighborhood of the great pueblo of Cia, which he calls Tria; also the Jemez, and in his explorations he discovered the famous sulphur springs of that locality. Returning from the mountain country of the Jemez, he came to San Gabriel by way of Santo Domingo, San Ildefonso, and San Juan, arriving at his seat of operations on the 10th.

On the 11th of August Oñate began the work of construction of the irrigation and supply ditches for the settlement of San Gabriel, and in this work he employed over one thousand five hundred of th natives. While this work was in progress, on the 18th, the last of the colonists and wagons arrived from the south, coming by way of the pueblo of San Marcos.[326] It was at this time that some of the soldiers and colonists became mutinous, apparently led by Captain Aguilar. Over forty-five men were concerned in the plot. The

and as he was led by Indian guides, living in the locality, it is but fair to presume that he passed by the present site of the capital of New Mexico and that there were no inhabited pueblos at the place at that time.

[326] The Queres name of this pueblo was Ya-tze, but the Tanos called it Kua-kaa, the same name as the one on the Arroyo Hondo, near Santa Fé. In 1680, at the time of the Pueblo revolt, it had six hundred inhabitants, according to Vetancurt, *Cronica*, p. 324: ''Tenia sesicientos cristianos, de nacion Queres.'' Escalante, however (*Carta*, par. 3), writes as follows: ''Dia 15 sitiaron á esta los Tanos de San Marcos, San Cristobal y Galisteo, los Queres de la Cienega, y los Pecos por la parte del sur.''

Mr. Bandelier says that ''it may be that there were both Queres and Tanos in this pueblo, but considers the village to have been Tanos, just as to-day Santo Domingo is counted among the Queres, although there are many Tanos among them, and Isleta among the Tiguas, although a good portion are Queres from Laguna.''

The name San Marcos was given to it in 1591 by Gaspar Castaño de Sosa. It was abandoned by its inhabitants during the siege of Santa Fé, in August, 1680.— *Diario de la Retirada de Otermin*, fol. 28. In 1692, when Diego de Vargas passed through it, it was in ruins, with only a few of the walls still standing and a small portion of the church edifice. In *Autos de Guerra de la Segunda Entrada*, fol. 138, we find: ''Y halle despoblado y se conservan algunos aposentos y paredes de los quarteles y viuyendas de el y asi mismo se hallan las paredes y cañon de la Yglesia buenas con las de el conuto.''

If there had been any inhabited pueblos or clusters of houses even in the immediate vicinity of the present site of Santa Fé, some one of the explorers would have mentioned the fact; we are entitled to this conclusion because they mention every other settlement within a radius of twenty-five miles of the place.

Indian Chief — Pueblo of San Juan

conspiracy was revealed to the commander, and owing to the tears and supplications of a majority of the colonists he granted a general pardon. Afterwards four men ran away with a band of horses, and Villagrá and Marquez went in pursuit; they overtook them, and hung two of the men and recovered the animals. Villagrá says that he went as far as Santa Barbara, and in this statement he is confirmed by the captain-general who says that they wrote to the viceroy from that place. It was not until the following November that Villagrá returned to San Gabriel.

In two weeks' time a fine chapel was constructed, which was formally dedicated on the 8th of September with great ceremonies, and concluding with a sham battle between the Christians and Moors. Villagrá says that during this particular time they were visited by many Indians from neighboring provinces, who came for the purpose of securing information as to the military strength of the Spaniards. On the 9th of September there was an assembling of all the native chieftains, and on this occasion Fr. Martinez apportioned [327] the pueblos into districts and over each appointed one

---

[327] See *ante*, p. 313, note 317 from Palacio, *Mexico, Tráves de los Siglos*. Mr. Bancroft, in writing of the names of the several tribes and their identity, says: "In the records of Oñate's conquest, and especially in the *Obediencia y Vassalaje* and distribution of the friars, the names are very numerous, and doubtless in many instances very inaccurate, as written or printed; yet I have deemed it advisable to preserve them, and for the convenience of reader and student I append them in compact form, adding all the names that appear in earlier narratives. . . Fortunately, the identity of groups or leading pueblos presents few difficulties, and in nearly every group a few names have survived to modern times. The towns in the sixteenth century occupied the same general range of territory as in the nineteenth, but most of them were destroyed in the seventeenth, and many of those remaining were moved from their original sites."

This list, compiled by Mr. Bancroft, is as nearly correct as is possible to be made, and the information therein is of so great importance that I have deemed it advisable to give it in full. Almost all of Bancroft's information was taken from the *Obediencias* of the *N. Mexico Traslado*. That which appears in parenthesis was taken from the *Ytinerario*, the *Historia* of Captain Villagrá, and other documents relating to the Oñate entrada. The notes of earlier entradas and comments are enclosed in brackets.

Mr. Bancroft says :

"Under care of Fr. Francisco de S. Miguel, prov. of the Pecos (Santiago) with the 7 pueblos of the eastern Cienega, and the Vaquero, or wild tribes, of that region to the Sierra Nevada, and the pueblos of the 'gran salina' behind the pueblo of Puaray; and besides the pueblos of Quanquiz, Hohota, Xonalus Xatol, Xaimela, Aggey, Cuza, Cicentetpi, Acoli, Abbo (Abó), Apena, Axauti, Amaxa, Couna, Dhiu, Alle, Atuyama, and Chein; and the three great pueblos of the Jumanas, or 'rayados' called in their language Tripuy, Genobey, Quelotetrey, and Pataotrey. In the *Obediencia* of Oct. 12th, we have also in the

of the friars who had come with the expedition. The poet historian relates that while the Indians readily submitted to the authority of the Spaniards, yet they informed Fr. Martinez that so far as the

S. E. region the prov. of Chealo with the pueblos of Acolocu, Cuzaya (Cuza above), Junetre, and Paaco; and in the *Obediencia* of Oct. 17th, those of Cueloce, Xenopue, Petasce, and Abó. (Coronado calls Pecos Cicuyé, Ciciuio, Cicuique, Ticuique, Tienique, or Acuique, not naming others in the region. Rodriguez mentions prov., or valleys, of Came with 6 pueblos, and Asay, or Osay, with 5, somewhere in the S. E. Espejo names the province of Tamos-, Tanos—one of its pueblos being called Cicuique, or Pecos; and also the prov. of Maguas, or Magrias, of 11 pueblos N. E. of Tiguas. Sayaque appears on Jeffrey's atlas). Galisteo is named in the *Ytin*. In all the eastern region of about 40 pueblos alluded to we have in modern times only the ruins Pecos, Galisteo, Abó, Gran Quivira (Tabira) and various scattered heaps of nameless ruins.

"Fr. Juan Claros, prov. of the Chiguas, or Tiguas, and pueblos of Napeya and Tuchiamas, and that of Pura with the 4 consecutive down the river, that of Poxen, Puaray (S. Antonio), Trimati, Guayotri, Acacafui, Henicohio, Vareato 'with all its subjects to Puaray up and down the Rio del Norte' (?); also the prov. of Xalay, the prov. of Mohoqui (?), and the province of the Atripuy down the river with its pueblos which are Preguey, Tuzahe, Aponitre, Vumahein, Quiapo, Trelaqueque, Cunquelipinoy, Calciati, Aquicato, Encaguiagualcaca, Quialpo, Trelagu, Pesquis, Ayqui, Yancomo, Teyaxa, Qualacu, (2nd pueblo coming from S. acc. to *Ytin*) Texa, Amo, on 'this side' (west) of the river; and on the other, Pencoana, Quiomaqui, Peixole, Zumaque, Teeytraan, Preguey (see above, repeated), Canocan, Peytre, Qui-Ubaco, Tohol, Cantensapue, Tercao, Polloca, Treyey, Queelquelu, Atepira, Trula, Treypual, Tecahanqualahamo, Pilopue, Penjeacu, Teypama (Teipana, or Socorro, 31. above Qualacu), and Trenaquel 'de la mesilla' which is the 1st pueblo coming from Mexico. (Which of these were the ones called Nueva Sevilla and S. Juan Baptista in the *Ytin*. does not appear). In the *Obed*. of July 7th the Chigua pueblos named are Paniete, Piaqui, Axoytre, Piamato, Quioyaco and Camitre, or at least these were under the captain of the Chiguas. (Niza's Totonteac may possibly have been the Tigua prov. Coronado wintered in Tiguex, Tihuex, or Tigueq, a prov. of 12 or 15 pueblos; and visited Tutahaco, a prov. of 8 pueblos down the river in the Isleta region; also 4 towns in the Socorro region not named, which were also mentioned without being named by Rodriguez and Espejo. R's visit 1st shows the name Puaray or Puara; and E. names the pueblo of Puara, Puala, or Poalas, one of 16 in the province of Tiguas. It is not probable that a single one of these 60 pueblos of the southern section of the Rio Grande valley is still standing, though there are a few of later origin).

"Fr. Juan de Rosas, prov. of the Cheres, or Cherechos (Hores) (Queres). The name Querechos is applied by Coronado and Espejo to wild tribes in the East and West with the pueblos of the Castixes, or S. Felipe and Comitre, Sto Domingo or Guipui, Alipoti, Chochiti or Cochiti; that of the Cienega de Carabajal; S. Marcos, S. Cristobal, Sta Ana, Ojana, Quipana, del Puerto, and Pueblo Quemado. In the *Obed*. of July 7th are also named Tamy, Acogiya, Cachichi, Yates and Tipoti. (Villagrá gives the Queres prov. to P. Zamora, omitting Rosas). (Coronado names Quirix, or Quivix, a prov. of 7 pueblos. Espejo calls it Quires with 5 pueblos. Castano calls it Quereses, naming one of the towns Sto Domingo, perhaps the same so called by Oñate, and also S. Marcos, S. Lucas, and S. Cristobal. Pueblos still standing in this region, the Rio Grande Valley, in about latitude 35° 30', retain the names of Sta Ana, S.

Holy Catholic faith was concerned they would adopt it, provided, after they had received proper instruction, they found it desirable. An exploring party was now organized under the command of

Felipe, Sto Domingo, and Cochití, some of them, perhaps, identical with those of the sixteenth century).

"Fr. Cristoval de Salazar, prov. of the Tepuas (Teguas, acc. to Villagrá) (Tehuas), with the pueblos of Triapi, Triaque, S. Ildefonso or Bove, Sta Clara, San Juan (de los Caballeros) or Caypa, S. Gabriel, Troomaxiaquino, Xiomato, Axol Camitria, Qiotraco, and the city of S. Francisco 'que se edifican.' (Coronado calls the prov. Yuque-Yunque with 6 towns; and his Ximera or Ximena, with Silos and other abandoned villages may have been in this region. Espejo calls the province or the Eastern part of it Ubates or Hubates. Of the 10 or 11 Tehua pueblos, the names of S. Juan, Sta Clara and S. Ildefonso still remain in this district, and of the same prov. are the towns of Nambe, Jojoaque and Tezuque).

"Fr. Francisco de Zamora, prov. of the Picuriés, with all the Apaches N. and West of the Sierra Nevada; also prov. of the Taos with pueblos in that region and upper valley of the Rio Grande. Taos was also called Tayberon and S. Miguel; and Picuriés was San. Buenaventura. (Coronado called Taos Braba, Uraba, or Uraba; and his Acha prov. in this region was possibly Picuríes).

"Fr. Alonzo de Lugo, prov. of the Emmes (Emes) (Jemes), and the pueblos of Yjar, Guayoguia, Mecastria, Quiusta, Ceca, Potre, Trea (Cia), Guatitruti, Catroo; and the Apades (Apaches) and Cocoyes of the sierra and region. In the *Obed.* of July 7th, the Emmes pueblos are called Yxcaguayo, Quiamera, Fia, Quinsta, Leeca, Poze, Fiapuze, Friyti, and Caatri. (If, as seems likely, these are different spellings of the same 9 pueblos, our confidence in the accuracy of these doc. is considerably shaken. Coronado mentions the prov. of Hemes with 7 towns, and that of Aguas Calientes with 3. Espejo calls the prov. that of the Emexes, Emeges, or Ameges. The pueblo of Jemes still stands, but not on its original site).

"Fr. Andres Corchado, prov. of Trias, or Trios, with pueblos of Tamaya, Yacco, Toajgua, and Pelchin. In the *Obed.* of July 7th are named Comitre and Ayquiyu with Triati and Pequen, perhaps in this region. Corchado's district lay westward from the 'gran pueblo' of Tria or S. Pedro y S. Pablo (Zia, Villagrá) (Cia, called Chia by Coronado. Perhaps the Tlascala of Rodriguez. Sia, or Siay, of Espejo, the capital of the prov. of Punames, Pumames or Cunames of 5 pueblos). Also Acoma, *Obed.* of Oct. 27th. (Possibly Niza's prov. of Acus or Marata. Coronado's Acuco, or Coco. Espejo's Acoma. If this pueblo could be located in the early times farther N. than its present site, say on the Puerco about Lat. 35 30, it would agree better with the records; but I find no evidence of a change, and the peculiarities of the peñol site render a change improbable, though not impossible). Also Zuñi, or Truni — *Obed.* of Nov. 9th — prov. of 6 pueblos, Aguicobi, or Aguscobi, Canabi, Coaqueria, Halonago, Macaqui, and Aguinsa. *Obed.* of Nov. 9th. (Niza's prov. of Cibola with 7 pueblos, one of them Ahacus. Coronado's Cibola, with 2 of the 7 towns named Granada and Muzaque, perhaps the Macaqui above. Espejo's Zuñi, Zuny, Ame, or Ami, one of the towns being Aquico). Also the prov. of Mohoce or Mohoqui — *Obed.* of Nov. 15th — with its pueblos of Mohoqui, Naybe, Xumupami, Cuanrabi, and Esperiez; the captains of which, perhaps confused with the pueblo names, were Pananma, Hoynigua, Xuynuxa, Patigua, and Aguatuyba. *Obed.* of Nov. 15th. (The modern names of the 7 Moqui towns — *Native Races*, i 528 — are Oraibe, Shumuthpa, Mushaiina, Ahlela, Gualpi, Siwinna, and Tegua; or acc. to Garces in the 18th century,

Captain Vicente Salvidar for the purpose of visiting the buffalo plains. There were fifty men in this expedition. Salvidar left San Gabriel on the 10th of September and was absent until the 8th of November, with the usual experiences accompanying the chasing of buffalo, and ascertaining nothing of consequence other than some traces of the expedition made by Bonilla and Humana. During the month following the departure of Salvidar, the captain-general made a tour of the salt lakes east of the Pecos, and also visited the Jumanos and Abó, all of whom rendered submission to his authority, whereupon he returned to the valley of the Rio Grande, arriving about the 20th of the month.

About a month after his return from the salinas country, Oñate started from the pueblo of Puara, on a trip to the west, being accompanied by Fr. Martinez. On the 27th of October he reached Acoma, where he received the submission of the chiefs and inhabitants of that noted pueblo. It was at this fortress that Oñate had a very narrow escape. A chief, according to Captain Villagrá, named Zutucapan, who had not been invited to the conference of September 9th, was violently opposed to his people giving in their submission to the Spaniards, and harangued the people from the azoteas of the pueblo. This chief, however, was overruled by others of more influence among the tribe, but there were a few who were active in support of the hostile cacique. These, numbering about a dozen, conceived the plan of having Oñate visit one of the pueblo's large kivas, where he was to be put to death. Oñate, a very cautious man, did not fall into the trap, for, although he was urgently invited to enter one of their sanctuaries, he declined to do so, and thus escaped being killed.

Acoma having given in its formal submission, the captain-general now proceeded to Zuñi, which place came under the Spanish yoke, according to Villagrá, from the 9th to the 15th of November. Here

Sesepaulaba, Masagneve, Janogualpa, Muqui, Concabe, and Muca or Oraibe. Coronado's Tusayan, Tucayan, Tuzan, Tusan, or Tucano with 7 towns. Espejo's Mohoce, or Mohace, with 5 towns, one of them Aguato, or Zaguato; other pueblos of Deziaguabos, Gaspe, Comupavi, Majanani, and Ollalla being mentioned in connection with this exped.)

"Other pueblos named in the *Obed.* of July 7th with no indication of locality, and not named in the distribution of friars, are Aychini, Baguacat, Xutis, Yucaopi, Acacagua, Ytrzica and Atica."

Oñate not only found the crosses which had been erected by Francisco Vasquez Coronado more than fifty years before but also met the Mexican Indians left by Coronado at that village. Of the explorations made by Oñate west of Zuñi we know very little; everywhere he was kindly received by the natives. When he was visiting the pueblos of Moqui, he sent out an expedition under Captains Farfan and Quesada in search of mines, which they located about thirty leagues to the west. Oñate had intended going to the ocean on this expedition, but soon after leaving he sent word to Juan Salvidar to turn over the command at San Gabriel to his brother Vicente, whenever the latter should return from his trip to the buffalo plains, and then to join his commander, bringing with him thirty men.

OÑATE MARCHES TO ZUÑI

On the 8th of November, Vicente Salvidar returned from the buffalo plains, and ten days later, Don Juan Salvidar started out to join Oñate, as he had been commanded. After Oñate left the pueblo of Acoma, the cacique, Zutucapan, still remained hostile and did everything in his power to persuade the inhabitants to make war upon the Spaniards when they should reappear. By his eloquence he succeeded in inducing the natives to share his views, and when Salvidar and his companions reached Acoma on their way to join Oñate, the Indians, as usual, came out to meet him, offering needed supplies and making every demonstration of friendship. No treachery was suspected by the Spaniards, and small parties were sent into different parts of the pueblo for the purpose of bringing out the stores which the Indians had given them. A loud shout was the first warning that Salvidar received of his peril; he wished to order a retreat, but another officer, whose name is not mentioned by Villagrá, strongly opposed this plan until it was too late and retreat was impossible. A tremendous conflict, lasting three hours, ensued. According to Villagrá, the caciques prominent in the battle were Zutucapan, Pilco, Amulco, Cotumbo, and Tempol; finally Salvidar fell, fighting in single combat with the chieftain Zutucapan. The cry of victory arose from the natives. Five Spaniards, driven to the edge of the

BATTLE OF ACOMA AND DEATH OF JUAN SALVIDAR

cliff, leaped over, four of them escaping with small bruises. Three others had escaped from the rocky height, and all joined Alférez Casas, who had been left in charge of the horses.

A council of the survivors was held, and Captain Tabora was sent to overtake the captain-general; two or three went to warn the friars in the outlying districts, and the remainder went back to San Gabriel.

In this battle, which took place on the 4th day of December, eleven lost their lives. The list as given in the account, which has been preserved, reveals the names of Captains Diego Nuñez and Felipe de Escalante, Alférez Pereyra, Araujo, Juan Camacho, Martin Ramirez, Juan de Segura, Pedro Robledo, Martin de Riveros, Sebastian Rodriguez, two servants, a mulatto, and an Indian, and the leader, Captain Juan de Salvidar. The wounded were Leon Zapata, Juan de Olague, Cavanillas, and the alguacil real, Las Casas, who was struck twice with stones.

When the messengers reached San Gabriel, bringing the news of the disaster, all was commotion. Funeral ceremonies were held and these were hardly concluded when Captain Tabora returned with the news that he had been unable to find Oñate. Alférez Casas volunteered for this service, and after many difficulties succeeded in finding him. The captain-general returned to his quarters and spent the night in prayer before a rude cross, and the following morning endeavored to console his men. He then proceeded to San Gabriel, where on the 21st day of December his arrival was celebrated with a te deum in the chapel which had been constructed.

The friars were called into council as to the best course to pursue against the rebellious natives; they were asked respecting the elements of a just war against the inhabitants of Acoma and it was decided to send Don Vicente Salvidar, with a substantial force, to avenge the death of his brother and his unfortunate companions. It was determined to assault and burn the town and that all who resisted must be taken prisoner and enslaved. Oñate selected seventy of his bravest soldiers for this enterprise, commanded by the captains Zubia, Romero, Aguilar, Farfan, Villagrá, and Marquez, Alférez Juan Cortés, and Juan Velarde as secretary.

Leaving San Gabriel on the 12th of January, 1599, on the 21st the Spaniards appeared before Acoma, Captain Villagrá having gone to Cia for supplies.[328]

At the pueblo the Indians celebrated with great rejoicing the results which had come from following the advice of their cacique, Zutucapan. It was believed that this victory was the beginning of greater successes which would crown the native arms in their efforts to drive out the invader. Giocombo, another prominent chief, who had not agreed with the course advocated by Zutucapan, now called together a council of the principal men of his tribe as well as representatives from adjoining nations. At this council it was agreed that war could not be averted. All declared themselves ready for the struggle, and preparations were at once begun for the safety of the women and children. Zutucapan, however, emboldened still further by his success, proclaimed his ability to hold the Rock of Acoma against any army that the Spaniards could bring. When the Spaniards under Salvidar appeared upon the plain, crowds of men and women were seen upon the walls of the pueblo, dancing stark naked; with great outbursts of defiance they heaped insults of every kind upon their enemies below them.

The Spaniards sent word to the chieftains to come down and answer for the murder of their companions, but their only reply was a continuance of their insulting actions.

The Spaniards pitched their camp upon the plain and made preparations for the assault. It was known that there were two places at which an ascent of the rock could be made. Salvidar determined to assault one of the peñoles with his main force, while a small but chosen band should hold themselves in readiness to ascend the other. All night long the sounds of revelry and rejoicing could be heard coming from the tops of the houses of the pueblo. The Spaniards quietly awaited the approach of dawn. On the morning of the 22nd of January the Indians began the battle with a great flight of arrows. What seemed to be the entire Spanish force was now sent by Salvidar to assault one of the entrances, at which point was soon

---

[328] Immediately upon the departure of Salvidar for Acoma, the people of San Gabriel became alarmed lest that village be attacked by the natives of the vicinity. Consequently they made great preparations for the defense of the capital, all of which is most graphically and minutely described by Captain Villagrá, who also refers to the heroic offer of Doña Eufemia to lead the women of the settlement in battle against the common enemy.

concentrated the entire native strength in opposition to the ascent. Meanwhile, with twelve men, who had been concealed during the previous night, he mounted the other peñol and gained the summit without serious effort. This force was quickly reënforced and during the entire day the conflict waged, both at the pass, which existed between the two plateaux, and at the entrance to the one not yet gained. During all of two days and a portion of a third the battle raged, in which there were many personal conflicts, desperate charges, and many acts of bravery on the part of Christian and savage. During the last day of the battle the pueblo was set on fire and hundreds killed each other or threw themselves from the cliff in their desperation. Finally, on the 24th, the entire pueblo was in possession of the Spaniards, which they proceeded to destroy, at the same time giving no quarter to the natives, who were ruthlessly slaughtered by the hundreds. Estimating the population of the pueblo at two thousand, the Spaniards say that only six hundred escaped the sword. These, under the leadership of a chief named Chumpo, surrendered, and came down upon the plain to settle.

With the fall of Acoma the regular documentary record ceases. Villagrá, in his poem, promised the king to continue his narration but it seems that this was never done.[329]

Oñate's prompt punishment of this tribe fixed his right and authority over all the country. Terrified by the courage of the Spaniards in thus successfully assaulting and subduing the strongest defenses and the most warlike tribe of the country, the natives felt that opposition was useless.

On the second of March the governor wrote to the viceroy telling him all that had happened, what he had accomplished, the lands he had conquered, and sent him samples of the products

---

[329] The account by Villagrá and that contained in the *Ytinerario* differ as to the termination of the battle of Acoma. Captain Villagrá implies that it lasted three days, when Chumpo and the six hundred natives surrendered. The *Ytinerario* intimates that the fight lasted from the evening of the 22nd to that of the following day, when the Indians surrendered, but the Spaniards did not occupy the Rock until the 24th, when the survivors of the Indians made further resistance; whereupon ''hizose la matanza y castigo de los mas dellos, á fuego y sangre; y de todo punto se asoló y quemó el pueblo.''

Oñate says that Acoma had about three thousand Indians ''al qual en castigo de su maldad y traicion . . . y para escarmiento á los demas, lo asole y abrase todo.''

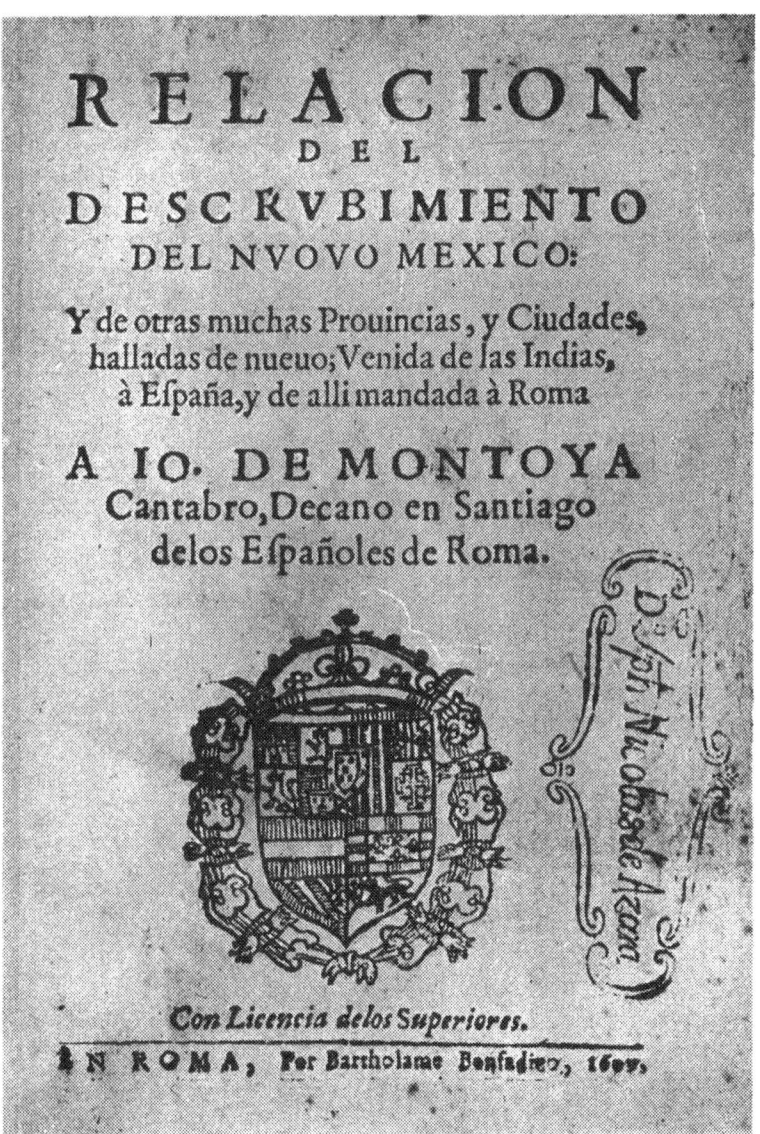

Fac-simile of Title Page of *Narrative of the Discovery of New Mexico*, by Fr. Montoya. Rome, 1602

From copy in John Gilmary Shea collection, Georgetown University, Washington, D. C.

THE CONQUEST OF NEW MEXICO   329

of the country. Oñate wanted to make further explorations to the west and advised that he be reënforced with five hundred men, which number was not too many to send to such a country, where it was possible for him to gain for the crown new worlds better and greater than those which Cortés had given him. Oñate sent this letter to the viceroy in charge of Captains Villagrá, Farfan, and Pinero, and also instructed them to make full explanations to the representative of the royal authority. At the same time, accompanied by an escort, Friars Martinez, Salazar, and Vergara went to New Spain for the purpose of securing more friars for the missions which had been and were to be established. On his journey Friar Salazar died. Fr. Martinez remained in Mexico, but Fr. Juan de Escalona came back as comisario along with Vergara and six or eight members of the Franciscan order. A force of seventy-one men, under Casas, also returned, being the force raised to complete the 200 which Oñate had promised to take with him. Later on the viceroy was ordered by the king to give Oñate all possible encouragement and support.

Everything now went well with the colonists; they seemed contented with the country as a home and the representatives of the church were satisfied with it as a field for their labors in the cause of Christianity.

The great majority of the colonists were favorable to a policy of extreme conciliation in dealing with the Indians. The captain-general, however, thought only of holding them in subjection, of reducing other pueblos, and making further explorations. The friars thought only of the salvation of souls, and regarded the army only as an aid and protection to them in their efforts for the faith. In the month of June, 1601, having become somewhat restless, for even though satisfied with his present achievements he was anxious for other and greater ones, accompanied by the friars, Velasco and Vergara, and guided by the Indian survivor of the force which had come into the country under Humana, he left San Gabriel, with a force of eighty men, and marched northeastward over the plains. His exact route is not known, but in all probability it was nearly the same as that followed

OÑATE MARCHES TO THE GREAT PLAINS

by Francisco Vasquez Coronado some sixty years before. At any rate he went a distance of more than two hundred leagues and reached, as he estimated, latitude 39° or 40°. While on this journey, Oñate fought a great battle with the Escanjaques, a thousand of whom were slain upon the very field where Humana had been killed. The battle was caused owing to Fr. Velasco's efforts to prevent the Escanjaques from destroying property belonging to the Quivira nation, the latter having fled from their towns upon the approach of Oñate's command.[330]

In the country where Oñate now found himself, large settlements were seen, and some of the exploring parties sent out by the captain-general claimed to have found utensils made of gold, which was said to be plentiful in an adjacent province. It is not certain that Oñate reached Quivira, but representatives of the people of that nation came to Oñate and wished to join him in his search for gold. But the captain-general thought it unwise to proceed further, owing to the smallness of his force, and retraced his steps to San Gabriel, which he reached in the early fall.

When Oñate arrived at San Gabriel he found the place almost deserted. Everybody almost, including colonists and friars, had returned to Nueva Vizcaya. Friar Escalona, who remained with Alférez Casas, awaiting the return of the governor, explained the situation in a letter to the comisario-general, which was carried south by the deserting colonists. In this letter Fr. Escalona said that the captain-general and his officers had sacked the pueblo villages; that he had not allowed any planting for the support of the garrison; that there had been a great drought, and that the natives were forced to live on wild seeds. A few settlers, fortunately, had planted some corn, thus saving the colony from actual starvation. These, he said, were the reasons why they had determined to retire to Nueva Vizcaya and await further orders as to their future conduct. The friars who left went under the orders of Fr. Escalona, the latter deeming it his duty, at the risk of his life, to remain.

---

[330] As to the facts connected with this expedition to Quivira, see Salmeron, *Relaciones*, 26-30; Niel, *Apunt.*, 91-4; Torquemada, *Monarquia Indiana*, i, 671-3; Posadas, *Noticias*, 216-217.

Nearly all of the authorities, including Salmeron, give the date as 1599, which is clearly erroneous.

Oñate was furious over this state of affairs and, with proof ready made and at hand, he began proceedings against those who had deserted, some of whom were condemned to death. He began the preparation of reports to the viceroy and his king to offset those of the friars, and despatched Vicente Salvidar to Mexico, with his letters and reports, and carrying also an order for the arrest of the deserters. Some time after this Fr. Escalona wrote to the provincial of his order that he and Fr. Velasco, a cousin of Oñate, proposed to leave the country; that their occupation as missionaries was useless, that Oñate's charges were false, and that no success for the colony could be hoped for until Oñate should be relieved of the government.

Oñate, however, through the efforts of Salvidar, and a vigorous correspondence with the heads of the Franciscan order, secured a return of the friars, and with them also came other settlers, in addition to those whom Salvidar forced to return, who acted with great cruelty, according to stories given out by the friars.[331]

The prosperity of the colony gradually returned, and the captain-general, having received reënforcements of troops, marched westward so far that he followed the Colorado river to its mouth. This was in 1604-5. He reached tide-water on the 23rd day of January, and on the 25th, with the friars who were with him, and nine men, went to the mouth of the great river. He found a fine harbor, which was called Puerto de la Conversion de San Pablo. Oñate now determined to return to San Gabriel, and although they were compelled to eat their horses, they arrived there safely on the 25th day of April, 1605.

Very little is definitely known of Oñate's acts in New Mexico after his return from the west in 1605. It is said that he went east six years later and discovered the Canibar lakes and a Rio Colorado,

---

[331] The letter of Fr. Escalona may be found in Torquemada's *Monarquia Indiana*, i, 673-4. It was written at San Gabriel. The frailes who left the country were San Miguel and Zamora of those who came with Oñate, and Lope Izquierdo and Gaston de Peralta, who came later. Velasco and Vergara were with Oñate on the expedition to Quivira; the others, Rosas, Lugo, Corchado, Claros, and San Buenaventura are of those who went to Santa Barbara and later came back.

Torquemada says that Fr. San Miguel wrote from Santa Barbara on Feb. 2, 1602, accusing Oñate of tyranny, falsehood, and general unfitness for his position.

or Palizade, probably Los Cadauchos, thus gaining a right to the eastern country.[332]

There seems to be little doubt that he was in New Mexico about that date, but it is generally conceded that he ceased to exercise the functions and authority of governor in the year 1608, and that his successor in office was Don Pedro de Peralta. According to the reports of the friars, at this time, more than eight thousand natives had been converted to the Christian religion, Fr. Alonzo Peinado having come as successor to Fr. Escobar, as comisario, and bringing with him eight or nine additional friars. Fr. Peinado was succeeded in 1614 by Fr. Estevan Perea. The names of the governors who succeeded Peralta are unknown, and for a dozen or more years after his rule the history of the country is almost a blank.[333]

The city of Santa Fé was founded some time between the years 1605 and 1616, in all probability in the first named year, but certainly not before the month of April.

FOUNDING OF THE CITY OF SANTA FÉ

Oñate returned to San Gabriel from his trip to the mouth of the Colorado river, as we have seen, on the 25th day of April, 1605. This date is given by Fr. Zarate-Salmeron and is confirmed by the inscription on the rock of the "Morro" or Inscription Rock, where it is stated that Oñate passed through there on the 16th day of April of the year "del descubrimiento de la Mar del Sur." Consequently there was no Spanish settlement at Santa Fé at that time.

All that has been said and published concerning the foundation of the present capital of New Mexico by Don Antonio de Espejo, in 1583, or by Don Francisco Vasquez Coronado, in 1540, or by an unknown founder, in 1550, is devoid of all historical basis. Espejo

---

[332] Barreiro, *Ojeada*, 7. Davis, in his *Conquest of New Mexico*, 276-7, makes the same statement, and he probably secured his information from Barreiro.

[333] Bancroft, H. H., *History of Arizona and New Mexico*, p. 158.

Calle, *Noticias*, p. 103, says that a new governor was appointed in 1608, with a salary of $2,000.

Vetancurt, *Cronica*, p. 96, says that in 1608 the king assumed the support of both the soldiers and the frailes, and that this probably put an end to the contract with Oñate.

Davis, W. W. H., *Spanish Conquest of New Mexico*, 420, found evidence in the Santa Fé Archives that Peralta was governor nine years after Oñate's coming, which would make it in 1607 or 1608. Davis made an error as to the date when Oñate came to New Mexico.

THE CONQUEST OF NEW MEXICO

founded no colonies whatever, and, as we have seen, was in no position, nor did he have the force, with which to found any settlement. Espejo may have been in the neighborhood of Santa Fé, but he nowhere mentions the fact even of any pueblo being located upon the present site of the capital; in fact, when he returned to Mexico, all the propositions which he made to the crown for the settlement of New Mexico had in view the establishment of a post at Acoma,[334] whereas the country of the Tanos, in which the site of Santa Fé was situated, is treated by him merely as one of the many ranges of sedentary tribes which might be brought under Spanish sway in course of time. The date of this proposal to the king was in 1584. It was never carried out, as Espejo died soon after. When Oñate came in 1598, he went directly to San Juan, established a camp there, and proceeded to found San Gabriel,[335] on the opposite bank of the Rio Grande. It is abundantly proven, by documentary evidence, that from San Gabriel the seat of government was moved to Santa Fé, and this appears to have been done in 1605.[336]

In the year 1617, as appears from a petition to the king by the cabildo of Santa Fé, in which aid was asked for the "nueva poblacion," although the friars had built eleven churches, converted 14,000 natives, and prepared as many more for conversion, there were only forty-eight soldiers and settlers in the province. In re-

---

[334] *Doc. de Indias*, vol. xv, pp. 156, 157.

[335] Oñate, *Discurso de las Jornadas*, pp. 256, 263.

[336] Posadas, Fr. Alonzo de, *Informe al Rey* (Ms): "La Villa de Santa Fé . . . descubriola el año de 1605 el Adelantado D. Juan de Oñate, llevando en su compania algunos soldados y religiosos de mi serafica religion, y por Presidente al padre predicador Fr. Francisco de Escobar."

Bandelier, A. F., *Final Report*, part i, pp. 124-125: "That site (Santa Fé) was deserted in the sixteenth century, the two pueblos of Tehua Indians that stood there once having been abandoned long previous to this date. Consequently an interval or vacant space of some thirty miles separated the northern Tehuas from their southern kinsmen, the Ta-ge-uing-ge or Tanos."

There is nowhere any mention of a pueblo at Santa Fé. There had been one formerly, as the ruins attest, but when the Spaniards came, it was in ruins. These ruins are now almost obliterated, and they are not those of the so-called "oldest house," opposite the chapel of San Miguel.

Bancroft, H. H., *History of Arizona and New Mexico*, pp. 158-159: "There are slight indications, if any, that Santa Fé was built on the site of a pueblo; and its identification with Cicuyé, Tiguex, or any other particular or prominent pueblo, has no foundation whatever. We have seen that Oñate's capital from 1598 was San Juan, and that preparations were made for building a city of San Francisco in that vicinity. Naturally, in the troubles that ensued, little if any progress was made, and after the controversies were past, it was deemed best to build the villa on a new site."

ply, the king, by royal cédula, dated May 20, 1620, ordered the viceroy to render all possible aid to the cabildo and the settlers.[337]

[337] Calle, *Noticias*, p. 103, says that the new governor, in 1608, was ordered to live at Santa Fé, and one or two authorities say that Oñate left Santa Fé for his western tour in 1604-05.

The city of Santa Fé — the City of the Holy Faith — lies in a very fertile sheltered valley about two miles from the mouth of the canyon of the Rio de Santa Fé, almost in the very heart of the wooded Sangre de Cristo range. Beyond all doubt it is the most picturesque, the most romantic town in the United States. Blessed by nature, hallowed by romance, the center of a region of the greatest archæological interest, it has many attractions for the sight-seer and the scientist.

The original and full name of New Mexico's capital is Villa Real de Santa Fé de San Francisco. It is the see of an archbishop of the Catholic church. It is the oldest capital in the United States. The thrilling and romantic incidents composing its history, the protracted and bloody struggles with hordes of savages, the capture and pillage by the Pueblos in 1680, the general massacre of the frailes of San Francisco, the flight of Governor Otermin and a few followers in the night for El Paso, the reserving of some of the handsomest Spanish maidens for the wives of Indian warriors, the destruction and desecration of the churches, the restoration of the worship of idols, the re-conquest by De Vargas, the terrible punishment visited upon the rebellious Pueblos, the change from Spanish to Mexican rule, the American occupation, the stirring scenes of the old Santa Fé Trail, the wild deeds of desperadoes, and the fabulous hazards at cards in those days prior to the advent of the railways, afford the material for an epic poem.

The old Palace, which was the official residence of the Spanish and Mexican governors for nearly three centuries, is a very quaint structure, and of great interest when the incidents connected with its history are known. The building is now occupied by the Historical Society of New Mexico, the Museum of New Mexico, and the Santa Fé School of American Archæology. There are relics of priceless value which may be seen in the collections of these several institutions, all installed in this old building.

The old San Miguel church, probably the oldest Christian church building in the United States, is situated in a part of the city, which is full of historic interest. The building is about seventy-four feet long by thirty in width, and is thirty-five feet high. The walls are built of adobe, and the roof, like those of all the old churches, was constructed of very strong rafters — *vigas* — supported by carved timbers at each end, the whole being covered originally with straight branches of poplar or willow, surmounted by a layer of adobe soil. The building was probably constructed shortly after 1605, probably during that year, as a large number of churches were built at that period under the direction of the friars. In the revolution of 1680 it was partially destroyed, though the walls remained standing. After the conquest by De Vargas it was repaired and completed in 1710. There is an inscription, plainly visible, on the great square *vigas* near the entrance which reads: "El Señor Marques de la Penuela hizo esta fabrica. El Alféres Real Don Agustin Flores Vergara su criado. Año de 1710."

There are two very fine paintings in this church building, one of the Archangel St. Michael and the Dragon of the Anunciation.

The oldest house in the city, which is undoubtedly of Pueblo Indian construction, and is supposed to antedate the coming of the Spaniards, is situated just northeast of the church of San Miguel. This building until about the beginning of the present century was two stories in height, the second story being

About this time serious controversies arose between the political and ecclesiastical authorities, the custodio assuming the right to issue

very low and the floor between the upper and lower rooms being adobe. Some years ago the upper story of the eastern portion fell and the entire second story was taken down when it was repaired (?).

The Cathedral of San Francisco de Assisi is a modern building. It was built upon the site of and over the former adobe parish church, under the auspices of the lamented Archbishop J. B. Lamy. There are many fine paintings in this edifice; behind the altar is a richly carved and painted *reredos*, erected by Governor Del Valle in 1761. Back of the altar of this cathedral are hung the old paintings, and beneath it are the remains of two Franciscan friars, who were murdered by Indians, as attested by the inscription upon a beam set into the massive wall. The remains of Archbishop Lamy also rest here.

On the east side of the main road entering the city from the north stand the ruins of the Garita, the only Spanish fortifications of which any remains now exist in New Mexico. It was built with two bastions, and occupies a prominent position on a hill. Under the Mexican government it was used as a customs house, and all wagons coming into the country over the Taos Trail and the Santa Fé Trail were stopped here, where the duties were paid. On the west side of the Garita, close to the wall, the four leaders of the revolution of 1837, Desiderio Montoya, Antonio Abad Montoya, General Chopon, and Alcalde Esquibel, were executed by command of General Manuel Armijo, in 1837. Near the Garita is the second oldest cemetery of the city, the oldest being that near the San Miguel church. The one at the Garita is surrounded by a high adobe wall. Many very celebrated historical characters and personages are buried here, but there are no stones marking the exact locality.

Guadalupe church is just south of the Rio Santa Fé. Owing to the modern appearance of the shingle roof and steeple, it often escapes attention, but this building is of great historical interest. The walls are very massive, and the carved supports of the *vigas* are the best specimens of this sort in New Mexico. Prior to the year 1883, for a long period, this church was only opened once a year, on Guadalupe day, December 12th, but in that year under the direction of Father De Fouri, it was renovated and has since been used principally by the English-speaking Catholics of the city. The altar-piece is a large group of pictures, about 14 feet high by 10 feet wide. The large central painting is of the virgin of Guadalupe, copied from the celebrated "imagen" in Mexico, and it is surrounded by four scenes in the well known legend, representing the appearances of the virgin to Juan Diego and the visits of the latter to the bishop; the whole surrounded by the representation of the Trinity. The church and the sacristy contain many interesting paintings, the most curious and valuable being one painted on a plate of copper, 28x18 inches in size, by Sebastian Salcedo, in 1779. This also represents the virgin of Guadalupe, a small portrait of Pope Benedict XIV being introduced. The statuette of the virgin standing in the crescent of the new moon is a beautiful specimen of wood carving.

The place of the assassination of Governor Perez is about two miles southwest of the Plaza on the Agua Fria road. It is now very appropriately marked by a neat stone monument erected by the Stephen Watts Kearny chapter of the Daughters of the American Revolution in 1901. It was here that the governor in the revolution of 1837, while retreating from the capital, was killed by an arrow shot by a Pueblo Indian from Santo Domingo. His assailants then forced Santiago Prada, by threats of death, to cut off his head, which was carried to the insurgent encampment near the Rosario chapel and treated with great indignity.

The Plaza, in the center of the city, is of historic interest. Here Juan de

excommunication against the governor, the latter claiming authority to appoint petty Indian officials at the missions, and both being

Oñate is supposed to have made his camp when he moved from San Gabriel on the Rio Grande in 1605; here General Kearny first floated the Stars and Stripes of the American government, in 1846, the place being marked by a stone also furnished by the Daughters of the American Revolution. In this Plaza the Indians burned the archives and sacred vessels of the church during the revolution of 1680, and here De Vargas entered in triumph twelve years later. A handsome monument in the center of the Plaza, erected by the people of New Mexico, commemorates the deeds of the soldiers who fell on New Mexican soil in the many Indian wars, the war of the rebellion, and a local organization of the women of the capital has placed near-by a drinking fountain, of bronze, in memory of Archbishop Lamy.

Rosario Chapel, in the cemetery of that name, commemorates the victory of De Vargas over the Pueblo Indians in 1692, and is the terminus of the annual historic De Vargas procession, which, with the two annual Corpus Cristi processions and the custom of celebrating Guadalupe day, Christmas eve, and other holidays by the lighting of numerous bonfires, is an echo of those ancient customs that gives Santa Fé a charm peculiarly its own.

The following is a translation of the entry in the journal of De Vargas relative to the chapel of San Miguel, which had been burned in 1680:

A. D. 1692, December, 18.

THE SAID GOVERNOR AND CAPTAIN-GENERAL DE VARGAS ORDERS THAT THE CAPTAIN AND GOVERNOR OF THE WALLED PUEBLO, AS ALSO ANTONIO BOLSAS AND TOGETHER GO TO EXAMINE THE HERMITAGE OF SAN MIGUEL, SO THAT IT BEING REPAIRED, IT MAY SERVE AS A CHURCH TILL THE COMING OF SUMMER

On the said day, month and year of the date, I, said Governor and Captain-General, very much grieved on account of the severity of the weather and the cold (suffered by the Indians) who in troops while away the time visiting the (ranch) huts in the plain. And, in order to act in everything with necessary prudence, I mounted on horseback, and with a few military officers and the captains Francisco Lucero de Godoy and Roque Madrid, I went to examine the church or hermitage which was used as a parish church for the Mexican Indians who lived in the said town (villa) under the title of the invocation of their patron, the Archangel San Miguel. And having examined it, though of small dimensions, and not for the accommodation of a great number; notwithstanding, on account of said inclemency of the weather, and the urgency of having a church in which should be celebrated the Divine Office and the Holy Sacrifice of the Mass, and in order that our Lady of the Conquest may have a becoming place, I, said Governor and Captain-General, recognized that it is proper to roof said walls, and to white-wash and repair its skylights (windows) in a manner that shall be the quickest, easiest, briefest and least laborious to said natives.

The parties alluded to being present, and the said governors of aforesaid pueblo, Joseph and Antonio Bolsas, I ordered that they should send said natives; having taken measures in respect to lumber aforesaid, and having offered them axes, and mules for its fast conveyance that those who were adapted to hewing said lumber should do so, and that those who were fit for the trade of masons in repairing said walls should be ordered in like manner, and that I, on my part, should have the Spaniards whom I had with me to assist thereat.

And that said work should be immediately executed, I went with them to the aforesaid pueblo, and being within their village square (plaza), I ordered the natives who were there in the manner before described. And I also exhorted

Ceremonial Dance — Pueblo of Cochití

charged with oppressive exactions of labor and tribute from the natives.

This matter was referred to the Audiencia, and drew out a reprimand and warning addressed to both parties. Fr. Geronimo Zarate-Salmeron came to New Mexico, probably after the Villa Real de Santa Fé had been established by the Spaniards. He was ardent in his missionary work, and for eight years "sacrificed himself to the Lord among the Pagans," toiling chiefly among the Jemez, of whom he says that he baptized 6,566, and in the language of which tribe he wrote a *doctrina*. This friar also served at Cia and Sandia, among the Queres, and once pacified the people of Acoma, after a revolt. Salmeron regarded, as did all his brothers in the order, the salvation of souls as paramount to everything in the settling of the new countries, and for the purpose of overcoming certain obstacles which he believed existed in the matter of salvation for the natives, he went to Mexico with his *Relaciones*.

In the year 1621 the missions, with over 16,000 converts, were formed into a "custodia de la Conversion de San Pablo." The first custodio was Fr. Alonzo de Benavides, who came from Mexico, bringing with him twenty-seven friars. According to Salmeron and Benavides, five years later, although 34,000 Indians had been baptized in the faith, yet only sixteen friars and three lay brothers were in the country. Requests were constantly being made for the sending of more friars, and, in 1627, the king ordered thirty new friars and a large number of lay brothers to be sent immediately. These came under the leadership of Fr. Estevan de Perea, from the provineia del Santo Evangelico, arriving in 1628-9. Vetancurt states that Fr. Tomás Manso was the custodio in the year 1629. This friar was procurador of New Mexico for twenty-five years, provincial of

---

them to go with cheerfulness to said labor, and that such it really was not, to make a house for God and His Most Blessed Mother, our Virgin lady, who was enclosed in a wagon; and that if a lady came they were obliged to furnish her with a house, and that such was their duty; and mine it was to issue such orders with much force, because the Lord our God might punish us, seeing that, being Christians, we did not make the church immediately, which they promised to accomplish, as I had ordered; and they afterward sent for the axes which I gave unto them immediately and a hide to make a ladder.

And for the authenticity of these proceedings, I have had an act thereof drawn up and signed it, with my secretary in civil and military affairs.

D. Diego de Vargas Zapata Lujan Ponce de Leon.　Roque de Madrid.
Before me, Antonio Balverde,　　　　　　　　　　　Joseph de Contreras.
Military and Civil Secretary.

his order in 1655, and later was consecrated bishop of Nicaragua, where he died. Other friars who came with Fr. Estevan de Perea were Fr. Garcia de San Francisco y Nuñiga, who founded Socorro and a pueblo of Mansos in 1659, dying in 1673 and buried at Senecú; Fr. Antonio de Arteaga, a companion of Fr. Garcia and the founder of Senecú; Fr. Francisco Letrado, who was a missionary among the Jumanos and the Zuñi and was killed by gentiles in 1632; Fr. Francisco Acevedo, who built churches at San Gregorio de Abó, Tenabó, and Tabira, dying in 1644. Fr. Francisco Porras and the frailes Gutierrez and de la Concepcion went among the Hopi, where many miracles were worked. Fr. Porras was poisoned on the 28th day of June, 1633. Fr. Geronimo de la Llana died at Quarac in 1659; Fr. Tomás de San Diego died at Oajaca the same year; and Fr. Juan Ramirez, who went to Acoma, where the arrows failed to touch him, and he worked many years, dying in Mexico in 1664; also Fr. Juan de la Torre, who became comisario-general of New Spain and bishop of Nicaragua, where he departed this life in 1663.

The names of two governors have come down to us as having ruled in New Mexico between the years 1621 and 1629; they are Felipe Zotylo and Manuel de Silva. At this period Fr. Benavides was custodio, and it was represented to the king of Spain that a bishopric [338] was necessary for New Mexico, where 500,000 gentiles had

[338] Bancroft, H. H., *History of Arizona and New Mexico*, note, p. 162, cites as authority the royal order of May 19, 1631, citing the demand of Comisario-general Sosa, *New Mex. Cédulas*, Ms., 1-2; also order of June 23, 1636, on the same subject, and adds that the pope had been asked to grant to some friar authority to confirm pending the election of a bishop. See also Bonilla, *Apuntes*, Ms., i; as early as 1596 the bishop of Guadalajara claims New Mexico as belonging to his bishopric, *N. Mex. Mem.*, 227.

During the time that Fr. Benavides was in New Mexico Don Francisco de Sylvia Nieto was the governor. A very well executed inscription on the Morro or Inscription Rock commemorates the passage of the Morro by this governor and another his return from the Zuñi pueblos, after having pacified them again and established the permanent missions. The inscription reads: "Aqui (effaced) nador Don Francisco . . . annuel de Silva Nieto (effaced) que lo ympucible tiene y á sujeto su braço yndubitable su balor con los carrso del Rei ñro Señor cosa que solo el puso en este efecto . . . De Agosto y seiscientos biente y nueve que (illegible) á Cuñi pase y la Fé Lleve,'' which, translated reads: ''Through here passed the Governor Francisco Manuel de Sylva Nieto, whose valor and unflinching arm have overcome the impossible with the carts of the King our Lord which he alone put in this state . . . August and six hundred and twenty-nine . . . to Zuñi passed and carried the faith thither.''

The other inscription reads: "El Capn Genl de Las Pro . . . del Nuebo Mexico for el Rey ñro Sr paso por aqui de buelta de los Pueblos de Zuñi á los 29 de Julio del año de 1629, y los puso en paz á su pedimiento

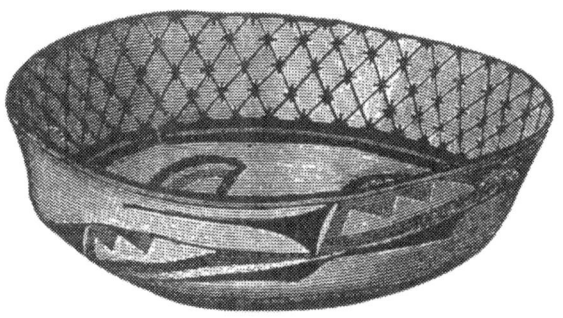

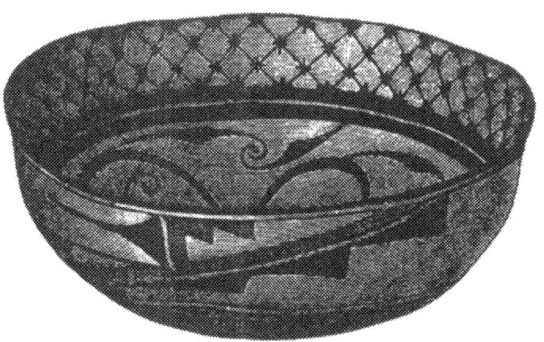

Courtesy Bureau American Ethnology
Pottery Bowls from Pueblo of Zuñi

been converted and 86,000 baptized, where over 100 friars were at work in 150 pueblos, where there were no clergymen and none authorized to administer the right of confirmation. A bishop would save much expense and would be easily supported by the tithes, particularly as rich mines had been found and the population was rapidly increasing. The viceroy was ordered to investigate and report on the desirability of this change; but long delays resulted and nothing was accomplished.

The most important authority of the events of this period is Fr. Benavides, who made a trip to Spain, and his report to the king, dated Madrid, 1630, while much colored and REPORT OF FR. ALONZO certainly exaggerated in many respects, DE BENAVIDES must be taken as a fair expression of conditions as they then existed in New Mexico. He says that there were about fifty friars, serving over sixty thousand natives who had accepted Christianity; that these lived in ninety pueblos, grouped into twenty-five conventos, or missions, and that each pueblo had its own church. This seems a most remarkable record for church building in such a country, and with so few Spaniards to supervise the construction of the edifices. It must be re-

pidiendole su fabor como basallos de su magd y de nuebo dieron la obidiencia todo lo qe hiso con el agasaxe selo y prudencia como tan chritianismo . . . tan par icular y gallardo soldado de inacabable y loada memo." Translated the inscription reads: "The Captain General of the Provinces of New Mexico for the King our Lord, passed through here on his return from the pueblos of Zuñi on the 29th day of July of the year 1629, and put them in peace at their request, begging him for his favor as vassals of his Majesty, and again they pledged obedience; all of which he performed with the zeal, gentleness, and prudence as so Christian . . . particular and gallant soldier of unending . . ."

Vetancurt in his *Cronica*, p. 300, states that Nieto was governor in 1629.

The journey to Zuñi, mentioned in the inscription, was undoubtedly for the purpose of establishing missions. In the year following, according to Vetancurt, *Menologio*, p. 53, the Zuñis revolted and killed the missionary. Bandelier says the date of the killing of the missionary was in 1630, but does not say why he differs with Vetancurt. The missionary was Fr. Francisco Letrado.

There is also an inscription of date 1636. Bancroft does not mention this governor, who Bandelier says was Francisco Martinez Baeza, and cites *Autos sobre Quexas contra los Religiosos del Nuevo Mexico*, Ms., 1636, as his authority.

The above inscription of 1636 is: "Pasamos por aqui el Sarjento Mayor y el Capitan Jua de Archuleta y el Aiudante Diego Martin . . . 1636." When General Simpson visited the Rock the word "Barba" followed the above and completed the inscription. Bandelier says that Diego Martin Barba was secretary to Governor Francisco Martinez Baeza in 1636; also that the sargento mayor was probably Francisco Gomez.

THE CONQUEST OF NEW MEXICO 341

membered that, as far as the record shows, no church building had been erected in New Mexico prior to 1598, when Oñate built one at San Gabriel, and in less than thirty-five years ninety had been constructed by these friars using the labor of the Indians for the purpose. The accuracy of Fr. Benavides's statement as to the number of churches and native converts may well be doubted.

Benavides refers to the church which had but recently been completed at Santa Fé; gives the number of the garrison at the capital, and refers to the tribute paid by the natives for their support.[339] He classifies the wandering tribes as Apaches de Gila, Apaches de Navajó, and Apaches Vaqueros, and says that these had given the Spaniards no trouble of any consequence. The friar personally visited the Apaches on the Gila,[340] and reports that at the time a missionary was among those Indians working with success. He goes into the details of the conversion of the Jumanos,[341] living 112 leagues east of the capital. He has something to say of Quivira and a tribe of Indians who lived east of the Jumanos, called the Aijaos. Bena-

[339] Benavides, *Memorial*, 1630, p. 26: "Villa de Santa Fé, cabeça deste Reino, adonde residan los gobernadores, y Españoles, que seran hasta dozientas y cin cuenta, aunque solos cinquenta se podran armar por falta de armas . . . á este presidio sustenta V. M. no con pagas de su caxa real, sino haziendo los encomenderos de aquellos pueblos, por mano del governador; el tributo que les dan los Indios, es cada casa una manta, que es una vara de lienço de algodon, y una fanega de maiz cada año, con que se sustentan los pobres Españoles; tendran de servuicio setecientas almas de suerte, que entre Españoles, mestizos, y Indios acerca mil almas."

These Indians, then living at the capital, had their houses in the immediate vicinity of the present chapel of San Miguel. As will be seen, they were not Pueblos, but Indians from New Spain. Some were "Mestizos."

[340] In the report of the friar the name Gila is first used. He says that the province was thirty leagues west from the Rio Grande (Senecú).

[341] Bancroft, H. H., *History of Arizona and New Mexico*, p. 163: The author recounts the miraculous conversion of the Jumanos . . . through the supernatural visits of Sister Luisa de la Asencion, an old nun of Carrion, Spain, who had the power of becoming young and beautiful, and of transporting herself in a state of trance to any part of the world where were souls to be saved.

In Spain Fr. Benavides found out that he was in error about the woman. He had an interview with Maria de Jesus, abbess of the convent of Agreda, who often since 1620 had been carried by the heavenly hosts to New Mexico to preach the faith. Sometimes she made the trip several times in twenty-four hours. Vetancurt, *Cronica*, p. 96, also speaks of this remarkable conversion of the Jumanos; he says that P. Juan de Salas and Diego Lopez went from San Antonio de Isleta after the miraculous operations of this lady.

Fr. Benavides never returned to New Mexico, but became archbishop of Goa, in Asia.

vides quite elaborately describes the manners and customs of the Apaches, and in this respect his report is very valuable.

Benavides, in his report, gives a classification of the pueblo Indians, which, while far from satisfactory, considering the information which he must have had as to their names and locations, must be taken as authentic.[342]

---

[342] Piros, or Picos, nation, southernmost of New Mexico; on both sides of the Rio Grande for 15 leagues, from Senecú to Sevilleta; 15 pueblos, 6,000 Indians, all baptized; 3 missions, Nra Sra del Socorro at Pilabó, San Antonio de Senecú and San Luis Obispo Sevilleta.

Taos nation, 7 leagues above Piros, 15 or 16 pueblos, 7,000 Indians, all baptized; 2 missions, San Antonio Sandia and San Antonio Isleta.

He calls this nation "Taos" which is clearly an error; he doubtless intended to say "Tiguas."

Queres nation, 4 leagues above the Tiguas (evidently in the preceding class which he calls "Taos," he meant "Tiguas") extending ten leagues from San Felipe and including Santa Ana on the west; 7 pueblos, 4,000 Indians, all baptized; 3 missions.

(This San Felipe of the Queres must not be confounded with a "Sant Felipe" mentioned by the companions of Chamuscado in 1582 when they gave certain testimony as to their journey into New Mexico. The latter pueblo was the first one met by these witnesses in 1581, on their way up the Rio Grande, and was a village of the Piros, probably near San Marcial, at least 160 miles farther south. The name Sant Felipe was afterwards forgotten. The pueblo at the foot of Ta-mi-ta was visited by Castaño in 1591, and it is possible that he gave it its name. Oñate refers to it by that name in 1598, in his *Jornadas*.)

The first church of San Felipe of the Queres was built by Fray Cristobal de Quiñones, who died at the pueblo in 1607, and he was buried in the church which he had founded,

Tompiros nation, ten leagues east of the Queres, extending 15 leagues from Chilili; 14 or 15 pueblos, over 10,000 Indians, all of whom were converted and most all of them baptized; six missions, one called San Isidori Numanas (Jumanas) (possibly); these lived near the Salinas. They actually lived to the east of the Piros and Tiguas.

Tanos nation, ten leagues northeast of the Tompiros, extending ten leagues; five pueblos and one mission; 4,000 Indians, all of whom had been baptized.

Pecos, pueblo of Jemez nation and language; 4 leagues north of the Tanos; 2,000 Indians and a mission.

(This is the earliest documentary proof that I have been able to find that there was a church building at Cicuyé or Pecos; it shows that the old church was built some time between 1598 and 1630.)

Villa de Santa Fé; seven leagues west of Pecos; capital; 250 Spaniards and 700 Indians. Mission church nearly completed.

(It will be noted that the church at Pecos was completed while that at Santa Fé was not.) This would show that the San Miguel chapel is of later construction than the old ruin at Pecos, but they were probably commenced about the same time. The Pecos church was much larger of the two.

Toas or Tevas nation, west of Santa Fé toward the Rio Grande, extending 10 or 12 leagues; 8 pueblos, including Santa Clara; 6,000 Indians; 3 missions, including San Ildefonso.

(These were Tehuas and, owing to the fact that the first settlement was at

THE CONQUEST OF NEW MEXICO 343

No complete list of the governors from 1630 down to the date of the Pueblo revolt has ever been obtained. No complete narrative of the events transpiring during this period will ever be secured, unless in the archives of Spain or Mexico are hereafter found copies of the records which were destroyed by the Indians at the time of the revolt. In the year 1640, Fernando de Arguello was the governor of New Mexico. Following him was Luis de Rosas; he was murdered in 1641 or 1642, and was succeeded by Valdéz, who was followed by Alonzo Pacheco de Heredia.[343] Arguello is named again as governor in 1645. During his administration a conspiracy on the part of the Indians of the Jemez nation

GOVERNORS OF NEW MEXICO — 1640-1680

San Gabriel, across the river from San Juan, these were the first Indians of New Mexico, after the coming of Oñate, who were baptized.)

Benavides refers to the Indians of Picuriés — Tehuas — as being 10 leagues up the river from San Ildefonso; that there were 2,000 of them, baptized, and the most savage in the province, and often miraculously restrained from killing the frailes.

Taos pueblo of same nation as the Picuriés, but differing somewhat in language, was seven leagues north of Picuriés and had 1,500 Indians who had been converted to the Christian faith owing to the fact that an Indian woman who opposed the Christian ideas of marriage had been killed by lightning; here was a mission and two frailes.

Acoma pueblo, twelve leagues west of Santa Ana, containing 2,000 Indians and which had been reduced in 1629, at which one friar was located. (This was the second time this pueblo had been ''reduced.'')

Zuñi nation, thirty leagues west of Acoma, extending nine or ten leagues, containing eleven or twelve pueblos and ten thousand converted Indians; there were two missions at Zuñi.

Moqui nation, thirty leagues west of Zuñi, containing ten thousand Indians, which Benavides claimed were being rapidly converted. (They never have been fully converted and are hostile to the priests to this day.)

[343] Davis, W. W. H., in his *Conquest of New Mexico*, gives a list of the governors of the territory, but it is very imperfect. The best authority, in my judgment, although his list is also somewhat misleading, is Mr. Bancroft, *History of Arizona and New Mexico*, pp. 164 et seq, together with notes, and the text is taken from his work. The list contained in Davis's *Conquest of New Mexico*, was originally prepared by David J. Miller, deceased, for many years official translator in the office of the surveyor general of New Mexico. Mr. Miller's list is found in the official reports of the United States Land Office, for the year 1862, at page 102. Mr. Miller secured most of his information from the Santa Fé Archives. The Miller list places Peralta in 1600-1608 et seq; Arguello, 1640; Concha, 1650; Avila y Pacheco in 1656; Villanuevo, Frecinio, in 1675; and Otermin in 1680-83.

Valdéz is named in a royal order. In 1681, Captain Juan Dominguez de Mendoza testified that, being now fifty years of age, he had come at the age of twelve with Governor Pacheco (that is, in 1643). Governor Otermin in 1682 stated that Governor Pacheco punished the murderers of Governor Rosas; this is soon after 1641-2.

was discovered. This was repressed with great severity by the governor. He caused twenty-nine Indians to be hanged, as they had already killed one Spaniard by the name of Diego Martinez Naranjo, and a very serious outbreak appeared imminent.[344] Luis de Guzman [345] held the office before 1650, and Hernando de Ugarte y la Concha in 1650. Juan de Samaniego [346] occupied the position in 1653, and three years later Enrique de Avila y Pacheco [347] had succeeded to the place. Bernardo Lopez de Mendizabal is named as having become involved in troubles with the Inquisition, and resigned as governor in 1660 or the year following. Don Diego de Peñalosa Briceño ruled in 1661-4.[348]

Next came Fernando de Villanueva, Juan de Medrano, and Juan de Miranda, the dates of whose incumbency of the office are not known. Juan Francisco Treviño seems to have ruled in 1675. Antonio Otermin was governor in 1679-83. Juan Dominguez testified in 1681 that he had known fourteen governors, in the past thirty-eight years, and it may be considered that the list which is given is fairly correct.[349]

[344] *Ynterrogatorio de Preguntas, 1681*, Ms.: The maestro de Campo Juan Dominguez Mendoza testified: ''Y en particular en el tiempo de D. Fernando de Arguello, que en el pueblo de Xemes ahorco por traidores confederados con los Apaches veinte y nueve Emes, despositando cantidad de ellos por el mismo delito, y haber muerto á Diego Martinez Naranjo.'' The Sargento Mayor Diego Lopez Zambrano states: ''Desde el Gobernador D. Fernando de Arguello, que ahorcó, azotó, y despositó mas de quarenta Yndios.'' This was the second time that Arguello had been governor and these events occurred between 1643 and 1646.

[345] Guijo, *Diario*, 154-5, says that such a man, who was ex-governor of New Mexico, was killed in a duel in Mexico in November, 1650.

In the *Ynterrogatorio*, etc., in the testimony of Mendoza, *supra*, we find: ''Y en el tiempo del Señor General Hernando de Ugarte y la Concha, se ahorcaron por traidores nueve de los dichos pueblos, confederados con los Apaches, Yndios Tiguas de la Ysleta, y del pueblo de Alameda, San Felipe, Cochití, y Xemes.'' This took place in 1650, and the conspiracy, according to the statements of the Indians themselves, was intended to embrace all of the pueblos, although not all of them had entered into the plot.— *Interrogatorios de Varios Indios*, 1681, fol. 135.

[346] Letter of the viceroy to the king, March 20, 1653, *N. Mex. Cédulas*, Ms., 8-9.

[347] According to Mr. D. J. Miller this name was found in a document of 1683.

[348] The only document ante-dating the Pueblo revolt, in the Santa Fé Archives, is signed by this governor. It is an order that the Indians be not employed in spinning and weaving without the governor's license; that the friendly Indians be well treated, but that wild tribes coming to trade be not admitted to the towns, but obliged to lodge outside. It is signed Diego de Peñalosa Briceño.

[349] Bancroft, H. H., *History of Arizona and New Mexico*, p. 167, and notes.

The Chapel of San Miguel, Santa Fé, N. M. From an old drawing, 1854

In the years of Fr. Benavides's stay in New Mexico, and prior to his departure for Spain, several missionary tours were made by various frailes into the eastern plains country, beyond the domains of the Jumanos. Prominent in these journeys were the frailes Salas, Estevan de Perea, Lopez, and Diego Ortega; these went as far to the southeast as the Nueces river. In 1634, Captain Alonzo Baca journeyed eastward three hundred leagues to the great river on the other side of which was the province of Quivira. Another expedition to the southeast was made in 1650 under the leadership of Captains Hernan Martin and Diego del Castillo; they went into the country of the Teyas; four years later another expedition was led by Diego de Guadalajara, who had a fight with the Cuitoas. About the middle of the century some trouble occurred at Taos, resulting in the migration eastward to the plains of certain prominent families; they fortified a place called Cuartalejo, and remained there until the governor sent Juan de Archuleta [350] to bring them back. Governor Peñalosa also claimed that he made a journey to Quivira, which has since proved to be without foundation in fact. A royal order of 1678 alluded to projects of exploring Quivira and Teguayo, and to conflicting reports on the geography and wealth of these and other distant provinces, calling for an investigation, and it was in reply that Fr. Posadas made his later report, which is the best authority on the outside regions.[351]

In the month of February, 1630, the frailes Arvide and Letrado [352]

Most authors begin Otermin's rule in '80; but Escalante says the great revolt was in the second year of his rule. Dominguez's testimony is found in Otermin, *Extractos*, Ms., 1395-6.

[350] Bancroft, H. H., *ibid*, p. 166.

[351] Bancroft, H. H., *ibid*, p. 166, says that this report contains very little on the history of New Mexico proper of which Posadas was custodio in 1660-4, and a missionary from 1650.

[352] The year of the death of Fr. Letrado is given by Vetancurt at 1632, *Menologio*, p. 53. Bandelier thinks this date erroneous, and says it occurred two years before; he says: ''In 1629, the Zuñi missions had been established, and Fray Francisco Letrado left at one of the pueblos as priest. The year after, on the 22nd of February, he was killed by the people, who thereupon fled to Thunder Mountain (Toyoalana), remaining at Thunder Mountain until 1635. This is stated in *Autos sobre restablecer las Misiones en los pueblos de los Zuñis*, 1636, Ms. The custodio of New Mexico says: 'Digo qe por quanto los Yndios del Peñol de Cquima de la Prouycia de Cuñi qe se abian alsado en tiempo del gouro Don Franco de Silua los quales Yndios.' Also: 'Y como los Yndios le la prouycia de Zuñi qe se alzaron y mataron á su ministro en tiempo de Dn Franco Silva, los quales Yndios dejó de paz Don Franco de la

were murdered by the gentile Zipias,[353] somewhere beyond the Zuñi country, and the year following Fr. Porras was poisoned by the Moquis.

In 1640-2 there were serious difficulties between the governor and the friars, the latter being accused of assuming, as jueces eclesiásticos and officials of the Inquisition, extraordinary and absolute powers, and even of having gone so far as to encourage a revolt, in connection with which Governor Rosas lost his life. Little is known of this controversy, but at the city of Mexico it was deemed very serious and seems to have been the beginning of the troubles that terminated in the Pueblo revolt of 1680. The friars were blamed, and special efforts were ordered to avoid a costly war, which it was thought could not be afforded in a province that yielded no return for an annual expenditure of sixty thousand pesos.[354]

About the year 1650 complaints of acts of oppression on the part of the governor were sent to Mexico and to Spain.[355]

The Teguas nation and the Pueblos of Cochití and Jemez conspired in 1650, with the Apaches as allies, to massacre or drive every Spaniard and priest from the country. The governor, Concha, promptly and energetically repressed this conspiracy, at its very inception. On Thursday night of Passion week, when the Christians would be assembled in their churches, the assassins were to rush

---

Mora que sucedió en el govierno y de poco tiempo á esta parte se ban reduziendo á sus pueblos.' ''

[353] Bandelier, A. F., *Final Report*, part ii, p. 381: When the Zuñi missions were first established, the missionaries heard of a tribe living in eastern Arizona who were called Zipias. The Zipias must have dwelt west of the Zuñis. In 1630 or 1632 Fray Martin de Arvide intended to visit them, but was murdered five days after the Zuñis had killed Fr. Francisco Letrado, their missionary.—Vetancurt, *Menologio*, p. 76. Bandelier says that the Tzipia Kue were well known to the Zuñis formerly; that they dwelt south of the Moquis.

[354] Bancroft, H. H., *History of Arizona and New Mexico*, note, p. 167, citing *Revilla Gigedo, Carta de 1793*, p. 441, says the matter was reported to the king in 1640, including an Indian revolt, as well as scandalous quarrels between the friars and the secular authorities. It appears that Governor Rosas was stabbed, perhaps while under arrest awaiting his residencia, by a man who accused him of intimacy with his wife, but the woman had been put in his way that an excuse for killing him might be found. Antonio Vaca is named as a leader in this movement.

[355] Bonilla, *Apuntes*, Ms. 1, *N. Mex. Ced.* Ms. 6, 8-9. The king in his cédula of September 22, 1650, notes these complaints and the popular discontent and strife leading to raids by the gentiles, and orders the viceroy to investigate and remedy the situation. The viceroy replied March 20, 1653, that he had given strict orders to the new governor; this was approved by the king, who ordered continued vigilance, June 20, 1654.

upon them in their devotions. Some Indians who had stolen horses were overtaken and confessed the design to murder the Spaniards. The governor, informed of this confession, ferreted out the principal leaders, and imprisoned them along with many others. To quell the turbulent spirit of the Indians, nine of the prisoners were hung and others sold into slavery for a period of ten years. The rebellion was crushed and the Indian spirit appeared to be broken. A Captain Vaca was the discoverer of this plot. A like result followed an uprising of the Piros, who ran away, joining the Apaches and killing five Spaniards [356] before they could be overpowered. Several of the Piros were later put to death for sorcery. Estevan Clemente, governor of the Salineros towns, was at the head of the next conspiracy to drive out the Spaniards. Don Estevan was hanged. The Taos Indians drew up on two deer-skins a plan for a general movement, but it was abandoned because the Moquis refused their aid.

Don Diego Dionisio de Peñalosa Briceño was the governor of New Mexico from 1661 to 1664, having been appointed in 1660. He was a native of Peru, an adventurer bent on achieving fame and fortune with the aid of his unlimited assurance and his attractive personality, by which alone he succeeded in obtaining his appointment from the viceroy. This governor visited Zuñi and the Moqui towns, heard of the great kingdom of Teguayo through a Jemez Indian, who had been a captive there, and also of Quivira and Tejas; also the Cerro Azul. He planned expeditions into these localities. He became involved in troubles with the friars, and particularly with the friar who represented the Inquisition. It is more than likely

---

[356] This occurred during the administration of Don Fernando de Villanueva: some Piros of Senecú killed the alcalde mayor of the jurisdiction of Socorro and four Spaniards in the Magdalena mountains. This massacre was at first attributed to the Apaches, but the participation of some of the Piros being detected, six of them were executed for the crime.

Ynterrogatorio de Preguntas, Ms. testimony of Juan Dominguez de Mendoza: "Y en particular en tiempo del Sr. General D. Fernando Villanueva en la Provincia de los Pyros por traidores y echizeros ahorcaron, y quemaron en el pueblo de Sena." Testimony of Diego Lopez Zambrano: "Y despuez aca se hizo otro castigo con los Pyros, por el mismo delito, gobernando el Señor General Fernando Villanueva, que se ahorcaron seis Yndios y otros fueron vendidos y depositados, porque á mas de sus delitos y conjuraciones, se hallaron en una emboscada com los enemigos los Apaches en la Sierra de la Magdalena, donde mataron cinco Españoles, y entre ellos al Alcalde Mayor, el cual lo mato uno de los seis Yndios Christianos que se ahorcaron llamado en su lengua el Tambulista."

that he returned to Mexico in 1664, where he was asking aid in order to send out expeditions to the north, and it is more than likely that while there he became involved with the holy office, by which he was put in prison. Just when this imprisonment began, we do not know, but it is certain that in 1668 he was forced to march bare-headed through the streets carrying a green candle, for having made blasphemous remarks against the holy office. During his incumbency there were established in New Mexico twenty-four additional missions, all of which was accomplished by the friars and not by the civil government.

When Peñalosa found that his proposals met with no favorable reception or consideration by the king and the viceroy, he went to London and Paris, where he attempted to organize a grand filibustering expedition against his former sovereign, freely resorting to falsehood, and claiming for himself the title of Condé de Santa Fé. Peñalosa died in 1687, and his efforts in the organization of the filibustering project are very closely allied with the expedition of La Salle in 1682-7.[357]

From about 1672 the various Apache [358] tribes became troublesome,

---

[357] Bancroft, H. H., *History of Arizona and New Mexico*, p. 169, and notes: "In France Peñalosa presented to the government what purported to be a narrative of an expedition to Quivira made by himself in 1662, written by Padre Freitas, one of the friars of his company, and sent to the Spanish king. He never made any such entrada or rendered any such report. The narrative was that of Oñate's expedition of 1601, slightly changed to suit his purposes in Paris. I made known this fraud in an earlier volume of this series, but have since received the work of Fernandes Duro, published two years before my volume, in which that investigator, by similar arguments, reached the same conclusions.

"The fictitious narrative, Freytas, *Relacion del Descubrimiento de Pais y Ciudad de Quivira*, given to the French minister in 1675, and claimed to have been sent to the king of Spain in 1663, was printed in Shea's *Expedition of Don Diego de Peñalosa*, New York, 1882, with Spanish and English text, with valuable notes and extracts from Margry and other authors respecting Peñalosa. Later, in 1882, appeared the work of Fernandes Duro, *Don Diego de Peñalosa y su descubrimiento del reino de Quivira*, a report to the Royal Academy of History. This author reproduces all of Shea's matter and adds much more on the same and kindred subjects. For his conclusion that the story was a fraud he relies largely, as I did, on the report of Padre Posadas (erroneously called Paredes by me from the printed edition, apparently not known to F. D.), who was custodio during Peñalosa's term of office and who mentions no such expedition. I did not see the Madrid work of '82 or know of its existence until after the publication of my volume. Prince devotes a chapter to this expedition, not recognizing its fictitious character."

[358] Bandelier, A. F., *Final Report*, part ii, p. 338. Hauicu (Hawaikúh) is an elongated polygon on a rocky promontory overlooking the plains that stretch out on the south side of the Zuñi river, and about fifteen miles southwest of the

destroying in their raids one of the Zuñi towns and six of the pueblos farther east. Several friars lost their lives. In 1675 it is related that four natives were hanged, forty-three or forty-seven whipped and enslaved, and many more imprisoned for having killed several missionaries and other Spaniards, besides bewitching the padre visitador, Andrés Duran. Seventy Tegua warriors came early one morning to Governor Treviño's residence with eggs, chickens, tobacco, beans, and skins, as a ransom for their countrymen, who were in prison. The governor, alarmed at their demands, consented to their release, and the Indians peacefully retired. These Indians told the governor that they would kill all the Spaniards or flee to the mountains and risk utter annihilation at the hands of the Apaches rather than see their sorcerers punished. Popé, who became prominent in the rebellion of the Pueblos later on, was connected with this affair in some manner, either as leader of those who were in jail or of those who came to rescue them. About this time the Apaches became especially active in their raids; all the wandering tribes were known to the Spaniards as Apaches except the Utes, who lived in the north, and with whom Governor Otermin was the first to enter into treaties. There is no documentary record of the Comanches until the following century.[359]

In 1676 the condition of affairs became very serious. Towns and churches had been destroyed and many Christians [360] killed by the

---
present Zuñi. This was the village first seen by Coronado and which he had to take by storm. Hauicu was occupied until 1672, when the Navajós surprised it, killing the resident missionary, Fray Pedro de Avila y Ayala, on the seventh of October.

Vetancurt places the massacre at Hawaikúh in 1670. A contemporaneous document places the date at October 7th, 1672. *Parecer del Fiscal*, September 5th, 1676 (Ms.): "Y lo que es mas que despues de haber muerto muchos cristianos sin reserbar á los Parbulos pasaron á dar muerte al Pe Fr. Pedro de Ayala, ministro en el pueblo de Auuico en el dia 7 de Octubre del año pasado de 1672."

[359] Bancroft, H. H., *History of Arizona and New Mexico*, p. 171.

[360] Bandelier, A. F., *Final Report*, part ii, p. 249: "In 1680 the Apaches had waged war so successfully against the Piros that there were remaining only four pueblos. This was due not only to the efforts of the missionaries to gather their flock into larger pueblos, but also to the danger to which these Indians were exposed from the Apaches of the 'Perillo' and the 'Xila' as the southern bands of that restless tribe were called. They harassed the Piros as much as the Navajós did the Jemez. All efforts at taming them utterly failed; for, although willing to make peace with the Spaniards, they persisted in preying upon the pueblos whom the Spaniards were bound to protect. . . The Apaches, on the 23rd day of January, 1675, surprised the pueblo of Senecú, killed its missionary, Fray Alonzo Gil de Avila, and slaughtered so many of the inhabitants of all

Apaches. The defensive force was only five men at each frontier station and these were but poorly armed or mounted. Reënforcements were absolutely necessary. The custodio, Fr. Francisco Ayeta,[361] had gone to Mexico and was preparing to start with a wagon train of supplies for the missionaries. He made earnest appeals for soldiers and horses, and the junta approved his request, and finally the train started from the City of Mexico on the last days of September, 1679. The relief arrived too late. The province had to be abandoned.

The historian Vetancurt gives a list, written in 1691, of the pueblo Indians in New Mexico, the several friars, and other valuable information.[362]

---

ages and both sexes that the survivors fled in dismay to Socorro, and the pueblo remained forever deserted.''

The oldest mention of this massacre is found in the *Paracer del Fiscal*, dated September 5, 1676 (Ms.): ''Pasaron qá dar muerte . . . y al Pe. Fr. Alonzo Gil de Avila, Ministro del pueblo de Zennecú en el dia 23 de Enero del año passado de 675.''

Fray Juan Alvarez, *Peticion al Gobernador Don Francisco Cubero y Valdes*, 1705, Ms.: ''Tambien el pueblo de Senecú, mattaron al Pe Fr. Alonzo Gil de Avila y destruieron lo mas de la gente indiana.''

Vetancurt says: ''Hoy esta el pueblo despoblado y arruinado en la tierra de los enemigos.''

The persistent hostilities of the Apaches caused the abandonment of Chilili and all the pueblos about the Salinas. This took place after 1669 and prior to 1676.

[361] Fray Francisco de Ayeta's report, or complaint, rather, is entitled *Memorial en Novere del Gobernador, Cabildo Justicia y Regimiento de la Uilla de Santa Fé, 1676* (Ms.) The *Paracer del Fiscal* of September 5, 1676, says: ''Por no pasar de cinco hombres Españoles los que hay en cada frontera, y ser solo diez los que han quedado en la cabecera, Villa de Santa Fé, estando muchos de los Españoles sin armas algunas, y casi todos sin caballos por haberselso llevado el enemigo.'' In the *Parecer del Fiscal*, we also find: ''Que á demas destruido totalmente poblaciones pasaron á poner fuego á las yglesias, llevandose los vasos sagrados, etc.''

Escalante, *Carta al Padre Morfi*, 1778, par. 2, says: ''Destruyeron los enemigos Apaches con casi continuas invasiones siete pueblos de los cuarenta y seis dichos, uno en la provinsia de Zuñi, que fue Jahuicú, y siete en el valle de las Salinas, que fueron Chilili, Tunque y Cuarac de Indios Tehuas, Abó, Jumancas y Tabira de Tompiros.''

The pueblo of Tajique was destroyed by the Apaches about this time. There is a statement to the effect that the last priest of Tajique escaped from the pueblo in company with two Spaniards. Vetancurt, *Cronica*, p. 324, says: ''Que administraba un religioso que escapo del rebellion con otros dos Españoles.'' This must have been four years before the rebellion of 1680, for Escalante, in his *Carta*, par. 2, says that Tajique was in ruins in 1680.

[362] Vetancurt, *Cronica*, 98 et seq. Missions of New Mexico in 1680:

Senecú (S. Antonio) 70 leagues above Guadalupe del Paso, founded in 1630 by P. Ant. Arteaga, succeeded by P. Garcia de Zuñiga, or San Francisco, who is buried there; Piros nation; convento of S. Antonio; vineyard; fish-stream.

NOTE 362 — Continued

Socorro (Nra Sra) 7 leagues above Senecú, of Piros nation; 600 inhabitants; founded by P. Garcia.

Alamillo (Sta Ana), 3 leagues above Socorro; 300 Piros.

Puaray, or Pururay (S. Bartolome, one league from Sandai (Alameda); 200 Tiguas; the name means "gusanos," or worms.

Sandia (S. Francisco) one league (from Puaray); 3,000 Tiguas; convent, where P. Estevan Perea is buried; he was the founder. Also the skull of P. Rodriguez is venerated.

S. Felipe, on the river on a height (apparently on east bank); 600 inhabitants with little pueblo of Sta Ana; of Zures (Queres) nation; convent founded by P. Cris. Quiñones, who, with P. Geronimo Pedraza, is buried here.

Santo Domingo, 2 leagues above San Felipe; 150 inhabitants; one of the best convents, where the archives are kept, and where in 1661 was celebrated an auto-de-fé, by order of the Inquisition. P. Juan de Escalona is buried here; padres in 1680, Talaban (once custodio), Lorenzana, and Montesdeoca.

Santa Fé, villa, 8 leagues from Santo Domingo; residence of the governor and soldiers, with four padres.

Tesuque (San Lorenzo), 2 leagues from Santa Fé, in a forest; 200 Tiguas (Tehuas); P. Juan Bautista Pio.

Nambé (S. Francisco) 3 leagues east of Tesuque, 5 leagues from Rio del Norte; 2 little settlements of Jacona and Cuya Mungué; 600 inhabitants; P. Tomas de Torres.

San Ildefonso, near the river and 2 leagues from Jacona, in a fertile tract, with 20 farms; 800 inhabitants; PP. Morales, Sanchez de Pro, and Fr. Luis.

Santa Clara, convento, on a height by the river; 300 inhabitants; a visita of San Ildefonso.

San Juan de los Caballeros, 300 inhabitants; visita of San Ildefonso. In sight are the buildings of the villa de San Gabriel, the 1st Spanish capital.

Picuriés (S. Lorenzo) 6 leagues from San Juan, on a height; 3,000 inhabitants. Fr. Ascencion de Zarate served and is buried here. P. Matias Rendon in 1680.

Tahos (S. Geronimo de Taos) 3 leagues from Picuries and 5 leagues from the river, in a fine valley; 2,000 inhabitants and some Spaniards; in 1631 P. Pedro Miranda de Avila was killed here; PP. Juan de Pedrosa and Antonio de Mora in 1680.

Acoma (San Estevan) east of Cia on a peñol one league in circumference, and thirty estados high; 1,500 inhabitants, converted by F. Juan Ramirez; in 1680 P. Lucas Maldonado.

Hemes (San Diego de Jemez) a large pueblo formed of five smaller ones, with 5,000 inhabitants; in charge of P. Juan de Jesus.

Alona (Purisima), 24 leagues from Acoma, with two visitas, called Mazquia and Ciquima; 1,500 inhabitants; P. Juan del Bal. (Zuñi province).

Aguico (Concepcion), 3 leagues west of Alona, with other small pueblos; 1,000 inhabitants; they revolted in 1632, and killed P. Francisco Letrado; in 1680, the padre escaped.

Aguatobi (San Bernardino), in Moqui province; 26 leagues from Zuñi; 800 inhabitants, converted by Fr. Francisco de Porras; much pumice stone. P. José de Figueroa or Concepcion in 1680.

Xongopavi (San Bartolomé), seven leagues from A. with a visita called Moxainabi, 500 inhabitants; P. José Trujillo in 1680.

Oraybi (San Francisco; others say San Miguel), farthest west of the Moqui towns, over seventy leagues from Santa Fé; had 14,000 gentiles, but a pestilence consumed them; 1,200 in a visita called Gualpi; PP. José de Espeleta and Augustin de Santa Maria.

NOTE 362 — Concluded

Cochití, 3 leagues from Santo Domingo; 300 inhabitants of Queres nation; the padre escaped in 1680.

Galisteo (Santa Cruz), 6 leagues from Cochití (?), with San Cristobal as a visita; 800 inhabitants of the Tanos nation; here once served P. Antonio de Aranda; in 1680 PP. Juan Bernal, custodio, and Domingo de Vera.

Pecos (Porciuncula), on the eastern or Quivira frontier, in a finely wooded country; has a magnificent church with six towers; population not given; P. Fernando de Velasco.

San Marcos, on the right toward the north 5 leagues from Santo Domingo; 600 inhabitants of the Queres nation; 2 visitas, San Lazaro and Cienega. P. Manuel Tinoco.

Chilili (Natividad), 3 leagues from San Lazaro; 500 Piros, converted by Padre Alonzo Peinado who is buried here; this is the first pueblo of the Salinas valley.

Quarac (Concepcion), 3 leagues from Chilili; 600 Tiguas speaking Piros language, converted by Padre Estevan de Perea; Padre Geronimo de la Llana is buried here.

Taxique (San Miguel), two leagues from Quarac; 300 inhabitants; the padre escaped in 1680.

Abbó (San Gregorio), in the Salinas valley, which is 10 leagues in circumference, and produced much excellent salt; 800 inhabitants; 2 visitas, Tenabó and Tabira; 15 leagues farther east are some Christian Jumanos served by the Padre of Quarac; P. Francisco de Acevedo is buried here.

Woman dancer — Corn dance — Santo Domingo

BIBLIOGRAPHY

Ayeta, Francisco	*Memorial al Virey*, 1676, Ms. In N. Mex. Docs.
Archivo de Santa Fé	Unbound Mss. at Washington, D. C., with Library of Congress.
Alegre, Franco. Javier	*Historia de la Compania de Jesus*, Mexico, 1841.
Bandelier, A. F.	*Investigations in the Southwest*, Final Report, part ii; *Aboriginal Ruins in the Valley of the Pecos; Historical Introduction.*
Bancroft, H. H.	*History of Arizona and New Mexico; Native Races; North Mexican States.*
Barreiro, Antonio	*Ojeada sobre Nuevo Mexico*, Puebla, 1832.
Benavides, Alonzo	*Memorial*, Madrid, 1630.
Bonilla, Antonio	*Apuntes sobre Nuevo Mexico*, 1776.
Calle, Juan Diaz	*Memorial y Noticias*, etc.
Castaño de Sosa	*Memorial del Descubrimiento*, in Pacheco, Doc. xv, 191.
Davis, W. W. H.	*The Spanish Conquest of New Mexico; El Gringo.*
Documentos para la Historia de Nuevo Mexico	Four Series, 20 volumes, Mexico, 1853, 1857.
Escalante, Silvestre Veles	*Carta*, in Arch De N. M., Carta de 1776 sobre Moqui, Ms.
Escalona	*Carta de Relacion.* In Torquemada.
Fernandes Duro, Sesareo	*Diego de Peñalosa*, Madrid, 1882.
Freytas, Nicolas	*Relacion del Descubrimiento de Quivira*; See Fernandes Duro and Shea, J. G. Diego de Peñalosa. Expedition.
Gomara, Franco Lopez	*Historia de Mexico*, Anvers, 1554.
Gregg, Josiah	*Commerce of the Prairies*, New York, 1844.
Guijo, J. M.	*Diario*, 1648-64, in Doc. Hist. Mex., 1st series, 1.
Herrera, Antonio	*Historia General*, Madrid, 1601. 4 vols.
Miller, David J.	*Historical Sketch of Santa Fé*, 1876.
Niel, Juan A.	*Apuntes*, in Doc. Hist. Mex., 3rd series, iv, 56.
Obediencia y Vassalaje	In Pacheco, Doc. xvi.
Pacheco, Joaquin F.	*Colecion de Documentos Inéditos*, Madrid, 1864.
Posadas, Alonzo	*Informe*, Doc. Hist. Mexico, 3rd series.
Ritch, W. G.	*Aztlan*, Santa Fé, 1882.
Salmeron, Geronimo Zarate	*Relaciones de Nuevo Mexico*, in Doc. Hist. Mexico, 3rd series, iv.
Shea, John Gilmary	*Expedition of Don Diego Peñalosa*, New York, 1882.
Torquemada, Juan de	*Monarquia Indiana*, Madrid, 1723, 3 volumes.
Vetancurt, Augustin	*Cronica*, etc., Mexico, 1697; *Menologio*, Mex., 1871.
Villagrá, Gaspar de	*Historia de Nuevo Mexico*, Alcala, 1610. Reprint, Mexico.
Zuñiga, Ignacio	*Ojeada*, etc., Mexico, 1835.

CHAPTER VIII

PUEBLO REBELLION AND INDEPENDENCE, 1680-1692 — OTERMIN, CRUZATE, DE VARGAS

THE Pueblos for a period of nearly half a century, and during the administration of fourteen Spanish governors, had made ineffectual attempts to free themselves from the yoke of the invaders. Filled with fear and alarm, the Spaniards were always on the alert, and the most unceasing vigilance on their part was always exercised and was required to prevent their expulsion from the country. Although these attempts had met with but poor success, all of them resulting in the death, enslavement, or punishment of the participants, still the Indian ardor remained undampened, although it appeared for a time that their spirit was broken. Each succeeding effort brought increased wisdom and cunning, and experience purchased by defeat.

Finally the oppression of the Spaniards reached such a height that the Indians resolved to bear it no longer, and it was determined, by a united and mighty effort to rid themselves of the oppressors forever. This led to the revolution of 1680, which resulted in the expulsion of the Spaniard, and independence on the part of the natives, although for upward of ten years the government spared no effort to reconquer the country.

Although the contemplated rebellion during the administration of Governor Concha had resulted in defeat, still the Indians continued the formation of new conspiracies, always discussed in their kivas. These efforts were advocated by some and opposed by others. Everywhere the Spaniard was regarded as a tyrant. The fetters which had been forged seemed to be tightly riveted. The native was required to render implicit obedience [363] and to pay heavy

---

[363] Bancroft, H. H., *History of Arizona and New Mexico*, pp. 174-5: ''Their complaints, however, in this direction are not known definitely. The Spaniards

VERDADERA
RELACION, DE LA GRAN
DIOSA CONVERSION QVE HA AVIDO EN EL
Nuevo Mexico. Embiada por el Padre Fray Eſtevan de Perea, Cuſtodio
de las Provincias del Nuevo Mexico, al muy Reverendo P. Fr. Franciſco
de Apodaca, Comiſſario General de toda la Nueva Eſpaña, de la
Orden de S. Franciſco, dandole cuenta del eſtado de aquellas
cóverſiones, y en particular de lo ſucedido en el deſpacho
que ſe hizo para aquellas partes.

¶ Con licencia del Señor Proviſor, y del ſeñor Alcalde. Don Alonſo de Bolaños.
Impreſſo en Sevilla, por Luys Eſtupiñan, en la Calle delas Palmas. Año de 1632.

Alieron deſta Ciudad de Mexico, a quatro de
Setiembre de 1628. años, doze ſoldados, diez y
nueve Sacerdotes, y dos Legos, Religioſos de
S. Franciſco, en compañia del P. Fr. Eſtevan de
Perea Cuſtodio, embiados de la Religioſiſsi-
ma Provincia del Santo Evangelio, con la li-
moſna, y expenſa de ſu Mageſtad, que có Ca-
tholico pecho, ſiédo ſu Ceptro como el Cadu-
ceo de Mercurio, vara vigilante tachonada de
ojos, para la conſervacion deſtas converſiones, en cuya defenſa gaſta la
mayor parte de ſus Reales haberes: vara al fin de la paz, y juſticia,
Con los ya referidos Religioſos fuerō otros nueve a coſta de la dicha
Provincia, todos con gallardo aliento, y eſpiritu diſpueſto a todo trance
de trabajos, y peligros, oprobrios, y afretas, por dar a conocer predicādo
el nombre de Ieſu Chriſto. Con toda alegria, y conformidad, caminarō
haſta el Valle de S. Bartholome, ſin ofrecerſe coſa particular. Aqui ſe re-
freſco la gente có algunos alivios para el deſavio con ḡ llegaron: y no lo
fue pequeño en eſta ocaſió, huyrſe de la manada treinta mulas à las ye-
guas cimarronas, ḡ con muchas diligencias ḡ ſe hizieren, no parecieron
las quinze. Aqui por ſer la vltima poblaciō, y neceſsitar de baſtimentos
para 150 leguas de deſpoblado, ḡ reſtā haſta el primer pueblo del nuevo
Mexico,

Fac-simile of Title Page of *Narrative* by Fr. Estevan de Perea,
Custodio of New Mexico, Order of St. Francis, 1632

From copy belonging to Mr. F. W. Hodge, Washington, D. C.

tribute in the products of their labor and personal service. The first attempt to unite all the pueblos in a common league against the Spaniards was made by the Taos Indians. Their method of communicating intelligence to their brethren was simple but effective. They obtained two deer-skins upon which they made drawings representing the manner of the proposed conspiracy, and its object. These skins were sent to all the pueblos, with an invitation to join in the attempt which would be made. The Moqui pueblos refused to join in the revolt and for this reason it was abandoned for the time being.

The second attempt to free themselves from the yoke of the invaders was inaugurated by Popé, a native of great ability and one who exercised a great influence among the Indians. He traveled over the country in every direction, picturing the wrongs they were suffering, and arousing a spirit of hatred against the friars and the Spaniards.

THE PUEBLO LEADERS, POPÉ, CATITI, TUPATU, AND JACA

---

in their later gathering of testimony ignored this element of secular oppression, if, as can hardly be doubted, it existed, and represented the revolt to be founded exclusively, as it was indeed largely, on religious grounds. The New Mexicans seem to have been more strongly attached than most American tribes to their aboriginal faith, and they had secretly continued so far as possible the practice of the old forms of worship. The friars had worked zealously to stamp out every vestige of the native rites; and the authorities had enforced the strictest compliance with Christian regulations, not hesitating to punish the slightest neglect, unbelief, relapse into paganism, so-called witchcraft, or chafing under missionary rule, with flogging, imprisonment, slavery, or even death. During the past thirty years large numbers of natives had been hanged for alleged sorcery, or communion with the devil, though generally accused also of projected rebellion or plotting with the Apaches. The influence of the native old men, or priests — sorcerers, the Spaniards called them — was still potent; the very superiority of the pueblo organization gave the patriotic conspirators an advantage; past failures had taught caution; and so skilfully was the movement managed that the premature outbreak a few days before the time agreed upon was hardly less successful and deadly than would have been the revolt as planned.''

Upon the return of the Spaniards everything was done that was possible to ascertain the causes which brought about the rebellion. Depositions of natives were taken during the ensuing fifteen years, all of which are recorded. The evidence shows a general agreement as to these causes, whether it comes from secular or ecclesiastical sources. The friars do not seem to have made any charges against the governor and his officers; everyone attributed the revolt to demoniac influences brought to bear upon a superstitious and idolatrous people. Vetancurt, *Cronica*, 103-4, *ibid*, *Menologio*, 119, says the revolt was prophesied six years in advance by a girl who had been miraculously raised from the dead, who said it was to be due to lack of respect for the friars. All suits against the friars were then dropped, but it was too late. A friar abroad also foretold the coming storm.

Popé was a San Juan Indian, but made the pueblo of Taos the center of his operations. He told the natives that their Great Father and Chief of all the Pueblos, he who had been their father since the flood, had commissioned him to order his countrymen to rebel against the invader and drive him from the land, so that they could live as their forefathers had done, free and independent. In order to wield a greater influence with them, he made them believe that this undertaking was the result of supernatural agencies, and that he held intercourse with the devil, who was lending every assistance possible in the work. Popé said that one day, while down in the kiva of Taos, there appeared unto him three figures of Indians who were always present there. They were named Caidit, Tilim, and Tlesime, who sent forth fire from every extremity of the body; they were messengers from the infernal regions; he had talked with them, had received their counsel, and he had been advised to unite all the Indians in a common league against the Spaniards. He had been directed to make a rope of the palmilla leaf, and tie in it the number of knots to represent the number of days before the uprising was to occur; that he must send this rope to all the pueblos in the kingdom, when each one should signify its approval of and union with the conspiracy by untying one of the knots. Popé, as he had been directed, caused the palmilla-leaf rope to be carried from pueblo to pueblo, by the fleetest young men, with an invitation to all to join in the enterprise, and threatening with death those who refused. Absolute secrecy was enjoined upon all. The rope was carried to every pueblo except the Piros.[364] These were not invited by Popé to participate in the rebellion. In this simple manner notice was given all over the province of what was to occur, and the time when it was to take place. The date fixed was the 13th of August, 1680.[365]

[364] *Interrogatorios de varios Indios,* 1681, fol. 125: "Que (Popé) cogio un mecate de palmilla, y marando en el unos nudos, que significaban los dias que faltaban, para la egecucion de la traicion, lo despachó por todos los pueblos hasta el de Isleta sin que quedase en todo el reyno, mas que el de la nacion de los Piros."

[365] Bancroft, H. H., *History of Arizona and New Mexico,* note p. 176, says: "Escalante, in print, makes the date the 18th, but my Ms. copy has it 13th, as do Gregg, Davis, and Miller, and some of the original correspondence makes it August 10th, the plot being revealed on the 8th. Otermin's narrative begins abruptly with the 10th and says nothing of preceding revelations. The knotted cord is mentioned by the original authorities. Davis's explanation that the

Popé was not alone in his efforts to arouse the Indians to a proper sense of the wrongs with which they were being inflicted. He was the leading spirit, but he had some very active co-laborers. These were Catiti, a half-breed Queres Indian, Tacu or Tu-pa-tú [366] of San Juan, Jaca of the Taos pueblo, and one from San Ildefonso, whose name was Francisco. Some of these men had cause of personal revenge, and all burned with a desire to rid themselves of the system of tyranny which had been their portion for nearly a hundred years. They had been whipped and imprisoned, enslaved and punished because they would not bow down and worship the unknown God of the invader, and they thirsted for vengeance.

Everything was conducted with great secrecy and every precaution taken to prevent the Spaniards knowing anything of their plans. A constant watch was kept upon those who were thought likely to divulge the plot, and no woman was let into the confidence of the conspirators. Popé's own son-in-law, Nicolas Bua, governor of the pueblo of San Juan, fell under suspicion, and, for fear he might inform the Spanish authorities at Santa Fé, he put him to death [367] with his own hands.

The Indians in south Santa Fé county, at San Lazaro and San Cristobal, revealed Popé's plot to Fr. Bernal, the custodio. Fr.

---

knots represented days before the rising, and that each pueblo consenting untied one knot, is not very clear.''

[366] Catiti belonged to the pueblo of Santo Domingo. Davis says that the Indians of San Juan were not hostile in the rebellion of 1680, and for that reason were thereafter known as ''de los Caballeros.'' This is a mistake; they were hostile; they were the most bitter and cruel of all; they also participated in the risings of 1694 and 1696.

[367] The best authority on the rebellion of 1680, is, of course, Otermin. His relation is cited as *Extractos de Doc. Hist. N. Mex., sacados de los autos existentes en el oficio del Supremo gobierno de esta corte, que sobre el Levantamiento del año de 1680 formó Don Antonio de Otermin, gobernador y capitan general del mismo reino.* This is found in *N. Mex. Doc. Hist.*, Ms., 1153-1728. This is a record of the movements of Otermin from August 10, 1680, to the spring of 1682. It is very voluminous. There is also a report by the fiscal in Mexico, which is but a résumé of the Otermin relation. In the same collection of *N. Mex. Docs.*, Ms., 514-81, are several important letters written at El Paso, in the months of August to December, 1680, by the Franciscan friars. In Vetancurt, *Cronica*, 94-114, and in his *Menologio*, the standard chronicle of the Franciscan provincia del Santo Evangelio, published in 1697, but written about 1691, before the re-conquest, there is much valuable information about the missions just prior to the revolt, and as to the friars who were murdered by the Indians. Escalante, *Carta*, 116 et seq., is also one of the best authorities on the subject, the author having searched the archives by order of his superior in 1778, and thus consulted, doubtless, much missionary correspondence in addition to the relation by Otermin. Davis, W. W. H., *The Spanish Conquest*

358 LEADING FACTS OF NEW MEXICAN HISTORY

Fernando de Velasco of Pecos also received a confession of the plot from one of his converts.[368] The Spanish alcalde at Taos sent word to Otermin at Santa Fé of the designs of the Indians and the gov-

of *New Mexico*, 287-335, gives a very satisfactory narrative, taken from a copy of Otermin's *Extractos* found at Santa Fé.
Other authorities are:
Niel, *Apuntes*, 103 et seq.
Villagutierre, *Hist. Conq. Itza.*, 204-9.
Davila, *Mem. Hist.*, pt. ii, 1-2.
Cavo, *Tres Siglos*, ii, 57-60.
Villaseñor, *Teatro*, ii, 419.
Mange, *Hist. Primeria*, 227-8.
Arch. N. Mex., 129.
Arlegui, *Cron. Zach.*, 249-50.
Davis, *El Gringo*, 75-80.
Prince, *Hist. Sketches*, 190-205.
Historical Society of New Mexico, *The Franciscan Martyrs of 1680*, bul. number 7. This is the funeral oration over the twenty-one Franciscan missionaries, killed by the Pueblo Indians, and was preached by Doctor Ysidro Sariñana y Cuenca, March 20, 1681. The list which it contains of those Christian martyrs is undoubtedly correct, as it comes from their brethren of the Order of St. Francis; and the statements of the sermon set at rest any doubts that existed as to the cause of the uprising, and show that it was principally religious. The memorial service was held in the cathedral of the City of Mexico in the presence of the viceroy of New Spain and other high officials. The sermon was published during the same year, with a preliminary address to the king by Francisco de Ayeta, Franciscan visitador of the custodia of New Mexico, and other documents of an introductory character.

[368] Bandelier, A. F., *Final Report*, p. 101 et seq., says: "When the Indian outbreak took place on the 10th of August, 1680, the Father Custodian of New Mexico, Fray Juan Bernal, resided at Galisteo, and he was one of the first priests killed by the Indians. With him perished Fray Juan Domingo de Vera; and in sight of the pueblo the Indians murdered Fray Manuel Tinoco, the priest of San Marcos, and Fray Fernando de Velasco, the missionary of Pecos. Both were coming to Galisteo from opposite directions to inform their superior of the designs of the natives. Several Spaniards also suffered death; as Galisteo was an 'Alcaldia Mayor,' of one of the several judicial districts into which New Mexico was divided, and although strictly an Indian pueblo, the lieutenant of the 'Alcalde Mayor,' Juan de Leyba, resided there with his family and a few other Spanish colonists.'' These were all killed. See *Diario del Sitio*, fol. 22, where we find: "El Teniente de Alcalde Mayor Juan de Leiba, el capitan José Nieto, Nicolas de Levba, y á todas las mugeres, y niños de sus familias.'' Details of this massacre are to be found in the *Diario de la Retirada*, fol. 33.

Otermin says: "Que se han alzado las Indios Tanos, y Pecos, Cienega y San Marcos, los cuales se dice haber muerto al R. P. Custodio F. Huan Bernal, y á los Padres predicadores Fr. Fernando de Velasco, Fr. Manuel Tinoco, y Fr. Domingo de Vera con el Teniente de Alcalde Mayor Juan de Leyva.''

In the *Diario de la Retirada*, fol. 323, it appears from the declaration of a Tanos Indian who was captured near San Marcos during the retreat to El Paso, that: "Hizo que habian muerto en el dicho pueblo de Galisteo á los padres al Padre Custodio, al Pe. Fr. Domingo de Vera, y en el campo á las vista del pueblo á los Padres Fr. Manuel Tinoco, ministros guardianes de Pecos, y S. Marcos.''

That Fr. Velasco had been warned by one of the Pecos Indians, who offered to save his life, is told as follows by the Custodian Fr. Salvador de San Antonio,

PUEBLO REBELLION AND INDEPENDENCE 359

ernor arrested two Indians from the nearby pueblo of Tesuque, who had been sent by the Tehuas to advise with the Tanos and Queres. Immediately upon receipt of the news from Taos Governor

and the other priests of New Mexico, *Protesta á Don Diego de Vargas*, December 18, 1693: "Dijo á su ministro el Padre Fray Fernando de Velasco; padre la gente se alza para matar á todos los Españoles, y religiosos; y asi, mira á donde quieres irte, que yo te daré mozetones para librarte, como de hecho lo hizo." This Indian who warned and attempted to save the priest was Juan Gé, afterwards Gobernador of Pecos in 1694, and murdered by the Taos Indians for his fidelity to the Spaniards. It seems that Fr. Velasco fled to Galisteo right into the jaws of death.

Vetancurt, in his *Cronica*, p. 323, says that there was a handsome temple at Galisteo at the time of the revolt.

Galisteo pueblo was a very important place at this time (1680). There were over one thousand native inhabitants. When the Spaniards had been expelled the inhabitants removed to Santa Fé, and were in turn driven out by De Vargas at the time of the re-conquest. In 1706 Governor Cubero established the pueblo again and gave it the name Nuestra Señora de los Remedios de Galisteo. It remained a very considerable Indian village until the latter part of the eighteenth century, when the Tanos, decimated by the hostilities of the Comanches and by small pox, removed to Santo Domingo, where their descendants still live, preserving the language of their ancestors and in part their tribal autonomy.

The ruins of the pueblo of Galisteo are a lot of low, red mounds, with walls protruding here and there. The site of the church and convent has not been determined upon, but undoubtedly they were outside the pueblo proper. It is possible that the church was built as early as 1617.

Inasmuch as the Indians of San Lazaro and San Cristobal were among the very first to carry fire, sword and death to the friars and Spaniards, a description of the ruins of these two pueblos, fast completely disappearing, will not be out of place here.

The Indian name for San Cristobal was Yam-p'ham-ba. The pueblo was east of Galisteo, on the borders of the basin in a very picturesque valley, surrounded with woods and having permanent water supply. At the time of the outbreak in 1680, it was a *visita* dependent upon the church at Galisteo, and in 1680 it had eight hundred inhabitants, according to Vetancurt. When the Spaniards had been driven out, the Indians of San Cristobal settled in the vicinity of San Juan de los Caballeros, south of the present pueblo of that name. The cause for their going to that locality is believed to have been the active hostility of the Pecos Indians, who at that time were a powerful and warlike nation. Escalante, in his *Carta al Padre Morfi*, par. 7, says: "Los Queres, Taos y Pecos, peleaban contra los Tehuas y Tanos." And in the *Relacion Anonima*, p. 127, it appears that: "Los Tanos, que cuando de sublevaron vivian en San Cristobal y en San Lazaro, dos pueblos situados en la parte austral de la villa de Santa Fé despues por las hostilidades de los Apaches y de Pecos y Queres se trasladaron y fundaron con los mismos nombres dos pueblos, tres leguas largas de San Juan."

Of those who went to the neighborhood of San Juan, most of their descendants are now among the Moquis.

The pueblo of San Cristobal was on one side of an arroyo which still bears that name. On the other side of this arroyo are also some ruins. The pueblo proper was built of stone, and the walls were about a foot in thickness, many of which are still standing. The church at San Cristobal was only a chapel, and some years since a part of the walls was still standing. The pueblo re-

Otermin despatched messengers in all directions warning the friars and settlers to flee to Isleta, while those living north were to come either to Santa Fé or to Santa Cruz de la Cañada. The Indian leaders having ascertained that their plans were known to the Spanish authorities immediately gave orders for prompt action, and by the orders of Popé the Taos, Picuriés, and Tehuas attacked the missions and farms of the northern pueblos before sunrise on the 10th of August, "Llevandolo todo á sangre y fuego."

On the 10th of August the Ensign Lucero and a soldier arrived at Santa Fé, advising the governor of the revolt of the Tehuas, that the alcalde mayor had collected the people at La Cañada de Santa Cruz, and that the Indians had gathered in force at the Santa Clara pueblo, across the Rio Grande. Immediately Otermin sent out Captain Francisco Gomez to reconnoitre, and on the 12th he returned confirming all the reports that had come in. Upon his return, all of those who had gathered at La Cañada were ordered to come to the capital, where, according to Escalante, they arrived in safety. Native scouts were sent to all parts, an order was sent to Lieutenant-General Alonso Garcia to send aid to the capital forth-

ceived its name from Castaño de Sosa, who visited it when he made his entrada. —*Memoria del Descubrimiento*, p. 247 et seq.

The pueblo of San Lazaro lies six miles west of Galisteo on the eastern slope of the Sierra del Real de Dolores, and on the banks of an arroyo called El Chorro. The Indian name of this pueblo was I-pe-ré. Its inhabitants were Tanos and it was abandoned after the revolt. The buildings at San Lazaro are about the same as those of San Cristobal and traces of the stone walls may yet be seen. It was built of stone and was not so large as either Galisteo or San Cristobal. The houses were evidently so built as partly to surround a sort of enclosure also built of stone; the latter was in a sort of depression, and inside are two sunken areas of small size, which may have been kivas. Bandelier does not think that these were kivas; he thinks that, possibly, inasmuch as these Indians were a pastoral people, and had flocks of sheep, they were used to herd these animals. If this is so the enclosures were built after Castaño de Sosa had visited them, because at that time they had no sheep. In the area occupied by these three pueblos there were living and subsisting off the products of the soil and their flocks not less than four thousand Indians.

There is not very much cultivable ground in the neighborhood of either of the three pueblos, but along the Galisteo river there is considerable irrigable land. The pueblos were not placed in very good position to resist attack from marauding tribes, although there seem to be traces of a double stone wall connecting several of the buildings of the pueblos. From the amount of stone now lying around the ruins it is safe to say that the pueblos were not over two stories in height. The ruin on the south bank of the Arroyo San Cristobal indicates that it belonged to the older class of pueblo structures, i. e., a compact, one-story building of many rooms. The chapel at San Cristobal was a structure about fifty by twenty-five feet; there are indications also that there were buildings attached to the chapel on the south.

The Pueblo of Cochití

PUEBLO REBELLION AND INDEPENDENCE 361

with, and the governor took immediate steps for the defense of his capital.

The Indians had resolved upon the utter destruction of the Spaniards. From the pueblo of San Felipe south, all were warned in time to escape, but in all the missions of the north, east and west, only the friar at Cochití, those at Santa Fé, and one in the province of Zuñi, survived the revolt. The number slain was over four hundred, including 21 [369] missionaries and 73 men capable of bearing arms. Those who escaped numbered 1,950, including eleven friars and 155 men capable of bearing arms.

---

[369] *The Franciscan Martyrs*; bulletin no. 8, Historical Society of New Mexico, pp. 10-11-12: "That Kingdom (New Mexico) was then, as the Governor says, in his letter of September 8th of last year, 'entirely foreign in character from the event which was so soon to occur, judging from the peace and tranquillity which prevailed.' He speaks of what appeared as the outward cloak of hypocrisy. Everything seemed to be peaceful outwardly; but inwardly all was rabid passion, instigated by the devil; for, on the 10th day of August, dedicated by our Holy Mother Church to the honor of the Most Glorious Spanish Protomartyr, St. Lawrence, the fury of the nefarious sacrilegious wickedness, which had been hidden in the quiver of the heart, suddenly broke forth.

"On this day, the venerable Padre Fray Juan Bautista Pio, a native of the City of Victoria in the Province of Alaba, having gone to celebrate the holy sacrifice of the Mass at the Pueblo of Tesuque, which is a mission of the City of Santa Fé, the Capital of that Kingdom, was killed by the Indians of that very pueblo.

"This is the death which is first mentioned in the authentic accounts of the conspiracy. If confederated cruelty was wickedly pursuing innocence it is clear that there had to be a Pio as the first target of the arrows which impiety and apostasy shot against the Christian Religion.

"Passing from sacrilege to robbery, they carried away the scanty supplies which the Convento had for its own subsistence, and like the wicked in the proverb, without knowing who pursued them, they fled to the mountains. *Fugite imius nemine persequente.*—Proverbs 28:1.

"On that same morning they killed in different and distant Conventos twenty other Religious.

"In Santa Cruz de Galisteo, the Reverend Fathers Fray Juan Bernal, the actual Custodian, and Fray Domingo de Vera, natives of the most noble City of Mexico.

"At San Bartolomé de Xongopavi, the Rev. Padre Fray Joseph de Truxillo, a man of exemplary virtues, the knowledge of which induced the higher Prelates to elect him First Guardian and Prelate of the Convento of San Cosme without the walls of this city, when it was erected as a memorial, under the title of Nuestra Señora de Consolacion.

"At the Convento of Porciuncula, the Rev. Padre Fray Fernando de Velasco, who had served thirty years as a missionary in that Holy Custodia; both of these latter being natives of Cadiz.

"In that of Nambé, the Reverend Padre Fray Thomas de Torres, a native of Tepozotlan.

"In that of Ildefonso, the Reverend Padre Fray Luis de Morales, a native of Ubeda or Baeza; and in company with him, the brother Fray Antonio Sanchez de Pro, a native of this city, who from the Order of the Descalces

On the 14th day of August the scouts who had been sent out by Otermin returned and reported that five hundred Indians from the pueblo of Pecos and the eastern pueblos were approaching the city, and on the following morning these appeared in the fields near the chapel of San Miguel, across the Santa Fé river, in that part of the town which was occupied by the Tlascaltec Indians who had come from New Spain and were living at the capital. A conference between a representative of the Indians and the Spanish officers was held, but the Indian was firm in his announcement that nothing would swerve the natives from their purpose of driving the Spaniards from the country. He said they had brought with them two crosses, one red and one white, the red, a token of war, the white indicating peace, but if the Spaniards chose the latter, they must immediately leave the country. They had killed God and Santa Maria and the king must yield. Otermin sent out a substantial force to meet the Indians, and soon followed in person. All day long the battle lasted, and just as the Spanish arms seemed crowned with victory, the army of Indians from the north appeared, and the governor was obliged to retire with his troops to protect the palace, where the women and children of the capital had taken refuge. The siege of the capital city lasted five days. There were over three

passed to the Observancia, with the object of going to serve in that Holy Custodia.

"In that of San Lorenzo de Picuriés, the Reverend Padre Fray Mathias Rendon.

"In that of San Gerónimo de Taos, the Reverend Padre Fray Antonio de Mora; both the last named being citizens of the City of Los Angeles; and in the same Convento de Taos, Brother Fray Juan de la Pedrosa, a native of Mexico.

"In that of San Marcos, the Reverend Padre Fray Manuel Tinoco, a son of the Province of San Miguel in Estremadura.

"In that of Santo Domingo, the Reverend Padres Fray Francisco Antonio Lorenzana, a native of Galicia; Fray Juan de Talaban, Custodio habitual, a native of Seville, who had been a missionary almost twenty years, and Fray Joseph de Montesdoca, a native of Queretaro.

"In that of San Diego de Jemez, the Reverend Padre Fray Juan de Jesus, a native of Granada.

"In that of San Estevan of Acoma, the Reverend Padre Fray Lucas Maldonado, Difinidor actual, a native of Tribugena.

"In that of the Purisima Concepcion of Alona, the Reverend Padre Fray Juan del Val, of the Kingdom of Castile.

"In that of Aguatubi, the Reverend Padre Fray Joseph de Figueroa, a native of Mexico.

"In that of Oraibi, the Reverend Padre Fray Joseph de Espeleta, Custodio habitual, a native of Estela in the Kingdom of Navarre, who had been thirty years a missionary, and the Reverend Padre Fray Agustin de Santa Maria, a native of Pasquaro."

PUEBLO REBELLION AND INDEPENDENCE 363

thousand Pueblo warriors, who quickly took and destroyed the suburbs of the city, in fact everything but the plaza and the royal houses. The church and convent were burned and the water supply cut off. The streets entering the plaza were all barricaded. Each day the number of besiegers increased, and it was evidently the purpose of the savages to starve out the Spaniards. The condition of the garrison was now becoming desperate; the horses and other animals were dying of thirst; provisions were becoming scarce, and starvation seemed soon to be their fate. There was no hope of succor from the Spaniards in the south, and the only hope of the garrison was to cut its way through the lines of the enemy. Otermin resolved upon this course, and made his preparations accordingly. On the morning of the 21st of August he abandoned his capital, or, as the record shows, marched to the relief of Isleta. Clothing to the value of eight thousand dollars was distributed, and the governor, garrison, women, and children, and three friars, Cadeña, Duran, and Farfan, about one thousand in all, began their march on foot, each carrying his own baggage, as the horses were barely sufficient for the sick and wounded.[370]

The Indians watched the Spaniards as they left the city, holding positions on the surrounding foot-hills; they did not attempt to interfere, content to see them leave and unwilling to risk their lives against the desperate courage of the governor and his band. Otermin proceeded by way of the old pueblo of Santo Domingo, where they found the bodies of the Frailes Lorenzana, Talaban, and Montesdoca, as well as those of five other Spaniards who had been murdered; thence they proceeded to San Felipe [371] and Sandia, whose Spanish inhabitants had escaped, though all these pueblos had been sacked and destroyed.[372]

GOVERNOR OTERMIN ABANDONS SANTA FÉ

---

[370] The friars who survived, as named in a letter of P. Fr. Sierra of September 4th, were PP. José Bonilla, Francisco Gomez de la Cadeña, Andrés Duran, Francisco Farfan, Nicolas Hurtado, Diego Mendoza, Francisco Muñoz, Diego Parraga, Antonio Sierra, Tomas Tobalina, and Juan Zavaleta.

Five captains are named as having been killed: Francisco Jimenez, Agustin Carbajal, Cristobal de Anaya, José Nieto, and Andrés Gomez.

[371] No massacre of friars or Spaniards occurred at San Felipe, but a few Indians who were faithful to the Spaniards were killed. All of the men of that pueblo joined those at Santo Domingo, with a few exceptions, and joined in the

[372] Bandelier, A. F., *Final Report*, p. 189-190: The pueblo of San Felipe in 1680 was ''constructed at the foot of the mesa of Ta-mi-ta. There the first

On the 27th day of August, Otermin reached the pueblo of Isleta, but the Spaniards and garrison who had resided at this pueblo had left thirteen days before and fled to the south to Fra Cristobal.[373]

committing of the murders there. At the time there was no resident friar at San Felipe, but the missionaries for the three Queres pueblos of Cochití, Santo Domingo, and San Felipe resided at the convent of Santo Domingo. The Indians of San Felipe also took part in the frightful slaughter of Spanish colonists that occurred in the ranches between the pueblo and Algodones. See *Interrogatorio de Varios Indios*, fol. 139; also *Diario de la Retirada*, 1680, Ms., fol. 31.

When Governor Otermin and his band of refugees came down from Santa Fé by way of the pueblo of Santo Domingo, the pueblo of San Felipe was abandoned by the Indians and many of the latter appeared upon the high mesa on the west side of the Rio Grande, watching the Spaniards as they came down the valley. As soon as the Spaniards had passed by the Indians re-occupied their homes.

church of San Felipe was built by Fray Cristobal de Quiñones, who died at the pueblo in 1607, and was buried in the temple which he had founded. The Queres occupied this pueblo until after 1683.''

Vetancurt, *Cronica*, p. 315, says that previous to the revolt San Felipe had a ''Capilla de Musicos.'' It is well established, says Bandelier, that many of the Pueblo Indians knew and performed church music in the seventeenth and eighteenth centuries.

When Diego de Vargas came in 1693, he found the people of San Felipe living on top of the Black Mesa which overlooks the site of the present pueblo. A church was built on this new site of the pueblo after 1694, the ruins of which may be seen today on the brink of the mesa. The present town of San Felipe was built in the beginning of the eighteenth century, and is the fourth town of the tribe bearing the name Kat-isht-ya. Not a vestige is left of the old pueblo at the foot of Ta-mi-ta; the village, the church, and the convent, all have been entirely obliterated by floods from the Arroyo Tun-que and the Rio Grande.

[373] After leaving San Felipe and Sandia pueblos, Otermin marched ''para la estancia de Da Luisa de Trugillo,'' three leagues distant from Sandia. Opposite to it stood the hacienda of the Lieutenant-General Alonzo Garcia. ''De este parage se marchó otras quatro leguas á la hacienda de los Gomez, sin ver mas enemigos y en todo este camino que hay desde el pueblo de Zandia hasta esta estancia, se hallaron todas disiertas robadas, asi de ganados como de las cosas de casa, siendo muchas las haciendas que hay de una y otra vanda del rio.'' The hacienda del Maestro de Campo Juan Dominguez de Mendoza lay ''en la jurisdiccion que llaman Atrisco tres leguas antes del pueblo de la Alameda.''— *Diario de las Retirada*, fol. 35, and, *Ynterrogatorio de Preguntas* (Mendoza's own testimony). According to the *Testimonio de Diligencias sobre la Fundacion de Albuquerque de Santa Maria de Grado, de Pujuaque y Galisteo* (1712, Ms.) there were, before the revolt of 1680, nineteen ranchos, haciendas, etc., of Spaniards in the vicinity of where Albuquerque now stands. See also *Peticion de los Vecinos de Albuquerque al Cabildo de Santa Fé*, 1708, Ms.

At the time of the revolt the pueblo of Isleta had about two thousand inhabitants. They were Tiguas. In 1629 it was a mission and had a resident friar. Its inhabitants did not participate in the uprising, owing to the fact that the Spanish settlers took refuge here as soon as the uprising began. Their position at the pueblo, however, could not be maintained, and they proceeded

When Otermin reached the pueblo of Alamillo,[374] above Socorro, he met Garcia who was returning from Fra Cristobal, having been overtaken by the messengers sent out by the governor.

Otermin was also reënforced by a command of thirty men under the Mæstro de Campo, Pedro de Leyba, who had come with Lieutenant General Garcia from Fra Cristobal, having met him about a league south of the pueblo of Alamillo. When Otermin and Garcia met, the latter was taken to task for having left Isleta and legal proceedings were taken against him on that account, but Garcia claimed that he had acted through necessity, believing that all of the Spaniards in the north had been slain. From Alamillo all continued southward to Fra Cristobal[375] where on the 16th of

south.— *Diario de la Retirada*, fol. 43, et seq. When Governor Otermin reached Isleta he found it abandoned. In the *Diario*, fol. 35, he says: "Y otro dia prosiguio su marcha para el dicho pueblo de la Ysleta, y pasando á el lo hallo despoblado de toda la gente y naturales, y sin persona ninguna asi religiosos como vecinos."

Old Isleta, the one abandoned after 1681, stood very near the site of the present village of the name; it was located on a sort of delta or island between the bed of a mountain arroyo and the Rio Grande, and it is owing to this peculiar location that it received its name of Isleta from the Spaniards.

[374] No mention is made of Alamillo by Juan de Oñate. The pueblo was situate a few miles south of La Joya on a bluff not far from the banks of the Rio Grande. It was called "Alamillo" because of the groves of cottonwood trees in the valley near by.

Bandelier, A. F., *Final Report*, pp. 239-240, says: "Until the uprising of 1680, Alamillo had a church dedicated to St. Anne, and its population in that year amounted to three hundred." It was a Piro pueblo. Some of the Indians from this pueblo joined the Spaniards in their retreat. The Maestro de Campo Francisco Gomez, says: "Saliendose todos con la fuerza que tenian siendo la mor cantidad y mejores soldados del rno, lleuvandose consigo la jente del puo de la Ysleta, Seuiletta y Alamillo, dexando los pueblos desiertos y despoblados."

[375] Before leaving Fra Cristobal for the north to meet Governor Otermin, Lieutenant-General Garcia wrote a letter to Padre Fr. Ayeta, then at El Paso, notifying him that he had received news from Governor Otermin. Padre Fr. Sierra also wrote a letter on the same date to Fr. Ayeta giving him the names of the padres who had been murdered and the names of those surviving.

Captain Sebastian Herrera and Fernando Chaves had been north to the country of the Utes, and returning were at Taos when the outbreak occurred; they escaped and reached the capital while the siege was in progress and proceeded south, joining Garcia at Isleta.

On the 31st day of August Padre Fr. Ayeta wrote to the viceroy that he had heard of the revolt and supposed that Governor Otermin and all the Spaniards in the north were dead. In this letter he states that the Maestro de Campo, Pedro de Leyba, had started north with twenty-seven men and supplies: thinks that a stand should be made at El Paso or the entire northern country would be lost to the government, and urges that if Otermin be killed Leyba succeed him; states also that twenty-seven friars had been killed. Later on, when the friar had received more authentic informaton, on September 11th,

September a council was held and it was determined not to return
to Santa Fé but to proceed south to San Lorenzo, about six miles

he again wrote to the viceroy, saying that relief and succor had reached Otermin; in this letter he gives the names and short biographies of the murdered friars.

Otermin, *Extractos*, etc. 1183-4: On the 22nd day of September the governor was able to cross the Rio Grande, having been prevented until that time by a great flood.

N. Mex. Docs., Ms., 541-58: Fr. Ayeta, writing to the comisario-general on December 20th, relates that at that time the army was encamped in three divisions on the Rio Grande; first, the governor, cabildo and five frailes at San Lorenzo; second, the camp of San Pedro de Alcantara with four friars, and third, the camp of Sacramento, under Fr. Alvaro Zavaleta as prelate. He states that the remainder of the friars are at the convent of Guadalupe, with Fr. Hurtado as custodio.

Bancroft, H. H., *History of Arizona and New Mexico*, note p. 182, has assembled a number of the legendary tales and traditions relative to the murder of the friars, none of which stories is mentioned by Escalante, and as to which I have found nothing in the testimony taken subsequent to the revolt, but these traditions may possibly have some foundation in fact, notwithstanding there is no documentary proof of the alleged occurrences. He says that it is related that the friar Jesus Morador of Jemez was taken from bed, bound naked on the back of a hog, and thus with blows and yells paraded through the pueblo, being afterwards himself ridden and spurred until death relieved his torture. Gregg in his *Commerce of the Prairies*, tells the same tale, but the padre belonged to the convento of Cia.

Now the truth of the killing of the friar at Jemez is told by Vetancurt in his *Cronica*, p. 319. The friars at Jemez were Fr. Juan de Jesus and Fr. Francisco Muñoz. The former was probably one of the very first to meet death. He was killed at Ginseua or San Diego de Jemez, very close to the Hot Springs, and was buried close to the wall of a kiva in the first square of the pueblo. The other missionary, Fr. Francisco Muñoz, with the Alcalde Mayor, Luis Granillo, and three soldiers, succeeded in escaping in the direction of Cia, hotly pursued by the savages. They were rescued by the Lieutenant-General Alonzo Garcia. Vetancurt says: ''Aqui, con sentimiento de muchos del pueblo que defendian á su ministro, que veneraban por padre y lo procuraron defender, sacaron á la plaza al reverendo Padre Fray Juan de Jesus . . . hincado de rodillas, con actos de amor de Dios, esperaba su santa voluntad con un Cristo en la mano, en interim que altercaban en su defensa; cuando uno de los que asistian, con una espada le paso los pechos.''

The remains of Fr. Juan de Jesus were exhumed by Diego de Vargas on the 8th of August, 1694. They were found in the first square of the pueblo close to a kiva, and showed that the body had been pierced by an arrow. The shaft of the arrow was found with the skeleton.—*Certificazion de los Huezos del Venerable Fray Juan de Jesus*, August 11, 1694, Ms. ''Entrando en la primera plaza donde se hallaba la estufa, que senalan á un lado de ella los dichos Indio é India, se halla enterado dicho cuerpo . . . se hallo al levantarlo por las espaldas y parte del espinazo, tener una punta de jara del tamaño de poco mas de un jeme, cuyo palo estaba al parecer en su mero color del que usan y traen los Indios para herir y matar, de dicho genero de flechas.''

The alcalde mayor, Luis Granillo, tells in *Diario de la Retirada*, fol. 50, how he and the three soldiers escaped and how they were rescued by the lieutenant-general Alonzo Garcia. The last named also states (fol. 42) that the Jemez Indians pursued the fugitives as far as the pueblo of Cia, and at folio 39 he says that he met them ''en el campo como una legua del pueblo.''

below the present town of Las Cruces, which place the refugees reached about the end of the month and where they encamped.

Here the Spaniards passed the winter, enduring great privations and suffering. Rude huts were built, with thatched roofs, the women of the several camps mixing the mud and plastering the walls. Most of the material was carried on the backs of the men, the governor himself and the friars assisting in this class of labor. Fr. Ayeta supplied them with ten beeves and as many fanegas of corn daily, but during a portion of the time the refugees were entirely destitute of provisions and lived on wild herbs, mesquite beans, and mescal. Many of them left for the south, going to Casas Grandes, Viscaya, and Sonora, looking for sustenance and quarters in which to live. The governor of the town of Parral issued a circular calling upon the inhabitants to send them supplies, but only a small amount was ever received. In the month of December, later than the 20th, Fr. Ayeta left for the City of Mexico, carrying with him a full report of the misfortunes which had befallen the people and also a petition for their relief. His mission was entirely successful. The viceroy immediately took steps for the relief of the refugees and also ordered that preparations be made for the re-conquest of the province.

Fr. Francisco Ayeta [376] came back early in 1681, still in charge of the interests of the vice-royalty and bringing with him abundant supplies, ammunition, and soldiers. It

FR. FRANCISCO AYETA RETURNS
FROM THE CITY OF MEXICO
WITH REËNFORCEMENTS

was at this time, the spring of 1682, that the present city of El Paso was founded, not the American city of that name, in the state of Texas, but the Mexican city known as Ciudad Juarez,[377] the name of which town was El Paso del Norte until a few years ago, when it was

[376] Otermin, *Extractos*, Ms., 1185-1205. In this is found a record of all that Fr. Francisco Ayeta did; the amount of money he had spent and the amount which had been taken from the king's treasury. Ayeta had an appointment as procurador-general of New Spain, and was ordered to the mother country; but the audiencia, prior to his leaving the city, in the spring of 1681, authorized him to proceed with his affairs in New Mexico.

[377] Several historians have thought and stated that El Paso was already a city or town at the time of the uprising of the pueblos, but this is a mistake. The convento of Guadalupe, which was in the vicinity of the ford of the Rio Grande, crossed by Oñate in 1598, was founded by Fray Garcia de Zuñiga in the year 1659. See ·*Auto de Fundacion de la Mision de Nuestra Señora de Guadalupe*, etc., Ms., fol. 13.

re-named for the great patriot of our sister republic. The place thus established became a sort of presidio and supply station for the re-conquest of New Mexico and the protection of its inhabitants.

The Indians did not pursue the Spaniards as far south as San Marcial, although some authors say they did. The pursuit was soon relinquished, and the great majority of the Indians went to Santa Fé, possession of which they immediately took, finishing the work of pillage and destruction which had been commenced during the siege. The churches and convent were burned, and while the fires were burning the Indians danced around the burning piles with the wildest demonstration of delight, crying aloud that the Christian God and Mary the Mother of the Spaniards were no more and that the God of the Indians alone lived. Dressing themselves in the vestments of the friars they rode around the town on horseback, crying aloud with joy. They established the four cardinal points for their visible church, erected stone enclosures in the public plaza around which they danced the *cachina* and made offerrings of flour, feathers, and the seed of the maguey plant, corn, tobacco, and other articles in order to propitiate the pagan deities. The Indians enjoined their children to observe these rites in the future. These ceremonies having been concluded, they proceeded to the Rio Santa Fé where they bathed, scrubbing themselves with amole that they might be cleansed of the Christian baptism which had been administered by the Spanish friars. The caciques ordered that the names of Jesus and Mary should not be mentioned in the pueblos; that every one should drop his baptismal name and that all should cast aside the wives who had been given them in marriage and take others suitable to their fancy. The kivas were ordered opened in place of the destroyed churches and the *cachina* dance was restored with all its forms and ceremonies. They were forbidden to speak the Spanish language.

PUEBLO INDEPENDENCE

The Indians, through their leaders, now began to take measures to unite in common league against the return of the Spaniards. They even made overtures to the wild tribes, and agreed to live and intermarry with the Apaches in return for assistance in keeping out the Spaniard. Popé made a tour throughout the entire country to see that everything was put in a proper state of defense

Residence of the Governor of the Pueblo of Tesuque

PUEBLO REBELLION AND INDEPENDENCE   369

to resist any attempt upon the part of the Christians to return. At every pueblo he saw to it that his decrees were enforced. On his tour, dressed in full Indian costume, he wore a bull's horn on his forehead. Everywhere he was received with great honor, and he invariably exacted the same attention and courtesies that had formerly been the custom when the governor and custodio visited the several pueblos. He not only threatened vengeance of the pagan gods on all who refused to obey his mandates, but, upon the slightest pretext, proceeded to execute that vengeance, often inflicting the death penalty. His rule became very oppressive. The most beautiful women he took for himself and his captains; excessive tribute was imposed for the support of his government. Jaca, Tacu, and Catiti usually accompanied him in his official inspections. Upon the occasion of his visit to the pueblo of Cia he rode upon a black mule; he made the inhabitants a speech, saying that in consequence of having expelled the Spaniards he had come to accompany them in the chase; that they would kill many deer, rabbits, and all other animals; they would have good crops of corn, pumpkins, and large bolls of cotton; that they need have no fear of the Spaniards as he had thrown up intrenchments on the three roads, and built strong walls that reached from the earth to the heavens, and if they should enter by any other road he would surround them with darkness, and take them without arms and put them to death. For some cause, not explained to the Indians by these pagan leaders, their prophecies failed of realization. Civil wars developed; there was an unprecedented drought; their deities did not respond when appealed to; the wild tribes were no longer friendly, and, taking advantage of the situation, began to raid and murder. Tribes became scattered, pueblos were abandoned, and others moved to different sites. Their lot was more barbarous than before the advent of the Spaniards. The Queres, Taos, and Pecos Indians waged bitter war upon the Tanos and the Tehuas. Popé was deposed by the Tanos and Tu-pa-tú was elected in his place. He continued in power until 1688 when Popé was again elected, but he soon died and Tu-pa-tú again was named as ruler.[378]

---

[378] Davis, W. W. H., *The Spanish Conquest of New Mexico*, p. 306, says: "Upon the arrival of Catiti at Santo Domingo he caused preparations to be made for the celebration of the *cachina* dance. It is related that the idols were brought out and the Indians assembled waiting for the ceremonies to begin,

Governor Otermin remained in camp at San Lorenzo for several months waiting for orders to undertake a re-conquest of the country
he had been forced [379] to abandon, and it was not
THE ENTRADA OF until November 5th, 1681, that his second entrada
OTERMIN IN 1681 was begun. It is recorded that there was much opposition to this attempt on his part, there being two parties among the soldiers, officers, colonists, and even the friars. Otermin experienced great difficulty in making proper preparations

when Catiti burst with a report like the sound of a gun, and was immediately carried off by the devil. Tu-pa-tú was also disposed of in the same manner.

The Yutas, as soon as they learned of the misfortunes of the Spaniards, waged ceaseless war upon the Jemez, Taos, and Picuriés, and especially on the Tehuas, upon whom they committed great ravages. They were also afflicted with hunger and pestilence. Niel, in his *Apuntes*, 103, 6, says that for seven years it rained ashes while for nine years no water fell, and the streams all dried up. The Tompiros were exterminated; very few Tiguas and Jemez survived; somewhat more of the Tehuas, Taos, and Pecos were left; and the Queres, protected by the walls of Santa Fé, suffered least of all. Finally the sacrifice of a virgin restored water to the bed of the Rio Grande, and thus life was saved, and their ''stubborn, insolent apostasy'' was confirmed. Niel also tells a curious story to the effect that of the Tanos, after the revolt, only half remained to quarrel with the other nations for supremacy, while the others, 4,000 men, women, and children, went away with their Spanish plunder to preserve themselves and let their cattle increase. They went via Zuñi to Moqui, and having induced that people to give them a home, gradually gained possession of the country and towns, reducing the original Moqui to complete subjection, extending their conquests far to the southwest and seating their young king, Trasquillo, on the throne at Oraibe. They brought with them many who had served the Spaniards, and learned from them all they could, instead of avoiding everything Spanish, like the other nations. Certain linguistic and other peculiarities of the different pueblos are sufficient, if not to give plausibilty to this story, at least to make it worth preserving here.

Arricivita, *Cron. Seraf.*, 199, says that the Tanos of Galisteo intrenched themselves at Santa Fé. See *ante*, this volume, p. 379. See also Bandelier, *Final Report*, Part ii, p. 90, who says, speaking of Santa Fé, the capital, that ''they [the Tehuas] also acknowledged that a Tanos village stood on the spot; but this may probably refer to the pueblo constructed after 1680 by the Tanos from Galisteo, on the ruins of the old 'palace' of Santa Fé.''

In the *Relacion Anonima*, Tercera Serie, p. 139, we find: ''Entro en el Pueblo de los Tanos y (de) Galisteo, puesto desde el alzmiento en las casas reales de dicha villa.'' Mr. Bandelier says that the *Relacion Anonima* was undoubtedly written by Fr. Escalante, who had before him the complete journal of De Vargas. The De Vargas journal, only fragments of which are now available, does not contain a description of Santa Fé as it existed in 1692 and 1693. Escalante in his letter to Padre Morfi, says: ''En Santa Fé estaban fortificados los Tanos de Galisteo;'' and there is also a description of the Tanos village at Santa Fé in the *Autos del Cabildo de Santa Fé*, Ms., 1703.

[379] Bancroft, H. H., *History of Arizona and New Mexico*, p. 186, says: ''Many believed that the opportunities for missionary work and colonization were better in the south than in the north; they had lost their property and their families or friends, and had not yet recovered from the terror of the massacre; they were in favor of utilizing the funds and forces lately received

PUEBLO REBELLION AND INDEPENDENCE 371

for this expedition, and in order to complete his outfit, he was compelled to ask assistance of the friars at El Paso. The Franciscan order supplied him with two thousand fanegas of corn, two thousand beef-cattle, besides ammunition, wagons, and other necessaries for the camp and his army. He had great trouble securing arms for the expedition. The old armor had become almost worthless and new armor was made of ox-hides. The inhabitants of the city of Santa Fé were filled with a desire to revenge themselves upon the Indians. On the 18th of September [380] they addressed a petition to Otermin requesting that their families be permitted to remain at San Lorenzo, and furnished with supplies during their absence. They set forth that the nearest point where corn could be procured was at the Casas Grandes, eighty leagues distant, where only two persons planted and that not more than two fanegas could be had there. The prayer of the petitioners was granted. A number of friars accompanied this second expedition. Otermin was the general-in-chief, Juan Dominguez de Mendoza, lieutenant-general. Francisco Javier was the military secretary, and Fr. Francisco Ayeta, the procurador-general. Another friar was Antonio Guerra. The sargentos mayores and captains were Juan Dominguez, Pedro Leiba, Nicolas Rodriguez, Juan and Diego Lucero de Godoy, Luis de Granillo, Alonso del Rio, Sebastian de Herrera, Diego Lopez Sembrano, Luis de Quintana, Pedro de Marquez, Roque de Madrid, Diego Dominguez, Ignacio and Cristoval Vaca, Felipe Romero, José Narváez, Francisco Anaya, Francisco Madrid, Antonio Marquez, Gonzalo Paredes, Salvador Olguin, Antonio Dominguez, Antonio de Avalos, Don José Chavez, and José Padilla. The armed force consisted of both infantry and cavalry; there were 146 soldiers, with 112 Indian allies, 975 horses, together with a supply train of ox-carts and pack mules.

to strengthen their position at El Paso, and of putting off the conquest to a more convenient season. Otermin himself may have been luke-warm in the cause, but if so the viceroy's instructions left him no choice. Captain Juan Dominguez de Mendoza, who had served in New Mexico from his boyhood, had retreated from Isleta with Garcia, and had succeeded the latter as lieutenant-general, was leader of the opposition, and legal proceedings had, on that account, been begun against him and others. This appears in the fiscal's report of 1682.—*N. Mex. Docs.*, Ms., 1623-1704. Most, if not all the friars, favored an experimental entrada at least, hoping that the natives, prompted to revolt and apostasy by the devil and a few sorcerers, had now seen the error of their ways, and would be eager for peace and pardon.''

[380] Davis, W. W. H., *The Spanish Conquest of New Mexico*, p. 308.

The army crossed the Rio Grande to the east side early on the morning of November 5th, and directed its course to the north. Good order was maintained on the march, the different divisions keeping in sight of each other, and about sunset a point called Estero Largo was reached, being in the vicinity of some salt marshes. Camp was made here for the night. From this camp smoke could be seen rising in different directions, being the signal fires of savages who were watching the movements of the Spaniards. The following day the army proceeded to Robledo, meeting with no opposition from the Indians. At this point began the march across the Jornada del Muerto, where for a distance of ninety miles water is not found except in small lakes, fed only by rain water. The governor now ordered a forced march of two days and one night to a point seven leagues from Fra Cristobal, the northern terminus of the Jornada. From this point all the soldiers were sent forward except a small camp guard, and the following day the army was in camp on the banks of the Rio Grande. Here the troops were paraded and the friars offered up solemn thanks to God for the safe passage of the desert. The following day the march was continued to Contadero. At this point signs of the Indians were seen, and a force of forty men and some Indians were sent out to reconnoiter. Otermin led this force in person. They crossed the river and visited the pueblo of Senecú.[381] It had the appearance of having been sacked. The church and convent were in ruins. The clappers had been taken from the bells in the church and cemetery, and the crosses in the latter and upon the plaza had been burned. In the vestry the head and crown of a crucifix and some "holy stones" were found lying upon the ground, having been desecrated by the Apaches. A small brass cannon which had been used for

---

[381] The pueblo of Senecú was better known than any of the Rio Grande pueblos. The most southerly church and convent were constructed here in 1626. Saint Anthony of Padua was made the patron of the place. So says Benavides in his *Memorial*, p. 16, and Vetancurt, in his *Cronica*, p. 309, also makes the same statement, but says it was founded in 1630.

The founders of the mission were Fr. Antonio de Arteaga, a Capuchin monk, and Fr. Garcia de Zuñiga. Benavides was an eye-witness of the events at this time as he was custodian of his order. He left New Mexico in 1628, so the mission and church must have been established before he left for Mexico. Here the grape was first introduced in New Mexico, for Vetancurt says, *Cronica*, p. 309: "Y una huerta, donde cogió uvas de sus viñas y hacia vino que repartia á los demas conventos."

the defense of the church, prior to the revolt, had been removed and thrown into the cemetery. Fr. Ayeta ordered the crosses found in the houses, the head and crown of the crucifix, and all the wooden ornaments of the altar to be collected, burnt, and the consecrated stones thrown into the river, so as to prevent their falling into the hands of the Indians. The bells were taken from the steeples and the cannon from the cemetery and placed in the wagons; this all accomplished, the pueblo was set on fire and entirely consumed. That night they re-crossed the river and joined the army at Contadero.

From the 26th day of November to the 4th of December, Otermin visited the southern group of pueblos, in addition to Senecú, those of San Pascual, Socorro, Alamillo, and Sevilleta. Every one of these pueblos had been abandoned by the inhabitants, the Piros, and all the ranches along the river had been pillaged. Everywhere were seen traces of the revolt against Christianity; the churches were burned, the images were broken, estufas had been rebuilt, showing a revival of the pagan rites of the savages, and these in turn had also been destroyed, probably by the Indians from the north or by the marauding Apaches.

Leaving the army at the pueblo of Sevilleta, Governor Otermin, with a force of sixty men, proceeded to the pueblo of Isleta, where he arrived early in the morning, and THE ARMY REACHES ISLETA seeing that the pueblo had not been abandoned, he began at once his preparations for an assault. He divided his command into four parts and began the attack simultaneously from as many points. The Indians were prepared and when they saw the Spaniards approaching, the war-cry was raised. Their resistance was feeble. The Spaniards easily secured possession of the plaza and being told by Otermin that every man would be put to death if they did not surrender at once, they laid down their arms. The pueblo contained 1,511 inhabitants, all of whom formally renewed their allegiance, and many children were offered for baptism. The Spaniards found that the church and convent had been burned and the body of the church had been used as a corral for stock. Otermin caused the entire population to assemble in the plaza, where he reprimanded them severely and gave them wholesome advice. They denied being guilty of the destruction of the buildings, but said it was owing to the commands of the leaders of the rebellion who had come with the Indians from the north who had compelled them to cast aside everything pertaining to the Christians and return to their ancient Indian customs and rites. The Indians were directed to deliver up everything which had belonged to the Christians and to the church, their dwellings being searched to see that nothing was concealed. The Spaniards found concealed the box in which the host was kept, a belt worn by the priest, five small bells used in saying mass, four candlesticks, three large bells, and a large number of other articles. The church property was delivered to Fr. Ayeta, and the remainder to the owners.

While the fight was in progress at Isleta two Indians made their escape, and it is believed that these had been sent out to notify the pueblos in all directions of the approach of the Spaniards. Otermin immediately sent out others notifying the Indians of his friendly intentions provided they would return to their allegiance to the Spanish authority.

On the 8th of December, the lieutenant-general Dominguez was despatched with seventy men to reconnoiter the pueblos in the north, and a few days afterwards the governor and the army followed up the Rio Grande, camping in sight of the pueblos of Alameda, Puara, and Sandia. All of these pueblos had been abandoned, except in each the Spaniards found large quantities of corn, all of which and the villages were burned by order of the governor.

On the 18th Dominguez returned, having visited San Felipe, Santo Domingo, and Cochití, all of which he found abandoned but no one of which did he destroy. At Cochití he met a large force of Indians who approached in battle array, but finally consented to parley. The chief professed the deepest penitence for his sins, shedding tears and promising to bring in all the Indians of these pueblos for purposes of receiving pardon and giving their allegiance. The chief did not keep his agreement, and the hostages which Dominguez held were permitted by him to depart. It afterwards developed that the penitence shown by the chief of Cochití was only a ruse to gain time so that other tribes might join the Indians at Cieneguilla for a combined attack upon the Spaniards. Otermin severely upbraided Dominguez for having failed to destroy the villages he had visited, for his failure to send reports, and for various other short-comings.

Otermin was desirous of gaining information as to the cause of the rebellion of the previous year and at once organized a tribunal for the examination of prisoners. The governor presided at this court, being assisted by Fr. Francisco Ayeta. Two soldiers, named Juan Lucero de Godoy and Juan Ruiz de Casares, who had knowledge of the Indian languages, acted as interpreters. The prisoners were brought before the tribunal but as they were heathens and could not be sworn until they had been first absolved, these rites were administered, whereupon they took the oath and gave their testimony. Among the witnesses were two half-breeds, who claimed to have been forced into the rebellion and who had voluntarily surrendered to the Spaniards. The record of the testimony taken by Otermin is very voluminous.

Governor Otermin now summoned a council of war for the purpose of determining upon the course to be pursued. Every officer in the army was requested to hand in his views in writing, and there was a great diversity of opinion. Some were in favor of advancing at all hazards, while others favored an immediate retreat. The majority favored falling back as far as Isleta, that pueblo having asked for protection. Friar Francisco Ayeta was asked to join in the council but declined, but gave his opinion at some length in writing, his advice being received with great consideration. It was his judgment that the expedition be immediately abandoned, and that the army return to San Lorenzo, inasmuch as the Indians were not disposed to make peace, and the force was entirely too small to compel them to do so. The time of year was not propitious for a campaign, as it was very cold and the men, owing to the severe exposures, were hardly able to perform their duties, and the horses and other animals were too much broken down to proceed further.

OTERMIN DECIDES TO RETURN TO EL PASO

Otermin finally resolved to fall back upon Isleta.[382] His de-

---

[382] Vetancurt, *Cronica*, p. 302, says: "En 22 de Julio, el año de 629, llegaron al convento de San Antonio de Isleta, donde estaba entonces el custodio, algunos cinquenta Xumanas á pedir religiosos que les ensenasen la ley del Evangelio."

Fray Juan de Salas is believed to have built the convent at Isleta, as ap-

parture was hastened by the arrival of a messenger bearing the information that a party of hostiles, led by the chief Tu-pa-tú, had appeared before the pueblo and threatened to burn it unless the inhabitants abandoned it immediately. Otermin at once sent the sargento-mayor Granillo, with a force of twenty men, to protect the pueblo until he should arrive with the army. Otermin marched at once and made his camp at a point opposite the pueblo on the 24th or 25th of December. At this place other witnesses were examined by Otermin and his court and evidence was soon produced showing that it was the intention of the hostiles to drive out the Spaniards if possible. Matters took a very serious turn when a large number of the inhabitants of Isleta fled and joined the hostiles under Tu-pa-tú. After this occurrence, although Otermin and Fr. Ayeta were apparently in favor of remaining, still they were not zealous in their work and every day was taken up in the taking of testimony of a sort that would lend color to the justness of the retreat which he had made up his mind to order.

On the first day of January, 1682, it was decided to march south to San Lorenzo. There was a number of Indians at Isleta still faithful and, not willing to remain to meet death at the hands of the hostiles, these accompanied the retreating army. Before leaving Otermin burned the pueblo, together with all the grain and supplies which could not be easily carried with the army.

Otermin left Isleta on the morning of the 2nd day of January, and his retreat down the river consumed nearly six weeks, as he arrived at Estero Largo, a point near El Paso, on the 11th day of February. Here the governor made out his report to the viceroy and attached to it the testimony which had been taken by him and upon which he relied for justification in ordering the retreat.[383]

pears from Vetancurt, *Cronica*, p. 311: "El convento es de claustros altos y bajos, que el venerable Padre Fray Juan de Salas edificó." This was some time about 1628. In 1643 Fr. Salas was priest at Cuaray.

Vetancurt says that the number of Indians who went south with Otermin from the pueblo of Isleta was 519. Escalante, *Carta al Padre Morfi*, par. 5, says the number was 385 and that 115 had fled during the time that Otermin had gone north on his second entrada.

[383] Bancroft, H. H., *History of Arizona and New Mexico*, pp. 190-191: "In this document he made known his plans for settlement and missionary work in the El Paso region, asked for more stringent regulations to keep the colony together and bring back fugitives of the past few years, and also for leave of absence to visit Parral for medical treatment.—Otermin, *Consulta al Virey*, II de Febrero, 1682. On the 25th of June the fiscal of the audiencia in

Ruins of the Mission at Jemez, N. M.

After Otermin's unsuccessful venture nothing seems to have been done by him looking to another entry of the country which he had lost. The Franciscan friars, however, were
EVENTS AT EL PASO — busy in the establishment of missions in
MISSIONS FOUNDED and around the region of El Paso. As a nucleus for their work they had the Indians of the Piros, Tompiros, and Tiguas nations, who had come south with Otermin and others who came later, and with these three missions were founded, Senecú, Socorro, and Isleta. The missions of Senecú and Socorro were composed of the Piros and Tompiros, and that of Isleta of Tiguas. It is believed that the rule of Otermin as governor terminated in the year of his return, for it is known that in the following year, 1683, Bartolomé de Estrada Ramirez, a "knight of the Order of Santiago," was captain-general and governor of New Mexico, but as to any of his official acts there is nothing of record that has been found.

In the month of August, 1683, Domingo Jironza Petriz de Cruzate became governor of New Mexico. He held the office for four years, became involved in some
RULE OF DON DOMINGO JIRONZA controversies with the governor of
PETRIZ DE CRUZATE Nueva Viscaya and was probably suspended from office by the viceroy. A historian of the times, and a nephew of the governor, says that Cruzate had been sent by his emperor, Carlos II, from Cadiz in 1680, as visitador of the Leaward Islands, with a force of fifty

---

Mexico made a report, in which, after a careful résumé of the entrada from the *autos*, he commented in severe terms on the acts of Dominguez de Mendoza, recommending criminal prosecution of that officer; and he also blamed Otermin for not having made a stand at Sandia or some other convenient point, since the large stores of maize destroyed in the southern pueblos and left undestroyed in the north would have sufficed to restore the horses and support the army until help or new orders could be received. The fiscal favored, however, the proposed settlement and presidio at El Paso, though the New Mexican soldiers should not be permitted to enlist in the southern presidial company; and he also approved strict measures to collect and keep together all fugitives of the colony, whether Spaniards or Indians. The governor's leave of absence was not granted."

The Indians from Isleta who accompanied Otermin south settled and established Isleta del Sur, in the present state of Texas, where there is today a pueblo of Tiguas. Northern Isleta remained vacant and in ruins until 1718, when it was repeopled with Tiguas who had returned from the Moquis, to whom the majority of the tribe had fled during the twelve years of independent pueblo domination, after the departure of Otermin in 1680.

men, holding the rank of captain, and carrying instructions to the viceroy to give him office in reward for his services in the wars against Portugal. He was made alcalde mayor of Meztitlan and soon thereafter was appointed to the governorship of New Mexico. Immediately upon his arrival at El Paso, Governor Cruzate began his preparations for entradas into the surrounding country. On the 29th day of November of 1683 he issued a formal order relative to an entrada into the country of the Jumanos and surrounding nations. Prior to this time the viceroy, in the month of September, had approved all of the governor's official acts, including the establishment of the presidio at El Paso, which contained fifty soldiers. He further ordered that the governor spare no effort, with the slightest possible expense, to regain the province of New Mexico. In the month of August, a force of fifty Spaniards, under command of Captain Roque Madrid, with one hundred Indian allies, was sent against the Apaches, with instructions to kill the men and capture the women and children. Don Pedro Ladron de Guevara is named as the military secretary of this expedition. In the month of September of the year following Cruzate issued orders for the arrest and return of all fugitives from his jurisdiction, and it is more than likely that his trouble with the governor of Nueva Viscaya grew out of this order or the acts of Cruzate's captains thereunder. If he was suspended from office, it was only for a period of less than two months, for in November of the same year, by an order of the viceroy, he was restored and maintained in his office with all its titles as held by his predecessor; while the governor of Nueva Viscaya, José de Neiva, was commanded to keep within the bounds of his own state and refrain from interfering with Cruzate in his governorship of New Mexico. It was in the month of September, 1685, also, that Juan Dominguez de Mendoza, who had been the lieutenant-general under Otermin, left El Paso for the City of Mexico, accompanied by several of the prominent officers of the garrison. These were the sargento-mayor, Juan Lucero de Godoy, Regidor Lazaro de Misquia, Baltazar Dominguez, Juan de Anaya, and the government secretary, Alfonso Rael de Aguilar. It is said that these men carried despatches from the Franciscan friars, which would indicate that there was some controversy at the time between them and the governor. On account of the desertion of Dominguez, Captain Alonzo Garcia was named as maestro de campo and lieutenant-general.

The despatches which Dominguez and his comrades carried to the City of Mexico were undoubtedly sent by the friars for the purpose of securing the removal of Cruzate from office. At any rate, shortly afterward, although he had within a few short months been restored to office by the viceroy, his suspension having come about through his difficulties with the governor of Nueva Viscaya, he was removed and Don Pedro Reneros de Posada appointed in his place. Reneros de Posada was exercising the duties of his office as early as the fall of 1686 and ruled until 1689. There is very little of record, so far as is now known, of the official acts of this governor. He made an entrada to the pueblos of the Queres, and according to one historian he was accused of inefficiency, all of which resulted in the reappointment of Cruzate.[384]

Governor Cruzate, again taking hold of the reins of government, immediately renewed the entrada and fought the Queres, with other tribes at the pueblo of Cia, killing six hundred of the Indians and capturing over seventy, who, with the exception of a very few old men who were shot in the plaza, were with the license of the king sold as slaves for a period of ten years.[385] In this battle of Cia

[384] Davis, W. W. H., *The Spanish Conquest of New Mexico*, note, p. 336. Mr. Davis makes some most remarkable statements in connection with what he says he found in the Santa Fé Archives, as appears from the note which is of sufficient importance to reproduce in full. No such information as he says he found is now in the archives nor has there been for many years, and no one of the persons who had control of them while they remained in Santa Fé, including Miller, Samuel Ellison, Bandelier, and others, ever found any paper containing the information that ''Cruzate was accompanied by Don Reneros de Posada and Juan de Oñate, a brave soldier,'' who ''said that he had made a visit to Zuñi, called the Buffalo province, during the reign of Phillip II. At the first arrival of himself and people in New Mexico, the inhabitants were much surprised, being astonshed at seeing white men, and at first believed them to be gods, and reported them as such. After the surprise had worn off, a cruel war broke out, the governor and most of the priests being killed, a few only escaping to the pueblo of El Paso. Among those who escaped was a Franciscan friar, who went to Mexico and carried with him an image of our Lady of Macana, which was preserved for a long time in the convent in that city.''

On this image of Nuestra Señora de la Macana there is a manuscript in *Papeles de Jesuitas*, no. 10, written in 1754, which informs us that in the great revolt of 1683 ('80) a chief raised his macana and cut off the head of an image of our Lady. Blood flowed from the wound; the devil hanged the impious wretch to a tree.

[385] Mange, *Hist. Pim.*, 288. On October 8, 1687, a town of the Queres (perhaps Cia) was attacked and fire set to the huts, many perishing in the

many of the Indians were burned to death in the flames which destroyed a portion of the pueblo rather than submit to captivity at the hands of the Spaniards. The following year, in 1690, Cruzate made preparations for another expedition to the north, but his plans were interrupted owing to a revolt of the Sumas, a tribe of Indians living near the presidio of El Paso, which demanded all his attention.

The success which had crowned the last martial efforts of Governor Cruzate in his conflicts with the apostate tribes was not known to his royal master until after he had named as his successor Don Diego de Vargas Zapata Lujan Ponce de Leon. When the reports from the viceroy reached the king relative to the deeds of Cruzate in the north, in July, 1691, he immediately instructed the viceroy that if De Vargas had not taken possession of the office, or if he was not ruling successfully, to give him another good office and retain Cruzate in his governorship. De Vargas, however, had already begun to discharge the duties of his office, and Cruzate, a few years later was made governor of Sonora. De Vargas was a man of decided energy and pronounced decision of character. When he arrived at El Paso, he was greatly

RECONQUEST BY DON DIEGO DE VARGAS — 1692-1700

---

flames; 10 were captured and sentenced to 10 years in the mines of Nueva Viscaya.—*Santa Fé Archives*, Ms. This was done by Reneros de Posada.

Escalante, *Carta*, 123, says that Reneros de Posada made his entrada to Cia in '88, nothing being accomplished except the taking of a few horses and cattle. In the year 1695, Reneros de Posada was alguacil mayor of the inquisition in the City of Mexico.—*Santa Fé Archives*, Ms.

There are some differences in the records as to the date of the battle of Cia, as fought by Cruzate. Davis and others give the date as 1688, and in the *Santa Fé Archives* are found papers which confirm this year. Escalante says it occurred in 1689. The viceroy reported the entrada to the king in 1690, after Vargas had been appointed governor, and the royal cedulas of July 16 and 21, 1691, express thanks and permit the enslavement of the captives but not their children or any Indian under 14 years of age.

In the *U. S. Land Office Reports of 1856*, p. 307-26, is printed a series of documents from the *Santa Fé Archives*, with translations. These are regarded as the original titles to the pueblo lands of several of the pueblo tribes. The papers are dated September 20-5, 1689. Each one consists of the formal statement under oath of Bartolomé Ojeda, one of the Indians captured at Cia, and who had taken a prominent part in the battle, to the effect that the natives of Jemez, San Juan, Picuriés, San Felipe, Pecos, Cochití, and Santo Domingo were so terrified by the event of "last year," that is, the defeat at Cia, that they would not revolt again or refuse to render allegiance. The governor then assigns the boundaries, four square leagues, measuring from the church, but sometimes by fixed landmarks.

PUEBLO REBELLION AND INDEPENDENCE 381

disappointed at the size of the army he could muster for his campaign against the Indians in the north. Three hundred armed men, including Indians, were all that he could muster, and yet he determined upon an immediate prosecution of his entrada. His plans, however, could not be carried out with the rapidity with which he had hoped, owing to the trouble with the Sumas [386] and other tribes living in the vicinity of El Paso, and it was not until the 21st day of August, 1692, that he set out for the north. Having settled the disturbances caused by the Sumas and Mansos Indians, De Vargas was very impatient to begin his march, and he set out upon his journey without waiting for the arrival of a force of fifty men from Parral, who had been ordered to his command by the viceroy. His entire force of armed men, in all probability, did not exceed two hundred, including Indian auxiliaries. The army was accompanied by the friars Francisco Corvera, Miguel Muñiz, and Cristobal Alonzo Barrosco.

De Vargas marched rapidly up the valley of the Rio Grande, passing all of the pueblos and finding nearly all of them in ruins. He stopped only for necessary rest and sleep, as he had determined to take the enemy by surprise and crush him before any defense could be made, and on the 9th of September all of the army and baggage was left at the Hacienda de Mejia with a guard of fourteen Spaniards and fifty Indians, under the command of Captain Rafael Tellez. De Vargas passed by Santo Domingo and Cochití, both of which pueblos he found abandoned, and in the early morning of the 13th of September the army appeared before Santa Fé, surrounding the town and cutting off both the water supply and all communication with the outside. The Tanos, who had come to Santa Fé from Galisteo after the evacuation by Otermin, had fortified the

---

[386] Bandelier, A. F., *Final Report*, part i, p. 87 et seq.: ''Geographically the Sumas appear to have been divided into two branches, one part of them hovering about the environs of El Paso, the other in possession of the fertile valley in which the ruins of Casas Grandes are situated.''

Ribas, *Historia de los Triumphos*, lib. vi, cap. i, p. 359, says: ''La nacion de los Batucos, caminando al Norte, tiene tambien por confinantes muchas Naciones de Gentiles amigos Cumupas, Buasdapas, Bapispes; y declinando al Oriente, á los Sumas.'' This historian wrote in 1645, and, as appears from the citation, the Sumas were then living in the northwestern part of the present state of Chihuahua.

They lived little better than the Apaches — *Estado de la Mision de San Lorenzo el Real*. The Sumas are mentioned by Benavides in his *Memorial*, p. 7, as early as 1630.

place with great strength. The inhabitants were very defiant, declaring they would perish rather than surrender, also stating that they would kill all the Spaniards together with any cowardly natives who might join them. De Vargas continued to parley and offer them full pardon, in which he was ably assisted by the friars, and before night the Tanos yielded without a blow being struck, and Santa Fé again became a loyal Spanish villa.[387]

Tu-pa-tú was the most powerful and influential of all the Indian chieftains after the death of Popé and Catiti. After the surrender of the Tanos this Indian appeared at the capital on horseback, clad in Spanish costume, and tendered his allegiance and that of the Tehuas. He informed De Vargas that the Queres, Jemez, Pecos, and Taos Indians would not recognize his authority and in all probability would offer strong resistance, but he was willing to accompany the governor on his march and would aid him in securing a peaceful surrender of the tribes named. The fifty soldiers whom the viceroy had sent from Parral had now arrived and joined De Vargas at Galisteo. The great pueblo of Pecos was abandoned by its inhabitants and although the governor endeavored to induce them to accept pardon for their past offenses, the negotiations being carried on for five days through a few who had been captured and acted as messengers, he was unable to secure their submission, and he returned to Santa Fé. On the 29th the governor started for the north, going by way of Pojoaque, Cañada de Santa Cruz, and passing by the Tanos pueblos of San Cristobal and San Lazaro, situate below the old pueblo of San Juan de los Caballeros. In his journey he also visited Tesuque, Nambé, Santa Clara, San Ildefonso, Cuyamungué, Picuriés, and finally reached the Pueblos of Taos. These ran away but were induced to return after being solicited by Tu-pa-tú. They revealed to the commander a plot which had been agreed upon by which the Spaniards were to be attacked from an ambush. These also joined the force of the governor as did also many Indians of other pueblos.

THE PUEBLOS SUBMIT WITHOUT CONFLICT

De Vargas now returned to Santa Fé, and on the 15th day of

---
[387] There is no foundation for the statement made by Davis in his *Spanish Conquest of New Mexico* that there was a great conflict, lasting all day. It is well established that there was no blood shed in the first De Vargas campaign.

PUEBLO REBELLION AND INDEPENDENCE 383

October sent a report to the viceroy that all the pueblos for thirty-six leagues had given in their submission; that the friars had baptized nearly a thousand children, and that to hold the country it would be necessary to establish permanent garrisons, and "to send less than 50 families and 100 soldiers would be like throwing a grain of salt into the sea."

In his letter to the king's representative in Mexico, De Vargas also recommended the sending of convict mechanics from Mexican jails who would serve as teachers and search for metals. The messenger bearing this report reached Mexico on the 21st of November and the following day there was a great celebration, the cathedral being illuminated by order of the viceroy.

The pueblo of Pecos sent in its allegiance two days after De Vargas had sent his report to the City of Mexico, and three days later the Indians of Cochití, San Marcos, and San Felipe were persuaded to re-occupy their pueblos. The pueblos of Santa Ana, Cia, Jemez, and Santo Domingo now surrendered, although there was a slight demonstration on the part of the Indians of Jemez.

Winter was now upon them and De Vargas, from the Hacienda de Mejia, sent all his artillery, horses which were disabled, Indian auxiliaries, ten settlers, and a party of rescued captives, to El Paso, accompanied by an escort of soldiers.[388]

On the 30th day of October, with a command of eighty-nine men, the general marched to Acoma, where he found the Indians prepared for defense of their pueblo. They did DE VARGAS MARCHES not believe that they would be pardoned for TO ACOMA AND ZUÑI the heinous offenses of which they had been guilty, and asked De Vargas to pass on to Zuñi and give them time in which to consider the matter of submission. Finally, however, the Indians yielded and De Vargas, the friars, and fifteen soldiers were admitted to the summit of the rock, where the ceremonies of submission were performed and a good many children baptized.

The commander now proceeded on his way to Zuñi, and arriving

[388] Siguenza says that these were mostly half-breeds; no Spaniards except a few women, with the children that had been born to them while in captivity, and who had been held by the rebellious Indians since 1680. According to the *Archivo N. Mex.* there were forty-three of these captives.

there, found that the inhabitants had abandoned the villages which they had lately built and retired to the summit of Thunder Mountain. While the Spaniards were at Zuñi their camp was attacked by the Apaches who drove off quite a number of the cattle, but the general was successful in his efforts to pacify the Zuñians who were restored to loyalty and the Holy Catholic faith on the 11th, about 300 children being baptized by the friars.[389] The friars were much impressed at finding that the Indians had preserved all of the sacred church vessels and all of the property of the martyred friars. This was the only pueblo that had preserved any respect for the teachings of Christianity. De Vargas left a guard at Zuñi and proceeded to the Moqui country, arriving at Aguatuvi on the nineteenth, and although the Indians had been advised by the Navajós not to trust the Spaniards, they gave in their submission on the day following. Their chief, Miguel, said that the other pueblos were hostile, but these also submitted with the exception of the pueblo of Oraibi, which was not visited by De Vargas. While here De Vargas received some alarming reports from Captain Tellez relative to raids being made by the Apaches, and he at once returned to Zuñi, from which place the entire army started for El Paso. On the way he was attacked by the Apaches, who wounded one of his men and secured some of his horses; one of the marauders was captured, baptized, and shot. On the 20th of December, De Vargas arrived at El Paso, and two days later the entire army under command of Captain Roque de Madrid. De Vargas presented to the president of the missionaries at El Paso the sacred vestments and church vessels which he had recovered at Zuñi. Thus ended the first entrada by De Vargas, the nominal submission of all the Indians having been received without the loss of a single drop of blood, except in the conflicts with the Apaches.

---

[389] The villages which the Zuñi had abandoned are now known as "Old Zuñi." This appellation is not correct. They were built between 1680 and 1692, during the absence of the Spaniards after the retreat of Otermin. The Navajós threatened to destroy their tribe and they abandoned the villages on the plain and retired to the summit of Thunder Mountain. It was here that De Vargas found them. It is known that they remained on the mesa for several years and returned to it in 1703, after having killed some Spaniards in revenge for excesses committed by them at the pueblo. They finally returned to the site of their present village in 1705. We find authority for this in Escalante, *Relacion*, p. 182.

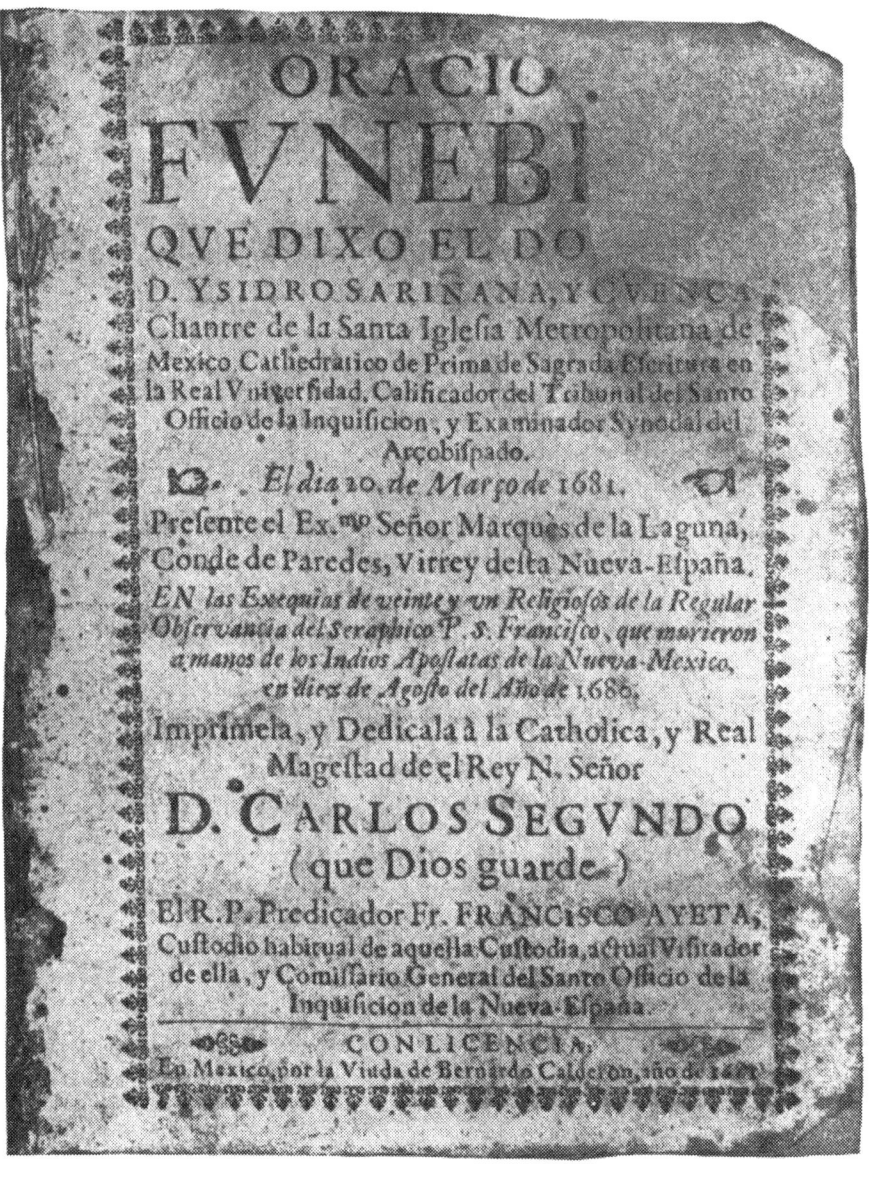

Fac-simile of Cover of Pamphlet containing funeral sermon delivered by Dr. Ysidro Sariñana y Cuenca at the City of Mexico, March 20, 1681

Original in possession of the New Mexico Historical Society

PUEBLO REBELLION AND INDEPENDENCE

The Indians of the province or kingdom of New Mexico, as has been seen, had formally submitted to the Spanish authority. De Vargas, on his return to El Paso, left no armed force or Spanish colonists at any point north of the region of El Paso. It can not be said, under these circumstances, that the authority of Spain had been firmly established, and subsequent events show this to have been the true condition of affairs after the general had retired to the presidio at El Paso. Upon receipt of the report made by De Vargas, the viceroy and his official advisers determined to supply De Vargas with the soldiers and colonists asked for by him. However, it required time to prepare for another entrada, to find the colonists and secure the soldiers and their necessary equipment. De Vargas, however, was impatient to proceed, and without waiting for the promised reënforcements, he assembled all the colonists he could induce to go with him at El Paso, about eight hundred persons in all, and with one hundred soldiers, on the 13th day of October, 1693, he set out on his march for the north. With him went seventeen friars under P. Fr. Salvador de San Antonio as custodio.[390]

ENTRADA BY DE VARGAS IN 1693

The officers of the expedition were Lieutenant-General Luis Granillo, second in command, and the colonists were under the charge and supervision of Captain Juan Paez Hurtado. Other officers were the captains Roque de Madrid, José Arias, Antonio Jorge, Lazaro de Misquia, Rafael Tellez Jiron, Juan de Dios Lucero de

---

[390] Davis, W. W. H., *The Spanish Conquest of New Mexico*, note, p. 373, says: "On the 24th day of November, 1692, by virtue of an order of the count of Galves, and the ministers of the Royal Junta, at Mexico, there was paid to Vargas the sum of $12,638.50, and on another order from the same officer, there were paid to him on the 8th of April, 1693, $29,783.62, in all $42,461.12, for the purpose of recruiting settlers for the Presidio of Santa Fé, and for their support for one year. Of this whole amount of forty-two thousand dollars and upward, it is alleged that De Vargas only expended seven thousand for the use of the emigrants; the remainder probably being spent for his private purposes.''

On the 14th day of September, according to the *Santa Fé Archives*, De Vargas published the fact that the 100 soldiers ordered by the viceroy to be enlisted for the garrison at Santa Fé should go north and that all of the original colonists who had fled from Santa Fé should go with them.

In 1698 proceedings were taken against De Vargas, and it appears that he enlisted these soldiers without expense to the royal treasury, by advancing each one $150.00, which was later deducted from their pay. It is also stated that he obtained at Zacatecas, Sombrerete, and Fresnillo 27 families

Godoy, Fernando Duran de Chavez, Adj. Gen'l Diego Varela, Adjutant Francisco de Anaya Almazan, and sergeant and secretary, Juan Ruiz. During this year, also, Alfonso Rael de Aguilar and Antonio Valverde appear as civil and military secretaries. There were over three thousand horses and mules. To each family there were given from ten to forty dollars for the purchase of necessaries on the journey. From whom these necessaries were to be purchased does not appear, nor is it apparent that coin was of any use in exchange or barter among the natives.

De Vargas pursued the same course up the river that he had taken on his previous journey. The colonists suffered greatly. Each person was allowed one pound of flour and a small amount of beef daily until they arrived at Luis Lopez, at which place the provisions were exhausted. Here it is related that they sold their arms and horses to the Indians for food. Thirty persons perished from hunger and exposure, and the march was so much retarded by the wagons — carts — carrying the effects of the colonists that the general was compelled to leave them behind to come up at leisure, while he pushed ahead with his troops. As the Spaniards passed the pueblos in the valley of the Rio Grande, they were received with coolness by the inhabitants. When the pueblo of Isleta was reached, less than a hundred miles south of the capital, De Vargas made camp and remained here for a time in order thoroughly to prepare for his march into the interior. He sent messengers to the pueblo of Cia, seeking information as to the condition of the country and such other news as might prove useful and valuable in his future operations. The messenger, upon his return, reported that the Indians at Santa Fé had been in council, had resolved to resist his advance, and had provided a great number of lances and arrows. Their plan was to make an attack upon the troops and the animals at the same time, hoping by thus dividing the attention of the Spaniards, to meet with success. The Pueblos had invited the Apaches to join them and these had agreed to do so. There was great scarcity of provisions in the country owing to the damage done to the crops by grasshoppers. He also reported that much division and dissension existed among the inhabitants of the pueblo of Cia, some being in favor of war, while others were very pronounced in their desire for peace. Being thus warned, De Vargas moved and acted with great caution.

It was made known to De Vargas that no sooner had he left the country the year before than his interpreter, one Pedro de Tapia, began telling the Indians that the moderation of De Vargas was all assumed and that it was his purpose, upon his return, when he had sufficient force to insure the execution of his demands and desires, to put to death all of the leading men who had taken part in the revolution of 1680. When the natives heard that he was approaching they feared that it was his design to carry this plan into effect.

Having made the necessary disposition of his forces to ward off any attack while on the march, De Vargas moved his command from Isleta and marched northward in the direction of Santa Fé, camping in the valley of the Rio Grande at a deserted Spanish hacienda, which he fortified. The day following he proceeded to the pueblo of San Felipe. Here the Indians formed in two lines, with a large cross between them, and upon his entry of the village he was received with friendly demonstrations. He told them that he had brought priests with him and that they must say mass according to the form of the Spaniards. In this they were satisfied and brought refreshments to him and his command.

At San Felipe he met some of the chiefs from the pueblo of Cochití, whom he told it was his intention to visit their pueblo and directed them to return and talk with the people, advising them of his friendliness and to come and see him the day after. De Vargas now sent Captain Cristobal with a number of cattle to the pueblos up the river to trade for grain and other provisions of which the army stood in great need. Four leagues from camp he met an old woman who told him that the Indians were assembling at a point about seven leagues from Santa Fé for the purpose of destroying the entire Spanish force. These Indians, she said, had sent two messengers to Cochití asking the assistance of that pueblo, but the latter, being divided in their opinions, had not yet determined upon the course they would pursue. Shortly afterwards he was informed that because the people of Cochití had refused to join with them, the Indians had returned to Santa Fé, where they were determined to resist any attempt upon the part of the Spaniards to enter the city. De Vargas now concluded to visit the pueblos of Santa Ana, Cia, and Cochití. He found the Indians from these pueblos assembled upon the high mesas which overlook the valley of the Rio Grande;

he found them friendly, baptized a few, obtained some provisions, and returned to his camp in the valley.

De Vargas now gave orders to move on to the capital, and, having reached the pueblo of Santo Domingo, which was deserted, on the march he met the governors of Tesuque, San Lazaro, and San Ildefonso. Luis Tu-pa-tú, the leader of all the Indians, was present and appeared much dejected. It was this Indian who had been appointed governor of all the pueblos by De Vargas the year before. Tu-pa-tú explained his dejection to De Vargas and repeated the story which had already come to the commander's ears that it was his intention upon his return to execute all the leaders of the rebellion of 1680. De Vargas soon convinced Tu-pa-tú that the interpreter had lied, but took pains to impress upon him that this second attempt to conspire for the destruction of the Spanish army and colonists merited the severest punishment, even to the extermination of every Indian in the kingdom.

Tu-pa-tú was now sent to Santa Fé and San Lazaro with instructions to inform the Indians that De Vargas had brought with him the images of Jesus and the Holy Mother, and a cross, and that he would not break the promise of pardon which he had made the previous year and that the images and cross were much better than the rites of their estufas. He also promised that when he met the interpreter, Pedro de Tapia, he would have him executed because of the deception which he had practiced upon them and him. Tu-pa-tú took with him a few goods for purposes of trade with the Indians, and on the fourth day returned with a good supply of corn, in addition to twelve mule-loads which the Indians of Santa Fé sent the general, as a present.

De Vargas left the pueblo of Santo Domingo in a heavy snow storm and in the evening camped at the ranch of Roque Madrid, situated within two leagues of Santa Fé. Here he was visited by a deputation of natives from Santa Fé, headed by the governor and the chief of Tesuque, all manifesting the greatest friendship and informing him that the report put in circulation by Pedro de Tapia had caused great commotion, but the old men and women would not believe him, saying that De Vargas was their father and would not injure them. Here De Vargas remained in camp until the 16th of December, when, under the original banner carried by Juan de

Oñate, he made a triumphal entry into the capital of the kingdom.[391]

---

[391] The following is a translation of the account of the entry by De Vargas on the 16th day of December, 1693:

"December 16, 1693.
"Entry into this town of Santa Fé, by said governor and captain-general:
"On the sixteenth day of the month of December, date and year above, I, the said governor and captain-general, about the eleventh hour of said day, made my entry into this town of Santa Fé, and coming in sight of the walled village where the Teguas and Tanos reside, with the squadron on the march and in company with the very illustrious corporation of this town and kingdom, its high sheriff and color-bearing alderman, the captain Don Bernardino Duran de Chaves, carrying the standard referred to in these acts and under which this land was conquered, we arrived at the square where we found the said natives congregated, the women apart from the men, all unarmed and abstaining from any hostile demonstration, but instead, behaving themselves with great composure, and, on proffering to them our greeting, saying 'Praise to Him' several times, they answered, 'Forever'; and seeing the approach on foot of the very reverend father custodian, Friar Salvador de San Antonio, and in his train the fifteen monks, priests and reverend father missionaries and the lay brothers of our father, St. Francis, chanting on their march divers psalms, I got down from my horse and my example was followed by the said corporation, corporals and officers of war and by the ensign of the royal standard in company with the said high sheriff and color-bearing alderman, all having gone out with the purpose of receiving the said reverend fathers, who, in union with their very reverend father custodian, came, singing in processional order, and when I made due obeisance as I was passing on my way to the entrance of said village and town, and the same thing was done by my followers, and in the middle of the square a cross had been raised, where all present knelt down and sang psalms and prayers, including the Te Deum and in conclusion the Litany of Our Lady and the said very reverend father custodian, atuning his voice, sang with such joy and fervor that almost every one without exception was duly moved by the happiness of hearing in such place the praises of our Lord God and His Most Holy Mother. And after he sang the hymn three times, I offered my congratulations to said very reverend father and the rest, telling them that notwithstanding the last year, at the time of my happy contest, I had given possession to the very reverend father president, Friar Francisco Corvera, who was one of the fathers who came at the time as chaplains to the said army, which said reverend father president had witnessed and accepted and in this manner and in the name of this order and in favor of his sacred religion would do it again and would grant it to him anew with great pleasure, considering the great resignation with which all, together with their very reverend father, do so heartily and freely agree to employ themselves in the administration of the Holy Sacrament in this said newly conquered kingdom; to which the said very reverend father answered, tendering his thanks for himself and all his order, and that by the use of said grant, invested and given by me, the said governor and captain-general, they had enough for the maintenance of their rights — much more than when they entered immediately in the administration of the missions above mentioned; and then I spoke to said corporation and told them I restored to them the possession of their town and that likewise they ought and should give me, the said governor and captain-general, testimonials of having taken the same, entering again therein and of the pacification of the said Indians and their submission to the Divine and Humane majesty; in the same manner, to the said natives in the plaza of said village, I told and repeated what Our Lord, the King had sent me on the news I gave his Royal Majesty of their

The population of the city assembled upon the plaza, the men being drawn up on one side, the women on the other. When the friars, who were in the rear of the army, approached the plaza they began chanting hymns and repeating prayers. The soldiers formed in open ranks to allow their passage, and when they arrived upon the plaza, they knelt down before a cross that had been erected by

---

surrender last year, with orders that this kingdom should be re-peopled; that with the information I had given of my having pardoned them and of their obedience which was the cause of said pardon, all his displeasure had vanished and he would call them again his chldren, and for that reason he had sent many priests in order that they might be Christians as they were, and that likewise he sent me with the soldiers they saw for the purpose of defending them against their enemies; that I came not to ask anything of them, but only for two things; that they should be Christians as they ought, hearing mass and saying their prayers, and their sons and women attending to the catechisms as the Spaniards did; and the second was that they might be safe from the Apaches and friendly with all, and that this was my sole object in coming, and not to ask or take away anything; and the said very reverend custodian assured them of my good heart and the good intentions which animated the Spaniards, which were not as they had supposed; that is I, the said captain-general, had come to kill them as they said, he would not have come, and so they should give no credit to anything but what I and their reverend father told them; besides I ordered them that if they had among them any bad and malicious Indian they should tie him up and bring him to me to ascertain the truth about what he said, and in case of falsehood I would order his instant execution, and that in this way we could live as brothers and be very happy; and after this talk we went away again, leaving them their village, to seek a more protected site, the soil being covered with snow, and only about midday I found in the outflows and slopes a table land and mountain susceptible to some repair, and therein I, the said governor and captain-general, established my camp, despising the dwelling place, a tower house which had been prepared for my occupation, having in the same a fire-place, which a resident told me belonged to said house and as such to himself; to which I replied he might repair the same; and in testimony whereof, regarding said entry, I sign my name in company with the very illustrious corporation and corporals and war officers; likewise the two secretaries who were present herein in said town.
    (SEAL)   "Dated ut supra.
        "DIEGO DE VARGAS ZAPATA LUJAN PONCE DE LEON
        "LORENZO DE MADRID
        "FERNANDO DE CHAVES
        "J. DE LEYBA
        "LAZARO DE MESQUIA
        "ROQUE MADRID
        "JOSEPH MIERA
        "XAVIER DE ORTEGA
            "Secretary of the Town Corporation
        "JUAN DE ALMAZAN
  "Before me: ANTONIO DE BALVERDE,
                "Secretary of Gov. and War.
"I attest the above:
    "ALFONZO RAEL DE AGUILAR,
"One of the Secretaries of Gov. and War of the Governor and Captain-general."

the Indians, celebrated the Te Deum and chanted the Litany. De Vargas now delivered an address to the assembled natives, in which the object of his second visit was explained to them and all that he said was confirmed by the friars.

The captain-general found the city of Santa Fé in about the same condition as when he left it the year before, the works and entrenchments being in good order. The inhabitants seemed to De Vargas to be polite but not enthusiastic, and to avoid any trouble or rupture between the Indians and the soldiers the latter were encamped upon a hill just outside the town.

De Vargas, always on his guard, made every effort to keep himself posted as to the real feelings of the Indians; reports were brought to him that the Indians of San Felipe, Santa Ana, and Cia were friendly, but the rest only awaited a favorable opportunity to show their hostility. The Pecos Indians were also friendly and kept the promise made the year before and advised De Vargas of the plans of the Indians and offered aid.

The captain-general now called upon the Indians for one hundred bags of corn, which were furnished, but later when he asked for two hundred more, they refused and declared their willingness to fight rather than comply. The Indians had been permitted to remain in possession of the town up to this time, but the weather had become so severe that the friars petitioned De Vargas to be permitted to occupy the old palace and the adjacent royal houses. The corporation also desired to take possession of the buildings occupied by the Tanos Indians, requesting that they be returned to the villages from which they had come to Santa Fé.

In the meantime there came many reports to De Vargas of the hatching of a conspiracy among the Indians. As a matter of precaution the captain-general permitted the town council to occupy the old palace but declined to accede to the request of the friars, saying that they must await the return of the men who had been sent to the mountains to cut timber for the repair of the chapel of San Miguel. Shortly these returned without the timber, saying that it was too cold for them to bring it in, and offered him the use of an estufa until warm weather, quite good enough they said for divine service. De Vargas now determined to take possession of the public buildings, and ordered the Tanos to vacate and return to their pueblos. It was now reported to De Vargas that the Picuriés and others had attempted to practice deception upon him by asking that the friars be distributed around among the different pueblos, thus assisting them in upholding and maintaining the Christian beliefs. The custodio and his companions presented a formal protest against this distribution, saying that while they were willing to sacrifice their lives, still they were not willing to go rashly and needlessly to certain destruction.[392] The Indians now heard of the announcement by Captain Arias that reënforcements to the number of 200 soldiers were on their way to New Mexico. In their meetings the leaders of the Indians pronounced this statement as false, that the Spaniards were few and helpless and urged immediate war. The order of the captain-general to the Tanos that they must give up the royal houses and retire to their villages at Galisteo brought matters to a crisis. On the 28th day of December the Tanos closed the entrance to the public plaza and made preparations for defense. De Vargas demanded that they surrender; they asked for a day's time in which to consider and then, with shouts of insult, declared their purpose to resist. The devil could help them, God and Mary were powerless, they cried, declaring that nothing but defeat would be the fate of the invader, who would be reduced to slavery and finally killed.

On the 29th of December, De Vargas, having caused prayers to be read for his courageous comrades, raised the picture of the Virgin upon the battle flag, and with STORMING OF THE CAPITAL his army advancing in two divisions, BY DE VARGAS assaulted the Indian defenses with great spirit. The Spaniards were met with great flights of arrows and stones; boiling water was hurled upon them as they endeavored to scale the works which the Span-

---

[392] Bancroft, H. H., *History of Arizona and New Mexico*, note, p. 204, says: "Dec. 18th, petition of the friars in Arch. N. Mex., 142-3. It is fol. 87 of the original ms., but only fol. 37-39 of this cuaderno still exist in the Arch. Sta. Fé, Ms. The friars who signed were as follows: Salvador de San Antonio, Juan Zavaleta, Francisco Corvera, Juan Alpuente, Juan Antonio del Corral, Juan Muñoz de Castro, Antonio Obregon, Juan Daza, Buenaventura Contreras, Antonio Carbonel, José Narváez Valverde, Diego Zeinos, Francisco de Jesus Maria Casanes, Geronimo Prieto, Antonio Bahamonde, Domingo de Jesus Maria and José Diez. The last five, with three others, Miguel Tircio, José Maria and Blas Navarro, who perhaps arrived a little later, were from the college of Santa Cruz de Queretaro, the rest being of the Province del Santo Evangelio, Mexico, who came to New Mexico in '93 and departed about

Carved Leather Horse Furniture of the Reconquistadores
From Collections of New Mexico Historical Society

iards themselves had erected years before. Finally the plaza gate was burned and the new kiva of the Indians captured. Tehua reënforcements now appeared and twice did the Spanish cavalry charge and scatter this new foe, but night was upon them and the captain-general was unable to do more than prevent the interference of this new enemy. Both sides were exhausted and glad that the darkness compelled a suspension of hostilities. The Indians had suffered severely, nine of their number having been slain. They were also much discouraged on account of the withdrawal from the scene of battle of the allies who had come the day of the battle, too late. The Indians determined to surrender; their governor hanged himself, and seventy of the Indians, including Antonio Bolsas, a leading spirit among them, were immediately executed. Four hundred women and children were taken and sold into slavery. De Vargas again planted his standard in the middle of the plaza, erected a cross at the entrance to the pueblo, and once more took possession in the name of his royal master. About three thousand bushels of corn, besides a large quantity of beans, wheat, and other provisions were seized and divided among the colonists.

These bloody events closed the year of 1693; they became the signal for a partial but still very formidable uprising of the Pueblos. The storming of the capital city, the Indian village which the Tanos had erected on the ruins of the old palace, was a necessary military measure. In truth, De Vargas had been too lenient; the Indians construed his forbearance into fear. The Tehuas who had come to the assistance of the Tanos had failed to raise the siege and now abandoned their village of Tesuque, as well as also the pueblos of Nambé, Pojoaque, Jacona, Cuyamungué, San Ildefonso, and the Tanos, who had settled near Santa Cruz, followed their example. All of these Indians assembled on the summit of Tu-yó, the Black Mesa of San Ildefonso. Matters looked anything but encouraging to the Spanish captain-general. Raids on the cattle and horses were frequent, their arms were broken and ammunition was scarce. The wooden cross was no longer a weapon of conquest. The Indians were always ready to attack the Spaniards whenever they left the walled protection of the presidio. The Indians of Pecos, Cia, Santa

---

'96, all but one, who "rubrico con su sangre la fe que predicaba."—*Espinosa, Cron.* '92, 282-4; *Arricivita, Cron. Seraf.*, 176, 199-200.

Ana, and San Felipe still remained faithful, but had all they could do to defend themselves against their angry neighbors. Juan Gé, chief of the Pecos, sent to De Vargas for aid against the rebels and the Apaches and Captain Roque Madrid was sent out with thirty men, but this was only a false alarm invented for the purpose of testing the good faith of De Vargas. On the 9th of January the captain-general marched to the abandoned villages of Tesuque and Nambé, and thence to the Black Mesa of San Ildefonso, where, as we have seen, the Tehuas and Tanos had assembled. They promised De Vargas to come to Santa Fé and make peace. They did not keep their promise and it was soon ascertained that it had been given merely for the purpose of gaining time for the formation of an alliance and a junction with the Indians of Picuriés, Jemez, and Taos.

De Vargas now sent word to Padre Farfan to come at once with ammunition and bring with him the colony of seventy families from El Paso. Again the captain-general determined to march to the mesa of San Ildefonso and offer peace and pardon to the assembled Indians. He was unsuccessful and returned to Santa Fé. Hostilities in all directions now became most frequent. The hostiles made every effort to secure aid from Acoma, Zuñi, and Moqui, and also to form alliances with the wandering Apache bands. De Vargas meanwhile kept on sending out raiding parties, taking captives, and obtaining large quantities of maize, whereupon the natives began the destruction of all the provisions of every kind which they could not move.

The captain-general was well aware that vigorous action must be taken and that he must act quickly. He therefore again marched against the mesa of San Ildefonso with one hundred and ten soldiers and many settlers and friendly Indians. On the fourth day of March, 1694, he began his attack, his two pieces of artillery bursting at the first discharge. He charged up the sides of the mesa in two divisions, but was repulsed, eight of his men being seriously wounded. Fifteen hostiles were killed in this fight, which lasted five hours. The captain-general now sent his wounded to Santa Fé, and on the eleventh repeated his assault with the same result. The following night the Indians came down off the mesa and attacked the Spaniards, but were repulsed. The siege lasted until the

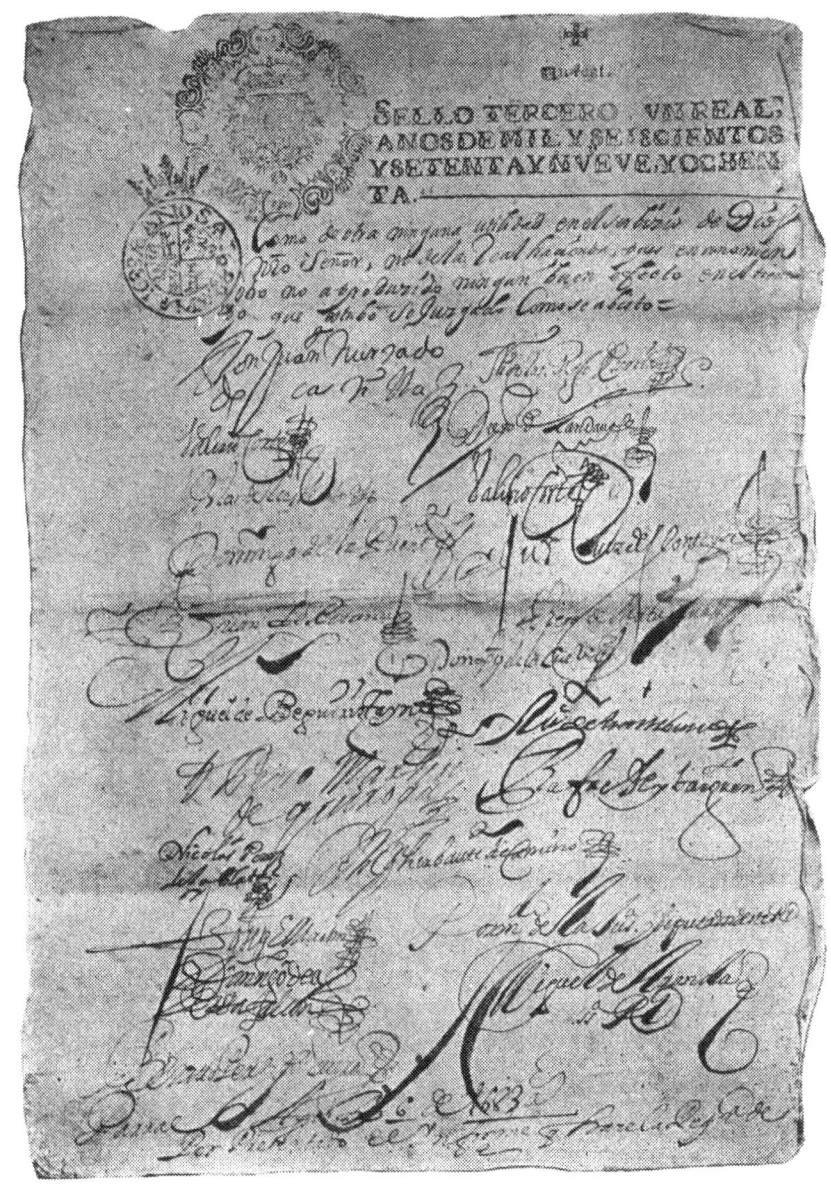

ac-simile of last page of Protest against Acts of Governor Cruzate as to South Boundary Line of New Mexico

19th and was then abandoned on account of the weather and the lack of ammunition. In these assaults the Indians lost about thirty. De Vargas now returned to Santa Fé, taking with him a large quantity of maize and one hundred horses and mules which he had recovered from the Indians.

The rebels of the pueblo of Cochití were said now to be intrenched with other Indians upon the mesa of Cieneguilla, and intending to attack the Spaniards at the most favorable opportunity. This information came to De Vargas from the Queres, who besought him to come to their assistance. Accordingly he left Santa Fé on the 12th day of April, with seventy soldiers and twenty armed colonists, and marched against the Potrero Viejo. He took the road to San Felipe where he was reënforced by about one hundred Indians from that village and from the pueblos of Santa Ana and Cia. Leaving San Felipe [393] on the day after his arrival, in the afternoon, he reached the Cañada de Cochití about midnight. He immediately held a council of war, and the war-captain of the pueblo of Cia, Bartolomé de Ojeda, described the cliff and the three trails leading to the summit. The enemy was prepared for the assault, as fires were burning along the upper edge of the mesa, showing that his position was well picketed. The Spanish camp had been pitched where it could not be seen from the Potrero.[394]

---

[393] *Autos de Guerra del Año de 1694*, fol. 86. De Vargas reached San Felipe on the 15th of April (fol. 88). Escalante in his *Relacion* gives incorrect dates and is very brief. He says: ''Y con la otra marchó para la Cienegui el de Cochití el dia 14 o 15 de April, é incorporandose con los dichos Queres amigos, en dos avances ganó la mesa.'' This is plainly an error as De Vargas gained the mesa at the first assault.

[394] *Ibid*, fol. 90-91: ''Hize alto por ser entre onze dela noche y hallarse avistado de la dcha messa y por no ser sentido del enemigo qe por sus lumbreras qe en ella tiene ser reconose tener puestas sus zentinelas, y asi para aguardar ora y rremudar cauallo la dcha gente hizo alto orilla de vna barranca y arroyo.'' April 17, fol. 91: ''Al salir de la luna y dos de la mañana hauydo aguardado á dha ora yo dho Gour y Cappn Genl y hauiendo resuelto y conferido con los dchos Cauos y el Cappan de los Queres y mi compadre Barme de Ojeda las suvidas qe la dha Messa de la Zieneguilla de Cochití tenia. Pues los Yndios reuveldes de dha nazion ye pueblo nueso de Cochití la Tenian Toda con sus trincheras y hoyos qe llaman trampas, para no obstante siendo ella por si sumante empiñada y derecha y juntamte toda de penas queria qe la hazia ynenpugnable se reconozio por el dho del dho Cappan Barme de Ojeda tener por vn constado dha messa vna suvida. Siendo la que esta mas fazil respecto de ser la que trajinan con sus vestias y ganados, de ser la mas corryte para por ella darsela al dho enemigo mucho dano, por podersele cojer las espaldas y la otra suvida tamuien la tenian estrabiada al otro frente para bajar al embudo y ojo de agua de donde se abastezen.'' This is a very correct description of

The captain-general divided his force into four parties. Captains Juan Olguin and Eusebio de Vargas, with forty men and one hundred Indians, under Bartolomé de Ojeda, took the long but easier trail that reaches the mesa from the southwest. This trail was used by the enemy in bringing sheep and horses to the summit. Captain Roque Madrid, with another detachment, was to storm the Potrero in front. Adjutant Barela, with ten soldiers, guarded the third trail, which descends to the little stream in the Cañada on the northern base of the cliff, while De Vargas personally took a position between the last two divisions, with only a small force of men. Captain Madrid had the difficult task, as the ascent from the east is very steep and over bare rocks. It was moonlight, and the enemy could inflict heavy loss by merely throwing stones upon the assailants.[395] About two o'clock in the morning of the 17th the advance began from the east, while the body guided by Ojeda had already begun to creep up in silence, all unnoticed by the enemy. The force under Madrid, however, was soon discovered, the Indians making a stubborn resistance. The Spaniards slowly advanced, replying with slow musketry firing of the period to the showers of stones and arrows from above. The handful of men on the north side of the Potrero also made demonstrations of an attack, and in this manner some of the enemy were diverted to that side, when suddenly the forty soldiers and the Indian allies appeared on top of the mesa in the rear.

The news of their arrival before the pueblo itself caused the defenders on the parapets to scatter at once; some sped to the rescue of their homes and families, but the majority fled through the forest. Some resistance was still offered at the pueblo, but it was fruitless, and by sunrise all was over. Twenty-one [396] Indians per-

the different ascents to the Potrero. The camp of the Spaniards must have been below the present settlement in the Cañada, probably near the ruins of Kua-pa.

[395] *Autos de Guerra del Año de 1694*, fol. 91: "Y diessen el dicho asalto mientras al mismo tiempo la daua al Cappan y Cauo Roque Madrid por la suvida dha y prinzipal de dha messa." The Adjutant, Diego Barela, occupied the foot of the northern trail, with ten soldiers. "Como asimismo para el asalto por dho rumbo y el otro trozo con las caualladas, quedando asimismo en la ladera y suvida de dha messa, yo dho Gounor &ca, para si el enemigo se despenase por ella ó bajada por dha banda qe es la qe tienen y asimismo para estar en dho puesto á socorrer los dhos referidos como el de la cauallada y tren."

[396] *Autos de Guerra*, etc., fol. 91-92: "Y en esta disposizion se zerro y se dio asalto, de suerte qe el eiemigo se pusso en arma, haziendo su rresistenza y

Reconquest of New Mexico by De Vargas. Ceremonies in Plaza, Santa Fé, N. M.

PUEBLO REBELLION AND INDEPENDENCE 397

ished in this engagement. On the side of the Spaniards four men were wounded, but none killed. Three hundred and forty-two women and children fell into the hands of De Vargas, together with seventy horses and more than nine hundred sheep. A portion of the spoils of battle was given to the Queres. A very considerable quantity of Indian corn was found in the pueblo which was of great value to the Spaniards, as provisions were very scarce. As yet there had been no season for planting, and the Indians took good care to conceal or remove their stores of grain. In order to facilitate the removal of this grain to Santa Fé, where the inhabitants were in great need of supplies, the captain-general ordered the captive Indians to shell it on the spot. This compelled him to remain on the Potrero longer than had been his purpose. By the 20th of April the corn was ready, and the bulk of the Spanish force was sent off to bring the beasts of burden and to reënforce Santa Fé, which, in the meantime, the Tehuas had attempted to surprise.

The captain-general was much concerned over the renewed efforts on the part of the Tehuas, and was anxious personally to return to Santa Fé. Meanwhile the Indian captives were kept under guard on the Potrero, and at night were confined in the kiva. De Vargas had only thirty-six men with him, as his Queres allies had left on the day of the assault to protect their own pueblos.[397] On the 21st,

bateria por la dha suvida donde me hallaba y el sussodho capitan, ofiziales de guerra y otros soldados de valor le correspondlan con repetidas cargas suviendo. . . A dha messa al mesmo tiempo que los dhos capitanes de campana y gennte de guerra amiga le zerraron las espaldas, cuya carga le obligo y berse por los dhos tres angulos y suvidas combattido, le obligo á la gennte de afuera á no aguardar la despedazassen y matassen la nuestra y asi se pusso en fuga, tomando diferentes veredas y brenas tenydo á si fauor las dhas peñas y estalaje pedregoso, y viendosse con el desemparo y fuga el dho enemigo de la dha gentte qe en su fauor hauia venido de socorro siguio la mesma fuga rretirrandose, dando algunas cargas qe los nuestros repararon con sus chimales y apoderados de la dha plaza y pueblo y messa, lo hizieron algunos de las cassas y trincheras por cuyas troneras algunos de los dhos reueldes tubieron lugar de herir á quatro de dho campo, aunque no peligro ninguno el perder la vida.'' Seven Indians were killed in the engagement, and one was suffocated in one of the lower rooms of the pueblo, by the Indian allies. ''Uno se quemó, pegandole fuego en vna cassa la gentte amiga sin aguadar á rromper la pader del sotano de ella á el qual se hauia bajado.'' Thirteen were taken with arms in their hands and executed on the spot.

[397] *Autos de Guerra,* fol. 94-104.

Bancroft, H. H., *History of Arizona and New Mexico,* p. 208-9: ''Vargas insisted on their burning the new pueblo and returning to their old home at Cochití. On the 20th or 21st the Spanish camp was suddenly attacked, and

at two o'clock in the afternoon, when the Spaniards thought themselves perfectly secure, the enemy suddenly made a furious attack upon the pueblo, having crept up from the west through a narrow pass where the cliffs behind the Potrero and the woods had concealed his approach. The Spaniards flew to arms and finally succeeded in beating off the enemy, with the loss, however, of one of their number and four of the Indians. During the confusion caused by the surprise of the attack more than one-half of the captive girls and boys escaped. This was the principal object of the Indian attack, and seeing that the Spaniards were determined in their resistance, and disheartened by the death of one of their principal leaders, they beat a precipitate retreat.[398]

On the 24th De Vargas evacuated the Potrero, taking with him his captives and his corn. Before leaving he set fire to the pueblo,[399] together with all the grain which he could not carry, "in order that the aforesaid rebellious enemy might not find any sustenance in it nor be able to take up his abode without being compelled to re-

---

150 of the captives were lost, two soldiers being killed, one of them accidentally, and Adjutant Francisco de Anaya de Almazan was drowned a few days later in crossing the river. The mesa pueblo was burned.''

[398] *Autos de Guerra*, fol. 105: ''Tubo el arrojo de dar suviendo por yno angostura en dha messa qe siendo tan ynmediatta fue repentina su entrrada con furioso alaridos y gruesso numero de gentte, qe se diuidieron entrando por los puestos de dhas dos Plazas y los demas de partte de afuera, zercando dho Pueblo y quartteles y aunque fue al parazer q los dos de la tarde la mesma seguridad de la ora tenia á la dha gentte desarmada sin sus queras.''

The leader of the Indians who lost his life was Juan Griego, a mestizo from San Juan. This shows that besides the Queres and those of San Marcos, there were Tehuas and perhaps Jemez in the conflict.

Escalante, in his *Relacion*, p. 160, also describes this affair: ''Cayeron en gran numero y cercaron el pueblo, pusieron á los nuestros en gran aprieto y como los nuestros eran tan pocos, atendian y solamente á defender las bocas calles del pueblo, y asi tuvieron lugar de huir ciento cincuenta de los prisioneros; lo cual visto por los rebeldes, se retiraron juzgando que ya habian librado á todos sus hijos y mugeres.'' Escalante says that only two of the Indians were killed.

[399] Bandelier, A. F., *Final Report*, p. 177: ''The condition of the ruins resembles that of a pueblo destroyed by fire and there is considerable charred corn to be seen. As in every other instance where I have compared the Spanish documents with the localities, and with current tales, I have found them to be of great accuracy, and in substantial agreement with the traditions of the people.''

Autos de Guerra, fol. 110: ''Y se pegue fuego á dho pueblo y Semillas qe en el hubiere para qe el dho enemigo rreuelde no logre en ella su susttentto ni mas hazer assisientto, sin que le queste de nuebo el trabajo de su rreedifizio y ejecuttado dho orden sali de dha messa con dho campo.''

build." The intentions of De Vargas were fully realized, for the Potrero Viejo was never again occupied.[400]

Arriving at Santa Fé, the captain-general devoted his time and attention to the distribution of lands and live stock, also distributing the slaves and posting guards, together with other measures for the protection of the settlers and the Indians who had given in their allegiance and remained friendly to the Spanish occupation. About this time a raid was made upon a grazing camp near Santa Fé, but the Indians were repulsed with loss. De Vargas, in the last days of May, again marched to the mesa of San Ildefonso where he had several fights, made a few captives, regained some animals, and returned to Santa Fé. The friendly Queres sent in some Jemez prisoners, two of whom were not shot, one because he promised to show the Spaniards the grave of a martyred friar and the other because of the intercession of the governor of the Pecos, Juan Gé. De Vargas gave to the friars two hundred sheep for the support of two missions which it was proposed to establish at Pecos and at Cia; he also gave them one hundred sheep for their own sustenance.

The capture of the Potrero Viejo, though a striking feat from a military standpoint, did not by any means at once bring the hostile Queres to the Spanish terms. They persisted in their hostile attitude for several months. The offensive power, however, of the tribe was broken and the villages of San Felipe, Santa Ana, and Cia were thereafter relieved of the annoyances to which they had been subjected. Still they continued to remain in arms as allies of the Jemez for some time and it was only in the late fall of 1694, after the Black Mesa of San Ildefonso had yielded to the Spanish soldiers, that Cochití was re-occupied by its inhabitants. The same happened with Santo Domingo. As has been said, since the destruction of the pueblo on the Potrero Viejo, the latter has ceased to be a place of refuge for the Queres of Cochití. In 1728 that tribe made an attempt at revolt, abandoning its village on the Rio Grande and retiring into the mountains with hostile intentions, but no extensive part

[400] Bandelier, A. F., *Final Report*, part ii, 178: "The ruins on its (Potrero Viejo) summit are frequently spoken of as the 'old pueblo of Cochití,' in the sense of the original home of that tribe. It will be seen that this is only partially correct. The oldest ruins on the mesa, which hardly attract attention, are those of a pre-historic Queres pueblo; the striking well preserved ones are those of a village built after the year 1683 and abandoned in April, 1694."

of the mesa was occupied by them on that occasion. They were prevailed upon by the Spanish governor to return, and their troubles were settled without bloodshed.[401]

On the 30th day of June, 1694, De Vargas marched northward, killing eleven Tehuas at the pueblo of Cuyamungué, the first day out. This point is about eleven miles north of Santa Fé on the main road to San Juan. After the fight at Cuyamungué the captain-general proceeded to Picuriés, which he found deserted, and reached the pueblo of Taos on the 3rd day of July. This pueblo was also deserted, but he found it protected by crosses, which the Indians believed the Spaniards would respect. De Vargas

DE VARGAS MAKES EXPEDITION TO TAOS

---

[401] There are a number of folk tales clustering around the Potrero Viejo and the Cañada de Cochití. The Indians firmly believe that in the walls of the cliff, at some barely accessible spot, ancient jars are concealed in a hole in the rocks, which jars are said to be filled with "treasure." Indian "treasure" differs from that of the white man. It is neither gold nor silver, but turquoises, both good and bad, provided they are green and blue; shell beads and fetiches. It is not the material or commercial price that gives these objects their value, but the superstitious importance attached to them in the eyes of aboriginal creeds and beliefs. The existence of such a deposit is not impossible, and were it ever recovered, would yield many objects worthy of ethnological or archæological collections. It is not likely, however, that the Indians will ever reveal its hiding place. Only an accident will ever discover this so-called "treasure."

In the walls of the Cañada, a few miles east of the Potrero, there is a niche or cave of inconsiderable dimensions, to which is attached much superstitious dread by the natives. They believe that this niche is the closed entrance to a grotto famous for the meeting of sorcerers. It is told and with the utmost gravity, that at the hour of midnight witches and wizards congregate about the place in great numbers. The witches appear disguised as crows, the wizards as buzzards and woodpeckers. They alight upon the trees and shrubs about the cave and scream, cackle, and croak until finally the rock opens and reveals a brilliantly lighted cavern. Then the bird shapes are discarded and their human shapes are assumed, minus the eyes which they have left at home, carefully concealed in some sacrificial *tinaja* or *olla*, and now they enter the cavern where the master of all evil — *el demonio* — is waiting for them. The solitary wanderer who has lost his way in these deserted places, hears the noise of their carousals until the day breaks in the east, when the junta breaks up, crows, turkey-buzzards, woodpeckers, and magpies cover the surrounding piñon trees, until at last they fly away, to sleep during the day and return again at night.

Another story connected with this place is that of an Indian hunter whose wife was a very successful witch. On a certain occasion she devised a plan to be rid of her husband, as he took no part in her evil doings. The plan failed through the faithlessness of the man who had been engaged to perform the crime, and whom the witch for that purpose had transformed into a deer. In place of the husband being killed, the latter killed the deer and the faithless spouse as well. The final result of the adventure was that the witch being killed the pueblo was relieved of great imaginary dangers, which the Indians dread more than real sources of injury.

The Condé de Galve, Viceroy of New Spain

PUEBLO REBELLION AND INDEPENDENCE 401

discovered that the people were in the mountains near-by and endeavored to negotiate with them, using Juan Gé, the Pecos governor, as intermediary, but he was not successful, and as a punishment for their conduct he sacked the pueblo and carried off a large amount of corn.[402]

The captain-general determined to return to Santa Fé by a roundabout way; he marched northward into the country of the Utes, across the Rio Grande, thence south to the Ojo Caliente,[403] Rio

[402] Bandelier, A. F., *Final Report*, part ii, p. 31: "Taos, built on both sides of the swift and cool Rio de Taos, is the only village of New Mexico, ancient or modern, so far discovered, the situation of which corresponds with Castañeda's description and location. He says, 'Valladolid is the last one in ascending towards the northeast.'

"Although the present buildings of Taos are not those of the Braba of the 16th century, they still preserve the appearance of the old village, and their position relative to the river and the valley is the same. Taos is, therefore, together with Acoma and some of the Moqui villages, one of the best preserved examples of antiquity so far as architecture is concerned."

[403] There is no indication that the pueblos near Ojo Caliente were inhabited at the time of the first coming of the Spaniards or since. It is not unlikely that when De Vargas, in 1694, passed by Ojo Caliente, he noticed the ruins, but mistook them for those of the former Spanish settlement at Chamita — San Gabriel. See *Relacion Sumaria de las Operaciones militares del Año de 1694*. Also Escalante Ms., *Relacion del Nuevo Mexico*.

The ruins at Ojo Caliente are claimed by the Tehua Indians to be those of their ancestors who lived there long before the coming of the Spaniard.

Bandelier, A. F., *Final Report*, part ii, p. 37 et seq., says: "Three of the largest pueblos of New Mexico, Colorado and Arizona lie on the banks of the Ojo Caliente stream, within a mile and a half of each other. One of them stands on the first low terrace above the creek on the east bank, and is called in the language of the Tehuas Ho-ui-ri. . . . the houses were unusually long; that is, they formed unusually large hollow rectangles. The three pueblos, Houiri Ho-mayo, opposite on the west bank, on a high promontory that rises at least one hundred feet over the stream, and Pose-uingge, the one immediately above the baths, are to a certain degree specimens of a kind which I have mentioned as 'one or two, seldom three, extensive buildings composing the village. These structures are so disposed as in most cases to surround an interior court.'

"Considerable interest attaches to the ruined sites at Ojo Caliente because the myth of Pose-yemo or Pose-ueve refers to one of them as the birth-place of that personage and the scene of his main achievements. Pose-ueve, which is the proper name in Tehua folk-lore, is the person around whom the Montezuma legend has gathered, or rather he has been taken as the figure-head for that modern fabrication.

"Pose-yemo — Moisture from Heaven — or Pose-ueve — he who walketh or cometh along strewing moisture in the morning — was the son of a girl of Pose-uingge. The story about his mother conceiving from a piñon nut that fell into her lap, may possibly be a genuine Indian legend. At all events, he remained, like the hero of the Zuñi folk-tale about the 'Poor boy of Pin-a-ua,' a wretched pauper for a long time, until the day came when a new cacique had to be chosen. Pose-ueve was proposed in jest to the medicine-men, and accepted, to the discomfiture of those who had intended to make a laughing-stock of the poor boy. At once he began to astonish all with prodigies, for which an

Chama, and San Juan. On the night of the 12th he was attacked by the Utes, on the San Antonio river, losing eight of his men. He

---

eagle was his principal helper. He soon became a great wizard, and the people of his village grew very rich in corn, turquoises, shells and other valuable objects. His fame spread, and he exercised a sort of power over many of the Pueblos, which, however, does not appear to have gone beyond that of a magician. . . . After remaining the great Shaman of the Tehuas for a long time he once went to the pueblo of Yuge-uingge (Chamita) in disguise. The people were on the point of celebrating one of their dances, and failed to recognize the powerful medicine-man. So he grew angry, and pronounced a dire curse on what he considered an ungrateful pueblo, returned to Pose-uingge, where he disappeared. Such is the Indian part of the tale. What is told of the wizard's journey to the south is a modern tradition. The Montezuma story as told to me by one of the Queres at Cochití, contains the details of his journey to the south. Another friend, a Tehua of San Juan, also stated to me that Pose-ueve went as far as the vicinity of El Paso del Norte in Chihuahua. He said he was accompanied by his sister, Navi-Tua, and that she followed him on Christmas. Christmas in Spanish is 'Pascua de Natividad,' and the word 'Navitua' is suspiciously like the Spanish word. The full details of the Montezuma legend, however, are found in a queer document, entitled *Historia de Montesuma* (Ms.), composed in Mexico in the year 1846, about the time of the breaking out of the Mexican war, which embodies, together with much nonsense purporting to be history, some of the original tales about Pose-ueve. Still many of the Pueblos of to-day believe it, and the name of Montezuma is familiar to all of them. Those 'who know,' however, members of esoteric societies, and principally the great Shamans, smile at the foreign importation and foreign dress, and discriminate between the Pose-ueve of their ancestors and later additions to his biography.''

The legend of Montezuma is as follows: Montezuma was born at the pueblo of Tehua-yo of a young virgin, to whom was given three piñones, one of them to be eaten by herself, and two reserved for the sustenance of herself and grandmother. From the one which she ate, this great monarch was conceived and brought forth, and who, through the will of the Great Spirit, upon arriving at years of discretion, gained distinction and renown. In youth he was not well thought of among his people or kindred. He was poor, and led a vagabond life, was unprepossessing in person, ''slobber-mouthed,'' and obnoxious in his habits. It happened during this period of his life that the *cacique* of his pueblo died, and that upon the assembling of the *principales* to elect a successor, they, after repeated councils, failing to agree, finally decreed that the young men of the pueblo should elect. The latter determined the choice by chance, and the honor fell upon the despised Montezuma. The office of *cacique*, it must be remembered, is one of great responsibility, and is sought to be filled by those noted for their knowledge of tribal lore, and for their wisdom and prudence. The selection, most naturally, was at first received with ridicule and derision. The despised youth, however, surprised and neutralized the revolting spirits by at once giving assurances that they should catch the small game with their hands, and the large game would deliver themselves to their control, as they would witness upon the first day of the next chase.

Near the dawn of the day upon which the latter had been designated, the Great Spirit, appearing to the new *cacique*, and finding him sad, spake encouragingly: ''Montezuma, why art thou cast down?'' Answering, he said: ''Great Father, my soul possesseth me in tribulation; this is the day appointed for the chase, and I, as *cacique*, must lead. I know not how it may come to pass among my people.'' And the Great Spirit, answering, said: ''Do not despair, thou shalt be successful. Go to thy cabin and search for the blanket

Fac-simile of Page from Journal of Don Diego de Vargas, containing entry relative to Ceremonies at time of Reconquest

PUEBLO REBELLION AND INDEPENDENCE 403

finally succeeded in repulsing the savages and pardoned them inasmuch as they claimed that they believed the Spanish force to be

and moccasins thy mother left thee before she died.'' He did as he was bidden, and found them, and they were adorned with turquoise. And the Great Spirit, further answering, said to him: ''The arms thy mother held for thee are upon the hither side, re-enter and search, and thou shalt find a strong bow, and a well-filled quiver made of lion-skin, and a head-dress, with a plume of eagle feathers.'' Whereupon the Great Spirit caused him to be washed and dressed, and he then placed in his hand a rattle made of the hoofs of many species of animals, captured in the chase, and further addressed him, commanding: ''Thou shalt sound this rattle to the east, west, north, and south as a charm and sign for all animals to surrender to thee upon approach, and which same shall be published by outcry, after the manner of thy people.''

And when this was done, the people thereof were amazed at the comely appearance of their youthful *cacique*, and they queried the verification of his astounding promises with a wondering interest, yielding obedience. The clan gathered at the kivas pursuant to out-cry, and were directed to prepare for the chase, that they might witness the supernatural powers of their young leader and hunter. Montezuma, entering upon the chase with his people, did as he had been commanded, by sounding his charm to the cardinal points. And it followed that game in abundance was captured, as promised, for their subsistence. And thus it was for eight days.

In further verification of the surprising powers of this *cacique*, he prophetically announced the coming of a great rain, and, in anticipation, commanded the people to repair their houses and to plant a greater breadth, that the harvest would be more bountiful. Some, doubting, failed to obey, and in consequence the houses were destroyed, although the harvest was abundant in the pueblo and in all the provinces round about.

With these experiences came confidence and enthusiasm, and renown in the adjacent provinces, and finally, general recognition, first as the great *cacique*, and then as Montezuma, the great monarch over all.

The same Great Spirit who had heretofore counseled and commanded him, viewing with pleasure the success and recognition received by young Montezuma, revealed to him that a great eagle would appear for him to ride in his exploration of his dominions, and eventually guide him to the place where he would found his future capital and metropolis. Eight days before starting, the Great Spirit selected Malinche, a maiden from the great pueblo of Zuñi, for the wife of Montezuma, and she was declared queen. All being ready, Montezuma, mounted upon his eagle throne, started upon his journey, as tradition has it, from the pueblo of Cicuyé (Pecos), accompanied by a large number of his people. To these were added many from other provinces, glad to accept service under so renowned a chief. Wherever he tarried for a time, he founded and peopled a pueblo from the hosts following him.

After the return of many vernal blooms, and after numerous moons of travel, the great monarch arrived at a lake, and where the guiding eagle alighted upon a prickly pear, growing upon a rock, near the edge of the lake, at the same time seizing a serpent with its beak. Such was the sign which had been revealed whereby it might be known that the site of the pueblo of Tenochtitlan, or the City of Mecitl, or Mexico, had been reached.

The tradition has it also that the Great Spirit gave to Montezuma the power to check water with keyes, which were handled by a *cacique* of great power, named Tlascala; that here where the site was revealed through the great eagle was founded and built, under Montezuma, the great pueblo of the tribes confederated as the Aztec Empire. This event was annually celebrated down to the coming of the children of the sun (Hernan Cortés), Malinche, the

hostile Indians dressed in Spanish clothes, they having had several experiences of this kind with their enemies.

Proceeding down the Chama river valley and the Rio Grande as far as San Ildefonso, he reconnoitered the Black Mesa, where the rebellious natives were still strongly posted; passing up the Rio de Pojoaque, he visited the pueblo of that name, as well as that of the Indians of Tesuque further on, and finally arrived at his capital on the 16th day of July, 1694.

The captain-general had visited the pueblo of Jemez in November, 1693, when they gave him promises of fidelity, but as soon as his back was turned, they began sending threatening messages to the pueblos of Cia and Santa Ana, also molesting the Indians of those villages by driving off their stock. Having now returned from his trip to the north, he determined to proceed against the Jemez. On his way to their pueblo, on the 21st day of July, he was notified that the Jemez and the Navajós had attempted to surprise Cia, killing four of the inhabitants, but had been finally driven off.

DE VARGAS MARCHES TO JEMEZ AND ATTACKS THE PUEBLO

De Vargas, as soon as he reached the friendly pueblos of Santa Ana and Cia, held a council with the leading men of both villages, and then marched with his force, said to have numbered one hundred and twenty Spaniards and some auxiliary natives, for the mesas above the San Diego canyon. He left Cia at eight o'clock at night, on the 23rd day of July, and at a distance of four leagues, near the junction of the two streams, divided his men into two parties. One of these, consisting of twenty-five Spanish soldiers under command of Eusebio de Vargas and the Indian allies, was to enter the gorge of San Diego and climb the mesa on a dizzy trail, so as to reach the rear of the highest plateau, while the main body, led by De Vargas himself, ascended from the southwest. The Spanish commander had ascertained that the Jemez had evacuated their village on the mesa, and retired to a still higher location north of it.[404] The operations were completely successful, and the Indians

empress, appearing sceptre in hand, all kneeling in homage in the presence of the emperor, who was seated upon a throne of gold.

[404] *Autos de Guerra*, July 23, 1694, fol. 60: ''Dijeron haver por las espaldas del peñol donde se han mudado los reveldes Xemes dejando su pueo de la messa vn camino qe por el sin ser senttida yndiana puede suvir y que para hazerlo y yr resguardada es prezisso mande con ella yr veynte y zinco

A Pecos Indian. From drawing made in 1849

were taken between two fires; but they offered a desperate resistance. The total number killed on this occasion amounted to eighty-four, five of whom perished in the flames, and seven threw themselves down the cliffs rather than surrender. De Vargas remained on the mesas until the 8th of August, removing gradually the considerable stores found in the villages, and the prisoners, who numbered three hundred and sixty-one. Then setting fire to both villages, he withdrew to San Diego and thence to Santa Fé. During his stay on the mesas he discovered a third pueblo, recently built by the people of Santo Domingo, who had joined the Jemez tribe upon the approach of the Spaniards. That village is said to have been situate three leagues farther north, so that, within a distance of about twelve miles from the southern extremity, three pueblos had been constructed between 1688 and 1694, all of which were abandoned after the latter year.[405]

From the spoils taken at the sacking of Jemez, De Vargas gave to Friar Alpuente 106 animals for his proposed mission at Cia. Before returning to Santa Fé, De Vargas went to the old pueblo of Jemez, where he recovered the remains of Fr. Juan de Jesus, killed in the revolt of 1680; these were taken to Santa Fé and were reinterred in the chapel at Santa Fé on the 11th of August.[406] About a week after De Vargas had returned to Santa Fé some of the

---

soldados con vn cauo y que el ressto de dho campo podia yr y suvir por la qe tienen dhos Yndios para bajar á sus milpas com oal dho puo de la messa qe han dejado qe sera su distanzia de poco mas de vna legua desde la dha messa y suvida para dho peñol.'' He marched (fol. 62) ''para el peñol poblado de los Xemes reveldes por las espaldas cuya trabesia seria de dos leguas largas para tomar el rrumbo y suvida de el . . . y hauydo endado al parezer de quatro leguas largas serian la vna de la noche quando se diuidio la dha gentte qe hauia de hazer dha ymbazon por dho rrumbo yendo el dho Capitan Evseuio de Vargas y ella la gentte y campo que quedaua commigo la haria por la suvida prinzipal de la messa del pueo despoblado.''

[405] *Ibid*, fol. 70 to 77.

Mr. Bandelier says, *Final Report*, part ii, p. 215: ''These historical facts warn the investigator not to take all the ruins in the Jemez region for those of pre-historic settlements. At least ten of them are those of villages that were abandoned only between 1598 and 1680, and three, perhaps four, those of pueblos built, occupied, and forsaken between 1688 and 1694. It is possible that some ruin may be a reconstruction of an ancient pueblo, or, it may be, built with material taken from some ancient ruin, so that the original character of the remains has become transformed by modern intrusion, especially in manufactured articles.''

San Diego de Jemez was re-occupied after 1694, and inhabited until June, 1696.

[406] *Certificazion de los Huezos del Venerable Pe Fray Juan de Jesus*, August

Jemez came to the capital asking pardon and attributing all their bad actions to the influence of one of their chiefs, Diego, whom they were willing to surrender. The offer was accepted and Diego, instead of being executed, was sentenced to slavery in the mines of Nueva Vizcaya for a period of ten years.

11, 1694 (Ms.). Prince and other historians state that the remains of Fr. Juan de Jesus were buried in the "parish church;" that an old Indian and his wife showed De Vargas where the friar had been buried in 1680.

The *Journal* of De Vargas contains the following entries relative to the removal of the remains of the Fr. Juan de Jesus to Santa Fé:

"On said tenth day of August, aforesaid date, having heard mass and the sermon, on the feast of the holy martyr San Lorenzo, of this day, the Rev. Father Vice-custodio Fr. Juan Muños de Castro and the other Reverend Fathers Missionaries Apostolic, came to bid me welcome, Governor and Captain-General as aforesaid, and presented their congratulations for my success and triumph, and most of all in that in which they were so interested, the vesture of the bones which were judged to be, and are undoubtedly considered to be those of the Rev. Father Juan de Jesus, missionary, who was Apostolic Preacher in the Convent of the Pueblo of Jemez, who, on the eleventh day of August, one thousand six hundred and eighty, was inhumanly killed. And having in my room said bones, with the skull, I exhibited and showed them to them in a box of medium size, with lock and key. They were arranged in two (parts), the first of damask mandarin of two colors, crimson and yellow, the other of Brittany, with a large ribbon, and in this form said bones were collected and enveloped in said box, the key thereof being given to the aforesaid Rev. Vice-custodio; and it appearing that it was his wish to bury them the next day, which is tomorrow, the eleventh of the month aforesaid; and they (meantime) remain in my said room, thence to be carried forth for interment.

"And for the authenticity of the aforesaid, I have signed, with my aforesaid secretary in military and civil affairs.

"D. Diego de Vargas Zapata Lujan Ponce de Leon.
"Before me, Alfonso Rael de Aguilar,
"Secretary in Civil and Military Affairs.

"On the eleventh day of said month of August, of the date (aforesaid) and year, to carry forth for burial the bones and skull which are judged to be those of the deceased missionary, Fr. Juan de Jesus, which are in my room where I sleep, there came the Rev. Father Commissary and Vice-custodian of said Kingdom, Fr. Juan Muños de Castro, in company with the other discreet fathers who are in this town (villa), and asked me, as did also Rev. Fathers, Missionaries, to proceed to the translation and interment of the bones and skull aforementioned, and that I should give them the certificate relating therein the circumstances in the manner narrated by me authentically in said acts, which I gave unto them immediately, and my civil and military secretary having transcribed it, I ordered it to be entered in said acts. And they proceeded to translate and inter said bones and skull, placed in said box, closed and fastened, in the chapel which is used as a parish church for this garrison; which they did on the gospel side of the high altar, I, said Governor and Captain-General, having been present with a concourse of soldiers and vassals who were present in this aforesaid town.

"Witness my hand, with that of my military and civil military secretary.
"D. Diego de Vargas Zapata Lujan Ponce de Leon.
"Before me,
"Alfonso Rael De Aguilar,
"Secretary in Military and Civil Affairs."

It now became necessary for the captain-general to take decided steps against the Tehuas and Tanos. Winter was coming on and he determined once more to attack the Indians of these tribes who still held the Black Mesa of San Ildefonso. With every soldier at his command, aided by 150 Queres and Jemez, De Vargas left Santa Fé on the 4th of September, assaulted the Indians upon the mesa, and was driven back with a loss of eleven men wounded, among them Captain Antonio Jorge of the Santa Fé garrison. The next day the native allies with some of the Spaniards marched up the slope, challenged the enemy, who were put to flight, two of their number being killed. The captain-general now devoted himself to cutting off the supplies of the Indians. Several times the Indians came down from the mesa and fought the Spaniards and their allies in the valley below, but each time met with defeat and retreated to their stronghold on the top of the mesa. They became discouraged, however, and finally, on the 8th, began to treat for peace, and pardon was granted them provided they return to their villages.

THE TEHUAS AND TANOS TREAT FOR PEACE

Inasmuch as the Jemez Indians had proved faithful allies in the campaign against the Tehuas and Tanos at San Ildefonso, De Vargas now restored to them their women and children, and on the 13th of September the chiefs of San Juan, San Cristobal, and San Lazaro reported to the captain-general that the Tehuas and Tanos had returned to their villages and were rapidly restoring their pueblos. De Vargas now appointed the regular pueblo officials, and in a few days started on a tour of inspection, finding everything to his satisfaction. During this tour De Vargas formally received the submission of and granted full pardon to the pueblos who had been in rebellion against his authority. By the end of the year the several friars were established in their missions, the Indians being occupied in the construction of churches and houses for their use and service.[407] The natives now seemed to have made up their minds

---

[407] Bancroft, H. H., *History of Arizona and New Mexico*, note, p. 212-213: ''The distribution was as follows: P. Francisco Corvera at San Ildefonso and Jacona; P. Geronimo at San Cristobal and (temporarily) at Santa Clara; P. Antonio Obregon at San Cristobal and San Lazaro; P. Diego Zeinos at Pecos; P. Juan Alpuente at Cia; P. Francisco J. M. Casanes at Jemez; P. Juan Muñoz de Castro, vice-custodio and com. de la inquisicion, at Santa Fé; P. José Diez at Tesuque; P. José Garcia Marin at Santa Clara; P. Antonio

to submit to the inevitable. De Vargas delivered over to them their women and children, whom he had distributed among the colonists as servants, causing much regret and opposition on the part of their masters. This policy made friends for the captain-general among the Indians, but was the cause of much trouble to De Vargas. Friar San Antonio, who had left for El Paso, resigned his office, and Fr. Francisco Vargas arrived as custodio in November, bringing with him four friars. In the meantime the governor sent south for three thousand fanegas of corn, wishing to relieve the Indians of excessive taxation for a time until the Indians should become more prosperous.[408]

In 1695 the colonists who had been brought to New Mexico by Friar Farfan settled in the new villa of Santa Cruz de la Cañada, which had been actually settled many years before, as we have records showing that Luis Quintana[409] was alcalde mayor of the village at the time of the revolt in 1680. In the new settlement, Fr. Moreño was the missionary. In his settlement were included the sites of the villages of San Cristobal and San Lazaro, which had been settled by the Tanos of Galisteo. It was urged by the friars that to deprive these Indians of their lands was very unjust on the part of De Vargas, and soon, before the friars in the several missions had been fairly installed, rumors of new troubles became very insistent and were circulated everywhere. The Indians had lost none of their hatred for the new condition of things and now that the friars were distributed and the forces of the enemy scattered, the Indians again began to think of driving the Spaniards out of the country. The Tehuas were specially prominent in these hidden conspiracies. The

Carbonel at San Felipe, Cochití and later Taos; P. Miguel Tirso at Santo Domingo; P. José Arbizu at San Cristobal; P. Antonio Moreno at Santa Fé (temporarily), La Cañada, and later Nambé; P. Antonio Acevedo at Nambé; P. Francisco Vargas, custodio.'' This leaves some of the original friars unaccounted for, and also one of the four who came in November, 1694.

[408] Bancroft, H. H., *History of Arizona and New Mexico*, p. 213: ''*Arch. N. Mex.*, 162-167: On January 10th, 1695, De Vargas wrote to the viceroy thanking him for the provisions — 3,000 fanegas of corn; and again, May 9th, on the trouble he had experienced in transporting the corn. *Arch de Santa Fé*, Ms. This, however, may not indicate that it was not purchased on De Vargas' account. It was charged later that only about 580 fanegas ever reached New Mexico, and much of that was wasted in the distribution.''

[409] At this founding of 1695 the villa was given the ''preeminencia de antiguedad'' over all the settlements of New Mexico, except Santa Fé. The poblaciones of Cerrillos and Bernalillo are also mentioned in the records of that year.

Fac-simile of Page of the Journal of Don Diego de Vargas, containing entry relative to ceremonies at time of Reconquest

Indians of San Cristobal and San Lazaro made their escape to the mountains, but returned as the other pueblos, who had promised aid, failed to join in a general movement.[410]

In the year 1696, a famine broke out desolating the colony. The people were very much distressed and were almost reduced to starvation. Every species of animals and herbs was used for food, and the people went into the mountains searching for them like wild beasts. In November of the preceding year the governor sent to the viceroy a petition of the cabildo and vecinos for relief, as all that they had sown had been consumed by the worms. The viceroy and junta in February following decided to send them two hundred cattle from Parral, with some arms and ammunition, at the same time warning them that they must learn to rely upon themselves and not upon the government for aid and assistance. The governor was charged with dereliction of duty in failing to distribute properly the stores of corn which had been sent up from Mexico; it is also stated that four of the colonists, driven by their suffering to desert, were captured and hanged by the governor without the consolations of religion. These statements were all supported by sworn testimony given a few years later in the City of Mexico.

THE FAMINE OF 1696

The friars, who doubtless had the best opportunities for understanding the real sentiments of the Indians, now looked for another general uprising. So satisfied were they of the hostile intentions of the Indians that on the 7th day of March the custodio wrote to the governor advising him of the imminent danger of a revolution, the defenseless condition of the several missions, the risks under which the friars were working, and the great damage which would inevitably result should the disaster of 1680 be repeated. He strongly insisted upon the placing of a guard of soldiers at each mission, but De Vargas, believing that the natives had submitted in good faith, paid no heed to the request of the custodio, although from different directions reports came in that the Indians had already committed outrages in the new churches. He told the friars that if they were fearful for their lives they might retire to the capital,

---

[410] *Arch. N. Mex.*, 168-9. May 31st, the settlers had been selling arms to the Indians, which was on this date forbidden by De Vargas. The friar at Pecos accidentally shot and killed an Indian, and was not blamed. The friar's name was Diego Zeinos.

and this course was pursued by some. The captain-general made a report to the viceroy in which he stated that all was quiet and the danger declared to exist by the friars was only imaginary. The language used by the governor in his report was regarded as an imputation upon their courage, and the friars who had come to Santa Fé quietly returned to their missions.

On the 4th day of June, 1696, the Indians of the pueblos of Taos and Picuriés, the Tehuas, the Queres of Santo Domingo and Cochití, as well as the Jemez, rose, killing five missionaries and twenty-one other Spaniards, and then fled to the mountains. The friar at the pueblo of Jemez had repeatedly warned De Vargas of the condition of affairs at his mission but De Vargas paid no attention to his reports. This priest, whose name was Fray Francisco de Jesus, also known as Fray Francisco de Casaus, was murdered and all of the Indians fled. They had no time to build a new pueblo on the mesa and only erected temporary shelters. Their first step was to secure help from the Navajós, from Acoma, and from Zuñi, and to make hostile demonstrations against the Indians of Cia, Santa Ana, and San Felipe. At Cia there was a small detachment of soldiers under the command of Captain Miguel de Lara, and he, together with the alcalde mayor of Bernalillo, Don Fernando Duran de Chavez, took the field against the superior numbers of the insurgents, starting on the 29th of June. A fierce conflict took place, partly in the San Diego canyon, partly at the ruins of the pueblo of San Juan, in which the Jemez and their allies were routed with the loss of thirty men. This defeat broke up the confederacy with Acoma and Zuñi, and caused the Jemez to flee to the Navajó country. When Captain Lara reconnoitered the mesas two months later, they were deserted. The Jemez remained among the Navajós for several years, finally returning to their old village and establishing themselves at or near the site of the present pueblo.[411]

THE UPRISING OF JUNE 4, 1696

[411] *Autos de Guerra*, 1696, fol. 7-94. The letters of Fernando Duran de Chavez and those of Captain Lara and of De Vargas' compadre, Bartolomé de Ojeda, give information as to this bloody battle. Ojeda states that the Indians lost forty killed, while Lara says that only twenty-eight fell. It is singular that Escalante, who had access to the official papers at Santa Fé, does not mention this battle, which was one of the most bloody of the war, and at the same time the most important, as it broke up the Jemez tribe and

Fac-simile of Page from the Journal of Don Diego de Vargas containing entry relative to the making of repairs on the chapel of San Miguel

Prior to the defeat of the combined forces of the Jemez, Acoma, and Zuñi as narrated, De Vargas left the capital for a tour of the deserted towns. Pecos, Tesuque, San Felipe, Santa Ana, and Cia had remained faithful, but as we have seen the Acomas and Zuñis had aided the rebels, not only actually participating in the outrages and conflicts but harboring the fugitives. The chief of Santo Domingo was captured on the 14th of June and immediately executed; several Indians who had gone to Pecos to stir up strife and secure the aid of that pueblo in the revolt, were also put to death at Pecos. On the 8th day of August, 1696, De Vargas marched to the pueblo of Acoma, having determined to punish the Indians for their part in the uprising and for the aid and

DE VARGAS MARCHES TO ACOMA comfort they had extended to those tribes which had been most prominent in the conspiracy. On the 15th he attacked the pueblo, captured five prisoners, one of them being the chief, but failed to reach the summit of the rock. Then he released the chief and endeavored to

frightened the Acomas and Zuñis to such a degree as to cause them to withdraw their aid. The Acomas lost eight men, while none of the Zuñis was slain.

The friars who lost their lives were Arbizú of San Cristobal, Carbonel of Taos, Corvera of San Ildefonso, Moreño of Nambé, and Casaus of Jemez. Corvera and Moreño were shut up in a cell at San Ildefonso and burned with the convent. Fr. Cisneros at Cochití had a narrow escape. Fr. Navarro of San Juan succeeded in escaping to La Cañada with the sacred vessels. According to Escalante, *Cron. Seraf.*, 260-86, Fr. Casaus at Jemez had foreseen his fate and asked the Indians to let him die at the foot of a certain cross. Summoned to attend a sick person, he was led into an ambush of Apaches, who killed him with clubs and stones at the chosen spot. He was the first martyr of the Queretaro college, and Espinosa gives an account of his life, including his miraculous transportation by an angel on muleback to visit unknown Texan tribes. Captain Lazaro Misquia, with Alf. José Dominguez and twelve soldiers, escaped from Taos and reached Santa Fé in nine days.

The Indians of San Felipe tell the story of the flight of Fr. Alonzo Ximenes de Cisneros, missionary at Cochití, from that village, on the night of June 4th, 1696, and his rescue by the Indians of San Felipe. The story is true in regard to the flight of the priest and the kind treatment extended to him by the people of Kat-isht-ya on the mesa; but the same cannot be said of the story of the siege which the pueblo is reported to have withstood afterwards. The Cochití Indians followed the friar, whom they intended to murder, for a short distance, but withdrew as soon as they saw he was beyond reach. Then they abandoned their pueblo and retired to the mountains, not to the Potrero Viejo, but to the more distant gorges and crests of the Valles range. The San Felipe pueblo was never directly threatened in 1696, and consequently the story of the blockade, and of the suffering from lack of water resulting from it and the miraculous intervention of the rescued friar, is without foundation.

See *Autos de Guerra del Año 1696*, Primer Cuaderno. Also Escalante, *Relacion*, pp. 172 and 174.

persuade the Indians, but was not successful, and finally shot the remaining four captives and withdrew. The friars Juan de Mata and Diego Chavarria were the chaplains of this expedition.

In the month of September, De Vargas proceeded against the Indians of the Taos pueblo, attacked them in a canyon not far from the village, and after several fights, in which his command suffered no injury, the Indians submitted and returned to the pueblo. The Tehuas of San Juan and their neighbors of Picuriés, in order to save the crops of that year, attempted to deceive the captain-general, but their plans were made known to De Vargas, and on the 26th of October, after a severe battle, eighty-four of their women and children were captured and given to his soldiers as servants after he had returned to Santa Fé. Upon his return to Santa Fé the captain-general made his report to the viceroy, from which it appears that all of the pueblos had submitted to his authority, with the exception of Acoma and the west, Pojoaque, Cuyamungué, and Santa Clara; there was also some doubt as to the loyalty of Santo Domingo and Cochití. Before the end of the year the friars of the college of Queretaro left for Mexico. At this time Captain Fernando Duran de Chavez was alcalde mayor of San Felipe and the "puesto de Españoles" of Bernalillo; Captain Roque Madrid was lieutenant-general of cavalry and alcalde mayor of "la villa nueva de los Mexicanos de Santa Cruz (de la Cañada):" Domingo de la Barreda was secretary of government and of war; Captain Alonso Rael de Aguilar, lieutenant-governor and captain-general in place of Luis Granillo. The cabildo of Santa Fé was the alcalde, Lorenzo de Madrid, Francisco Romero de Pedrada, Lazaro de Misquia, Diego Montoya, Jose Garcia Jurado; clerk, Lucero de Godoy.

As a result of this war, as we have seen, many pueblos were abandoned and a great many of the Indians lost their lives, mainly from sickness and exposure. Others left their old villages and joined the Apaches and Navajós, so that during this year there was a great diminution of the native population. The Spaniards, meanwhile, constantly increased in numbers.

BIBLIOGRAPHY

Archivo de Santa Fé	*Unbound Mss.* at Washington, D. C., in Library of Congress.
Archivo N. Mexico	*Archivo General de Mexico*, printed in 1856.
Bancroft, H. H.	*History of Arizona and New Mexico.*
Bandelier, A. F.	*Final Report*, parts i and ii.
Benavides, Alonzo	*Memorial*, Madrid, 1630.
Davis, W. W. H.	*The Spanish Conquest of New Mexico.*
Documentos para la Historia de Nuevo Mexico	*Four Series*, 20 volumes, Mexico, 1853, 1857.
Escalante, Silvestre Veles	*Carta*, in *Archivo N. Mex.*
Gregg, Josiah	*Commerce of the Prairies*, New York, 1844.
Mange, Juan M.	*Historia de la Pimeria Alta*, in *Doc. Hist. Mex.*, 4th series, i, 226.
Otermin, Antonio de	*Extractos.*
Prince, L. Bradford	*Historical Sketches.*
U. S. Land Office Reports	Printed at Washington in 1856; is translation of part of the *Archivo de Santa Fé*.
Siguenza y Góngora	*Mercurio Volante*, etc.

CHAPTER IX

ONE HUNDRED AND TWENTY-TWO YEARS OF SPANISH RULE,
1700-1822

THE term of office of De Vargas expired in 1696, and the king named Don Pedro Rodriguez Cubero to succeed him. On account of his successes De Vargas had fully expected a re-appointment at the hands of his royal master, but his application came too late. De Vargas made strong protest to the viceroy, but the representative of the crown sustained his successor, who proceeded to New Mexico and took possession of his office on the 2nd day of July, 1697.[412] The action of the viceroy in sustaining Cubero did not reach the king until nearly three years had elapsed. This delay is not accountable, for it appears that when the king was apprized of the situation, he made public his acknowledgment of the thanks and appreciation of the crown and gave to De Vargas the choice of titles between marqués and condé, and also gave him a re-appointment, which was to take effect three years later upon the expiration of the term of office of Cubero, or sooner, if the office should become vacant.[413] In this royal order everything that had been done by the viceroy was also approved,[414] and it was further ordered that the garrison at Santa Fé be strengthened to a maxi-

---
[412] According to the *Arch. N. Mex.*, p. 174, the date was July 4th. The acts of the viceroy in connection with the re-conquest were approved by a royal cedula of January 26, 1699.

[413] June 15, 1699, in *N. Mex. Cedulas*, Ms., 29-33.

[414] Davis, W. W. H., *Conquest of New Mexico*, p. 414, says: "In the year 1695 the corporation of Santa Fé, and the regiment in garrison there, presented charges to the viceroy against De Vargas, for peculation." As stated by Bancroft, *History of Arizona and New Mexico*, note, p. 218, this is an error; the charges were preferred at a later date by the cabildo, or corporation of Santa Fé.

Typical Zuñi Indians

mum of one hundred men, and that additional families should be sent to the province from Mexico.

From the very beginning De Vargas had incurred the displeasure of the cabildo of Santa Fé. As has been seen, De Vargas had enjoyed the full confidence of the viceroy, the condé de Galve, and, in the administration of the affairs of the province, he had seen fit, in many ways, to ignore the minor civil and military officials. His policy of restoring Indian captives to their several pueblos also gave great dissatisfaction to the settlers, who were thus deprived of their slaves. Upon the arrival of Cubero, the cabildo again took up the quarrel with De Vargas and filed formal charges against him. He was accused of the embezzlement of money which had been given him for the purpose of supporting the colonists. On account of his having ordered the execution of the Tanos captives at Santa Fé, it was declared that he had provoked the hostilities of 1694-6. The famine of 1695-6 was laid at his door, inasmuch as it was charged that by the mismanagement of the ex-governor and his failure properly to distribute the remaining portion of the food supply, the famine had been brought upon them. He was charged with having sold a portion of this food supply in the south for his own private gain. He was charged with oppression in having driven out of the country the members of families who were likely to testify against him. Don Juan Paez Hurtado, afterwards a governor of New Mexico, was declared to have been an accomplice of De Vargas.[415]

[DE VARGAS IS PLACED IN PRISON AT SANTA FÉ BY GOVERNOR CUBERO]

Governor Cubero felt very unkindly toward De Vargas, largely on account of the position taken by the latter, who gave up his office very unwillingly upon the arrival of Cubero. The cabildo of Santa Fé knew that Cubero was the foe of De Vargas. Cubero gratified his enmity and that of the officials of the cabildo by finding De Vargas guilty as charged. He was fined four thousand pesos as costs of the suit, all of his property was confiscated, and he was confined in prison for nearly three years. In fact, at the very time that he was publicly thanked by his king and offered the title of

---

[415] Bancroft, H. H., *History of Arizona and New Mexico*, note, p. 219, says: "The charges in detail are recited in the original documents, still preserved, though not complete, in the *Arch. Sta. Fé.*" These documents are now in the custody of the government at Washington.

marqués or condé, De Vargas was an inmate of the jail at the capital of the province.[416]

The fact that De Vargas was so closely guarded, was not allowed to present his case to the viceroy, and the other harsh treatment administered by Cubero would seem to indicate a pronounced animus on the part of the latter. Upon his arrival at the city of Mexico De Vargas succeeded in having the charges against him fully investigated; this was done by royal order and, as a result, he was fully exonerated and his re-appointment as governor remained valid. The cabildo, having heard of the results of the investigation and the re-appointment of De Vargas, petitioned the king against permitting his return; but the king by a cedula of October 10, 1701, ordered an investigation, and immediately the cabildo recognized the position in which they had placed themselves and retracted the accusations they had made.[417]

During the period of De Vargas's imprisonment many settlers came to New Mexico. There were also many soldiers who came

---

[416] The cabildo filed its charges against De Vargas in the month of October, 1697. On the 20th day of that month, Governor Cubero issued orders to Captain Luis Granillo, at El Paso, to arrest Hurtado and send him to Santa Fé. At the same time Captain Antonio Valverde, Alf. Martin Urioste, and Adj. Félix Martinez were exiled from the province. Hurtado, it was charged, had defrauded the colonists of half of the money allotted to them by the crown; of collecting $100.00 each for 38 colonists who never came to New Mexico; of employing individuals for the purpose of impersonating colonists, for each of whom he collected $100.00, and subsequently filling their places with negroes, and finally of collecting $100.00 several times on account of one person assuming different names. He was also charged with the theft of a box containing $7,000.00, and of aiding and abetting Governor De Vargas in his illegal and oppressive acts.

Bancroft, H. H., *History of Arizona and New Mexico*, p. 220, says: "Few, even of his own family, were allowed to see him, and every precaution was taken to prevent the sending of any written communication to Mexico or Spain. Padre Vargas, the custodian, visited Mexico and obtained an order for the prisoner's release under bonds to defend himself before the viceroy; but Don Diego refused to accept liberty on such conditions, claiming that to give bonds would be degrading to a man of his rank and services, especially in view of the king's recent orders in his favor. At last came an order for his release without conditions and he started for Mexico in July, 1700."

[417] Bancroft, H. H., *Ibid*, p. 220, says: "It would perhaps be going too far to declare Don Diego entirely innocent; the cabildo, however, later retracted its accusations, attributing all the blame to Cubero; and the chronicler, a Franciscan, who can hardly be suspected of prejudice in Vargas' favor, states — doubtless reflecting the views of his order — that Don Diego, while somewhat over-enthusiastic, disposed to promise more than he could perform, and to ignore in his reports many of the difficulties and dangers in New Mexico, never gave the Spaniards any just cause of enmity, but rather merited their love as a protector."

Fac-simile of Page from the Journal of Don Diego de Vargas, containing entry relative to the burial of the remains of Fr. Juan de Jesus, murdered in the revolt of 1680

at this time, and in all probability the total population of Spaniards in New Mexico was not less than 1,500. There is very little, from the standpoint of interest, which may be said of the rule of Cubero. In July, 1699, he visited the pueblos in the west, and the Moquis, who never had any regard for the Spaniards, sent representatives to Cubero, agreeing to rebuild the churches which had been destroyed and to receive the Franciscan missionaries.[418]

The Queres who had fled from the pueblos of Cieneguilla, Santo Domingo, and Cochití, built a new pueblo on a stream called Cubero.[419] The vast plain in that vicinity is also known as the Cubero plain, and was doubtless so named because of the visit of Cubero at this time; this pueblo was known as San José de la Laguna.[420]

[418] Niel, *Apuntias*, 108-9, says that Moqui was visited at this time.

[419] The new pueblo of the Queres submitted; also those of Acoma and Zuñi as well.

Bandelier, A. F., *Investigations in the Southwest*, Final Report, part ii, p. 314, says: "Nine miles northeast of the pueblo of Laguna, and fourteen north of Acoma, the little town of Cubero stands in the corner of a plain that extends along the southern base of the dark mesas above which the Sierra de San Mateo rises as from a pedestal. This plain is fertile, and about fifteen miles long from west to east, and five to six broad. In its northeastern corner the Picacho stands up like a black tusk. There are a number of ruins on the plain around Cubero. The largest one was a pueblo capable of sheltering a few hundred souls, with pottery of the coarsely glazed kind, some corrugated and indented ware, and a sprinkling of the ancient black and white and red and black. Excavations have revealed cells of the usual size and form, and more pottery. Whether this ruin, which seems to belong to the class of those on the Rio Grande and about the Salines, is claimed by the people of Acoma as one of their former pueblos or not, I am unable to say.

"Remains of detached houses, all built of stones, are common on the Cubero plain, and the pottery with which these ruins are covered is of the distinctively ancient type. At the Rinconada de San José, on the western extremity of the plain, at the foot of a mesa the eastern front of which bends around in a semicircle, I found fifteen of these dwellings, similar in size and in arrangement to the clusters which I have already described in the vicinity of Socorro and of Abó. In most cases the walls of the houses could be easily traced. There my attention was for the first time directed to this class of ruins, and my suspicions awakened that they might represent a peculiar type, and were not, as I at first supposed, ancient summer-houses of the inhabitants of communal dwellings."

[420] Hodge, F. W., *Handbook of American Indians*, part i, p. 752: "A Keresan tribe whose principal pueblo, which bears the same popular name, is situated on the south bank of San José river, Valencia county, N. Mex., about 45 miles west of Alburquerque. It was formerly the seat of a Spanish mission, dating from its establishment as a pueblo in July, 1699, and having Acoma as a visita after 1782. The lands of the Lagunas consist of a Spanish Grant of 125,225 acres, mostly of desert land. The Laguna people are composed of 19 clans, as follows, those marked with X being extinct: Kohaia (Bear), Ohshahch (Sun), Chopi (Badger), Tyami (Eagle), Skursha (Water-snake), Sqowi (Rattlesnake), Tsushki (Coyote), Yaka (Corn, divided into Kochinish-yaka, or Yellow-corn,

In October of the same year, a chief of the Moqui, of Oraibe, Espeleta by name, paid a visit to the governor at Santa Fé, proposing a treaty of peace, with the proviso that his nation, like the Spaniards retain their own religion.[421]

---

and Kukinish-yaka, or Red-corn), Sits (Water), Tsina (Turkey), Kakhan (Wolf), Hatsi (Earth)X, Mokaiqch (Mountain-lion)X, Shawiti (Parrot), Shuwimi (Turquoise), Shiaska (Chapparal-cock), Kurtsi (Antelope), Meyo (Lizard), Hapai (Oak). Most of the clans constitute phratal groups, as follows: (1) Bear, Badger, Coyote, Wolf; (2) Mountain-lion and Oak; (3) Water-snake, Rattlesnake, Lizard, and Earth; (4) Antelope and Water. According to Laguna tradition, the Bear, Eagle, Water, Turkey, and Corn clans, together with some members of the Coyote clan, came originally from Acoma; the Badger, Parrot, Chapparal-cock, and Antelope clans, and some members of the Coyote clan, came from Zuñi; the Sun people originated probably in San Felipe; the Water-snake in Sia; the Rattlesnake probably in Oraibi; the Wolf and Turquoise in Sandia; the Earth clan in Jemez; the Mountain-lion and Oak people claim to have come from Mt. Taylor; the Lizard clan is of unknown origin. Laguna, therefore, is not only the most recent of the New Mexican pueblos, but its inhabitants are of mixed origin, being composed of at least four linguistic stocks — Keresan, Tanoan, Shoshonean, and Zuñian. It is said that formerly the people were divided into two social groups, or phratries, known as Kapaits and Kayomasho, but these are now practically political parties, one progressive, the other conservative. Until 1871 the tribe occupied, except during the summer season, the single pueblo of Laguna, but this village is gradually becoming depopulated, the inhabitants establishing permanent residences in the former summer villages of Casa Blanca, Cubero, Hasatch, Paguate, Encinál, Santa Ana, Paraje, Tsiama, and Puertecito. Of these, Paguate is the oldest and most populous, containing 350 to 400 inhabitants in 1891. Former villages were Shinats and Shunaiki. The Laguna people numbered 1,384 in 1905, in 1910, 1,583."

[421] Bancroft, H. H., *History of Arizona and New Mexico*, pp. 221-222, says: "At the same time (May, 1700) Espeleta, chief of Oraibe, sent for Padre Juan Garaicochea to come and baptize children. The friar set out at once with Alcalde José Lopez Naranjo, and went to Aguatuvi, where he baptized 73 young Moquis. On account of a pretended rumor that the messengers to Santa Fé had been killed, he was not permitted to visit Oraibe or the other pueblos at this time; but Espeleta promised to notify him soon when they were ready for another visit, Garaicochea returning to Zuñi and reporting to the governor on June 9th. In October the Moquis were again heard from, when Espeleta came in person to Santa Fé with 20 companions, and with somewhat modified views. He now proposed a simple treaty of peace, his nation, like Spain, to retain its own religion. Cubero could offer peace only on condition of conversion to Christianity. Then the Moqui chief proposed as an ultimatum that the padres should visit one pueblo each year for six years to baptize, but postponed permanent residence till the end of that period. This scheme was likewise rejected, and Espeleta went home for further deliberation."

Bandelier, A. F., *Final Report*, part ii, pp. 371-372: "On the 11th of October of the same year (1700) one of the leading chiefs of Oraybe appeared at Santa Fé with twenty other delegates and presented themselves to the governor, Pedro Rodriguez Cubero, as a formal embassy from the Moquis not as subjects and vassals of the crown, but as delegates of a foreign power sent to conclude a treaty of peace and amity. This Cubero could not entertain; still he negotiated with them for a long while, until finally the Moquis, seeing that the governor would not recede from his position, seemingly yielded consent to

Fac-simile of Page from the Journal of Don Diego de Vargas

Within a year after the visit of the Oraibe chieftain to Santa Fé the Moquis of the pueblos other than those of Aguatuvi fell upon the people of that pueblo and utterly destroyed it for the reason that the inhabitants had received the missionary, Fr. Garaicoechea, and had repaired or rebuilt the convent and mission which had been destroyed in the rebellion of a few years previous. All of the Moquis had given in their allegiance to Spain anew, in 1692, and Cubero, regarding them as vassals and subjects of the Spanish crown, would entertain none of the proposals [422] made by Espeleta.

DESTRUCTION OF THE PUEBLO OF AGUATUVI

The submission of the pueblos at the close of the seventeenth century was comparatively complete. The power of the Spaniard was everywhere in evidence. During the entire period of one hundred years which followed, the pueblos gave little, if any, trouble. They were demoralized, tired of revolts, which seemingly availed them nothing and always resulted in disaster. There were some local troubles,[423] but nothing of a serious character disturbed the Span-

everything that was asked. With these false promises they were suffered to return, and Cubero indulged the hope that he had completely gained his point.

"In the meantime Ahua-tuyba had virtually become again a Christianized pueblo. In the last days of the year 1700, or in the beginning of 1701, the Moquis of the other pueblos fell upon the unsuspecting village at night. The men were mostly killed, stifled in their estufas, it is said; the women and children were dragged into captivity, and the houses were burnt. The exact date of this butchery I have not been able to find, as nearly all the papers concerning the administration of Cubero have disappeared from the archives at Santa Fé; since that time Ahua-tuyba has belonged to the class of ruined historical pueblos."

[422] *Relacion*, p. 179. The proposition made by Espeleta is unique. It was as follows: "Respondió Espeleta, que el venia á nombre de todos los Moquiños, y qe estos en consulta generál, habian resuelto admitir que entrasen los religiosos á bautizar los parvulos de cada pueblo de la provincia; sucesivamente en seis años, entrando el primer año el primer pueblo, y regrasandose concluidos los bautismos, y el siguiente año al segundo pueblo, y de este modo entrando y saliendo hasta llegar á Oraibe y completar los dichos seis años, y concluidos estos del modo dicho se rendirián todos los Moquiños y admitirian de asiento á los ministros."

Mr. Bancroft thinks that this slaughter never occurred, but detailed reference is made to it in a *Parecer* of the clergy of New Mexico, bearing date 1722. In it the destruction of Aguatuvi is explicitly stated. There existed at Santa Fé, in 1713, a collection of testimonies taken on the occurrence, and described as follows: "Yten vn Quaderno de autos sobre la notisia de lo susedido en el puo de Aguatubi de la proa de Moqui autorisadas de Pedro de Morales en 63 fojas." It is mentioned in Ynbentario de los Papeles que se hallan en el Archibo del Cabildo justizia reximiento de esta villa de Santa Fé, 1713, Ms.

[423] Bancroft, H. H., *History of Arizona and New Mexico*, pp. 225-226, says: "In the spring of 1702 there were alarming rumors from various quarters, rest-

iard except raids from the Navajós, Apaches, Comanches, and other wild tribes. In 1701, after the destruction of Aguatuvi, Governor Cubero marched against the Moquis, killing a few and capturing a great many, but the captives were all released, as this was deemed good policy.

In the month of August, 1703, Governor Cubero, having learned that De Vargas was on his way from Mexico to assume the duties of governor, to which office he had been appoint-
RETURN OF DE VARGAS ed, fearing that De Vargas would take revenge upon him for the many acts of cruelty which he had suffered at his hands, under the feigned statement that he was going upon a campaign against the Indians, left Santa Fé and never returned. Later he was named as governor of Maracaibo, but died in Mexico some time in the year following. De Vargas, now marqués de la Nava de Braziñas, arrived at Santa Fé in November, 1703, and on the 10th of the month assumed the office of governor and captain-general for a second time. The Franciscans urged him to reëstablish the mission at Zuñi, the Fr. Garaicoechea having kept in touch with the internal affairs of that pueblo; but De Vargas declined to grant the request, or at least found no opportunity during his brief incumbency to give the matter attention. In March, of the following year, De Vargas began a campaign

ing largely on statements of Apaches, who seem in these times to have been willing witnesses against the town Indians. Cubero made a tour among the pueblos to investigate and administer warnings, but he found slight ground for alarm. It appeared, however, that the Moquis, or perhaps Tehua fugitives in the Moqui towns, were trying to incite the Zuñis and others to revolt; and it was decided to send Captain Juan de Uribarri with a force to make investigations, and to leave Captain Medina and nineteen men as a garrison at Zuñi. This was probably done, but, all being quiet, the escolta was soon reduced. The remaining soldiers behaved badly, and three Spanish exiles from Santa Fé much worse, treating the Indians harshly, and living publicly with native women. The padre complained; the governor failed to provide any remedy, and, on March 4, 1703, the Indians killed the three Spaniards, Valdés, Palomino, and Lucero, fleeing, some to the peñol, others to Moqui. The soldiers seem to have run away. Padre Garaicoechea was not molested, and wrote that only seven Indians were concerned in the affair; but evidently in his missionary zeal and sympathy for the natives he underrated the danger. The governor, justifying his course by the viceroy's orders to use gentle means, sent Captain Madrid to bring away the friar, and Zuñi, like the Moqui towns, was left to the aborigines.''

Arch. N. Mex., 180-6. Fr. Miranda, who was located at Acoma, wrote to Cubero that all the Zuñi property had been stolen; that Fr. Garaicoechea's life was threatened and that the Indians of Acoma and Cia wished to go to his rescue.

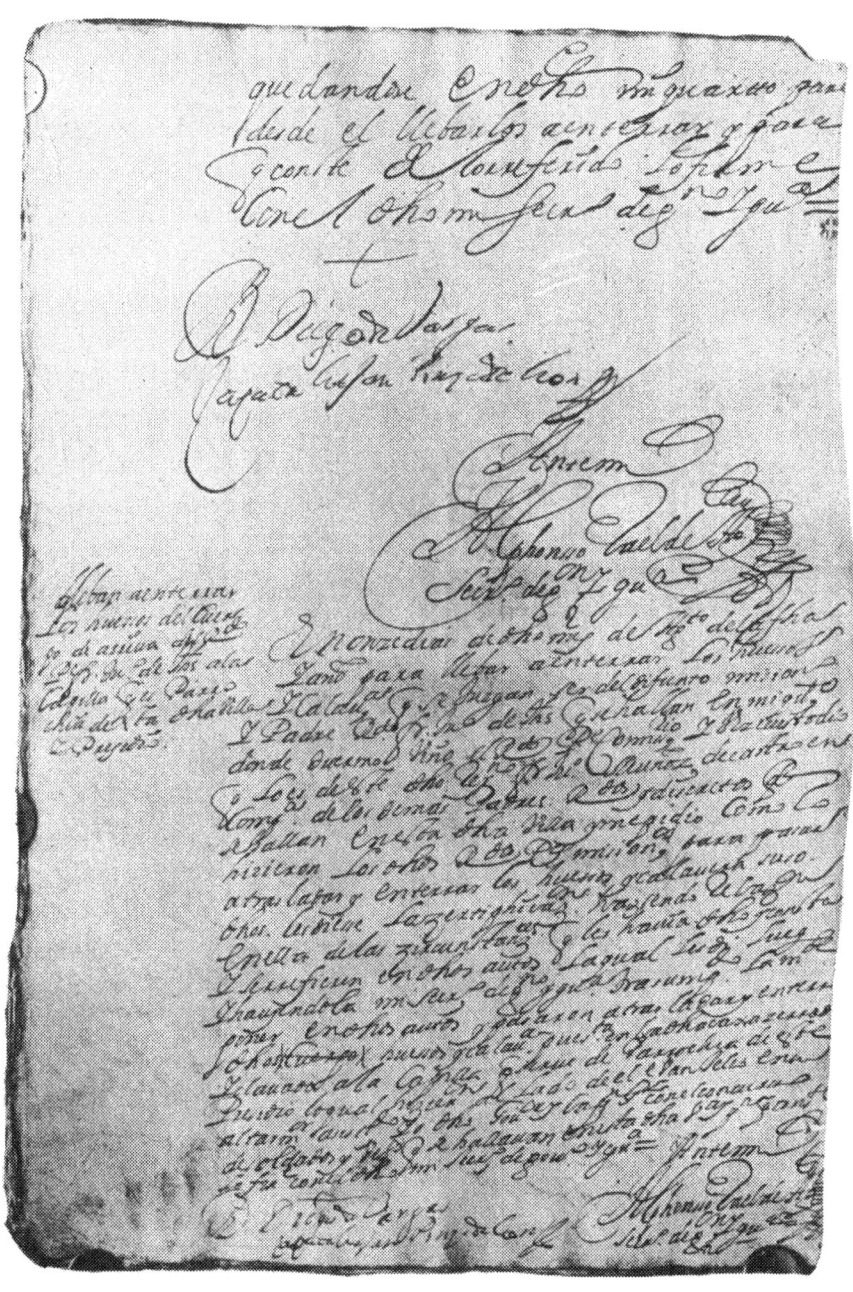

Fac-simile of Page of the Journal of Don Diego de Vargas, containing entry relative to the burial of the remains of Fr. Juan de Jesus, killed in the revolt of 1680 at Jemez

SPANISH RULE, 1700 TO 1822   421

against the Apaches but was taken suddenly ill in the Sandia mountains and died at Bernalillo on the 4th of April. His remains were taken to the capital and buried under the altar in the parish church.[424]

Don Juan Paez Hurtado, an intimate friend of De Vargas and for whose arrest, several years previous, Cubero had issued an order, upon a charge of embezzlement of funds belonging to the colonists, now lieutenant-general of the province, served as acting governor until the 10th day of March, 1705.

DON JUAN PAEZ HURTADO
GOVERNOR AD INTERIM

On the date last mentioned, Don Francisco Cuervo y Valdés assumed the office of governor ad interim, having been appointed by the viceroy, Don Francisco Fernandez [425] de la Cueva Enriquez, Duke of Alburquerque. The new governor found the affairs of the province in a very bad state. The Apaches and Navajós were constantly raiding the settlers and the friendly pueblos. The Moquis still refused to receive the missionaries, some of the Zuñis were on their peñol, and the soldiers stood in great need of clothing and supplies. The governor made frequent appeals for aid, but only a small supply of arms and ammunition was sent to New Mexico for his use. The viceroy notified his royal master of the fact of his having appointed Cuervo to the governorship by a letter written

DON FRANCISCO CUERVO Y VALDES APPOINTED GOVERNOR BY THE VICEROY

---

[424] Upon the site of the old parish church was begun, under the supervision of Archbishop J. B. Lamy, soon after his coming to New Mexico, the construction of the present cathedral at Santa Fé. This building has never been completed. Every year a procession is had, at which an image of the Virgin Mary, claimed by some to be the same one which De Vargas carried into the battle fought by him at Santa Fé at the time of the re-conquest, is carried at the head of the procession, from the Cathedral to the Chapel of Rosario. On the eve of the battle De Vargas made a vow that if he was successful in his battle with the Indians this image should be carried from the principal church to the chapel which he erected on the battlefield later on, and it is said that this vow has been kept every year since.

[425] The Duke of Alburquerque was the 34th viceroy of New Spain; he was the second of his title to hold the office; he arrived at Vera Cruz on the 6th day of October, 1702, and assumed control of the government on the twenty-seventh of the following month. He enjoyed the confidence of Felipe V, and continued in the viceroyalty until the year 1710, when he was succeeded by Don Fernando de Alencastre Noroña y Silva, duke of Linares and marqués of Valdefuentes.

on the 11th of October, 1704. Governor Cuervo was a knight of Santiago and had been a treasury official at Guadalajára.

In 1706 Governor Cuervo informed the viceroy that he had founded the new villa of Alburquerque, and had named the same in his honor, the population at that time consisting of thirty families; that he had re-settled Santa Maria — formerly Santa Cruz — de Galisteo, with eighteen Tanos families from Tesuque; had transferred some Tehua families to the old pueblo of Pojoaque, and had re-founded with twenty-nine families the old

CITY OF ALBURQUERQUE
FOUNDED BY CUERVO

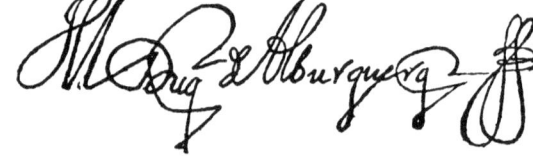

Facsimile of signature of the Duke of Alburquerque

Villa de La Cañada. The governor was taken to task by the viceroy for founding the Villa de Alburquerque without authority and he was ordered to change the name to San Felipe de Alburquerque, instead of San Francisco, in honor of the king, Felipe V. During Cuervo's rule, small garrisons were maintained at Santa Clara, Cochití, Jemez, and Laguna.[426] All of the cavalry at El Paso was brought to Santa Fé. In the year 1706, Juan de Uribarri, who had been a captain, was made a general and conducted a campaign against the Indians on the buffalo plains. At Jicarilla,[427] thirty-seven leagues

---

[426] *Arch. Santa Fé*, Ms. Upon his arrival, or soon thereafter, Cuervo ordered an inspection of the Spanish troops in the province, from which it appeared that there were 74 at Santa Fé, 37 at Bernalillo, and 82 at La Cañada.

Fr. Juan Alvarez was custodio of the Franciscans; Fr. Juan de Zavaleta was comisario of the sancto oficio. Captain Valverde was lieutenant-general and commander at El Paso. Juan Paez Hurtado and Juan de Uribarri were named as generals; Lorenzo de Madrid, maestro de campo; captains, Félix Martinez, Juan Lucero Godoy, Diego de Medina, and Alf. Juan Roque Gutierrez; alcalde, Captain Diego Arias de Quiros; alguacil mayor, Antonio Aguilar; regidores, Captain Antonio Montoya, Captain Antonio Lucero, Francisco Romero de Pedraza, Alf. Martin Hurtado; escribano, Cristobal Gongora, all at Santa Fé. At Bernalillo, captains, Fernando Chavez, Diego Montoya, Manuel Vaca, Alf. Cristobal Jaramillo, sergeant, Juan Gonzales. At La Cañada (Santa Cruz), captains, Silvestre Pacheco, Miguel Tenorio, José de Atienza, Nicolas Ortiz, and sergeant, Bartolo Malabato.

[427] Hodge, F. W., *Handbook of American Indians*, p. 631, part i: "An Athapascan tribe, first so called by the Spaniards because of their expertness in

northeast of Taos, he was kindly received by the Apaches, who conducted him to Cuartaléjo, naming the province San Luis. During the last year of the rule of Cuervo trouble again arose between the Moquis and the Zuñis, the latter having again become good Christians. Several detachments of soldiers were sent to the Zuñi country, and finally, in April, 1707, a junta of officers at the pueblo of Cia, which was attended by the governor, determined to withdraw all the frontier garrisons to Santa Fé.[428]

the making of basketry. They apparently formed a part of the Vaqueros of early Spanish chronicles, although, according to their creation legend, they have occupied from the earliest period the mountainous region of S. E. Colorado and N. New Mexico, their range at various periods extending eastward to W. Kansas and Oklahoma, and into N. W. Texas. The Arkansas, Rio Grande, and Canadian rivers figure in their genesis myth, but their traditions seem to center about Taos and the head of the Arkansas river. They regard the kindred Mescaleros and also the Navajó as enemies, and, according to Mooney, their alliances and blood mixture have been with the Ute and Taos. In language they are more closely related to the Mescaleros than to the Navajó or the Arizona Apache. The Jicarillas were first mentioned by this name early in the eighteenth century. Later, their different bands were designated Carlanes, Calchufines, Quartelejos, etc., after their habitat or chieftains. The Spaniards established a mission among them within a few leagues of Taos, N. Mex., in 1733, which prospered only for a short time. They were regarded as a worthless people by both the Spanish settlers of New Mexico and their American successors, in raids for plunder the worst of the Apache tribes, more treacherous and cruel and less brave and energetic warriors than the Ute, but equally fond of intoxicants. While they sometimes planted on a small scale, they regarded theft as a natural means of support. The governor of New Mexico in 1853 induced 250 of the tribe to settle on the Rio Puerco, but failure to ratify the treaty caused them to go on the warpath, maintaining hostility until their defeat by the United States troops in 1854. Henceforward they were nominally at peace, although committing many petty thefts. In 1870 they resided on the Maxwell Grant in New Mexico, the sale of which necessitated their removal. In 1872 and again in 1878 an attempt was made to move them south to Ft. Stanton, but most of them were permitted to go to the Tierra Amarilla, on the north confines of the territory, on a reservation of 900 square miles, set aside in 1874. Their annuities being suspended in 1878 on account of their refusal to move southward in accordance with an act of congress of that year, they resorted to thieving. In 1880 the act of 1878 was repealed, and a new reservation was set aside on the Rio Navajó, to which they were removed. Here they remained until 1883, when they were transferred to Ft. Stanton, but in 1887 were again returned to the reservation set aside for them in the Tierra Amarilla region by executive order of February 11 of that year, where they have since resided. Of this reservation 129,313.35 acres have been allotted to the Indians and 280.44 acres reserved for mission, school and agency purposes; the remainder is unallotted. Their population in 1905 was 795.''

[428] Bancroft, H. H., *History of Arizona and New Mexico*, p. 229: ''The Moquis often attacked the Zuñis, who were now for the time good Christians, and to protect whom Captain Juan Roque Gutierrez was sent in April, 1706, with eight men. With this aid the Zuñis went to Moqui in May, killed two of the old foe, and recovered 70 animals. Captain Tomás Holguin was sent with a new reënforcement, and in September surrounded the Tehua pueblo between

Governor Cuervo was succeeded in the governorship by the admiral, Don José Chacon Medina Salazar y Villaseñor, marqués de la Penuela, who had received his appointment from the king in 1705 and who governed the province until the year 1712. Governor Chacon also had some trouble with the Moquis, and he sent some of the Zuñi chieftains to Moqui exhorting them to peace and submission. Nothing was accomplished, however, other than a raid upon Zuñi led by Tanos and Tehua Indians. This governor rebuilt the chapel of San Miguel, erected about one hundred years previous during the time of Oñate, and destroyed by the Indians in the revolt of 1680.[429]

DON JOSÉ CHACON MEDINA SALAZAR Y VILLASEÑOR, MARQUÉS DE LA PENUELA, NAMED GOVERNOR

In the year 1709 a war was waged with the Navajós, who were constantly raiding the villages of the friendly Pueblos. All of the pueblos of the Jemez Indians [430] were sacked by this marauding tribe in the month of June of that year. Governor Chacón insti-

---

Walpi and Oraibi, forcing the Indians, after a fight, to sue for peace and give hostages; but the Tanos and other reënforcements arrived, attacked the Spaniards and allies as they retired, and drove them back to Zuñi, the hostages being shot. Presently the Zuñis — now under Fr. Miranda, who came occasionally from Acoma — asked to have their escolta removed, a request which aroused fears of a general rising in the west.''

[429] On the rafters in this chapel is carved the following inscription: ''El Señor Marquéz de la Penuela hizo esta fabrica; el Alferes Real Don Agustin Flores Vergara, su criado. Año de 1710.'' *Translation*: ''His Lordship, the Marquis de la Penuela, erected this building; the Royal Ensign Don Agustin Flores Vergara, his servant. A. D. 1710.''

Prince, L. B., *Historical Sketches of New Mexico*, p. 224, says: ''At this period all the principal churches in the 'kingdom' were rebuilt, including many that are now standing. The register of deaths — Libro de Difuntos — of the mission of San Diego, of Jemez, commences in August, 1720, when Francisco Carlos Joseph Delgado, 'Preacher of the Holy Office of the Inquisition,' was the priest in charge.''

The great church at Santa Cruz, which was the center of an enormous parish in the north, has records anterior to 1720; and its register of marriages, with a curious pen picture of the marriage of the Blessed Virgin to Saint Joseph as a frontispiece, bears date 1726, the first part being written by Padre Predicador Fray Manuel de Sopeña. The baptismal register in the church at Alburquerque commences in 1743.

[430] F. W. Hodge, in *Handbook of American Indians*, part i, pp. 629-630: ''A village on the north bank of the Jemez river, about twenty miles northwest of Bernalillo, N. Mex. According to tradition the Jemez had their origin in the north at a lagoon called Uabunatota (apparently identical with the Shipapulima and Cibobe of other Pueblo tribes), whence they slowly drifted into the valleys of the upper tributaries of the Rio Jemez — the Guadalupe and San Diego — where they resided in a number of villages, and finally into the sandy valley of

Don Francisco Fernandez de la Cueva Enriquez, Duke of Alburquerque, Viceroy of New Spain, 1702-1711

tuted a most vigorous campaign against them, defeating them in a decisive battle, after which they were compelled to make a treaty of peace.

Little seems to have been recorded during the years following the campaign against the Navajós, other than the activity of the members of the Franciscan order, led by Padre Peña, in an effort to compel the Indians to abandon the rites which they performed in their estufas or kivas. The Franciscans also made complaint to

the Jemez proper, which they now occupy, their habitat being bounded on the south by the range of the west division of the Rio Grande Keresan tribes — the Sia and Santa Ana. Castañeda, the chronicler of Coronado's expedition of 1541, speaks of seven pueblos of the Jemez tribe in addition to three others in the province of Aguas Calientes, identified by Simpson with the Jemez Hot Springs region. Espejo in 1583 also mentions that seven villages were occupied by the Jemez, while in 1598 Oñate heard of eleven but saw only eight. In the opinion of Bandelier, it is probable that ten pueblos were inhabited by the tribe in the early part of the 16th century.

"Following is a list of the pueblos formerly occupied by the Jemez people so far as known. The names include those given by Oñate, which may be identical with some of the others: Amushhungkwa, Astialakwa, Bulitzequa, Catroo, Ceca, Guatitrutri, Guayoguia, Gyusiwa, Hanakwa, Kiashita, Kiatsukwa, Mecastria, Nokyuntseleta, Nonyishagi, Ostyalkwa, Patoqua, Pebulikwa, Pekwilligi, Potre, Seshiuqua, Setoqua, Towakwa, Trea, Tyajuindena, Tyasoliwa, Uuhatzaa, Wabakwa, Yjar, Zolatungzezhii.

"Doubtless the reason for the division of the tribe into so many lesser village communities instead of aggregating in a single pueblo for defense against the persistent aggressiveness of the Navajó, according to Bandelier, was the fact that cultivable areas in the sandy valley of the Jemez and its lower tributaries are small and at somewhat considerable distances from one another; but another and perhaps more significant reason was that the Navajó were apparently not troublesome to the Pueblos at the time of the Spanish conquest. On the establishment of Spanish missions in this section and the introduction of improved methods of utilizing water for irrigation, however, the Jemez were induced to abandon their pueblos one by one, until about the year 1622 they became consolidated into the two settlements of Gyusiwa and probably Astialakwa, mainly through the efforts of the Fray Martin de Arvide. These pueblos are supposed to have been the seats of the missions of San Diego and San Joseph, respectively, and both contained chapels probably from 1618. Astialakwa was permanently abandoned prior to the Pueblo revolt of 1680, but in the meantime another pueblo (probably Patoqua) seems to have been established, which became the mission of San Juan de los Jemez. About the middle of the 17th century the Jemez conspired with the Navajó against the Spaniards, but the outbreak plotted was suppressed by the hanging of twenty-nine of the Jemez. A few years later the Jemez were again confederated with the Navajó and some Tigua against the Spaniards, but the contemplated rebellion was again quelled, the Navajó soon resuming their hostility toward the village dwellers. In the revolt of the Pueblos in August, 1680, the Jemez took a prominent part. . ."

The Jemez, who fled to the Navajó country at the time of the revolt in 1696, remained there several years, but finally returned to their former home and constructed their present village which is called Walatoa, "Village of the Bear." In 1728, 108 of the inhabitants died of pestilence. In 1782 Jemez was made a visita of the mission of Sia. The Jemez now number about 500.

the authorities in Mexico of abuses on the part of the governor and the alcaldes in making the Indians perform menial services. These complaints were answered by an order from the viceroy against forcing the Indians to work without being paid.[431]

Several royal orders, in regard to the affairs of New Mexico, were issued about this time, but none of them were of any historic significance.[432] The Marquis de la Penuela[433] retired as governor of New Mexico after the expiration of his term of office, and Don Juan Ignacio Flores Mogollon, who had been commissioned by Felipe V, at Madrid, assumed the office on October 5, 1712, and continued to rule until 1715. His salary, as fixed by the king, was two thousand dollars per annum. He was accused of malfeasance in office, but he was not tried until several years had elapsed. He was relieved of his position by royal order, October 5, 1715. His trial was had at Santa Fé, in 1721, long after he had left the province, and the finding of the court was sent to the viceroy for confirmation, the costs

JUAN IGNACIO FLORES MOGOLLON IS APPOINTED GOVERNOR

---

[431] Bandelier, A. F., *Investigations in the Southwest*, part i, p. 192: "The first great step in this direction was the promulgation of the celebrated 'New Laws and Ordinances for the Government of the Indies,' finally established in 1543, by which the aborigines were declared direct vassals of the crown. Stipulations in their favor, as, for instance, enfranchisement from personal servitude and from compulsory labor, became the subject of subsequent modifications and local changes, but the disposition first announced, that of direct vassalage, remained a fixed dogma in Spanish American law."

Ibid, pp. 194-6: "In New Mexico, there were no mines until after 1725, and compulsory labor on the part of Indians even after that date was limited to service in the missions, and, by abuse of authority, to personal attendance upon higher magistrates. The latter was time and again severely checked, and strong penalties threatened the governor who ventured to infringe the royal decrees prohibiting personal service to him and to his assistants. The solicitude of royal officers went so far as to abolish, in 1784, any and all personal services for church matters; a measure that called forth well grounded and effective protests."— Fr. Santiago Fernandes de Sierra, *Memorial*, Ms.

[432] Bancroft, H. H., *History of Arizona and New Mexico*, p. 231: "The soldiers had asked for an increase in pay, the friars for reënforcements, and Governor Cuervo had reported his great achievements in town founding; the cédulas were routine replies, ordering the viceroy to investigate and report, but always to look out for the welfare of the northern province. The sum total of information seems to be that there were thirty-four padres in the field, which number the viceroy deemed sufficient, though he was authorized by the king to increase the missionary force whenever it might be deemed best."

[433] Prince, L. B., in his *Historical Sketches*, p. 224, says that the marquis de la Penuela was succeeded by the duke of Linares. This is impossible, as that functionary in the beginning of the year 1711 had only assumed the duties of viceroy of New Spain.

being adjudged against him. The officer charged with their collection reported that neither the accused nor any of his property could be found. There was a revolt of the Sumas [434] Indians the first year of the new governor's incumbency. This tribe lived in the neighborhood of El Paso, and were very hostile to the Spaniards for a long period. These Indians had been conquered immediately following the Pueblo revolt of 1680. Governor Mogollon sent a force, commanded by Captain Valverde, against them. They were reduced in short order and compelled to settle at the Realito de San Lorenzo. In the following year occurred some trouble with the Indians of Acoma and Laguna, caused by the zealous acts of the fraile in charge of the mission. It was claimed that these Indians had determined to kill the Fr. Delgado, but it was impossible to ascertain the truth or falsity of the report.

In the month of October, 1713, a force under the command of Captain Serna, consisting of four hundred men, soldiers and colon-

---

[434] Bandelier, A. F., *Final Report*, part i, pp. 87-8 (note), says: ''That the Sumas lived about the Pass of the North at a very early date is certain. They are mentioned as forming a part of the first mission there, under the name of Zumanas, by Fray Garcia de San Francisco, *Auto de Fundacion*, 1659: 'Por aver ido, á dha custta los Capitanes y ancianos de la gentilidad, de los indios Mansos y Zumanas, á suplicarme; les bajase á predicar el SS evango de nro Sr. Jesuxpto.' At a still earlier date, in 1630, the Sumas are mentioned by Benavides, *Memorial*, p. 7. Vetancurt, *Cronica de la Provincia del Santo Evangelio de Mexico* (edition of 1871, p. 308), speaks of the Zumas and Zumanas as living somewhat below El Paso. Of their original numbers I have no idea. They became very turbulent after the uprising of 1680 and as early as 1681 there were signs of trouble. *Autos que se ysieron sobre clamar los Vesinos de este Reino para Salir á Mejorarse de Puesto, 1681*, Ms. . . Several settlements of Sumas were formed by the Spaniards around El Paso, but only one remained, San Lorenzo del Real. In 1744 it had but fifty Indian families, in 1765 only twenty-one. Current tradition among the Mansos of El Paso attributes their decline to the smallpox. It is certain that between 1693 and 1709 severe epidemics prevailed among the Indians at El Paso.

''In the documents forming the acts of the prosecution against the Mansos Indians when the latter, induced by the Sumas, rose against the Spaniards in 1684, there is mention of a ceremony performed by the Sumas. *Declaracion de Juan del Espiritu Santo* (fol. 21): 'Y llebandole de buelta á la Rancheria, les hallo á todos Juntos en Rueda, y con un cuchillo clauado en medio de ella en el suelo.' This ceremony appears to have been connected with their customs of war. Among the Pueblos I never heard of a similar practice, but it is said that the Apaches have some performance of that kind.

''In regard to the customs of the Sumas of the Rio Grande, little is positively known. . . Among the many bad habits charged to the Sumas, in general terms, the use of the Peyote is specially mentioned. This herb has a very bad reputation in the southwest among Indians and Spaniards.''

They were known as ''gente mui viciosa,'' and from accounts of their ceremonies and customs after using the ''Peyote'' were entitled to be known as of that class.

ists, and Indian allies, defeated the Navajós in their own country, and in addition, the Faraon tribe of Apaches were warned against the commission of further depredations. In 1714, the Utes and Taos were engaged in constant warfare, but quiet was restored through the efforts of Governor Mogollon, who compelled a restitution of all stolen property. The Navajó again raided the Jemez and in a campaign conducted by Captain Madrid the Navajó was forced to retire to his home in the northwest.

A junta of civil, military, and missionary authorities was held for the purpose of deliberating upon two questions which seemed to be of prime importance. One, whether the Christian Indians should be allowed to carry firearms; two, whether the converted natives should be permitted to paint themselves. It does not appear just how these questions were determined by the junta, although the frailes seemed to have been divided in their opinions upon the two subjects. This junta was held on the 6th day of July, 1714.[435] In the following year, Captain Juan Paez Hurtado, with a force of 250 men, conducted a campaign against the Apaches on the Colorado river, but nothing worthy of note was accomplished. The Moquis, as usual, were constantly causing trouble and no less than five juntas de guerra were held at Santa Fé on their account.

It appears that in June, 1713, an Indian named Naranjo was refused permission to visit the Moquis, but in December two natives of Zuñi, through Padre Irazabal, obtained the license and were given letters. They found the Moquis eager for peace and alliance with the Zuñis, but the controlling element under the chief of Oraibe had no desire for the friendship of the Spaniards. In the month of March, 1715, a Moqui appeared at the capital with favorable reports, and was sent back with assurances of good will. Later on, in May, a chief of Oraibe came to make further investigations, reporting

---

[435] Bancroft, H. H., *History of Arizona and New Mexico*, p. 222: "First, should the Christian Indians be deprived of fire-arms? The military favored such a policy, but the friars opposed it, both to avoid offence and afford the converts protection; and the governor at last ordered the arms taken away except in the case of natives especially trustworthy. Second, should the converts be allowed to paint themselves and wear skin caps, thus causing themselves to be suspected of crimes committed by gentiles, or enabling them to commit offences attributed to gentiles? Governor Flores and his officers, with some of the padres, were in favor of forbidding the custom; but the rest of the friars took an opposite view, holding that no Christian Indian had ever been known to use his paint for a disguise to cover crime."

Chapel of our Lady of Guadalupe, Santa Fé, 1850

that a grand junta of all the towns had decided on peace and Christianity. This chief was sent back with gifts, and in July eight Moquis came to announce that after harvest the formal arrangements for submission would be completed. Thus all went well so long as the Moquis were the ambassadors; but when the governor sent messengers of his own choosing, the truth came out that the pretended ambassadors were traders, who had invented all their reports to account for their visits and insure their own safety, the Moqui nation being as hostile as ever.[436]

Captain Félix Martinez, by appointment of the viceroy, assumed the office as acting governor, or possibly governor ad interim, on the 30th day of October, 1715. He immediately began suits at law against his predecessor and kept him in jail for two or three years. Captain Martinez was a soldier under De Vargas, and became a captain during the governorship of the Marquis de la Penuela. He was a man of very quarrelsome disposition and was forced to resign in 1712, but three years later he received a new appointment from the king as captain for life and *regidor perpetuo* of the villa. During his rule of two years two campaigns are recorded, one against the Moquis and the other against the Utes and Comanches. The governor led the army in person against the Moquis, having a force of sixty-eight men, together with the custodio, Fr. Camargo, the cabildo of Santa Fé, and a force of settlers from the towns of Alburquerque and Santa Cruz. Before the first battle began, commissioners were sent forward from Zuñi who found a portion of the Moqui towns willing to give in their submission, but the people of Walpi and those of the Tanos pueblo refused. Two battles occurred in the month of September, the Indians being defeated, but the army satisfied itself with destroying some of the corn-fields and then retreated to Santa Fé. On this expedition Governor Martinez visited "El Morro," Inscription Rock, as appears from the record cut in the stone, as follows: "In the year 1716, upon the 26th day of August, passed by this place Don Félix Martinez, governor and captain-general of this kingdom, for the purpose of reducing and uniting Moqui." On another part of the rock are the inscriptions

CAPTAIN FÉLIX MARTINEZ IS NAMED GOVERNOR AD INTERIM

---

[436] Bancroft, H. H., *History of Arizona and New Mexico*, p. 233.

of some of the companions of the governor, as follows: "Juan Garcia de la Revas, Chief Alcalde, and the first elected, of the town of Santa Fé, in the year 1716, on the 26th of August. By the hand of Bartolo Fernandez, Antonio Fernandez." The return to Santa Fé was made on the 8th of October, 1716.[437]

During the time that Governor Martinez was at Zuñi and Moqui the Utes and Comanches attacked the town of Taos, some other pueblos and some of the Spanish settlements near by. Captain Serna was sent with a substantial force and attacked the Indians at the Cerro de San Antonio, thirty leagues north of Santa Fé. The hostiles were decisively defeated, many of them being killed and all their own captives being taken by the Spanish captain. It afterwards developed that these captives were divided between Don Félix and his brother and sold in Nueva Viscaya, the Indians being told that they had died of the smallpox. In a memorial of 1722, all of the officers and soldiers stated that the province was in great peril during the rule of Martinez.[438]

In the year 1716, the viceroy of Mexico, through private sources, received many complaints concerning the conduct in office of Governor Martinez, and forthwith ordered Captain Antonio Valverde y Cosio to proceed from El Paso, assume the governorship and investigate the charges against Martinez which had reached him. Valverde did not reach Santa Fé until the 9th of December of that year, and on his arrival was received by Martinez, but the latter refused to give up his office or to place the records in Valverde's hands. Under the order of the viceroy, however, he was compelled to go to Mexico, and, placing the government in the hands of Captain Juan Paez Hurtado, he started for the City of Mexico on the 20th day of January, 1717.[439]

ANTONIO VALVERDE Y COSIO, GOVERNOR AD INTERIM

---

[437] *Arch. N. Mex.*, pp. 206-7. The governor accomplished nothing and the truth which he concealed in his diary of the expedition came out later in his residencia.

In *Moqui, Noticias*, Ms., 671-4, it appears that the Moquis at first pretended to be well disposed but required time for deliberation, but actually spent the time allowed — 5 days — in preparing for war. This expedition is mentioned by Fernandez Duro, *Noticias*, p. 137.

[438] *Arch. Sta. Fé*, Ms.: "Con su insaciable y voraz coaicia, robos y engaños manifestos, estuvo pendiente de un cabello para una total asolacion."

[439] Bancroft, H. H., *History of Arizona and New Mexico*, p. 235: "Valverde was ordered to accompany him to El Paso, but feigned illness, and took refuge with a friend, Padre Tagle, at the convent of San Yldefonso. As to resulting

Viceroys of New Spain

1. Don Fernando de Alencastre Noroña y Silva, Duke of Linares, 1711-1716.
2. Don Baltazar de Zuñiga, Marqués de Valero, Duke of Arion, 1716-1722.
3. Don Juan de Acuña, Marqués de Casa-Fuerte, 1722-1734.
4. Don Juan Antonio de Vizarrón y Eguiarreta, Archbishop of Mexico, 1734-1740.

Governor Valverde was very active in the performance of the duties of his office. In the year 1719 he led an expedition, consisting of one hundred and five Spaniards and thirty Indians, and a force

complications between Hurtado and Valverde, I have found no record, but suppose that the former ruled but a few months, and that before the end of 1717, as soon as orders could be returned from Mexico, Valverde assumed the office, which he held for four or five years.''

A tradition has come down to the descendants, now living, of Captain Sebastian Martin, that, in the year 1717, the Comanches were on the warpath and the lives of the Spanish settlers were in great danger at all times. Two daughters of Captain Martin were the wives of Spanish captains, Don Juan de Padilla and Don Carlos Fernandez; these men were famous in those days as spirited soldiers and intrepid Indian fighters. Of all the Indian tribes, the Comanche was the most aggressive, and its warriors were constantly committing depredations and carrying into captivity the children of the settlers. Finally it was determined to make a campaign against the marauders, and a general junta was held at Santa Fé. The officers selected to command the expedition were Don Juan de Padilla, first, Don Carlos Fernandez, second, and Don Pedro Pino, of Santa Fé, third. A majority of the soldiers were equipped with firearms but many had only machetes, lances, and bows and arrows. The first night out the expedition camped at the pueblo of Pecos, whence they marched to the Llano Estacado by way of Anton Chico. Many buffalo were on the plains in those days. Finally they came to a beautiful valley, where the scouts and trailers had led them. They were informed that the dreaded Comanches were only a few leagues ahead. Arrangements for a night march were made and the enemy was attacked at sunrise.

In those days the Spaniards wore their hair long, similar to the Indians, but tied in the back. Before starting all the men painted their faces red with almagre and let their hair down in order to look like Indians as much as possible. At dawn they found the Comanche camp; hundreds of tepees were in sight. A charge was ordered, and giving the war-cry of ''Santiago,'' the Spaniards charged and surprised the enemy. The Indians thought at first that the Spaniards were a returning war-party of their own people, but they were soon undeceived. The slaughter was terrible. Hundreds perished and seven hundred Indians were taken prisoners. Most of the Spanish captives were there and were liberated. The Comanches numbered hundreds, and had been in camp some time awaiting the return of war-parties that were raiding the country settled by the Spaniards. Only a few escaped this massacre.

The victorious Spaniards now started on the homeward march, and, arriving at the pueblo of Pecos, sent messengers ahead to Santa Fé to announce the success of the expedition to Governor Valverde. When the messenger arrived the captain-general and all the people were at the chapel of San Miguel, which had only recently been rebuilt. The governor announced to the people the good tidings which had been received and nearly every resident of the city went out to meet the returning soldiers, who, on their arrival, went to the parish church, where a Te Deum was sung.

What disposition was to be made of the Indian captives was a serious problem. It was finally determined to send them to Cuba, which was done by order of the queen of Spain. It did not take long for the climate of Cuba to do the work of extermination. In a few years there was not one Comanche of the lot left to tell the tale. Until a few years since there were letters in the possession of the Pino family giving full accounts of what was done with the prisoners.

The story of this campaign was written in verse by one of the members of the expedition and to this day, in some places in New Mexico, a play based upon the story is acted in a manner very similar to the matachines.

of Apaches under Captain Carlana, against the Utes and Comanches. He traveled north and east, exploring the areas now comprising the states of Colorado and Kansas, and going farther north, as he believed, than Coronado,[440] in 1541. This expedition left Santa Fé on the 15th of September, the Fr. Juan Pino accompanying it as chaplain. The Apaches who accompanied this expedition joined it at the Nepesta or Arkansas river.[441] On this stream Valverde became advised of a battle between the Apaches and the French, the latter being aided by the Pawnees [442] and the Jumanos.[443]

About this time the viceroy sent an order to Governor Valverde commanding him to establish a presidio of twenty-five men at Cuartelejo, some 130 leagues from Santa Fé,[444] a council of war, however, decided that this was impossible of execution as twenty-five men was entirely too small a force for the purpose. In 1718 complaint

[440] Valverde y Cosio (Antonio), *Diario y Derrotero*, 1719, Ms., in the *Pinart Col.* and cited by Mr. Bancroft, in note on page 236, *History of Arizona and New Mexico*. This diary states that the officers and men suffered terribly from poison-oak; that the best remedy found was the chewing of chocolate and the application of the saliva to the affected parts.

[441] These were the Apaches of Cuartelejo, Jicarillas, residing in the 17th and 18th centuries in the valley of Beaver creek, Scott county, Kansas. The district was called Quartelejo by Capt. Juan Uribarri, who on taking possession of it in 1706, named it the province of San Luis, giving the name Santo Domingo to the Indian rancheria.

[442] It is said that the French had given these Indians firearms. They were Pawnees, and the Spanish knew them as Pananas.
Escalante, *Carta*, p. 125, says that in the year 1719 a company under Captain Villasur was sent to find these Indians, 300 leagues northeast of Santa Fé. He reached the river on which their towns stood, but the Pananas attacked him in the night-time with guns, killing Villasur, Fr. Juan Mingues, and almost all of the command, including the French guide.

[443] Bandelier, A. F., *Investigations in the Southwest*, Final Report, part i, note, p. 212: "The earliest advance on the part of the French towards New Mexico, so far as known, is reported as having taken place in 1700. The French were said to have destroyed a village of the Jumanos. This, however, is not certain. I find it in the *Relacion Anonima de la Reconquista del Nuevo Mexico* (p. 180). The news was brought by an Apache from the plains. Certain it is that in 1702 the Governor Pedro Rodriguez Cubero made an expedition to the Jumanos. See *Libro de Difuntos de Pecos* (Ms.), 1695 to 1706. In case this aggression be true, it must have come from Texas or Louisiana. In 1720, the Spaniards made a reconnoissance with fifty men as far as the Arkansas, but they were surprised by the French and some Pawnees and nearly all perished. In 1748 it is officially stated that the French traded with the Comanches at the place called Quartelejo, north or northeast of Mora."

[444] *Arch. Sta. Fé*, Ms. At this time captain, Villasur was lieutenant-general. The alcaldes mayores were Alf. Cristobal Torres at La Cañada; captain, Luis Garcia at Alburquerque, Bernalillo, Santa Ana, Cia, and Jemez; captain, Alonzo Garcia, Isleta; captain, Antonio Uribarri, at Laguna, Acoma, Halona, and the entire region of the Zuñis; captain, Alfonso Rael de Aguilar, at Pecos and Galisteo, and captain, Miguel Tenorio de Alba at San Geronimo de Taos.

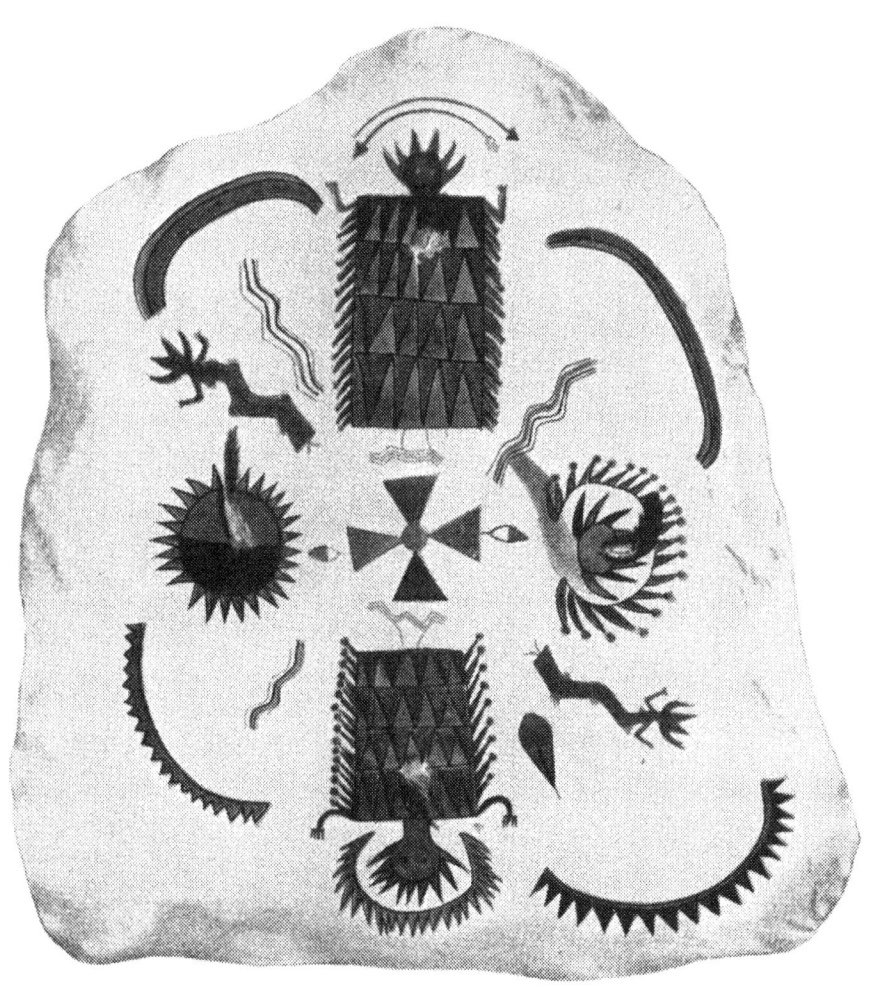

APACHE MEDICINE SHIRT

was made against the alcalde mayor of Cochití, Miguel de Vaca, charging him with maltreating and otherwise abusing the Indians of that pueblo. An investigation was had and Governor Valverde issued an order upon the subject of treatment of the natives by the Spanish officials.[445] About this time a dispute arose between the bishop of Durango and the archbishop of Mexico on the ecclesiastical jurisdiction of New Mexico. This fact appears in an order of February 11, 1719.[446] Governor Valverde made a tour of inspection of every pueblo and Spanish settlement in the province during the last two years of his tenure of office, and also received a royal order commanding an investigation of the management of Captain Félix Martinez and other commanders of the presidios in New Mexico.[447]

Some historians name Don Juan de Estrada y Austria as a governor of New Mexico. "It is perhaps true," says Mr. Bancroft, but

DON JUAN DE ESTRADA Y AUSTRIA ACTING GOVERNOR

that historian failed to find any original record of his presence and acting in that capacity. He came to New Mexico in 1721 for the purpose of investigating the charges and counter-charges in the controversies which had existed between Governors Mogollon and Martinez. He came as juez de residencia, and it is possible that, in that capacity, he may have held, as well, the position of acting governor, although the officers of the garrison at Santa Fé signed a memorial of praise in favor of Governor Valverde [448] and delivered the same to his successor, Don

---

[445] *New Mexico Cédulas*, Ms., 42-4.
[446] *N. Mexico Cédulas*, Ms., 44-5.
[447] Bancroft, H. H., *History of Arizona and New Mexico*, note, p. 237, says: "In a letter of Feb., 1886, Dr. J. F. Snyder, of Virginia, Cass Co., Ill., informs me that a massacre of Spaniards by the Missouris, mistaken for Pawnees by the victims, in 1720, is mentioned in all the early histories of the region. . .
It would seem that the expedition must have been that of Villasur, or one sent out after Valverde's return, and in consequence of his reports about the French." It is possible that Villasur, says Mr. Bancroft, reached the Missouri; but it is strange that such a disaster has left no definite trace in the archives.
The Missouris belonged to the Siouan family. About the beginning of the eighteenth century the French found them on the left bank of the Missouri river, near the mouth of Grand river. They dwelt here until about the year 1800.
[448] In this memorial there is no reference made to Don Juan de Estrada. Governor Valverde seems to have enjoyed the confidence of all the settlers and officers and soldiers, as well. He is accredited with all kinds of good conduct. He built, at his own cost, a church and chapel at the capital, and a chapel at San Ildefonso. After relinquishing his office, he returned to El Paso.

Juan Domingo de Bustamante. The principal act of Estrada was to preside over the trial of Governor Mogollon, and if he acted in an executive as well as judicial capacity, his term was very short, for Governor Bustamante assumed the office on the 2nd of March, 1722, and held the position until the year 1731.[449]

Governor Bustamante had been in office but a few months when a visitador-general, from the City of Mexico, Captain Antonio Cobian Busto, arrived at the capital for the purpose of making an investigation of the affairs of the province.

ADMINISTRATION OF GOVERNOR
JUAN DOMINGO DE BUSTAMANTE

Shortly after the arrival of the visitador-general, a convention was held at Santa Fé, being attended by all the principal men of the province. The order of Franciscans was present, represented by the leading members of the order, who were Fr. Juan de Tagle, comisario del Sancto Oficio and visitador, Fr. Juan de la Cruz, custodio and juez eclesiástica, Fr. Juan Sanchez, Fr. Diego Espinosa de los Monteros, Fr. Juan de Mirabal, Fr. Juan Antonio de Celi, Fr. Manuel de Sopeña, Fr. Carlos Delgado, Fr. Juan del Pino, Fr. Francisco Irazabal, Fr. Domingo de Araos, Fr. Francisco Antonio Perez, comisario del Sancto Oficio, Fr. José Antonio Guerra, guardian of the Convent at Santa Fé. This junta was held for the purpose of explaining to the visitador-general, who would make report to the king, why the country from Chihuahua to New Mexico was not fully settled by Spaniards. The convention found a reason in the small number and poverty of the settlers, and the fear of Indian raids. The convention proposed as a remedy the establishment of a presidio of fifty soldiers and two hundred settlers at Socorro, and another presidio of fifty soldiers at Aguatuvi. It was sought to explain to the representative of the crown that the country was rich in metals and well adapted to agriculture and the raising of stock, and that any expenditure of money by the government would be a good investment.[450]

---

[449] During the first year of Bustamante's rule, Miguel Enriquez was secretary; Juan Paez Hurtado and Antonio Becerro Nieto were generals. Captain Francisco Bueno de Bohorquez y Corcuera was the alcalde mayor of the capital, and among the principal officers of presidios were the Captains Ignacio de Roybal, Diego Arias de Quiros and Lieutenant Francisco Montes y Vigil, many of whose lineal descendants are still living in the counties of Santa Fé and Rio Arriba.

[450] *Arch. Santa Fé*, Ms.

In the year 1723 an order from the king was received prohibiting trade with the French in the province of Louisiana. Governor Bustamante also issued orders regulating traffic with the gentile tribes.[451] Under these orders the people of New Mexico were permitted to trade with the gentiles who came to Taos and to Pecos; prior to this order the people had gone out upon the plains to meet the Indians for purposes of trade. In the year 1724 the Utes raided the Jemez country and the Comanches attacked the Jicarilla Apaches, forcing them to give up half of their women and children, and thereafter killing every one except sixty-nine men, two women, and three boys, all of whom were mortally wounded. It was thought by the frailes that inasmuch as the Jicarillas were Christians and the Comanches had been notified of the fact, war upon the Comanches was justifiable. This seems to have been the view taken by Governor Bustamante, for he sent Captain Juan Paez Hurtado, at the head of one hundred men, to take revenge upon them, but as to the outcome of this expedition the records reveal nothing.

The activities of the French were a constant source of apprehension on the part of the Spanish authorities, and when, in 1727, Governor Bustamante learned that the French had taken Cuartelejo, he promptly notified the viceroy and proposed that an expedition be sent out to ascertain what the French had done, and asked for troops for this purpose. It does not appear that Bustamante's proposal was ever carried out, although every effort was made to ascertain from the Indians of the plains just what the French were doing.

"In these and later years," says Mr. Bancroft, "there was a complicated controversy between the missionary and episcopal authorities. The bishop of Durango claimed New Mexico as part of his bishopric, insisting upon his right to appoint a vicar and control ecclesiastic matters in the province, which the friars refused to recognize. Bishop Crespo, in his *visita* of 1725, reached El Paso, and exercised his functions without much opposition; but in August, 1730, when he extended his tour to Santa Fé, though he administered the rite of confirmation there and at a few other towns, at some of the missions he was not permitted to do so, the friars objecting by instruction to the custodio, Padre Andrés

CONTROVERSY BETWEEN THE BISHOP OF DURANGO AND THE FRANCISCANS

---

[451] *Arch. Santa Fé.* This order was made upon the 3rd of April, 1723. The royal order as to trade with Louisiana came about because of some New Mexico traders having gone to Louisiana and bought $12,000 worth of goods.

Varo, and he, of course, obeying the instructions of his superior in Mexico. The bishop also appointed Don Santiago Roybal as juez eclesiástico, whose authority was only partially recognized. Crespo began legal proceedings against the Franciscan authorities in Mexico, and besides demanding recognition of his episcopal rights, he made serious charges against the New Mexican friars, alleging that they did not properly administer the sacraments; that they did not learn the native language; that the neophytes rather than confess through an interpreter, who might reveal their secrets, did not confess at all, except in *articulo mortis*; that of 30 padres provided for, only 24 were serving; that the failure to reduce the Moquis was their fault; that some of them neglected their duties, and others by their conduct caused scandal; and that tithes were not properly collected or expended.

"These charges, especially those connected with ignorance of the native language, were supported by the formal testimony of twenty-four prominent officials and residents, taken by the governor at Santa Fé in June, 1731. Details of the suit are too bulky and complicated for notice here. There was a royal order of 1729 favorable to the bishop, and another of 1731 to some extent favoring the position of the Franciscans; but the decision in 1733 was in substance that, pending a final decision on the great principles involved, the bishop had, and might exercise, jurisdiction in New Mexico; and, as we shall see, he did make a *visita* in 1737. In Spain the case came up on appeal in 1736, and a main feature of the friars' plea was the claim that the testimony against them was false, having been given by bad men, moved by prejudice against the padres, who had opposed their sinful customs. To prove this, they produced the evidence, taken by the vice-custodio, Padre José Antonio Guerrero, in July, 1731, of another set of officials and citizens, to the effect that the missionaries had performed every duty in the most exemplary and zealous manner, though it was not pretended that they knew the native dialects. Counter-charges were also made that the governor and his officials abused the Indians, forcing them to work without pay. The record from which I take this information was printed in 1738, when no permanent decision had been reached." [452]

---

[425] Bancroft, H. H., *History of Arizona and New Mexico*, pp. 240-241. In a note to the above brief resume of this controversy, citing *Crespo, Memorial ajustado que de orden del consejo supremo de Indias se ha hecho del pleyto, que siguió el Illmo. Sor. Don Benito Crespo, obispo que fue de Durango, y lo continua el Illmo. Sor. Don Martin de Elizacoechea, su sucesor en dicho obispando. Con la religion de N. P. S. Francisco, de la Regular Observencia, y su procurador general de las Indias. Sobre visitar, y exercer los actos de la jurisdicion diocesana en la custodia del Nuevo Mexico en la Nueva España, poner vicario foraneo, y otras cosas*, Madrid, 1738, fol. 64 i, says: "The padres accused of neglect, so far as named, were PP. Ant. Gabaldon of Nambé, Juan de la Cruz of S. Juan, Carlos Delgado of Isleta, Manuel Sopeña of Sta Clara, José Yrigoyen

The rule of Governor Bustamante closed in the year 1731. He was tried on charges of illegal trade, found guilty, and forced to pay the costs of his trial. All in all, Governor Bustamante's administration was very successful.

Gervasio Cruzat y Góngora succeeded Bustamante in the governorship of the province. He held the office continuously for the full term of five years. Very little, other than the establishment of a mission among the Jicarilla Apaches, is of record concerning the events of this period.[453] During the time that Cruzat occupied the gubernatorial office he visited all parts of the province. When the bishop of Durango made his *visita*, he, also, was at Inscription Rock, as appears from a memorial cut in the stone, as follows: "On the 28th day of September, of the year 1737, arrived at this place the Illustrious Don Martin Elizacochea, bishop of Durango; and on the 29th left for Zuñi." This bishop was the successor to Bishop Crespo, both of which dignitaries prosecuted the case against the Franciscans, the latter before the Council of the Indies in Spain. At the time of his visit to El Morro he was accompanied by the bachelor Don Juan Ignacio de Arrasain, whose name appears on the rock on the same date. General Juan Paez Hurtado, the year previous, had been at

RULE OF GOVERNOR GERVASIO CRUZAT Y GÓNGORA

---

of S. Ildefonso, Domingo Araos of Sta Ana, Ant. Miranda of Cia, Pedro Montano of Jemez, Juan Mirabal of Taos, and Juan Ant. Hereiza of Picuriés. Some of the witnesses against the padres were Capt. Juan Gonzales, alc. Mayor of Alburquerque; Diego de Torres, lieut.-alc. m. of Sta Clara; Juan Paez Hurtado; Ramon Garcia, alc. m. of Bernalillo; and Miguel Vega, alc. m. of Taos. Witnesses in favor of the padres included Capt. Nuñez de Haro, Capt. Ant. de Uribarri, Capt. Sebastian Martin, Capt. Alonso Rael de Aguilar, Andrés Montoya, alc. m. of S. Felipe, Capt. Nicolás Ortiz Niño, and some of the opposing witnesses on certain points. P. Juan Mig. Menchero was in N. Mex. as visitador, and took some part in this affair. The bishop's visits, both in '25 and '30, are said to have produced copious rains, and thus greatly benefited the province. The marriage of Manuel Armijo and Maria Francisca Vaca, which the Jues ecles. tried to prevent, figured largely in the testimony."

[453] This mission was near Las Trampas, about ten miles from Taos. Villaseñor, *Teatro*, ii, 420.

Bancroft, H. H., *History of Arizona and New Mexico*, p. 242, note, says: "There were 130 Ind. at this mission in '34, but few or none were left in '48. In '33 an Ind. greatly excited the wrath of P. Montaño at Alburquerque by presenting himself during service without a cloak and with braided hair, being sustained in the ensuing quarrel by his grandfather. The padre complained through the custodio, P. José Ant. Guerrero, to the governor and declared that the grandfather should be shut up in a dungeon with shackles for his impious conduct.— *Arch. Sta. Fé.*, Ms."

El Morro as appears from the following inscription thereon: "On the 14th day of July, of the year 1736, Gen. Juan Paez Hurtado, Inspector, passed by this place, and in his company Corporal Joseph Armenta, Antonio Sandoval Martinez, Alonso Barela, Marcos Duran, Francisco Barela, Luis Pacheco, Antonio de Salas, Roque Gomez.''

Don Enrique de Olavide y Micheleña was named by the viceroy as successor to Governor Cruzat on May 17, 1736, but it does not appear with certainty that he took possession of his office until the following year. During his rule Olavide also visited all of the pueblos and settlements, and, as he came to a pueblo, it was his custom to have the fact officially announced, calling upon all persons to come forward with complaints, if any they had. This governor ruled until the year 1739

ENRIQUE DE OLAVIDE Y MICHELEÑA, GOVERNOR AD INTERIM

On the 12th day of May, 1737, the king appointed Don Gaspar Domingo de Mendoza governor of New Mexico, but he did not assume the duties of his position until the month of January, 1739. He continued to exercise the functions of the office until 1743. Shortly after his accession to the office a small party of Frenchmen came by way of Jicarilla and Taos.[454]

DON GASPAR DOMINGO DE MENDOZA IS NAMED AS GOVERNOR

---

[454] Bandelier, A. F., *Investigations in the Southwest*, Final Report, part i, p. 212, note, says: ''The first immigration into New Mexico (aside from the three deserters from the expedition of La Salle, among them the famous L'Archeveque who came to New Mexico about 1693) took place in 1739, when nine French Canadians made their appearance, and two of them remained in New Mexico. One of these, named Luis Maria Colons (?), attempted to foment an insurrection among the Pueblos against the Spaniards, for which he was shot at Santa Fé, on October 19, 1743. *Causa fuliminado criminalmente contra Luis Maria Colons, moro criolo de las Colonias de Franzia de la parte de la Probinzia de Canadá en 31 de Mayo del Año de 1743*, Ms.''

Bancroft, *History of Arizona and New Mexico*, note, p. 243, says: ''Mention of the arrival of 9 Frenchmen is made in *Arch. Sta. Fé*, Ms. Of the 2 who remained, one, Jean d'Alay, married and became a good citizen and barber of Santa Fé; the other, Louis Marie, became involved in troubles, and was shot in the plaza in Mendoza's time. *Codallos y Rabal, Testimonio*, etc., in *Arch. Sta. Fé*. The French criminal sentenced to death, 'sacado el corazon por las espaldas' is mentioned by the gov. in a letter of '43, *N. Mex. Docs.*, Ms., 691. According to this the Frenchmen came in 1739. They are also mentioned in *Menchero, Declaracion*, Ms., 726, who says that for their country a settlement near Isleta was named Canadá. Salvador, *Consulta*, 662-3, says they were on the way to settle in the west; and Villaseñor, *Teatro*, ii, 416, tells us that they were settled at a place near Alburquerque called Cañada, and later Limpia Concepcion,

In the year 1743, the frailes Delgado and Pino visited Moqui and brought back with them 441 Tiguas, who, prior to the revolt of 1680, had lived in the pueblos of Sandia, Alameda, and Pajarito. The Franciscans desired a re-establishment of these pueblos, but Governor Mendoza would not act without special instructions from the viceroy. The governor was blamed for not aiding in the projects of the missionaries, and one of the frailes says that twice as many converts might have been made at Moqui had their efforts been seconded by the governor and his officers. These Tiguas were settled in various pueblos and were given the sum of two thousand dollars in live stock and other property. Mendoza's rule ended in 1743, and the records show no complaints other than those made by the friars.

The next governor was Don Joaquin Codallos y Rabal, who ruled slightly over his full term from 1743 to 1749. Colonel Francisco de la Rocha was appointed in 1747, but declined to serve on account of his age and infirmities.[455] The viceroy wished to appoint a substitute, but the king would not allow it, and named Don Tomás Velez Cachupin as governor, who took command in May, 1749, and ruled till 1754.

JOAQUIN CODALLOS Y RABAL APPOINTED GOVERNOR

During the administration of Governor Codallos, in 1747, the viceroy instructed him to institute a campaign in the west, in the region of Zuñi, Acoma, and Moqui. The garrisons from Janos,[456] Corodeguachi,[457] and Guevavi[458] were ordered to co-operate with a force from Santa Fé. The several southern presidios, under this order, executed the movement

ADMINISTRATION OF DON TOMÁS VELEZ CACHUPIN

---

or Fuenclara. According to records of land grants, published with trans. in *U. S. Land Office Reps.*, '56, pp. 291-8, it appears that the settlement of Tomé Dominguez was founded in 1739, by some 30 settlers who received lands.''

[455] Bancroft, H. H., *Ibid*, note, p. 244, says: ''The viceroy in a report of November 8, '47, notified the king of Rocha's inability to serve, and the king in an order of Jan. 20, '49, forbids the appointment of a substitute.— *N. Mex. Céd.*, Ms., 54-5. The king in this cédula says nothing of a new appointment, and if at that time he had appointed Cachupin the latter could not have been at Santa Fé so early as May, '49; so that after all C. may have been the substitute confirmed by the king.'' Governor Codallos was a major in the army.

Davis and Prince says that Güemes y Horcasitas ruled in 1747. Güemes y Horcasitas was viceroy of New Spain.

[456] The most southerly band of the Apaches, a tribe now extinct, inhabiting a part of Chihuahua, Mexico, between Casas Grandes, Chihuahua, and Fronteras. They received their name from the presidio Janos located in northwest Chihuahua.

and reached Acoma, but the governor with his force from Santa Fé did not join them, owing to a campaign against the Comanches, who were raiding the friendly pueblos and settlers on the north and east of the capital. The viceroy was very angry over the failure of this campaign, although he later accepted the governor's explanation. In the same year, Fr. J. Miguel Menchero came to New Mexico again as visitador, and, accompanied from El Paso by a large party, turned west from the Jornada del Muerto, reached the upper waters of the Gila, and thence north to Acoma. The same year thirty-three Frenchmen visited the Comanches at Rio de Jicarilla and sold them firearms.[459] It was believed that in this party were some who had visited New Mexico before, and that the French entertained hostile designs upon the Spanish province.

The Franciscans had been very much exercised over the possible necessity of being compelled to surrender the Moqui field to the Jesuits. As has been said, the former complained of lack of assistance from the governor in their efforts to bring the Moquis to the

---

Bandelier says that after 1684 the tribe was composed of Lipan, Mescalero, and other Apache stragglers, together with renegade Suma, Toboso, Tarahumare, and Opata Indians and Spanish captives. Missions were established among them at an early date at Janos and Carretas, but were abandoned on account of constant Apache raids. The Jesuit missionaries of the first half of the 18th century frequently mention them, but nothing is known of their customs or language. See Kino (1690) in *Doc. Hist. Mex.*, 4th s., i, 230, 1856.

[457] Mr. Hodge, *Handbook of American Indians*, p. 350, says that Corodeguachi was an Opata pueblo on the headwaters of the Sonora river, in the northeastern part of Sonora, about 25 miles below the boundary of Arizona. It was the seat of the Spanish mission of Santa Rosa, founded in 1653, and of the presidio of Fronteras, established in 1690. In 1689 the mission was abandoned on account of the hostilities of the Janos, Jocome, Suma, and Apache; and owing to Apache depredations in more recent times the settlement was deserted on several occasions, once as late as 1847.

[458] *Ibid.* A former Sobaipuri settlement and the seat of a Spanish mission established about 1720-32, situated on the west bank of Rio Santa Cruz, below Tubac, at or near the present Nogales, Arizona-Sonora boundary. In 1750 it was plundered by the Indians and abandoned, but was re-occupied two years later as a mission under the protection of Tubac. In 1760-64 Guevavi contained 111 natives; in 1772, 86, and with its *visitas* (Calabazas, Jamac, Sonoita, and Tumacocori), 337. It was abandoned before 1784.

[459] Bandelier, A. F., *Investigations in the Southwest*, part i, p. 212: "The savage Indian grasped the utility of the horse and of firearms with much greater vigor than sedentary tribes, and the complaint is often heard that the Apaches, as well as the Comanches, were better armed and better equipped than the few Spanish soldiers who pretended to defend New Mexico against their incursions."

Antonio Bonilla, *Apuntes Históricos sobre el Nuevo Mexico, 1776*, Ms., p. 124, says: "Los Cumanches . . . no les intimidan las armas de fuego, porque las usan y manejan con mas destreza que sus maestros."

Viceroys of New Spain, 1740-1760

1. Don Pedro de Castro Figueroa, Duke de la Conquista, 1740-1741.
2. Don Juan Francisco de Guëmes y Horcasitas, Condé de Revillagigedo, 1746-55.
3. Don Agustin de Ahumada y Villaon, Marqués de las Amarillas, 1755-1760.
4. Don Francisco Cajigal de la Vega, 1760.

SPANISH RULE, 1700 TO 1822 441

Christian faith, and great was their joy upon being notified of the royal order by which the viceroy was compelled to render them all the assistance possible. Thus, the Franciscans, who were known as *padres azules*, won their fight for supremacy.[460]

The Franciscans endeavored to make converts of the Navajós, but in this they made a complete failure.[461] They did not establish missions in the Navajó country proper but in the region of Acoma, at Cebolleta [462] and Encinal, in which were installed the frailes Juan de Lezaun and Manuel Bermejo.

During the rule of Governor Codallos a fierce battle had been

[460] Bancroft, H. H., *History of Arizona and New Mexico*, p. 246: "Meanwhile the king was induced to change his mind and to believe that he had been grossly deceived respecting the geographical situation of Moqui, the hostility and power of its people, and the vain efforts of the soldiers and friars to reduce them. Surely if two missionaries could go alone, without a cent of expense to the royal treasury and bring out 441 converts, the Moquiños could neither be so far off from New Mexico, nor so confirmed in their apostasy, as had been represented."

Ibid, p. 247: "The Navajós attracted still more attention than the Moquiños. Padres Delgado and Irigoyen started in March, 1744, by way of Jemez for the Navajó country and found the Indians apparently eager to become Christians and receive missionaries, 4,000 of them being 'interviewed.'"

[461] Bancroft, H. H., *History of Arizona and New Mexico*, p. 248, says: "All went well for a brief time, but in the spring of 1750 there was trouble, which Lieutenant-governor Bernardo Antonio de Bustamante, with the vice-custodio, Padre Manuel de San Juan Nepomuceno de Trigo, went to investigate. Then the real state of affairs became apparent. Padre Menchero had been liberal with his gifts, and still more so with promises of more; hence his success in bringing Navajós to Cebolleta. But they said they had not received half the gifts promised, and their present padres — against whom they had no complaint — were too poor to make any gifts at all. What, then, had they gained by the change? At any rate, pueblo life and Christianity had no charms for them, and they were determined not to remain. They would still be friends of the Spaniards and trade with them and would always welcome the friars, who might even baptize and teach their children; perhaps the little ones might grow up to like a different life, but as for themselves, they had been born free, like the deer, to go where they pleased, and they were too old to learn new ways. Indeed they took a very sensible view of the situation. Thus stood the matter in 1750 and the Navajó conversion was a failure." See also letters of PP. Delgado and Irigoyen, in *N. Mex. Doc.*, Ms., 692-704-777, etc.

[462] Hodge, F. W., *Handbook of American Indians*, p. 225: "Cebolleta (Span. 'tender onion'). A place on Pojuate river in the northeast corner of Valencia county, New Mexico, at which, in 1746, a temporary settlement of 400 or 500 Navajó was made by Father Juan M. Menchero. A mission was established there in 1749, but in the following year the Navajó grew tired of sedentary life, and Cebolleta, together with Encinal, which was established at the same time, was abandoned. In 1804 a request from the Navajó to re-settle at Cebolleta was refused by the Spanish authorities. It is now a Mexican town. Cebolleta mountain and the Cebolleta land grant take their name from the settlement."

N. Mex. Doc., 1090-1134: The troubles of 1750, with official record of the

fought with the Comanches and some allied Utes a short distance beyond the town of Abiquiú, in which, according to the record, one hundred and seven Indians were slain, two hundred and six captured, with nearly one thousand horses.[463]

Governor Cachupin, also, marched against the Comanches in 1751, and in a fierce engagement succeeded in killing one hundred and one and capturing forty-four. This battle brought forth a letter of strong commendation from the viceroy, who reported the facts to the king.[464]

---

investigation and report of Fr. Trigo are found under title *Infórme sobre las Misiones de la Cebolleta y Encinal y sus acaecimientos en este Año de 1750*, Ms.

Fr. Carlos Delgado, in his report, *Infórme que hizo el R. P. á N. R. P. Jimeno sobre las execrables hostilidades y tiraniás de los gobernadores y alcaldes mayores contra los indios en consternacion de la custodio, año de 1750*, Ms., found in *N. Mex. Doc.*, 99-128, dated March 27, 1750, from Tlatelcolco, Mexico, gives voice to the beliefs of the members of his order as to the conduct of the civil and military authorities at this time. He says: "The alcaldes are creatures of the governor, appointed on condition of making all they can and dividing with the governor. From each pueblo they take a squad of 30 or 40 Indians to do all their work of tilling the soil, making adobes and buildings; others are employed to trade with gentiles and drive live-stock to Chihuahua, none receiving other pay than an occasional handful of tobacco or glass beads. Those left at the pueblos have to weave each year for their oppressors 400 *mantas* and 400 *sábanas*, besides tilling their own *milpas*. When harvest time comes they are forced to transport nearly all their maize to the villas and sell it on credit, the payment of worthless trinkets being in three instalments, *tarde, mal, y nunca*. The Indian women are used for the gratification of lust. Once, in the padre's presence, a woman came to upbraid the governor for taking her daughter, whereupon he gave her a buffalo-skin to make it all right. Any slight disobedience is punished by the stocks and flogging. In his visits to the gentiles the padre has found apostates generally covered with scars and refusing to be Christians again at such cost. On an unsupported charge of stealing 3 ears of corn an Indian was shot by orders of a captain. On a march three Indians who were footsore and could not keep up were killed and their children sold as slaves for the commander's profit."

[463] It seems rather remarkable that within three months after this fight, as reported, and within a very short time after some of the Utes who had been captured had been tried and shot at Santa Fé, this governor should have received 600 Comanches at Taos, on their assurance that they had taken no part in the war. Later on a junta was held at Santa Fé to determine whether the Comanches should be permitted to attend the fairs at Taos. See Codallos y Rabal, *Testimonio á la letra sobre Comanches, 1748*, Ms., Arch Sta. Fé.

[464] *Arch. Sta. Fé*, Ms. This engagement followed a raid upon the settlement of Galisteo. Cachupin led a force of 164 men and lost but one in the battle. Forty of the captives were released with the women and children, but 4 were held as hostages for the return of prisoners who had been taken at previous raids by these hostiles.

Mr. Bancroft, p. 256, *History of Arizona and New Mexico*, thinks "it may be well, however, to bear in mind, that according to the friars, who were particularly bitter against Cachupin, the governor's reports had often no foundation in fact."

SPANISH RULE, 1700 TO 1822 443

It is easily seen that little was accomplished by the Spaniards during the first half of the eighteenth century. There was almost constant warfare between them and the Comanches, Utes, and other tribes of the plains. There were controversies between the secular priesthood and the mendicant order of Franciscans. The province was visited three times by the bishop of Durango, but in almost any aspect the period may be deemed to have been unprogressive. There were political and official quarrels; there were prosecutions which failed of their purpose. The missions did not thrive. A constant source of trouble was the question of the conversion of the Moquis. There were many Indian campaigns, resulting, according to reports, in most instances, favorable to the Spanish arms, but the plains tribes were not subdued. Idolatrous worship was not abandoned by the Pueblos; it was concealed. The Indians, according to the friars, were constantly abused and harshly treated by the Spanish authorities. Statistics and general information relative to the condition of the province has been preserved to us by historians of the period.[465] The population at this time, according to Bonilla, was, Spaniards, 3,779, Christian Indians, 12,142, and about 1,400 Spaniards and the same number of Indians at El Paso. The city of Santa Fé contained a population of 965 Spaniards and 570 Indians; Santa Cruz de la Cañada, 1,205 Spaniards and 580 Indians, including the mission and the adjacent ranchos. The town of Alburquerque, with its suburb of Atrisco and mission, had a population of 500 Spaniards and 200 Indians.[466]

---
[465] Menchero, Juan Miguel, *Declaracion, 1744*, in *N. Mex. Doc.*, Ms., 704-73.
Bonilla, *Apuntes*, Ms., 376-81.
Villaseñor, *Teatro*, ii, 409-23.

[466] Bancroft, H. H., in a note, p. 252-253, *History of Arizona and New Mexico*, gives a comparative resume of the statistics of the period as taken by him from Menchero, Bonilla and Villaseñor, stating that what appears in brackets is from Bonilla; in parentheses from Menchero; the rest chiefly from Villaseñor, as follows:

"Santa Fé, villa [965 Span., 570 Ind.], 300 (127) Span. fam. and a few Ind. under a curate (2 PP., M.). Sta Cruz de la Cañada, villa [1,205 Span., 580 Ind., including mission and ranchos], 260 (100) fam.; 1 padre; new church being built in '44. Alburquerque, villa, with suburb of Atrisco and mission [500 Span., 200 Ind.], 100 fam., 1 padre. Concepción, or Fuenclara, Span. settlement of 50 Fam., under padre of Isleta. M. calls it Gracia Real or later Canadá, from the Canadians who settled here in '40; not mentioned by B. It was probably the Tomé of '39. The following ranchos are named by M. and V., their pop. being included in B.'s figures; Chama, 17 fam., and Sta. Rosa Abiquiú, 20 fam., under padre of San Ildefonso; Ojo Caliente, 46 fam., and 4 other ranchos 10 fam., under padre of Taos; Soledad, 40 fam., under padre of

Governor Capuchin retired in 1754 and was succeeded by Don Francisco Antonio Marin del Valle. During Del Valle's rule the province was visited by the bishop of Durango, Pedro Tamaron, who during the months of April, May, June, and July, 1760, confirmed 11,271 persons, together with 2,973 in the El Paso district. There were sixty-four people in the bishop's party, including the padre custodio and a guard of twenty-two soldiers. It is recorded that the bishop's carriage was overturned, but his Grace fell on top of the custodio and escaped unhurt. The pueblo of Pecos was visited, where hundreds were confirmed. No other event of consequence occurred during the rule of del Valle, and late

DON FRANCISCO ANTONIO MARIN DEL VALLE, GOVERNOR, AD INTERIM

San Juan, 71; Embudo, 8 fam., under padre of Picuriés; Bocas, 10 fam., under padre of Sta. Ana; and Alameda, 8 fam., under padre of Alburquerque. Few of these are named by V.

"Missions, each with one padre, including some ranchos of Span.; Taos [125 Span., 541 Ind.], 80 (170) fam.; with an alcalde mayor; the mission of Jicarilla, 5 l. N., being abandoned in '44. Picuriés [64,322], 80 fam. S. Juan [346,404], 60 fam. Sta. Cruz included in La Cañada. S. Ildefonso and its visita, Sta. Clara [89,631], 100 fam. Tesuque and Pujuaque [507 Ind.], 50 and 18 (30) fam. both visitas of Santa Fé. Nambé [100,350], 50 fam. Pecos (1,000 Ind.) 125 fam; curate, V.; 2 padres, M. fine church and convent. Galisteo [350 Ind.], 50 fam.; ranchos. Cochití [25,400], 85 (80) fam.; ranchos. Sto. Domingo [300 Ind.], 50, (40) fam. S. Felipe [70,400], 60 (70) fam.; ranchos. Jemes [574 Ind.], 100 fam. Sta. Ana [100,606], 50 fam.; on Rio Bernalillo. Cia [100,606], 50 fam.; 2 ranchos. Laguna [401 Ind.], 60 fam.; 3 ranchos. Acoma [750 Ind.], 110 fam. Zuñi [2,000 Ind.], 150 fam.; 2 padres. Isleta [100,250], 80 fam. Sandia, not founded until '48, and not mentioned by M. or V. B. gives it a pop. of 400 Ind. in '49.

"Tomé, or Valencia — called by V. Genizaros, made up of ill-treated neophytes is mentioned by M. as a settlement of 40 Ind. fam. who were captives of the Apaches and Comanches, sold to the Span., and released from servitude by the gov. in '40 to form this visita of Isleta, being 2 L. s. of that mission. The El Paso establishments, presidio and five missions, not included in the figures of my text, included about 220 Spanish families and 330 Indian fam. [1,428 Span., 1,431 Ind. in '49. *Bonilla*]. Villaseñor tells us there were a few unprofitable and abandoned mines in the country; the Ind. rode horseback and saluted the Span. with 'Ave Maria'; the route up the river to Alburquerque was infested with savages; and there was some trade with El Pazo, where fairs were held.

"In '48 P. Juan José Perez Mirabal was custodio; Man. Zambrano vice-custodio and ex-visitador; Man Sopeña discreto and min. of Sta. Clara; Ant. Gabaldón ex-visitador, discreto, and min. of Santa Cruz; Juan Anto. Ereiza ex-vice cust. at S. Ildefonso; Ant. Zamora at Nambé; Juan Martinez, sec.; Toledo at Zuñi; Irigoyen at Alburquerque; and Delgado at Isleta. *Arch. Sta. Fé.* Additional padres named by Menchero in the reports of '50, some of them doubtful, were Andrés Varo, cust. Pedro Pino, Man. Bermejo, Mig. Colluela, José Urquiros, José Tello, Marcelino Alburn, Ant. Roa, Fran. Concepcion Gonzales, Trigo Guzman.''

in the year 1760 he was succeeded by Don Mateo Antonio de Mendoza, who served only a few months when he was succeeded by Don Manuel Portillo Urrisola, whose administration lasted until the first of February, 1762.

During the rule of this governor the Comanches were again active in their depredations, and in an expedition led by himself, he defeated them in an engagement near Taos, killing, as the governor reported, four hundred of the hostiles. At the close of the administration of his predecessor, del Valle, this same band of Comanches had made a raid upon the Spanish settlements near Taos, killed all the men and carried off fifty women, with a loss of forty-nine of their own force. The defeat administered by Urrisola he hoped would settle the Comanche question, but his successor was averse to such warlike methods and the country still continued at the mercy of the Comanche marauder and murderer.[467]

THE RULE OF DON MANUEL PORTILLO URRISOLA

According to Bishop Tamaron, at the very time that Governor Urrisola was engaged in his campaign against the Comanches, his successor was on the way from Mexico, having been appointed on the 5th of March, 1761. Great opposition to Governor Cachupin had been made by the Franciscans, who believed him to be their enemy, but the king ordered the viceroy to put him in office without delay. Governor Cachupin was the first of the captains-general to make any pronounced effort in a search for mines. He sent expeditions into the northwest, into the Gunnison country, for that purpose. During his rule a trial was had, at La Cañada, of certain persons living at Abiquiú, who were charged with witchcraft. The alcalde mayor was Don Carlos Fernandez, a brave soldier and great Indian fighter. It will be seen that this trial, the defendants being Indians, was had before the civil authorities of the province and not by the ecclesiastics. The Inquisition had no manner of sway over the Indians of New Mexico. References to *autos de fe*, in which Indians are represented as being the victims, are absolutely untrue.

TOMÁS VELEZ CACHUPIN AGAIN APPOINTED GOVERNOR

---

[467] Tamaron, Pedro, *Visita del Obispo de Durango*, Ms., 141-4.

Not only the laws of the Indies, but the official declarations of the Holy Office, bear witness to this fact.[468] A most eminent authority tells us that crimes committed with Indians were visited by this tribunal upon those who perpetrated them, but it never interfered nor was permitted to interfere in matters of faith or belief of the aborigines. Cases of witchcraft were disposed of by the civil or military authorities, as the case might be, for it was considered that an Indian could not be held responsible for his creed in the same degree as the European or his American offspring, and the principle of patience and leniency adopted in legislation also prevailed in religion.[469]

---

[468] Bandelier, A. F., *Investigations in the Southwest*, Final Report, part i, p. 215, in a note says: "The great documentary historian of Mexico, Don Joaquin Garcia Ycazbalceta, has called attention to this in his *Bibliografiá Mexicana del Siglo XVI*, p. 377. He refers to the cédula of Charles V of October 15, 1538, and to Law No. 35, tit. i. lib. vi of the *Recopilacion de Indias*. Here follows the text of this law (fol. 192, vol. ii.), 'Por estar prohibido á los Inquisidores Apostolicos el proceder contra Indios, compete su castigo á los ordinarios Eclesiásticos, y deben ser obedecidos y cumplidos sus mandamientos, y contra los hechieros, que matan con hechizos y usan de otros maleficios procederán nuestras justicias reales.' In confirmation see *Carta Patente del Padre Custodio Fray Joseph Lopez Tello, communicando una Instruccion del Santo Tribunal de la Inquisicion*, April 22, 1715, Ms. The instruction is issued by three inquisitors and the secretary: 'Esto es porque los delitos Yndios no tocan al Sto Oricio, si los que en materia de fé se cometen con ellos ó Yndios.'"

[469] Bandelier, A. F., *Ibid.*, p. 215-216. Mr. Bandelier says that the prohibition to the Inquisition to meddle with Indian matters is due to Phillip II, and the *cédula* bears date February 23, 1575. It is in harmony with the ordinances of 1573. *Ordenanzas para Descubrimientos*, etc., p. 182: "Los Predicadores, con la mayor solenidad que podieren y con mucha caridad, les comiencen á persuadir, quieran entender las cosas de la Santa Fee católica, y sedlas comiencen á enseñar con mucha prudencia y discrecion por el orden questa dicho en el libro primero, en el Título de la Santa Fee católica, usando de los medios mas suaves que podieren para los aficionar á que la quieran aprender; para lo cual no comenzarán reprehendiendoles sus vicios ni idolatrías, ni quiténdoles las mugeres ni sus ídolos. Porque no se escandalizen ni tengan enemistad con la doctrina cristiana, sino enseñensele primero, y despues que esten instruidos en ella, les persuaden á que de su propria voluntad dexen aquello ques contrario á nuestra Sancta Fee católica y doctrina evangélica." This is so far as the idols are concerned an abrogation of decrees of Charles V, June 26, 1523, of the empress, August 23, 1538, and of the king (then prince regent) himself, August 8, 1551. See *Recopilacion*, vol. i, fol. 2.

Mr. Bandelier says that he had in his possession a number of witchcraft trials from New Mexico, beginning with 1704, and that all were conducted by the civil authorities of the province.

The witchcraft trial at La Cañada resulted in the condemnation of those who had been brought to trial. There are over 100 pages of testimony, and the defendants were condemned to "become servants" of certain Spanish families. A detachment of troops was sent to Abiquiú to destroy relics of supposed idolatrous worship, including a stone with hieroglyphics, etc.

The last of the New Mexico governors to hold the title of captain-general was Captain Pedro Fermín de Mendinueta, knight of Santiago, succeeding Governor Cachupin in 1767. The only event occurring during the first year of his rule was a great flood in the Rio Santa Fé, the course of the river being turned into the Rio Chiquito, now known as Water street. In the year 1771 a treaty with the Comanches was made and the governor, in announcing the treaty to the people of the province, urges the greatest care in treating the Indians strictly in conformity with the provisions of the contract. The governor desired the establishment of a new presidio at Taos, and a law which would require the settlers to live in compact pueblos like the Indians. He gave this advice for the reason that the force at Santa Fé was insufficient to protect so great an area, apt to be raided by the Indians at any time. A new presidio was established at Robledo, consisting of thirty soldiers from Santa Fé and a like number of citizen auxiliaries from the district of El Paso. It was intended to make secure as possible the highway from El Paso to the capital, and eventually to reëstablish the ruined pueblos of Senecú, Socorro, Alamillo, and Sevilleta.

DON PEDRO FERMÍN DE MENDINUETA IS APPOINTED GOVERNOR

"The conquest or conversion of the Moquis," says Mr. Bancroft, "was a matter still kept in view, though for about twenty years no practical efforts in that direction are recorded, down to 1774-6, when the project was revived in connection with the California expeditions from Sonora." In fact there was a great revival of interest so far as the conversion of the Moquis was concerned. Fr. Escalante, in 1774 or 1775, visited Moqui, where he spent eight days in a vain effort to reach the Rio Grande de Cosinas beyond. He recommended that the Moquis should be reduced by force of arms and a presidio established at Oraibe.[470] Fr. Francisco Garcés, starting from a point on the Gila river, at its junction with the Colorado, followed up the latter stream into the Mohave country, and thence marched east to the land of the Moquis. He found the Moquis very inhospitable, and, after passing two nights in the court-yard, wrote a letter to the fraile at Zuñi, and returned by way of the Mohave district to Bac. While at Moqui, Fr. Garcés visited Oraibe and one other pueblo,

---

[470] Escalante, *Carta de 1776 sobre Moqui*, in *N. Mex. Doc.*, Ms., 985-1013.

and, in his report, gives a good description of the towns and the people. He met a Zuñi Indian who could speak Spanish, as could also some of the Moquis.[471]

In the year 1776, in the form of a report, Lieutenant-Colonel Antonio Bonilla [472] wrote a history of New Mexico up to this time, giving also his views as to what should be done by the government to avert impending dangers. He was of the opinion that as a frontier out-post among gentile tribes, the holding of the province had an importance far beyond its direct value as a Spanish possession, since if it were lost the savage hordes would direct their whole force against Nueva Viscaya and Sonora. For that reason, if for no other, a vigorous warfare should be waged by veteran troops from New Mexico as a centre.

It was also in this year that the northern provinces of Mexico were organized as the Internal Provinces, under the Caballero de Croix as commanding general, independent of the viceroy. This change deprived the governor of New Mexico of his title as captain-general. In November of 1777 there was a battle between the Comanches and the Apaches, the latter losing thirty killed and forty horses. The governor, alive to the situation, was ordered to make peace, if possible, with the Comanches, and use them as an ally in his campaigns against the Apaches.[473]

In the year 1778, Governor Mendinueta retired from his post and left, as acting governor, Don Francisco Trebol Navarro, who filled the position only a few months, and was relieved in the fall of the year by Lientenant-Colonel Juan Bautista de Anza as political and

---

[471] Garces, *Carta*, found in *N. Mex. Doc.*, Ms., 828-30.

[472] Bonilla, *Apuntes Historicos*, Ms. found in *N. Mex. Doc.*, 327-81.

[473] Bancroft, H. H., *History of Arizona and New Mexico*, note p. 264: "On the 14th of March, 1778, Governor Mendinueta wrote a letter of instructions for his successor dealing largely with Indian affairs. He mentions the fact that Galisteo and Pecos as frontier posts require special care. Says that the Yutas have been at peace, and pains should be taken to keep them so, no attention to be paid to petty offenses. The Navajós are at peace, but are said to join the Gileño Apaches in their raids. There should be no peace, with the Apaches, always war. The Comanches should be drawn to peace, but never trusted, for their custom is to be at peace with the Taos and at war with other parts. In the *Arch. Sta. Fé*, Ms. are several communications from Croix and Rubio to the governor on the subject of Indian policy. In the same year Fr. Escalante writes upon Teguayo, which is in the Yuta country, shown by ruins and pottery to have been once the home of pueblo Indians; also on Quivira, which is nothing more wonderful than the Panana or Pawnee villages. *Doc. Hist. Mex.*, 3rd ser., iv. 124-6."

Viceroys of New Spain, 1760-1794

1. Don Joaquin de Montserrat, Marqués de Cruillas, 1760-1766.
2. Don Matias Galvez, 1783-1785.
3. Don Juan Vicente de Guëmes Pacheco de Padilla, Condé de Revillagigedo, 1789-1794.
4. Don Manuel Antonio Flores, 1788.

SPANISH RULE, 1700 TO 1822

military governor. This governor was a native of Sonora, of excellent ability, and a soldier of wide experience in warfare with the Indian tribes. In 1774 he conducted an expedition to California, reaching the junction of the Gila and Colorado rivers February 7, 1774. On February 9th, having been entertained by the Yuma Indians, he crossed the Colorado, being the first white man to cross into Alta California. As has been noted elsewhere in this volume, the river had been crossed by Melchior Diaz in 1540, and by Father Kino in 1701. It was also crossed by Fr. Garcés, in 1771, but all of these crossed into Lower California. Having crossed the river, Anza celebrated the event by firing a salvo and setting off some rockets, which pleased the Indians very much by their flight through the air, though the sound of guns frightened them so that they threw themselves on the ground. The Colorado was crossed at a point above its junction with the Gila, and he says that at the time the season of greatest drouth was present, and that the river was only three and one-half feet deep and five hundred and seventy feet wide. He gives an excellent description of the river and its surroundings, the San Dionisio of Fr. Kino, a Yuma rancheria, now the town of Yuma, Arizona; the Purple Hills ten miles to the northwest, through whose gorge the Colorado emerges into the open valley; the large peak to the northwest which he named Cabeza del Gigante, now called Castle Dome; a lesser peak fifteen miles to the north, which, on account of its shape, he named La Campana, now Chimney Peak. He also named a narrow strait below the junction of the Gila Puerto de la Concepcion, which place, during the rule of Anza in New Mexico, became the mission of La Purisima Concepcion, and upon which is the site of the present Fort Yuma.

COLONEL JUAN BAUTISTA DE ANZA SUCCEEDS MENDINUETA

The governor was a great friend of the comandante of the Provincias Internas, Croix, but with all his knowledge of Indian affairs and his undoubted energy as an executive, he was unable to accomplish much for the province or better its affairs. A campaign against the Comanches was begun shortly after his coming to his capital. In this expedition he led a command of six hundred and forty-five men, including eighty-five soldiers and two hundred and fifty-nine Indians, and in a battle ninety-five leagues northeast of Santa Fé, defeated and killed the celebrated Comanche chief, Cuerno Verde, with four of his leading sub-chiefs, his chief medicine men, his eldest son and thirty-two of his warriors.[474]

Upon his return from this highly successful campaign, and there is no doubt as to the veracity of the reports, Governor Anza tried his hand upon the Moquis, visited them and found them in a woeful condition. When Escalante visited the pueblos of Moqui in 1775, there were 7,494 souls, but now, through a drouth of three years, pestilence and famine had done their work and there were only seven hundred and ninety-eight left.[475]

The Moqui chief of Oraibe declined to receive any assistance from the Spaniards, but told his people that they were free to go with the governor and become Christians if they cared to do so. Only thirty

---

[474] Cuerno Verde led many successful Comanche raids against the Spanish settlers in the valley of the Rio Grande in the latter part of the 18th century. The Greenhorn Mountains in Colorado and the river of the same name were named for this chieftain.

Anza, Juan B., *Diario de la Expedicion que sale a praoticár contra la Nacion Comancha, 1779*, Ms., in *N. Mex. Doc.*, 861-922, preceded by letter of Governor Anza to Commanding General Croix and the answer of the latter thanking him. The campaign was in August and September, 1779; 200 Yutas and Apaches accompanied the army as allies, and in the battle thirty women and five hundred horses were captured. The army proceeded and returned by way of Taos, and passed by the present towns of Alamosa and Salida.

[475] In *N. Mex. Doc.*, Ms., 922-1022, we find in *Moqui, Providencias tomadas á consequencia de los avisos comunicados por Anza, 1779*, that there had been a failure of crops, and it was believed that owing to their condition, the time was favorable for their conversion, as they were in danger of starvation. Many of the Moquis, it was said, had abandoned their pueblos, seeking food in the mountains and among the Navajos. It was feared that if something was not done now they would quit pueblo life and join the Navajós. Says Mr. Bancroft: "Anza wrote repeatedly to Croix on the prospects, enclosing letters from the padres, and advising that an effort should be made either to establish missionaries at the towns, which would require some additional force, or to induce the natives to migrate en masse and settle in new pueblos nearer the Spanish centres." Governor Anza, in September, 1780, left the capital for the Moqui country, accompanied by the frailes Fernandez and Garciá, and visited all of the towns, two of which were completely abandoned. Of 30,000 sheep only 300 remained, and there were but five horses and no cattle. Only 500 fanegas of corn and beans could be expected from the coming crop. They had been constantly raided by the Utes and Navajos and some of the Moqui believed that all this trouble had come upon them because of their treatment of Fr. Garcés, in 1776. The chief of Oraibe was offered a load of provisions to relieve immediate wants, but "he proudly declined the gift" says Mr. Bancroft, "as he had nothing to offer in return. He refused to listen to the friars, and in reply to Anza's exhortations declared that as his nation was apparently doomed to annihilation, the few who remained were resolved to die in their own homes and in their own faith."

families were willing to accept the offer of the governor, including the chief of Walpi.⁴⁷⁶ Mr. Bancroft was unable to find any record of what became of these converts, but believed that with them, and some others later, was founded the pueblo of Moquino, in the Laguna region. This pestilence — the smallpox — also carried off five thousand and twenty-five of the Pueblo Indians, and the governor, as a consequence, reduced the number of missions to twenty, which provoked much protest from the Franciscans. By this reduction the missions of Jemez, Santa Ana, Acoma, Nambé, Tesuque, Pecos, San Felipe, and San Ildefonso were made visitas. The frailes were very much displeased at the action of the government in making this reduction, and were constant in their efforts to secure more salaries, an increase of missionaries, and the right to collect parochial taxes, but all without success.

On the 10th of August, 1789, Governor Anza was notified from El Paso that his successor, Don Fernando de la Concha, was on his way to the capital. Concha had probably been appointed the year previous but he did not arrive at Santa Fé until after the middle of the year 1789.⁴⁷⁷

FERNANDO DE LA CONCHA APPOINTED GOVERNOR

The archives do not reveal much of interest during the term of office of Governor de la Concha, nor during that of his successor, Lieutenant-Colonel Fernando Chacon. Indian affairs constitute all that is of interest and even as to these there is not much worth recording. The Spaniards seem to have been enjoying peace with all the tribes of the plains, except the Apaches, against whom constant warfare was waged, the authorities in New Mexico co-operating with those of the neighboring provinces to the south. In May, 1793, the Indians held a meeting at the pueblo of San Ildefonso, which gave rise to some apprehension on the part of the authorities, resulting in some arrests and a long investigation, as a result of which nothing was definitely proven, although a number of the Indians were publicly whipped and some of them condemned to imprisonment for several months in chains.

---

⁴⁷⁶ Anza, Juan B., *Diario de la expedicion que hace á la provincia de Moqui*, Ms., original in the Pinart Collection. Anza only remained at Moqui four days, leaving on the 24th of September and reaching Santa Fé on the 1st of October.

⁴⁷⁷ Gomez, *Diario*, 214-16, says that Lieutenant-Colonel Manuel Flon came from Spain in 1785 with a commission as governor; he never assumed the office.

In the month of July, 1794, it was known at El Paso that de la Concha's successor, Don Fernando Chacon, had been appointed and was on his way to the capital. Lieutenant Francisco Javier de Uranga was named as lieutenant-governor at El Paso, in the same year. During this period the Navajós were on friendly terms with the Spaniards but were at war with the Apaches. Notwithstanding the peaceful relationship at that time existing between the settlers and the Navajós, Governor Chacon maintained spies among them, who constantly watched their movements and reported regularly to headquarters at Santa Fé. It was the custom in these times, whenever a hostile Indian was killed, to bring his ears to the governor's palace, thereby receiving a reward, and General Nava made complaint that of five hostile Apaches who had been killed the ears had not been brought to him as proofs, "que es la práctica que se observa en esta provincia." The Apaches were very persistent in depredations upon the settlers of the Rio Grande valley, having made a raid upon the town of Alburquerque. On account of this raid, Lieutenant Canuelas, with a force of one hundred and sixty men, was sent against them. Governor Chacon made official inspection of all the presidios and visited many pueblos and missions, but nothing of importance seems to have been discovered. The Apaches still continuing their warfare upon the settlers, Governor Chacon determined upon a vigorous campaign against them,[478] and in the month of May, 1800, with a force of five hundred men, proceeded down the valley and after a short campaign twenty of their principal chiefs gave in their submission and surrendered a number of animals which had been stolen during their previous raids in the valley. Another expedition, however, became necessary as this peace was quickly broken, and Lieutenant José Manrique[479] was despatched to the San Mateo and Magdalena mountains with a force of two hundred and fifty men, accomplishing nothing, however, other than the recovery of some stock which had been stolen.

During all this period of occupation under Spanish rule, New Mexico was the extreme outpost of authority and colonization.

---
[478] *Arch. Sta Fé*, Ms.
[479] *Ibid.*

Everything that was not raised in the province was brought in by way of the long routes to the south, through Durango and Chihuahua, but the time was soon to come, when, by the opening of communication with the states of the American Union, to the east, New Mexico itself was to become a great point of trade and distribution for the northern states of Mexico.

The principal industries of the province at the beginning of the nineteenth century were agriculture, stock-raising, and barter.[480] Crops were raised principally by the application of water upon the valley lands through irrigating ditches, acequias, as they were called by the settlers. Indian corn, wheat, and beans were the principal crops in and around Santa Fé, the Santa Cruz, and upper Rio Grande valleys, and at Taos; there was also raised, in and about the Rio Abajo, as the valley adjacent to Alburquerque was known, some fruit and some cotton; also an inferior kind of tobacco, called *punche*, although by an official order, in the latter portion of the eighteenth century, the raising of this substitute for tobacco was prohibited. Of live stock, sheep formed the principal element, large numbers of these animals being produced, both for their wool and the meat. Some cattle were raised but not many, and horses were always scarce on account of the numbers sold to and stolen by the Indians of the plains. A great many mules were also raised and of *burros*, a small jackass, there was a great plenty. In fact the *burro* was and is still the pack animal of the native. There were very few manufactories or manufactures, beyond the preparation of skins of animals for home use or sale in the southern markets. Cotton cloth was woven at some of the pueblos in the valley of the Rio Grande, and also coarse woollen blankets were made by the pueblo Indians.

NEW MEXICAN INDUSTRIES AT THE BEGINNING OF THE 19TH CENTURY

Every year in the month of July or August the people of the province would journey to Taos, where a fair was held. Here they met the Comanches and other wild Indians for purposes of barter and trade. Hundreds of Indians came to this outpost of Spanish civilization bringing deer-skins, buffalo hides, to-

THE ANNUAL FAIR AT TAOS

---

[480] Even at this time there was no mining of any consequence, although the existence of mineral and some *placers* were known to the Spaniards.

gether with Indian captives to trade for knives, horses, beads, all sorts of trinkets, and to a limited extent, blankets.

After the fair at Taos had closed, the traders and merchants came south, and just before the beginning of each year, proceeded in great caravans to Chihuahua, THE TRADE WITH CHIHUAHUA where they exchanged the skins, hides, Indian servants, blankets, and other products of the province for cloths, groceries, and other articles needed in New Mexico for consumption or for trade with the Indians of the plains. The departure [481] and return of the *caravanas* were the great events of the year. Up to this time there was no trade with the French of Louisiana [482] or with the Spaniards of Texas.

There was no coin or other money in New Mexico at this time, and the traders for their accounts invented a system of "imaginary" currency, which included four kinds of dollars — *pesos de plata*,

---

[481] Bancroft, H. H., *History of Arizona and New Mexico*, p. 277: "The value of each year's exports was estimated by the comandante general in 1788 at $30,000. . . In 1776 the governor delayed the publication of an important bando till the people had returned from their 'ordinaria anual salida'; and the provincial in 1788 explains the impossibility of obtaining reports from New Mexico until the people come down to the January fair."

[482] *Arch. Sta. Fé.* In August, 1789, M. Louis Blanc, commander at Natchidoches wrote to General Ugarte urging the opening of trade between New Mexico and Louisiana, by establishing a presidio among the Jumanos. He said that this would prevent smuggling and tend to keep peace with the Indian tribes like the Osages; that the journey with freight was only forty days, through a very fertile country all of which was known to him by reports from a man named Pierre Vial who had recently made the trip. This letter was sent to Governor Concha for his consideration and report.

Morfi, *Desórdenes*, Ms., contains the best general presentment of the country's commercial condition and needs, explaining the system of imaginary money and giving instances of enormous profits which were made.

Revilla Gigedo, *Carta de '93*, 444, paints a vivid picture of conditions then existing. He says, comparing the settlers with the Indians: "No son mejoras respectivamente las costumbres de los vecinos españoles y demas castas, cuyas poblaciones consisten en casas ó ranchos dispersos, donde no tienes testigos que descubran los vicios y la disolucion en que se prostituyen, imitando á los indios en la vida ociosa, y reduciéndose todos sus afanes y comercio á la permuta usuraria de semillas y frutos, y á la benta que hacen ellos en la villa de Chihuahua, adonde bajan en cordon cada año y se proveen de los generos, efectos, y utensilios para sus vestuarios, atenciones domesticas, y labores del campo."

Arch. Sta. Fé. On October 25th, 1788, General Ugarte made a long report on the trade with New Mexico, recommending the encouragement of the industries of the province of Chihuahua, now being abandoned on account of the decadence in mining; also the sending of artisan instructors to New Mexico, exemption from taxes, etc., so as to increase manufactures and give the province a balance of money.

worth eight reales; *pesos de proyecto*, six reales; *pesos antiguous*, four reales; and *pesos de la tierra*, two reales. "The beauty of this system," says Mr. Bancroft, "was that the traders always bought for the cheap pesos and sold for the dearer kinds, all being 'dollars' to the Indians. Through this system, the natives, through debt, became practically slaves, besides losing their land, and the poor settlers were hardly less the victims of commercial oppression."[483]

POPULATION OF NEW MEXICO IN 1800

At the close of the century the Spanish population of New Mexico had increased much more than double in fifty years. Details of the population of the province from 1760 to 1799 are given by Mr. Bancroft in a table, which is here reproduced, as follows:

Mr. Bancroft's table of population in New Mexico — 1750-1800:

SETTLEMENTS	1760		1788	1793		1798		1799	
	Span.	Ind.	Total	Span.	Ind.	Span.	Ind.	Span.	Ind.
Alburquerque	1814	.....	2146	1650	.....	2279	.....	4020	603
Santa Fé	1285	.....	2244	2419	.....	.....	.....	4194	314
La Cañada	1515	316	1076	1650	.....	2594	.....	7351	1079
Abiquiú	617	166	1181	1147	216	1573	176	.....	.....
Taos	160	505	578	403	518	789	531	1351	782
Picuriés	208	328	212	1310	254	566	251	.....	.....
San Juan	575	316	1566	2173	260	1971	202	.....	.....
Santa Clara	277	257	452	635	139	1840	193	.....	.....
San Ildefonso	30	484	.....	.....	240	225	251	.....	.....
Pojoaque	.....	99	368	308	53	220	79	.....	.....
Nambé	118	204	.....	.....	155	20	178	.....	.....
Tesuque	.....	232	.....	200	138	148	155	.....	.....
Pecos and Galisteo	.....	599	.....	.....	152	150	180	.....	.....
Cochití	140	450	.....	400	720	425	505	.....	.....
Santo Domingo	.....	424	608	.....	650	257	1488	.....	.....
San Felipe	.....	458	.....	.....	532	434	282	.....	.....
Jemez	.....	373	.....	375	485	314	272	398	1166
Cia	.....	568	1035	.....	275	.....	262	.....	.....
Santa Ana	.....	404	.....	.....	356	84	634	.....	.....
Sandia (Alameda)	222	201	596	810	304	384	236	1490	1513
Isleta, Tomé, Belen	620	304	2103	2680	410	1771	603	.....	.....
Acoma	.....	1052	.....	10	820	.....	757	.....	.....
Laguna	85	600	1368	6	668	15	802	15	1559
Zuñi	.....	664	1617	10	1935	7	2716	7	2716
Total	7666	9104	17153	16156	9275	16065	10762	18826	9732
El Paso District	3588	1394	4927	3622	1900	.....	.....	4943	637
Grand Total	11254	10498	22080	19778	11175	.....	.....	23769	10369

The five reports embodied in the table are as follows: Tamaron, *Visita*,

---

[483] Bancroft, H. H., *History of Arizona and New Mexico*, p. 278: "While the settlers and Pueblo Indians were always in debt to the traders, the latter in

1760, Ms., in which the bishop expresses the opinion that the padron of Sta. Fé does not show more than half the real population. *Ilzrbe (Joaquin) Estado de las Missiones*, 1788, Ms., in Pinart col., the writer — provincial of the Sto. Evangelio province — stating that there were 18 missions (the omissions in his list as per table showing the consolidation effected by Anza), 11 annexes, 24 padres (who are named), 5,508 fam., and for the year 1,254 baptisms, 438 marriages, and 647 deaths, this author making no distinction of races; *Revilla Gigedo, Carta de 1793, sobre misiones*, 441-2. The report of the custodio, P. Fran. Osio, for '98, as given in *Meline's 2,000 Miles*, 208-9.

Governor Chacon relinquished his office in the spring of 1805 and was succeeded by Colonel Joaquin del Real Alencastre, who held the office until 1812, although it appears that Alberto Mainez served as acting governor during a part of the years 1807-8. Subsequent to the creation of the office of comandante-general of the Provincias Internas, there was always a governor or an acting governor at Santa Fé, subordinate to the comandante-general. That a given person appears in the records as acting governor does not necessarily imply that the office of governor was not occupied; if, for any reason, the governor left the province, some person served in his place as acting governor. This system has led to some confusion among writers in making up the list of persons who have occupied the position of executive in New Mexico. It was much so in these times as it is in the present, for when the governor of New Mexico today is absent from the territory, the secretary performs the duties of the executive, but, officially, is secretary acting as

COLONEL JOAQUIN DEL REAL ALENCASTRE APPOINTED GOVERNOR

---

turn were debtors to or agents for Chihuahua merchants, who thus monopolized all the profits, and nothing was left for New Mexico, except for certain traders, who as alcaldes mayores utilized their political authority for private gain. Padre Morfi's proposed remedy for these evils was the encouragement of home manufactures by sending artisan teachers and machinery to the province, with a view to render the inhabitants independent of Chihuahua. His plan was to send criminals of the better class, whose offences were chiefly due to drink and the temptations of a city, from Mexico to the far north, and through them to reform the New Mexican industrial system.

"The prices to be paid for some animals and other articles of trade were sometimes fixed by executive order. As early as 1754, Governor Valle determined that the price of a horse should be fixed at 12 to 15 skins, just what sort of skins does not appear; that a piece of cotton cloth, weighing 10 arrobas, was exchangeable for two pack-horses or an iron knife for a skin.

"Under no subterfuge or on any account whatsoever were the settlers in his time permitted to sell to the Indians, mares, mules, asses, or offensive weapons. The wild tribes to the east and northeast of New Mexico obtained horses and fire-arms as far to the east as Illinois."

Fac-simile of Muster Roll of Spanish Garrison at Santa Fé, 1760

governor and is not governor, nor is he entitled, officially, to be designated as such.

During the winter of the year 1804-5, while Chacon was still executive, the Navajós were very troublesome, and in an active campaign waged against this tribe, led by Lieutenant Narbona, a battle was fought in the canyon de Chelly, a Navajó stronghold, in which ninety warriors were slain, together with twenty-five women and children, besides capturing thirty-six with thirty women and children, losing only one friendly Indian chief (a Zuñi) and sixty-four wounded.[484] Narbona was a fearless officer and had been sent to New Mexico from the presidio at Chihuahua. There was a number of battles during 1804-5 with this tribe, and finally, late in the latter year, while Alencastre was governor, a treaty of peace was made with the Spaniards. The terms of this treaty had been prepared by Governor Chacon, but the treaty was not made until after Chacon had been superseded by Colonel Alencastre. In the earlier days of the campaign which terminated in this treaty Governor Chacon, in person, led the Spaniards against the hostiles.[485]

---

[484] Matthews — Chelly — pronounced *shay-ee*, frequently *shay*; Spanish corruption of Navajó *Tsé-'gi* or *tseyí*, "among the cliffs." A canyon on the Navajó reservation in northeastern Arizona, in which are numerous cliff-dwellings. Cortéz in 1799 gave the name (Chellé) to a Navahó settlement, but this is true only in so far as the canyon contains numerous scattered hogans or huts.

[485] Pino, Pedro Bautista, *Noticias Historicas*, etc., p. 85: "La guerra que por espacio de tres años nos hicieran con la mayor tenacidad y sin fruto alguno los ha convertido tambien en pacificos; comenzo por los años de 1803 y 1804, siendo gobernador D. Fernando Chacon. Salió éste en persona á campaña, y á sus órdenes el capitan D. José Francisco Pino, D. Antonio Vargas, y D. Nicolás Tarin; fueron felices en las primeras acciones de guerra; mas no por esto cedian los navajoes. Retirose el Sr. Chacon de su gobierno, y continuó la campaña el teniente veterano Narvona, que de órden del Sr. Salceed, comandante general, vino al socorro de la provincia para unirse con los capitanes de Milicias D. Lorenzo Gutierrez, y D. Bartolomé Baca, que se hallaban peleando. Al fin, despues de muchas y muy sangrientas acciones y de haber perdido los Navajóes hasta su capital Chellé (que la tenian atrincherada y provista asombrosamente de gente y armas) pidieron la paz en 1805; siendo gobernador D. Joaquin del Real Alencastre, y renovaron la alianza que habian mantenido años antes con nosotros."

Among the *Arch. Sta. Fé*, Ms., on March 25, 1805, Governor Chacon recites the terms to be given the Navajós. They should make no claim to Cebolleta — which they had abandoned many years before — nor shall they make any claim to any live-stock in the possession of the Spaniards; for their two captives four women might be exchanged; for purposes of grazing they must not go beyond the canyon of Juan Tafoya, Rio del Oso, and San Mateo; should they commit any depredations they shall be punished by force of arms, unless the property which they steal shall be returned, and when they come to Santa Fé they shall

According to Major Zebulon M. Pike, in the year 1806, Lieutenant Melgares was sent from Chihuahua with a force of one hundred cavalry to join five hundred militiamen in an expedition to the buffalo plains. In his book, reference to which will be made later on in this volume, Major Pike says that this expedition was the most important ever sent out of the province of New Mexico; and in fact the only one directed to the northeastward, except that mentioned by the Abbé Raynal, in his history of the Indies, to the Pawnees. Says Pike:[486]

EXPEDITION TO BUFFALO PLAINS UNDER MELGARES

"In the year 1806 our affairs with Spain began to wear a very serious aspect, and the troops of the two governments almost came to actual hostilities on the frontiers of Texas and the Orleans territory; at this time, when matters bore every appearance of coming to a crisis, I was fitting out for my expedition from St. Louis, when some of the Spanish emissaries in that country transmitted the information to Major Merior, and the Spanish council at that place, who immediately forwarded the information to Captian Sebastian Rodriguez, the then commandant of Nacogdoches, who forwarded it to Colonel Cordero, by whom it was transmitted to the seat of government. This information was personally communicated to me, as an instance of the rapid means they possessed of conveying intelligence relative to the occurrences transacting on our frontiers. The expedition was then determined on; and had three objects in view; first, to descend the Red river, in order if they met our expedition to intercept and turn it back; or should Major Sparks and Mr. Freeman have missed the party from Nacogdoches, under the command of Captain Viana, to oblige them to return, and not penetrate further into the country, or make them prisoners of war.

"Secondly, to explore and examine all the internal parts of the country, from the frontiers of the province of New Mexico to the Missouri, between the La Plate and Kansas rivers.

expect no gifts except sustenance; they shall also give up four thousand sheep, one hundred and fifty cattle, and sixty horses which they had stolen

Pino, Pedro Bautista, *ibid*, also reiers to a Lieutenant Lopez who defeated the Navajó at Chaca: "Debe hacerse tambien mencion del teniente D. Vicente Lopez, hijo de aquella provincia, y servidor de ella desde su tierna edad con las armas en la mano y baston; pues en este tiempo, comandando una partida de vecinos armados, derrotó estas mesas de Chacá á los enemigos. Este y los demas servicios se le pagaron tan mal, que el año de 1808, hallandose en otra campaña resultó suspenso por una intriga, segun opinion en toda la provincia, sin conocimiento del gobernador; el comandante general, despues de haberle oido, ofreció hacerle justicia; ignoro si despues de mi ausencia ha tenido el interesado esta justa satisfaccion."

[486] Pike, Major Z. M., *Exploratory Travels*, etc., pp. 182-183, note.

SPANISH RULE, 1700 TO 1822

"Thirdly, to visit the Ietans, Pawnee republic, Grand Pawnees, Pawnee Mahaws and Kansas. To the head chief of each of these nations, the commanding officer bore flags, a commission, grand medal, four mules; and with all of them he had to renew the chain of ancient amity, which was said to have existed between their father, his most catholic majesty, and his children, the red people.

"The commanding officers also bore positive orders to oblige all parties or persons in the above specified countries, either to retire from them into the acknowledged territories of the United States, or to make prisoners of them, and conduct them into the province of New Mexico.

"Lieut. Don Facundo Melgares, the officer selected from the five internal provinces to command this expedition, was an European and his uncle was at that time one of the royal judges of the kingdom of New Spain. He had distinguished himself in several long expeditions against the Apaches and other Indian nations, with whom the Spaniards were at war; added to these circumstances, he was a man of immense fortune, and generous in its disposal, almost to profusion; possessed a liberal education, a high sense of honour, and a disposition formed for military enterprize.

"This officer marched from the province of Biscay, with one hundred dragoons of the regular service, and at Santa Fé, the place where the expedition was fitted out, he was joined by five hundred of the mounted militia of that province, and completely equipped with ammnuition, etc., for six months; each man leading with him (by order) two horses and one mule. The whole number of their beasts was two thousand and seventy-five. They descended the Red River two hundred and thirty-three leagues. Met the grand bands of the Ietans, held councils with them; then struck off to the northeast, and crossed the country to the Arkansas, where Lieutenant Melgares left two hundred and forty of his men, with the lame and tired horses, whilst he proceeded on with the rest to the Pawnee republic. Here he was met by the chiefs and warriors of the Grand Pawnees; held councils with the two nations, and presented them with flags, medals, etc., which were designed for them. He did not proceed on to the execution of his missions with the Pawnees,[487] Mahaws, and Kansas, as he represented to me, from the poverty of their horses, and the discontent of his own men; but as I conceive, from the suspicion and discontent which began to arise between the

---

[487] The Spaniards knew the Pawnees well. At the time of the expedition under Melgares they were a very large nation, and resided on the Platte and Kansas rivers. They were divided into three distinct nations. The village of the Grand Pawnees was on the Platte, the Pawnee Loups on one of its branches. Their language was like that of the Sioux; they were tall and of commanding figure; had high cheek bones, clearly indicating their Asiatic origin. Their government was a hereditary aristocracy, the father handing his chieftainship down to his son.

Spaniards and the Indians. The former wishing to revenge the death of Villanueve and his party, whilst the latter possessed all the suspicions of conscious villany, deserving punishment.

"Melgares took with him all the traders he found there from our country, some of whom, being sent to Natchitoches, were in abject poverty at that place on my arrival, and applied to me for means to return to St. Louis. Lieutenant Melgares returned to Santa Fé in October, when his militia was disbanded; but he remained in the vicinity of that place until we were brought in, when with his dragoons he became our escort to the seat of government."

The Spanish government at this time was undoubtedly laying claim to the portions of the country east and northeast of the boundaries of the province of New Mexico. If not actually laying claim, the action of Melgares in giving Spanish flags to the Indian chiefs would seem to indicate that by this act, if it ever became necessary to make proof, they could easily assert that they had given the protection of the Spanish government to the Indians and had driven out all of the traders and others who were citizens of, or who had come from, the territories of the United States.[488]

---

[488] Major Pike says that all of the notes which he took at his own grand council with the Pawnee nation were seized by Governor Alencastre, together with all of his speeches to the several Indian nations. He says that when Melgares left the Pawnees he gave them several Spanish flags, one of which was unfurled at the door of the chief on the day of his meeting with the grand council; and that, amongst the various demands and charges that he made was one to deliver the Spanish flag to him and that a flag of the United States be received and hoisted in its place. Pike says that probably "this was carrying the pride of nations a little too far, as there had so lately been a large force of Spanish cavalry at the village, which had made a great impression on the minds of the young men, as to their power, consequence, etc.," which Pike's appearance with twenty men (infantry) was by no means calculated to remove. The Pawnee chiefs replied to Pike's argument, but said nothing about the flag, and Pike again demanded that the flag be given to him, saying that it was impossible for the nation to have two fathers; that they must either be children of the Spaniards or acknowledge their American father. After a silence of some time, an old man arose, went to the door, and took down the Spanish flag, and brought it in and laid it at the feet of Pike and received from the American officer the flag of his country. This was elevated on a staff which had lately borne the standard of his catholic majesty. This gave great satisfaction to the Osage and Kansas Indians who were present at the council, both of whom decidedly avowed themselves to be under the American protection. When Pike saw that every face in the council was clouded with sorrow, as if some great national calamity was about to befall them, he took up the contested colors, and told them, that as they had now shown themselves dutiful children in acknowledging their great American father, he had no desire to embarrass them with the Spaniards, for it was the wish of the Americans, that their red brethren should remain peaceably around their own fires, and not embroil themselves in any disputes between the white people; and that for fear the Spaniards might return there in force, Pike gave them back the Spanish flag, but with an

SPANISH RULE, 1700 TO 1822   461

From the standpoint of history the rule of Alencastre is one of the most important in the annals of New Mexico. From the year 1803 to 1819 the question of boundary between the possessions of the United States and Spanish territory was not determined. The American was little behind the Spaniard in making claims, the one claiming to the Arkansas and the other east to the Missouri. When the question was finally determined, in 1819, the Spanish claim that the Arkansas from the mountains down to longitude 23°, became the permanent dividing line. As a revenue producing area, at that time, the Spaniards were not favorably impressed with anything east of the Arkansas, and did not hesitate to accept the settlement as made.

In 1805-6 the relations between the United States and Spain were under great strain. The Louisiana Purchase had been consummated, but the limits of the grant, especially toward the southwest, were disputed, and much jealousy was manifest on both sides. The American and the Spaniard both claimed Red river, and the latter, as we have seen, was claiming dominion far to the east and northeast of that stream.

In the month of May, 1806, the American government sent out an expedition under command of Captain Sparks, who was instructed to ascend Red river, "to the country of the Pawnee Indians." After reaching the country of this tribe, he was to purchase horses for use in transporting his command to the "top of the mountains," which, it was believed, lay to the west about three hundred miles. Sparks was met, while on Red river, by the Spaniards under Melgares, and compelled to turn back. Just at this time in the history of the United States, the country was much agitated over the intrigues of Aaron Burr. It was believed by many that Burr desired a secession of the country to the west of the Alleghenies and that an invasion of the northern provinces of Spain was contemplated. General James

THE EXPEDITION UNDER
MAJOR ZEBULON M. PIKE

injunction that it should never be hoisted during his stay. There was great applause at this, and the charge was strictly attended to by the Indians. Pike was something of a diplomat. There were over four hundred Pawnee warriors present at this council. Pike says that at the time the Pawnees were decidedly under Spanish influence and "should a war commence tomorrow, would all be in their (Spanish) interests." Pike says that Melgares took some of the Pawnees to Chihuahua.

Wilkinson was the commander-in-chief of the army of the United States, and, at the time, was governor of the territory of Louisiana. It was thought that some bond of union between Wilkinson and Burr existed. The country was in a high state of alarm over the supposed designs of Burr, and Wilkinson was under great suspicion in some quarters. He was afterwards acquitted of any complicity in the plot. Major Pike, then a lieutenant, was a friend of Wilkinson, and it was from him and not from the American secretary of war that the orders for the expedition came. It was said, at the time, that Pike was an emissary of Burr and Wilkinson, and that the expedition was all in the interest of Burr and his enterprises. Pike, upon his return, promptly denounced his calumniators, and a reading of his journal [489] dispels at once any suspicion of his fidelity to his country. In point of daring adventure and enduring fortitude the journey of Pike is not surpassed in the annals of American history. Without provisions of any consequence, with a handful of men, in the dead of winter, marched this intrepid American soldier into the heart of the Rocky mountains, eight hundred miles from the American frontier. Indeed they were a band of heroes; emaciated, half clothed, half frozen, they pierced the fierce canyons of the Sangre de Cristo. But why did he cross these mountains from the Arkansas? [490] The exact line of his

[489] Pike, Zebulon Montgomery, Major 6th Reg. U. S. Inf., *Exploratory Travels through the Western Territories of North America*, etc. In the year 1808, Pike secured a copyright for a book, the title of which was, "An account of Expedition to the Sources of the Mississippi, and through the western parts of Louisiana, to the sources of the Arkansaw, Kansas, La Platte and Pierre Juan rivers. Performed by order of the Government of the United States, during the years 1805, 1806 and 1807. And a tour through the interior parts of New Spain, when conducted through these provinces by order of the captain-general in the year 1807. By Major Z. M. Pike." This book was printed by John Binns, of Philadelphia, and was published by C. & A. Conrad & Co., of Philadelphia. The date of publication is 1810. The book contained a portrait of Pike. The text is full of errors and the book, a cramped octavo, is quite unworthy of the great story it contains. Copies of this publication are found only in very old libraries or in the hands of lovers or dealers in rare old books.

In the year 1811 the work was re-published in London, in quarto form, on hand-made paper, by Longman, Hurst, Rees, Orme and Brown. The text is changed somewhat from the American edition, but it is an improvement upon the work of Binns in every respect. It was undoubtedly an authorized edition. This edition is also very rare, copies only being found in the hands of collectors or in the old libraries.

[490] Many of the stories about Major Pike are untrue. Nearly everyone believes that he climbed the peak bearing his name. He did not. His diary shows that he failed to do so. He probably climbed Cheyenne mountain. Major

march is not easily traced. One cannot identify the streams mentioned, inasmuch as the Spanish general confiscated his notes and Pike was compelled subsequently to use Spanish maps in the preparation of his journal and book. On the 28th of January, 1807, Pike reached the San Luis valley at a point on the Rio Grande near where the town of Alamosa now stands. He followed down the Rio Grande to the Conéjos and, upon the south bank of that stream, at a point five or six miles above its junction with the Rio Grande, built his fort. The Spanish records all indicate that the prairie opposite the mineral springs and high hill on the south bank of the Conéjos was the spot where the American flag first floated in New Mexico. Pike was at once a picturesque and bold figure. There is no doubt that Pike had further instructions than those which appear of record, and in this fact may be found an explanation for his conduct. There was every probability of war with Spain, in which case a strategic demonstration upon the headwaters of Red river, or upon those of the Rio Grande, even with his small force, might be important. It was also necessary, should certain events occur, that a line of march to the capital of New Mexico be known. When Pike reached the Rio Del Norte, or Rio Grande, as he says, he believed he was on Red river, and his plan was to descend that stream in boats or rafts to Natchidoches, and on that account he sought a suitable spot for a fortified camp,[491] where the necessary

---

Long was the first to ascend Pike's Peak. It is also supposed that Pike had many encounters with the Indians of the plains. This is untrue. There is also a belief that mining was at this time being prosecuted by the Spaniards in what is now the state of Colorado. This is also untrue. As a matter of fact there was not a man of European birth or ancestry in the limits of that state as now constituted.

[491] Pike, Major Z. M., *Ibid*, page 231, note: "The stockade was situated in a small prairie, on the west fork of the Rio del Norte. The south flank joining the edge of the river (which at that place was not fordable), the east and west curtains were flanked by bastions in the N. E. and N. W. angles, which likewise flanked the curtain of the north side of the work. The stockade from the centre of the angles of the bastions was thirty-six feet square. There were heavy cottonwood logs about two feet in diameter, laid up all round about six feet, after which lighter ones until we made it twelve feet in height; these logs were joined together by a lap of about two feet at each end. We then dug a small ditch on the inside all around, making it perpendicular on the internal side, and sloping next the work; in this ditch we planted small stakes of about six inches diameter, sharpened at the upper end to a nice point, slanted them over the top of the work, giving them about two and a half feet projection. We then secured them below and above in that position, which formed a small pointed frieze, which must have been removed before the works could have been scaled. Lastly, we had dug a ditch round the whole four feet wide and let the

preparations might be made, and to which the remainder of his command, some of them having been left behind, might be brought as soon as possible.

Pike's instructions were to be very cautious as he approached the Spanish frontier. As before stated, he must have had some sort of instructions not appearing in the record, for it is peculiar that when he built his fort he built it on the Spanish side of Red river. Accompanying Pike was Dr. J. H. Robinson,[492] who had in his possession a bill against a man named Baptiste La Lande,[493] given him by William Morrison, a merchant of Kaskaskia, Illinois, for collection. Pike was desirous of extending his explorations into Spanish territory, or at least to learn the geographic situation of his fort, so far as the capital of New Mexico was concerned. So, under the pretext of collecting this account, in the dead of winter, Pike despatched Dr. Robinson for Santa Fé, the doctor leaving the fort on the 7th day of February. All of the actions of Pike after reaching the San Luis valley are mysterious. It may or it may not be true that Pike believed he was on the Red river. There were Spanish maps available to him, prior to his departure on this expedition, which show with comparative accuracy the relative courses and positions of the Arkansas, the Rio Grande, and the Red river, but Pike may still have been ignorant of the fact that he was on the Rio Grande. When Dr. Robinson left the fort he started to the west

water into it; the earth taken out being thrown against the work, formed an excellent rampart against small arms, three or four feet high. Our mode of getting in was to crawl over the ditch on a plank, and into a small hole sunk below the level of the work near the river for that purpose. Our port-holes we pierced about eight feet from the ground, and a platform prepared to shoot from.''

[492] The command consisted of Capt. Z. M. Pike, Dr. John H. Robinson, Serg. William E. Meek, Corporal Jeremiah Jackson, privates Henry Kennerman, John Brown, Jacob Carter, Thomas Dougherty, William Gorden, Theodore Miller, Hugh Menaugh, Jacob Mountjoy, Alex. Roy, John Sparks, Patrick Smith, Freegift Stout, and Baroney Vasquez, as interpreter.

Meek, Jackson, Carter, Dougherty, Miller, Sparks, Smith, and Vasquez were left on the Arkansas, and were not at the stockade at the time Pike and his companions delivered themselves into the hands of the Spanish officers, Salteo and Fernandez.

[493] In 1804 William Morrison of Kaskaskia, sent La Lande, a creole trader, up the Platte, instructing him to carry his goods to Santa Fé, with a view to test the commercial prospects in that direction. Obeying his instructions, La Lande succeeded in being arrested by the Spaniards and carried to the capital. The New Mexicans liked the goods, and Baptiste liked the country so well that he determined to settle there, and even forgot to account to Morrison for the consignment. Pike met La Lande at Santa Fé.

Viceroys of New Spain, 1794-1803
1. Don Bernardo de Galvés.
2. Don Felix Berenguer de Marquina, 1800-1803.
3. Don Miguel Jose de Azanza, 1798-1800.
4. Don Miguel de la Grua Talamanca y Branciforte, Marqués de Branciforte, 1794-1798.

on his journey to Santa Fé, all of which indicates an ignorance of the country. It is difficult, too, to understand the doctor's actions. He had no interest in the claim against La Lande, for the collection of which he went to Santa Fé. Why then, upon his arrival, did he represent himself as a Frenchman, who had accompanied a hunting party and tell the story that Salcedo wrote to Wilkinson in his letter of May 20, 1807; whether he expected to return, and, if so, how; and why did Pike deny that he belonged to his force? All this is mysterious, unless we accept the idea that Pike really was engaged in reconnoitering the Spanish frontier.[494]

Ten days later a Spanish dragoon and an Indian made their appearance at the fort. Pike regarded them as spies. From these Pike learned that Dr. Robinson had reached Santa Fé in safety; they noted the construction of the stockade, its location, ascertained

[494] Major Pike says, *Ibid*, p. 232, note: "The demands which Dr. Robinson had on persons in New Mexico, although originally legitimate, were in some degree spurious in his hands; the circumstances were as follows: In the year 1804 William Morrison, Esq., an enterprising merchant of Kaskaskias, sent a man by the name of Baptiste La Lande, a Creole of the country of Missouri and of La Platte, directing him, if possible to push into Santa Fé. He sent in Indians, and the Spaniards came out with horses and carried him and his goods into the province. Finding that he sold the goods high, had land offered him, and that the women were kind, he concluded to expatriate himself, and convert the property of Morrison to his own benefit. When I was about to sail, Morrison conceiving that it was possible I might meet some Spanish factors on the Red river, intrusted me with the claim, in order if they were acquainted with La Lande, I might negotiate the affair with some of them. When on the frontiers, the idea suggested itself to us of making this claim a pretext for Robinson to visit Santa Fé. We therefore gave it the proper appearance, and he marched for that place. Our views were to gain a knowledge of the country, the prospect of trade, force, &c, whilst at the same time our treaties with Spain guaranteed to him, as a citizen of the United States, the right of seeking the recovery of all just debts, dues or demands, before the legal and authorized tribunals of the country, as a franchised inhabitant of the same, as specified in the 22nd article of the treaty.

"As it was uncertain whether this gentleman would ever join me again, I at that time committed the following testimonial of respect for his good qualities to paper, which I do not at this time feel any disposition to efface.

"He has had the benefit of a liberal education, without having spent his time as too many of our gentlemen do in college, in skimming over the surfaces of science, without ever endeavouring to make themselves masters of the solid foundation; but he had studied and reasoned. With these qualifications he possessed a liberality of mind too great ever to reject an hypothesis, because it was not agreeable to the dogmas of the schools; or adopt it, because it had all the eclat of novelty. His soul could conceive great actions, and his hand was ready to achieve them; in short, it may be truly said, that nothing was above his genius, nor anything so minute that he conceived it entirely unworthy of consideration. As a gentleman and companion in dangers, difficulties and hardships, I, in particular, and the expedition in general, owe much to his exertions.''

from Pike that it was his intention to descend the river to Nachidoches, and rode away. Ten days more having elapsed, a force of fifty dragoons and fifty militia, under Lieutenants Ignacio Saltelo and Bartolomé Fernandez, arrived who informed Pike that he was not on Red river but on the Rio del Norte; whereupon Pike at once lowered his flag. The Spaniards were most courteous and kind and supplied the explorers with food and blankets. Presently the officers notified Pike [495] that he must go to Santa Fé, and on the 27th of February they started, leaving a portion of the Spanish force behind to bring in the eight explorers left on the Arkansas and who had not as yet reached the fort.

The route from Pike's stockade seems to have been across the mountains to the Chama river, and down that stream past the Ojo Caliente [496] and San Juan. The people were uniformly [497] courteous and kind, but were much surprised at the wearing apparel of

[495] The commanding officer, Lieutenant Saltelo, after having breakfasted with Pike, addressed him as follows: "Sir, the governor of New Mexico, being informed that you had missed your route, ordered me to offer you in his name mules, horses, money, or whatever you may stand in need of, to conduct you to the head of Red river; as from Santa Fé, to where it is sometimes navigable, is eight days' journey; and we have guides and the routes of the traders to conduct us."

"What," interrupted Pike, "is not this the Red river?" "No, sir, it is the Rio del Norte." Saltelo added that "he had provided one hundred mules and horses to take in my party and baggage, and stated how anxious his excellency was to see me at Santa Fé." Pike then stated to him the absence of his sergeant, the situation of the rest of his party and that his own orders would not permit or justify his entering the Spanish territories; but the lieutenant urged still further until Pike began to feel himself a "little heated in the argument" and told him that he would not go until the arrival of his sergeant, with the remainder of his party. The mildness of the Spaniard induced Pike, as he says, "to tell him that he would march, but must leave two men in order to meet the sergeant and party to instruct him as to coming in, as he would never do so without a fight, unless ordered."

[496] Pike gives a description of the village of Ojo Caliente which he says was situated on the eastern branch of a creek of that name; and at a distance presents to the eye a square enclosure of mud walls, the houses forming the wall. "They are flat on the top, or with extremely little ascent on one side,

[497] Major Pike says: "We were frequently stopped on our march by the women, who invited us into their houses to eat, and in every place where we halted a moment, there was a contest who should be our hosts. My poor lads who had been frozen were conducted home by old men, who would cause their daughters to dress their feet, provide their victuals and drink, and at night give them the best bed in the house. The whole of their conduct brought to my recollection the hospitality of the ancient patriarchs, and caused me to sigh with regret at the corruption of that noble principle by the polish of modern ages."

While stopping at San Juan, Pike met a priest, who was a "great natural-

SPANISH RULE, 1700 TO 1822

the Americans. Baptiste La Lande and another Frenchman tried to gain the confidence of Pike, but the latter regarded them as spies. The party arrived at Santa Fé on the 3rd of March.

Upon the arrival of the party at the capital they were taken before Governor Alencastre, who informed Major Pike that he and his men must appear before General Salcedo at Chihuahua. Pike denied that Dr. Robinson was a member of his party and at-

---

where there are spouts to carry off the water of the melting snow and rain when it falls. . . From this village the Ietans drove off two thousand horses at one time, when at war with the Spaniards. . . I was shown the ruins of several old villages, which had been taken and destroyed by the Ietans.''

This stream is permanent, running through a valley not over half a mile in breadth, and watering a long, narrow strip of irrigable land.

Major Pike speaks of several old villages pointed out to him ''which had been taken and destroyed by the 'Ietans.' These ruins were those of villages destroyed by the Utes in 1747, or they were the ruins of three large communal dwellings which lie on the banks of this stream. The names of the pueblos were, in the Tehua language, Houiri, Ho-mayo, and Pose-uinggee. They were the largest pueblos, in their time, of any in New Mexico or Arizona. Large jars filled with meal, and skeletons have been unearthed from these ruins within the past fifty years. In the ruin of Pose-uingge, in every room that has been excavated, human skeletons have been found. They were in every imaginable posture, and with the skulls fractured or crushed ''

Major Pike uses the word ''Ietans,'' evidently naming them as a particular nation of Indians. Mr. Mooney, in *17th Report, B. A. E.*, 167, 1898, explains the true application of this word. He says: ''The Ute of the mountain region at the headwaters of the Platte and the Arkansaw, being a powerful and aggressive tribe, were well known to all the Indians of the plains, who usually called them by some form of their proper name, *Yútawáts*, or, in its root form, *Yuta*, whence we get Eutaw, Utah, and Ute. Among the Kiowa the name becomes *Iătä (-go)*, while the Siouan tribes seem to have nasalized it so that the early French traders wrote it as Ayutan, Iatan, or Ietan. By prefixing the French article it became L'Iatan, and afterward Aliatan, while by misreading of the manuscript word we get Jatan, Jetan and finally Tetau. Moreover, as the early traders and explorers knew but little of the mountain tribes, they frequently confounded those of the same generic stock, so that almost any of these forms may mean Shoshoni, Ute, or Comanche, according to the general context of the description.''

---

ist.'' Pike secured the esteem of this worthy father, who, on being informed that Pike had with him some astronomical instruments, expressed a desire to see them; all that Pike had was a sextant and a large glass which magnified considerably, calculated for the day or night, the remainder of his instruments being with Sergeant Meek. On an examination of the sextant, and being shown the effect of it, in the reflection of the sun, the worthy father appeared much surprised, as did also hundreds who were present. Pike was impressed with the fact that a man who appeared a perfect master of the ancient languages, a botanist, mineralogist, and chemist, should be so ignorant of the powers of reflection, and the first principles of mathematics; but the father explained the enigma by informing Pike of the care of the Spanish government in preventing any branch of science being made a pursuit, which would have a tendency to extend the views of the subjects of the provinces to the geography of their

tempted to prevent an examination of his papers,[498] and believed that he had been sadly "deceived" when the governor very shrewdly forestalled his efforts and secured possession of the notes and papers.[499] The governor assured Pike that he was not a prisoner, but the American officer insisted on receiving a certificate that he was obliged to go to Chihuahua.

Major Pike and party, after a dinner given by the governor in their honor, left the capital,[500] Pike riding with the governor in his coach drawn by six mules. The military escort [501] was under com-

country, or any other subject which might bring to view a comparison of their local advantages and situations with those of other countries.

[498] Pike says that he had understood the doctor had been sent forty-five leagues from Santa Fé under a strong guard, and the haughty and unfriendly reception of the governor induced him to believe that war must have been declared, and that if it were known Doctor Robinson accompanied him, he would be treated with great severity. "I was correct," says Pike, "in saying he was not attached to my party, for he was only a volunteer, and could not properly be said to be one of my command."

[499] Major Pike gave all of his important papers to the several members of his command, and showed his trunk, containing the remainder to Alencastre, who, seemingly satisfied, returned the trunk. Pike then, fearing that his men would become intoxicated, collected his papers from them, fearing that they might lose or give them up. Next morning Governor Alencastre again called for the trunk and Pike learned something of Spanish wit and cunning.

[500] Pike gives a short description of Santa Fé as he saw it. He says: "Santa Fé is situated along the banks of a small creek, which comes down from the mountains, and runs west to the Rio del Norte. The length of the town on the creek may be estimated at one mile, and it is but three streets in width. Its appearance from a distance struck my mind with the same effect as a fleet of flat-bottomed boats, such as are seen in the spring and fall seasons descending the Ohio river. There are two churches, the magnificence of whose steeples forms a striking contrast to the miserable appearance of the other buildings. On the north side of the town is the square of soldiers' houses, one hundred and twenty, or one hundred and forty on each flank. The public square is in the center of the town, on the north side of which is situated the palace, as they term it, or government house, with the quarters for guards, &c., the other is occupied by the clergy, and public officers. In general, the houses have a shed before their front, some of which have a flooring of brick; this occasions the streets to be very narrow, being, in general, about twenty-five feet. The supposed population is four thousand five hundred souls."

[501] Pike is full of praise for Captains Almanza and Melgares. In his diary he mentions a number of the towns and villages from Santa Fé south. Among the rest "Sibilleta," which he describes as a fine and regular village on the east side of the Rio Grande. Prince calls this place Cebolleta; he errs. Bancroft says he has found no record of its founding, nor is it mentioned in statistical list. This place is now known as La Joya. It was the principal settlement of the colonizers of the Sevilleta de la Joya grant, made to the settlers by the Spanish government.

Pike mentions the fact that at Santo Domingo were found rich paintings in the church; that there was a fine bridge at San Felipe. At this place he met Fr. Rubi with whom he became very well acquainted. Fr. Rubi showed Pike a statistical table, on which he had in a regular manner taken the whole province

mand of Captain Antonio Almanza, and the route was by way of La Bajada, Santo Domingo, and thence down the valley of the Rio Grande to Alburquerque and Isleta further on. At this point Lieutenant Melgares, commanding a detachment of dragoons, took charge of the party, conducting them to El Paso, and thence to Chihuahua, where the Americans were treated most courteously by General Salcedo, who insisted, however, on retaining all of Pike's papers. Pike and his companions were finally sent home through Coahuila and Texas, leaving Chihuahua at the end of the month of April, and reaching Natchidoches in July. Pike was afterwards commissioned a brigadier general and lost his life at the taking of Toronto in 1813. The congress of the United States, through a committee appointed on the 15th of November, 1808, made a report [502] in relation to Pike's expedition.

of New Mexico by villages, beginning at Taos on the northwest, and ending with Valencia on the south; giving their latitude, longitude, population, whether savages or Spaniards, civilized or barbarous, Christians or Pagans; numbers, name of the nation, when converted, how governed, military force, clergy, salary, etc., etc., in short a complete geographical and historical sketch of the province. Pike desired a copy of this but noticed that Captain Almanza was much surprised at the father having shown it to him.

At Alburquerque, Pike was entertained by Fr. Ambrosio Guerra, who led him into his hall, from thence, after taking some refreshment, into an inner apartment, where he ordered his adopted children of the female sex to appear, when they came in by turns. They were Indians of various nations — Spanish, French, and finally two young girls ''who, from their complexion, I conceived to be English; on perceiving I noticed them,'' says Pike, ''he ordered the rest to retire, many of whom were beautiful, and directed these two to sit down on the sofa beside me. Thus situated, he told me that they had been taken to the east by the Ietans, passed from one nation to the other until he purchased them (at that time infants) but they could recollect neither names nor language. Concluding they were my country women, he ordered them to embrace me as a mark of their friendship, to which they appeared nothing loath. We then sat down to dinner, which consisted of various dishes, excellent wines, and to crown all, we were waited upon by half a dozen of those beautiful girls, who like Hebe at the feast of the gods, converted our wine into nectar, and with their ambrosial breath shed incense on our cups.''

[502] *Report of Committee*, H. R., December 16, 1808: ''The Committee of the House of Representatives of the United States, to whom was referred the resolution to inquire, Whether any, and if any, what compensation ought to be made to Captain Zebulon M. Pike and his companions, for their services in exploring the Mississippi river, in their late expedition to the sources of the Osage, Arkansaw and La Platte rivers, and in their tour through New Spain: *Report*: That it appears by the documents accompanying this Report, that the objects of each of the exploring expeditions, together with the instructions for executing them were communicated to and approved by the President of the United States; that the conduct of Captain Pike in each of the expeditions also met with the approbation of the President, and that the information obtained and communicated to the executive on the subjects of his instructions, and

During the rule of Governor Alencastre a census of the province was taken, a report of which, signed by the governor, shows a population, not including El Paso and its surroundings, of Spaniards: male, 10,390; female, 10,236; total, 20,626; Pueblo Indians: male, 4,094; female, 4,078; total, 8,172. Total population, 28,798, exclusive of the wild tribes.

Don Alberto Mainez seems to have performed the duties of governor in the years 1807-8, but it is more than likely that he merely acted as such for the next regularly on the list of executives of the province is Lieutenant-Colonel José Manrique, who ruled during the years 1810-14. Mainez again occupied the position in 1815-17, Don Pedro Maria de Allande in 1816-18, and Don Facundo Melgares, in 1818-22, he being the last governor under Spain, and was succeeded on the 5th day of July, 1822, by Don Francisco Javier Chavez, as jefe político, ruling in 1822-3, although Antonio Vizcarra also held the office for a time prior to 1822.

On the 11th of August, 1810, all of the alcaldes and leading men of the province, there being no ayuntamientos, assembled at Santa Fé, for the purpose of selecting a delegate to the Spanish Córtes. The presiding officer of the meeting was Don José Manrique, governor of New Mexico. Those present at the junta were José Pino, captain of militia and ex-alcalde of Alburquerque, Don Antonio Ortiz, alférez real, Don Diego Montoya, first alcalde of Santa Fé, Captain José Garciá de Mora, who represented Santa Cruz de la Cañada, Don José Miguel Tafoya, second alcalde of Santa Fé, who had been for twenty-nine years a corporal in the *compania veterana*, Don José Antonio Chavez, first alcalde of Alburquerque, Don Manuel Garcia, for twenty-four years the alcalde at La Cañada and partido, Don Miguel Antonio Vaca, second alcalde of Alburquerque, Don Cleto

DON PEDRO BAUTISTA PINO DELEGATE IN THE SPANISH CÓRTES

---

particularly in relation to the source of the Mississippi, and the natives in that quarter, and the country generally, as well on the Upper Mississippi as that between the Arkansaw and the Missouri, and on the borders of the latter extensive river to its source, and the country adjacent, is highly interesting in a political, geographical, and historical view; and that although no special encouragement was given to the individuals who performed these laborious and dangerous expeditions, yet it was but reasonable to them, should they fortunately succeed in their objects, to expect some reward from government. That the zeal, perseverance, and intelligence of Captain Pike as commander, have been meritorious, and the conduct of the individuals generally, who composed

Miera y Pacheco, alcalde of San Carlos de la Alameda and Don Tomás Ortiz, the alcalde of Taos.[503] There were three candidates, Don Antonio Ortiz, Don Rafael Ortiz, and Don Pedro Bautista Pino, and the last named was chosen by lot. Provided with instructions, not only from the convention that had chosen him, but from many prominent men [504] of the province, he left New Mexico for Spain on the 14th day of October, 1811, being, as he believed, the first native-born New Mexican to visit Spain. He had to pay the expenses of his journey, but the patriotic people contributed the sum of nine thousand dollars as a donation to the cause of the king of Spain. To raise this sum, it is said some citizens "sacrificed the liberty of their sons."

Don Pedro Bautista Pino was a most distinguished gentleman, a soldier and a scholar as well. He was probably the ablest statesman ever born in New Mexico during Spanish rule.[505] Pino was a descendant of two of the re-conquerors of New Mexico, who served under De Vargas, and was married to the descendant of one of the most distinguished families of his country.

There were many valiant cavaliers accompanying De Vargas when he entered the country for its re-conquest, after the Pueblo uprising of 1680. Not the least of these was Captain Nicolás Ortiz Niño Ladron de Guevara. He was a most adventurous spirit, whom a restless love of enterprise induced to join the expedition

---
the parties respectively, has been faithful, and their exertions arduous. The Committee, therefore, are of the opinion that compensation ought to be made by law to Captain Pike and his companions."

[503] This "junta" was held pursuant to the decree of the "Junta central de las Españas," February 14, 1810, which provided for a "diputado" from the province of New Mexico.

[504] Padre Francisco Osio, for twenty-six years chaplain at Santa Fé, furnished a *Prospecto ó plan sobre diferentes solicitudes*. Don Mariano de la Peña, a very prominent man of his time, gave some suggestions in writing, as did also Don Ignacio Sanchez Vergara, the alcalde of Jemez, Don José Gutierrez, Captain. Bartolomé Vaca, afterwards governor of New Mexico, and Don Juan José Silva.

[505] There is no record of Pino's labors in the Córtes other than his report of November, 1812, published at Cadiz the same year, and 37 years later at Mexico with additions by D. Antonio Barreiro in 1839, and annotated by Don José Augustin de Escudero for the *Comision de Estadistica Militar* of the Republic of Mexico. To this work we are indebted for almost all the information of the period, containing as it does a complete description of the province, its institutions, conditions, and needs. Pino was a descendant of a long line of patriots and soldiers, and his sons and grandsons were alike men of the same mold and lofty character.

under the great Spanish captain-general. The story of the life of Ortiz is as brilliant and exciting as a fairy tale, and his remarkable adventures served to develop a bold and courageous character. While yet a boy, he had won the favor of his king by winning from the Moors the city of Guevara, by which exploit he secured from his royal master the addition to his name, Niño Ladron de Guevara.

Captain Nicolás Ortiz Niño Ladron de Guevara brought with him to New Mexico his wife and family, and all were present at the ceremonies had at the time of the entry into the city of Santa Fé. His wife was Maria Ana Garcia Coronado. There were several children, of whom the eldest was also Nicolás Ortiz Niño Ladron de Guevara. The latter married Doña Juana Baca, also a descendant of one of the re-conquistadores. Of this marriage there were three children, Nicolás Ortiz Niño Ladron de Guevara, 3rd, Francisco, and Toribio Ortiz Niño Ladron de Guevara. The eldest married Gertrudis Paez Hurtado, the daughter of a famous soldier and governor and captain-general of the province. Of this marriage there were two children, Juan Antonio and Antonio José. The last named married Rosa de Bustamante, daughter of Don Pedro de Bustamante, governor and captain-general of the province, of which union there were five children, among them a daughter, Ana Gertrudis Ortiz Niño Ladron de Guevara, who became the wife of Juan Domingo Baca. There were twelve children of this marriage, one of whom, Ana Maria, married Don Pedro Bautista Pino. The fruit of this marriage was Don Facundo Pino, Don Miguel E. Pino, and Don Nicolás Pino, all of whom were prominent in the affairs of New Mexico during the years of Mexican rule, and whose names will appear later in the history of the American occupation period, and also during the Civil War period of our country.

Don Pedro was not able to accomplish much in his capacity as delegate from the province, and after his return from abroad a statement of what he had accomplished was embodied in a charming couplet, as follows: *Don Pedro Pino fue; Don Pedro Pino vino.*

His *Exposicion,* as he termed his report to the king, is fairly accurate in its statements as to the history of New Mexico during the preceding two centuries of Spanish rule. He endeavored to impress upon the king the danger of aggression from the Americans co-operating with the Indians of the plains. To meet this, Pino

Major Zebulon M. Pike, U. S. A.

SPANISH RULE, 1700 TO 1822

favored and demanded not only a reorganization of the military service, including payment to the citizen soldiery, but the establishment of five new garrisons on the north and east, transferring soldiers from the south for that purpose. He says that the American people, advised as to the neglect of New Mexico by the mother country, were trying in various ways, by offers of liberal and protecting laws, advantageous commerce and other attractive measures, to secure the assistance of the people of New Mexico with a view of joining the province to Louisiana which had been but lately acquired from the French. He also said that the Americans now had much influence with the Indians and had succeeded in making them believe that the Spaniards were not invincible. Through the influence of the clergy in New Mexico, Pino embodied in his report a request for a separate bishopric, with a college and a system of schools to be supported by the tithes. He also asked for a civil and criminal audiencia at Chihuahua, that of Guadalajara being too far away to be of any practical benefit to New Mexico. The establishment of the bishopric was ordered the following year, but other than this small attention seems to have been given to his demands. Pino was reëlected for the years 1820-21, and the sum of six thousand dollars was sent to Mexico to pay his expenses, but on reaching Vera Cruz, he could obtain of this sum only enough to pay the expenses of his journey to that point. He wrote a letter to the Córtes, explaining why he did not come, and complained that the decrees of that body in response to his *Exposicion*, though confirmed by royal order of May 9, 1813, had not been carried into effect. On his former trip to Spain he was accompanied by his grandson, Juan de los Reyes Vaca y Pino, a youth of eleven years, the retired soldier Salvador Leiva y Chavez, and Bartolomé Fernandes, clerk, who died on the voyage.

During the last years of Spanish rule, the population nearly doubled. The Pueblo Indians made a very slight increase in their numbers, according to the report of the custodio, P. José Pedro Rubi, there being in the year 1821 nine thousand and thirty-four of the latter. The report of Governor Melgares in 1819 and 1820 gives the Spanish population at twenty-eight thousand four hundred and thirty-six. There are several

THE LAST YEARS OF SPANISH RULE

statements of the population of the country between 1800 and 1821 but, of course, no one of them can be deemed accurate, except possibly the enumeration of the citizens living in towns and villages. The city of Santa Fé had, possibly, including the dwellers in the immediate vicinity, six thousand souls, but the records are so meagre and there are so many discrepancies and differences that it is safe to say that no single report is based upon any census accurately taken.[506]

Relative to the commercial conditions of the province as they existed during the last years of Spanish rule, deriving almost all of his information upon the subject from the *Santa Fé Archives*, Pino's *Exposicion*, and Pike's book, Mr. Bancroft says that commercial conditions continued to exist as they had before.[507] Each fall the caravans left for El Paso and Chihuahua; at El Paso, to a greater extent than before, the companies were divided, small parties seeking different markets; that large flocks of sheep were now driven from the province is noted by Governor Chacon, in his report of 1803. At this time there was no custom house in the province,[508] all duties being paid in the south.

Down to about the year 1798 no coin was in circulation in New Mexico, but later on the salaries of officers and soldiers were paid

---

[506] According to the official reports, the Spanish population of the leading towns, including the outlying ranchos, in 1805-1820, was as follows: Santa Fé, 3,741, 6,038; La Cañada, 2,188, 2,633; Alburquerque, 4,294, 2,564; San Juan de los Caballeros, 1,888, 2,125; Abiquiú, 1,218, 2,182 (3,029 in 1821); Belen, 1,588, 2,103 (1,756 in 1821); Taos, 1,337, 1,252; Santa Clara, 967, 1,116; Isleta, 378, 2,324; Picuriés, 17, 1,041. In 1821 Socorro is given with a population of 1,580. The largest Indian pueblos in 1820-21 were, Taos, 751; San Ildefonso, 527; Cochití, 653; Santa Ana, 527; Laguna, 950; Acoma, 829; Zuñi, 1,597; and Isleta, 513. Humboldt says Santa Fé had a population in 1803 of 3,600, Alburquerque, 6,000, Taos, 8,900. Pike says Santa Fé had 4,500 in 1807, and Pino, in 1811, says the capital had 5,000. According to Pino, the pueblo of Pecos had but 30 fighting men in 1811, and in 1820 its population was only 58.

El Paso, according to an official census, in 1822, had 8,383, of which there were 161 married couples, single men, 2,267, single women, 3,173, widowers, 305, widows, 417, farmers, 2,072, artisans, 681, laborers, 269, teachers, 8, priests, 2, and total valuation of property, $234,018.—*Arch. Sta. Fé*, Ms.

[507] *Arch. Sta. Fé.* In April, 1806, General Salcedo, comandante at Chihuahua, issued an order demanding that trade with the Indians must be encouraged.

[508] *Diario de Mex.*, i, 353. The viceroy gives out a decree in behalf of the trade of New Mexico.

The report of Governor Chacon, of 1803, is found in the *Arch. Sta. Fé*. He says that everybody trades in his own way, often a very bad way. Pino describes the outfitting of the caravans from La Joya and says that a small force leaving that place in 1809 was attacked by Indians, with a loss of several killed and 300 horses.

in coin, but this did not furnish a medium in any way sufficient for the needs of the country. There was a duty upon tobacco, and none was raised in New Mexico, except by the padres for home consumption. The total value of imports, according to Pino, who gives an official report to the consulate at Vera Cruz in 1804, was $112,000 in a year, while the exports, chiefly wool, wine, and peltries, were only $60,000, leaving a balance of trade against New Mexico of $52,000. The imports included $61,000 of European goods, $7,000 Asiatic, $34,000 American and only $10,000 of horses and mules. Governor Chacon, however, in his report of August 28, 1803, says that 600 horses and mules were sent away annually. He also notes that books on agriculture and stock-raising were much needed. All the official reports made during these years sound the praises of the country as to its agricultural advantages. There were a few Spanish artisans in the province, but almost all of the mechanical and other work was performed by Indians.

In 1803, in his report, Governor Chacon says that copper is abundant, but no mines are worked, as does also Pino, who says there are also mines of gold and silver. Pike, in 1807, refers to a copper mine, west of the Rio Grande, in latitude 34°, yielding 20,000 muleloads of metal annually; that vessels of wrought copper are among the exports of the country. This must have been the Santa Rita mine, as Bartlett says it was worked in 1804. This mine was discovered in 1800 by Lieutenant-Colonel Carrisco, through the aid of an Indian. In 1804 it was sold to Don Francisco Manuel Elguea, of Chihuahua, who at once commenced extensive developments, and found the metal of such fine quality that the entire output was contracted to the royal mint for coinage purposes. The metal was transported to the City of Mexico by pack-mules and wagons, 100 mules, carrying three hundred pounds each, being constantly employed. There is very little of record which shows any mining done in New Mexico during Spanish rule.

In matters of education for the people very little was done during this period. Colleges and public schools, there were none. There were a few private teachers in the larger towns. There were no lawyers in the province. There was one doctor, the garrison surgeon, at Santa Fé. As to the social habits and customs of the people, there is nothing worth recording. Major Pike says something as to the habits of the people, but his stay was of so short duration that his observations on this subject are of little value. He saw nothing of the inner life of the best families of the province, and what he says of the plain people and lower classes was gleaned from a few hours of conversation and association with a class who could not and would not communicate anything to him.[509]

Pino says that at this time the government and administration of justice were military, the governor also being military chief. There were no ayuntamientos or other municipal bodies, no courts, no taxes, or municipal funds. Each of the eight alcaldes gave attention to all matters of local concern, being responsible only to the governor, an appeal from whose decision might be taken to the audiencia of Guadalajara. Pino demanded an audiencia at Chihuahua. The governor had no legal adviser, nor was there a notary in the province. In the administration of the affairs of his office, the governor was assisted by two lieutenants and two alféreces.[510]

---

[509] Pike, Z. M., *Explorations*, etc., p. 259. On the trip from Santa Fé to Chihuahua, Pike was frequently entertained — in a way — and from some of these entertainments he drew some of his conclusions, which, it would seem, were entirely unwarranted. Pike says that Melgares possessed none of the haughty Castilian pride, but much of the urbanity of the Frenchman, and declares that he was one of the few officers or citizens whom he found loyal to the king of Spain, and yet, by innuendo, he seeks to throw aspersions upon the character and customs of the native people by calling attention to one of Melgares's honest efforts to make his journey to Chihuahua as pleasant as possible. When the command had reached a point south of Alburquerque, and while yet in charge of Lieutenant 'Almanza, they met Melgares near San Fernandez. The latter, knowing Pike's temperament and disposition evidently much better than Pike understood the manner of providing entertainment for the ''stranger within their gates,'' proposed giving a *baille* for Pike and his companions, and to make sure of the attendance, the notice being very short, Melgares sent out a notice to the alcaldes of several small villages near-by, as follows: ''Send this evening six or eight of your handsomest young girls to the village of St. Fernandez, where I propose giving a fandango, for the entertainment of the American officers arrived today,'' signed, Don Facundo. As Pike says, this order was punctually obeyed, but to one who has any knowledge whatever of the customs of the people there is no cause for Pike's saying, as he did, that the order ''portrays more clearly than a chapter of observations the degraded state of the common people.''

[510] Pino, Pedro Bautista, *Noticias de Nuevo Mexico*, p. 25, cap. vi: ''Toda la provincia está dividida en ocho alcaidias servidas por sus vecinos, sin sueldo, y sujetas á un gobernador político y militar, que residen en la capital de Santa Fé, sin asesor ni aun escribano, porque no lo hay en toda la provincia. Tiene como por ayudantes dos tenientes y dos alféreces.

''De las determinaciones de este gobernador, no hay mas apelaciones en lo civil y criminal, que á la audiencia de Guadalajara, distante como 500 leguas. En lo militar, estuvo muchos años sujeta al vireinato de México (800 leguas), hasta que se estableció la comandancia general de provincias internas en Chihuahua (240 leguas).

''No se ha podido nunca pensar en impuestos municipales. . . Tampoco

The alcaldes received no pay. At El Paso there was a lieutenant of the governor who received two thousand dollars salary. The salary of the governor was four thousand dollars per annum.

Mr. Pino says that the roads in the province were good; that the highway from New Mexico to the United States was beautiful, crossing the great plains, following in its course many of the rivers along whose banks were many views of magnificent scenery.[512]

The military force of the province, as supported by the royal government, consisted of one hundred and twenty-one men, which formed the garrison or veteran company at Santa Fé, of which thirty-nine were cavalry, moving to various parts of the province, when ordered, or occasion demanded; twelve were guards at the capital, seven were stationed at La Joya de Sevilleta, and the remainder was scattered over the province with the citizen soldiery. The pay of a regular soldier was two hundred and forty dollars.

In his *Exposicion*, Pino calls the attention of the Spanish government to the fact that the people of New Mexico had always maintained a force of approximately one thousand five hundred men, citizen soldiers, which the settlers had furnished without pay, and had armed and equipped them, at no cost to the royal treasury, thus saving to the king $43,090,000 in the 118 years preceding the making of his report. Pino demanded that the militia be paid as in other provinces, and that five presidios should be established or transferred from the south. But nothing was ever done.

In the year 1808, three companies of citizen soldiers were organ-

---

ha habido hasta ahora un cuerpo autorizado para promover así el establecimiento de una caja ó cajas de provincias, como para representar á nombre de ellas lo conveniente á su prosperidad.

"Los pueblos del Paso son gobernados por un teniente de gobernador militar, con sueldo de 2,000 duros."

[512] Pino, Pedro Bautista, *Ibid*, p. 17. On the the subject of roads — caminos — Mr. Pino says: "Los caminos del interior de este territorio, son en lo general cómodos, porque los mas van á las orillas de los rios, y por poblaciones donde hay mucha hospilidad; todos son carreteros, menos el que conduce á Taos por la ruta de la cañada, pues una sierra elevandísima apenas dá paso por sus desfiladeros á los caballos; todos son seguros, y el viajero no camina con el temor de que unsaltador le quite sus intereses ó de la muerte.

"El Camino que conduce á los Estados Unidos por la ruta del Missuri, es muy hermoso, pues va por llanuras inmensas, y en su mayor parte por márgenes de rios que presentan vistas de suma variabilidad; en el espacio de mas de 250 leguas no se encuentra poblacion, y solo se ven numerosas naciones de gentiles, hasta que se ariba á las primeras poblaciones del Norte — América en el condado de Jefferson; anualmente andan este camino caravanas de anglo-americanos."

ized. They were commanded by Captains Lorenzo Gutierrez, José Francisco Pino, and Bartolomé Vaca, sixty-one men in each company, but up to the time of the making of his report, says Mr. Pino, they had received no pay.

The twenty-six "poblaciones" of Indians and the one hundred and two "plazas españoles," which formed the province at the time Mr. Pino was elected delegate to the Spanish cortés, pertained to the diocese of Durango. The spiritual wants of these people were administered to by twenty-two "religiosos" of the order of St. Francis. These frailes lived principally at the places where there was a large Spanish population. There was one secular priest at Santa Fé, and there, as at Alburquerque and Santa Cruz, the frailes were supported by fees; the others by their sínodos of $330 from the royal treasury. At this period complaint is again made against the frailes, for in 1810 Protector-General Andrade appointed Felipe Sandoval a "protector partidario" of the Indians in New Mexico. Sandoval made a report to his superior in which he stated that the frailes were content with simply saying mass, and that the neophytes were in reality deprived of spiritual instruction. The bishop of Durango sent a reprimand to the Franciscans and the vice-custodio, Fr. Alvarez, called upon the members of the order for a defense. Naturally they denied the accusations, declaring that the "protector" was only influenced by evil motives and was a thief. No bishop visited the province after 1760, and therefore there were no confirmations. Pino, in his report, demanded that his province be erected into a separate bishopric, saying that although he was fifty years of age he had never seen a bishop until he came to Spain in 1812. He also demanded that the royal order providing for a college be carried out as well. Accordingly, on the 26th of January, 1813, the erection of a bishopric and the establishment of the colleges were decreed by the córtes, but practically nothing was done under Spanish rule.[513] Pino complained of this in his letter to the córtes after his second election as deputy.

THE FRANCISCAN MISSIONS

---

[513] Pino, Pedro Bautista, *Ibid*, p. 31, on the subject of church government at that time, says: "Las 26 poblaciones de indios y las 102 plazas de españoles que forman el todo de la provincia, pertenecen en lo espiritual á la diócesis de Durango. Son administradas por 22 religiosos del orden de San Francisco de la provincia de México; y solo en un pueblo del Paso y la capital, son clérigos sus parrocos. Gozan renta por el erario, á excepcion de los de las villas de Albur-

Major Pike says, it will be remembered, that Captain Melgares was one of the few officers and citizens whom he met, who was loyal to his king. It is true that during this period the Mexicans had fondly indulged the hope that the Spanish yoke might be removed. Prior to 1810 murmurs were heard on all sides. They penetrated far into the northern provinces. In that year came the first struggle for independence under Hidalgo.[514] It was quickly suppressed; but the spirit of independence had penetrated and was strong among the people. Too often the Spaniard had made the Mexican feel that he was not of pure Castilian blood. The revolutionary attempt, under Hidalgo, commencing September 16, 1810, did little other than to stir up the flames of revolution which were to burst out at a

---

querque, Santa Cruz de la Cañada y la capital, que no tienen mas renta que las obvenciones ó pié de altar.

"Las distancias que hay de los pueblos donde residen los párrocos á las plazas de habitantes españoles, deben llamar atencion, pues siendo algunas de 8 y 10 leguas, ni pueden concurrir á oir misa en un mismo pueblo, ni puede el párroco decir dos misas en un dia con tan largo viaje, ni pueden tener vicarios, porque no alcanzan las rentas ó sínodos señalados puramente para la administracion espiritual de aquellos pueblos, cuya dotacion fué hecha sin contar en aquel tiempo con aquellas 102 plazas que la necesidad obligó á construir desde el año de 1780 para conservar el todo de la provincia.

"Hace mas de 50 años que se sabe si hay obispo, ni se ha visto ninguno en aquella provincia en todo este tiempo; por consiguiente, se hallan sin cumplir las soberanas disposiciones y lo prevenido en la disciplina eclesiástica. Son infinitos los males que sufren aquellos habitantes por esta falta tan grave de su primado pastor. Se hallan sin confirmar todos los nacidos en dichos 50 años; y los pobres que quieren contraer matrimonio con sus parientas por medio de dispensa, no lo pueden verificar por los crecidos costos en el dilatado viaje de mas de 400 leguas que hay á Durango; de aquí proviene que muchos, estrechados del amor, viven amancebados y con familia, dolo, y otros que se sufren por la falta referida. Es bien doloroso, por cierto, que entregando aquella provincia todos los años de 9 á 10,000 duros de sus diezmos, no haya podido conseguir el los 50 años ver la cara á su obispo; yo que cuento mas de edad, nunca supe, cómo se vestian hasta que vine á Cádiz."

Mr. Pino was very friendly to the Franciscans, for, as is seen above, he tells of the great difficulties under which all have labored, and in his report relative to the establishment of the *colegio de religiosos*, he says further: "Como la religion de S. Francisco ha sido la conquistadora, digamoslo así, y ha sido ella sola en lo espiritual, están los habitantes tan acostumbrados á ver este hábito, que cualquiera otro no seria quizá bien admitido. En este concepto, convendrian fuesen los 12 religiosos de la misma órden, y aun el primer obispo; y aquí tiene V. M. allanadas todas las dificudades por la misma provincia sobre los dos primeros establecimientos."

[514] Don Miguel Hidalgo y Costilla, patriot priest of Mexico, raised the standard of revolt in his parish of Dolores, September, 1810. At first he was successful, but on the 21st of March, 1811, he was captured, while trying to escape to the United States. After trial and degradation from his priestly offices, he was shot on the 31st of July, 1811. A monument to his memory was erected in the city of Chihuahua.

later day. It does not appear that this first attempt or the execution of the great Hidalgo at Chihuahua in 1811 made much if any impression upon the people of New Mexico. The province was so far removed from the center of revolutionary plans and operation that scarcely a ripple of excitement was caused by the stirring events in the south at that period. It seems that the people of New Mexico were content to await the issue, or else, kept in ignorance of the course of events by the royalist officials, they did not know of the revolution until after it was suppressed.

Melgares was the last of the Spanish governors. In the official newspaper in the City of Mexico, of March 7, 1819, the office of governor of New Mexico was declared vacant, and aspirants were notified to send in their petitions, and Melgares, in the documents of 1819-20, is called governor *ad interim.* In 1822 he was succeeded by Don Francisco Javier Chavez, who ruled for a brief period, 1822-23, when he was succeeded by Colonel Antonio Viscarra. On the 28th day of September, 1821, Mexico had declared its independence of the mother country, and shortly afterwards had succeeded in making it a reality. This, of necessity, caused an entire change in the relations of New Mexico, a part of the empire under Iturbide,[515] and a republic after his fall. The cry of Dolores had not been in vain.

The news of Iturbide's accession was received with great demonstrations of joy in New Mexico. "It was on September 11th," says Mr. Bancroft, "that the 'dulce voz de libertad' was first heard, and lovers of the country and religion swore to the independence at Santa Fé; and on December 26th — dia glorioso! Dia de admiracion, y dia tan eternal para los Nuevos Mexicos, que de padres á hijos se ira trasmitiendo hasta la mas remota posteridad! — came news of Iturbide's entry into Mexico. Dozens of citizens received communications in writing and print by the mail of that day, which they

---

[515] Agustin Iturbide was a native of Valladolid province, who entered the militia and rose to a colonelcy. In 1820, as military chief, he succeeded in combining the various Mexican parties, and drove the Spanish viceroy and army from the country. He was hailed as "Liberator," and shortly, in May, 1822, had himself proclaimed emperor. But his arbitrary rule and the general desire for a republic united his late allies against him, and in less than a year he was compelled to abdicate and submit to banishment. In 1824 he imprudently returned unheralded, being thereupon arrested and executed by the republican authorities.

Zuñi Fetiches of the Chase

read aloud to the crowd at the postoffice, the governor reading a patriotic address from the city of Tepic, with a poetic effusion of that 'liberalísimo europeo' Don Pedro Negrete, on listening to which, all, from the 'tierno parvulito' to the 'trémulo anciano,' were beside themselves with joy, and filled the air with *vivas*, as Melgares shouted, 'New Mexicans, this is the occasion for showing the heroic patriotism that inflames you; let your sentiments of liberty and gratitude be published abroad, and let us show tyrants that although we live at the very extremity of North America we love the holy religion of our fathers; that we cherish and protect the desired union between Spaniards of both hemispheres; and that, with our last drop of blood, we will sustain the sacred independence of the Mexican empire!' The 6th of January, 1822, was set apart for a formal celebration, which should, if possible, excel that of Tepic. At dawn the salutes of artillery and the marching of processions began; and with the dawn of the next day, ended the grand *baille* at the palacio. Never did Santa Fé behold such a splendid display. The *independientisimo* postmaster, Juan Bautista Vigil, excelled himself in painting decorations; the *excesivo independiente* alcalde, Pedro Armendaris, led a triumphant *paseo*; and a grand *loa de tres garantias* was performed, by Alférez Santiago Abréu representing independence, Curate and Vicar Juan Tomás Terrazas, religion, and Chaplain Francisco Osio, the union. All through the day and night the villa was painted red with independence or death, and Governor Melgares wrote a flaming account of the whole affair for the *Gaçeta Imperial*.[516] Doubtless Don Facundo, realizing the side on which his bread was buttered, saw to it that nothing was lost in telling the story; and presumably the fall of Iturbide, a little later, was celebrated with equal enthusiasm.''

---

[516] Melgares, Facundo, *Demonstraciones que para solemnizar la Independencia del Imperio hizo la Ciudad de Sta. Fé*, 1822. In *Gaçeta Imperial*, March 23, 26, 1822, ii., 85-93.

On September 10, 1822, New Mexico was made one of the five Provincias Internas under a comandante general at Chihuahua, corresponding to the earlier intendencia; that is, there was practically no change in New Mexico. *Mex., Mem. Guerra*, 1823, p. 25. In Bancroft, *Hist. Arizona and N. M.*, note, p. 309.

List of Spanish governors and captains general of New Mexico:

Juan de Oñate, 1598-1608.
Pedro de Peralta, 1608-.
Felipe Zotylo, (1621-8).
Manuel Silva, 1629.
Fernando de Argüello, 1640 (?)
Juan Paez Hurtado, acting, 1717.
Antonio Valverde y Cosio, ad interim, 1717-22.
Juan de Estrada y Austria (?), ad interim, 1721 (?).

NOTE 516 — Concluded

Luis de Rosas, 1641.
——— Valdéz, (1642).
Alonso Pacheco de Heredia, 1643.
Fernando de Argüello, 1645.
Luis de Guzman, (1647).
Hernando de Ugarte y la Concha, 1650.
Juan de Samaniego, 1653-4.
Enrique de Avila y Pacheco, 1656.
Bernardo Lopez de Mendizibal, to 1661.
Diego de Penaloza Briceño, 1661-4.
Fernando de Villanueva.
Juan de Medrano.
Juan de Miranda.
Juan Francisco de Treviño, 1675.
Antonio Otermin, 1679-83.
Domingo Jironza Petriz Cruzate, 1683-6.
Pedro Reneros de Posada, 1686-9.
Domingo Jironza Petriz Cruzate, 1689-91.
Diego de Vargas, Zapata Lujan, Ponce de Leon, 1691-7.
Pedro Rodriguez Cubero, 1697-1703.
Diego de Vargas, Zapata Lujan, Ponce de Leon, 1703-4.
Juan Paez Hurtado, acting, 1704-5.
Francisco Cuervo y Valdés, ad interim, 1705-7.
José Chacon Medina Salazar y Villaseñor, marqués de la Penuela, 1707-12.
Juan Ignacio Flores Mogollon, 1712-15.
Félix Martinez, ad interim, 1715-17.

Juan Domingo de Bustamante, 1722-31.
Gervasio Cruzat y Góngora, 1731-6.
Enrique de Olavide y Micheleña, ad interim, 1736-9.
Gaspar Domingo de Mendoza, 1739-43.
Joaquin Codallos y Rabal, 1744-9.
Francisco de la Rocha (appointed), 1747.
Tomás Velez Cachupin, 1749-54.
Francisco Antonio Marin del Valle, 1754-60.
Mateo Antonio de Mendoza, acting, 1760.
Manuel Portillo Urrisola, acting, 1761-2.
Tomás Velez Cachupin, 1762-7.
Pedro Fermin de Mendinueta, 1767-78.
Francisco Trebol Navarro, acting 1778.
Juan Bautista de Anza, 1778-89.
Manuel Flon (appointed), 1785.
Fernando de la Concha, 1789-94.
Fernando Chacon, 1794-1805.
Joaquin Real Alencaster, 1805-8.
Alberto Mainez, acting, 1807-8.
José Manrique, 1810-14.
Pedro Maria de Allande, 1816-18.
Facundo Melgares, 1818-22.
Under the Mexican Empire—Iturbide
Francisco Javier Chavez, 1822-3.
Antonio Vizcarra, 1822-23.

Old church at Laguna, N. M.

BIBLIOGRAPHY

Archivo de Santa Fé	*Unbound Mss.* at Washington, D. C., Library of Congress.
Archivo, N. Mex.	*Archivo General de Mexico*, printed in 1856.
Archivo, Gen. de Mex.	*Doc. Hist. Mex.*
Aleman	*Disertaciones*, Mexico, 1844-9. 3 vols.
Alegre, Fran. Javier	*Historia de la Compania de Jesus*, Mex., 1841.
Anza, Juan B.	*Carta de 1776. Diario de la Expedicion á Moqui, 1780.* Ms. *Diario de una Expedicion contra la nacion Comanche, 1779.* Ms. in *New Mex. Doc.*, 861. *Expedicion de Anza y muerté de "Cuerno Verde," 1779.* Ms.
Arricivita, J. D.	*Cronica Seráfica y Apostólica*, Madrid, 1792.
Bancroft, H. H.	*History of Arizona and New Mexico.*
Bandelier, A. F.	*Investigations in the Southwest*, Final Rep., parts i and ii; *Historical Introduction.*
Bartlett, John R.	*Personal Narrative of Explorations, 1850-3*, N. Y., 1854, 2 vols.
Bonilla, Antonio	*Apuntes sobre N. Mex., 1775*, in *N. Mex., Cédulas.*
Davis, W. W. H.	*The Spanish Conquest of New Mexico; El Gringo.*
Documentos para la Historia de Nuevo Mexico	*Four Series*, 20 vols., Mexico, 1853-1857.
Diario de Mexico	Mexico, 1805-10, 13 vols.
Fernandes Duro, C.	*Don Diego de Peñalosa*, Madrid, 1882.
Gaçeta Imperial de Mexico	Mexico, 1821-3.
Galvez, Condé de	*Instruction á Ugárte*, 1786.
Garcés, Francisco	*Diario y Derrotero, 1775-6*, in *Doc. Hist. Mex.*, 2nd series, i, 226.
Gregg, Josiah	*Commerce of the Prairies*, N. Y., 1844.
Guëmes y Horcasitas	*Medios para la pacificacion de los Comanches*, Ms., 1746.
Hurtado, Juan Paez	*Campaña contra los Apaches, 1715*, Ms.
Melgares, Facundo	*Demonstraciones*, in *Gaceta Imperial, 1822.*
Meline, James F.	*Two Thousand Miles on Horseback*, N. Y., 1867.
Menchero, J. M.	*Informe, 1749*, Ms.
Moqui	*Juntas de Guerra*, Ms., in *N. Mex. Doc.*, 922.
Morfi, Juan A.	*Viaje*, etc., *y Diario de N. Mex., 1777*, in *Doc. Hist. Mex.*, 3rd series, iv, 305.
Niel, Juan A.	*Apuntes*, in *Doc. Hist. Mex.*, 3rd series, iv, 56.
Pattie, James Ohio	*Personal Narrative, Western Travels*, vol. xix.
Pike, Z. M.	*Account of Travels*, Phil., 1810, London, 1811.
Pino, Pedro B.	*Noticias*, etc., *Hist. of N. M.*, Mex., 1849.
Prince, L. B.	*Historical Sketches, N. Mexico.*
Ritch, W. G.	*Aztlan*, Boston, 1875, Leg. Blue Book, Sta. Fé, 1882.
Tamaron, Pedro	*Visita del Obispando de Durango, 1765.*
Vargas, Diego de, etc.	*Journal.*
Villaseñor y Sanchez, J. A.	*Teatro Americano*, Mex., 1746.

INDEX

INDEX

ABIQUIU, pueblo of, mentioned, battle with Comanches near, 440
Abó, pass of, mentioned, 271
Abó, San Gregorio de, pueblo of, mentioned, 338
Aborigines, number of, public domain, language, character, customs, 6
Abuses, by Spaniards, complaints made by Franciscans, 354, 357, note 367; 443
Acevedo, Fr. Francisco, churches built by, death of, 338
Acochis, definition, 207; mentioned, 234
Acoma, pueblo of, visited by Alvarado, 199; description, 199, note 215; history of, 199, note 215; peace with Alvarado, 202; mentioned, 148; visited by Oñate, 324; conspiracy to kill Oñate, 324; battles at, 327; visited by Espejo, 278; visited by De Vargas, submission, 383; garrison at, recommended by Espejo, 289; battle of, Oñate's soldiers killed, 327; De Vargas visits, 411; expedition to, 439
Acus, pueblo of, mentioned, 148
Adrian VI, Pope, mentioned, 254
Aguas Zarcas, springs, Fr. Rodriguez, 258
Aguatuvi, pueblo of, destruction of, 419, note 421
Aguilar, Captain Alonzo Rael de, lieutenant-governor and captain-general, mentioned, note 452
Alamillo, pueblo of, visited by Otermin, 373
Alarcon, Hernando, cited, 157, note 168; cited, death of Estevan, 159, note 172; expedition of, 179, note 197; mentioned, 179 *et seq.*; report, 179, 183, note 201
Alburquerque, city of, founded by, 422; population of, 1751, 443, note 466

Alburquerque, Duke of, mentioned, 421, note 425; appoints Cuervo governor, 421, 422
Alcaraz, Diego de, meets Cabeza de Vaca, 107; mentioned, 114
Aleman, Juan, mentioned, 214, note 226
Alencaster, Colonel Joaquin de Real, governor of New Mexico, 456; expedition under Melgares, 458; Pike taken before, 467; population during rule of, 470
Allande, Pedro Maria de, governor of New Mexico, 470
Alvarado, Hernando, officer Coronado expedition, leaves Hawaikúh, passes Acoma, reaches Tiguex, 203; official account of his journey, 202, note 216; sends messenger to Coronado, marches to Cicuyé, 203; meets El Turco, 206; goes to Cicuyé, arrests Bigotes and cacique, 207; takes them to Tiguex, province rises, 207; goes to buffalo plains, sees buffalos, reports to Coronado, 204; visits Taos, 230
Alvarado, Pedro de, biography, 166; claims of, 166; joins Alarcon's fleet, 184
America, South and Central, explorations in, mentioned, 274
Amole, mentioned, 103, note 109
Andrés, Francisco, Mexican Indian with Fr. Rodriguez, mentioned, 258
Andrés, Indian left by Coronado at Hawaikúh, mentioned, 279
Antiquities, Jemez Plateau, cited, 26, note 10; origin of name of, 27, note 11
Antonio, de Guadalajara, Indian left by Coronado at Hawaikúh, mentioned, 279
Anza, Juan Bautista de, governor of New Mexico, 1778, biography, 449; campaign against Comanches, 450, death of Cuerno Verde, 450, note

474; visits Moqui, famine, deaths, 450, note 475; missions reduced, list of, friars displeased, 451, note 476

Apaches, mentioned, 16; de Navajú, 16; tribal groups, numbers, location, 48, 49, note 31; derivation of term, 49; assists Valverde against Comanches, 432, note 441; battle with French, 432, note 442; raids of, 420, note 423; De Vargas campaign against, 1703, 421; warned by Mogollon, 428; campaign against by Hurtado, 428; troubles and classification by Fr. Benavides, 341; conspiracies, 346, 348; raids on Zuñi by, 348, 349; raids in valley of Rio Grande and on Alburquerque, 452; campaign against by governor Chacon, 452, note 478, 479

Apalachee, province of, 64; location of town of, 68, note 61

Aparicio, historian, cited, 255, note 269; cited as to number in Espejo's entrada, 265, note 280

Arbadaos, Indians, mentioned, 92

Archæology, American School of, Santa Fé, excavations by, 12

Archæology, science, study of, 4

Archæological Institute of America, papers of, cited, 35, note 19

Architecture, communal houses, mentioned, 9

Archives, Santa Fé, destruction of by Governor Pyle, 239, note 256; only document in prior to 1680, 344, note 348

Archuleta, Juan de, brings families from Cuartalejo to Taos, 345

Arellano, Tristan de, officer Coronado expedition, 184; left in command of army, 184; starts for Cibola, 194; arrival, 205; return to Tiguex, 228, note 245; crosses Pecos river on return, 229, note 245; leaves Tiguex to find Coronado, 234; reaches Cicuyé, Indians hostile, arrival of Coronado, return to Tiguex, 234

Arguello, Fernando de, governor of New Mexico, 343, note 343; conspiracy at Jemez, 343; hangs Indians, 344, note 344

Arkansas river, mentioned, 223

Arteaga, Fr. Antonio de, founder of Senecú, 338

Arts, of Pajaritans, first inhabitants of communal houses, glazing, pottery, 30, note 16

Arvide, Fr., murdered, 345, note 352

Asa, people, clan of Hopi, mentioned, 43

Asay, Osay, Zuñi, heard of by Rodriguez, 258

Asuncion, Fr. Juan de la, expedition of, 139, 164

Atayos, Indians, described, 118, note 126

Athapascan, stock, mentioned, 9; race, Navajó, Apache, enemies of Pueblo, description, 49, note 31

Audiencia, of Seville, Cabeza de Vaca, seat in, 116

Auté, location of, 71, note 65

Autos de fe, mentioned, 446, note 468

Avavares, Indians, mentioned, 90

Avila, Pedro de, revolt at Suya, goes to Culiacan, detained by Saavedra, 238

Avila y Pacheco, Don Enrique de, governor of New Mexico, 344

Awatobi, pueblo of Moqui, called Zaguato, visited by Espejo, 280, note 289

Ayeta, Fr. Francisco, mentioned, goes to City of Mexico, secures relief, 350; his report, note 361; reports revolt of 1680, 365, note 375; returns from City of Mexico, 367, note 376; with Otermin's second entrada, 371; founds city of El Paso, 367; brings missionaries to New Mexico, 350, note 361

Ayolas, mentioned, 115

BACA, CAPTAIN ALONZO, expedition beyond Quivira, 345; discovers plot of Tehuas, Cochití and Jemez Indians to revolt, 347

Baca, Captain Bartolomé, mentioned, 471, note 504

Bad Thing, myth, described, 91, note 92

Baird, Spencer F., secretary Smithsonian Institution, mentioned, 6

Bancroft, H. H., historian, mentioned xii; cited, 7, note 1; 8, note 2; 48, note 30; 57, note 45; 141, note 149; 164, note 179; 183, note 200; 206, note 220; 219, note 234; 220, note 236; 227, note 243; 256, note 270; 258, note 273; 275, note 286; 276, note 287; 281, notes 290, 291; 284, note 292; 292, note 300; 299, note 304; 301, note 305; 309, note 312; 310, note 313; Pueblo villages in 16th century, 321, note 327; cited,

INDEX 489

332, note 333; 333, note 336 as to city of Santa Fé; cited, 338, note 338; 341, note 341; 344, note 349; 345, notes 350, 351; 346, note 354; 348, note 357; 349, note 359; 354, note 363; 356, note 365; 366, note 375; 376, note 383; 392, note 392; 397, note 397; 407, note 407; 408, note 408; 415, note 415; 416, note 417; 419, notes 422, 423, 428; 426, note 432; 428, note 435; 429, note 436; 430, note 439; 433, note 447; quoted as to controversy between bishop and Franciscans, 435, 436, note 425; 437, note 453; 438, note 454; 439, note 455; 441, notes 460, 461; 443, note 466 as to population in 1750; 448, note 473; 454, note 481; 445, note 483 table of population, 1750-1800; commercial conditions, 474, note 506; quoted as to succession of Iturbide, 480, 481

Bandelier, Adolph F., historian, archæologist, ethnologist, mentioned, xii; Indian creeds, 8, note 3; pioneer explorer of Rito de los Frijoles, 28, note 11; Tarahumares, 34, note 18; mentioned, 35, note 19; cited, 38, note 21; Indian customs, 40, note 24; cited, 42, notes 26, 27; 48, note 29; 73, note 69; mentioned, 89, note 92; Bad Thing myth, note 92; mentioned, 107, note 114; primahaitu, 108, note 118; Spanish justice, 109, note 119; mines, 111, note 119; slavery, 112, note 119; Cabeza de Vaca in Paraguay, 116, note 125; character of Cabeza de Vaca, 117, note 125; his route, 121; route of Coronado, 122; argument as to route of Cabeza de Vaca, 123-132; notes 133-138; expeditions of Cortés, 138, note 142; efforts of Mendoza, 139, notes 145-147; Mendoza's letter about Fr. Marcos, 142, note 151; cited, 145, note 152; 146, note 154; Opatas, 147, note 156; Cibola, description of, 153, note 165; death of Estevan, 159, note 171; City of Mexico, 162, note 175; Alarcon's voyage, 183, note 200; route of Coronado, 185, note 202; Tutahaco, 205, note 219; Cochití, 218, note 230; Quiviras, 226, note 243; Yugeuingege, 229, note 246; Braba, Taos, 230, note 247; range of Piros, 231, notes 249, 250; N. M. Archives, employment, 241, note 256; Puara, 257, note 272; Tobosos, 267, note 283; Espejo's estimates as to population, 276, note 288; estimate of Benavides, 277, note 288; copy of Villagrá, 302, note 306; turquoise mines, 314, note 318; Yuqueyunque, 316, note 321; San Ildefonso, 319, note 324; old pueblo at Santa Fé, 333, note 336; Zipias, 346, note 353; Hawaikúh, 348, note 358; Apaches, wars with Piros, 349, note 360; Pueblo Rebellion, 1680, 358, note 368; San Felipe, 363, note 372; Alamillo, church at, 365, note 374; Sumas, 381, notes 386, 434; ruins on Potrero Viejo, 398, notes 399, 400; Taos, 401, note 402; ruins at Ojo Caliente, 401, note 403; Jemez ruins, 405, note 405; town of Cubero, 417, note 419; Oraybe, 418, note 421; compulsory labor by Indians, 426, note 431; French in New Mexico, 432, notes 443, 454; Indians, horses, use of fire-arms, 440, note 459; inquisition did not deal with Indians, 446, note 468

Bandelier, Mrs. Fanny, cited, 60, note 48; 63, note 51; 68, note 60; 80, note 75; 86, note 85; 91, notes 91, 92

Banuelos, mentioned, 306

Barela, Adjutant, under De Vargas, battle of Potrero Viejo, 396

Barreda, Domingo de la, mentioned, 412

Barrionuevo, Captain, under Coronado, 229, note 246; visits Taos, 230, note 247; Braba, 230, note 247; kivas described, 233

Bartlett, J. R., *Personal Narrative*, cited, 147, note 155

Bay of Caballos, description, 72, note 66

Belen, town of, mentioned, 232

Beltran, Fr., mentioned, 263; leaves Zuñi for Mexico, 281; goes to Durango, 282; report to viceroy, 286

Benavides, Fr. Alonzo, historian, mentioned, 16; custodio, 337; asks for bishopric, report, 338, note 338; classifies tribes, visits Apaches, Jumanos, manners and customs of Apaches, 341, note 339; goes to Spain, archbishop of Goa, 341, note 339

Bermejo, Fr. Manuel, mentioned, Navajó mission, Encinal, 441, note 461

Bernal, Fr., Pueblo plot revealed to, 357, note 368; death of, 361, note 369
Bernalillo, town of, mentioned, 225; old pueblo near, 263, note 279
Bibliography, 51, 135, 161, 249, 264, 300, 353, 413, 483
Black Mesa, San Ildefonso, Indians assemble at, 393, 394; battle at, 394, 407; friars killed at, 411, note 411
Bolsas, Antonio, Indian chief, shot by De Vargas, Santa Fé, 393
Bonilla, Captain Francisco Leiva, expedition of, 298, quarrels with Humana, slain, 299
Bonilla, Lieut. Col., Apuntes, report, views of, 448, note 472
Bonito, Pueblo, described, 25
Braba, Taos, 230, note 247
Brower, J. V., *Memoirs*, cited, Cicuyé, 298, note 214; location of Quivira Indians, 227, note 243
Bua, Nicolas, San Juan Indian, governor, son-in-law of Popé, killed by Popé, 357
Buffalo, first mentioned by Cabeza de Vaca, 88
Bureau, American Ethnology, cited, 32, note 17
Bustamente, Pedro, soldier with Fr. Rodriguez, 257; his account of the expedition, 258, note 273
Bustamente, Juan Domingo de, governor of New Mexico, 434, note 449; French take Cuartalejo, 435, report, 435; trial, 437
Busto, Captain Antonio Cobian, visitador-general, 434; holds convention at Santa Fé, 434

CABEZA DE VACA, ALVAR NUÑEZ, survivor Narvaéz expedition, 54; report, 55, 56; goes to Spain, presented at court, 57; bibliography, 57, note 47; journeys inland from Tampa Bay, experiences, fights, 63, 67; given command at boat by Narvaéz, 73; passes mouth of Mississippi, 76; wrecked, wanderings, localities, 77; Dorantes and Castillo, 77; winter on island, 79; heals sick, 82; escapes to mainland, experiences with Indians, 84; fate of Narvaéz, 86; other companions, 87; his captivity and experiences with wandering tribes, 88 *et seq.*; piñon nuts, 98; great river from north, 99, note 98;
meets fixed habitations, 100; further wanderings, 102, notes 103, 104, 105; coral beads and turquoises, 102; reaches settlements, Village of Hearts, 103, note 110; City of Mexico, Mendoza, tells story to, 104-115; asks king for governorship of Florida, 115; captain-general, 116; charges against, 116; trial, 116; end of, 116; route discussed by authorities, 118 *et seq*
Cachupin, Tomas Veles, governor of New Mexico, 439; campaign against Comanches, 442, note 463; quarrels with Franciscans, 443; re-appointed, 445; visits Gunnison, 445; trials for witchcraft, 445, note 469
Campo, Portuguese, left behind by Coronado, 238, note 254
Canadian river, mentioned, 226
Capoques, language, 82
Caravallo, alcalde of Narvaéz expedition, 66
Cardenas, Lope de, officer Coronado expedition, 205; fight at Tiguex, 208; rape of Indian woman, 208; massacre of Indians, 209; punished, 209, note 224; consequences of massacre, 211; siege of Tiguex, 214; returns from Suya, report, Alcarez, 238
Casa Blanca, 48, note 29
Castañeda, Pedro de Naçera, historian, biography, 173, note 190; cited, 174, note 191; 186, note 204; 195, 196, notes 210, 211; Grand Canyon, 198, note 213; Cicuyé, description, 203, note 217; Tiguex, description, 204, note 218; cited, 214, note 226; death of Estevan, 158, note 190; cited, 219, notes 233, 235; Alvarado visits Taos, 230; cited as to petition of soldiers for return to New Spain, 237, note 252; cited, Indians left at Hawaikúh, 239, note 255; biography, 247, note 261; quoted, 283, note 292
Castaño de Sosa, his entrada, 292, note 299; list of persons, 292, note 300; visits pueblos, his explorations, 293, 294, 297; his arrest by Captain Morlete, 298
Castillo, survivor Narvaéz expedition, 117
Castillo, Captain Diego, expedition to Teyas Indians, 345
Cathedral, at Santa Fé, site, built by, 421, note 424

INDEX 491

Catiti, Indian chief, 357, note 366; 369, note 378; death of, 370, note 378
Cebolleta, Navajó mission, 441, note 460
Census, earliest of the Pueblo Indians, 277, note 288; Vetancurt's statement, 277, note 288. See *Population*
Cerro Azul, 347
Chacan, mentioned, 102
Chacon, Don Fernando, governor of New Mexico, 452; Indian campaigns, 452, notes 478, 479
Chacon, Don José Medina Salazar Villaseñor, governor of New Mexico, Marqués de la Penuela, administration of, 424; raids upon Zuñi, 424; rebuilds chapel of San Miguel, 424, note 429; campaign against Navajós, 425
Chalchuitl, mentioned, 122
Chamita, site of Oñate's capital, 317, note 323; called San Pedro de Chama by De Vargas, 317
Chamuscado, Francisco Sanchez, explorer, with Fr. Rodriquez, 256; names of his soldiers, 256, note 270; his explorations, 256-257; visits pueblo of Puara, 257, note 272; returns to San Bartolomé, death of, 258
Charlevoix, Letters of, mentioned, 116, note 125
Chavarria, Fr. Diego, mentioned, 412
Chavez, Don Fernando Duran de, officer with De Vargas, alcalde of Bernalillo, fought with Jemez Indians, 410, note 411; alcalde of San Felipe, 412
Chavez, Don Francisco Javier, governor of New Mexico, 470
Chavez, Don José Antonio, alcalde of Alburquerque, 470
Chelly, Canyon de, mentioned, 43; battle at, 457; definition, pronunciation, 457, note 484
Cherokee Indians, mentioned as mound-builders, 9
Chichilticalli, 185; Coronado camps at, 185, note 203; mentioned, 246
Chihuahua, trade with, 474, note 508; route through by Oñate, 310
Chupadero, pueblo of, ruins, 17
Cia, pueblo of, 217, note 229; Espejo cited, note 229; Espejo visits, 278; battle of, 379, note 385; junta at, 423; mentioned, 395
Cicuyé, pueblo of, visited by Alvarado, 203; description, 203, note 217; Indians in revolt at, 229; Castaño de Sosa visits, 293
Ciudad Rodrigo, Fr. Antonio de, mentioned, 139
Cliff Palace, mentioned, 46, note 29
Cliff Dwellings, location of, distinctions, 42-45; antiquity, 46. See *Habitations*
Climate, pre-historic conditions as to, 29, note 13
Cochití, pueblo of, Indians conspire with Tehuas, 346. See *Bandelier*
Cocopas, Indians, met by Alarcon, 180, note 199
Codallos y Rabal, Don Joaquin, governor of New Mexico, administration of, 439, note 455; battle with Comanches and Utes, 442, note 463
Comanches, Indians, origin, Shoshonean, range, 50, note 32; records, 349, note 359; raids by, 420; battle with, 430; expedition against, 431; expedition of Padilla and Fernandez, 431, note 439; raids by, 435; campaign against by Cachupin, 439; French sell them arms, 440, 442; attack Galisteo, note 464; expedition against by Governor Urrisola, 445; battle between them and Apaches, 448; recommended as allies against the Apaches, 448; killing of Cuerno Verde, 450, note 474
Compostela, 115
Concepcion, Fr. de la, mentioned, missionary among Hopi, 338
Concha, Don Fernando de la, governor of New Mexico, administration of, 451; Indian campaigns, Indians at San Ildefonso, trouble feared, 451
Conchos, Indians, 256; met by Espejo, 266
Conchos, river, mentioned, 256; Espejo returns by way of, 282
Condé de Coruña, mentioned, 285; instructions from king as to contracts for entradas, 286, note 295
Copper bell, given to Cabeza de Vaca, 97, note 97
Corodeguachi, pueblo of, 439, note 457; Opata pueblo, note 457
Coronado, Don Francisco Vasquez, governor of Nueva Galicia, 141; goes with Fr. Marcos to Culiacan, 142; letter to Mendoza, 159, note 174; biography, 177, note 189; journey to Cibola, 184, 185, 186; battle of

Hawaikúh, 186, note 204, 187; letter to Mendoza describing battle, 189, note 205; Pedro de Tovar goes to Moqui, 192; letter to Mendoza, 194; Cardenas to Grand Canyon, 197; Indians from Cicuyé, 198; Alvarado to Cicuyé, 199; Lope de Cardenas to Tiguex, 205; goes to Tutahaco, 205, note 219; siege of Tiguex, 214; visits Cicuyé, 217; sends Tovar to Sonora, 218, note 231; his expedition to Quivira, 219-223; erects cross, 228, note 243; returns to Tiguex; captain makes trip down river 80 leagues, thrown from horse, 235, note 251; starts on return for Mexico, 238, notes 253, 254; meets Juan Gallego with reënforcements, 246; reaches New Galicia, 246; arrives City of Mexico, sees Mendoza, gives up position, accusations against, 247

Coronado Expedition, officers of, 173-174; equipment, 174, note 191; departure of, 175, note 194; Chiametla, 177; death of Lope de Samaniego, 177, note 195; route, 176, note 194; march of, description, 212, siege of Tiguex, 214. See *Coronado*

Cortés, Hernando, marqués del Valle, mentioned, 55; protests from, 163; note 177; claims of, 163, note 179; relations with Mendoza, 169; entertains Cabeza de Vaca, 115; titles, 137; expeditions of, 138

Cortés, Juan, 306

Cortes, Spanish, 470; delegate Pino's labors at, 471, note 505

Council of the Indies, protests before, 166

Cows, 100, note 100; 101, note 102

Cruz, Fr. Juan de la, 241, note 257

Cruzate, Don Domingo Jironza Petriz de, governor of New Mexico, biography, his entrada. 377, 378; his administration, 377-380

Cruzate y Gongora, Don Gervasio, governor of New Mexico, his administration, 437, 438

Cuartalejo, location of, 432, note 441; presidio ordered established at, 432; council of war decides adversely, 432

Cubero, Don Pedro Rodriguez, governor of New Mexico, administration of, troubles with De Vargas, 414, notes 414, 415; population during rule of, 417; visits Moquis, 417, note 419; hears of return of De Vargas, leaves Santa Fé, governor of Maracaibo, death of, 420

Cubero, town and plain of, 417, note 419

Cuerno Verde, Comanche chief, 450, note 474

Cuervo y Valdes, Don Francisco, governor of New Mexico, his administration, 421; named by the Duke of Alburquerque, founds city of that name, 422; campaign of Juan de Uribarri upon the buffalo plains, 422, 423

Cueva Enriquez, Don Francisco Fernández de la, Duke of Alburquerque, 421, note 425; city of Alburquerque named for him by Governor Cuervo, 422; name ordered changed by the duke, 422

Cuitaos, Indians, fight with Guadalajara, 345

Cushing, Frank H., cited, 133, note 140

Cuyamungue, pueblo of, visited by De Vargas, battle at, 400

DAVIS, W. W. H., historian, cited, 54, notes 37, 38; 66, note 56; 68, notes 59, 61; 71, note 65; 72, note 66; 76, note 73; 118, note 126; 146, note 153, route of Fr. Marcos; 227, note 243

De la Cerda, Alvaro, Captain, Narvaéz expedition, 60

De la Croix, Internal Provinces organized, 448; commanding general, deprived New Mexico of office of captain-general, 448, 449, 456

Delgado, Fr. Carlos, mentioned, 427; 436, note 425; report of against official tyranny, 442, note 462

Del Valle, Don Francisco Antonio Marin, governor of New Mexico, administration of, 444; visit of bishop Tamaron, 444

Descalona, Fr. Luis, left behind by Coronado, 239, notes 254, 256; biography, 241, note 257; Cicuyé, 242

De Soto, Hernando, mentioned, 165

De Vargas, Don Diego Zapata Lujan Ponce de Leon, governor of New Mexico, the reconquest, 380; character, marches against Sumas from El Paso, 380, 381; flying entry into New Mexico, reaches Santa Fé, his reception, incidents of trip, 381, 382;

goes to northern pueblos, returns to Santa Fé, reports to viceroy, asks for reënforcements, sends horses, etc., to El Paso, marches to Zuñi and Acoma, 383; Apache attack, returns from Acoma, returns to El Paso, 384; entrada of 1693, officers of, 385, note 390; marches up Rio Grande, finds change in sentiment among Indians, 386; meets Indians at San Felipe, 387; journey to Santa Fé, entry and reception, ceremonies, 387, 388, note 391; calls for supplies from Indians, conspiracies renewed, 391; Indians close gates of city, storming of city, 392; Indians surrender, chief and others executed in plaza, 393; sends to El Paso for aid, sends out raiding parties, marches against Black Mesa, 394; marches on Potrero Viejo, battle of, 395, 396, notes 393, 394, 395; Indian losses, 396, note 396; Spanish camp attacked, 398; result, 398, notes 398, 399; sets fire to pueblo, returns to Santa Fé, 399, note 400; marches northward, battle at Cuyamungue, reaches Taos, pueblo is sacked, 400, 401, note 402; marches to the Ute country, Ojo Caliente, battle on San Antonio river, 402, 403, 404; returns to Santa Fé, marches to Jemez, attacks pueblo, 404, note 404; sacks Jemez, recovers remains of Fr. Juan de Jesus, 405, returns to Santa Fé, 405, note 406; entry in journal as to burial of bones of Fr. Juan de Jesus, note 406; Indians ask peace, pardon granted, natives submit, 407, 408; famine of 1696, 409; uprising of 1696, murder of friars, battle of Canyon de San Diego, defeat of Indians, 410, note 411; marches to Acoma, attacks pueblo, fails, 411, note 411; fight at Taos, Picuriés, return to Santa Fé, 412; De Vargas arrested by Governor Cubero, fined, in jail, 415, 416, notes 416, 417; reappointed, 420, campaign against Apaches, death and burial, 420, 421, note 424

De Vargas, Eusebio, mentioned, 396

Diaz, Bernal, historian, cited, 53, note 35

Diaz, Melchior, mentioned, 55; Cabeza de Vaca meets, 109, note 119, 113; arrives at Chiametla, report to Fr. Marcos, 178; leaves Cibola, 295; joins Arellano, 194; reaches Colorado river, 194; hears of Alarcon, finds letters, journeys to coast, 196, note 211; death of, 196, note 212

Doc. de Indies, cited, 171, note 188; 202, note 216; 286, note 295. See *Pacheco y Cardenas*, and *Pacheco, Joaquin F.*, and *Pacheco, Doc.*

Doc. Inédit. See *Pacheco, Doc.*

Doña Ana, town of, mentioned, 9

Dorantes, Andrés, survivor Narvaéz expedition, 55, note 39, biography; helped prepare map with Cabeza de Vaca, 56, note 45; mentioned, 73; fight with Indians, 75; meeting with Cabeza de Vaca, 85; mentioned, 89; deer hearts, 103; mentioned, 132, 133

Duran, Fr. Andrés, bewitched, 349

Duran, Fr. Rodrigo, with Oñate, 307

Durango, bishop of, disputes with, 435; visits province, 437, note 452

ELIZACOCHEA, DON MARTIN, bishop of Durango, visits New Mexico, 436, note 425; inscription on El Morro, 437

El Paso, city of, mentioned, Fr. Rodriguez reaches, 256; founded, 367; missions near, 371, note 379; Otermin returns to, 375, 376, note 383; missions founded, Senecú, Socorro and Isleta, 377; mentioned, 378; Juan Dominguez de Mendoza leaves, 378; De Vargas arrives at, 381, 384, presents vestments to Franciscans, 384; De Vargas leaves for 2nd entrada, 385; settlers at, 394; Poseueve myth, 402, note 403; mentioned, 408; mentioned, relative to Fr. Menchero's visit, 440; population in district of, confirmations by Bishop Tamaron, 1760, 444; mentioned, 452; population, 1800, 455; Pike taken to, 469; mentioned, 470; caravans left for, 474; lieutenant-governor at, 477

El Pueblito, near Yunque Yunque, 317, note 323

Enchanted Mesa, mentioned, 200, note 215

Escalante, Fr., visits Moqui, recommendations as to Oraibe, 447, note 470

Escalona and Barrundo, cited, 257, note 271; mines mentioned by, 258, note 273

Escalona, Fr. Juan de, letters to captain-general about Oñate, 330, note 331; writes to provincial, 331

Escobar, Fr. mentioned, comisario, 332

Espejo, Don Antonio de, mentioned, 265, his entrada, 265 et seq.; soldiers with, 265, note 280; note 281; starts for north, meets Conchos and Tobosos, Jumanos, 266, note 282; tell him of Spaniards and negro, Estevan, 269; passes up Rio Grande, visits many pueblos, population of, 273, 274; arrives at Puara; death of friars confirmed, 275, notes 284, 285 and 286; visits many pueblos, estimates of population, 276, note 288; visits Acoma, Zuñi and Moqui, 278; finds Indians left by Coronado, 279; finds mines, 281, note 290; returns and goes to the Rio Grande, visits pueblos in north, returns, goes home by way of the Pecos river, 282; escorted by Jumanos to the Concho, 282; arrives at San Bartolomé, makes report to king, 282; report as to mines, 286; makes application for right to colonize, 288, 289, note 297; no expedition organized by, 290

Espeleta, chief of Oraibe, 418, notes 421, 422

Estevan, survivor Narvaéz expedition, birthplace, 55, note 39; mentioned, 83, 91, 100, 103, 120; lives in tradition of Zuñis, 133; note 140; instructed to go with Fr. Marcos, his orders, 143, 144; starts north, with instructions from Fr. Marcos, 145, 146, notes 153, 154; mentioned, 150; reaches Cibola, robbed and killed, 151; manner of death, 156, note 167; authorities differ, 157, 158, note 169; Coronado's letter as to death of, 159, note 174

Estevan, Indian, governor, conspirator, hanged, 347, note 356

Estrada y Austria, Don Juan, acting governor, no record of, 433, note 448; came as juez de residencia, 433, 434

Ethnology, Bureau of, investigations by, founded, contributions to, 6, 7

FAMINE OF 1696, 409; friars expected uprising, 409

Faraon Apaches, mentioned, warned, 428

Farfan, Captain, joins Oñate, 309; wrote comedy, 312; goes in search of mines, 325; selected to be leader in attack on Acoma, 326; sent to city of Mexico by Oñate, 329

Fernandes Duro, author, cited, 304, note 307

Fernandez, Don Carlos, captain, Indian fighter, traditions, 431, note 435

Figueroa, Antonio de, friend of Oñate, mentioned, 306; partner in Oñate's entrada, 306

Flag, American, first floated in New Mexico, 463, note 491

Flagstaff, town of, cliff-dwellings near, 46, note 29

Flon, Colonel Manuel, commissioned governor of New Mexico, did not qualify, 451, note 477

Franciscan Martyrs, list of, 358, notes 367, 368, 369; sermon over, 361, note 369

Franciscans, Order of, send Fr. Asuncion beyond New Galicia, 139, note 144; proud of Fr. Marcos, 162, 163; mentioned, 243; character of members of order, 243, 244, 252, 254, 258, 260, 261, 281, 289; mentioned, with Oñate, 307, 309; missions definitely located by Oñate, 313, 314; Fr. Martinez apportions districts, 321, note 327; additional friars come to Oñate, 329; opposed to policy of Oñate, 331; mentioned, 332; by 1617, number of churches built by and converts, 333; missions in 1621, formed into a custodia under Fr. Benavides, 337; additional friars arrive under Fr. Estevan Perea, 337, 338; names of, 338; report of Fr. Benavides, 340, 341, 342, note 342; journeys by to the eastern plains, 345; death of Fr. Letrado, note 352; difficulties between friars and officials, 346, note 354; Fr. Ayeta, his report, 350, note 361; missions in 1680, 350, note 362; their labors against Indian paganism, 354, 355, note 363; rebellion of 1680, plot of revealed to Fr. Bernal, his death, 357; list of friars killed, 358, notes 367, 368, 369; bodies of friars found at Santo Domingo, 363; list of friars who survived the massacre, 363, note 370; Fr. Ayeta goes to city of Mexico with report of revolt, 367, note 376; list accompanying Otermin's second entrada, 371; despatches from to Mexico, in 1685,

378; vestments presented to by De Vargas, recovered at Zuñi, 384; ceremonies and incidents connected with entry of De Vargas into Santa Fé, 1693, 389, note 391; ask De Vargas for old palace, Santa Fé, 391; remains of Fr. Juan de Jesus recovered and taken to Santa Fé, 405, note 406; friars established in their missions after re-conquest, 407, note 407; list of, note 407; De Vargas advised by friars of danger of second revolution, 409; revolt of 1696, friars killed, 410, note 411; Fr. Garaicochea, 419, 420; mentioned, 422, note 426; efforts of Fr. Peña, 425; junta of friars and civil authorities, 428, note 435; junta of friars at Santa Fé, 434; controversy with bishop of Durango, 435, 436; anxious about order of Jesuits as to Moqui, 440; padres azules win their contest, 441; controversies between Franciscans and secular priests, 443, list of friars, 1750, note 466; conversion of the Moquis by, 447, note by Fr. Escalante, 470; experiences of Major Pike with, 467, note 497, notes 501, 502; missions in 1810, complaints, 478, note 513; Pino's request for a college, 479, note 513

Francisco, Indian of San Ildefonso, leader in pueblo revolt, 357

French, earliest advance into New Mexico, 432, notes 440, 441, 443, 454

GALISTEO, PUEBLO OF, group, names of, 259, note 275; Fr. Bernal killed at, 358, note 368; a Tanos pueblo, 381; they come to Santa Fé, 381

Gallatin, Albert, mentioned, 4

Gallego, Juan, officer Coronado expedition, 174, 194, 246

Gallegos, Hernan, soldier with Fr. Rodriguez, 257, 258, note 273

Gallinas river, 220, note 236

Garaicochea, Fr., 420, note 423

Garcés, Fr., 449, visits, Moqui, 447, note 471

Garcia, Alonzo, Lieutenant-general, 360, 365, note 375

Garcia de Mora, Captain José, soldier, 470; member of junta of 1910, 471, note 503

Garcia, Don Manuel, 470

Gaspar de Mexico, met by Espejo, 279

Gatschet, cited, *Migration Legend*, 69, note 61

Gomez, Captain Francisco, officer under Otermin, 360

Gonzales de Mendoza, Don Pedro, father-in-law of Espejo, goes to Spain, 289

Gourds, veneration of, origin, 95, note 96

Governors and captains-general, New Mexico, 1822, list, 481, 482

Granillo, Luis, Lieutenant-general, under De Vargas, 385

Gran Quivira, origin of name, 231, note 250

Grand Canyon of Colorado, discovered by, description, 197, note 213

Grapes, first introduced into New Mexico, 372, note 381

Gregg, Josiah, cited, Oñate's petition, 304, note 308

Guadalajara, Captain Diego de, expedition of, battle with the Cuitaos, 345

Guerra, Fr. Ambrosio, entertains Major Pike, 469, note 501

Guerra, Fr. Antonio, with Otermin, 371

Guerra, Juan, mentioned, helps Oñate financially, 307

Guevara, Diego de, officer with Coronado, 217

Guevara, Juan de, 306

Guevavi, settlement, mentioned, 440, note 456

Guipuy, pueblo of, location, destroyed, 42, note 27

Gutierrez, Captain Lorenzo, 457, note 485

Gutierrez, Fr., missionary among Hopi, 338

Guzman, Don Luis de, governor of New Mexico, 344, note 345

Guzman, Nuño de, governor of New Galicia, 112; character of, 137; conquers Sinaloa, founded settlements, 137

HABITATIONS, location, reasons for, 40, note 24; classification, 9, 10; styles of, 10, note 4; occupation, 11; location of ancient districts, 11, note 5. See *Houses*

Hacienda de Mejia, De Vargas leaves baggage at, 381; sends escort with captives to El Paso, 383, note 388

Hakluyt, R., *Voyages*, cited, 67, note 58; 71, note 66; 139, note 143; 146, note 154

Han, language, 93
Handbook of American Indians, cited, 49; Apaches, note 31; 180, Cocopas, note 199; 266, note 282
Harrington, J. P., cited, reseemblance of Kiowa and Tanonan languages, 32, note 17
Hawaikúh, pueblo of, 152, note 165; Estevan slain here, 159; Coronado orders advance on, 186; kiva at, 186, note 204; battle of, 187; mentioned, 199, 205, 211; Bandelier's description of, 348, note 358; occupied until 1672, 349, note 358
Haxa, mentioned, 221
Hayden Survey, mentioned, 6
Haynes, Quiviras, 227, note 243
Heredia, Alonzo Pacheco de, governor of New Mexico, 343, note 343
Herrera, historian, cited, 69, note 61; 80, note 74; 139, note 146; 254, note 266
Hewett, Dr. Edgar L., archæologist, cited, 10, note 4; 11, note 5; 12, Puyé, note 6; quoted, 13, 14, 15, 16, 17, 18, 19, 20; cited, 26, note 10; 27, note 11; 28, note 12; 29, notes 13, 14; 30, notes 15, 16; glazing, note, 16; 31, note 17; 35, note 19; 38, notes 20, 22; ancestors of Pueblos, 39, note 23; 48, note 29
Hidalgo y Costilla, Don Miguel, Mexican patriot, 479, note 514
History, aboriginal, divisions of, 9
Hodge, F. W., ethnologist, historian, 49, Apaches, note 31; cited, 53, notes 33, 34; 54, notes 36, 37, 38; 55, notes 39, 40; Juan Ortiz, survivor Narvaéz expedition, 56; Cabeza de Vaca narrative, notes 41, 42; character of Cabeza de Vaca, 57, note 46; bibliography of Relacion of Alvar Nuñez Cabeza de Vaca, 57, note 47; cited, 60, note 48; 64, notes 52, 53; 68, note 59; 70, note 64; 71, note 65; 72, notes 67, 68; 73, note 69; 75, notes 71, 72; 82, notes 77, 78; Malhado Island, 83, note 80; cited, 86, note 86; 89, note 88; 90, note 89; 92, note 93; 93, note 95; gourds, rattles, 95, note 96; origin of copper bell, 97, note 97; Pimahaitu, 108, note 118; route of Cabeza de Vaca, 119, note 128; colophon of Relacion, 134, note 141; First Discovered City of Cibola, 152, note 165; Cocopas, 180, note 199; Acoma, people of, 200, note 215; Querechos, 220, note 237; route of Coronado, 224, note 241; note 243; bridge over Pecos, 229, note 245; language of the Piro, 232, note 250; date of death of Fr. Padilla, 245, note 259; biography of Castañeda, 247, note 261; Jumanos Indians, 266, note 282; note 283; Jicarilla Apaches, 422, 423, note 427; origin of the Jemez, 424, note 430; Corodeguachi, 440, note 457; Cebolleta, 441, note 462
Hopi, mentioned, 43; 44, note 28, names of all the Hopi pueblos; first visited by Spaniards, 44, note 28; missions established, 44, note 28
Houses, communal, southern limit, 9; detached type, 9; social organization, 29, note 14
Humana, Juan de, accompanies Bonilla, 298, 299, note 304
Hungo Pavie, pueblo of, 45
Hurtado, Juan Paez, governor of New Mexico, De Vargas entrada, 1693, in charge of colonists, 385; accomplice of De Vargas, 415, note 415; lieutenant-general, 421; governor ad interim, 421; name on Inscription Rock, 437

IBARRA, FRANCISCO DE, expedition of, 283, 284, note 293; mentioned, 285
Icazbalceta, J. G., historian, cited, 175, details of Coronado expedition, note 193
Ietans, Indians, 467, note 496
Indian tribes met by Cabeza de Vaca, 93, 94, note 95
Inhabitants, first, of New Mexico, 7, 8; theories, 8, note 2; customs, ceremonies, kinship, origin, 8, note 3; epoch of, 9; relationship, 31, note 17; disappearance of, 33, 34; remnants found, 34; ruins, districts where found, 11, note 5
Inquisition, mentioned, 445, 446, note 468
Inscription Rock, visited by Governor Martinez, 429; by bishop of Durango and Hurtado, 266, 437; inscriptions on, 275, 281
Internal Provinces, established, 448
Investigations, Indian, New Mexico, advent of railways assisted, 4
Irala, lieutenant-governor, mentioned, 116, note 125
Irigoyen, Fr., mentioned, 461, note 460

Irrigation, ditches at Tschirege, Puyé, 19
Isleta, pueblo of, 364, note 373; Otermin reaches, 373; fight at, 374; inhabitants join Tu-pa-tu, 376, note 382; De Vargas camps at, 386
Iturbide, Don Agustin, biography, 480, note 515

JACA, pueblo Indian chief, Taos pueblo, 357
Janos, Apaches, 439, note 456
Jaramillo, lieutenant, route to Quivira, mentioned, 224, note 241; mentioned, 226; cited, 228, note 244; mentioned, 237, note 252; cited, 238, note 254; 218, note 231; 221, note 239
Javier de Uranga, lieutenant-governor, mentioned, 452
Jefferson, Thomas, president, mentioned, 4
Jemez, pueblo of, visited by Espejo, 278; population of, 278; Fr. De Lugo sent to, 323, note 327; mentioned by Benavides, 342, note 342; conspiracy, 1650, 346; Vetancurt's list, 351, note 362; 362, note 369; bones of Fr. Juan de Jesus, 366, note 375; mentioned, 382, 383; De Vargas marches to, 404; battle, 405, note 405; De Vargas recovers bones of Fr. Juan de Jesus, 405, note 406; entry in journal of De Vargas as to, 406, note 406; mentioned, 407, note 407; uprising of 1696, warning from the friar, Francisco de Jesus, friar killed, battle at, 410, note 411; pueblos sacked by the Navajós, 424, description and origin of, 424, note 430; mentioned, 428; Utes raid, 435; made a visita account small-pox, 451; population, 1750-1800, 455
Jesuits, Order of, mentioned, 252, note 262; mentioned, 440
Jesus, Fr. Francisco de, murdered at Jemez, 410, note 411
Jicarillas, Apaches, history of, 422, note 427
Jimenez, town of, mentioned, 255
Jimenes, Fortuno, pilot, mentioned, 138
José, Indian with Humana, mentioned, 299, note 304
Jumanos, tribe of Indians, met by Cabeza de Vaca, 122; by Espejo, 266, note 282; monograph of Mr. Hodge, 269, 270, 271, note 283; Benavides says, 273, 341, note 341; mentioned, 345; Fr. Ayeta's report, 352, note 361
Junta, 1714, Indians, 428, note, 435; as to Indian raids, 1731, 434; to elect delegate to Cortes, 470, 471, notes 503, 504
Justice, of Spaniards, 110, 111, 112, note 119

KERESAN STOCK, mentioned, 9
Keres. See *Queres*
Kino, Father, mentioned, 449
Kivas, description, ceremonies, 30, note 15

LADRON DE GUEVARA, DON PEDRO, 378
Laguna, San José de, pueblo of, description, founding of, 417, note 419; trouble with Indians of, 427
LaLande, Baptiste, creole trader, mentioned, 464, note 493, 465; regarded as spy by Pike, 467
Lara, Captain Miguel de, battle of Canyon de San Diego, 410, note 411
La Salle, mentioned, Peñalosa story, 348, note 357
Las Casas, Fr. Bartolomé, biography, 141, note 150
Letrado, Fr. Francisco, 338, mentioned, killed by the Indians, note 338; date of death of, 345, note 352
Leyba, Captain Pedro de, 365, note 375; mentioned, 371
Lewis and Clark, expedition of, mentioned, 4
Little Bird, pueblo of, definition, 22
Llana, Fr. Geronimo de la, death of, 338
Llanos de San Francisco, buffalo plains, Aguas Zarcas, 258
Lomas y Colmenares, Juan Bautista de, asks for concession, 290, 291; contract approved by viceroy, nothing done, 291
Lopez, Fr. Francisco, 256; his companions, route to New Mexico, 257; martyrdom, 259, 260; came from Andalusia, 260, note 276; burial place, 260; re-burial by Fr. Estevan de Perea, 261, note 278
Lopez de Mendizibal, Don Bernardo, governor of New Mexico, 344
Los Cerrillos, mentioned, 102, note 106
Lucero y Godoy, Juan, with Otermin, 371; goes to City of Mexico, 378
Lucero de Godoy, Diego, with Otermin, 371
Luis Lopez, De Vargas stops at, 386

Lummis, Charles F., cited, Acoma, 200, note 215

MACANA, OUR LADY OF, story, 379, note 384
Madrid, Captain Roque, mentioned, campaign against Apaches, 1683, 378; arrival at El Paso, in command of De Vargas's army, 384; officer second De Vargas entrada, 385; mentioned, 394; commands division at Potrero Viejo, 396, note 395; lieut. gen. of cavalry and alcalde mayor of La Cañada, 412
Magdalena, mountains, Lieut. Manrique, campaign against Apaches, 452, note 479
Magrias, Indians, Espejo visits, 276, note 287
Mainez, Don Alberto, governor of New Mexico, 470
Maldonado, Captain Rodrigo, officer under Coronado, 216
Maldonado, friend of Oñate, member of Audiencia, 306
Maldonado, Captain Alonzo de Castillo, 55; citizen of Salamanca, note 39; mentioned, 79; cures the sick, 90; mentioned, 100; sees Indian with buckle of sword-belt, 104; became resident of City of Mexico, 117
Malhado, Island of, 80, 83, note 80; 118, note 126
Maliacones, Indians, mentioned, 94
Manrique, Lieutenant-colonel, governor of New Mexico, 470; member of junta of 1810, 470; campaign against Apaches, 452, note 479
Manso, Fr. Tomas, custodio, 337; biography, 338
Marata, kingdom of, mentioned, 148, note 157; mentioned, passed by Alvarado, 199
Mariames, Indians, mentioned, 94
Marquez, Fr. Diego, mentioned, 287; captured by the English, 287
Martin, Cristobal, 287, 288, note 296
Martin, Captain Sebastian, tradition, 431, note 439
Martin, Captain Hernan, 345
Martinez, Fr. Diego, mentioned, 309; apportions pueblos into districts, 321; mentioned, 322, 323, 324; goes to Mexico for friars, remains there, 329
Martinez, Captain Felix, governor, 1715, 429; campaign against Moquis, name on inscription rock, 429; mentioned, 430, 433; investigation of, 433; alderman of Santa Fé for life, 429
Matsaki, pueblo of, 211; described, note 225
Medrano, Juan de, governor of New Mexico, 344
McElmo, canyon, cliff-dwellings in, 44
Melgares, Captain Facundo, expedition of, 458; biography, 459; escorts Pike to Chihuahua, 469, note 501; governor of New Mexico, 480; mentioned, 481, note 516
Menchero, Fr. Miguel, 440, visits Gila River and pueblo of Acoma, 440; statistics by, 443, note 466
Mendieta, historian, cited, 139, note 144; 140, note 148
Mendinueta, Don Pedro Fermín de, governor of New Mexico, 447; knight of Santiago, 447; makes treaty with Comanches, 447
Mendoza, Don Antonio, viceroy of New Spain, mentioned, 55, 115, 141; selects Fr. Marcos, 142, note 151; letter from Coronado, 159, note 174; mentioned, 162, 169, 171; organization of Coronado expedition, 171, et seq.; departure of expedition, 176; sends Alarcon by sea, 179, note 188; letter to from Coronado, 189, notes 205, 206, 207; Coronado's return, his reception by, 247
Mendoza, Diego Bercerra de, mentioned, 138
Mendoza, Diego Hurtado de, mentioned, 147
Mesa, Black, 393; battle at, 394; mentioned, 399; battle at, defeat of De Vargas, treaty of peace, 407
Mesa Verde, 48, note 29
Mesilla Valley, Fr. Rodriguez passes through, 256
Mexico, independence, 480; demonstration at Santa Fé, 481, note 516
Mexico, city of, mentioned, 162; population of in 1540, 162, notes 175, 176
Miera, y Pacheco, Don Cleto, Alcalde, member of junta, 471, note 503
Migrations, of families, 9
Mines, mentioned by Chamuscado, 258, note 273; found by Espejo, 281, note 290; no mines worked until 1725, 111, note 119; report of Governor Chacon 1803, 475; Pike refers to, 475; Santa Rita mine discovered, history of, 475

Mindeleff, C., cited, 42, note 27
Miranda, Don Juan de, governor of New Mexico, 344
Missions, Franciscan, 321, note 327; 441, 451; in 1810, 478, note 513
Missouri, Indians, 433, note 447
Mogollon, Don Juan Ignacio Flores, governor of New Mexico, administration of, 426, 428
Money, no circulating medium, 454
Mongolian race, mentioned, 8
Montezuma, legend of, 402, note 403
Montezuma, castle, 48, note 29
Montoya, Don Diego, alcalde of Santa Fé, 470
Mooney, James, ethnologist, Kiowa vocabulary mentioned, 32, note 17
Moqui, pueblos of, 148, note 157; 192, note 208; 423, note 428; Moqui diplomacy, 429, note 436, 439; conversion of, 447, note 470; 450, note 475; De Vargas visits, 384; mentioned, 417, note 418; 418, 419
Morlete, Captain Juan, 298, note 302
Morrison, William, mentioned, 464, note 493
Morse, Rev. J., mentioned, 4
Mota Padilla, historian, cited, 163, note 176; 177, note 195; 186, note 204; 196, note 212; 209, note 224; siege of Tiguex, 216, note 228; 235, note 251; 241, note 257; 254, note 264
Mound-builders, 9

NAMBÉ, PUEBLO OF, De Vargas visits, 382; mentioned, 393
Narbona, Captain, Navajó campaign, Canyon de Chelly, 457
Narvaéz, Pamfilo de, Expedition of, 1527, 53-76; biography, 53, notes 33, 34, 35
Naufragios, cited, 65, note 54; 70, note 62; 126, note 133; 129, note 135; 130, note 136
Navajó, Indians, mentioned, 5; enemies of Pueblos, 48; Benavides' classification, 341; pueblos join, 412; defeat of by Captain Serna, 428; missions near, 441, note 462; troublesome, 457; campaign against by Narbona, 457, note 485
Navajú, settlement, location, 15
Navarro, Don Francisco Trebol, acting governor, New Mexico, 448
Navawí, pueblo of, location, 22
Neiva, Don José de, governor of New Viscaya, 378
New Mexico, origin of name, 283, 284;
mentioned, 286, 291, 292; conquest of, 301, 308, 309, 311; first capital of, 315, notes 319, 320, 321; missions in, 321, note 327; end of Oñate's rule in, 332; conflicting stories as to capital of, 332, 333; date of establishment of capital at Santa Fé, 333, note 336; capital of, 334, note 337; arrival of friars in, 1627, 337; friars in, 338; governors in 1621, 1629, 338, note 338; no complete list of governors, 343, note 343; governors of, testimony of Juan Dominguez, 344, notes 348, 349; mentioned, 345; governor Peñalosa, 347; missions established, 1664, 348; pueblo Indians in, by Vetancurt, 350, note 362; Spaniards driven out of by Pueblos, 361 et seq., mentioned, 377; reconquest by De Vargas, 380 et seq., Governor Cubero arrives in, 414; De Vargas returns to, 420; governors of, 421 et seq.; visit of Bishop Crespo, 435; visit of bishop of Durango, Elizacochea, 437; French designs upon, 440; visit of Tamaron, bishop of Durango, 444; industries of, 453, 454; trade with Chihuahua, 454, 455; population in 1800, 455; Pike's expedition into, 461, notes 491, 492, 495; governors of, 470; delegate from to Spanish Cortes, 470, 471, notes 503, 504, 505; last of Spanish rule in, 473 et seq.; commercial conditions in, 474, 475; mines in, 475; education in, 475; character of administration, 476; military force in, 477, 478; Franciscan missions in, 478, note 513; last Spanish governor, 480; Mexican governors, 480; list of governors 1598 to 1823, 481, 482
Niza, Fr. Marcos de, vice commissioner-general, 139, note 147, note 148; biography of, 140, 141; Mendoza selects, 142, note 151; leaves Culiacan, 144; journey to Cibola, 145 et seq., route of, 147, note 155; reaches Gila river, 150, note 162; hears of death of Estevan, 151; proceeds to Cibola, sees city of Hawaikúh, 152, note 165; names province St. Francis, 154; return journey, 155 et seq., reports to provincial, 156; mentioned, 157, 158; Bandelier, as to route of, 160, note 174; returns to City of Mexico, his reception, report, 162, 163; veracity of, 163, note 178, 173; report of

Salvidar as to, 178; mentioned, 185; Coronado's report as to, 190, note 206; maledictions of soldiers, 186; returns to Mexico with Gallego, 194

Nueva Andalucia, name given New Mexico by Espejo, 289, note 297

Nueva Galicia, mentioned, conquered by Guzman, 137; mentioned, 139, note 144; Coronado, governor of, 141; Guzman, governor of, 170

OJEDA, BARTOLOMÉ, Indian, officer under De Vargas, Potrero Viejo, 396, 397, canyon de Jemez, 410, note 411

Ojo Caliente, pueblo of, 401, note 403; Pike's description of, 466, note 496

Olavide y Michaleña, Don Enrique, governor of New Mexico, administration of, 438

Olguin, Captain Juan, Potrero Viejo, 396

Oñate, Don Cristobal, lieutenant-governor, 310

Oñate, Don Juan de, entrada of, 301-331; Bandelier, use of Villagra's history of New Mexico, 302, note 306; contract signed, 304; delays, 306 et seq.; copy of decree in favor of Oñate, 304, note 309; leaves San Bartolomé, 309; Franciscans join, names of, 309; first explorer of Chihuahua, 310; names of colonists, 310, note 313; reaches Rio Grande, takes possession of New Mexico, 311, note 314; marches up Rio Grande, 312 et seq.; visits pueblos, 313; conference at Santo Domingo, 313, 314; establishes capital, 315, notes 319, 320; explorations of, 319; irrigation ditches, plot of Aguilar, 320, 321; chapel constructed, 321; friars distributed, 321, 322, note 327; Acoma, 324; Zuñi, 325; finds Mexican Indians left by Coronado, 325; battle at Acoma, death of Juan Salvidar, 325 et seq.; reports to viceroy, 328; marches to great plains, 329, 330; returns to San Gabriel, trouble with friars, 330, 331; founds city of Santa Fé, 332; visits Inscription Rock, 332

Opatas, Indians, 147, note 156

Oraibe, pueblo of, 418, note 421. See Hopi, Moqui

Orders, mendicant, division of, 253, note 262

Ortiz, Don Antonio, candidate for delegate to Spanish cortes, 471, note 503

Ortiz, Don Rafael, candidate for delegate to Spanish Cortes, 471, note 503

Ortiz, Don Tomas, alcalde of Taos, 471, note 503

Ortiz, Juan, survivor Narvaéz expedition, 55, note 40

Otermin, Don Antonio, governor of New Mexico, 344; receives word of the revolt of the Pueblos, 358; sends out messengers, 360; report of scouts to, 362; Indians appear, battle, siege of Santa Fé, abandons city, 362, 363; marches down the Rio Grande valley, 364; reënforced by Leyba, 365; reaches region of Mesilla valley, 367; entrada of 1681, 370, 371 et seq.; reaches Isleta, 374; burns pueblos, 374; decides return to El Paso, 375; end of rule of, 377, note 383

Otero, Miguel A., governor of New Mexico, archives, 241, note 256

Otowi, pueblo of, 25, 26, 27; traditions of, 27

Ovando, Francisco de, killed, 215

Oviedo, historian, cited, 56; biography, 56, note 42; cited, 66, note 55; 107, note 114; 138, note 142

Oviedo, Lope de, Narvaéz expedition, 83, 84, 85

PACHECO Y CARDENAS, 166, note 180; 171, note 188. See Doc. Inédit.

Padilla, Fr. Juan de, mentioned, 193; journey of with Alvarado, 199, 200, note 216; with Coronado to Quivira, 226; remains behind on return of Coronado to Mexico, 238, note 254; courage of, 239, note 256; biography and character of, 240, 241, note 257; returns to Quivira, his martyrdom, 244, 245

Pajaritans, symbolism, culture, 28, note 12; arts, customs, kivas, clans, 30, note 15; Awanyu, emblem, 32, 33; migrations from, 34

Pajarito plateau, mentioned, 11, 13, 15; ruins on, 20 et seq.; pioneer explorations on, 28, note 11

Palacio, historian, 308, note 311

Pantoja, Captain Juan, under Narvaéz, 60, note 48

Paraguay, Indians of, 116

Pariembos, Indians, mentioned, 116, note 125

Passaguates, Indians met by Espejo, 266

Patarabueyes, Indians, 266, note 282. See *Jumanos*
Pecos, pueblo of, Coronado arrives at, 219, note 236, 224; Arellano arrives with army, 229, note 245, 234; Fr. Escalona goes to, 242, 243; Fr. Padilla leaves, 244; mentioned, 254; Espejo visits, 282; Castaño de Sosa, visits, 293; attacks the pueblo, supplies taken, 293; mentioned, population, Benavides, 342, note 342; Porciuncola, 352, note 362; Vetancurt's list, mentioned, 359, note 368; Indians from attack Santa Fé, 362; mentioned, 369, 382; sends in allegiance to De Vargas, 383; Indians of, friendly, 391, 411; Santo Domingo chief killed at, 411; 444, population, note 466; mission at made a visita, account deaths by small-pox, 451; population, 1800, 455, note, table; population in 1828, 474, note 506
Pecos river, Coronado reaches, 219; builds bridge, notes 234, 236; Bandelier says was Canadian, 224; Arellano crosses, 229, note 245; return route of Espejo down the, 282; called Rio de las Vacas, 282; Salado of Castaño de Sosa, 293
Pedernal Peak, mentioned, 27
Peiñado, Fr., mentioned, 332
Peña, Fr., mentioned, his activities, 425
Peñsalosa, Briceéo, Don Diego Dionisio, governor of New Mexico, 347, 348, note 357
Pe-ra-ge, pueblo of, location, 27
Peralta, Don Pedro de, governor of New Mexico, 332, note 333
Perea, Fr. Estevan, comisario, 1614, 332; brings 30 friars, 337; makes journey to the great plains, 345
Petatlan, mentioned, 106, note 112
Picuriés, pueblo of, visited by Oñate, 319; Fr. Zamora at, 323, note 327; Benavides mentions, 343, note 342, 351; Vetancurt's list, population of, note 362; Indians of attack ranches in 1680, 360; Fr. Rendon, murdered at, 1680, 362, note 368; mentioned as to land grant to, 380, note 385; De Vargas visits, 382; mentioned, 394; De Vargas visits in 1694, 400; population, 444, note 466
Piedras Verdes, mentioned, 46, note 29
Pike, Major Zebulon M., expedition of, 461 *et seq.*, notes 489, 490, 491, 492, 494, 495; description of Santa Fé, 468, note 500; compensation to by congress, 469, note 502
Pimahaitu, language, 108, note 118
Pininicangwi, pueblo of, 16
Pino, Fr. Juan, mentioned, 432
Pino, Don José, alcalde of Alburquerque, mentioned, 470
Pino, Don Pedro Bautista, delegate to Spanish cortes, biography, labors, family, views of, 470, 471, 472, note 505
Pintado pueblo of, 23, 24, 25
Piros Indians, 232; Hodge's monograph, 232, note 250; uprising of, 347; executions of, note 356
Plata, Rio de la, mentioned, 116
Pobares, Francisco, killed, Tiguex, 215
Pojoaque, pueblo of, de Vargas visits, 382
Policy of Spaniards, 252, 253, note 262
Po-pé, Indian, San Juan pueblo, mentioned, 349; leader of Pueblo rebellion of 1680, 355 *et seq.*, note 364; co-conspirators, 357; kills son-in-law, 357; tours country, 368, 369, note 378; death of, 369
Population, Indians, Espejo, 276, note 288
Porras, Fr. Francisco, death of, 338
Posadas, Fr., mentioned, report, 345, note 351
Pose-ueve, legend of, 401, note 403
Potrero Viejo, battle of, 395, note 394; folk tales, 400, note 401. See *De Vargas*
Pottery, ancient, similarity to present day, 40, note 23
Powell, Major J. W., mentioned, 6
Pow-ho-ge, clans of, 27
Prince, Dr. L. Bradford, cited, 66, note 56; 67, note 59; 69, note 61; 71, notes 65, 66; 75, note 71; 118, note 126; 122, note 131; 133, note 139; 227, note 243
Puara, pueblo of, Fr. Rodriguez visits, 257, note 272; location of, 261, note 279
Pueblos, ruined, abandonment, 41, notes 24, 25, 26, and 27
Pueblo Indians, total number of, 42, note 27; classification of, 342; Benavides, list, note 342; rebellion and independence, 354 *et seq.*; final submission of, 412
Puerto de la conversion de San Pablo, 331

Punames, Indians, visited by Espejo, 278
Pu-yé, ruins of, excavations at, 12, note 6; description of, 13, 14, 15
QUALACU, PUEBLO OF, mentioned, 231, note 250
Quarac, pueblo of, mentioned, Fr. De la Llana died at, 338
Querechos, Indians, 220, note 237
Queres, Indians, described by Bandelier, 218, note 230; visited by Espejo, 277; by Castaño de Sosa, 296; aid De Vargas, 407; refugees built Cubero, 417, notes 419, 420
Quivira, province of, mentioned, 219; Coronado's description of, 222, note 240; Fr. Padilla returns to, 238, note 254; 245, note 258; mentioned by Rio de Losa, 286

RAMIREZ, DON BARTOLOMÉ DE ESTRADA, governor of New Mexico, 377
Ramirez, Fr. Juan, mentioned, 338; death of, 338
Red House, Chichilticalli, mentioned, 185, note 203
Reneros de Posada, Don Pedro, governor of New Mexico, 379, 380, note 385
Revolt, of Pueblo Indians, 354 et seq. See *Pueblo Indians, De Vargas, Otermin, Cruzate, Po-pé.*
Rio de Losa, Don Rodrigo de, captain-general Nueva Galicia, mentioned, report to viceroy, 285, 286, note 294
Rito de los Frijoles, 35, note 19, 37, 38
Robinson, Dr. J. H., mentioned, companion of Major Pike, 464, 465, note 494
Rocha, Don Francisco de la, governor of New Mexico, declined to serve, 439, note 455
Rodriguez, Fr. Agustin, explorations by, 255, 262; best account of, 258, note 273; death of and companions, 259, 260, note 274; burial place of, 260; Torquemada's story of, 260, note 276; mentioned, 265; news of death of confirmed to Espejo, 275
Rodriguez, Nicolas, 371
Rosas, Don Luis de, governor of New Mexico, administration of, murdered, 343, note 343
Ruins, pueblo, classification of, 10; districts, 11, note 5. See *Habitations*

SAAVEDRA, HERNANDARIAS, officer Coronado expedition, 238
Sacrifices, in kivas, 30, note 15
Salado, river, Pecos, 293
Salazar, Fr. Cristoval, 307
Salvidar, Don Juan, nephew of Oñate, son of Juan Salvidar, 306; maestro de campo, 310; searches for Abó, 312; mentioned, 313, 324; turns command over to brother, 325; battle at Acoma, death of, 326
Salvidar, Juan de, officer Coronado expedition, 178; report to Mendoza, 178; massacre of Indians, 217
Salvidar, Vicente, son of Juan Salvidar, 306; sargento mayor, 310; mentioned, 312; expedition to buffalo plains, 324; mentioned, 325; returns from buffalo plains, 325; takes command, 325; commands forces to Acoma, 326; massacre of Indians, Acoma, 328, note 329; goes to Mexico, 331, secures return of friars, note 331
Samaniego, Lope de, officer Coronado expedition, death of, 177, note 195
Samaniego, Don Juan, governor of New Mexico, 344, note 346
San Antonio, Fr. Salvador de, custodio, 385, note 390
San Bartolomé, town of, mentioned, Fr. Rodriguez and companions leave, 256; mentioned, 258; Espejo leaves, 265, note 281; Espejo returns to, 282
Sanchez, Alonzo, mentioned, chief, 299, note 304
San Cristobal, pueblo of, visited by Castaño de Sosa, 296; ruins of, location, 297; Indians of reveal pueblo plot, 357; Indian name of, description of, 359, note 368
San Diego, Fr. Tomas de, mentioned, death of, 338
San Felipe de Nuevo Mexico, name in early documents, 284
San Felipe, pueblo of, mentioned, 363, note 371; description of, note 372
San Felipe, name for San Marcial, given by Fr. Rodriguez, 256; Piro village, called Tre-na-quel, visited by one of Coronado's captains, 256
San Francisco y Nuñiga, Fr. Garcia, founder of Socorro, burial place, 338
San Gabriel, capital, 315, note 320; mentioned, 326; defenses at, 327, note 328

INDEX 503

San Gregorio, town of, same as San Bartolomé, 255
San Ildefonso, Black Mesa of, Indians assemble at, name of Tulyó, 393; De Vargas marches to, 394; battle at, 394, 395, 399; yields to De Vargas, 399; Indians still held, 404; De Vargas attacks, treaty of peace at, 407
San Ildefonso, pueblo of, visited by Oñate, Bové, 314, 319, note 324; friars cremated, note 324; visited by De Vargas, 382; De Vargas meets governor of, 388; abandoned by Tehuas, 393; mentioned, 404; Fr. Corvera, killed at, 411, note 411
San Juan, location of, Oñate arrives at, 314, 315, 316, note 321, 322; mentioned, 320; Fr. Salazar located at, 323, note 327; mentioned, 333; population of, 1691, 351, note 361; Popé, native of, 356; governor of, 357; most hostile of all in revolt of 1680, 357, note 366
San Lazaro, pueblo of, Tanos, 360, description of, note 368
San Lorenzo, mentioned, 366
San Lucas, pueblo of, visited by Castaño de Sosa, 296
San Marcial, mentioned, 256
San Marcos, pueblo of, visited by Castaño de Sosa, 296; mines near, 297; mentioned, 314; turquoise mines near, note 318; Oñate visits, 319; Tanos pueblo, 320, note 326; name given by, abandoned, 320, note 326
San Mateo, mentioned, expedition to, 452
San Miguel de Culiacan, mentioned, 55, 107, note 116; Fr. Marcos and Estevan go to, 143; Fr. Marcos leaves, 144; Castañeda wrote history at, 174, note 190; mentioned, 176; description of, 178, note 196
San Miguel, chapel of, Santa Fé, 333, note 336; 334, note 337; entry in journal of De Vargas concerning, 336, note 337; Benavides' report, 342, note 342; Indians near, revolt of 1680, 362; rebuilt by Marqués de la Peñuela, 424, note 429; mentioned, 431, note 439
San Pascual, pueblo of, visited by Otermin, 373
San Pedro, valley of, mentioned, 149
Santa Barbola, town of. See *San Bartolomé*
Santa Clara, pueblo of, mentioned, 382

Santa Clara, canyon de, mentioned, 15
Santa Cruz, de la Cañada, settlement of, alcalde mayor of, visited by De Vargas, 408
Santa Maria, Fr. Juan, martyrdom of, story of, 259, 260; biography, 260, note 276
Santa Fé, city of, founded, 332, 334, note 337; mentioned, 341, 352, note 361; mentioned, 358, 360, 361; battle at, 362, 363; Otermin abandons, 363; mentioned, 371, 381; De Vargas enters, 382; mentioned, 388; De Vargas' entry, ceremonies, 389, note 391; mentioned, 395, 397, 399, 400, 401, 405; bones of Fr. Juan de Jesus taken to, 405; re-interment of bones, 406, note 406; mentioned, 407, 412; garrison at strengthened, 414, note 414; mentioned, 415; Moqui chieftains come to, 419, note 422; mentioned, 420; garrisons taken to, 423; mentioned, 429; convention at, 434; bishop of Durango visits, 435; flood at, 447; mentioned, 451; population of, 1800, 455; mentioned, 465; Major Pike taken to, 467; junta at, 1810, 470, 471, note 503; one doctor at, 475; celebration at, 480
Santa Rita, copper mine, 475, discovered by, 475
Santo Domingo, pueblo of, mentioned, visited by Castaño de Sosa, 297; Oñate holds conference at, 313; Fr. Juan de Rosas at, 322, note 327; Auto de fe celebrated at, Fr. Escalona buried here; also Frs. Talaban, Lorenzana and Montesdoca, 351, note 362; those killed in 1680 at, 362, note 369; Lieut.-gen. Dominguez visits, 374; surrenders to De Vargas, 383; mentioned, 399; pueblo of near Cochití, 405
Saurez de Peralta, cited, 169, note 183; 246, note 260
Schoolcraft, James, mentioned, 4
Selden, Ft., mentioned, 9
Senecú, pueblo of, 372, description of, note 381
Seven Cities of Cibola, mentioned, 137, 152, note 165; almost forgotten, 253
Sevilleta, pueblo of, visited by Otermin, 373
Simpson, Gen. J. H., cited, 23, 24, 25; 226, note 242; location of Quivira, note 243

Smith, Buckingham, historian, cited, 41, note 25; cited, 53, note 34; 56, note 44; 61, note 49; 66, note 56; 67, note 59; 70, note 63; 71, note 66; 75, note 71; 93, note 94; 108, note 117; 116, note 125

Socorro, pueblo of, called Pilabó, 231, note 249; mentioned, 365; visited by Otermin, 373

Spain, last days of rule of, 473 et seq.

Spruce-Tree House, mentioned, 46, note 29

Squier and Davis, mentioned, 6

Stocks, Indian, in New Mexico, 9

St. Peter and St. Paul, Arkansas river, 223

Sumas Indians, 381, note 386; revolt of, 427, note 434

Sylva, Manuel de, governor of New Mexico, 338, note 338

TABIRA, PUEBLO OF, mentioned, Fr. Acevedo built church at, 338; Indians of mentioned, 350, note 361; Fr. Acevedo buried at, 352, note 361; erroneously called Gran Quivira, 231, note 249; 232, note 249

Tabora, Captain, mentioned, 326

Ta-cú, San Juan Indian, Tu-pa-tú, 357

Tafoya, Don José Miguel, alcalde of Santa Fé, 470

Tamaron, Don Pedro, bishop of Durango, 443, 444

Tanonan stock, mentioned, 9

Tanos nation, mentioned, 259, note 275; visited by Espejo, 282; mentioned, 320, note 326; location of, 342, note 342; mentioned, 359, note 368; war waged on by Queres, 369; 370, note 378; came to Santa Fé, 381; gave up city, 382; they sue for peace, 407; mentioned, 408

Taos, pueblo of, visited by Alvarado, 230, by Castaño de Sosa, 294, note 301; by Oñate, called Tayberon, 319; mentioned, 342, note 342; news of Pueblo rebellion from, 359; mentioned, 382; death of Fr. Carbonel at, 411, note 411; mentioned as to traders, 435; Comanches raid, 445; annual fairs at, 453, 454; population, table of, 455; 474, note 506

Tapia, Pedro de, traitor, 387

Tarahumares, Indians, cliff dwellers, 46, note 29; Bandelier as to, 34, note 18

Tayberon, Taos, 319

Tehuas nation, seven villages, 277, note 287; 320, note 326; 322, note 327; 342, note 342; population, number, note 342; conspire with Jemez, 346; 350, note 361; mentioned in revolt of 1680, 359; war waged on by Queres, 369; mentioned, 370, note 378; mentioned, 394, 397, 400; fight with, 412

Tellez, Captain Rafael, 381

Tenabó, pueblo of, church built by Fr. Acevedo, 338

Teodoro, Greek, lost, 75, note 71

Tesuque, pueblo of, 15; Indians of arrested by Otermin, 359; mission of city of Santa Fé, Fr. Pio killed at, 361, note 369; De Vargas visited, 382, De Vargas meets governor of, 388; abandoned, 393; Fr. José Diez, located at, 407, note 407; mentioned, 411

Thunder Mountain, 384, note 389

Tiguex, province of, Alvarado arrives at, description of, 202, note 216; mentioned, 203, 204; Castañeda's account of, 204, note 218; mentioned, 205; Coronado reaches, 206, 234, note 220; mentioned, 207, 212; siege of, 214, 215, 216, note 228; mentioned, 221; Coronado returns to, 228; Arrellano arrives at, 229; mentioned, 230; Coronado leaves for Mexico, 239; mentioned, 254

Tiguex, river of, 229, note 245

Tizon, river, 195

Tlascala, pueblo of, 257

Tobosos, Indians, 267, note 283

Torre, Fr. Juan de la, bishop of Nicaragua, death of, 338

Totonteac, province of, Moqui, 148, note 157

Tovar, Don Pedro de, standard-bearer under Coronado, 173; wounded at Hawaikúh, 189; visits Tusayan, 192, note 208

Trenaquel, pueblo of, 231, note 250

Treviño, Don Juan Francisco, governor of New Mexico, 1675, 344

Tsankawi, pueblo of, Place of Round Cactus, 20, 21

Tscherege, pueblo of, description of, 22, 23

Tu-pa-tu, leader of revolt of 1680, 357, note 366; mentioned, 369, death of, note 378; mentioned, 382; De Vargas has conference with, 388

Turk, El Turco, Coronado meets, 206; mentioned, 207, 218, 219, note 239;

mentioned, 223, 228; strangled, 225, notes 241, 244
Turquoise mines, near pueblo of San Marcos, description of, 314, note 318
Tutahaco, pueblo of, Coronado visits, 205; mentioned, 204, note 218
Tu-yó, definition, 14; description, 15
Ty-u-on-yi, pueblo of, 37; description, kivas, excavations at, 37, 38

UBATES, Indians, mentioned, 282
Ugarte y la Concha, Don Hernando, governor of New Mexico, 1650, 344
Ulloa, Francisco, expedition of, 164
Ulloa y Lemos, inspector, 307
Urribari, Juan de, 422
Urrisola, Don Manuel Portillo, governor of New Mexico, 1760, 445
Ute, Indians, Otermin makes treaty with, 349; war with Pueblos, 370, note 378; attack town of Taos, 430; Valverde leads expedition against, 431; battle with near Abiquiú, 442, note 463

VACA, CAPTAIN MIGUEL DE, alcalde of Cochití, charges against, 433
Vaca, Don Miguel, alcalde of Alburquerque, 470
Vacapa, mentioned, 145, note, 152
Valdéz, governor of New Mexico, 343
Valverde y Cosio, Don Antonio, governor of New Mexico, 430, 431, 432, 433
Velasco, Don Luis de, viceroy of New Spain, 304
Velasco, Fr., death of, 358, note 368
Vetancurt, historian, cited, 245, note 258; 315, note 318; 320, note 326; 332, note 333; 340, says Nieto was governor in 1629, note 338; 341, note 341; massacre at Hawaikúh, 349, note 358; missions of New Mexico, 1680, 350, 351, note 362
Victorio, Fr. Antonio, 185
Villagrá, Captain Gaspar de, cited and quoted as to pueblo of Puara, 262, note 279; Castaño de Sosa's entrada, 298, note 303; historian, mentioned, quoted, first canto, 302, note 306; biography, 303, note 306; mentioned, 312; cited, 317, note 322; cited, 321, 324, 325, 328, note 329
Villanueva, Don Fernando, governor of New Mexico, 344
Villasur, Captain, 432, note 442; 433, note 447

Viscarra, Colonel Antonio, governor of New Mexico, 470
Visita, definition, 253, note 262

WALPI, pueblo of. See *Moqui*
Washington, Col. J. M., 23, note 8
We-je-gi, pueblo of, description, 25
Windsor, Justin, historian, cited, 56, note 43
Winship, George Parker, historian, cited, 149, note 159; 160, 163; official report of Fr. Marcos, 152, note 164; Fr. Marcos' credit with Mendoza, 156, note 166; orders to Estevan, 156, 157, note 167; 158, note 169; 162, 163, notes 177, 178; De Soto, 165, note 180; Cortés to Spain, 169, notes 184, 185; cited, 171, note 187; 175, note 192; Culiacan, 178, note 196; route of Coronado, 185, note 202; 227, note 243; Fr. Padilla, 245, note 258; Coronado's return to Mexico, quoted, 246, 247, note 260
Witchcraft, trials, 445, note 467

XABE, Quivira Indian, 219
Xuares, Fr., comisario Narvaéz expedition, 65

YGUAZES, Indians, 87, note 87
Ysopete, Quivira Indian, 219
Yuma, Indians, met by Melchior Diaz, 194, note 209
Yunque Yunque, pueblo of, visited by Barrionuevo, 229, note 246; capital founded by Oñate, 316, note 321

ZARATE-SALMERON, FR. GERONIMO, place of death of Estevan, 160; as to date of founding of Santa Fé, 332; career in New Mexico, 337; cited, 259, note 274; Puara, 261, note 279; cited, 275, note 284; cited, 302, note 305; Oñate's expedition to Quivira, cited, 330, note 330
Zaragosa, Juston, cited, 168, note 181
Zipias, Indians, 346, note 353
Zotylo, Don Felipe, governor of New Mexico, 338, note 338
Zuñi, pueblo of, mentioned, 9; Marata, 148; *First Discovered City of*, 152, note 165, 186; not visited by Chamuscado, 258; Espejo visits, 278; returns to from Moqui, 281; Oñate visits, 324, 325; extent, population, etc., Benavides' report, 343, note

342; missions established at, 345, note 352; visited by Peñalosa, 347; Vetancurt's list, Alona, 351, note 362; one friar at survived the revolt of 1680, 361; De Vargas goes to, 383, finds villages abandoned, natives on Thunder Mountain, 384, note 389; recovers church vestments, etc., 384; in revolt of 1696, 410; De Vargas urged to establish mission at, declined, Zuñi abandoned by friars, 420, note 423; Tanos raid upon, 424, note 428; mentioned, 439; population, 1754, 444, note 466; mentioned, 447; population, table, 1760-1800, 455; Indians of, aid against Navajós, 457

Zuñian stock, mentioned, 9

www.ingramcontent.com/pod-product-compliance
Lightning Source LLC
Chambersburg PA
CBHW071428300426
44114CB00013B/1354